DISTRIBUTED OBJECT MANAGEMENT

IWDOM WAS ORGANIZED WITH THE FINANCIAL SPONSORSHIP OF

University of Alberta

Canadian Information Processing Society Edmonton Section

OBJECT MANAGEMENT GROUP

Alberta TECHNOLOGY, RESEARCH AND TELECOMMUNICATIONS

IN COOPERATION WITH

acm

IEEE

IEEE Computer Society

DISTRIBUTED OBJECT MANAGEMENT

M. Tamer Özsu
Umeshwar Dayal
Patrick Valduriez

Morgan Kaufmann Publishers
San Mateo, California

Senior Editor: Bruce M. Spatz
Production Manager: Yonie Overton
Assistant Editor: Douglas Sery
Type Design, Cover: Patty King
Composition: Edward W. Sznyter, Babel Press
Proofreader: Fran Taylor
Printer: R.R. Donnelley & Sons

Editorial Offices:
Morgan Kaufmann Publishers
2929 Campus Drive, Suite 260
San Mateo, CA 94403

98 97 96 95 94 5 4 3 2 1

Library of Congress Cataloging-in-Publication Data

Distributed object management / M. Tamer Özsu, Umeshwar Dayal, Patrick Valduriez.
p. cm.
Edited collection of papers presented at the International Workshop on Distributed Object Management, held in August of 1992 at the University of Alberta, Canada.
Includes bibliographical references and index.
ISBN 1-55860-256-9
1. Object-oriented data bases--Congresses. I. Özsu, M. Tamer, 1951- . II. Dayal, Umeshwar. III. Valduriez, Patrick. IV. International Workshop on Distributed Object Management (1992 : University of Alberta)
QA76.9.D3D585 1994
005.75'8--dc20 93-31654
CIP

CONTENTS

PART 2. OBJECT AND STORAGE MANAGEMENT

PART 3. DISTRIBUTION AND QUERY PROCESSING

PART 4. TRANSACTION PROCESSING AND CONCURRENCY CONTROL

PREFACE

Distribution and object-orientation are expected to be important features of next generation database management systems (DBMSs). Research on distributed DBMSs during the past decade has made an impact on today's commercial products. Although object-oriented DBMS (OODBMS) technology is more recent and less mature, second generation systems have started to appear. The synthesis of these two technologies is essential since applications that require OODBMS technology typically arise in distributed environments.

These observations have led us to organize the **International Workshop on Distributed Object Management (IWDOM)** to address the theory and practice of developing distributed OODBMSs. IWDOM was organized in Edmonton, Canada on the University of Alberta campus between August 19–21, 1992. The objective was to take note of the state-of-the-art in distributed object management technology and to identify the issues that need to be resolved. The recent developments in standards-related activities, notably the release of the CORBA specifications by the Object Management Group, contributed to the timeliness and importance of the Workshop.

IWDOM was the third in a series of workshops dedicated to OODBMSs. While the first two (at Pacific Grove, California in 1986 and at Bad Munster am Stein-Ebernburg, Germany in 1988) were general in their coverage, this one was exclusively devoted to *distributed object management*. The current volume includes most of the papers that were presented at the workshop. We were not able to get the final versions of two presentations to include in this book.

The papers that were presented at IWDOM cover a wide spectrum of issues related to distributed object management. The topics that were covered include system architecture, object management techniques, object models, design issues, transaction management and concurrency control, implementation considerations, security, system integration, and interoperability. In the current volume, we have organized these papers into six groups — system architecture, object and storage management, distribution and query processing, transaction management and concurrency control, operating system support, and interoperability. In addition, we wrote an introductory paper that introduces the topic and puts the other papers in their proper context. We believe that the book provides a fairly complete coverage of the state-of-the-art in distributed object management.

All the papers included here were revised by the authors following the presentations and discussions at the Workshop. This has allowed the authors to point out similarities and differences of their work with others presented at the Workshop. We have chosen not to attempt to revise the authors' terminology to enforce consistency in the use of terms (most notably in the interchangable use of "object-oriented DBMS", "objectbase", "persistent object base" and others). This, would have been, perhaps, a worthwhile exercise, but given the current turmoil in terminology (and the difficulty in getting researchers to agree on a common set of terms), it would have delayed the publication of this book considerably. We have opted for timeliness at the expense of some diversity in terminology.

Acknowledgements

We have received excellent support in organizing IWDOM. The University of Alberta and the Edmonton Section of the Canadian Information Processing Society (CIPS) were early supporters. We received further financial assistance from Object Management Group and Alberta Technology, Research and Telecommunicatins. We gratefully acknowledge their support as well as the cooperation of ACM and IEEE Computer Society.

The workshop organization was chaired by M. Tamer Özsu assisted by Jasbir Dhaliwal as the local arrangements chair and Brenda Holt (both from the University of Alberta) who ran the workshop secretariat. Brenda, together with graduate students, Iqbal Ghorawalla and Youping Niu also handled the editing of the final versions of the papers and generated the composite index. Their help is greatly appreciated. The organization of the Workshop also benefitted greatly from the assistance provided by the graduate students in the Laboratory for Database Systems Research of University of Alberta (Ana Dominguez, Boman Irani, Anna Lipka, Adriana Munoz, Youping Niu, Randal Peters, and John Shillington). In addition to their organizational assistance, the notes that they took during the discussions formed the basis of the workshop summary that we published in *ACM SIGMOD Record* (March 1993).

Technical success of IWDOM is the result of excellent work by the Program Committee. The Committee was co-chaired by Umesh Dayal and Patrick Valduriez and consisted of Rakesh Agrawal (IBM Almaden), Alex Buchmann (University of Darmstadt), Stefano Ceri (Politecnico di Milano), Klaus Dittrich (University of Zurich), Frank Manola (GTE Laboratories), Sylvia Osborn (University of Western Ontario), M. Tamer Özsu (University of Alberta), Marc Shapiro (INRIA), Fernando Velez (O2 Technology), and Stan Zdonik (Brown University). The Program Committee reviewed over 50 full and short papers (position statements) which were received in response to the Call for Papers. Of these, 17 papers were accepted for regular presentation and 11 were accepted for short presentation at the Workshop. We were very fortunate in that Malcolm Atkinson (University of Glasgow) and Craig Schaffert (DEC Cambridge Research Laboratory) agreed to give invited talks. The Program Committee also extended invitations to a number of researchers who had expressed an interest by submitting position papers. Altogether, there were close to 60 participants from various object communities: object-oriented databases, object-oriented programming languages and programming environments, and object-oriented operating systems. This diversity gave the workshop a unique flavor in that it provided an opportunity for cross-fertilization of ideas between these communities.

Finally, we gratefully acknowledge the assistance of the following colleagues and their institutions in distributing the workshop notices: Amr El Abbadi (University of California, Santa Barbara), Malcolm Atkinson (University of Glasgow), José Blakeley (Texas

Instruments), Chin-Chen Chang, (National Chung Cheng University, Taiwan), Ahmed Elmagarmid (Purdue University), Hector Hernandez (New Mexico State University), Sushil Jajodia (George Mason University), Yahiko Kambayashi (Kyoto University, Japan), Vijay Kumar (University of Missouri-Kansas City), Yoon-Joon Lee (KAIST, Korea), Toh Wang Ling (National University of Singapore), Shamkant Navathe (Georgia Institute of Technology), William Perrizo (North Dakota State University), Krithi Ramamritham (University of Massachusetts, Amherst), Ron Sacks-Davis (RMIT, Australia), Avi Silberschatz (University of Texas at Austin), and Craig Thompson (Texas Instruments).

M. Tamer Özsu
Umeshwar Dayal
Patrick Valduriez

An Introduction to Distributed Object Management

M. Tamer Özsu
University of Alberta
Department of Computing Science
Edmonton, Alberta
Canada T6G 2H1

Umeshwar Dayal
Hewlett-Packard Laboratories
1501 Page Mill Road
Palo Alto, CA 94304
U.S.A.

Patrick Valduriez
INRIA Rocquencourt
78153 Le Chesnay Cedex
France

Abstract

Object-oriented data management systems (OODBMSs) are expected to meet the requirements of new application domains which have a need for functionality beyond those provided by relational database systems. In addition, most of these application domains require the management of distributed artifacts. Therefore, next generation OODBMSs are likely to be distributed systems. This paper provides an overview of distributed object management issues and provides an introduction to the other papers included in this volume.

1 INTRODUCTION

Relational database systems have been very successful in meeting the requirements of traditional business applications. Some of the features of the relational systems which make them suitable for these applications become too restrictive when these systems are put to use in other application domains that are more complex than traditional business applications (e.g., office information systems, engineering databases, artificial intelligence applications, medical imaging systems, geographical information processing systems, biological information systems). Some of the more important shortcomings of the relational model in meeting the requirements of these applications can be listed as follows:

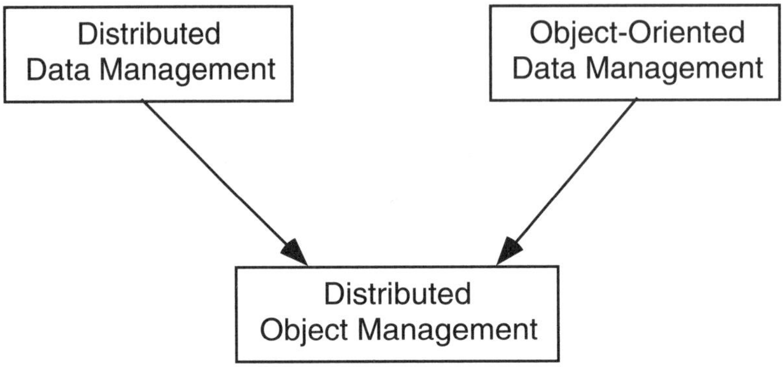

Figure 1: Technologies Contributing to DOM

1. Relational systems deal with a single object type: a relation. A relation is used to model different real-world objects, but the semantics of this association is not part of the database. Furthermore, the attributes of a relation may come only from simple and fixed data type domains (numeric, character, and, sometimes, date types). The advanced applications cited above require explicit storage and manipulation of more abstract types (e.g., images, design documents) and the ability for the users to define their own application-specific types. Therefore, a rich type system supporting user-defined abstract types is required.

2. The relational model structures data in a relatively simple and flat manner. These applications require more complex object structures with nested objects (e.g., a vehicle object containing an engine object).

3. Relational systems provide a declarative and (arguably) simple language for accessing the data. The applications mentioned above require richer languages which overcome the well-known "impedance mismatch" problem. This problem arises because of the differences in the level of abstraction between the relational languages and the programming languages with which they interact.

Object-oriented technology is now a topic of intense study as the major candidate to successfully meet the requirements of advanced applications that require data management services. However, a close study of these applications reveals that they are distributed in nature and require data management support in a distributed environment. Thus, these systems require the development of distributed object management systems (DOMs). The purpose of this paper is to provide an overview of the issues that need to be addressed in the development of this technology.

Even though the work on OODBMSs is relatively new, there has been more than a decade of work in relational distributed DBMSs. It is possible that the lessons learned in that process would be useful in developing distributed OODBMSs. In fact, we view distributed OODBMSs as the merger of the relational distributed DBMS and the OODBMS technologies (Figure 1). Therefore, we start with a review of distributed data management in the Section 2 and object-orientation in Section 3, before we embark on a discussion of issues that arise in developing distributed OODBMSs in Section 4.

2 DISTRIBUTED DATA MANAGEMENT

A distributed database is a collection of multiple, logically interrelated databases distributed over a computer network [Özsu and Valduriez, 1991a]. A distributed DBMS is then defined as the software system that permits the management of the distributed database and makes the distribution transparent to the users. This definition is based on the following implicit assumptions [Özsu and Valduriez, 1991b]:

1. Data is stored at a number of sites. Each site is assumed to logically consist of a single processor.
2. The processors at these sites are interconnected by a computer network rather than a multiprocessor configuration.
3. The distributed database is a "database", not some "collection" of files that can be individually stored at each node of a computer network.
4. The system has the full functionality of a DBMS. It is neither, as indicated above, a distributed file system, nor purely a transaction processing system.

The last two assumptions indicate that the system has to be a fully-functional DBMS. The first two assumptions make the distinction between *distributed DBMS* and *parallel DBMS*. As indicated in [Özsu and Valduriez, 1993], next generation DBMSs will relax many of these assumptions due to technological developments — especially the emergence of affordable multiprocessors and high-speed networks — and the increasing use of client-server mode of computing. Thus, next generation systems will include parallel database servers connected to high speed networks which link them and other repositories to client machines that run application code and participate in the execution of database requests. It is within this context that object-oriented systems should be viewed. Even though our emphasis in this paper and in this volume is predominantly on distributed object-oriented DBMS, there has been some work on implementing these systems on top of parallel architectures as well (e.g., Bubba [Boral et al., 1990]).

Distributed DBMSs provide transparent access to a physically distributed database. User queries and transactions access the database based on *external schemas* (ES) defined over a *global conceptual schema* (GCS) which is partitioned and stored at different sites forming the *local conceptual schemas* (LCS) at those sites. The LCS at a given site is then mapped to a *local internal schema* (LIS) which describes the physical organization of data at that site (Figure 2).

Transparency, in this context, can be viewed as the extension of the well-known *data independence* concept to distributed systems. The following transparencies have to be provided by the distributed DBMS in order to achieve full data independence in a distributed environment: *network* (or *distribution*) *transparency* which hides the existence of the network and the distribution of data, *replication transparency* which masks the existence of physical copies of logical data items, and *fragmentation transparency* which prevents the user from having to deal with the partitioning of database objects.

Various distributed DBMS modules cooperate to provide the functionality described above. **Distributed query processors** partition global queries to a set of sub-queries that can execute at each site. This partitioning is done transparently, using the location information in the distributed database directory. Distributed processors also optimize the distributed

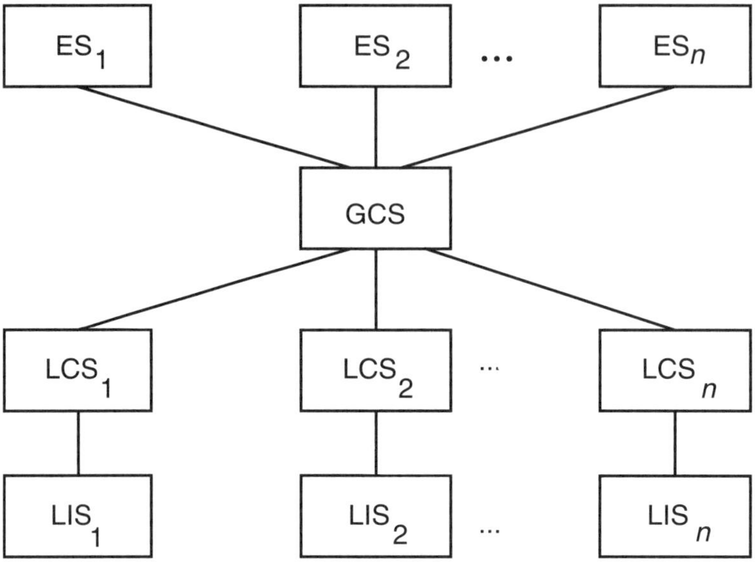

Figure 2: Datalogical Distributed DBMS Architecture

operation of binary operators (e.g., join, union). This partitioning of a given global query introduces *intra-query parallelism* that contributes to improved performance. The inherent parallelism in a distributed system enable queries to be submitted at a number of sites giving rise to *inter-query parallelism*. Further optimization (access path selection) of each sub-query is done at each site where it is executed.

Transactional accesses are managed by **global transaction managers** with the help of **schedulers** for synchronization and **local recovery managers** for reliability. The placement and operation of the schedulers are dependent upon the concurrency control algorithms that are implemented. The most common algorithm is some form of two-phase locking. Transaction managers are designed to specifically support a particular transaction model (see Section 4.4 for more discussion of models). They participate in the execution of an atomic commit protocol (usually two-phase commit) to provide transaction atomicity. Local recovery managers participate in the execution of the atomic commit protocol in addition to implementing reliability protocols (to ensure durability) and recovery routines.

3 OBJECT-ORIENTED DATA MANAGEMENT

What constitutes an object-oriented database system is a topic of considerable discussion. Contrary to the relational model, there is no universally accepted and formally specified object model. There are a number of features that are common to most model specifications, but the exact semantics of these features are different in each model. In this paper, we will review the fundamental concepts assuming a fairly conventional object model.

Object-oriented database systems combine the features of object-oriented programming languages with those of database management systems. The former contributes the notions

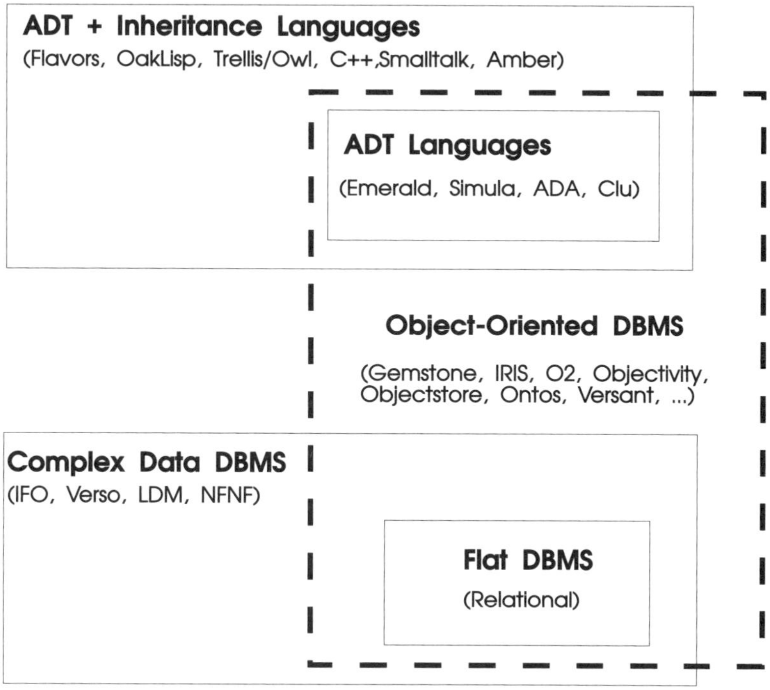

Figure 3: Merging of Technologies

of types and instances, object identity, encapsulation, inheritance and navigational access, whereas the latter provides support for persistence, concurrency control, recovery, consistency, and query access. Figure 3 shows the merger of these technologies in producing an OODBMS.

All object-oriented DBMSs are built around the fundamental concept of an *object*. An object represents a real entity in the system that is being modeled. It is an abstraction defined by (a) a unique *object identifier*, (2) a set of *instance variables* (attributes) which define the *state* of the object, and (3) an interface in terms of *methods* (operations) which manipulate the object. Some object models (e.g., OODAPLEX [Dayal, 1989] and TIGUKAT [Peters et al., 1992]) take a behavioral approach and define a set of behaviors which are the only means of accessing and manipulating objects. In these models, there are no instance variables or methods, there are only *behaviors*. In either case, the structure and implementation of objects are hidden and cannot be accessed by others. The only way of accessing objects is by their *interface* which is either the set of behaviors or the set of instance variables and methods. This is a fundamental feature of object-orientation and is called *encapsulation*. Encapsulation provides data abstraction and data independence.

Object identity (OID) is another fundamental feature of object models since they form the foundation of object comparisons and referencing. An OID is an *invariant* property of an object which distinguishes it logically and physically from all other objects. It is unique to each object and independent of the object's state. In some object models OID equality is the only comparison primitive; for other types of comparisons, the type definer is expected to specify the semantics of comparison. In other models, comparisons with respect to object states is allowed (e.g., shallow and deep equality). OIDs also form the basis of *referential sharing* where multiple objects contain the OID of another object as the value of one of their instance variables. These objects are also known as *composite objects*.

Object models also differ in how they deal with types, classes and collections. A *type* defines a template for all the objects of that type. It provides a common representation for all objects of that type and a set of operations on those objects. A *class* is a grouping of all object instances of a given type. It is the *extent* of the associated type. A *collection* is a user-defined grouping of objects which differs from a class in that it can be heterogeneous and objects need to be inserted into it explicityly by users. In most conventional systems a class is not separated from a type and serves both as a type specification and as an extent of that type. Beeri argues that there is use for both of classes and collections and that they should be supported in an object model [Beeri, 1990]. Collections provide for a clear closure semantics of the query models and facilitate definition of user views. Some of the recent models (e.g., TIGUKAT [Peters et al., 1992]) separate types and classes and also provide collections.

Object-oriented systems provide extensibility by allowing user-defined types to be defined that will be managed by the system. Typically, these types are defined based on predefined types. This is the process of subtyping. A type `A` is a *subtype* of another type `B` if it inherits all the behaviors (or instance variables and methods) of `B` and possibly more. It is possible for a type to be subtypes of more than one type, in which case the model supports *multiple subtyping*.

What we called subtyping above has commonly been called *inheritance*. In models where there is no distinction between a type and a class, subtyping and inheritance can be used interchangeably. In models which separate the two, however, inheritance is associated with code sharing, and is, therefore, treated as an implementation concept, whereas subtyping is considered a behavioral concept. Subtyping indicates a relationship between types. In the above example, `A` **is-a** `B`, resulting in *substitutability*: an instance of a subtype can be substituted in place of an instance of any of its supertypes in any expression. If this separation is made between subtyping (as a behavioral concept) and inheritance (as an implementation concept for code sharing), one gets a clear separation of concepts. However, merging the two makes sense in models where the class and type concepts are not separated.

The fundamental feature that database technology contributes to OODBMSs is *persistence*, which is the property of objects to exist beyond the duration of the process that creates them. Two important properties of persistence have been identified [Atkinson, 1993]:

1. **Persistence independence.** The semantics of a program is not changed by the longevity of the objects to which it is applied.

2. **Persistence orthogonality.** Any object of any type can be made persistent.

A number of different persistence models have been adopted in various OODBMSs. Most straightforward persistence model is to attach persistence to objects, thereby making an object persistent only if it is declared as such. This model provides persistence orthogonality and it can also support persistence independence if the OODBMS treats persistent and transient objects uniformly. A second model is to associate persistence with the grouping construct (e.g., a collection). In this case, an object is persistent if it is placed in a collection which is declared to be persistent. A third model is to associate persistence with types. Thus an object is persistent if its type is declared to be persistent. To provide persistence orthogonality in this model, it is necessary to define the persistent (transient) dual of each transient (persistent) type (e.g., have both a `TransientInteger` and a `PersistentInteger` type). Finally, persistence can be associated with reachability. In this case, the type semilattice has a persistent root and any object that is reachable (by following the subtype and instance_of relationships) from that root is persistent.

Management of persistence is another important issue. One of the questions is the duration of persistence. There have been some research projects which treat all objects as persistent (without a clear deletion semantics). In these systems, objects are considered to be permanently persistent. More realistically, however, the two alternatives are (a) objects are persistent until they are explicitly deleted, or (b) objects are persistent until they are unreachable from any other object (i.e., no object holds reference to them any longer). In the latter case, garbage collection routines take care of reclaiming the storage (distributed versions of these algorithms are discussed later in this paper). A second question that arises is with respect to how objects are shared. Two alternatives have been identified. First is what is called the workspace model where objects, when they are brought into memory, are copied into the requesting application's address space. Thus, the objects are checked-out of the database buffers and need to be checked-in later when the application releases them. In the second model, persistent objects reside in shared database buffers and the OODBMS accesses them on behalf of each application.

In this section we provided an overview of the more important object-oriented concepts. This was not meant to be a complete tutorial; much better ones are available. We have, hopefully, established a platform upon which the distributed object management concepts can be presented in the subsequent sections.

4 DISTRIBUTED OBJECT MANAGEMENT

Distributed object management has the same objective with regards to object-oriented data management as the traditional database systems had for relational databases: transparent management of "objects" that are distributed across a number of sites. Thus users have an integrated, "single image" view of the objectbase (Figure 4) while it is physically distributed among a number of sites (Figure 5).

Maintaining such an environment requires that problems similar to those of relational distributed databases be addressed, with the additional opportunities and difficulties posed by object-orientation. In the remainder, we will review these issues and indicate some of the approaches.

4.1 ARCHITECTURE

The first step that system developers seem to take, on the way to providing true distribution by peer-to-peer communication, is to develop client-server systems. This was true in relational distributed DBMSs, and it certainly seems to be true for OODBMSs as well. Most of the existing OODBMSs are *multiple client-single server* architectures where the

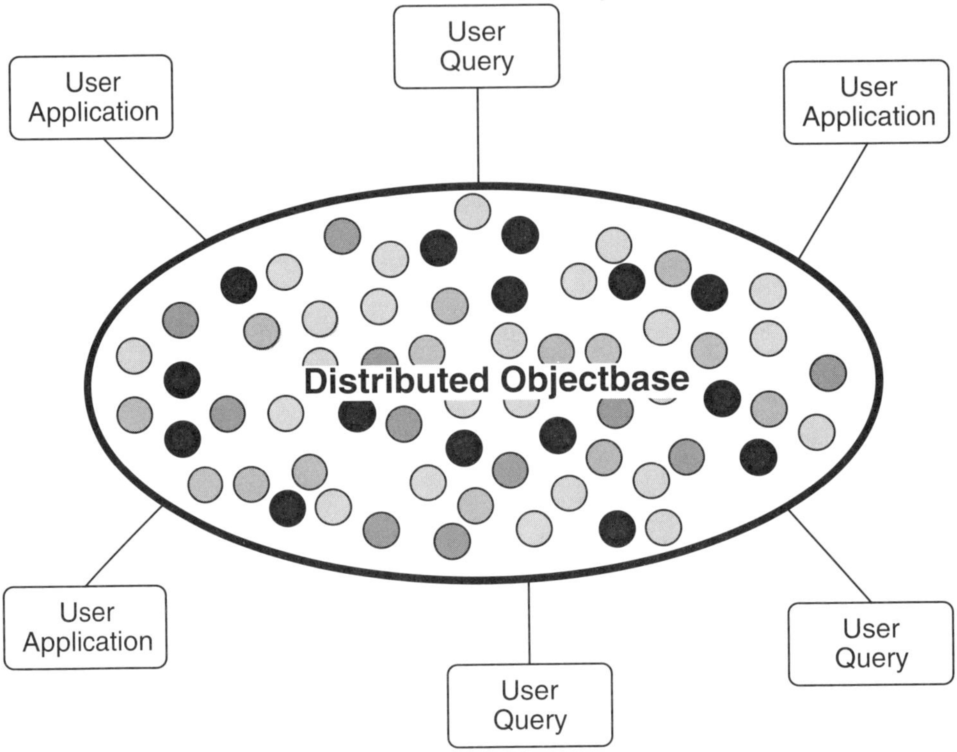

Figure 4: Transparent Access to Objectbase

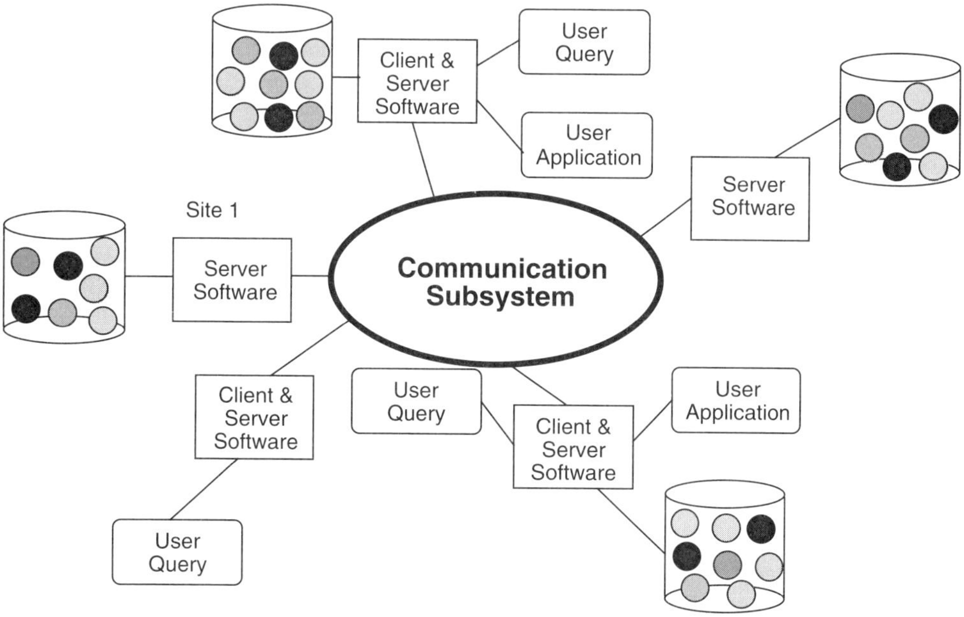

Figure 5: Distribution of Objectbase

objectbase is stored at and managed by a single server which provides services to a number of clients. Such systems are usually called *data shipping* systems [Franklin and Carey, 1993] to differentiate them from distributed systems that provide simple print server services, etc.

The design of data shipping client-server systems requires the resolution of a number of design issues. One issue is the communication mechanism between the clients and the server. The two alternatives are remote procedure calls (RPC) and message passing. The relative merits of these schemes have been discussed extensively in literature (e.g., see [Stankovic, 1982]). In Section 4.6, we provide a brief overview and comparison among them. A second important design issue is to determine the functions to be provided by the clients and the server. This is at least partly dependent upon the the resolution of a third issue, namely the unit of communication between the clients and the server. Two alternatives exist which result in two types of client-server architectures. The first alternative is that the clients request "objects" from the server which retrieves them from the database and returns them to the requesting client. These systems are called *object servers* (Figure 6). In object servers, the server undertakes most of the object management services with the client providing basically an execution environment for the applications as well as providing some level of object management functionality. The optimization of user queries and the synchronization of user transactions are all performed in the server with the client receiving the resulting objects. Object manager serves a number of functions. First and foremost, it provides a context for method execution. The replication of the object manager in both the server and the client enables methods to be executed at both the server and the clients. The execution of methods in the client may invoke the execution of other methods which may not have been shipped to the server with the object. The optimization of method executions of this type is an important research problem which is addressed

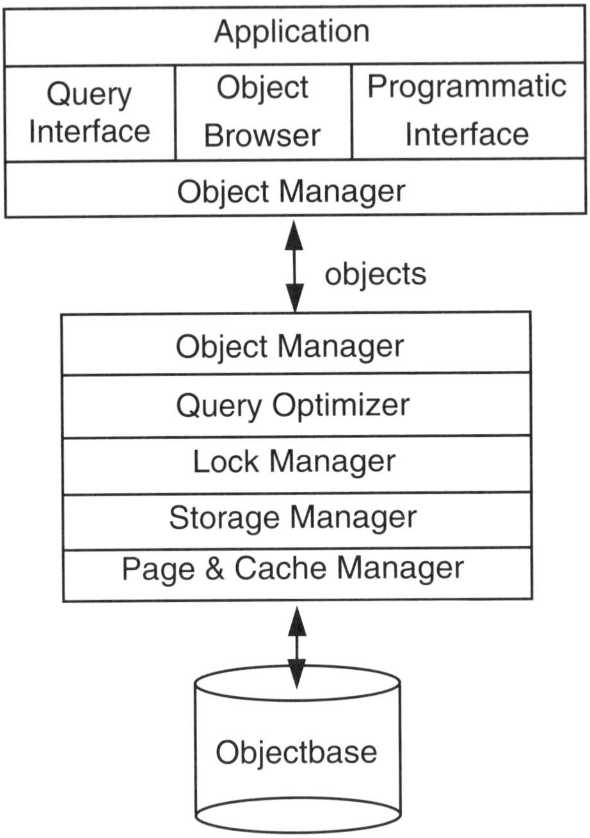

Figure 6: Object Server Architecture

in [Maier et al., 1993]. Object manager also deals with the implementation of the object identifier (logical, physical, or virtual), the deletion of objects (either explicit deletion or garbage collection). At the server, it also provides support for object clustering and access methods.

An alternative organization is a *page server* client-server architecture where the unit of transfer between the servers and the clients are physical units of data such as pages or segments rather than objects Figure 7). Page server architectures split the object processing services between the clients and the servers. In fact, the servers do not deal with objects anymore, instead acting as "value-added" storage managers.

Early performance studies (e.g., [DeWitt et al., 1990]) indicate that page server architectures perform better than object server architectures. Further studies on these designs are necessary before a definitive conclusion can be reached, however. It would be interesting to repeat the performance studies in multiple client-multiple server environments with different job mixes (query versus navigational access) and with different storage system designs taking into account different buffer management policies.

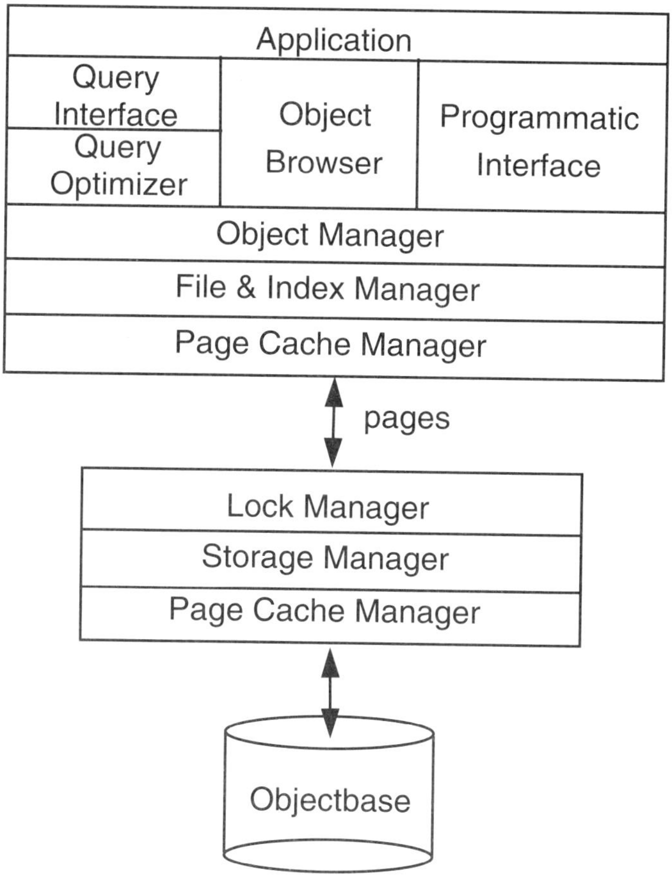

Figure 7: Page Server Architecture

A final design issue that we address relates to caching policies. There has been some work done in this regard ([Carey et al., 1991; Franklin and Carey, 1993]). Here we summarize the results of [Franklin and Carey, 1993]. This study considers data shipping, multiple client-single server, page server architectures. It compares the performance of three types of caching algorithms: (1) *server-based two-phase locking* where data pages are cached to the clients, but locks are managed by the server; (2) *optimistic two-phase locking* (O2PL) where both data pages and locks are cached and the detection of conflicts of locks cached at multiple clients are deferred until transaction commit time; and (3) *callback locking* (CL) where both data pages and locks are cached at the clients, but locks are obtained (if they are not already cached) from the server before the data pages can be accessed. Four versions of O2PL are analyzed: one which invalidates the cached data pages if there is a conflict (O2PL-I), one which propagates the changes to the cached copies (O2PL-P), one which dynamically chooses between invalidation and propagation (O2PL-D), and an improved version of O2PL-D (O2PL-ND) which is proposed by the authors. For callback locking, two variants are considered: callback-read which allows for caching of read-locks only, and callback-all which allows caching of both the read- and write-locks. The throughput of these algorithms are compared with respect to four different workloads. Simply stated, the results indicate that callback-read performs as well or slightly better than callback-all in most situations. Furthermore, the O2PL-ND algorithm performs close to O2PL-I when invalidation is the right choice and close to O2PL-P when propagation is the right choice. It always performs better than O2PL-D and slightly better than the callback algorithms.

The client-server architectures that we have discussed above are relatively traditional ones. An interesting proposal that is included in [Atkinson, 1993] is to construct a distributed persistent object system as a substrate to the various components (operating systems, DBMSs, persistent programming languages, etc) that are used to develop large-scale, long-lived applications. The proposal is motivated by two observations: (1) development of these types of applications can be greatly aided if a persistent programming language is used, since this reduces the number of mappings that the programmer has to deal with, and (2) many of these components that are used in developing these systems, "despite the fact that they service very different needs, have a substantial number of sub-components serving common functional requirements." These activities are identified as persistence, stability, recovery, concurrency, scheduling, space administration, protection, accounting, resource allocation and control, naming, binding programs to data (see Figure 6 in [Atkinson, 1993]). The paper identifies four possible architectural approaches to supporting the development of persistent application systems: (1) ignore it and hope that it will be taken care of by market forces or that it will go away; (2) make sure that all of the components employ common standards for all the common activities; (3) provide a software layer on top of these components that hides their differences; and (4) provide a common substrate that provides these common functions. Atkinson's proposal is to follow the last approach and develop what is called a *scalable persistent foundation* (SPF). The architecture of such a system is depicted in Figure 8 of [Atkinson, 1993].

Open system architectures for DOMs have been the topic of some study. One such effort, carried out at Texas Instruments and supported by DARPA, concentrates on the definition of an architectural framework of an open OODBMS and on the description of the design space for these systems [Wells and Blakeley, 1993]. The system employs a computational model where objects exist in a universe of objects partitioned into environments according to certain criteria (e.g., address space) that are transparent to applications. The architecture consists of a *meta-architecture* consisting of a collection of glue modules and definitions providing the infrastructure for extending the operations of programming languages, and an extensible collection of policy performers (PPs). The meta-architecture contains a collection of address space managers, communications and translation managers for transferring objects between multiple address spaces (if there are more than one), a data dictionary, and a meta-architecture support module that provides the extension mechanism and defines the interface conventions to which policy modules must adhere. The PP modules that are instantiated in a particular open OODBMS may vary, but the full set includes transaction, distribution, replication, index, object query processor, version, configuration, dependency (for consistency and derived objects), persistence, access control, and gateway (for access to objects in foreign databases) policy performers. There is on-going work in most of these PPs except for the replication, access control and gateway PPs.

4.2 OBJECT DISTRIBUTION AND MIGRATION

The two important aspects of distribution design are fragmentation and allocation. Distribution design in the object-oriented world brings new complexities. Conceptually, objects encapsulate behaviors (methods) together with state. In reality, behaviors are implemented on types and shared by all instance objects of that type. Therefore, the location of objects with respect to their types becomes an issue. Objects can be co-located with their types, in which case different types of objects are located at different sites. Alternatively, objects of one type can be located at different sites. This is similar to horizontal partitioning in relational database systems (called *horizontal class partitioning* in [Karlapalem et al., 1993]). In this case, types may be duplicated at each site where there is an instance of that type, or the type specification may be stored at one site and remote processing of objects is supported as described below. The final alternative is to partition the type specification by dividing its behaviors (or instance variables and methods) into different fragments (called *vertical class partitioning* in [Karlapalem et al., 1993]) and distributing the objects in that manner. Again, in this case, there is a need for remote object processing.

Replication adds a new dimension to the design problem. Individual objects, classes of objects or collections of objects (or all) can be units of replication. Undoubtedly, the decision is at least partially object model dependent. Whether or not type specifications are located at each site can also be considered as a replication problem.

In horizontal and vertical partitioning, it is possible that the objects are not located at the site where the behaviors or methods (usually implemented as functions) that operate on them. This problem is addressed within the context of interoperable systems in [Fang et al., 1993], but the same techniques are applicable in general. Four alternatives can be identified: (1) local function – local argument, (2) local function – remote argument, (2) remote function – local argument, and (4) remote function – remote argument. The paper discusses solutions to all of these alternatives. Access to remote arguments is accomplished by creating surrogates in the local database that point to their remote counterparts. Local or remote functions operate on these surrogates. In the case of local stored functions applied to remote objects that do not have their counterparts in the remote component, new local function values are created as surrogates are created.

4.2.1 Storage Management and Object Clustering

An object model is essentially conceptual and should provide high physical data independence in order to increase programmer productivity. The mapping of this conceptual model to a physical storage is a classical database problem. In the case of OODBMSs, two kinds of relationships exist between types (or classes, depending upon the object model): subtyping or inheritance (e.g., an employee is a person) and composition (e.g., an employee works in a department). By providing a good approximation of object access, these relationships are essential to guide the physical clustering of persistent objects. Object clustering refers to the grouping of objects in physical containers (i.e., disk extents) according to common properties, such as the same value of an attribute or subobjects of the same object. Thus, fast access to clustered objects can be obtained.

Object clustering is difficult for two reasons. First, it is not orthogonal to object identity implementation, i.e, logical vs. physical OID. Logical OIDs incur more overhead (an indirection table) but enable vertical partitioning of classes. Physical OIDs yield more efficient direct object access but require each object to contain all inherited attributes. Second, the clustering of complex objects along the composition relationship is more involved because of object sharing (objects with multiple parents).

Given a class graph, there are three basic storage models for object clustering [Valduriez et al., 1986]. The *decomposition storage model* (DSM) partitions each object class in binary relations (OID, attribute) and therefore relies on logical OID. The advantage of DSM is simplicity. The *normalized storage model* (NSM) stores each class as a separate relation. It can be used with logical or physical OID. However, only logical OID allow the vertical partitioning of objects along the inheritance relationship [Kim et al., 1987]. The *direct storage model* enables multi-class clustering of complex objects based on the composition relationship. This model generalizes the techniques of hierarchical and network databases and works best with physical OID [Benzaken and Delobel, 1991]. This model can capture object access locality and is therefore potentially superior for well-known access patterns. The major difficulty, however, is to be able to recluster an object whose parent it is grouped with has been deleted.

In a distributed system, both DSM and NSM are straightforward using horizontal partitioning. Goblin [Kersten et al., 1993] implements DSM as a basis for a distributed OODBMS with large main memory. DSM provides flexibility and its performance disadvantage is compensated by the use of large main memory and caching. Eos [Gruber and Amsaleg, 1993] implements the direct storage model in a distributed single-level store architecture where each object has a physical system-wide OID. The Eos grouping mechanism is based on the concept of most relevant composition links and solves the problem of multiparent shared objects. When an object moves to a different node, it gets a new OID. To avoid the indirection of forwarders, references to the object are subsequently changed as part of the garbage collection process without any overhead. The grouping mechanism is dynamic to achieve load balancing and cope with the evolutions of the object graph.

4.2.2 Distributed Garbage Collection

An advantage of object-based systems is that objects can refer to other objects using object identity. As programs modify objects and remove references, a persistent object may become unreachable from the persistent roots of the system when there is no more reference to it. Such an object is garbage and should be de-allocated by the garbage collector. In relational DBMSs, there is no need for automatic garbage collection since object references are supported by join values. However, cascading updates as specified by referential integrity constraints are a simple form of "manual" garbage collection. In more general operating system or programming language contexts, manual garbage collection is typically error-prone. Therefore, the generality of distributed object-based systems calls for automatic distributed garbage collection.

There are two basic techniques for garbage collection: *reference counting* and *tracing*. With reference counting, each object carries a count of the number of references to it. When the number reaches zero, the object is garbage and can be de-allocated. Thus, garbage collection is done during object update. With tracing, garbage collection is a periodic process which walks the object graph and detects unreachable objects.

Reference counting seems to be the most suited for distributed systems [Bevan, 1987]. However, dealing with garbage cycles is difficult (the count of the cycle root can never be zero). Furthermore, the basic problem is that maintaining a strong invariant (equality of the count with the actual number of references) is difficult in the presence of failures.

Tracing is potentially more fault-tolerant because each execution of the collector starts from the root [Dijkstra et al., 1978]. However, most distributed tracing algorithms are usually very complex because they try to detect the minimal set of reachable objects. This is difficult and costly in the case of distributed cycles and a global service is needed to synchronize the local collectors.

However, when the assumptions are weakened, simpler protocols are possible. For instance, with the assumptions of fail-stop crashes only and that messages are either lost or delivered in finite time, [Shapiro et al., 1990] proposes an algorithm with tracing and local garbage collection but no global service. Nevertheless, as in most solutions, the detection of inter-space cycles of garbage remains an open issue.

4.2.3 Object Migration

One aspect of distributed systems is that objects move, from time to time, between sites. This raises a number of issues in object management systems. First is the unit of migration. In systems where the state is separated from the methods, it is possible to consider moving the object's state without moving the methods. The counterpart of this scenario in purely behavioral systems is the fragmentation of an object according to its behaviors. In either case, the application of methods to an object requires the invocation of remote procedures. This is an issue that we discussed above under object distribution. Other systems (e.g. [Dollimore et al., 1993]) consider the object as the unit of distribution. Even then, the migration of individual objects may move them away from their type specifications and one has to decide whether types are duplicated at every site where instances reside or whether the types are accessed remotely when behaviors or methods are applied to objects.

Another issue is that the movements of the objects have to be tracked so that they can be found in their new locations. A common way of tracking objects is to leave *surrogates* [Hwang, 1987; Liskov et al., 1993] or *proxy objects* [Dickman, 1993b]. These are place-holder objects left at the previous site of the object, pointing to its new location. Accesses to the proxy objects are directed transparently by the system to the objects themselves at the new sites. The migration of objects can be accomplished based on the state that they are in [Dollimore et al., 1993]. Objects can be in one of four states: ready, active, waiting, or suspended. Ready objects are those that are not currently invoked (or have not received a message) but are ready to be invoked (to receive a message). Active objects are those which are currently involved in an activity in response to an invocation or a message. Waiting objects are those which have invoked (or have sent a message to) another object and are waiting for a response and suspended objects are temporarily unavailable for invocation. Objects in active or waiting state are not allowed to migrate since the activity they are currently involved in would be broken. The migration involves two steps: (1) shipping the object from the source to the destination, and (2) creating a proxy at the source, replacing the original object.

Two related issues have to be addressed here. One relates to the maintenance of the system directory. As objects move, the system directory needs to be updated to reflect the new location. This may be done lazily whenever a surrogate or proxy object redirects an invocation rather than eagerly at the time of the movement. The second issue is that in a highly dynamic environment where objects move frequently, the surrogate or proxy chains may become quite long. It is useful for the system to transparently compact these chains from time to time. However, the result of compaction needs to be reflected in the directory and it may not be possible to accomplish that lazily.

Another important migration issue arises with respect to the movement of composite objects. The shipping of a composite object may involve shipping other objects referenced by the composite object (called the composition graph). A lazy migration strategy is employed in [Dollimore et al., 1993]. Three alternatives are considered for the migration of classes (types): (1) the source code is moved and recompiled at the destination, (2) the compiled version of a class is migrated just like any other object, or (3) the source code of the class definition is moved, but not its compiled operations for which a lazy migration strategy is used.

4.3 QUERY PROCESSING

In distributed relational database systems, query processing consists largely of generating, and executing, a low-cost plan for decomposing the query into operations that are shipped to various nodes, sequencing these operations, and piecing the results of these operations to construct the query's result. Since data movement across nodes of the distributed system is a key factor contributing to the cost of query processing, the plan consists of *bulk* operations that operate on and move sets of records, instead of one record at a time.

The same considerations carry over to distributed object systems. However, unlike relational systems, objects are not always implemented as flat records. Objects may have complex states consisting of many subobjects distributed over several nodes, and objects may reference other objects. Performing an operation over a collection of complex objects typically requires accessing these distributed pieces of state and following embedded references among the subobjects. A naive implementation of the operation, for example one that tries to access each piece of state for one object at a time, may incur unacceptable performance costs due to navigating across the network, following inter-object references, and making remote procedure calls. How to efficiently assemble the fragments of several distributed objects' state necessary to processing a query is addressed in [Maier et al., 1993].

In earlier work, the *assembly* operation had been introduced for use in centralized object systems [Keller et al., 1991]. This operation efficiently assembles the fragments of objects' states required for a particular processing step, and returns them as a complex object in memory. It translates the disk representations of complex objects into readily traversable memory representations. Efficiency is achieved by reordering disk accesses to exploit the physical locations of objects, sharing of subobjects, clustering and selectivity information, and data already present in database buffers. The assembly operation resembles a functional join in that it links objects based on inter-object references.

In [Maier et al., 1993], several strategies for implementing a distributed assembly operation are discussed. One strategy involves shipping all data to a central site for processing. This is straightforward to implement, but could be inefficient in general. A second strategy involves doing simple operations (e.g., selections, local assembly) at remote sites, then shipping all data to a central site for final assembly. This strategy also requires fairly simple control, since all communication occurs through the central site. The third strategy is significantly more complicated: perform complex operations (e.g., joins, complete assembly of remote objects) at remote sites, and then ship the results to the central site for final assembly. A distributed object system may include some or all of these strategies.

4.4 TRANSACTION MANAGEMENT

The transaction concept has been used effectively in traditional database systems to synchronize concurrent accesses to a shared database and to provide reliable access in the face of failures. A transaction is an atomic unit of work against the database. ACID properties of transactions (atomicity, consistency, isolation, and durability) guarantee correct concurrent execution as well as reliability [Bernstein et al., 1987; Gray and Reuter, 1992].

It is commonly accepted that the traditional flat transaction model would not meet the requirements of the advanced application domains that object-oriented data management technology would serve. Some of the considerations are that transactions in these domains are longer in duration requiring interactions with the user or the application program during its execution. In the case of object-oriented systems, transactions do not consist of simple read/write operations, necessitating, instead, synchronization algorithms that deal with complex operations on abstract (and possibly complex) objects. In some application domains, the fundamental transaction synchronization paradigm based on competition among transactions for access to resources has to change to one of cooperation among transactions in accomplishing a common task. This is the case, for example, in cooperative work environments.

In [Martin and Pedersen, 1993] four example applications are considered to argue the point. These examples are (1) collaborative work in an office environment (the "shared desk top" metaphor), (2) a concurrent `make` facility, (3) editing a large document, (4) a CASE environment, and (5) cooperative arrangement of meeting rooms. A number of extensions to the traditional transaction model are identified from these examples categorized as those that *preserve transaction isolation* and those that *isolate cooperation*. The former class of extensions provide transaction properties more flexibly by capturing application semantics while the latter allow localized cooperation between a group of transactions. To preserve isolation, three specific extensions are proposed:

1. use of semantics-based concurrency control using commutativity of operations on objects;
2. identification of the layers of abstraction of a concurrent activity so that low level ordering dependencies can be ignored if higher level operations commute;

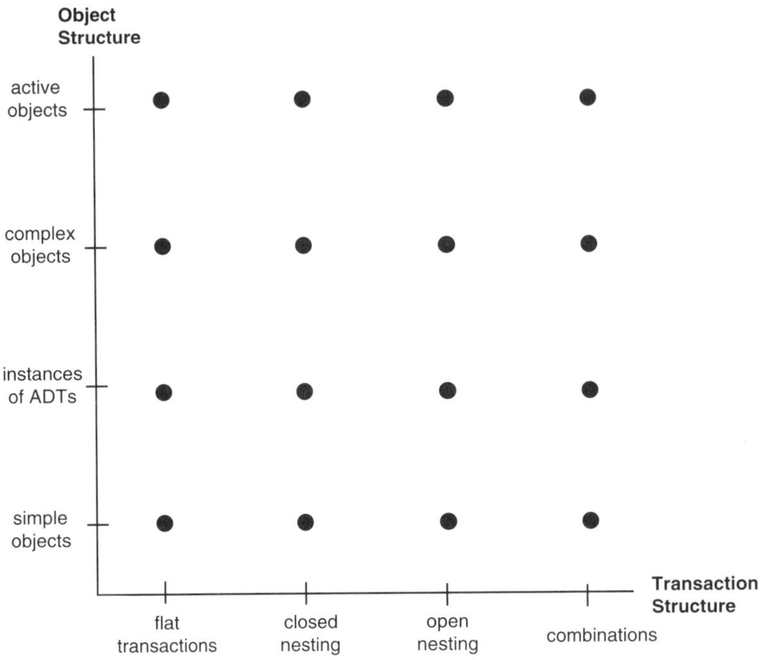

Figure 8: Transaction Model Alternatives

3. separation of the boundaries for failure atomicity and serializability to provide more flexibility.

To support isolation cooperation, the concept of *cooperative atomicity* is introduced. A group of concurrent activities is externally viewed as a single action and synchronized with respect to the group as a whole. Internally, the group of cooperating activities synchronize their own accesses to shared data.

There are a number of ways to characterize transaction management systems. In [Buchmann et al., 1992] these systems are characterized along two dimensions: transaction model and consistency definition. Transaction model is represented by transaction structure and the structure of objects that they operate on (Figure 8).

Each of the points in Figure 8 needs to be mapped to a correctness criterion. Serializability is the most common one of these, but there are others which provide more concurrency. It is not easy, however, to characterize these criteria. In [Ramamritham and Chrysanthis, 1993], the authors develop a taxonomy of correctness criteria and the formal specification of different classes using ACTA [Chrysanthis and Ramamritham, 1990]. The taxonomy follows two dimensions: *database consistency requirements*, and *transaction correctness properties*. Under database consistency requirements, two issues are considered. The first is the unit of consistency, which specifies the sphere of application of the consistency criteria. If the consistency unit is the complete database, then all of the objects in the database have to be locally as well as mutually consistent. The consistency unit can be (location-independent or location-dependent) subsets of the database where mutual consistency is required only for objects in the same subset. Finally, the consistency unit may be specified as individual objects wherein each object in the database is expected to be locally consistent. The second issue that is covered under database consistency requirements is consistency maintenance. The questions that are addressed are "When is a consistency requirement expected to hold?" and "If a consistency requirement does not hold at a point it is supposed to, how is it restored?" Three alternative responses to the first question are identified: at activity boundaries, at specific points of time, and at specific database sates. Two responses to the second question are possible. One is that no restoration of consistency is possible if it does not hold at the point it is supposed to. The second is that consistency is restored in a deferred manner.

The second dimension of the taxonomy is transaction correctness properties. These properties can be presented with respect to four criteria: correctness of transaction results, correctness of transaction structure, correctness of data access related transaction behavior, and correctness of temporal behavior of transactions.

Using the characterization of Figure 8 and the classification of correctness criteria given in [Ramamritham and Chrysanthis, 1993], it is possible to identify a large number of transaction management systems. For example, the point at the lower left-hand corner of the figure (flat transactions on simple objects) coupled with serializability characterizes many of the traditional transaction managers. This point is very well-studied and well-understood. However, object-oriented DBMSs, especially if they have active capabilities (see next section), require transaction managers that reside in the upper right-hand corner of Figure 8 and use correctness criteria that are significantly more relaxed than serializability. The move to that point is not straightforward.

There have been a number of studies along the axes of Figure 8. Of special interest are those studies that deal with nested transaction models and those that operate on abstract data types and on complex objects. Early studies on using a semantics-based correctness criterion to deal with operations on abstract data types are discussed in [Weihl, 1989a] and [Herlihy and Weihl, 1988]. These studies use the commutativity relationship among abstract operations defined over abstract data types to synchronize transactions. The consequence is that the degree of concurrency increases since read-write or write-write operations may commute and may, therefore, be allowed to execute concurrently (e.g., the `enqueue` and `dequeue` operations on a queue commute, and can execute concurrently, even though they correspond to a write-read pair). In [Nakajima, 1993], the work of Weihl is extended. Weihl defines two commutativity-based conflict relations (forward commutativity and backward commutativity) as well as describing concurrency control algorithms to enforce them. These two relations are somewhat difficult to work with since they are quite independent because one depends on the latest committed history while the other depends on the current history (consequently, one is not a subset of the other) and since they require different recovery algorithms. Thus, one or the other has to be chosen for enforcement even though each permit certain operation histories that the other one rejects. Nakajima defines a *general commutative relation* which is a superset of both the forward and the backward commutativity relations [Nakajima, 1993]. To support this generality, the paper argues for the use of multiversion objects since they enable access, at the same time, to both the latest committed states of objects and to their current states. The paper describes concurrency control and recovery algorithms to enforce general commutativity. It also provides a high level discussion of the cost of the approach, but no detailed performance evaluation is provided.

A more general transactional model for supporting advanced applications in distributed object systems is described in [Dayal, 1993]. Instead of the cooperative applications considered in [Martin and Pedersen, 1993], the problem considered is that of automating long duration activities in complex enterprises. Such activities typically have weaker atomicity and consistency requirements than ACID transactions. Shared data resources cannot be locked for the entire duration of an activity. Also, complete rollback on failure and restart are unacceptable. Instead, an activity must be thought of as a collection of steps that can commit and release resources before the end of the activity. An activity may be partially rolled back, with committed steps being compensated for, and rolled forward. The *Activity/Transaction Model* of [Dayal et al., 1991; Dayal, 1993] describes the structure and semantics of activities.

4.5 ACTIVE DISTRIBUTED OBJECTS

Active systems are systems that monitor events of interest, and trigger an appropriate response when an event of interest is detected. Recently, active database systems have become a very active area of research and development [Dayal et al., 1988a; Stonebraker et al., 1990a; Widom and Finkelstein, 1990]. Traditional passive database systems only execute queries or transactions that are explicitly submitted by a user or application. Active database systems, by contrast, store and implement *Event-Condition-Action* rules: when the event is detected, a condition is evaluated; if the condition is satisfied, the action is executed. In active, object database systems, the events of interest typically involve the invocation of operations on objects. Some systems also support other types of events, such as temporal events and transaction events, and composite events that are constructed from simpler events using operations such as disjunction or sequence. Conditions are typically predicates over database states; and actions are arbitrary operations against the database or calls to application programs.

In a distributed active system, rule processing is distributed. The component events of a composite event may occur at different nodes; an event detected at one node may trigger conditions or actions at some other nodes; or, the condition and action may themselves involve distributed operations. Some work has been reported on the semantics of, and protocols for, distributed active databases [Ceri and Widom, 1992]. In that paper, a notion of correctness was defined, in which a distributed execution of rules is deemed correct if it is equivalent to a sequential execution at a single node, However, that work was restricted to relational database systems and simple events.

In [Jagadish and Shmueli, 1993], a formal model for specifying and reasoning about composite events in a distributed active object database system is introduced. A number of operations for constructing composite events are described. In this model, the basic events are points in time. An object event history is a sequence of basic events against a single object. Composite events then are predicates defined over object event histories. A trigger is an event (basic or composite) together with a procedure (the action). The notion of *s-correctness* is introduced as the correctness criterion for distributed execution. It specifies that in a distributed execution, all objects behave as if they were part of a centralized system, i.e., all objects see the same object event histories as in some centralized execution. A number of protocols for ensuring s-correctness are described. These involve centralizing the checking for s-correctness or using the underlying transaction facilities (e.g., object-level locking, optimistic concurrency control), treating events as transactions, to enforce s-correctness.

4.6 OPERATING SYSTEM SUPPORT ISSUES

The problems of building relational DBMSs on top of current operating systems (OSs) has long been recognized within the database community (see, for example, [Gray, 1979; Stonebraker, 1981; Christmann et al., 1987]). The operating system community has also been discussing the difficulty of supporting, with a single set of operating system abstractions, multiple applications with potentially conflicting demands [Kiczales et al., 1992]. The problem is not that OSs provide one set of abstractions, but that they provide a single *implementation* for each of these abstractions. Thus, when a DBMS requires a different implementation for an OS abstraction (such as a file system), the options are limited: either the implementation has to be modified (if there is access to the source code), or the DBMS implementer has to re-implement the abstraction (in some closed OSs, the entire set of abstractions may need to be re-implemented). Clearly, these are not acceptable solutions. The recent movement towards microkernel architectures has the positive effect of reducing the set of abstractions that are implemented within the operating system kernel. The end result is that it is easier to re-implement some of the abstractions that are provided outside the kernel at the user level.

In distributed systems, the situation is further complicated by communication network considerations. Typically, distributed operating systems implement their own communication primitives (for performance reasons), ignoring the standard services offered by the communication protocols. However, a fundamental problem associated with avoiding the standardization efforts is the two-track approach that is being followed. Using the operating system in different networking environments can result in major re-work to accommodate the idiosyncrasies of each individual network architecture. On the other hand, network protocol standardization attempts typically treat the issue in isolation, without sufficient consideration for integration with operating systems. Thus, in distributed environments, the issue is considerably more complicated. We do not intend to go into details of all of these issues; interested readers can refer to above cited literature as well as [Özsu and Valduriez, 1991a]. The above discussion is sufficient to highlight the difficulties.

Object-orientation raises additional issues as well as providing new opportunities to deal with these issues. On the one hand, problems related to providing object management support have to be solved. On the other hand, the uniform use of object-oriented technology in both the DBMS and the OS can overcome some of the difficulties in integrating (or interfacing) them.

One of the major architectural issues is determining where the object management support will be located within the OS. There are three readily identifiable alternatives. The first alternative is to place object management support outside the OS kernel in the user space. The result is an object support layer not unlike the scalable persistent foundation that Atkinson proposes [Atkinson, 1993]. In this case, the OS kernel is not object-oriented and applications that do not require object support can access the kernel directly through kernel calls. Applications (such as OODBMSs, object-oriented programming environments, object-oriented user interfaces, etc) that require a level of object support can be built on top of the object management layer. The second alternative is to put the object management support inside the operating system kernel without the kernel being object-oriented. In this case, the object management services are provided (without exception) to all OS users, but the OS kernel is not developed in an object-oriented fashion. This alternative uniformly provides object management support to all applications and requires them to access kernel services using the particular interface (e.g., messages, invocation, behavior application) the object model supports. A final alternative is to provide object management support at a much lower level and develop the OS kernel using the object-oriented paradigm.

Each of these alternatives have obvious advantages and disadvantages, particularly in terms of their performance implications and the ease with which they can support the development of object-oriented data managers. There are active research projects investigating the design and development of object-oriented operating systems (e.g., [Shapiro, 1993; Cabrera and Jul, 1992]). As a result, some of the issues are fairly well understood; but there are many others that the researchers are uncertain about.

Another fundamental question that needs to be addressed is the nature of object management support that needs to be provided by the object-oriented OS to OODBMSs. [Kulkarni et al, 1993] identifies the following OS requirements: (1) OS has to deal with differing and dynamic resource requirements of applications; (2) the storage hierarchy must be utilized effectively; (3) support should be provided for a variety of cooperation patterns that have different optimizations; (4) cooperation should not be impeded by the heterogeneity of the environment; and (5) the support for interface specification should enable integration of event management. How these requirements can be realized is an open research topic. Dickman argues that the following features of the Bellerophon [Dickman, 1993b] system architecture are well-suited to support an OODBMS: lightweight references, a class-structured object table, and a hybrid garbage collection algorithm. The references in Bellerophon are lightweight resulting in substantial reduction of the space overhead on reference passing while at the same time reducing the CPU overhead of marshalling a reference. It is claimed that this is advantageous for OODBMSs since "constructing additional indices is somewhat eased by having cheap and easily copied references. Furthermore, the transient objects involved in query handling will pass many references to persistent objects as arguments and results; the overhead involved in this is also reduced by the use of small references within the object pools." Bellerophon maintains a local object table at each site (with references to local objects and proxies) which is organized according to classes. Thus, each local object table implicitly contains a "complete set of local class indices" that may be used by the OODBMS in executing queries. Finally, Bellerophon implements a multi-layered hybrid garbage collection algorithm with local and distributed garbage collectors. The efficiency of this hybrid approach as well as the effective garbage collection of transient data is claimed to be advantageous for OODBMSs.

The use of object-orientation in the design and development of both the OS and the OODBMS is expected to assist in properly their "seamless" integration. Even though there is significant promise in this approach, their "object-orientation" may be quite different. For example, operating systems typically implement hardware and software resources as objects; thus objects are *system resources* which are large but have simple consistency specifications. There are few types in the system each usually having a few instances (e.g., there are only a few printers, a limited number of processes, etc). In databases, very large amounts of simple and complex *data* are the objects; they are persistent and have more sophisticated integrity constraints.

The parallel work on object-oriented operating systems and object-oriented database systems should provide us with a better insight into these issues. On the one hand, we learn more about the object management support requirements of OODBMSs; on the other hand, we are learning what set of support services can be efficiently provided by operating systems.

4.7 MULTI-OBJECTBASES AND INTEROPERABILITY

Object-oriented technology plays a dual role in providing interoperability among autonomous, distributed and possibly heterogeneous data repositories. On the one hand, object-oriented DBMSs are yet another form of data repository adding to the complexity. On the other hand, object-orientation, with its encapsulation and abstraction capabilities, may assist in providing interoperability. It is the latter role that is the topic of discussion in this section.

Semantic heterogeneity among data objects is a long-standing problem in multidatabases. When object-oriented DBMSs are included as repositories in multidatabases, the issue surfaces as heterogeneity among types, requiring the definition of mappings between type definitions. In [Chomicki and Litwin, 1993], the problem is dealt with by providing a declarative language in which derived objects, derived types and derived functions can be defined from "base" types, objects and functions in various object-oriented DBMSs. These derived objects are like views, and are not instantiated.

A very similar problem is addressed in [Bratsberg, 1993] but somewhat differently. Bratsberg proposes to separate the extensional and intensional dimensions of classes and defining separate hierarchies for each. Consequently, a class has semantics similar to views (and in this sense there is some similarity with Chomicki and Litwin's work) and the problem of class integration becomes a subset of the problem of schema evolution (evolution of class hierarchies). Class integration is accomplished by connecting two extent graphs (corresponding to two classes) by proper extent propagations. A second problem is the integration of properties which defines the relationships between the properties of the classes that are to be integrated. The paper discusses various ways in which these relationships can be defined and relates this approach to those based on object-oriented views.

There are a number of ways that object-orientation can play a role in assisting interoperability. A common approach is to define a common object model that can be used to represent various objects from different repositories. In this context, it is useful to recall that this is one of the alternatives that Atkinson proposes to deal with the development of applications over heterogeneous and autonomous components (see Section 4.1). Even though the exact features of a "canonical" model that can serve this purpose are yet to be universally agreed upon, there have been a number of model proposals. There are a number of such models defined in this volume [Manola and Heiler, 1993; Castellanos et al., 1993; Kelter, 1993]. A popular approach is to define an object model that is powerful enough to model others (i.e., is a superset of other models) [Castellanos et al., 1993; Kelter, 1993]. An interesting modeling approach is to define a "RISC" object model [Manola and Heiler, 1993] which establishes a common denominator for the description of other data models and via which integration and interoperability can be established. The potential components of such a model are defined in the paper. Some of these are explicit primitives for describing basic object model components such as methods, state, OIDs, and interfaces. The model should also permit the definition of various dispatching and delegation mechanisms, should contain type constructors, a generalized view mechanism and the ability to directly manipulate interface specifications (to describe various variants of type systems).

Another alternative discussed in [Tirri et al., 1993] is to use composite objects to integrate data from various data sources. Some of these data sources may be full-function DBMSs while others may not have DBMS functionality (file systems, etc). The data residing at each data source is viewed as a fragment of a composite object and a set of methods is defined to manipulate these fragments as a single entity. These objects are referred to as *fragment objects* (Figure 1 in [Tirri et al., 1993]) and allow loose integration of data in a bottom-up fashion. One fragment per data source is defined and a number of these fragments are integrated into a federated composite object. Two mappings (translation routines) are defined between a data source and the corresponding federated object fragment: `fragment_to_data` and `data_to_fragment` with obvious semantics. Once created, the federated objects can be accessed via methods that can read and/or update parts of the federated object.

The CORBA standard from Object Management Group (OMG) [OMG, 1991] is one of the standardization efforts to deal with interoperability. It establishes a shared conceptual base, similar to Atkinson's scalable persistent foundation, but CORBA has additional functionality such as a common object model and a common model of interaction between object-oriented components. The common object model is *abstract* and includes objects, values (object names and handles), operations, signatures, types and classes. It defines a high-level interface language to this base.

5 CONCLUSIONS

In this paper we provide an overview of distributed object management technology and the issues that need to be addressed in developing it. In addition to providing an introduction to the topic, the paper serves as a road map for the rest of the book providing a context for the rest of the papers in this volume.

PART 1
SYSTEM ARCHITECTURE

Persistent Foundations for Scalable Multi-Paradigmal Systems

Malcolm Atkinson
University of Glasgow
Department of Computing Science
Glasgow, G12 8QQ
Scotland

Abstract

Problems with the inconsistent behaviour of system construction components for building large and long-lived application systems are identified. They make the programmer's task harder and the user's world more confusing in the same way that the disharmonies between programming languages and databases did. Persistent programming languages overcame those disharmonies.

This paper challenges researchers to design and build a common substrate to the construction components. The construction components would be re-built using the substrate to achieve consistent behaviour. Application systems would then use this new family of construction components. The substrate, called the Scalable Persistent Foundation promises several advantages: consistent application system behaviour even when under stress, accelerated application system building and maintenance, genuine longevity of application systems and improved operational efficiency.

The search for a design and implementation of this foundation will provoke debate about what behaviour, in the context of distribution, overload, failure, change, concurrency, transactions, safety, security, etc. is wanted.

Experiments using short-lived computations and small-scale systems are rarely useful in predicting large-scale and long-term behaviour. Therefore large-scale apparatus and long-term experimental procedures are required.

1 INTRODUCTION

The concept of persistence was introduced [Atkinson et al., 1982] as a means of simplifying the task of programming. In essence the task of programming had not been simplified by the introduction of database systems as intended,[1] instead *application programmers* had an increasingly difficult conceptual task managing the eternal triangle (see Figure 1). They had to match a mapping between the modelled system and the programs with a pair of mappings: the mapping from modelled system to database and thence from database to program. If users are to be convinced that the system is operating correctly then the operations on a database conducted directly and those conducted via the program have to appear consistent.

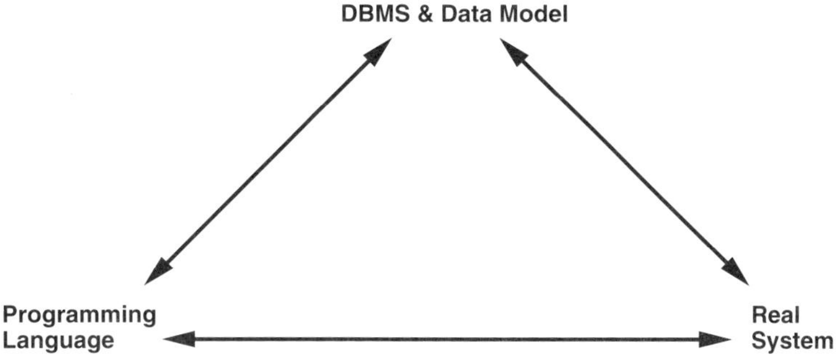

Figure 1: A programmer has to keep three mappings consistent

Achieving this consistency for a few simple programs operating against a *simple* (relational?) database was moderately easy provided the mappings were simple. As soon as there were many programs or the models, programs and mappings became complex, this illusion of consistency became almost unachievable.

In the previous case there are two *constructional components* used to build the application: the programming language and the DBMS. If only one constructional component, a *persistent programming language* is used only one mapping is maintained—a considerable simplification of the conceptual context. This is illustrated in Figure 2 and further described in Section 2. Persistent systems were proposed that used automated data management techniques to maintain the one model across all the time scales encountered. Medium-scale demonstrations showed that programming was simplified and that application systems using them were easier to understand. A summary of relevant work is given in Section 4.

Fundamental to the implementation of all persistent systems is the management of identity (references) and a consistent treatment of program and data. In order to have simple semantics and the potential for large system construction, programs must have the same semantics however long they have been stored in the system and whatever the lifetime of the data on which they operate. An illustration of the engineering issues these requirements raise

[1] Other benefits had been achieved, such as a basis for physical independence and a methodology for large system construction by incrementally binding programs to the central repository of data, which we revisit later in this paper.

Figure 2: Persistence Requires a Single Mapping

is given in Section 5. The challenges encountered are typical of any database management system.

It can be argued that any persistent programming language provides an object-oriented database, though some definitions of object-orientation would restrict the set of persistent programming languages (PPLs) that provide OODBs to those with inclusion polymorphism), i.e. subtyping or bounded parametric polymorphism [Cardelli and Wegner, 1985]. Certainly the experiences of trying to implement persistent programming languages has relevance to object-oriented systems and vice versa. On the other hand some object-oriented database systems are not true persistent systems as they require different treatment of long-lived and short-lived data. The code to manipulate a long-lived object's data is different in some respects from code applied to transient data or the types available in the two contexts differ. This re-introduces the dual model problems; essentially there are now lots of little triangles to manage rather than one big one.

A major concern in large-scale and long-lived system construction is safety. This requires protection which in most persistent programming languages is provided via a strong type system (that is a type system that cannot be evaded, not necessarily an entirely static one). The strength of this protection depends on a closed world. Any chink might let in a malevolent or erroneous piece of code. Realisation of the full potential of persistent systems requires a transformation in application system building habits that cannot be incremental. These issues are further described in Section 6.

The author has recently been involved in the construction of a large system (HMS), distributed over several hospitals and designed to support health care management [Atkinson and England, 1990]. It is probably typical of many large application systems in that it was built using a variety of construction components. One of these was a tailored scripting and control language with persistent tables [Perihelion, 1992]. But other construction components, for example, a relational system, filing systems, an operating system and a distributed window manager, were also in use. The intention is that for all application programmers (domain experts) and all end-users the illusion of a seamless consistent single system operating on a single HMS model would be maintained. Significant effort was invested by the HMS team who constructed the HMS system software to automate data movement, update propagation, conflicting change notification, distributed databases and queries. This is successful for *most* of the time. The problem is that the illusion is not permanently maintained. The moment a system failure occurs, for example the windowing system mysteriously loses a font on one machine or all the machines in a room stop when a fan fails, the illusion of a consistent system fails catastrophically. It requires a guru with a black belt[2] in systems software to organise a restart quickly i.e. with only a moderate amount of file copying, keyboard activity, etc. The distributed and duplicated databases recover themselves and the scripts still run but other parts of the system don't recover.

[2]Matters are usually made *much* worse when a would-be-guru with a green belt attempts to intervene!

It is informative to consider why this is so. An attempt is made to identify the cause of the problem in Section 7. It can be seen as a consequence of attempting to use in combination construction components with different semantics for their preservation and management of data. It is argued that such construction components inevitably have different semantics for their persistence and hence that problems will arise whenever they are stressed. This problem will be manifest in any application system built from heterogeneous construction components, particularly those that are distributed.

An examination of the task of building a complete DBMS for whatever model, a well-engineered PPL or an operating system reveals a certain commonality. It is proposed that by identifying that common substrate and by implementing that once as a low-level persistent language with well defined semantics the problem of inconsistent behaviour from construction components will be overcome. A simple solution is not feasible whereby total applications are re-implemented in this persistent language for two reasons:

- existing investment is lost, particularly: the training of programmers, the existing data and the existing software; and
- different construction components and paradigms may be best for different parts of an application.

A two-level architecture, Scalable Persistent Foundations (SPF), is therefore proposed (see Section 8) whereby the traditional construction components are *all re-implemented* in a common persistent programming language, call it LLPL. These components then exhibit their familiar behaviour except with respect to persistence where they all exhibit a common semantics. The applications are then built out of these re-implemented construction components, LLPL and any other components that are made possible by the new architecture such as a variety of programming languages, all of which will have become PPLs, new software engineering tools and extensive libraries relevant to persistent application programming.

This architecture is proposed because:

1. it is more likely to yield understandable contexts for application programming and predictable application system behaviour for users and programmers than alternative architectures;
2. it is necessary if the data currently being committed to Object-Oriented Databases and Persistent System stores is to remain useable over typical application system life-times;
3. it is expected to provide a basis for building construction components more economically, in research initially and when proven, in industry;
4. the attempt to identify its properties will focus the discussion on what common behaviour is required irrespective of whether it is achieved by this or some other architecture;
5. it will draw research in operating systems, database systems, persistent languages and distributed systems into a collaborative effort towards achieving a common goal; and
6. a clearly identified substrate would result in sharply defined demands on hardware architectures, network protocols and operating system micro-kernels.

It is a complete inversion of the approach to disharmony being advocated elsewhere [OMG, 1991]. In those approaches a layer is placed *above* the construction components to try to hide their intrinsic behaviour and expose a consistent composite behaviour. This is a natural short-term approach and is valuable as a mechanism for developing collaborative working in the software industry [OMG, 1991] but the extent to which consistent behaviour and long-term persistence can be achieved in this way is limited, while it does little if anything to simplify the application programmer's task.

The claims of an alternative architecture cannot be trivially evaluated. In the case of a putative architecture for large-scale, long-lived and distributed-application systems this is particularly true. A radically different architecture requires an investigation on the scale of large science to validate its claims. Such an experiment is proposed here (see Section 14). It is an example of a new requirement for experimental facilities and large-scale coordinated research in computing science.

The remainder of this paper is presented in two parts:

1. a brief survey (Sections 2 to 7) of current work in persistent languages aimed at providing the reader with entry points to that work and at filling in the background that motivates the SPF proposal; and

2. a development of the SPF idea, identifying some of the major questions and requirements, leading to a sketch of the proposed experiment and the way in which it might be conducted (see Sections 8 to 14).

This attempt to bring together all the issues concerned with a complete persistent architecture inevitably treats each individual issue cursorily. But it is the juxtaposition of all these issues that is the real challenge for the large and long-term persistent architecture. Individually they may be difficult challenges but not intractable. Consistent and feasible solutions to carefully chosen subsets can also be envisaged but where is the research that tackles the whole problem, by this or any other architecture?

2 PERSISTENCE DEFINED

This section and the following five are an introduction to the issues explored by persistent programming research over the last twelve years. Readers familiar with these issues may wish to skip to Section 8.

Persistent systems make *uniform* provision for the storage and use of data irrespective of those data's lifetimes.

For example, if particular data, say relations, can be created and stored for very long periods then it should be possible to have similar data that is short-lived, as a local variable in a procedure perhaps. Similarly, if a datum such as a list or tree can be created and used within a program's execution it should also be given the potential for a longer useful lifetime.

Two principles guide the provision of persistence:

1. **Persistence Independence**: The semantics of all or part of a program is not changed by changes in the longevity of the data to which it is applied; and

2. **Persistence Orthogonality**: The same facilities for persistence are accorded to data irrespective of the type of that data.

These principles arise from the original motive for providing persistence. Persistence is intended to make it much easier to build application software that works with combinations of short-term and long-lived data. Initially the need was recognized in the context of building CAD systems. In that context, sophisticated programs manipulate complex data which models some aspects of an artefact (electrical circuit, diesel engine, digital chip, aircraft, etc.) on behalf of designers. During a calculation or a design session there is much transitory data, but the design is of enduring interest, in the examples given measured in years or decades. Usually there is the added complication of many programs, each modelling different aspects of the common design.

Programmers are already challenged to build adequate models of the real artefact. Consider for a moment the design of a diesel engine. The shape of the cylinder and piston has to be modelled. The structure, stresses and heat flow in the cylinder head has to be modelled. The injection, mixing of the fuel and the chemistry and physics of its explosion has to be modelled. Interfaces have to be provided that enable designers to visualize this total system and adjust its parameters, e.g. the shape of the piston, and assess aspects of its manufacture and performance.

Building tools to make and manipulate such models just once is enough effort for any application programming team. They should be able to build them with data structures appropriate for the task in hand, i.e. manipulating the model and making it simulate the real system. Lumbering those programmers with the additional intellectual task of moving that data in and out of some long-term repository, organising its reliable storage and worst still requiring them to map it to a different stored form based on a different data model is clearly an impediment to their work.

The principles follow in consequence. If persistence were provided non-orthogonally then the "natural" model would sooner or later use some data structure whose type had limited persistence. If it only existed transiently within executions the programmers would need to remember to always translate it to something else whenever they stored a designer's work. If it had only long-term storage rights they would find themselves having to build some equivalent to hold the related data that was generated during calculations.

If program had different semantics depending on the longevity of the data on which it worked programmers would continually have to write two versions of their code, one that worked correctly when the data came from earlier design sessions and one for the data recently created. Then they have to contrive to use the correct mixtures of code according to the sources of data in any given calculation.

It is boring to re-iterate the case for these principles, however, it is necessary. Systems appear today, which as a short cut to the market place or in the pursuit of local rather than global economies, fail to comply with the principles and generate the programming problems caricatured in the preceding two paragraphs: object-oriented systems where the data types available in objects aren't identical with those used in the language(s) in which program (methods, procedures, programs) are written; object-oriented systems in which the data has to be explicitly fetched from the database; object-oriented systems which have different name spaces in their long-term repositories from those in programs; and object-oriented systems which present a different semantics when viewed via their query language from the semantics they present to programmers. The motivation for these object-oriented systems is to facilitate the construction of large and sophisticated applications such as the ones illustrated above. If the market place is rational, those where these fundamental flaws are obvious will be a short-lived novelty as they will soon be found out. We should be concerned about those where the flaws are less obvious and the cases where the market is irrational through ignorance. There the investments made in application building on shaky foundations may be very substantial and totally wasted.

There are many consequences of the two principles of persistence. For example the principle of persistence independence ultimately requires that type checking should not be any different if data is generated by one program, stored for an arbitrary period and then used in another program. Persistence independence also forbids constructs which expect programmers to explicitly organise data movement and requires that constructs used to organise concurrency, transactions and recovery are equally available for short-term and long-lived data.

The main consequence of persistence orthogonality is that all types have to be supported over the full range of lifetimes. This includes the recursive types [Hoare, 1975] which have references in their implementations. In consequence providing long-lived and reliable identity was one of the principle challenges facing PPL implementors from the beginning.

3 PERSISTENT APPLICATION SYSTEMS

Persistent Application Systems (PAS) are a class of applications in which the provision of good quality persistence is a prerequisite for their success. The health care and diesel engine design examples already given are indicative of their general form. Other examples are: support for the work of a city engineer's office, support for the operational management of a power distribution network, computer integrated manufacturing, scientific databases built and maintained by an extensive group of scientists and geographic information systems. PAS are systems where computers (together with communications and other technology) are deployed to support *cooperative* human activity. The people involved are attempting to construct and/or operate some complex system (the target) and use a shared computer model to help them do it.

The shared model is important as:

1. it represents the state of the target and it is easier to get useful information from the model than the target;
2. it allows people to communicate with others as they input details into the model and others extract them, not necessarily in the same combinations or in the same form;
3. it supports analysis, experiment and consistency checking; and
4. in the operational management, control and manufacturing contexts at least may be the intermediary, implementing in the target system operations that humans have performed on the model.

Communication is often the most significant of these when assessing the impact of a PAS on an organization. That communication takes place in both space (to someone in some other place) and in time (to someone trying to find out what was done hours or even decades later). Builders of PAS have a responsibility to recognize and honour both these forms of communication requirement.

The trend in PAS is towards much more sophisticated models requiring very large amounts of program. At the same time the scope of a typical PAS is broadening, larger and more disparate groups are to be supported in a wider range of cooperative work. Finally, the groups of people do not operate in isolation, but interact with other groups, hence PAS must interact with other PAS on their behalf. The requirements of a group change, groups split and merge, and consequently a PAS must also have the ability to evolve, adapt, merge and split.

Our long-term goal must therefore be to make it easier to build and maintain such PAS. To cope with the volumes of program and data, the very long time scales and the ability to evolve that they require.

4 SURVEY OF PERSISTENT PROGRAMMING SYSTEMS

The requirements for persistent programming languages were first published in 1978 [Atkinson, 1978]. An initial implementation of a data type complete PPL was achieved by 1981 [Atkinson et al., 1982; Atkinson et al., 1983b; Atkinson et al., 1983c]. A fuller story of the development of a variety of persistent languages can be obtained by reading the references of "Figure 1 History of Persistent Programming" in [Atkinson, 1989].

Important landmarks in the development of these languages were:

1. development and exploitation of persistent procedures [Atkinson and Morrison, 1985] which have provided the basis for encapsulation and protection, active and object-oriented models and incremental system construction;
2. a recognition of the rôle played by dynamic and incremental binding [Atkinson et al., 1988];
3. the provision of a construct to hold an extensible set of bindings and to localise dynamic binding, so that incremental system development is safely achievable [Dearle, 1989]; and
4. the development of type-safe linguistic reflection [Stemple et al., 1992].

A general issue in these languages, partly driven by research into programming languages and partly by the special needs of persistence, is the development of type systems which are further discussed in Section 6. The relationship of PPLs with database programming languages has been surveyed [Atkinson and Buneman, 1987].

There are a number of workshops and conferences where current work on persistent languages may be found, these are summarised in Table 1.

5 ENGINEERING PERSISTENT SYSTEMS

Several challenges have been encountered while trying to produce well engineered PPLs and associated programming environments. Mechanisms had to be developed for incremental binding between existing data[3] and new programs. To prevent this invalidating the type system, incremental checking of the structural equivalence of types had to be implemented with sufficient efficiency to accommodate relatively rare dynamic binding events during

[3] Henceforth in this paper it is assumed that procedures, abstract data types and other values which contain code are **all** included as first class values in the type system. Hence "data" will normally mean all data including the data that is program such as procedures.

Event	Proceedings
POS1	Data Types and Persistence, Atkinson, Morrison & Buneman (eds), Springer-Verlag, 1988
POS3	Persistent Object Stores, Rosenberg & Koch (eds), Springer-Verlag, 1989
POS4	Implementing Persistent Object Bases, Dearle, Shaw & Zdonik (eds), Morgan Kaufmann, 1990
POS5	To be announced, Albano & Morrison (eds), Springer- Verlag, 1992
DBPL1	Advances in Database Programming Languages, Bancilhon & Buneman (eds), ACM Press with Addison-Wesley, 1990
DBPL2	Database Programming Languages, Hull, Morrison & Stemple (eds), Morgan Kaufmann, 1989
DBPL3	Proceedings of the Third Int. Workshop on DBPLs, Kanellakis & Schmidt (eds), Morgan Kaufmann, 1991
Bremen	Security and Persistence, Rosenberg & Keedy (eds), Springer-Verlag, 1990
HICSS22	Persistent Programming Systems Sections in Proceedings of the Twenty Second Hawaii International Conference on Systems Sciences, Shriver, IEEE Press, 1989
HICSS25	Architectural and Operating Systems for Persistent Object Systems & Persistent Object Systems Sections in Proceedings of the Twenty Fifth Hawaii International Conference on Systems Sciences, Shriver, IEEE Press, 1992
IWOOOS2	Proceedings of the Int. Workshop on Object-Orientation in Operating Systems, Cabrera, Russo & Shapiro (eds), Palo Alto, IEEE Computer Society Press, 1991
IWOOOS3	Proceedings of the Int. Workshop on Object-Orientation in Operating Systems, Lea & Jul (eds), Dourdan, France, IEEE Press, 1992

Table 1: Sources of Papers on Persistence

execution [Connor et al., 1990a]. Representing and storing all the types that may occur is an interesting problem; polymorphic procedures, ADTs and the data they produce are examples [Morrison et al., 1991].

Perhaps the most challenging problem is to implement a store that meets the following combination of requirements:

- manage the various memories and storage devices, allocating and recovering space, giving the illusion of an indefinitely large store;
- provide stable references (needed to implement all recursive types [Hoare, 1975] and to provide persistent block retention semantics for procedures [Johnston, 1971]);
- provide a reliable store that offers recovery after various kinds of failure [Brown, 1988];
- provide mechanisms for concurrent use of data; and
- provide a transactional mechanism to allow programs to voluntarily withdraw updates that they have grouped together and to control their release of revised information.

Many solutions to parts of the problem exist. For exampling swizzling can be combined with various disc block copying strategies to provide the references and the recovery over large stores [Moss, 1989]. In this case reasonably explicable recovery is provided but the transaction and concurrency mechanisms are likely to exhibit phantom recovery and locking. An extreme example is the simple provision of recovery and transactions by manipulating the paging mechanism [Wilson et al., 1992]. Remember that when paging or block copying is used the copies and recovery and therefore probably the locking are of whole pages. Consequently items co-resident with objects in use will be locked and recovered. This generates locking and recovery effects that are nothing to do with the logic of programs or data, but are coincidences generated by the placement and usage patterns. Such phenomena subvert the intended goal of freeing the programming task from distracting anomalies.

These anomalies can be entirely unpredictable in the higher-order languages. For example, a procedure collected from a library may have been the result of some earlier procedure application and contain encapsulated data, probably stored in a remnant of the generating procedure's activation record. The user of the procedure from the library doesn't wish to know about its life history. Even if that is known there is nothing the programmer can do to predict a lock on or recovery of the activation record, let alone program around such events. Furthermore, several procedures could have been generated in the original activation and these will interact on their common hidden data even if they are used in different transactions. Lock interferance here may be intentional or one of the coincidences just described. How can the application programmer be informed as to which kind of event has really occurred? It may be tempting to ignore the problem, arguing that the application program is only delayed until the lock clears. But if the system is stressed these problems may occur often leading to deadlocks or performance degradation which will become the concern of the hapless programmer.

Pursuing the details of these challenges is not appropriate in this paper. For recent work the reader is referred to [Brown and Rosenberg, 1990; Brown et al., 1992; Zezula and Rabitti, 1992; Vaughan and Dearle, 1992; Wilson et al., 1992; Wolczko, 1992].

6 PERSISTENT TYPE SYSTEMS

In persistent programming languages the type system has three rôles:

1. to describe data so that its use and interpretation may be better understood by programmers;
2. to limit the programs that may be written in order to make programming safer; and
3. to describe data so that its properties are communicated from the programmer to the compiler and onward to the run-time support and storage machinery so that they may store and manipulate it more efficiently.

Type systems are languages for describing types and the mechanisms whereby sentences in those languages are interpreted. *Types* are denoted by expressions in the type algebra provided by the type system. *Variables* have types which denote the subset of values they may hold. Each *value* has a type. It is useful to note how this vocabulary relates to that used in databases [Nikhil, 1988]; see Table 2.

Programming Languages	Databases
Type System	Data Model
Type	Schema
Variable	Database
Value	Instantaneous DB Extent

Table 2: Vocabulary Equivalences between Databases and Programming Languages

There are many conflicting forces influencing the designer of a type system, as shown in Figure 3.

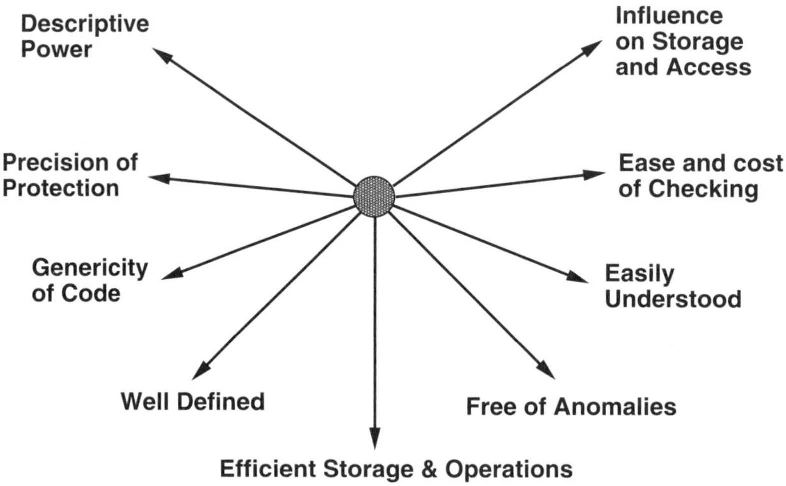

Figure 3: Forces Influencing Type System Design

Research into type systems has attempted to make program parts more re-usable through the use of various kinds of polymorphism [Cardelli and Wegner, 1985]. In the context of persistent languages this has been developed as universal parametric polymorphism [Morrison et al., 1990] and various forms of inclusion polymorphism providing subtyping and inheritance [Curien and Ghelli, 1992; Castagna et al., 1992; Albano et al., 1991]. Recently Connor has analysed the options for resolving some of the difficulties that occur when sharing, update and inclusion polymorphism are combined [Connor et al., 1991] and developed a model of bounded parametric polymorphism [Connor and Morrison, 1992] which solves the type information loss problem encountered in subtyping. Quest [Cardelli, 1990], Modula-3 [Cardelli et al., 1989] and TYCOON [Matthes, 1992; Matthes and Schmidt, 1992] are also developing practical and sophisticated typing systems.

The advantage of these more sophisticated type systems is that they allow more programs to be written by being more precise about the exact restrictions placed on the combination of operations and data. This not only allows for more re-usable code but it also enables better type description from the programmer's point of view. The expressions in the type algebra may now describe a set of possible values and their usage very precisely and may also be given a suggestive name and used by name in other type expressions. Furthermore these expressions may be parametric and so describe a way of combining types with which they are parameterised. This allows application specific or general purpose structures to be named. For example:

type Set [ElementType] **is** ...
...
type Students **is** Set[Student]
type Staff **is** Set[Employee]
...

In the above example the structure *Set* was named and later it was used to name two set types *Students* and *Staff*.

Abstract data types are used to completely encapsulate data, making the operations on it precisely limited to those provided. In Napier88 the type **any** is used to denote an infinite discriminated union type so that limits may be placed on type checking. This allows incremental matching of types; essential when they reach the scale encountered in schemata.[4] Any operation that projects a value out of **any** will invoke further typechecking. Other significant uses of **any** are:

1. to allow code to be written which will handle data not yet specified;
2. to provide an interface for type enquiry when generating type-safe code that provides type dependent behaviour via reflection [Dearle and Brown, 1988; Kirby, 1992; Stemple et al., 1992];
3. to act as place holders for parts of schemata that are yet to be specified while code operates against the parts already defined.

The type **env** in Napier88 denotes an updateable set of bindings [Dearle, 1989]. Each binding holds an identifier, a locality in which a value may reside, the type constraining that value and constancy information. Thus the **env** values in the language act as the locus of incremental construction as additional bindings are added to them. To permit safe incrementality the type requirements of any identifier being introduced into scope are verified dynamically. If the data made accessible in this way are large and/or the introduction occurs in the outer scopes of programs then the cost of dynamic checks is relatively small. As the constructional tools now run in a persistent environment it is also possible to perform the introduction and verification earlier, e.g. this leads to early feedback to programmers, to further reduction in text input and checking costs, and to novel program structures [Kirby et al., 1992; Farkas et al., 1992].

A recurring interest in the type system research for persistent languages is the appropriate treatment of bulk types [Atkinson and Buneman, 1987]. These types describe regular structures such as: sets, relations, finite maps, sequences and trees. The description is advantageous to programmers as it identifies the regularity and this may then be exploited via an algebra of bulk operations. The description is also advantageous to implementors as the scale and regularity make optimisation both possible and worthwhile. Questions

[4] A particular program is usually concerned only with data described by some small subgraph of the schema against which it runs

arise about the form of these types, the extent to which they should be built-in and their prerequisites such as equality and order [Atkinson et al., 1991; Matthes and Schmidt, 1991]. Consistent notations may be provided over such types with the power and convenience of query languages but with a natural and consistent relationship with the rest of the programming language [Trinder, 1991].

The repertoire of constructs available in type systems would appear to offer similar descriptive power to that in the data models. The ability to declare new parametric constructs should allow all semantic description to be captured. These claims are difficult to verify since equivalent care in developing and presenting definitions has to be taken and assessment of the efficacy of descriptions in communication with humans is difficult. Valid comparisons also require supporting tools and real applications.

For recent work the reader is referred to [Connor et al., 1989; Connor et al., 1990b; Ohori et al., 1990; Connor et al., 1990a; Atkinson et al., 1991; Connor et al., 1991; Connor, 1991; Connor and Morrison, 1992].

7 USING MULTIPLE SYSTEM COMPONENTS

The target of the research considered here is to better support the construction, maintenance and operation of PAS (see Section 3). It is informative to consider their present support. This comprises a number of construction components: operating system, user interface management system (UIMS), various DBMS, various programming languages, a communications system, etc. Consequently, for the programmer or user the PAS looks more complex than the eternal triangle (see Figure 1). A more realistic current structure is shown in Figure 4.

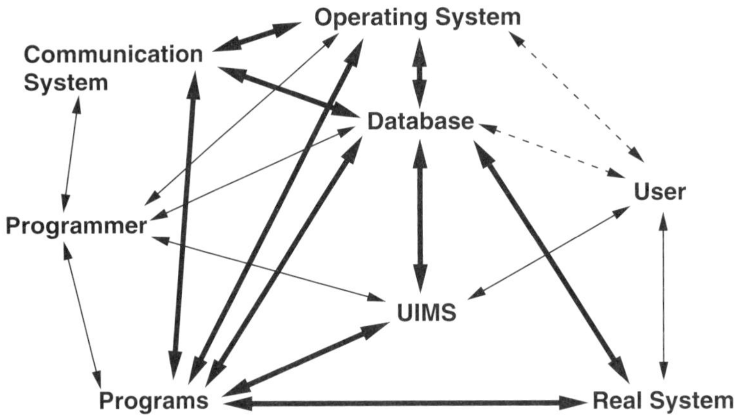

Figure 4: Structure of a Typical PAS

The heavy arrows denote mapping or relationships that have to be understood and maintained by programmers, the light arrows denote the components each class of person has to understand and the interrupted arrows are undesirable awareness by users of construction components. As explained above these intrude into the user's awareness due to the failure modes of the PAS. An alternative view depicting the method of constructing a PAS is shown in Figure 5. This shows part of the cause of the problem. The various constructional components that support the PAS are designed and built independently, guided by different research and industrial cultures. During their construction little consideration was given to consistency which would aid interworking with other construction components. Large and complex PAS need a multiplicity of construction components. Therefore a strategy saying that only one generalised component can be used is doomed from the start.[5]

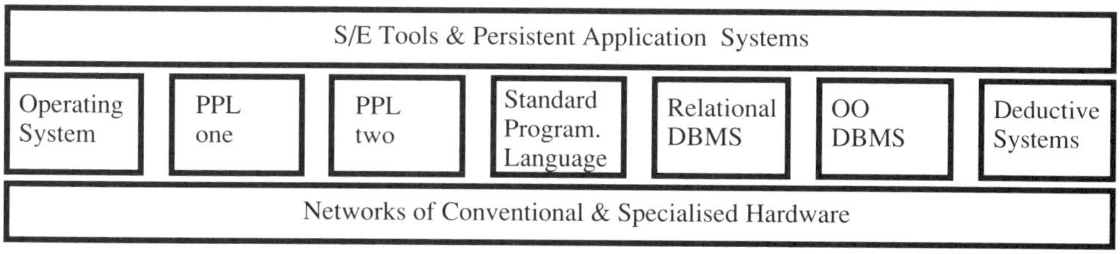

Figure 5: Complex PAS Support

The multiplicity of construction components serve three purposes:

1. they identify and provide services and subsystems that are useful, capturing particular ways of handling *different* parts of the computational and constructional processes;
2. as such they each embody the accumulated understanding of how to perform *their* part of the PAS task and hence it is a significant economy to re-use them; and
3. they provide a means of dividing the labour of building PAS so that subsidiary industries may make the construction components and recover their cost over many PAS.

Figure 6 exposes a property of the implementation of the construction components themselves. Many of them, despite the fact that they service very different needs, have a substantial number of sub-components serving common functional requirements. These repeated sub-components are just those that deal with the provision of generalised persistence, such as recovery, concurrency, distribution, accounting, etc. They typically account for a large part of the construction component (95% in the case of System R [King, 1980]). It is marginal differences in the behaviour of sub-components that purport to provide the same service that cause the problems when systems are under stress, whereas differences in the special part of each construction component are precisely those that are useful. The replicated common functionality can also be seen as unnecessary repetition of work that would be better amortised over many construction components.

The model of PAS so far presented is a simplification. It omits to distinguish several types of programmer[6] and system builder and ignores the fact that many additional construction components are built within the PAS or for a family of PAS[7] using the original construction components. Similarly the construction components themselves may often be built out of

[5] It is about as sensible as saying all buildings will be built using only concrete, albeit very good concrete, denying the use of windows, doors, lifts, etc.

[6] Those that provide generic packages and those that work with high levels of domain specific knowledge are examples.

[7] For example, a shape modelling solid geometry package and a fluid dynamics package, in the diesel engine design PAS.

Operating System	Relational DBMS	Persistent PL	O-O DBMS	
Files, Directories Shell, Processes	Relations, Schemata, QLs	Types, Values, Operations	Objects, Sets, O-OQLs	Special Parts
Persistence, Stability, Recovery, Concurrency, Scheduling, Space Admin., Protection, Accounting, Resource Alloc. & Control, Naming, Binding Programs to Data	Persistence, Stability, Recovery, Concurrency, Scheduling, Space Admin., Protection, Accounting, Resource Alloc. & Control, Naming, Binding Programs to Data	Persistence, Stability, Recovery, Concurrency, Scheduling, Space Admin., Protection, Accounting, Resource Alloc. & Control, Naming, Binding Programs to Data	Persistence, Stability, Recovery, Concurrency, Scheduling, Space Admin., Protection, Accounting, Resource Alloc. & Control, Naming, Binding Programs to Data	COMMON PARTS

Figure 6: Undesirable Replication of Effort

other families of construction components, so the decomposition may be recursive. The construction and the relationships are indeed more complex but the simplified picture will suffice for most of the arguments in this paper.

8 A SCALABLE PERSISTENT ARCHITECTURE

Figure 7 depicts the illusion of a single coherent PAS that is desirable to present to the user.

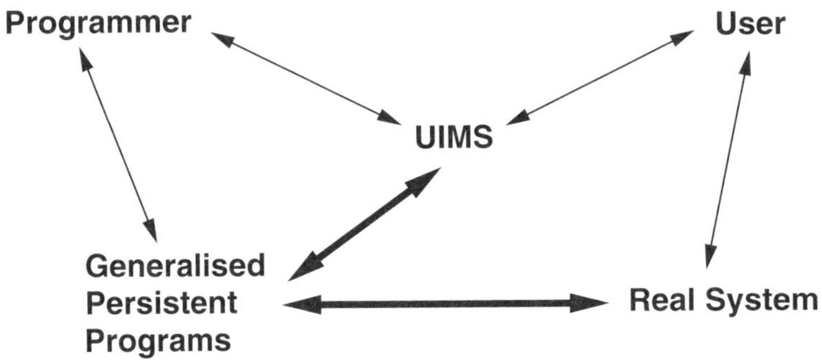

Figure 7: The Goal of Simpler PAS

The UIMS has remained distinct as it may play a major rôle in allowing users to work with many PAS and will certainly develop independently. It will however be changed by and will exploit good quality mechanisms for persistence. For example it will store its fonts and user profiles in the reliable store provided. The application programmer, particularly those that work in the domain specific end of the work should now be given a simple[8] environment in which to program.

A challenge for computing science research is to establish the best architecture for the construction of PAS, call it a Scalable Persistent Architecture. Four lines of response are possible:

Laissez faire Ignore the problem either hoping it will go away or be resolved by market forces;

Obtain Standard Behaviour Coerce *all* the construction component providers to adopt a precise common standard for *all* the issues in the common parts;

Arrange a Cover Up Provide a "veneer" that hides *all* the inconsistencies; or

Simplify Components Provide a common substrate that provides most of the critical functionality of construction components but leaves them able to exhibit their essential differences when they have been re-written using this substrate.

The OMG [OMG, 1991] initiative is adopting the second policy. Their call for common service specifications is however a step in the direction of the fourth policy. Clearly any research programme that makes significant progress on the fourth policy will, *inter alia*, benefit the second policy. The cover up policy is a caricature of many of the efforts in interoperability and heterogeneous system technology [Landers and Rosenberg, 1982]. It has the advantage that some of the uniformity of behaviour can be obtained with relatively little effort compared with the second and fourth policies. However, to get truly uniform behaviour may take a very thick "veneer" or may even be unachievable given the behaviour of underlying systems. It does however offer the best promise for short- and medium-term results, as it avoids re-implementation of large constructional components, and will remain important technology for managing PAS transitions and for interworking between PAS where strongly coupled behaviour is not required and inconsistency will be expected and tolerated.

This paper espouses the fourth policy for reasons given above (see Section 1) and because it is believed that in the long term it will give best PAS behaviour and performance and will significantly encourage the provision of more useful construction components. The proposed architecture is shown in Figure 8 modulo the caveat about simplification that was given above and with the reminder that the particular construction components actually shown are illustrative examples.

The important new system component proposed by this architecture is the Scalable Persistent Foundation (SPF). This provides all the common services needed by programmers building construction components but is not normally used directly by application programmers. Its facilities are exercised via one interface called LLPL (Low-Level Persistent Language). Once the actual facilities to be provided by SPF through LLPL have been precisely identified it would be constructed to very high engineering standards, possibly on top of a micro-kernel platform. In order to achieve the goal of longevity for PAS the commitments made by the SPF definition must be sufficiently independent of particular technology that they can be kept for many decades.

[8] In the sense of free of distractions, as it will probably be rich in available construction components — only some of which are relevant to any given programmer.

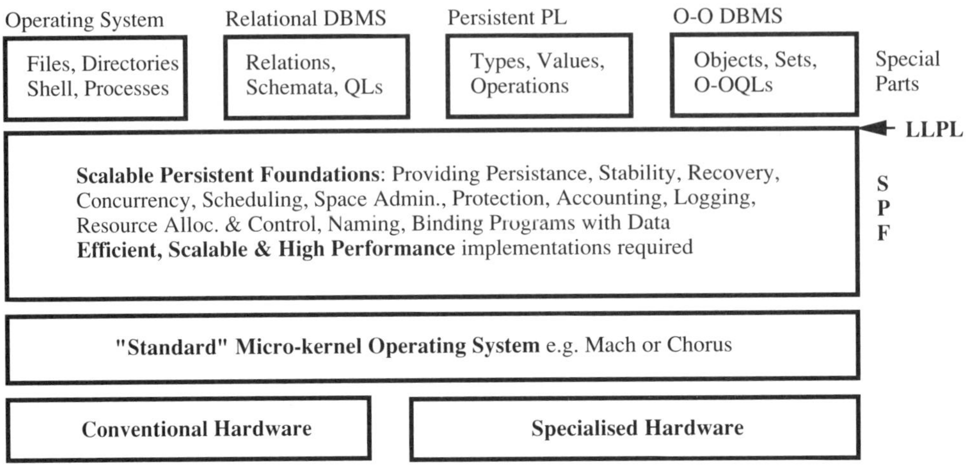

Figure 8: Common PAS Support

The remaining sections of this paper begin the discussion of the form that SPF and LLPL should take. The only strong statement this paper makes about the architecture is that this common substrate should be identified and built. It does not claim to have a definitive list of its required functions. Nor does it claim to specify any one of those functions, these are matters for research and debate. What is clear is that:

- the maximum gain from the SPF is achieved if it offers significant functionality to the construction component builders;
- there is a minimum functionality necessary to ensure reasonably consistent construction component behaviour, which would be enforced, i.e. there would be no direct access to the micro-kernel from construction components; and
- there is a maximum enforced functionality tolerable before it starts impeding the construction components from meeting their validly different goals.

A possible outcome of this research is that it will discover that there are no realistic SPF because the minimum functionality exceeds the maximum functionality as defined above. If this is a problem that is encountered it may be relieved by building SPF for useful subsets of constructional components.

9 ACHIEVING REASONABLE LONGEVITY

An example of a PAS given in Section 3 was a system supporting the work of city engineers. The main sewers of Paris were built by Napolean's engineers about 180 years ago. In contrast files I have constructed with various applications on my computer in the last three years are no longer useable as the technology moved on and the application packages didn't. Today we mostly store data indirectly, via some applications package and its direct use and interpretation is extremely difficult. Imagine the consternation in a city engineer's office if the data about the sewers (or any other service) became inaccessible after only twenty years.

Yet more and more of the data within PAS are being stored in forms that are only known to programs and are virtually meaningless without the corresponding code. The trend towards object-oriented systems (persistent programming for that matter) exacerbates this problem. Now the code and data are intimately bound together and with proper encapsulation the data are not even accessible without the code. So in the future, in order to achieve reasonable longevity, not only the data values but also all the code will need to migrate across the successive technologies that support the SPF and hence the PAS.

The old solutions will no longer work. Old databases and files were moved forward by effective data translation technology, for example EXPRESS [Shu et al., 1977]. This will no longer be possible because humans are no longer aware of the precise formats in use (they are the results of decisions by applications programmers compounded with those of construction component builders, for example compiler writers) and it is no longer straightforward to locate all the data. In any case, if that data were translated the programs (e.g. methods in objects) would no longer function correctly. They too would need translation to the equivalent code. But these translations have to be done in tandem while preserving the bindings between program and data.

No technology is available at present that can perform this, but, unless we postulate that contrary to previous experience computer technology will stop developing, this technology is an essential prerequisite of persistence over moderate timescales. SPF has to guarantee such longevity.

How might this be achieved? If the LLPL ensured that all data (including program) was stored with a sufficient description this would suffice. The interface that it provided could require this whenever types and code were deposited. The additional information could normally be provided by compilers and other constructional components and would not be a further burden on applications programmers. The volume of data involved is small since it could be factored out of individual items and be reachable by reference or context.

The challenge is to identify precisely what extra data is needed and to find ways of expressing it that are independent of the current computer architectures so that there is confidence that equivalent code and representations can always be found. A similar architectural independence was required for ANDF/TDF [Defence Research Agency, 1991; Defence Research Agency, 1992]. In the case of code, reverse translation is not possible, so it will be necessary to store some intermediary form of code from which the executable code can be regenerated.

10 SAFETY REQUIREMENTS

Another prerequisite is that the data be adequately protected against accident and malevolence. The relative merits of various forms of protection have been discussed elsewhere [Brown et al., 1990]. At the very least the fundamental properties of the data managed by the SPF and on which the SPF depends for its correct functioning must be inviolable.

For example, the SPF will need to distinguish between persistent references[9] and the scalar (bit pattern data) so that the integrity of references and of space allocation can be maintained under changing circumstances. The LLPL interface must not allow a program to present an arbitrary bit pattern as a reference or to overwrite a location constrained to hold references

[9] At least the subset that can traverse space management boundaries.

without ensuring the replacement is a valid reference and that any protocols needed for space and reference management have been completed.

Similarly code must be distinguished from the scalar data and references. It is clear that fundamental damage could be done if an LLPL implementation were ever to let a sequence of references or scalars be executed as code. Furthermore any code cannot be let into the SPF domain; it must have been checked that it complies with any rules that are not checked dynamically.

Consequently, at the very least, for safety the SPF/LLPL must ensure that scalar data, references and code are immiscible. That is, there must be no operations available in the LLPL interface that could violate their separation.

But this leaves a problem; a major class of construction components, the compilers or linkers, need to generate code.[10] Conventional compilers overcome this problem by creating files as some kind of scalar data that happens to have the same bit pattern as the required code. The file is then re-opened as an executable program. This is not a safe operation — the file appears to have changed type and the operation could have been applied to a file not produced by a compiler.

In order to perform this operation in a persistent store or any other context that relies on type checking to preserve safety and integrity it is necessary to supply the compiler with "magic" which is a small amount of trustworthy code that takes the data in a form that the compiler was able to produce, e.g. a vector of integers into which the compiler was able to write, and turns it into a form which is no longer available for read and write operations but is now susceptible to execute operations [Atkinson and Morrison, 1987]. This provides a minimum foundation for reflection [Stemple et al., 1992] which then allows the system to become populated with code. All the constructional tools will then use this reflection as they enable people to build constructional components and PAS.

One way in which this reflective magic could be provided is for LLPL to include operations which take code, in the form output by compilers, and transform it to the form required in the store. It could, at the same time, verify that the necessary information for longevity had been provided as the ANDF [Defence Research Agency, 1991] installers do.

The minimal protection considered above could be extended towards a more complete and modern type system (see Section 6). The problem here is to be certain that this did not unduely restrict the efficiency with which the construction components could store data. For example, if a language that uses LLPL as its target traditionally packs records and vectors, or an image handling package wishes to compress the data they should be able to do this. The choice of the appropriate level of types in LLPL and the extent, above the minimum given above that they are mandatory is a major design issue. However, the type information can provide the framework for providing the information needed for data longevity.

If a more sophisticated type system is used then the magic needs to be extended to include a mechanism for introducing new types, or more precisely new identification via type algebraic expressions of types, into the SPF. Again this can be part of the reflection mechanisms accessible through LLPL.

---

[10]This is just a special, but obvious case; there is a problem creating any new value and placing it in the store — it has to be denoted in some way before it can be put in the store.

11 DISTRIBUTION AND ITS VISIBILITY

Consider the traditional requirements of a distributed system as categorized under various forms of transparency [APM, 1989]:

- *Access transparency* enables local and remote data to be used with exactly the same operations;
- *Location transparency* enables objects to be used without knowledge of their location;
- *Concurrency transparency* enables several processes to operate concurrently on shared data without interference between them;
- *Replication transparency* enables multiple instances of data to be used to increase reliability and performance without knowledge of the replicas by users or application programs;
- *Failure transparency* enables the concealment of faults, allowing users and application programs to complete tasks despite the failure of hardware or software components;
- *Migration transparency* allows the movement of data within a system without affecting the operation of users or application programs;
- *Performance transparency* allows the system to be reconfigured to improve performance as loads vary; and
- *Scaling transparency* allows the system and applications to expand in scale without change to the system structure or the application algorithms.

However few if any of these transparencies are wanted *all the time* by the implementors of construction components. A few examples are offered. Remember that in all these examples we are considering the needs of computer science experts writing highly tuned construction components, other programmers may always need the transparencies and even the experts may accept them as a useful simplification much of the time.

- *Access transparency* may be undesirable when a program wishes to evaluate *a priori* whether the cost or delay of an operation may be unacceptable;
- *Location transparency* is undesirable when optimisers wish to arrange operations and code to be co-located, and programs organizing reliability will want to arrange for replicas to be stored in widely separated locations;
- *Concurrency transparency* will be inappropriate since the construction components will need to mediate their own concurrency regimes and process interaction is essential for prompt communication;
- *Replication transparency* is often provided in particular ways by construction components which will therefore need access to the replicas and will use this access for optimisation;
- *Failure transparency* is undesirable when the construction component is required to inform its users of the cause when it is unable to perform a service on schedule; and
- *Migration transparency* is also contraindicated when construction components are themselves attempting to optimise operations.

Whenever a transparency is usually appropriate the normal operations provided by LLPL should provide it. However, *enquiry operations* are necessary which allow the construction component to see behind the transparency mechanism. Design of these enquiry operations and identification of the information they should reveal is a research issue. It may also be desirable to provide operations that allow the construction component to give advice or even specify object attributes like locality. Both classes of operation would obviously need to be handled with care and may not be available to all programmers. They need to use information and interfaces that are sufficiently independent of current hardware and the particular implementation of SPF so that the programs still operate as the technology changes.

12 ACCOMMODATING CHANGE

A particular feature of any PAS is that it is continuously subject to change. There are external pressures for change on the PAS such as new organizational requirements, repairs and new domain specific techniques. A set of measurements on the HMS system showed very high rates of change [Sjøberg, 1992b].

There are also changes in the supporting technology. In some ways the SPF must protect the construction components and the PAS from untoward effects of change but nevertheless allow them to exploit significant progress.

The challenge is to:

- ensure that all the necessary consequences of any change are propagated; and
- avoid all unnecessary propagation of the consequences of change.

It is necessary that the SPF will be well designed to support change. For example the incremental binding described with the type **env** (see Section 6), reflection and inclusion polymorphism all allow certain kinds of system evolution without the changes impacting program and data that are not directly using the changed parts. Reflection and type **any** can be combined to automate some consequential changes. Tools can be built that assist the programmer in keeping track of the consequences of changes [Sjøberg, 1992a].

These mechanisms are necessary but not sufficient to meet the changes that PAS will encounter. For example, it is likely that new base types will be supported by underlying (specialist) hardware, e.g. to represent and process images. To utilize such facilities LLPL will need to be extensible with new base types and operations without these perturbing existing code. The need to accommodate changes of support architecture, value representations and instruction sets below the SPF has already been introduced.

13 STANDARD PROGRAMMING LANGUAGE ISSUES

Several issues have been addressed specifically in the preceding sections, this section identifies a few of the general issues that must also be considered.

One obvious requirement is a requirement for high performance. This should be addressed in two ways. The measures of performance established for SPF should take account of its ability to perform all its operations including stability operations, etc. and accommodation of change. Indeed any short- term performance measures may be misleading. Another set of enquiry operations and perhaps advisory operations should be provided in LLPL so that construction components can enquire about the expected performance and indicate preferences about the treatment of code or objects. Of course, the final implementation of SPF should be particularly well-engineered with high quality optimised code generation available through LLPL.

It is necessary to decide whether the language provided via LLPL is higher order. A higher-order language would probably assist significantly with the coding of construction components and the SPF already has to accommodate code as data. If it is a higher-order language then components requiring fast execution and compilers using LLPL[11] as their route to code generation should be able to avoid any overheads of the provisions for higher-order code if they do not use it.

The exact primitives for transactions and concurrency need to be chosen so that common regimes, such as serialisability, are easily obtained but other mechanisms may also be efficiently supported. A promising set of primitives has been suggested for ACTA [Ramamritham and Chrysanthis, 1993] and its use is being investigated as CACS [Stemple and Morrison, 1992]. Other languages, such as Concurrent CLU [Liskov et al., 1981; Hamilton, 1984; Cooper and Hamilton, 1985] and Argus [Liskov, 1984], have explored different concurrency provision.

The primitives for distribution have also to be chosen. Candidates may be found in Emerald [Black et al., 1987], Argus [Liskov, 1984], Hermes [Strom et al., 1991] and Guide [Riveill, 1992].

A major choice is the level of type system that should be provided. Some aspects of this choice have already been considered (see Section 10). Additionally we may consider their effectiveness in aiding construction component implementation. If a high-level type system were provided, then a dialect of the language that inhibited the transgression of transparencies might also be useful for direct use by application programmers. This may be expecting too much of one language. At the very least it would be necessary to guarantee that any overheads introduced by the advanced type system could be avoided by compilers and other construction components that only used simple types.

This is an incomplete[12] list of the design aspects of SPF/LLPL that have yet to be addressed. The challenge is to meet all the requirements reasonably well rather than some of them exceptionally well at the expense of ignoring others. It is also necessary to restrict the language features so that the language is easily understood and can be precisely defined.

14 SUMMARY OF ISSUES

The achievements of persistence have been surveyed. These suggest that it might be possible to continue the process of integration and provide a much simpler and more reliable basis for application programming. The present construction components all exhibit different behaviour with respect to persistence particularly when stressed. This leads to difficulties building PAS and the resulting PAS have unsatisfactory behaviours that force users to become aware of some of the construction components.

[11] In an efficient binary form.

[12] For example, accounting and resource usage control have been omitted.

A new architecture, SPF, which arranges that all the construction components rest on a common substrate and which ensures certain consistencies is proposed. This is an inversion of the approach currently used to obtain interoperability where a layer of software is placed over the construction components that attempts to translate their existing behaviour into consistent behaviour.

It is argued that the SPF approach is the only approach that will obtain completely consistent behaviour and that it also has the advantage of reducing the cost of building construction components. Its advantages however, can only be realized in the longer term.

Research into the design of SPF is proposed as a means of identifying the common goals of the persistence, distributed object management and distributed operating systems communities. This identification of the required common behaviour is of value whether it is realized via the OMG's common services, the interoperability surface layers or SPF's common substrate.

An experiment is necessary to evaluate the efficacy of the SPF architecture; specifically that the SPF architecture gives a better environment in which to build, maintain and operate PAS than the interoperability inversion or the attempts to straitjacket all the construction components into a common behaviour without the benefit of the substrate. This research cannot be conducted entirely on a small scale and by minor perturbations of the existing research and commercial systems. Perturbations will not accomplish the change in structure. Small scale experiments will not exercise the architecture in relevant ways and will not yield measurements of behaviour over lifetimes that approximate the target longevity.

An experimental plan is therefore proposed.

1. Develop an agreed design of SPF and LLPL, during this phase prototypical experiments would be necessary to test specific constructs, their use and implementation.
2. Build a well-engineered version of SPF and LLPL ensuring they are adequately equipped with instrumentation.
3. Re-build a selection of major construction components to a high standard on top of SPF.
4. Run experiments building and operating realistic PAS using these revised components. Measure and analyse their behaviour when they operate over significant volumes of data under typical loads for a sufficiently long period that independent and typical application programmers take the PAS through several evolutionary steps.

The first phase requires a collaborative effort from the distributed object management community, the operating systems community and the persistent programming researchers as rival designs are proposed and reviewed. It would conclude with one design[13] being chosen which had probably already been taken to a prototype stage.

Phase 2 would commence with the construction of the foundation which can be considered as an experimental apparatus. Much of the quality software production and its subsequent maintenance should be subcontracted to the industry's leading experts in each technology. Similarly the long term maintenance should be contracted to such companies.[14]

---

[13] If resources permit, continuing the experiment with two rival designs would test the architecture's sensitivity to design details, explore a larger application space and add the spice of rivalry.

[14] This is analogous to specialist companies building and maintaining a particle accelerator — physicist do not have to dig their own tunnels, build their own vacuum pumps and make their own

During phase 3 the standard construction components and tools would be re-implemented using the SPF. Again this should be mostly subcontracted — for example a relational system should be set up by a company already expert in building relational systems.[15] At the same time researchers would begin to use SPF to build new construction components and extend libraries giving new variations of persistent behaviour.

During phase 4 groups of computer scientists would "book time" on the SPF and construction components to run experiments. These would vary between those that operated some artificial PAS that characterised some perceived property of PASs and the operation of actual PAS with independent application programmers and users.[16] In both cases the instrumentation would be used to obtain measurements of relevant properties from any level of the system and on any scale from the measurement of changes in PAS structure and code to the measurement of data movements across various interfaces. The experimenters would be expected to establish in advance the possible outcomes and the way in which the experiment would test some relevant hypothesis or provide data to guide the improved design of the SPF, construction components or PASs. This phase is illustrated in Figure 9.

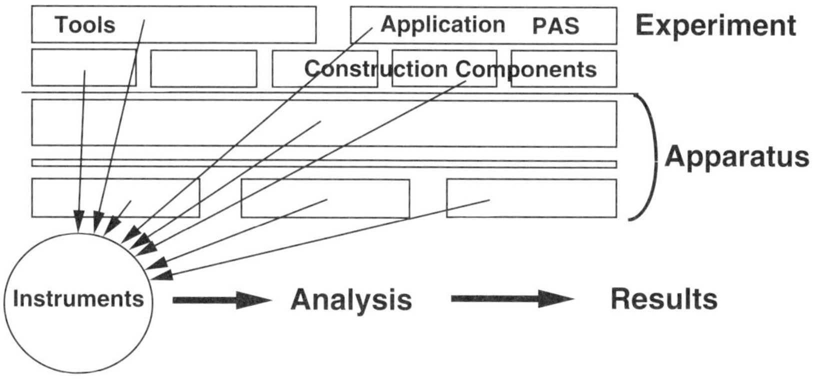

Figure 9: The Form of a Typical Experiment in Phase 4

To obtain relevant measurements the PAS may need to be operated for many years, with a large and geographically extensive network. The whole experimental plan needs to be executed as a large, long-term and well-funded programme. This is, however, worthwhile as it will answer questions that cannot be answered with smaller scale experiments. These may be important answers as architectures may otherwise be limited to evolve by a succession of minor perturbations. In computing science we are not limited by the constraints of Darwinian evolution, we can intervene and try a new architecture.

superconducting magnets — though they are rightly involved in their design and in verifying that performance goals are met.

[15]This would develop and propagate ideas about SPF and provide expert criticism as well as producing necessary experimental apparatus.

[16]For example the astronomical data processing suggested by [Kersten et al., 1992]

50 Acknowledgements

The European Community supported parts of this work through two ESPRIT projects: FIDE, Basic Research Action 3070 and $FIDE_2$, Basic Research Action 6309. The author is grateful to the programme committee of IWDOM92 for the invitation to prepare and present this paper, particularly to Tamer Özsu who showed both forbearance and kind hospitality. He also readily acknowledges the considerable help given in preparing the paper by João Lopes and Paul Philbrow.

Distribution and Persistence in the Open Object-Oriented Database System

David L. Wells
Texas Instruments Incorporated
P.O. Box 655474, MS 238
Dallas, TX 75265
U.S.A.

José A. Blakeley
Texas Instruments Incorporated
P.O. Box 655474, MS 238
Dallas, TX 75265
U.S.A.

Abstract

Distribution is the ability of a system to manipulate and transfer objects located in separate address spaces. Persistence is a special case of distribution when the address spaces involved are virtual memory and secondary storage. This paper describes our approach to unifying the concepts of persistence and distribution in the Open OODB.

1 INTRODUCTION

The Open Object Oriented Database (Open OODB) project is developing an open, extensible architecture for constructing a family of OODBs. By abstracting orthogonal dimensions of database functionality, the Open OODB system will allow tailoring each of these dimensions for particular applications within a common, incrementally improvable framework, and will also serve as a shared platform for research. The Open OODB project goals are to describe the design space of OODBs; build an architectural framework that enables configuring independently useful modules to form an OODB; verify the suitability of this open approach by implementing an OODB to these specifications; and determine areas where consensus exists or is possible. Database functionality (such as transactions, persistence, versioning, etc.) is provided via an extensible set of seamless behavioral extensions of the objects and operations from application programming languages such as C++ and Lisp. The extension model allows developers to instantiate Open OODBs with different collections of extensions as needed, and allows researchers to experiment with alternative semantics for the various database extensions (e.g., different versioning or transaction models). Seamlessness aids this process in several ways: it allows application developers to ignore irrelevant details that often require up to 30% of the application code [Atkinson, 1983], it allows new extensions to be applied to existing programs, and it encourages minimalist extensions that can be widely applied.

There is a large intersection between the Open OODB project goals and the goals of Atkinson's *Scalable Persistent Foundation* (SPF) which proposes the development of a common substrate on which to build large, reliable, and persistent applications [Atkinson, 1993]. Atkinson's SPF represents the intersection of functionality available in many systems including database management systems, persistent programming languages, and operating systems. Open OODB can be seen as a first step in the direction of building such a shared SPF resource by abstracting orthogonal functionality provided by database management systems and persistent programming languages [Wells et al., 1992].

Two extensions supported by Open OODB are persistence and distribution of objects and computation. These extensions are closely related in both semantics and implementation mechanisms. The remainder of this paper discusses how we model persistence and distribution as seamless extensions to programming languages, and the common mechanisms that we use to support these two extensions.

2 COMPUTATIONAL MODEL

Open OODB's computational model is based on transparently extending the behavior of normal operations (events) in application programming languages [Wells et al., 1992]. In this computational model, objects reside in a *universe of objects* partitioned into *environments* by a collection of *environmental attributes* not normally visible to applications. Environments and the *boundaries* between them are used to identify circumstances in which extensions will be required. An example of an environmental attribute is the address space in which an object resides; an extension of the application's language is required to operate on an object in a remote address space. Objects are monitored by *sentries* that trap extended events and invoke *policy performers* (PPs) which implement the extended behavior. Persistence and distribution are instances of policy performers.

3 ARCHITECTURE

The Open OODB *system architecture* is divided into (1) a *meta-architecture* consisting of a collection of *glue* modules and definitions providing the infrastructure for specifying and implementing event extensions and normalizing interfaces among modules, and (2) an extensible collection of policy performers.

The meta architecture contains a collection of **address space managers (ASM)**, each of which controls one address space. At least one ASM must allow execution of events. If more than one address space exists, there must be **communications** and **translation** mechanisms to effect object transfer between them. A **data dictionary** serves as a globally known repository of system, object, and type information. A **meta-architecture support** module provides the *extension* mechanism and defines necessary *interface* conventions to which policy performers must adhere.

Extension	Policy Performer Module
Transactions and controlled sharing	Transaction PP
Distributed (remote) access to objects	Distribution PP
Replicated/partitioned objects	Replication PP*
Indexed sets of objects	Index PP
Object queries	Object Query Processor
Versions of objects	Version PP
Configurations of objects	Configuration PP
Consistency and derived objects	Dependency PP
Object persistence and naming	Persistence PP
Security control over objects	Access Control PP*
Access to objects in foreign databases	Gateway PP*

Table 1: Mapping extended behavior to policy performers.

The set of policy performers in any Open OODB instantiation is flexible; the actual set being determined by the subset of functional requirements being addressed by the instantiation. Since the model supports different extensions, it is possible that systems other than OODBs could be configured in this way. The collection of policy performers for a fully configured Open OODB [Wells, 1991a] is summarized in Table 1. Policy performers marked with an asterisk will not be supported in the current implementation of Open OODB.

4 DISTRIBUTION AND PERSISTENCE EXTENSIONS

In Open OODB, the concepts of persistence and distribution are strongly influenced by our goal of seamlessness. Both concepts are supported by the same mechanisms, and in fact are much more closely related than is the case in most distributed databases. Persistence refers to the ability of objects to exist beyond the lifetime of the program that created them. As described in [Wells et al., 1992], these models vary in their type system, how and when objects may become persistent, how permanent persistent objects must be, transaction model, versioning of objects and when versions may be created, and whether performance tuning hooks are exposed to applications [Wells, 1991b]. However, this paper concentrates on their commonalities rather than their differences. Distribution is the ability of objects to reside in, and be manipulated from, separate address spaces. Clearly, many kinds of distribution exist, including remote servers, distributed (fragmented) storage, remote computation as supported by RPCs, and distributed, parallel computation.

Objects can become persistent in the workspace in which they are created; in LISP environments, any object reachable from a symbol continues to exist beyond its creating program's life as long as the environment itself exists. However, because in most language/operating system combinations, a program's address space is purged at program termination, persistence generally requires the use of a separate address space(s) to hold persistent results. This in turn requires a way to make connections between references within a program and objects outside the program's address space and a way to transfer objects between two spaces. Because of the way Open OODB abstracts the concept of an Address Space Manager (Section 5.1), we are able to distribute objects (for the purposes of persistence) to any address space, regardless of whether that address space is computational or long-term storage.

The persistence extension is built on top of distribution which is responsible for moving objects and messages among address spaces in response to object reference faults. Object faults may occur on either remote or persistent objects. Particular persistence and distribution policies determine whether local or remote method execution should be applied. It is possible to create persistence in a system with NO long-term storage by distributing replicas of persistent objects to a sufficient number of transient stores that maintain a quorum of these replicas. Persistence and distribution PPs use separate transaction PPs to provide desired levels of atomicity, concurrency control, isolation, and durability. The support of persistence and distribution by a single set of mechanisms is desirable because any improvement to a mechanism benefits both extensions.

5 MECHANISMS

The mechanisms of interest are: (1) the address space manager abstraction, (2) support for distributed transactions, (3) treatment of OIDs and references as types, (4) unified naming conventions for distribution and persistence, (5) the ability to suspend and restart the implementation of event extensions, and (6) pragmas to support transparent performance tuning.

5.1 ADDRESS SPACE MANAGER ABSTRACTION

Objects reside in some address space. Address space implementations vary in their representation of objects and their addressing schemes, which allow them to satisfy different functional and performance needs. For example, virtual memories support computation; relational databases support associative access and long term storage; file systems support sequential and perhaps indexed or random access; and archives support long-term storage and recovery. Open OODB can contain address spaces of any of these types (and perhaps others). To allow uniform access to objects from outside an address space, Open OODB defines a module called an Address Space Manager (ASM), which supports mappings between global identifiers and addressing conventions local to an individual address space (see Section 5.3).

The address space manager abstraction is orthogonal to physical address spaces. Several address spaces can exist within a single virtual memory; for example a server cache and an application workspace. An address space can also span machine boundaries such as in a client-server model. In this case, the client and server are typically on separate machines, but from the perspective of the OODB, they form a single ASM.

5.2 DISTRIBUTED TRANSACTION MANAGEMENT

Because Open OODB supports a variety of ASMs within a single system instantiation, it must be possible to not only support distributed transactions, but to do so in a way that allows the use of heterogeneous ASMs. This means that coordination of distributed commit and deadlock detection/prevention must be handled outside of the ASMs via a Transaction Policy Performer, since to do otherwise would require ASMs to know details of other ASMs: this is unreasonable to expect. To participate in a distributed transaction, an ASM must export an interface including `prepare-for-commit`, `commit`, and `waits-for`; the first two being used in two-phase commit, the latter reporting the local waits-for graph for use by a distributed deadlock detector. ASMs not exporting this interface cannot participate in distributed transactions. An ASM that internally supports distribution is compatible with this scheme; it simply appears to the outside world as a single, non-distributed ASM.

5.3 OBJECT IDENTIFIERS AND REFERENCES

Object identifiers (OIDs) and *references* to objects are manipulated by all Open OODB modules. A reference consists of an OID that names the object and a mechanism for mapping the OID to the object's state. An object's state is stored in one or more physical storage locations; the actual collection of storage locations is a function of the object's type, its current representation, and the memory management policies of the address space(s) in which it resides. Many behavioral extensions are modeled or implemented in terms of references to objects rather than operations directed at the objects.

Reference implementations vary on the representation of OIDs, and the semantics of pointer following and identity comparison operators. Usually, reference implementations are fixed by the language compiler as a simple resolution to a set of storage locations. However, resolving a reference may be a fairly complex operation outside the norm of resolving an address to a memory location. For example, maintenance of replicas modifies identity comparisons. An application holding references to two different replicas of an object should see them as identical, yet the mechanism maintaining replica consistency has to be aware of their difference. References are modeled as a type lattice having subtypes particular to various extensions of reference semantics.

To make it possible for objects and references to be shared, there is one form of OID called a *global identifier (GID)* that can be interpreted in any environment in which it may be encountered. To allow address space independence and to allow ASMs to locally relocate objects, Open OODB uses a mapping scheme that first determines the current address space of the object globally and then allows the object's current ASM to locate the object locally in its own idiosyncratic manner. Objects can be created in any address space (not necessarily the address space of the creating program).

5.4 NAMING

There are a variety of naming schemes that can be employed in Open OODB. However, because of the lack of distinction between persistence and distribution, it is important that the same naming protocol be used for both.

5.5 CONTINUABLE POLICIES

Policy performers must have the capability to suspend or delay the execution of a policy and then restart (transparently) on demand. When fetching objects, maintaining indices, creating versions, and many other activities of an OODB, it is often impractical or impossible to perform the entire operation at one time. For instance, incremental object retrieval may be more efficient than eager retrieval when concurrent users access disjoint parts of a graph. Similarly, during automatic index maintenance, an index cannot be maintained when a side-effecting method on an indexed object is trapped because such a side-effect has not occurred yet. In this case, index maintenance needs to be suspended and reactivated at a later time.

5.6 PRAGMAS

Pragmas are parameters to policy performers specifying optional or alternative behavior. An example of this is a prefetching request that states that it would be desirable to fetch objects with certain characteristics, but that failure to perform this action should not result in an exception. Since pragmas need not be satisfied, the recipient of a pragma has substantial freedom about how to respond. This allows the policy receiving a pragma to treat it as a suggestion to be balanced with other suggestions to obtain globally optimal behavior, to reduce the actions taken in response to a pragma due to resource limitations or scheduling conflicts, or even to ignore the pragma as unintelligible. The use of pragmas allows applications to provide hints to influence the behavior of an extension, but to continue to operate even if the attempt is unsuccessful. Thus, pragmas must be outside the semantic interface of a module.

6 STATUS AND CONCLUSIONS

The current Open OODB prototype contains implementations of several policy performers including concurrency control based on two-phase locking, atomic transactions, query processing, version and configuration management, and persistence policies for CLOS and C++ objects. The current implementations of the query processor, and the version and configuration management modules are detachable from the rest of the Open OODB. We have coupled our query processor with a commercial C++-based OODB and with the Exodus storage manager, which provides initial evidence that it is possible to enhance the capabilities of an OODB with modules developed independently. The Exodus server is being modified (at the University of Wisconsin) to expose distributed commit support as sketched in this paper. We have ASM implementations based on Unix files and relational DBMSs, translation for CLOS and C++ objects, and CLOS implementations of sentries and policy performers. We are currently experimenting with implementations of sentries and policy performers in C++.

Acknowledgements

This research is sponsored by the Defense Advanced Research Projects Agency under DARPA Order No. 7558 and managed by the US Army CECOM, under contract DAAB07-90-C-B920. The views and conclusions contained in this document are those of the authors and should not be interpreted as necessarily representing the official policies, either expressed or implied, of the Defense Advanced Research Projects Agency or the United States Government.

Client-Server Caching Revisited

Michael J. Franklin
University of Wisconsin
Department of Computer Sciences
Madison, WI 53706
U.S.A.

Michael J. Carey
University of Wisconsin
Department of Computer Sciences
Madison, WI 53706
U.S.A.

Abstract

The caching of data and/or locks at client workstations is an effective technique for improving the performance of a client-server database system. This paper extends an earlier performance study of client-server caching in several ways. The first is a re-examination of heuristics for deciding dynamically between propagating changes or invalidating remote copies of data pages in order to maintain cache consistency. The second is a study of the "Callback Locking" family of caching algorithms. These algorithms are of interest because they provide an alternative to the optimistic techniques used in the earlier study and because they have recently begun to find use in commercial systems. In addition, the performance of the caching algorithms is examined in light of current trends in processor and network speeds and in the presence of data contention.

1 INTRODUCTION

Object-Oriented Database Management Systems (OODBMS) are typically designed for use in networks of high-performance workstations and servers. As a result, most OODBMS products and research prototypes have adopted a variant of a *client-server* software architecture known as *data shipping*. In a data shipping system, client processes send requests for specific data items to servers, and servers respond with the requested items (and possibly others). Data shipping systems are particularly well-suited for use in workstation-based environments since they allow a DBMS to perform much of its work on client workstations, thus exploiting the workstations' processing and memory resources and offloading shared server machines. Data shipping systems can be categorized as *page servers*, in which clients and servers interact using physical units of data such as pages or segments, and *object servers*, which send logical units of data such as objects or tuples between clients and servers [DeWitt et al., 1990] . Many recent systems (e.g., ObServer [Hornick and Zdonik, 1987], O_2 [Deux et al., 1990], EXODUS [EXODUS Project, 1991; Franklin et al., 1992b], and ObjectStore [Lamb et al., 1991]) have adopted the page server approach due its relative simplicity and potential performance advantages compared to an object server approach.

Caching data and locks at client workstations is an important technique for improving the performance of client-server database systems. Data and locks can be cached both within a single transaction (*intra-transaction caching*) and across transaction boundaries (*inter-transaction caching*). Intra-transaction caching is easily implemented; it requires only that a client can manage its own buffer pool and can keep track of the locks it has obtained. Due to this simplicity, all of the algorithms investigated in this study perform intra-transaction caching of both data and locks. On the other hand, inter-transaction data caching requires additional mechanisms to ensure the consistency of cached data pages, and inter-transaction lock caching requires full-function lock management on clients and protocols for distributed lock management. In this study, we concentrate on the performance tradeoffs of inter-transaction caching. For the remainder of the paper, use the term "caching" to refer exclusively to inter-transaction caching at client workstations. Also, for concreteness, this study concentrates on page server architectures; however, many of the results are also applicable to object server systems.

1.1 PREVIOUS WORK

Several previous studies have shown that the caching of data and locks can have substantial performance benefits [Wilkinson and Neimat, 1990; Carey et al., 1991; Wang and Rowe, 1991]. These benefits can result from: (1) reducing reliance on the server, thus offloading a potential bottleneck and reducing communication, (2) allowing better utilization of the CPU and memory resources that are available on clients, and (3) increasing the scalability of the system in terms of the impact of adding client workstations. However, caching also has the potential to degrade performance due to the overhead of maintaining cache consistency. This overhead can manifest itself in several forms: (1) increased communication, (2) increased load on the server CPU, (3) additional path length, and (4) extra load placed on clients. Also, some algorithms may postpone the discovery of data conflicts, resulting in increased transaction abort rates.

In an earlier paper [Carey et al., 1991] we investigated the performance implications of inter-transaction data and lock caching. In that paper, five locking-based algorithms were compared: an algorithm that performed no caching, one that cached data (but not locks), and three variants of an *Optimistic Two-Phase Locking* (O2PL) algorithm that allowed caching of data pages and an optimistic form of lock caching. With O2PL, locks are obtained only locally at clients during transaction execution and then, prior to commit, locks on all copies of updated pages are obtained at remote sites in order to ensure consistency. This form of lock caching is optimistic in the sense that a local lock at one site does not guarantee the absence of conflicting local locks at other sites. The three O2PL-based algorithms differed in the actions that they performed at the remote sites once locks were obtained. One variant, called O2PL!Invalidate (O2PL-I), always removed the copies from the remote sites. The second variant, O2PL!Propagate (O2PL-P), always sent new copies of the updated pages to the remote sites, thereby preserving replication. The third variant, O2PL!Dynamic (O2PL-D), was an adaptive algorithm that used a simple heuristic to choose between invalidation and propagation on a copy-by-copy basis.

In the previous study, a number of conclusions were reached about the relative merits of these alternative caching algorithms. These include the following: (1) All of the caching algorithms were shown to have much higher performance than the non-caching algorithm in most of the workloads examined; (2) The optimistic caching of locks in addition to the caching of data was found to improve performance except in a workload with extremely high data contention and in some cases where the O2PL-P algorithm performed excessive update propagation; (3) The invalidation-based version of O2PL (O2PL-I) typically had the highest throughput; (4) The propagate version of O2PL (O2PL-P) was found to have significant performance advantages for certain types of data sharing, but also displayed a high degree of volatility, especially with regard to client buffer pool sizes; (5) The dynamic O2PL algorithm (O2PL-D) was seen to approach, but not quite equal, the performance of the better of the static O2PL algorithms over a wide range of workloads.

1.2 EXTENSIONS TO THE PREVIOUS STUDY

In this paper, we extend the results of the previous study in the following ways:

1. *A Better Adaptive Heuristic*: As stated above, the O2PL-Dynamic algorithm usually approached, but never met or exceeded the performance level of the better of the two static O2PL algorithms for a given workload. Thus, the first issue addressed here is to find a better heuristic for the adaptive algorithm.

2. *Callback Locking*: An alternative method for maintaining cache consistency is *Callback Locking* [Howard et al., 1988; Lamb et al., 1991; Wang and Rowe, 1991]. Callback locking allows clients to cache both data pages and locks, but unlike O2PL, lock caching is not optimistic — sites are not allowed to simultaneously hold conflicting locks.

3. *System Parameter and Workload Changes*: Current trends in hardware technology have the potential to shift the performance bottlenecks in the system and may alter the comparative advantages of the caching algorithms. For example, CPU speeds are increasing dramatically while disk speeds are not; network technology has been improving, but most installed networks have yet to catch up. In this study, we examine the effects of these changes by increasing the speeds of the client and server CPUs compared to the earlier study, and by examining the effect of two different network bandwidths. We also use an additional workload to help examine the performance of the caching algorithms in the presence of high data contention.

The remainder of the paper is structured as follows: Section 2 describes the three types of cache consistency algorithms that are investigated in this study. Section 3 describes the simulation model and workloads. Section 4 presents the experiments and results. Section 5 discusses related work, and Section 6 presents conclusions.

2 OVERVIEW OF CACHING ALGORITHMS

The algorithms of this study fall into three families: Server-based 2PL, Optimistic 2PL (O2PL), and Callback Locking. These are described in the following sections.

2.1 SERVER-BASED TWO-PHASE LOCKING

Server-based 2PL schemes are derived from *primary-copy* concurrency control algorithms, with the server's copy of each page being treated as the primary copy of that page. Client transactions must obtain the proper lock from the server before they are allowed to access a data item. Clients are not allowed to cache locks across transaction boundaries. In this study we use a variant called Caching 2PL (*C2PL*) which allows *data pages* to be cached at clients across transaction boundaries. Consistency is maintained using a "check-on-access" policy. When a transaction requests a read lock for a page that is cached at its client, it sends the Log Sequence Number (LSN) found on its copy of the page along with the lock request. When the server responds to the lock request, it includes an up-to-date copy of the page along with the response if it determines that the site's copy is no longer current. In C2PL, deadlock detection is performed exclusively at the server. Deadlocks are resolved by aborting the youngest transaction involved in the deadlock. An algorithm similar to C2PL is currently used in the EXODUS storage manager.

2.2 OPTIMISTIC TWO-PHASE LOCKING (O2PL)

The O2PL schemes allow inter-transaction caching of data pages and and an optimistic form of lock caching. They are based on a *read-one, write-all* concurrency control protocol for replicated data in distributed databases, which was studied in [Carey and Livny, 1991]. The O2PL algorithms are "optimistic" in the sense that they defer the detection of conflicts among locks cached at multiple sites until transaction commit time. In these algorithms, each client has its own local lock manager from which the proper lock must be obtained before a transaction can access a data item at that client. A non-two-phase read lock (i.e., latch) is obtained briefly at the server when a data item is in the process of being prepared for shipment to a client, thus ensuring that the client is given a transaction-consistent copy of the page. The server is responsible for keeping track of where pages are cached in the system. Clients inform the server when they drop a page from their buffer pool by piggybacking that information on the next message that they send to the server. Thus, the server's copy information is conservative, as there may be some delay before the server learns that a page is no longer cached at a client.

When an updating transaction is ready to enter its commit phase, it sends a message to the server containing a copy of each page that it has updated. The server then acquires exclusive locks on these pages on behalf of the transaction. Once these locks have been acquired at the server, the server sends a message to each client that has cached copies of any of the updated pages. These remote clients obtain exclusive locks on their local copies of the updated pages on behalf of the committing transaction. Once all the required locks have been obtained, variant-specific actions are taken. O2PL!Invalidate (*O2PL-I*) invalidates the remote cached copies of data pages, while O2PL!Propagate (*O2PL-P*) propagates the new values of data items to remote caching sites; O2PL!Dynamic (*O2PL-D*) chooses between invalidation and propagation on a per-copy basis. All sites that propagate one or more new page values must participate in a two-phase commit protocol with the server to ensure atomicity. Invalidation does not require a two-phase commit, as it does not result in the updating of any data that remains valid at the site.

With O2PL, each client maintains a local waits-for graph which is used to detect deadlocks that are local to the client. Global deadlocks are detected using a centralized algorithm *a la* [Stonebraker, 1979]. The server periodically requests local waits-for graphs from the clients and combines them to build a global waits-for graph. Deadlocks involving consistency actions can be detected early. When a conflict is detected between exclusive locks for two consistency actions or between a consistency action lock and a write lock, it is known that a deadlock has occurred or will shortly occur, so the deadlock can be resolved immediately [Carey and Livny, 1991]. As in the server-based case, deadlocks are resolved by aborting the youngest transaction.

2.3 CALLBACK LOCKING

The third family of caching algorithms studied is Callback Locking. Callback Locking allows caching of data pages and non-optimistic caching of locks. In contrast to the O2PL algorithms, with Callback Locking clients must obtain a lock from the server immediately (rather than at commit time) prior to accessing a data page, if they don't have the proper lock cached locally. When a client requests a lock that conflicts with one or more locks that are currently cached at other clients, the server "calls back" the conflicting locks by sending requests to the sites which have those locks cached. The lock request is granted only when the server has determined that all conflicting locks have been released. As a result, transactions do not need to perform consistency maintenance actions during the commit phase. In this study, we analyze two Callback Locking variants: Callback-Read (CB-Read), which allows inter-transaction caching of read locks only, and Callback-All (CB-All), which allows inter-transaction caching of read locks and write locks.

As in the O2PL algorithms, the server keeps track of which sites have copies of pages in their cache. CB-Read, which caches only read locks works as follows. When a request for a write lock on a page arrives at the server, the server issues callback requests to all sites (except the requester) that have a cached copy of the page. At a client, such a callback request is treated as a request for an exclusive lock on the specified page. If the request can not be granted immediately (due to a lock conflict), the client responds to the server saying that the page is currently in use. When the callback request is granted at the client, the page is removed from the client's buffer and an acknowledgement message is sent to the server. When all callbacks have been acknowledged to the server, the server grants a write lock on the page to the requesting client. Any subsequent read or write lock requests for the page will be blocked at the server until the write lock is released by the holding transaction. At the end of the transaction, the client sends copies of the updated pages to the server and releases its write locks; retaining copies of the pages (and hence, implicit read locks on the pages) in its cache.

The CB-All algorithm works similarly to CB-Read, except that write locks are kept at the clients rather than at the server and are not released at the end of a transaction. The server's copy information is augmented to allow a copy at a site to be designated as an *exclusive copy*, and clients also keep track of which of their pages are cached exclusively. If a read request for a page arrives at the server and an exclusive copy of the page is currently held at some site, a downgrade request is sent to that site. A downgrade request is similar to a callback request, but rather than removing the page from its buffer, the client simply notes that it no longer has an exclusive copy of the page; in effect it downgrades its cached write lock to a read lock. Non-exclusive copies are treated as in the CB-Read algorithm. As in CB-Read, clients send copies of pages dirtied by a transaction to the server when the transaction commits. However, in CB-All this is done only to to simplify recovery, as no other sites can access a page while it is exclusively cached at another site.

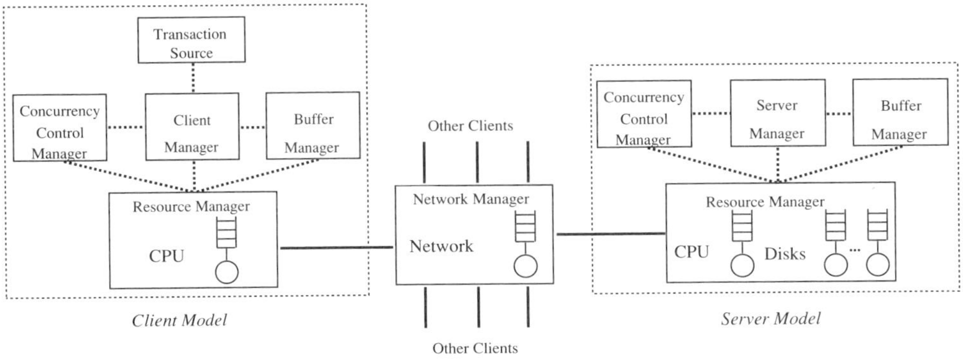

Figure 1: Model of a Client-Server DBMS

Callback algorithms were originally introduced to maintain cache consistency in distributed file systems such as Andrew [Howard et al., 1988] and Sprite [Nelson et al., 1988], which provide a weaker form of consistency than that required by database systems. More recently, a Callback Locking algorithm that provides transaction serializability has been employed in the ObjectStore OODBMS. An algorithm similar to CB-Read was studied in [Wang and Rowe, 1991]. That algorithm differed from CB-Read with regard to deadlock detection — it considered all cached locks to be in-use for the purpose of computing the waits-for graph at the server. This could cause aborts due to phantom deadlocks; especially with large client caches. To avoid this problem, CB-Read (and CB-All) adopt a convention from ObjectStore: copy sites always respond to a callback request immediately, even if the page is currently in use at the site. This allows deadlock detection to be performed with accurate information.

2.4 SUMMARY OF THE ALGORITHMS

We now briefly summarize the three types of algorithms that are investigated in this study. All of the algorithms allow caching of data pages. C2PL does not allow caching of locks — it uses check-on-access to ensure the consistency of accessed data. The O2PL algorithms allow an optimistic form of lock caching: locks are obtained locally at clients during transaction execution, deferring global acquisition of locks until the commit phase. The three O2PL variants use invalidation and/or propagation to maintain consistency. The Callback Locking algorithms allow true inter-transaction caching of locks, but they require non-cached locks to be obtained at the server immediately during transaction execution. The Callback Locking algorithms of this study are invalidation-based.

3 A CLIENT-SERVER CACHING MODEL

3.1 THE SYSTEM MODEL[1]

Figure 1 shows the structure of our simulation model, which was constructed using the DeNet discrete event simulation language [Livny, 1988]. It consists of components that model diskless client workstations and a server machine (with disks) that are connected

[1]A more detailed description of the model can be found in [Carey et al., 1991].

Parameter	Meaning	Setting
ClientCPU	Instruction rate of client CPU	15 MIPS
ServerCPU	Instruction rate of server CPU	30 MIPS
ClientBufSize	Per-client buffer size	5% or 25% of DB size
ServerBufSize	Server buffer size	50% of DB size
ServerDisks	Number of disks at server	2 disks
MinDiskTime	Minimum disk access time	10 millisecond
MaxDiskTime	Maximum disk access time	30 milliseconds
NetworkBandwidth	Network bandwidth	8 or 80 Mbits per sec
PageSize	Size of a page	4,096 bytes
DatabaseSize	Size of database in pages	1250 (5 MBytes)
NumClients	Number of client workstations	1 to 25
FixedMsgInst	Fixed no. of instructions per message	20,000 instructions
PerByteMsgInst	No. of addl. instructions per msg. byte	2.44 instructions
ControlMsgSize	Size in bytes of a control message	256 bytes
LockInst	No. of instructions per lock/unlock pair	300 instructions
RegisterCopyInst	No. of inst. to register/unregister a copy	300 instructions
DiskOverheadInst	CPU Overhead for performing disk I/O	5000 instructions
DeadlockInterval	Global deadlock detection frequency	1 second (if needed)

Table 1: System and Overhead Parameters

over a simple network. Each client site consists of a *buffer manager* that uses an LRU page replacement policy, a *concurrency control manager* that is used either as a simple lock cache or as a full-function lock manager (depending on the cache consistency algorithm in use), a *resource manager* that provides CPU service and access to the network, and a *client manager* that coordinates the execution of transactions at the client. Each client also has a module called the *Transaction Source* which submits transactions to the client according to the workload model described in the following section. Transactions are represented as page reference strings and are submitted to the client one at a time; upon completion of a transaction, the source waits for a specified think time and then submits a new transaction. When a transaction aborts, it is resubmitted with the same page reference string. The number of client machines is a parameter to the model. The server is modeled similarly to the clients, but with the following differences: the Resource Manager manages disks as well as a CPU, the Concurrency Control Manager has the ability to store information about the location of page copies in the system and also manages locks, there is a *server manager* component that coordinates the operation of the server (analogous to the client's client manager), and there is no "transaction source" module (since all transactions originate at client workstations).

Table 1 describes the parameters that are used to specify the resources and overheads of the system and shows the settings used in this study. The simulated CPUs of the system are managed using a two-level priority scheme. System CPU requests, such as those for message and disk handling, are given priority over user (transaction) requests. System requests are handled using a FIFO queueing discipline, while a processor-sharing discipline is employed for user requests. Each disk has a FIFO queue of requests; the disk used to service a particular request is chosen uniformly from among all the disks at the server. The disk access time is drawn from a uniform distribution between a specified minimum and maximum. A very simple network model is used in the simulator's *network manager* component; the network is modeled as a FIFO server with a specified bandwidth. We did not model the details of the operation of a specific type of network (e.g., Ethernet, token

Parameter	Meaning
TransSize	Mean number of pages accessed per transaction
HotBounds	Page bounds of hot range
ColdBounds	Page bounds of cold range
HotAccProb	Prob. of accessing a page in the hot range
HotWrtProb	Prob. of writing to a page in the hot range
ColdWrtProb	Prob. of writing to a page in the cold range
PerPageInst	Mean no. of CPU instructions per page on read (doubled on write)
ThinkTime	Mean think time between client transactions

Table 2: Workload Parameter Meanings

ring, etc.). Rather, the approach we took was to separate the CPU costs of messages from the on-the-wire costs of messages, and to allow the on-the-wire message costs to be adjusted using the bandwidth parameter. The CPU cost for managing the protocol for a send or a receive of a message is modeled as a fixed number of instructions per message plus a charge per message byte.

3.2 WORKLOADS

Our simulation model provides a simple but flexible mechanism for describing workloads. The access pattern for each client can be specified separately using the parameters shown in Table 2. Transactions are represented as a string of page access requests in which some accesses are for reads and others are for writes. Two ranges of database pages can be specified: a hot range and a cold range. The probability of a page access being to a page in the hot range is specified; the remainder of the accesses are directed to cold range pages. For both ranges, the probability that an access to a page in the range will be a write access (in addition to a read access) is specified. The parameters also allow the specification of an average number of instructions to be performed at the client for each page access, once the proper lock has been obtained. This number is doubled for write accesses.

Table 3 summarizes the workloads that are used in this study. The HOTCOLD workload has a high degree of locality per client and a moderate amount of sharing and data contention among clients. The FEED workload represents a situation such as a stock quotation system in which one site produces data while the other sites consume it. UNIFORM is a low-locality, moderate write probability workload which is used to examine the consistency algorithms in a case where caching is not expected to pay off significantly. Finally, HICON is a workload with varying degrees of data contention. It is similar to skewed workloads that are often used to study shared-disk transaction processing systems, and it is introduced here to investigate the effects of data contention on the various algorithms.

4 EXPERIMENTS AND RESULTS

In this section we present the results of the performance studies of the new heuristic for the adaptive O2PL algorithm and of the Callback Locking algorithms. For most experiments the main metric presented is throughput, measured in transactions per second. Where necessary, auxiliary performance measures are also discussed. An additional metric that is used in several of the experiments is the number of messages sent per committed transactions. This metric is computed by taking the total number of messages sent during the simulation runs

Parameter	HOTCOLD	FEED	UNIFORM	HICON
TransSize	20 pages	5 pages	20 pages	20 pages
HotBounds	p to p+49, $p = 50(n-1)+1$	1 to 50	-	1 to 250
ColdBounds	rest of DB	rest of DB	whole DB	rest of DB
HotAccProb	0.8	0.8	-	0.8
ColdAccProb	0.2	0.2	1.0	0.2
HotWrtProb	0.2	1.0/0.0	-	0.0 to 0.5
ColdWrtProb	0.2	0.0/0.0	0.2	0.2
PerPageInst	30,000	30,000	30,000	30,000
ThinkTime	0	0	0	0

Table 3: Workload Parameter Settings for Client n

(by clients and the server) and dividing by the number transaction commits that occur during the simulation run. Results are presented for two different network bandwidths called "slow" (8 Mbits/sec) and "fast" (80 Mbits/sec); these correspond to slightly discounted bandwidths of Ethernet and FDDI technology, respectively.

4.1 A NEW ADAPTIVE HEURISTIC

As described earlier, the heuristic for the dynamic O2PL algorithm used in [Carey et al., 1991] generally performed well, but was never able to match the performance of the better of the other two O2PL algorithms for a given workload (except in a workload with no data contention, where all O2PL algorithms performed identically). The original O2PL-D algorithm uses a simple heuristic to determine whether to use invalidation or propagation in order to ensure that a site does not retain an out-of-date copy of a page. It initially propagates updates, invalidating copies on a subsequent consistency operation if it detects that the preceding page propagation was wasted. Specifically, O2PL-D will propagate a new copy of a page if both: *(1) the page is resident at the site when the consistency operation is attempted*, and *(2) if the page was previously propagated to the site, then the page has been re-accessed since that propagation.* In the initial study, it was found that the algorithm's willingness to err on the side of propagation resulted in its performance being somewhat lower than that of O2PL-I in most cases. The new heuristic, therefore, was designed to instead err on the side of invalidation if a mistake was to be made. In the new dynamic algorithm, O2PL-ND (for "New Dynamic"), an updated copy of a page will be propagated to a site only if conditions 1 and 2 of O2PL-D hold plus *(3) the page was previously invalidated at that site and that invalidation was a mistake.* The new condition ensures that O2PL-ND will invalidate a page at a site at least once before propagating it to that site.

In order to implement the new condition, it is necessary to have a mechanism for determining that an invalidation was a mistake. This is not straightforward since invalidating a page removes the page and its buffer control information from the site, leaving no place to store information about the invalidation. To solve this problem we use a structure called the *invalidate window*. The invalidate window is a list of the last n distinct pages that have been invalidated at the site. The window size, n, is a parameter of the O2PL-ND algorithm. When a page is invalidated at a site, its page number is placed at the front of the invalidate window on that site. If the window is full and the page does not already appear in the window, then the entry at the end is pushed out of the window to make room for the new entry. If the page already appears in the window, it is simply moved from its present location to the front. When a transaction's page access request results in a page being brought into the site's buffer pool, the invalidate window is checked and if the page appears in the window, the page is marked as having had a mistaken invalidation applied to it.[2] The page remains marked as long as it resides in the client's buffer.

Except for the different heuristic, the O2PL-ND algorithm works much like O2PL-D. When a consistency action request arrives at a client, the client obtains exclusive locks on its copies of the affected pages. The client then checks the remaining two conditions for propagation for each page and if both conditions are met the client will decide to receive a new copy of the page. The client retains its locks on those pages it has chosen to propagate and invalidates (also releasing its locks on) the other pages affected by the consistency request. The client then sends a message to inform the server of its decision(s). If all decisions were to invalidate, then the client is finished with the consistency action. Otherwise, this message acts as the acknowledgement in the first phase of a two-phase commit protocol. When the server has heard from all involved clients, it sends copies of the necessary pages to those sites that requested them. This message serves as the second phase of the commit protocol. Upon receipt of the new page copies, the clients install them in their buffer pools and release the locks on those pages. The receipt of a propagated page copy at a client does not affect the LRU status of the page at that site.

The performance of the new heuristic was examined using the HOTCOLD, FEED, and UNIFORM workloads. In all of the experiments described here, the O2PL-ND algorithm was run with a window size of 20 pages. An early concern with the new heuristic was its potential sensitivity to the window size. A series of tests using the parameters from [Carey et al., 1991] found that in all cases but one, the algorithm was insensitive to the window size within a range of 10 to 100 pages (0.8% to 8% of the database size). The exception case and the reasons for the insensitivity of the algorithm in the other cases will be discussed in the following sections.

4.1.1 Experiment 1 : The HOTCOLD Workload

Figure 2 shows the throughput for the HOTCOLD workload using the slow network and a client buffer size of 5% of the database size (62 pages). This case shows a clear example of how the new heuristic of O2PL-ND can improve performance over the heuristic used by the original O2PL-D algorithm. O2PL-ND performs as well as O2PL-I, the better of the static O2PL algorithms in this case, while O2PL-D tracks the lower performance of O2PL-P. All of the algorithms eventually become disk-bound in this case. In this experiment, all of the O2PL algorithms outperform the C2PL algorithm prior to reaching the disk bottleneck. This is due to the additional latency incurred by C2PL's heavy reliance on messages. The similarity of O2PL-D's performance to that of O2PL-P in this case is due to the fact that O2PL-D will propagate a page once to a site before it detects that it should have invalidated the page. Since the client buffer pool is relatively small in this experiment, O2PL-P performs only slightly more propagations than O2PL-D, as an unused page is likely to be pushed out of the buffer pool by the LRU page replacement algorithm. About 80% of the propagations go unused for both O2PL-P and O2PL-D (that is, these propagated pages are not accessed

[2] Marking the page at this time limits the algorithm's sensitivity to the window size. If the window was checked at consistency maintenance time, then a small window size could result in useful pages being invalidated because they have been "pushed out of the window" even while they were being used at the client.

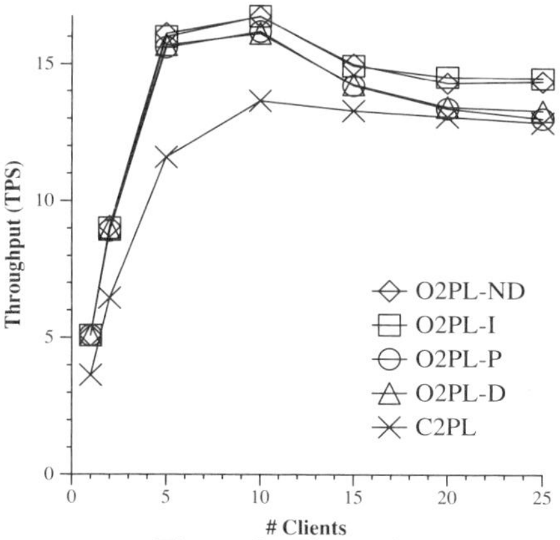

Figure 2: Throughput
(HOTCOLD, 5% Cli Buffers, Slow Net)

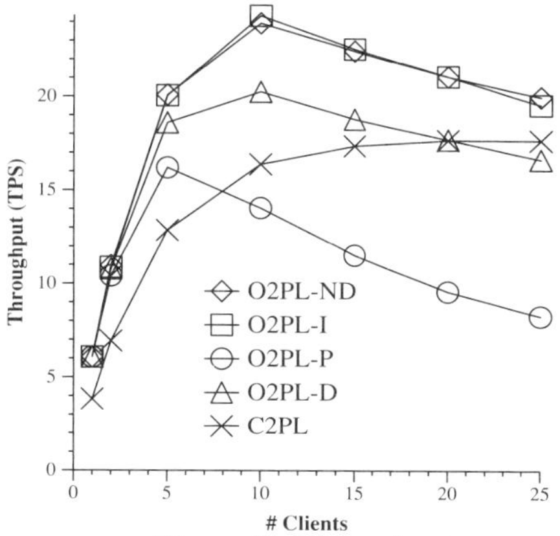

Figure 3: Throughput
(HOTCOLD, 25% Cli Buffers, Slow Net)

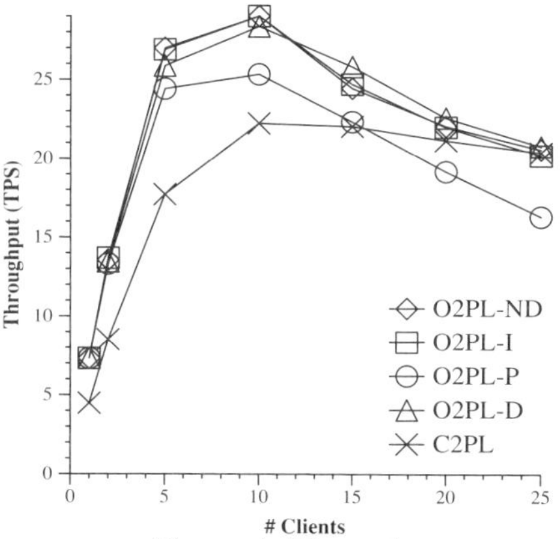

Figure 4: Throughput
(HOTCOLD, 25% Cli Buffers, Fast Net)

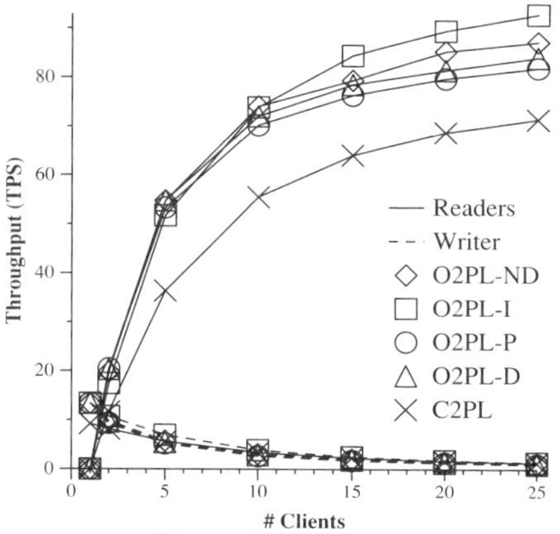

Figure 5: Throughput
(FEED, 5% Cli Buffers, Slow Net)

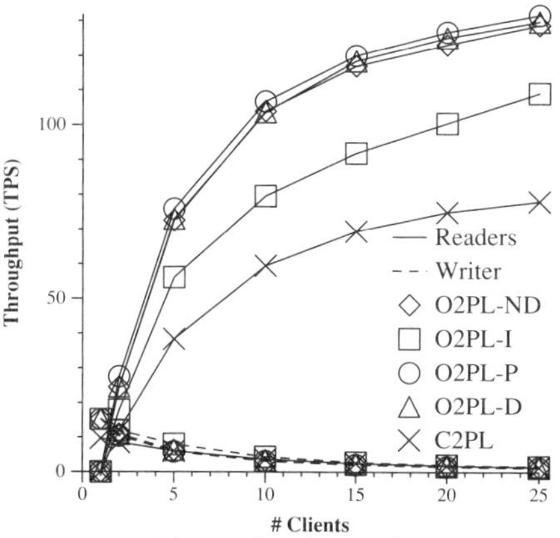

Figure 6: Throughput
(FEED, 25% Cli Buffers, Slow Net)

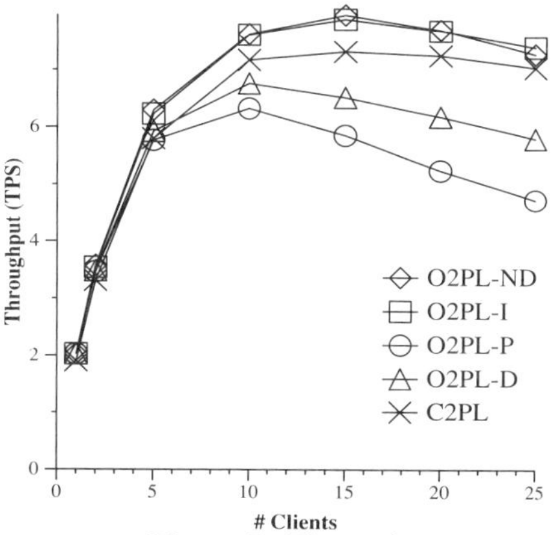

Figure 7: Throughput
(UNIFORM, 25% Cli Buffers, Slow Net)

before they are forced out of the buffer pool or another consistency action arrives for the page).

The lower performance of O2PL-P and O2PL-D, as compared to O2PL-I and O2PL-ND, is due to both messages and disk I/O. The additional messages are due to the propagations just described. As was seen in [Carey et al., 1991], the additional disk I/O is caused by slightly lower server and client buffer hit rates. These lower hit rates result from the fact that with propagation of updates, pages are removed from the client buffers only when they are aged out. Aged-out pages are not likely to be found in the server buffer pool if they are needed (thus lowering the server buffer hit rate), and propagated pages take up valuable space in the small client buffer pool if they are not needed (thus lowering the client hit rate).

The O2PL-ND algorithm performs similarly to O2PL-I mainly because the majority of its consistency operations are invalidates. This is because the invalidation window is small relative to the database size. As the invalidate window size is increased O2PL-ND becomes more like the original O2PL-D algorithm. Sensitivity tests showed that while the number of propagations per committed transaction increases with the window size, it remains quite small in the range of window sizes tested (10 to 100) and the number of useless propagations grows slowly and smoothly with the invalidate window size in that range. Therefore, there is reasonable room for error in choosing the window size as long as it is kept well below the size of the database.

Figure 3 shows the throughput results for the HOTCOLD workload and slow network when the client buffer size is increased to 25% of the database size (312 pages). This case shows the effect of the updated system parameter settings used in this study. In [Carey et al., 1991], which used slower CPUs and a faster network, O2PL-D achieved performance much closer to that of O2PL-I for this case. The earlier parameter settings were based on the intuition that the network itself would not ever be a bottleneck. However, the continuing disparity in the performance increases of CPUs and installed networks has increased the likelihood of a network bottleneck arising. The effect of these technology trends is an increase in the relative cost of useless propagations and as a result, the relative performance of O2PL-D suffers. These trends also exacerbate the performance problems incurred by O2PL-P. In this case, O2PL-P and O2PL-D become network-bound, while O2PL-I and O2PL-ND approach a disk bottleneck at 25 clients. In terms of the new heuristic, the results in this case are similar to those for the 5% client buffer case; O2PL-ND closely matches the performance of O2PL-I because the vast majority of its consistency operations are invalidations. Furthermore, nearly all of the invalidations are the result of pages not being in the invalidate window (condition 3), so the invalidate window is effective in avoiding even the single mistake that is made by O2PL-D.

We now turn to the throughput results for the HOTCOLD workload using the fast network. When the smaller client buffer pool size is used (not shown), the results are similar to those of the slow network case (Figure 2) in that O2PL-I and O2PL-ND have similar performance, while O2PL-P and O2PL-D have similar but lower performance. However, due to the fast network, the performance differences among the O2PL algorithms are primarily driven by disk I/O requirements. When the larger client buffer size is used in conjunction with the fast network (shown in Figure 4), the original dynamic algorithm performs significantly better than O2PL-P because it performs many fewer propagations than O2PL-P. O2PL-P becomes CPU-bound at the server due to message processing overhead, while all other algorithms eventually become disk-bound. At 15 clients and beyond, O2PL-D matches and even slightly exceeds the performance of O2PL-I and O2PL-ND. This is due to the fact that

O2PL-D has a better client hit rate than these other algorithms, and thus requires fewer disk I/Os per transaction. Its improved hit rate is due to the fact that O2PL-D performs more than twice as many useful propagations as O2PL-ND. Of course, O2PL-D also performs many more wasted propagations than O2PL-ND, but the overhead of these propagations is not high enough here to cause O2PL-D to become network or server CPU-bound and the large buffer-pool size ensures that hot range pages will remain in the client buffer pool despite the wasted propagations.

4.1.2 Experiment 2: The FEED Workload [3]

In the FEED workload, client 1 reads and writes data pages, while all other clients only read data pages, and thus, there is a flow of information from client 1 to the others. In contrast to the HOTCOLD workload, where propagation is generally a bad idea, the FEED workload was shown in [Carey et al., 1991] to benefit from propagation. This result also holds in general in this study, however, an exception arises in the case with small client buffer sizes and the slow network (Figure 5). In this case, O2PL-I has the highest reader throughput at 15 clients and beyond, while O2PL-P has the lowest reader throughput of the O2PL algorithms. The dynamic algorithms fall roughly between the two static ones, with O2PL-ND having a slight advantage. This ordering is due to the combination of the slow network, which makes propagations expensive, and the small buffer pool, which causes propagations to be wasted. For the O2PL algorithms that do propagation, 53% to 60% of the propagations actually prove to be useful. Moreover, due to the small client buffer pools, many of these propagations are used only once before the page is thrown out. A propagation costs a page-sized message. On the other hand, a propagation that is used exactly once saves only a smaller control message (the page request message that would be required to obtain the page from the server). Thus, if many "useful" propagations are used only once before being thrown out of the buffer pool or re-propagated to, the net effect of a small majority of useful propagations can be a reduction in the number of messages but an increase in the demand for network bandwidth. This is the effect seen in Figure 5.

The FEED workload with small client buffer pools was the only situation examined where the invalidate window size of O2PL-ND made a noticeable performance difference within the range of 10 to 100 pages. In fact, differences are only noticed at window sizes of 50 and smaller, as a window size of 50 pages allows all pages that are updated by the FEED workload to fit in the window. The sensitivity in this case results from the combination of the small client buffer pools and the small number of pages that are updated in the FEED workload. Because of the small buffer pools, hot region pages are often removed by being aged out rather than invalidated. If the window size is less than 50, an aged-out page may not have an entry in the window when it is re-referenced because its entry was pushed out by invalidations of other pages. Therefore, a hot page that is marked as recently invalidated, but then aged out, can lose its marking on a subsequent re-reference. A window size of 50 avoids this problem for the FEED workload, since only 50 pages are ever updated. Therefore a small decrease in the window size raises the possibility of losing the markings of aged-out pages. While the algorithm is sensitive to the window size in this case, its performance is bracketed by O2PL-I (i.e., a window size of 0) and O2PL-D (i.e., a window size of 50). In this test, at 10 clients and beyond, O2PL-ND (window size = 20) chooses to invalidate remote copies about 40% of the time, while O2PL-D chooses to invalidate only about 15% of the time.

[3] Due to space limitations, we report results only for the slow network case here.

Figure 6 shows the throughput of the FEED workload with the slow network when the client buffer pool size is increased to 25% of the database size. As in the previous case, all of the algorithms approach a network bottleneck; in this case however, O2PL-P significantly outperforms O2PL-I. The larger buffer pools allow all of the clients to keep their 50 hot range pages in memory, so many fewer of O2PL-P's propagations are wasted due to pages being forced out of the buffer pool. As a result, O2PL-I sends more page requests to the server than O2PL-P, which results in increased path length for transactions under O2PL-I. This additional path length includes additional messages (O2PL-I sends about 6 messages per transaction versus about 3 per transaction for O2PL-P), and additional lock requests at the server. The two dynamic algorithms have nearly identical performance in this case; they are slightly worse than O2PL-P but much better than O2PL-I. O2PL-D and O2PL-ND perform similarly because O2PL-ND's additional condition for propagation almost always holds here. Due to the large client buffer size, hot range pages are aged out of the buffer pool very infrequently — they are removed mainly as the result of invalidations. Invalidated hot pages are likely to be re-referenced quickly, and if so, they will still be in the invalidate window when the re-reference occurs. Therefore, in this case, a small invalidate window is sufficient to detect invalidated hot pages, so O2PL-ND is fairly insensitive to the invalidate window size.

4.1.3 Experiment 3: The UNIFORM Workload

So far we have investigated one workload where invalidation is advantageous and one in which propagation performs well. We now briefly examine the UNIFORM workload, in which caching is not expected to provide much of a performance benefit. In [Carey et al., 1991], there was very little performance difference among the algorithms when the UNIFORM workload was run with the 5% client buffer pool size. Here, this holds only for the fast network case. In the slow network case with the small client buffer pools (not shown), O2PL-P and O2PL-D perform noticeably below the level of the other O2PL algorithms due to the message costs for wasted propagations. More significant differences arise when the client buffer size is increased to 25%. As shown in Figure 7, when the slow network is used, O2PL-I and O2PL-ND perform similarly, and both are much better than O2PL-P and O2PL-D. In this workload, propagations do not generally turn out to be useful (e.g., fewer than 15% of O2PL-P's propagations are useful in this case) because the workload's lack of locality means that pages are likely to be aged out of the buffer pool or updated elsewhere before they are accessed again at a site. Therefore, doing fewer propagations results in sending fewer messages and better performance in this case. O2PL-P and O2PL-D approach a network bottleneck at 25 clients, while the other algorithms become disk-bound. When the fast network is used (not shown), the network becomes less of a factor as the disk becomes the main bottleneck. In this case, O2PL-I and O2PL-ND have a slight performance advantage due to better server and client buffer hit rates that result from their use of invalidations.

4.1.4 Summary

The experiments presented in Sections 4.1.1 thru 4.1.3 show that the new heuristic for the dynamic algorithm performs as well as the static O2PL-I algorithm in cases where invalidation is the correct approach, which O2PL-D was unable to do. In addition, it retains the performance advantages of the O2PL-D heuristic in cases where propagation is advantageous. Though the new heuristic never significantly outperformed the better of the static algorithms in any of the cases tested, it was shown to be a reasonable choice even in situations with static locality.

4.2 CALLBACK LOCKING

In this section, we study the performance of the two Callback Locking algorithms: CB-Read and CB-All. For comparison purposes, we also show the performance of O2PL-ND and C2PL. Experiments were run with client buffer pool sizes of 5% and 25% of the database size. Results are shown only for the 25% case since the important aspects of the performance of the CB algorithms are slightly more pronounced (but not qualitatively different) in the large client buffer pool case.

4.2.1 Experiment 4: The HOTCOLD Workload

Figure 8 shows the results of the HOTCOLD workload using the slow network and a client buffer pool size of 25%. The C2PL algorithm has the lowest throughput due to the combination of high message requirements (shown in Figure 9) and its higher disk requirements (compared the others) due to lower buffer hit rates. In general, the CB algorithms both perform at a somewhat lower level than O2PL-ND, which has the highest throughput overall. These results are driven primarily by the message requirements of the algorithms, as the disk requirements of the two CB algorithms and the O2PL-ND algorithm are nearly identical. This is because the CB algorithms are invalidation-based, and O2PL-ND chooses to use invalidation for over 90% of its consistency operations. As shown in Figure 9, the CB algorithms send significantly more messages per commit than O2PL-ND. The difference between CB-Read and O2PL-ND is due to the fact that CB-Read performs consistency operations on a per-page basis, while O2PL-ND performs consistency operations only at the end of the execution phase. O2PL-ND saves messages by sending fewer requests to the server for consistency actions (one per transaction versus as many as one per write for CB-Read) and, to a lesser extent, by grouping multiple consistency requests for the same client in a single message. In contrast to CB-Read, CB-All is allowed to cache write locks; this is the reason for its sending fewer messages than CB-Read when small numbers of clients are present. However, beyond 10 clients the caching of write locks results in a net increase in messages. For the CB algorithms, the advantage of caching a write lock is that a request for a lock on a site where it is already cached saves one round trip message with the server. However, the penalty for caching a write lock that conflicts with a read request at a different site is also a round trip message with the server. In the HOTCOLD workload, caching write locks becomes a losing proposition when the number of clients is sufficient to make it more likely that a page will be read at some remote site before it is re-written at a site with a cached write lock. When the fast network is used (not shown), all of the algorithms eventually become disk-bound so the messaging effects discussed in the slow network case eventually have no impact on the throughput. As a result, CB-Read, CB-All and O2PL-ND all have similar performance.

4.2.2 Experiment 5: The FEED Workload

The reader and writer throughput results for the FEED workload with the slow network are shown in Figure 10. O2PL-ND has the best reader throughput prior to 10 clients, while CB-Read and CB-All have the best reader throughput beyond 10 clients. The writer throughput is similar for all of the algorithms at 5 clients and beyond. O2PL-ND and CB-All have better writer throughput when there are 0 or 1 reader sites. Once again, the throughput results are driven by the message requirements of the algorithms. Figure 11 shows the messages sent per commit averaged over the writer and all of the readers for

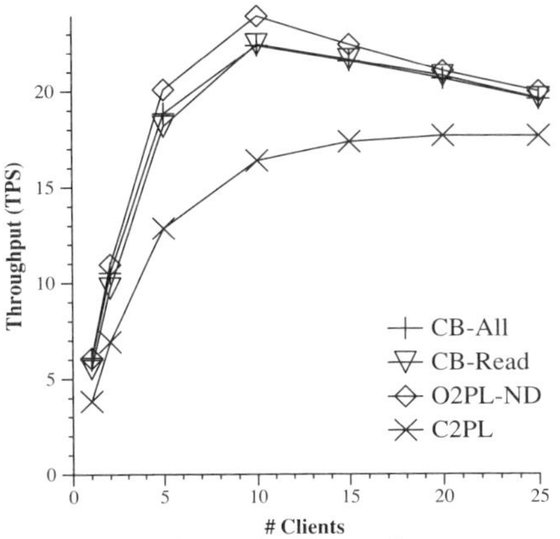

Figure 8: Throughput
(HOTCOLD, 25% Cli Buffers, Slow Net)

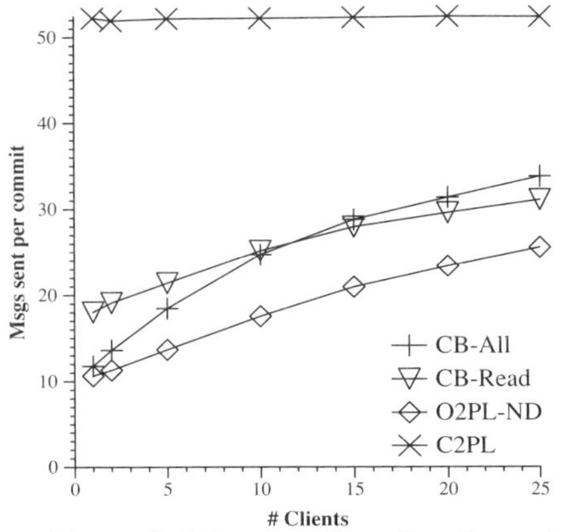

Figure 9: Messages Sent Per Commit
(HOTCOLD, 25% Cli Buffers, Slow Net)

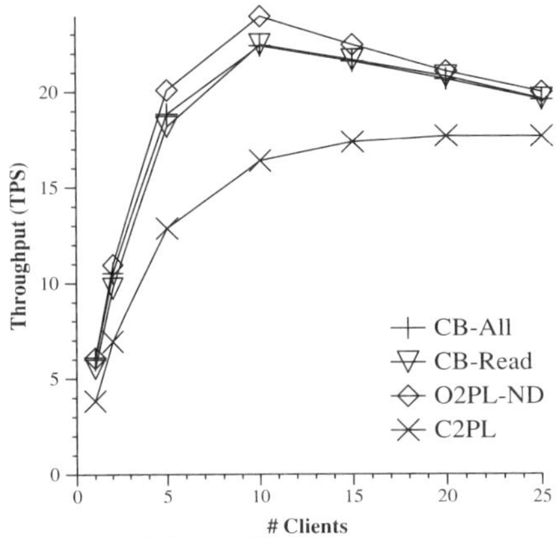

Figure 10: Throughput
(FEED, 25% Cli Buffers, Slow Net)

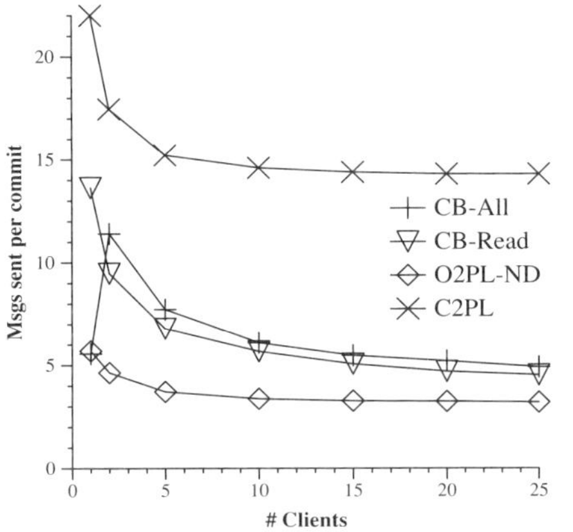

Figure 11: Messages Sent Per Commit
(FEED, 25% Cli Buffers)

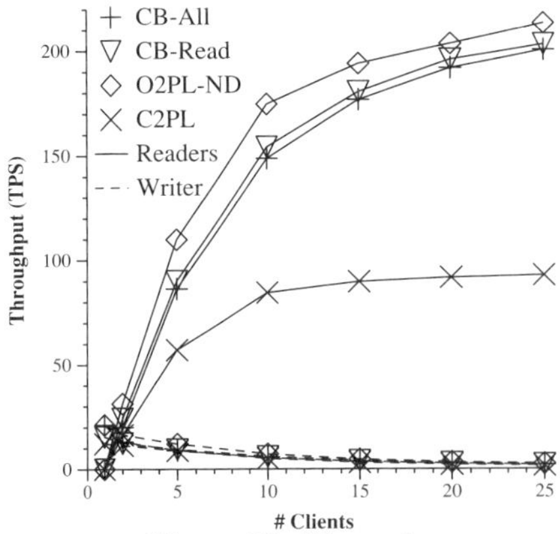

Figure 12: Throughput
(FEED, 25% Cli Buffers, Fast Net)

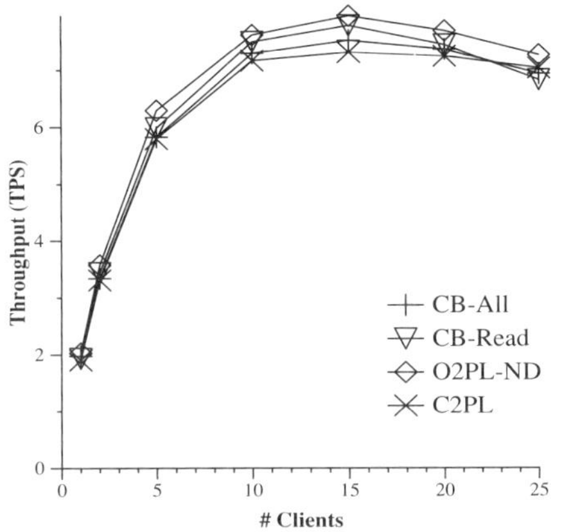

Figure 13: Throughput
(UNIFORM, 25% Cli Buffers, Slow Net)

each of the algorithms.[4] O2PL-ND's higher initial reader throughput is due to its lower message requirements, which result from its reduced consistency message requirements (as described previously) and a better client buffer hit rate due to propagations. All of the algorithms except for C2PL approach a network bottleneck at 15 clients and beyond. As the network becomes saturated, the cost of wasted propagations performed by O2PL-ND cause its reader performance to suffer compared to the callback algorithms. In terms of the callback algorithms, the writer site in CB-Read has to request every write lock from the server, while in the CB-All algorithm, the writer has to request write locks that have been called back (virtually all write locks at five clients and beyond). CB-All also requires extra messages for readers to callback the write locks that are cached at the writer site. As a result, CB-All's writer site receives and sends up to 6 times more messages per commit than CB-Read's writer site in this case. The callback requests for write locks are the cause of the difference in the message requirements for the CB algorithms seen in Figure 11. Furthermore, there is little or no benefit to caching write locks here, as the updated pages are in the hot region of all of the readers and are thus likely to be read at reader clients. The C2PL algorithm has the highest message requirements for reader sites, as such sites must send a message to the server for each page accessed. Many of these messages are small, so their main impact on C2PL is an increase in server and client CPU requirements.

The throughput results for the FEED workload with the fast network are shown in Figure 12. Again, in this case, all of the algorithms except for C2PL approach (but do not quite reach) a disk bottleneck at 25 clients. C2PL eventually becomes server CPU-bound due to lock requests that are sent to the server. The propagations performed by O2PL-ND give it a better buffer hit rate at the reader clients. However, this translates to only a slight reduction in disk reads compared to the callback algorithms, as hot pages missed at clients due to invalidations are likely to be in the server's buffer pool. Thus, in the range of clients studied, the relative performance of the algorithms is still largely dictated by the message characteristics as described for the slow network case. With the fast network, the size of the messages is less important. Therefore the relative performance of the algorithms is more in line with the message counts shown in Figure 12.

4.2.3 Experiment 6: The UNIFORM Workload

The results for the UNIFORM workload using the slow network are shown in Figure 13. None of the algorithms hits a resource bottleneck in the range of clients shown. O2PL-ND achieves the highest throughput across the range of client populations, with the callback algorithms performing below O2PL-ND but better than C2PL through most of the range. CB-Read performs slightly better than CB-All because caching write locks is costly due to the lack of locality and the low write probability. The decline in throughput for the three lock caching algorithms is due to their increased message requirements for consistency operations in this low-locality workload. At 15 clients and beyond, all three of the lock caching algorithms send more messages than C2PL, which does not cache locks. While C2PL's message requirements per commit remain constant as clients are added, the lock caching algorithms are forced to send consistency operations (e.g., invalidations or callbacks) to more sites. C2PL's lower performance through most of the range is due to its higher disk requirements resulting from low client and server buffer hit rates. The reason that the algorithms do not quite reach a bottleneck in this case is a higher level

[4] Since client number 1 is the writer site, the data points for one client in Figure 11 show the messages per writer transaction in the absence of conflicting readers.

of data contention than was seen in the other workloads. When the fast network is used (not shown), the network effects are removed as all algorithms eventually approach a disk bottleneck. Therefore, the lock caching algorithms perform similarly, and slightly better than C2PL due to buffering characteristics.

4.2.4 Experiment 7: The HICON workload

The final workload examined in this paper is the HICON workload. While we do not expect high data contention to be typical for client-server DBMS applications, we use this workload to examine the robustness of the algorithms in the presence of data contention and to gain a better understanding of their different approaches to detecting conflicts. As described in Section 3.2, this workload has a 250 page hot range that is shared by all clients. The write probability for hot range pages is varied from 0% to 50% in order to study different levels of data contention. In this section we briefly describe the HICON results, using the fast network and large client buffer pools. Figure 14 shows the throughput for HICON with a hot write probability of 5%. In the range of 1 to 5 clients, the lock caching algorithms perform similarly and C2PL has the lowest performance. C2PL's lower performance in this range is due to its significantly higher message requirements here. These results are latency-based, as no bottlenecks develop in this range — in fact, no resource bottlenecks are reached by any of the algorithms in this experiment. At 10 clients and beyond, the effects of increased data contention become apparent; O2PL-ND's performance suffers and it has the lowest utilization of all three major system resources (disk, server CPU, and network). O2PL-ND has a somewhat higher level of blocking for concurrency control than the other algorithms (e.g., at 15 clients, approximately 42% of its transactions are blocked at any given time versus approximately 37% for the callback algorithms and 35% for C2PL). O2PL-ND has a higher blocking level because it detects global deadlocks using periodic detection, while the other algorithms detect deadlocks immediately at the server. All of the algorithms suffer from increased blocking as clients are added. In addition, the lock caching algorithms suffer from increasing message costs due to consistency messages as clients are added. These two factors account for the thrashing behavior seen in Figure 14. Again, in this workload, the caching of write locks causes CB-All to send more messages than CB-Read. C2PL performs best at 25 clients because at that point it sends the fewest messages. C2PL's message requirements remain fairly constant as clients are added to the system, while the other algorithms all incur an increase in messages for consistency operations as clients are added. The slight downturn in performance seen for C2PL beyond 15 clients is due to data contention.

Figure 15 shows the throughput of the algorithms when the hot write probability is increased to 10%. Here, the trends seen in the 5% write probability case are even more pronounced. C2PL becomes the highest performing algorithm at 15 clients and beyond, and O2PL-ND performs at a much lower level than the other algorithms. C2PL sends fewer messages per transaction than the other algorithms at fifteen clients and beyond in this case. An increase in data contention causes all of the algorithms to exhibit thrashing behavior beyond 10 clients. In this case, the thrashing is due not only to additional blocking, but also to a significant number of aborts. For example, at 20 clients, O2PL-ND performs nearly 0.6 aborts per committed transaction, while the other algorithms perform about 0.3 aborts per commit. In all of the HICON experiments, O2PL-ND was found to have a significantly higher abort rate than the other three algorithms. This is due to the fact that it resolves write-write conflicts using aborts, whereas the other three algorithms resolve them using

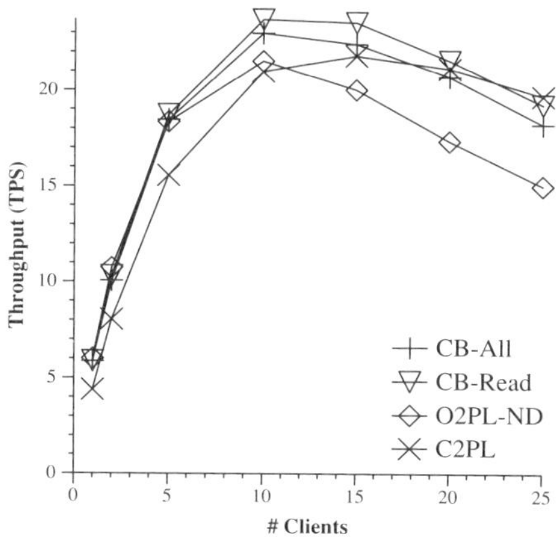

Figure 14: Throughput
(5% HICON, 25% Cli Buffers, Fast Net)

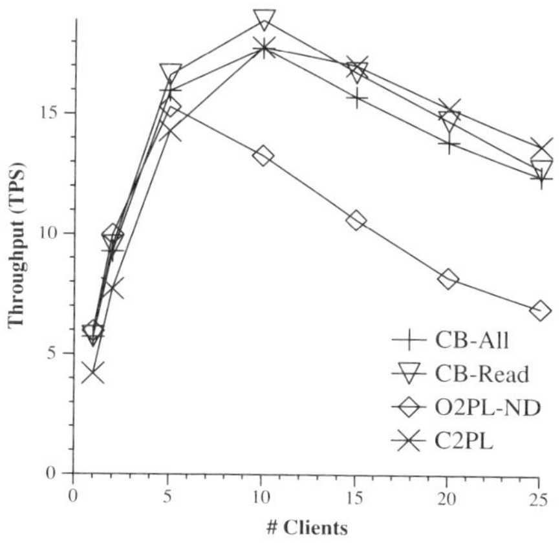

Figure 15: Throughput
(10% HICON, 25% Cli Buffers, Fast Net)

blocking. The trends seen in these two cases become more pronounced as the hot write probability is increased beyond the two cases shown here. An interesting effect that appears with higher write probabilities (e.g., HICON with write probabilities of 25% and 50%) is that in some cases, O2PL-ND actually has fewer blocked transactions than the other algorithms. This effect arises because of its higher abort rate, which at high contention levels acts as a throttle on the blocking level. However, the net result is that O2PL-ND performs worse relative to the other algorithms as the hot write probability is increased.

4.2.5 Summary

The results described in Sections 4.2.1-4.2.4 show that the CB algorithms have similar (but often slightly lower) performance to O2PL-ND. The CB algorithms typically have higher message requirements than O2PL-ND because they perform consistency maintenance on a per-page basis. Therefore, they perform below the level of O2PL-ND in situations where network usage plays a large factor in determining performance. However, in situations where disk I/O is the dominant factor, they perform comparably to O2PL-ND. The caching of write locks (by CB-All) decreased message traffic only in cases with few clients or limited data contention, and resulted in additional message costs in most other cases. The CB algorithms performed much better than C2PL under most workloads, while retaining the lower (compared to O2PL-ND) abort rate of that algorithm. This is because the CB algorithms cache locks across transactions without using optimistic techniques. The combination of pessimism and the ability to perform deadlock detection locally at the server allow the CB algorithms to be much more robust in the presence of data contention than O2PL-ND. C2PL had the best performance under very high data contention because it has a low abort rate and fast deadlock detection (similar to CB) together with message requirements that remain constant as client sites are added to the system. However, in all other cases, C2PL performed below the level of the CB algorithms and the better of the O2PL algorithms.

5 RELATED WORK [5]

5.1 DYNAMIC ALGORITHMS

We are unaware of any other work investigating dynamic algorithms for choosing between propagation and invalidation to maintain cache consistency in a client-server DBMS environment. Similar problems have been addressed in work on Non-Uniform Memory Access (NUMA) architectures, however. In such systems, an access to a data object that is located in a remote memory can result in migrating the data object to the requesting site (invalidation), replicating the object (propagation), or simply accessing the object remotely using the hardware support of a shared-memory multiprocessor. These issues are addressed in Munin [Carter et al., 1991] by allowing the programmer to annotate data declarations with a designation of the sharing properties of each variable. These annotations serve as hints to Munin in deciding among propagation and invalidation, making replication decisions, etc. DUnX [LaRowe et al., 1991] uses a parameterized policy which chooses dynamically among page replacement options based on reference histories. The parameters allow a user to adjust the level of dynamism of the algorithms. [LaRowe et al., 1991] demonstrated that it was possible to find a set of default parameter settings that provided good performance over a range of NUMA workloads.

5.2 CALLBACK LOCKING

A Callback Locking algorithm for client-server database systems was studied in [Wang and Rowe, 1991]. That study compared the callback algorithm with a caching 2PL algorithm (similar to C2PL) and two variants of a "no-wait" locking algorithm that allowed clients to access cached objects before receiving a lock response from the server. The results of that study showed that if network delay was taken into account, Callback Locking was the best among the algorithms studied when locality was high or data contention was low, with caching 2PL being better in high conflict situations. These results mostly agree with those presented in Section 4.2, but there are several differences between the two studies. First, the workload model used in [Wang and Rowe, 1991] provided a notion of locality that was more dynamic than that of this study but was not as flexible in terms of the nature of data sharing among clients. [Wang and Rowe, 1991] did not study the implications of caching write locks, and did not examine algorithms that have lower message requirements such as O2PL-ND. Also, as described in Section 2.3, the Callback Locking algorithm in [Wang and Rowe, 1991] differed from CB-Read in its method of detecting deadlocks.

An area that is closely related to client-server caching is work on using Distributed Shared Virtual Memory (DSM) to support database systems [Bellew et al., 1990]. DSM is a technique that implements the abstraction of a system-wide single-level store in a distributed system [Li and Hudak, 1989]. Three algorithms for maintaining cache consistency were studied in [Bellew et al., 1990], one of which was a 2PL variant that used callbacks. The callback algorithm was compared to several broadcast-based algorithms using a simulation model that had an inexpensive broadcast facility. Given this facility, the callback-style algorithm typically had lower performance than one of the broadcast algorithms. Several related algorithms for the shared-disk environment have been investigated in [Dan and Yu, 1992]. These algorithms include shared-disk equivalents of the C2PL, CB-Read and

[5] In this section we discuss work related to the specific issues that were addressed in this study. For work related to client-server caching in general see [Carey et al., 1991].

CB-All algorithms. An algorithm that was similar to CB-Read (i.e., it retained only read locks) was shown to perform relatively well in that study.

As mentioned earlier, callback algorithms were initially developed for use in distributed file systems. The Andrew File System [Howard et al., 1988] uses a callback scheme to inform sites of pending modifications to files that they have cached. This scheme does not guarantee consistent updates, however. Files that must be kept consistent, such as directories, are handled by simply not allowing them to be updated at cached sites. Sprite [Nelson et al., 1988] provides consistent updates, but it does so by disallowing caching for files that are open for write access. This is done using a callback mechanism that informs sites that a file is no longer cachable.

6 CONCLUSIONS

In this paper, we have extended the results of the earlier client-server caching study of [Carey et al., 1991]. A new heuristic for the dynamic O2PL algorithm was shown to perform as well as a static invalidation-based O2PL algorithm in cases where invalidation is the correct approach — which the heuristic of [Carey et al., 1991] was unable to do. In addition, it retains the performance advantages of the earlier heuristic in cases where propagation is advantageous. The heuristic uses a fixed window size parameter, but it was found to be fairly insensitive to the exact size of the window as long as the window size was kept small in proportion to the database size. The advantages of the new heuristic were more significant than were seen with the parameters of [Carey et al., 1991], as the greater disparity between CPU speeds and network bandwidth here (when the slow network was used) increased the negative effects of bad propagations compared to what was seen in that study. Two variants of Callback Locking were described and studied: CB-Read, which caches only read locks, and CB-All, which caches both read and write locks. CB-Read was found to perform as well as or slightly better than CB-All in many situations, because the caching of write locks caused a net increase in messages except in cases with small client populations or minimal data contention. Both CB algorithms were seen to have slightly lower performance than O2PL-ND (which typically sent fewer messages) in situations where network usage plays a large factor in determining performance but their performance was similar to that of O2PL-ND in cases where disk I/O was the dominant factor. However, the CB algorithms were seen to have a lower abort rate than O2PL-ND, and were much more robust than O2PL-ND in the presence of data contention. A low abort rate is particularly important in a workstation-based environment, as the abort of a complex transaction is likely to be less acceptable to users than the abort of a simple transaction (e.g., in a transaction processing environment). Finally, C2PL, which does not cache locks, was found to be the best algorithm for workloads with very high data contention, but performed below the level of the CB algorithms and O2PL-ND in all other cases.

The results of this study have led us to choose CB-Read for implementation in the EXODUS system. This choice is due to its combination of good performance, low abort rate, and relative ease of implementation. This implementation effort is currently under way. In addition, a number of issues remain to be addressed in the area of cache consistency algorithms. In particular, mixed workloads and workloads with dynamic properties should be studied to better demonstrate the effectiveness of the adaptive algorithms. In addition, it should be possible to devise adaptive versions of the callback algorithms that perform better in situations where propagation is appropriate. It should also be possible to devise algorithms that are adaptive in terms of lock caching as well as data caching, in order to handle high contention "hot spot" data. Finally, we are investigating ways of more fully exploiting the memory and processing power of the workstations in a client-server database system. A first step in this direction is described in [Franklin et al., 1992a].

Acknowledgements

We thank Miron Livny and Beau Shekita for providing insight into the performance of client-server systems. We also thank Dave Maier and the database reading group at OGI for providing helpful comments on an earlier version of this paper. This work was partially supported by DARPA under contract DAAB07-92-C-Q508, by the National Science Foundation under grant IRI-8657323, and by a research grant from IBM.

Distributed Object Management in Thor

Barbara Liskov
Massachusetts Institute of Technology
Laboratory for Computer Science
Cambridge, MA 02139
U.S.A.

Mark Day
Massachusetts Institute of Technology
Laboratory for Computer Science
Cambridge, MA 02139
U.S.A.

Liuba Shrira
Massachusetts Institute of Technology
Laboratory for Computer Science
Cambridge, MA 02139
U.S.A.

Abstract

Thoris a new object-oriented database management system (OODBMS), intended to be used in heterogeneous distributed systems to allow programs written in different programming languages to share objects in a convenient manner. Thor objects are persistent in spite of failures, are highly likely to be accessible whenever they are needed, and can be structured to reflect the kinds of information of interest to users. Thor combines the advantages of the object-oriented approach with those of database systems: users can store and manipulate objects that capture the semantics of their applications, and can also access objects via queries.

Thor is an ongoing project, and this paper is a snapshot: we describe our first design and a partial implementation of that design. This design is primarily concerned with issues related to the implementation of an OODBMS as a distributed system.

1 INTRODUCTION

Distributed systems contain different kinds of computers, and users write programs in different programming languages. The programs have persistent data that they need to share. This paper describes a new system called Thor that is intended to provide a convenient sharing mechanism.

Thor allows users to store and manipulate objects that capture the semantics of their applications. Users can access these objects by high level path names, by navigation, and also by means of queries.

Thor provides users with a universe of persistent objects. Objects in the universe can refer to one another, so that useful object structures, such as graphs and trees, can be constructed. All accesses to Thor objects occur within atomic transactions so that objects can remain consistent in spite of concurrency and failures.

To support heterogeneity Thor provides a language-independent type system that allows programs written in different programming languages to share data. The type system is hierarchical to support program evolution. Thor objects are abstract and encapsulated: each object has operations (or methods) that can be used to interact with it. Users can extend the type system by defining new, abstract types. A type is defined by a specification; specifications are independent both of any programming language used to access the type's objects and of the language used to implement the new type.

Thor provides a persistent root and high-level path names that can be used to name objects relative to the root. The root provides the basis for persistence: All objects accessible (directly or indirectly) from the root persist. If a persistent object ceases to be accessible, it will be garbage collected. Persistent objects are stored reliably, so that with high probability they will not be lost in the case of failures, and they are highly-available, so that they are highly likely to be accessible when needed. High availability and reliability are supported by a novel implementation strategy based on replication. In addition, Thor supports secure sharing by allowing users to define access control for objects.

Thor is a distributed system in which objects are stored at server nodes that are distinct from the machines where client programs reside. Nevertheless, it will provide clients with fast access to objects. Thor front ends run at client machines to cache and prefetch objects and to run operations on objects locally, thus reducing delay as observed by the clients. This architecture provides high performance and also scalability, since front ends offload work from the servers and extra servers can be added to accommodate increased load.

The Thor data model is a unique synthesis of ideas from programming languages and databases. Unlike many systems [Atkinson et al., 1983a; Richardson and Carey, 1987; Weinreb et al., 1988; Nettles and Wing, 1992], it is language-independent rather than being embedded in a particular programming language. It provides access to object through both navigation and queries (as opposed to conventional database systems (e.g., [Stonebraker et al., 1990]) that support only queries). Furthermore, it supports full indexing for queries over sets of abstract objects, as opposed to the more limited techniques in [Bertino and Kim, 1989; Maier and Stein, 1986; Stonebraker et al., 1990; Zdonik, 1988]. Concurrency control and recovery are provided for individual objects (unlike many other systems such as [Atkinson et al., 1983a, Haskin et al., 1987]); furthermore programmers can control the granularity of concurrency control and recovery (the techniques in [Weihl and Liskov, 1985] are being extended here). Unlike all other systems, it provides highly-available access to persistent objects. Finally, its implementation is fully distributed; not only are clients separated from servers, but the servers themselves are distributed.

Thor is an ongoing project, and this paper is a snapshot: we describe our first design and a partial implementation of that design. That design emphasizes issues related to the implementation of an OODBMS as a distributed system. We are currently working on a second design and a different implementation.

In the next section, we sketch the basic system architecture. Subsequent sections discuss the elements of this architecture in more detail.

2 SYSTEM ARCHITECTURE

Thor is intended to run in an environment of computing nodes connected by a network. Some of these nodes are Thor servers, which store the objects in the Thor universe. Others are client nodes where users of Thor run their programs. Although it is possible that a single node might act as both a server and a client, the common case is for client and server nodes to be distinct; we assume this separation in the remainder of this discussion.

The Thor system runs on both clients and servers. It runs front ends (FEs) at the client nodes, and back ends (BEs) and object repositories (ORs) at the servers. Users always interact with Thor via an FE, which typically resides at the user's workstation. The FE makes use of BEs and ORs to carry out client requests. The FEs and BEs understand types and perform operations. The ORs are concerned only with managing the storage for the persistent objects.

Every persistent object resides at one of the ORs. Usually this is the OR selected when it first became persistent. An object can move from one OR to another under user control, although we expect this to be rare. Each OR runs at one or more servers, and its objects are replicated at those servers (see Section 2.4).

There are two major obstacles to achieving good performance in such a distributed system: (1) the delay inherent in having clients and servers at distinct nodes, and (2) high load at servers, which slows down their response to requests. Below we discuss our approach to overcoming these obstacles.

When a user asks the FE to perform an operation on an object, the system will not run well if doing the operation always involves a remote access, e.g., to the OR that stores the object. The delay is not so bad if the operation involves a significant amount of computation. More typically, however, operations will be short relative to the network delay, so we would like to avoid the delay.

The situation is especially difficult in Thor because we assume that there are many servers and the servers are geographically distributed. Although we expect most objects used in a client application to reside at a single OR that is physically close to the client node (e.g., on the same local area net), an application might use objects from several ORs, some of which are far away from the client.

Delay can be masked in one of two ways: by caching objects at the FE, so that operations can usually be executed at the FE without the need for remote access, or by combining a number of calls into a larger "combined operation" that can be performed at an OR, so that the cost of the remote access can be amortized across several calls.

The other performance issue is reducing the load at the servers. Work in distributed file systems has shown that servers are the critical resource in a distributed system like ours, and that the way to improve system performance is to offload work from servers to clients [Howard et al., 1988; Nelson et al., 1988]. The analog in our system is again caching at the FEs and running the operations there.

Therefore we do most client requests at the FEs. FEs cache copies of objects from the ORs. When a client executes an operation, the FE runs it, fetching objects from the ORs if necessary. We hope that fetching will usually not be necessary because the objects that are needed are already cached at the FE. We discuss techniques that improve the likelihood of hitting in the cache in Section 2.1.

In our first design, all operations run at FEs (with the exception of queries as discussed further in Section 2.5). Ultimately, however, we may run some operations at servers, in the BEs; this will allow us to use the "combined operations" method of improving performance. (For example, an operation to look up a multipart pathname could run at the BE.) We have yet to do a detailed design of BEs, so we do not discuss them further in this paper.

2.1 CLIENTS AND FRONT ENDS

In this section and subsequent sections, we present our first design for Thor and describe a partial implementation of that design (called TH and described in detail in section 3). To distinguish between capabilities that have been implemented and those that have only been designed, we use the present tense in describing the former and the future tense in describing the latter.

2.1.1 Starting Up

As mentioned, clients always interact with Thor via an FE. When a client program begins a session with Thor, the first step is to create or connect to an FE for the client. Each FE acts on behalf of a single client principal (although it could be used by several client processes). An FE will be authenticated, both in its own right, and on behalf of the client principal, to the ORs with which it interacts; we plan to use the Kerberos authentication service [Steiner et al., 1988] for this. Limiting an FE to a single client principal helps in satisfying our security requirement.

Usually the FE resides at the client workstation but it could run elsewhere, e.g., if the client machine is very small, or its system is inadequately secure. Typically, the client program runs in a separate address space from the FE, so that errors in the client program cannot cause the FE to malfunction. However, if client programs are written in a type-safe language, such as ML [Milner et al., 1990] or CLU [Liskov et al., 1981], we can run them in the same address space as the FE. Such an organization will provide better performance because it avoids the cost of inter-process calls. To reduce delay when the client and FE run in different processes, we plan to investigate client "combined operations" as a way of amortizing the cost of the FE call over a larger unit of work. Combined operations might be extracted from the client code by means of a preprocessor.

As part of starting a session, a client will be able to indicate an initial "setup." This setup will initialize the cache at the FE to contain useful objects (e.g., a part of the database for the client application and implementations of the types used by the application) so that we can avoid a lengthy startup transient. We are investigating means for users to indicate what such a setup should be. The client would not be delayed until the entire setup arrives at the FE; rather, the FE will use the setup information to prefetch information in the background.

2.1.2 Computation at the Front End

The client program interacts with Thor by executing Thor commands, e.g., to start and terminate transactions, and to run operations. In our prototype, each client transaction is carried out at a single FE; we plan to investigate multi-FE transactions later, and we will also look at the question of having Thor be a player in a larger environment in which transactions span many databases.

Client programs typically refer to objects by means of *handles*. These are names created by the FE and given to the client program whenever an operation called by a client returns a reference to an object. Handles are meaningful only with respect to an FE, and only for the duration of the current session.

When a client calls an operation, the FE begins by doing type-checking: the arguments (handles and values) must be of the types expected by that operation. This type checking takes account of the type hierarchy: if a formal is of type T, the corresponding actual argument must be of some type S, where S is a subtype of T. Then the FE runs the operation; that operation may call other operations, but these calls do not need to be type-checked because the checking was done at compile time.

2.1.3 Interacting with the Object Repositories

In running the operation, the FE may discover (in a way that we describe shortly) that some required item (e.g., an object, or the code of an operation) is not in its cache. In this case it must fetch that item from an OR. A fetch returns a *block* containing the requested object and also a number of other objects that are related to it. In other words, we do not fetch single objects, but rather we fetch them in groups.

Fetching in groups is important because it can enable us to "prime" the cache by filling it with objects that are likely to be used shortly; it also gives us a way of dealing with small objects effectively. One of the major challenges of the implementation is getting the blocks right so that the objects brought over really are likely to be used. We are planning to investigate a number of *prefetching* strategies. Some of these are fairly static, e.g., when an object is stored at an OR, it is stored close to related objects on disk; a block could thus contain objects that are close to one another on disk. An example of a more dynamic strategy is to have the FE indicate in the fetch command other items of interest, e.g., if the required object x refers to n others, the FE could indicate that the i-th and the k-th are also of interest. An interesting research question is how an FE might know what other objects are of interest: does this information come from a client combined operation, or is there some other way that a client, or a Thor program (coded in our implementation language), indicates this?

A block need not be sent to the FE as a single unit, but rather it can be streamed across (as in Mercury [Liskov et al., 1988]). As the objects arrive at an FE, they are copied into the FE virtual memory space, and any object references they contain, which are expressed in OR terms as *orefs* (see Section 2.2), are changed to FE virtual memory addresses, i.e., we are "swizzling" pointers. Our scheme here has similarities to Mneme [Moss, 1990] and also to other object-oriented systems such as [Kaehler and Krasner, 1990]. If we encounter a reference to an object that does not reside at the FE, we create a *surrogate* for it.[1] The surrogate contains within it the object's OR and oref so that if we need to fetch it later, we know where to find it. A surrogate is only large enough to hold the information to find the real object, not large enough to hold the object. When an object for which there is a surrogate arrives at the FE, we modify the surrogate to refer to the object; this link will be snapped at the next FE garbage collection.

Using a surrogate is what causes the FE to "discover" that an object is not present in the cache, causing an "object fault" to occur. The FE will be able to avoid such faults by prefetching. For example, if it creates a handle for an object, and that object is a surrogate, it will be able to prefetch the object, its type information, and its code, if necessary, since it is reasonable to assume that these items will be needed shortly. This prefetching will be able to take place in the background, without incurring a delay that is visible to the client.

As operations run, they may create new objects. Some of these objects never become persistent; they are used during the session only as temporaries. Such objects reside entirely at the FE. Other new objects become persistent (by having references to them stored into persistent objects). Newly persistent objects are sent to ORs when the transaction that made them persistent commits. Unless specifically instructed otherwise at commit time, Thor stores each newly persistent object at the OR of the object that was modified to make it persistent, and stores the new object "close" to the modified object or components of the modified object so that subsequent fetches will work well.

Non-persistent objects have neither orefs nor oids (see Section 2.2); if the objects become permanent, orefs and oids are assigned at the ORs during the commit where the objects become permanent. The result of a successful commit includes information allowing a front end to fix up its copies of those objects to include the new data.

The roots of the FE are the handles that have been given to the client. The client can optionally inform the FE of its current set of handles, either by listing the handles it still has or by listing the handles that it has determined it will not use in the future. When so informed, the FE runs a garbage collector that discards all objects not accessible from the client's current handles. The FE will eventually have a true garbage collector that runs whenever there is no more free space. Since prefetching may bring over large numbers of reachable but unused objects, reclaiming inaccessible objects may not free enough space at the FE. We may also need to *shrink* (that is, convert to surrogates) some accessible objects that have not been used recently. We are investigating policies governing what objects to shrink or discard as part of our work on prefetching strategies [Day, 1993].

2.2 OBJECT REPOSITORIES

The ORs provide storage for persistent objects. They send copies of objects to FEs in response to fetch commands, and they commit transactions in response to FE commands as described in Section 2.3. Periodically, an OR will do garbage collection and discard any inaccessible objects as discussed below.

[1] A surrogate in Thor is similar to a proxy object in Bellerophon [Dickman, 1992] although some details of implementation are different because Bellerophon and Thor make different assumptions about the structure of the underlying distributed system. A Thor surrogate is also conceptually similar to a surrogate as used in [Fang et al., 1993] although again the details are different.

2.2.1 Fetching and Segments

An OR's persistent objects are stored on disk, which is organized into *segments*. Segments are variable length; each will be allocated contiguously on disk. Each segment is intended to contain a group of related objects, i.e., a *cluster* [Gruber and Amsaleg, 1993]. When asked to fetch an object, an OR responds by sending a block, as previously described. Currently a block (the unit sent) is identical to a segment (the unit stored), but we plan to experiment with more sophisticated mappings between segments and blocks.[2]

Our goals for the fetch command are (1) to limit the number of disk accesses required to carry it out, and (2) to respond with a block of related objects so that future fetches can be avoided. A fetch command identifies the required object by giving its oref. An oref is a name local to that particular OR. We divide an oref into two parts: a segment id, or *sid* for short, and an object number. The sid is used to locate the disk storage for the object's segment by looking it up in the sid-table; we hope to keep this table in primary memory. Then the entire segment is read from disk (unless it is already in primary memory). The segment includes a table mapping the object number to an offset within the segment. This second level of mapping allows an object to move within the segment and change size without affecting its oref.

We can ensure that at most one disk read per fetch is needed by simply stopping the construction of a block at any time that another disk read would be needed. As long as we have the object that was actually requested, we need not send any other objects. Note that the OR will be able to keep information about relationships between segments; once a segment has been fetched, it will be able to prefetch a related segment from disk so that a subsequent fetch may be able to avoid any disk accesses.

Disk performance at the OR will improve if objects are clustered well. Quite a bit of work has been done on clustering strategies [Benzaken and Delobel, 1991; Chang, 1989; Cheng and Hurson, 1991; Shannon and Snodgrass, 1991; Tsangaris and Naughton, 1991; Gruber and Amsaleg, 1993]. Our system is somewhat different from others, however, because objects will be written to segments in the background as explained in Section 2.4. Therefore, we will be able to reorganize segments on the fly if this turns out to be a good thing to do. We plan to experiment with techniques for evaluating the placement of objects in segment and reorganizing segments (for example, as in [Palmer and Zdonik, 1990]).

2.2.2 Mobility and Identity

As mentioned earlier, every object has a unique identity. As long as an object stays at the same OR where it first became persistent, the ⟨OR-id, oref⟩ is a sufficiently unique name (where the OR-id is a unique name for the OR). However, if the object moves (which we expect to be rare), it may be referred to by more than one such name (e.g., its name relative to the old OR and its name relative to the new one). To ensure that the relative names will resolve to the same object, we assign each object an OR-independent unique id called an *oid* when it becomes persistent.

When an object moves from one OR to another, it will leave behind an *OR-surrogate* at the old OR. This surrogate contains the ⟨OR-id, oref⟩ for the object at its new OR. A chaining technique like this is described in [Fowler, 1985]. We believe such a technique will be

[2] Building a block from one or more segments is similar to *assembly* as described in [Maier et al., 1993].

suitable for our system, both because we expect chains to be short, and because ORs will be highly available, so the probability of an FE being unable to access an object because an OR on the path to the object is inaccessible is very small. An alternative to the chaining technique that is also feasible is to use a highly-available location service [Hwang, 1987].

In addition to surrogates caused by mobile objects, references from an object at one OR to an object at another OR make use of OR-surrogates. Whenever an object containing a reference to such a surrogate moves to an FE, we will endeavor to prefetch the surrogate itself. The goal is to ensure that by the time the FE needs to follow the reference, it knows which OR to ask for the object.

2.2.3 Roots

Recall that persistence is based on reachability from the root of Thor. The root names a top-level directory that (conceptually) contains an entry for each OR. The top-level directory is not stored in Thor; instead we find ORs via external systems such as network name servers. Each OR contains a second-level directory.

The OR garbage collector will make use of three kinds of roots: the OR directory, a table for each FE that is currently using the OR, and a table for other ORs. The FE and OR tables contain lists of references used at the respective FEs and ORs. The garbage collector will discard any objects not accessible from these roots. FE references will be discarded when FEs terminate (at the end of client sessions), and also as a result of FE communications (e.g., after an FE garbage collects, it will inform ORs of what references it contains). To determine what to do with references from other ORs, we will use a distributed garbage collection technique. We are currently developing a distributed garbage collection algorithm based on [Hughes, 1985; Ladin, 1989; Shapiro et al., 1990]. We have not decided what local method to use, but we are investigating a generational scheme with several spaces at each OR.

The FE table that acts as a root for garbage collection must contain the orefs of all local objects that might be in use at the FE. In this way we will be able to avoid nasty surprises, e.g., in which an object relied on by the client is discarded by the FE garbage collector because it is thought to be persistent, and is also discarded by the OR garbage collector because it is no longer persistent (due to the activities of some other client). We will fill the FE table lazily, as transactions commit that could cause objects to become apparently unreachable [Maheshwari, 1992].

2.3 TRANSACTIONS

So far we have not discussed how we achieve the atomicity properties—serializability and totality—of transactions. Totality is easy to achieve: all modifications are made at FEs and are installed in phase 2 of two-phase commit [Eswaran et al, 1976] only if phase 1 is successful. Serializability is more difficult. The problem is that operations are performed at FEs, yet we need to coordinate concurrent transactions (from different FEs) at the ORs. One way to do this would be to have FEs set locks at the ORs, but this would obviate the advantages of FE caching since it would require communication with ORs even when there is a cache hit. Therefore we use an optimistic scheme [Kung and Robinson, 1981] that works as follows.

Every persistent object has a version number v# that is advanced each time a transaction that modifies the object commits. Each object contains its current v#, which is copied to the FE along with the object. While a transaction runs at the FE, the FE keeps track of what objects it reads and modifies. When the client requests a commit, the FE sends the v#s of all the objects read by the committing transaction, and the v#s and new versions of all the objects modified by the transaction, to an OR.

If all objects used by the transaction reside at that OR, committing can be done locally there; otherwise we need to do two-phase commit. (To make it more likely that transactions concern just one OR, Thor stores objects at ORs where related objects reside.) This OR acts as the coordinator of two-phase commit; the participants are the ORs that manage the objects that were read and modified by the committing transaction. In phase one, each participant OR checks the v#s used by the committing transaction against the actual v#s of its objects; if any do not match, the transaction must abort. If all participants agree to commit, the coordinator selects a new v# larger than any of the current ones, and this is written into all the modified objects along with their new versions in phase 2 (this information is actually written to a log as explained in Section 2.4). Thus what we have is an optimistic scheme using backward validation. The FE is informed about the new v# in the reply from the coordinator; it can then update the v#s it has stored for the modified objects.

We hope to run two-phase commit without requiring any disk I/O. This will be possible because our replication algorithm allows us to keep log records in volatile memory (see Section 2.4). However, in phase 1 we do need access to the version numbers of the objects used by the transaction. If ORs have very large volatile caches, the necessary information is highly likely to be in primary memory; otherwise, v#s can be stored in the FE tables.

2.3.1 Reducing Aborts

Although this concurrency control scheme is correct, it has the problem (as do all optimistic schemes) of possibly leading to aborts that need not have happened in a pessimistic scheme such as locking. Aborts in our system can come from two places: stale data in caches, and actual conflicts between concurrent transactions. To solve the first problem, we use *invalidation*: the OR notifies FEs when objects in their caches become stale as a result of transaction commits. ORs use the information in their FE tables to determine what invalidations are required. The front end receiving an invalidation message shrinks the stale objects back to surrogates, causing them to be refetched if needed. If the objects have been read by an active transaction, the transaction is aborted before shrinking the objects.

We are looking at two ways to reduce the problems of concurrent transactions. Our plan in both approaches is to move from an optimistic scheme to a locking scheme when there is contention, because locking is known to work better in such a case [Agrawal et al., 1987]. The first possibility is to switch from optimistic concurrency control to locking for objects that are hot spots. The OR would determine when this happens (e.g., because there had been contention at the object) and how long the object continues to be "hot". For hot objects, FEs would request locks before doing operations. The second possibility is to do lazy locking, in which the FEs do not wait to obtain locks, but instead notify the ORs about them in the background. The information thus obtained could be used to abort transactions early when there are conflicts (so that less work would be lost), to change which transactions abort (e.g., we could abort a writer if its commit would invalidate a concurrent reader), and to order commits intelligently (e.g., delaying commits of writers if they would invalidate concurrent readers).

Note that we use objects as a basis of concurrency control rather than pages or segments as has been done in most other systems [Deux et al., 1990; Haskin et al., 1987] because using a larger granularity can lead to false deadlocks and spurious conflicts. In addition, we plan to provide implementors of Thor objects with the ability to control the granularity of locking, as is done in Argus [Weihl and Liskov, 1985]. User control can lead to better performance by decreasing conflicts and improving concurrency. The scheme for indexes discussed in [Liskov, 1992] is an example.

2.4 REPLICATION

We are planning to use a primary copy scheme for replication [Oki and Liskov, 1988]. This scheme is an adaptation of one that we have been using in our work on the Harp file system [Liskov et al., 1991a]. Harp is a replicated Unix file system that is intended to be used via a network file server such as NFS. Our motivation for building the file system was partly that such a service would be useful and partly to make sure that our replication method would be satisfactory. Our performance measurements to date have been encouraging; our replicated system performs slightly better than an unreplicated system on standard benchmarks.

Our primary copy scheme will work as follows: As mentioned, each OR will reside at a number of servers; the OR's objects will have multiple copies at these servers. For each object, one of the servers that has a copy of that object will act as the *primary*; others with copies will act as *backups*. Actually, objects will be distributed in units of segments; a server will act as a primary (or backup) for all the objects in a segment. The primary will handle all FE interactions (fetches and commits) for that object. It will maintain a log in which it records information about commits, e.g., the new versions and v#s of modified objects, and will force the log to the backups at appropriate places, e.g., at transaction prepare or commit. If the primary fails, the backups and other servers of the OR will carry out a view change [El Abbadi et al., 1985; El Abbadi and Toueg, 1986] and one of the backups will become the new primary.

All servers will have uninterruptible power supplies (UPS's) in addition to disks; the UPS's protect against power failures, which are the most likely cause of a simultaneous server crash. The UPS's will allow us to view a record (such as a commit record) as safely recorded in the log as soon as it resides in volatile memory at the primary and backups; the log will be written to disk in the background. Thus forcing a record to the log will require one message roundtrip; since the primary and backups are typically located close to one another, this time is usually shorter than a disk write. Records will not need to be kept in the log indefinitely: only those records whose effects have not yet been recorded on disk at the primary and backups will need to be saved. Thus, the log typically will be short.

When there is a failure, the view change algorithm will select a new primary and backups for the object and will define the initial state of the new view. The initial state is guaranteed to contain the log records of all prepared and committed transaction. This guarantee follows from the fact that log records are forced at critical points (prepares and commits) and because views will always overlap in at least one member. Therefore, the needed log records will be known to at least one member of the new view. Other members of the new view will be brought up to date by sending them any of these records they do not already have. Since logs will be short (as discussed above), bringing the other members of the view up to date will not take long, so failover is fast.

When there is a recovery, the recovering node is likely to be very out of date (especially if it has been down for a long time). In this case we will bring it up to date before doing the view change, in parallel with running the current view. Only when its state is almost current will we do the view change; at this point little information needs to be exchanged and again we will have fast failover.

One of the interesting implications of our replication method is that it will speed up two-phase commit, since no writing to disk is required. In addition, since information in the log is moved to disk in the background, the OR will be able to take the time to organize segments as they are changed. For example, new objects can be added to the appropriate segments, and if objects in a segment grow, we will be able to reorganize the space to accommodate this. Therefore, we should be able to put the right objects together in segments and thus obtain the benefits of reading entire segments.

2.5 QUERIES AND INDEXES

The ability to identify objects by means of queries is an important property of Thor. Queries introduce two new problems: (1) how to maintain indexes when the set being indexed contains objects of abstract, user-defined types, and (2) where to run the query.

Efficient index maintenance requires some way of recognizing when a particular change to an object indicates that a particular index must change. In a database system, changes that affect indexes are easy to recognize, since these are just inserts into indexed sets, and updates of tuples in indexed sets. When sets contain abstract objects, however, the system no longer knows what constitutes an update, and furthermore objects in an indexed set may contain references to other objects whose modifications can affect an index for the set. We are currently investigating techniques for solving these problems [Hwang, 1993]. Note that the solution must take account of distribution: Changes to objects happen at FEs but indexes are stored at ORs, and furthermore the right kind of concurrency control must be in place.

We are also investigating several ways of running queries. If the set being queried is large and the query results in a small number of selected objects, it is desirable to run the query at the OR. However, if the queried set is not large, or if the query results in lots of matches, or if many queries are run on the same set, it may be better to move the set (or possibly just its index) to the FE and run the query there.

Ultimately we plan to use a flexible approach in which the FE decides where to run the query based on information available to it at that time. When a set object is used at an FE, meta-data about the set is sent to the FE, but the elements of the set are not. The meta-data includes information about indexes so that the FE can make decisions about how to carry out the query most effectively. If the FE decides to run the query at the OR, it sends a "match" command to the OR indicating what index to use and what index value or values are of interest. The OR responds by creating a new set containing the object that matched and either sending a reference to it to the FE, or sending the new set to the FE. (It will be possible to stream the elements of the new set to the FE so that the FE code can start to use them before they all arrive.) Alternatively, the FE can request that an index be sent to it, or that the set elements be sent (again the elements can be streamed).

If the indexed set is distributed, i.e., its elements are stored at more than one OR, the index will be distributed so that it has a component at each OR where there are elements. The component will store the portion of the entire index that concerns the elements at its OR. This organization will allow the FE to do the "matches" at the different ORs in parallel; it will also allow for easy index maintenance as the set and its elements change.

3 STATUS AND PLANS

We have implemented a partial prototype of Thor, called TH. TH is implemented in Argus [Liskov, 1988]. It is a distributed system in which clients run at different nodes than ORs, and there are several ORs. We have built a veneer for Emacs Lisp [Lewis and LaLiberte, 1990] and Argus, and have written both a toy hypertext application and a toy mail system on top of Emacs and TH. Several members of our group use a shared calendar system (of local origin) called ical; we plan to implement a version of this system to run on top of TH. We are currently designing veneers for C++ [Stroustrup, 1987] and CLOS [DeMichiel and Gabriel, 1987] and are working with groups who have other real applications to test TH.

Abstract types in TH are defined in a stylized dialect of Argus, and all objects are implemented in terms of a single underlying primitive object type called f_obj. An f_obj is a variable-length heterogeneous array: it is essentially an Argus array with tagged elements. A slot in an f_obj can hold an integer, boolean, character, string, or reference. There is also a field for "self" that allows an object to refer to itself before it has been allocated. References are constrained to occupy the same space at the FE (where they are 32-bit VM addresses) and at the OR (where they are 32-bit orefs). References that require more bits are done by an indirection through a surrogate, in a style similar to that of Mneme [Moss, 1990].

Argus stable storage was useful for getting the system up quickly, but our research version of Argus limited the size of databases that we could build in TH. We have moved most persistent store management into TH, delegating the details of disk storage to the Unix filesystem for now.

TH does not implement our full design. The following features of Thor are not yet in TH: replication, control of disk storage, real programming and specification languages for Thor types, security and access control, distributed garbage collection, queries, and indexes. In Thor, code is stored at the ORs and fetched to the FEs, but TH statically links code into FEs.

We plan to add distributed garbage collection, queries and indexes, and object mobility to TH. We also expect to compile our Thor language into TH abstract type definitions (that is, in one mode the compiler will produce the appropriate stylized Argus code as the object code). However, we do not plan to implement replication, disk management, or access control in TH. It seems unlikely that we will attempt to implement code objects in TH.

Implementing TH has allowed us to firm up and test some of our implementation decisions. We plan to use TH as a test bed for studying various research issues, e.g., prefetching mechanisms, indexing mechanisms, and distributed garbage collection techniques. TH will also be used as a basis for some applications so that we can get a better understanding of how well our design meets the needs of users.

We plan to begin implementing a full prototype of Thor soon. Performance and portability are important goals of this implementation. We are likely to implement it in either Modula-3 or C++. We will use Recoverable Virtual Memory [Mashburn and Satyanarayanan, 1992] as our initial storage manager, then move to using our replication scheme.

We are also working now on the design of the Thor implementation and specification languages, and at various extensions to the Thor model. For example, we are looking at triggers and constraints, and considering support for very long transactions.

Acknowledgements

Thor is a joint research project carried out by the authors and a number of others. Members of this team include Atul Adya, Boaz Ben-Zvi, Dorothy Curtis, Sanjay Ghemawat, Robert Gruber, Deborah Hwang, Paul Johnson, Umesh Maheshwari, and Andrew Myers. In addition, the design has benefited from conversations with Stan Zdonik and David Langworthy.

This research was supported in part by the Advanced Research Projects Agency of the Department of Defense, monitored by the Office of Naval Research under contract N00014-91-J-4136 and in part by the National Science Foundation under Grant CCR-8822158.

Database Security Issues in Distributed Object-Oriented Databases

G. Matunda Nyanchama
The University of Western Ontario
Department of Computer Science
London, Ontario
Canada N6A 5B7

Sylvia L. Osborn
The University of Western Ontario
Department of Computer Science
London, Ontario
Canada N6A 5B7

Abstract

Distributed object oriented databases combine properties and capabilities of database systems, such as querying, object oriented models with complex nested object structures and inheritance hierarchies, and distribution of processing over a network. Each of these contributing technologies poses its own challenges for the maintenance of discretionary and mandatory access control. This paper explores these security issues for distributed object oriented database systems.

1 INTRODUCTION

Database security addresses the issues of *confidentiality, integrity* and *denial of service*. Object-Oriented Database System security research is an active area, a trend sure to continue as OODBSs establish their presence in the marketplace. Distributed OODBS security is the next step.

Object security in a distributed environment is affected by the architecture (distribution strategies), the enforced security policies and threats in the communication channels. Many questions arise: Are the distributed OODBS homogeneous or heterogeneous? Do they cover single or multiple domains? Is the security policy uniformly applied, and if not, how is a global view presented? Is distribution based on information sensitivity? How are communication specific threats such as the data modification and/or destruction, masquerade, network failure, etc. handled? What are the query processing strategies? Are there any inherent OODBS properties that can be exploited for security in the distributed environment?

2 OBJECT ORIENTED DATABASE SECURITY

Much of the research in OODBS security has concentrated on access control: mandatory access control (MAC) and discretionary access control (DAC).

MAC is most widely implemented as multilevel security (MLS), in which database objects are assigned sensitivity levels while subjects are assigned corresponding clearance levels. In general, these security levels are partially ordered. Given any two such levels, one dominates the other, they are equal, or they are incomparable. The Bell and LaPadula model for security, the most widely used model for multilevel security multilevel security, has rules governing the reading and writing of objects based on a subject's clearance level: the simple security and *–properties.

In an OODBS the database entities include *classes, instances* and *instance variables* or any arbitrary collections of such entities. These can either be *single-level* or *multilevel*. A multilevel entity contains information at different sensitivity levels while a single level entity has information at only one security level. The MAC security policy must address how to handle both *multilevel* and *single-level* entities. The security policy must state the *granularity of authorization*: the class, the instance or the instance variable. Access can also be based on any arbitrary collection of objects as long as it is possible to determine the sensitivity level of the collection.

The policy must state whether or not methods have classifications. It must specify method invocation rules based on the clearance of the invoker compared to that of the method. It must determine the difference in the invocation of methods that return object states, those that alter object states as well as those that invoke other methods. The last case, which we call the *method invocation chain*, may have far reaching overall effects which may involve alternately invoking *read* and *write* methods. This overall effect of method invocation must be determined to ensure that the invocation sequence is secure.

Considering the inheritance hierarchy, what is the classification of a subclass with respect to its superclass or the sensitivity of inherited properties within a subclass with respect to the sensitivity within the superclass? There seems to be consensus [Thuraisingham, 1989; Keefe et al., 1989; Nyanchama and Osborn 1991; Lunt, 1990; Petrie et al., 1990; Varadharan and Black, 1991] that the classification of both classes and their properties in a subclass should dominate that in the superclass.

The MAC policy must also state whether or not the sensitivity levels of composite objects or their collections are imposed (static) or derived (dynamic) from those of their components (members). Multilevel rules governing these require that the sensitivity of a composite (set) object dominate that of its components (members). While this is true when given the sensitivity of components (members), it is not sufficient to guard against *aggregation*: where the information content of two or more objects taken together is greater than the sum of information of the parts. Aggregation is a major research concern in computer security. Static determination of security levels for composite objects and sets may limit the impact of aggregation but this is only feasible in cases where it is possible to "predict" that such a composite (set) object may be constituted in the future. On the other hand, *dynamic derivation* of sensitivity levels of composite and set objects is flexible and can be "computed" at execution time. How much a system employs the static approach in combination with the dynamic one, is a matter of the security policy.

With DAC, access control to information is determined on an individual basis. Access to a certain object or a collection of objects can be confined to an individual or group of individuals. A discretionary security policy deals with ownership and granting of access rights. It is distinguished from MAC in that subjects with access rights can pass them on to third parties, a factor which makes it susceptible to *trojan horse* attacks. As in MAC, a DAC security policy must state what the granularity of authorization is.[1] This can be, as in the case of MAC, the *class, instance, instance variable* or any *arbitrary collection* of objects in the database. Another DAC policy issue is the manner of specification of authorizations, i.e., whether it is explicit or implicit [Rabitti et al., 1991]. Implicit determination of authorizations reduces the complexity of these specifications and can be done for the class (hence applicable to its instances) and/or the composite object (hence applicable to its components). The inheritance hierarchy, however, must be treated differently. A special authorization (call it inheritance authorization) must be granted to facilitate the subclassing mechanism. This is a problem yet to be addressed exhaustively.

3 THREATS IN A DISTRIBUTED ENVIRONMENT

Threats to database information in a distributed environment include those to stand-alone systems (unauthorized access, unauthorized modification, denial of service) as well as those that arise due to the introduction of distribution. In a distributed environment, these problems include risks due to the communication network, object partitioning, network partitioning, replication (if any) etc.

Communication Authenticity. Communication in OODBS is via message passing which may be sent across a communication network. Authentication assures the authenticity of the communicating entities as well as the information exchanged. There are several forms of authentication including: *originating site authentication, sender authentication, message content authentication, and non-repudiation.*

Originating site authentication involves establishing the identity of the originating site and its authorization to communicate with the receiving site. *Sender Authentication* is a means of establishing the identity of the sender and the validation of the access rights to the receiver object. Before method invocation at the receiver, we must ensure that not only does that sender have the access rights to the request, but also that it is a valid sender in the database, hence preventing *masquerading*. How can authentication information be built into the OODBS message paradigm? Should a mere confirmation of sender identity suffice or would arbitration be required? Some check field in the sender identity may assure sender authenticity. Object identities (OIDs) in transit must also be protected. Tampering with OIDs may be an ideal chance for a masquerade. Not only should we authenticate sender identity, we should also detect any tampering of these identities. *Message Content Authentication* must also be carried out. Cryptographic techniques or use of capabilities [Tanenbaum et al., 1990] can guarantee non-tampering of message content.

Non-Repudiation ensures that neither sender nor receiver can deny sending or receiving some message. This scheme ensures secure communication between any two database entities once they have been authenticated. Traditionally, non-repudiation employs digital signatures. It can also be used with arbitration where all communication between any two entities must be "registered" with the arbitrator.

[1] Note that the granularity of authorization may be selected independently of whether the protection mode employs mandatory or discretionary access control or both. In other words, the three are orthogonal [Nyanchama and Osborn, 1991].

How can authentication be built into distributed OODBS? Given that cryptography has been successfully employed for communication security, is it feasible to utilize it within the OODBS paradigm? Should it prove feasible, how about the concerns for the cost of Public key cryptography?

Management of Security Information. How is the Trusted Computer Base (TCB) [Department of Defence, 1985] partitioned among sites? Ideally, security information must be distributed along with the objects it pertains to. What is the distribution unit of this information: the class, the instance or the instance variable? What partition strategy eases the task of design and verification of the TCB? Should the *management* of this information be centralized or distributed? What are the advantages of either strategy? Which strategy is better applicable to distributed OODBS? Should objects migrate, how do we ensure that the migration also involves correct migration of the security information with the object? In what cases can such migration be rejected on grounds of security?

On **replication,** issues of consistency arise. Just as the data in the copies must be kept consistent, so also must the security information. The transaction model and commit protocols provide a means of ensuring the required consistency. Where distribution is sensitivity-based, then replication must be sensitive to this too. Information that is required to be located at a site of a certain level of integrity must have all its copies located at sites of the required integrity level.

4 OBJECTS IN A DISTRIBUTED ENVIRONMENT

In relational databases, distribution is achieved either by vertical or horizontal partitioning of tables (relations). Horizontal distribution partitions tables and locates whole tuples in different locations. A union operation is used to reconstruct the original table. Vertical partitioning splits tuples and distributes components on different sites whose reconstruction is possible via a join operation using some key.

An analogy in OODBS would distribute whole objects to different sites for the "horizontal" case, while different attributes of objects may be distributed to different sites for the latter case. Reconstruction of these objects depends on the OID and the *is-part-of* relationship. Other issues of concern to security are the nature of databases involved in the distribution. Are such databases homogeneous or heterogeneous? Does distribution cover different domains?[2] If so, are there suitable translation mechanisms that provide a uniform view of security?

In a *homogeneous environment*, where the data representation is uniform, the task is to provide a unified security policy applicable to the distributed environment as in any distributed case. A global TCB, concept must be in place. Should the TCB be distributed among sites? If so, how do we compose its global view from the partitions?

In the *heterogeneous* case, there is a need to provide a *global view* of the database information: or *model unification*. There must be *translation mechanisms* between the different

[2] We use domain here to refer to an administration. If distribution covers only one domain, we can expect a uniform enforcement of one security policy. On the other hand, if distribution covers different administrations (domains), then there may be different security policies enforced which will require a means of unifying them.

data models and/or the data manipulation languages. Just as there is a global view of data, there must be a *global TCB* concept enforced as a result of some security policy. We also require an accurate translation of both the representation of the security information and the mechanisms for its management in different models into this global view. The translation and unifying mechanisms must be accurate and trusted to ensure correctness and prevent leakage. It must present a uniform concept of the granularity of access.

For *multiple domain* distributed systems, the important issue is that of the security policies, aside from the questions of homogeneity and heterogeneity. A *global security policy* is required that unifies the domain-specific policies. Issues of a unified security policy concern whether protection is achieved via discretionary and/or mandatory security. It must address how to realize a unified concept of the unit of authorization across the different domains: how to map security levels (in case of MAC) from one domain into the unified view, etc. For multilevel security, associating security levels of one domain to another results in (1) the security levels from the two domains being incomparable, (2) the set of security levels in one domain being a subset of those in another domain, (3) the set of security levels overlapping or (4) the set of security levels being the same. The translation mechanisms must be both accurate and trusted and must implement a uniform concept of global security.

Sensitivity-based distribution offers the advantages of *isolation, ease of design, implementation* and *verification* [MacEwen, 1987]. Is there a strategic (optimal?) object distribution in particular circumstances that exploits these advantages? For instance, how will multilevel objects fit into a sensitivity distribution strategy?

5 QUERY PROCESSING

In relational systems, prevalent queries involve *join, project* and *select* constructs. Similar operations must be considered for OODBS. The query processing facility must not only maintain the security information of the objects involved in queries, but must be trusted too. In *join-like operations*, the overriding problem is *aggregation* where the result of join ends up with less strict sensitivity than that desirable. Aggregation is less of a problem in *select-like* and *project-like* queries. Despite the fact that contexts may be used to reduce the impact of aggregation in a database, they are not sufficient to eliminate its threat to security. Moreover, contexts must be specified statically which makes it difficult to anticipate all possible object combinations in the future. Can any OODBS features be used to minimize aggregation? How do we ensure security sensitive processing in the navigation tools for objects?

6 RELATED WORK

[Cole, 1990] discusses issues of security in a distributed environment in relation to the standardization of the Open Distributed Processing standard. This discussion offers good insight into corresponding concerns for distributed object-oriented databases. [Varadharan and Black, 1991] addresses multilevel information security in a distributed OODBS with reference to a particular model.

7 CONCLUSION

In this paper we have raised major issues that affect object security in a distributed environment in view of *architecture*: homogeneity, heterogeneity and multiple domains; *distribution*: authentication and non-repudiation; *query processing*: aggregation and its impact on project and join-like combinations of objects. The questions that remain are whether there are inherent properties of OODBS that can be utilized to circumvent security threats in a distributed environment.

PART 2
OBJECT AND STORAGE MANAGEMENT

Object Storage Management in Goblin

Martin L. Kersten
CWI
Kruislaan 413
1098 SJ, Amsterdam
The Netherlands

Sander Plomp
CWI
Kruislaan 413
1098 SJ, Amsterdam
The Netherlands

Carel A. van den Berg
CWI
Kruislaan 413
1098 SJ, Amsterdam
The Netherlands

Abstract

Goblin is a distributed OODBMS under development within our group to explore techniques for dynamic query optimization and efficient language interworking on a shared nothing computer architecture. Its three-level storage scheme for complex objects is one of the novelties being researched. The basis is formed by an extensible, unconventional storage scheme for attribute collections with multiple incarnations, called Binary Association Tables (BAT). The structural relationships for a specific database schema are described by Class Administration Table (CAT). Finally, the mapping from schema to database instantiation is administered by Redistribution Administration Tables (RAT), which includes the partitioning and distribution aspects. This paper provides an introduction to this storage scheme, the distribution of objects, and the rationale behind the choices made.

1 INTRODUCTION

A challenging research goal is to develop DBMS architectures that can easily be adapted to a changing hardware environment and to changing requirements of an application domain. Such systems, called extensible DBMSs [Carey et al., 1986b; Graefe and DeWitt, 1987;

Stonebraker and Rowe, 1990; Haas et al., 1990], provide hooks at various software levels to change the system's internals. For example, new data structures and access paths are readily included at the physical level, ease of access to domain specific libraries is provided, and the rule base governing query plan generation can be enhanced.

Extensible object-oriented database systems pose many problems to the system designer, such as how to cope with additional data model semantics, how to parameterize the query optimizer, how to deal with the impedance mismatch between DBMS and host language, how to quickly capitalize on emerging hardware characteristics, etc. Thus, research in this area requires a flexible platform for experimentation. The Goblin DBPL and DBMS developed in our group aims to fill this gap.

Goblin provides object-oriented database management facilities using a network of workstations. It has been under development since 1990 after we finished the design and implementation of a full-fledged distributed main memory DBMS, called PRISMA, which is a relational DBMS running on a single multicomputer of 100 M68020 processors with 1.5 gigabyte dynamic RAM [Kersten et al., 1988; vdBerg and Kersten, 1991; Apers et al., 1992].

The experiences gained within the PRISMA implementation and the preliminary studies for Goblin led to increased design and implementation efforts towards our next generation DBMS. In the first phase of the Goblin project we have studied dynamic query optimization and processing schemes using discrete event simulations on queueing networks [vdBerg et al., 1991], prototype implementations of the core algorithms [Kersten et al., 1990], and analytical models to predict effectiveness under different data distributions [vdBerg and Kersten, 1992]. Currently, two prototype implementations are under development for a network of SPARCs running SUN/OS and a network of Intel-386 machines running the Amoeba distributed operating system [Mullender and Tanenbaum, 1986]. This paper is focussed on the design of its object storage management scheme, which is based on the following general observations and goals:

- *The database is memory resident.* In Goblin we focus on loosely coupled multiprocessors with sufficient (combined) main-memory to keep the database hot set and the intermediates for query processing memory resident. This assumption continues the thread started in 1986 with PRISMA and aligns with market expectations for cheap computer systems with an abundance of main memory.

- *Bulk object management.* In Goblin we purposely focus on handling (large) collections of objects, because it is the operation on bulk data with order independent semantics that has proven to be a decisive factor in the exploitation of parallelism. Fast navigational access to a single object is a focus of (more) efficient OOPL implementations.

- *Multiple object incarnations.* In Goblin we recognize that object representations strongly depend on their role within the query processing strategy. Alternative representations are often used for version management (deltas), for search operations (path-indices), and for application controlled fast access (pointer swizzling). Moreover, we assume that in most situations objects are not clustered optimally, nor necessarily produced at the best location, which implies object transport (linearization and compression) for most queries. Therefore, we aim for an object storage and distribution scheme that supports concurrent use of multiple incarnations and that automatically selects the best among the supported alternatives.

- *Object caching strategy.* In Goblin we expect parallelism to be exploited effectively in query dominant environments with local updates. This means that portions of the object space can be replicated on demand, while their contents are kept synchronized using a read-one-write-all protocol using the facilities of the underlying operating system.
- *Cooperative distributed operating system.* In Goblin we do not aim for a (re-)implementation of basic distributed operating facilities, such as memory mapped files, persistent storage, network management, concurrency control primitives, and caching. Instead, we focus on mechanisms to advise a cooperative underlying operating system on how to optimize its resource allocation.

The storage scheme described in the sequel is a three-level storage hierarchy for complex objects. The basis is formed by an extensible, unconventional storage scheme for attribute collections with multiple incarnations, called Binary Association Tables. The Class Administration Table describe the structural relationships between object components for a specific database schema. Finally, the mapping from schema to database instance is administered by a Redistribution Administration Table, which includes the partitioning and distribution information.

Our medium term goal is to analyse the performance aspects of this storage strategy using our distributed operating systems platforms. In particular, the management of multiple object incarnations and the proper liaison with the operating system have high priority.

The remainder of this paper is organized as follows. In Section 2 we set the context for this research with a short introduction to the Goblin DBPL and system architecture. Section 3 introduces a model of the storage management problem to be dealt with in a OODBMS. Section 4 describes the lower level storage structures for dealing with attribute collections, called BATs. Section 5 provides the details of the high-level storage management, which links BATs into object classes, called CATs. Section 6 describes the partitioning and distribution scheme for CATs, called RATs. Finally, Section 7 summarizes the implementation status and future research activities.

2 SYSTEM OVERVIEW

To understand the rationale for the storage management scheme derived in Sections 3-6 we give a short introduction into three aspects of the Goblin project. In Section 2.1 we introduce the Goblin DBPL and its data model using an illustrative program fragment. Section 2.2 provides an overview of the Goblin architecture and its dynamic query optimization process.

2.1 A SAMPLE PROGRAM

The Goblin DBPL includes features commonly encountered in this area, such as classes, inheritance, active database support, extensible typing scheme, nested transactions, etc. The data model is similar in many aspects to O_2 [Deux et al., 1990] where a distinction is made between values and objects. However, objects in Goblin are automatically classified by attributes and methods, which can selectively be added to or removed from objects (!).

Furthermore, we designed a full-fledged programming language to describe applications, instead of an add-on language to C(++), such as $Jasmin/C$ [Aoshima et al., 1990] or CO_2. The rationale is to obtain a simpler language for extracting parallelism by forbidding

```
TYPE Fingerprint = IMAGE(200,200);
TYPE Person = TUPLE(STR name;
          OID address;
          INT age;
          Fingerprint lefthand[5],righthand[5]);
TYPE Crime = TUPLE(STR crime; INT sentence);

VOID Person.answer()
{   printf("Suspect of crime %s %s\n", SELF.name, SELF.address);}

CLASS persons TYPE Person;
CLASS criminals TYPE persons + (SET(Crime) criminal_record);

FLOAT match(Fingerprint f,m) {...}
VOID main(Fingerprint m; INT age_low, age_high)
{
    SELECT [ person p WHERE p.age >= age_low && p.age<= age_high]{
          FLOAT l= [ match(m,f) FROM p.lefthand f].max();
          FLOAT r= [ match(m,f) FROM p.righthand f].max();
          IF( l IN 0.4..0.6 && confirm(p.lefthand,m)) l= 0.6;
          IF( r IN 0.4..0.6 && confirm(p.righthand,m)) r= 0.6;
          IF( l>= 0.6  || r >= 0.6) p.answer()
}   }
```

Figure 1: A sample Goblin program

address arithmetic and to replace sequential for-loops by bulk data operations. The language does, however, provide an open interface towards routines written in other (imperative) programming languages. The interface to these routines is described by an ADT formalism including optimization guidelines for the rule driven query optimizer. The language is described at length in [Kersten, 1991] and [Kersten et al., 1992].

An illustrative program fragment is shown in Figure 1. It describes a small police information system about persons and criminals. For persons we keep track of fingerprints, which are arrays of 200 × 200 pixel images. Criminals form a subclass of persons, who have been convicted for a series of crimes.

A so called *targeted function* `answer` is defined for values of type `Person`. Its appearance is similar to a method definition for classes and it can be applied like a method, but its receiver is a value rather than an object. Furthermore, the semantics of targeted function body aligns with those of a method. That is, the function behaves as a (sub)transaction, which can be aborted to recover the original state of the target. Moreover, targeted functions used for retrieval purposes ensure that the target is safeguarded against side-effects.

The function **match** is a heuristic function, which determines the correlation between a fingerprint mark left at the crime scene and a fingerprint stored in the database. The details are left to the imagination of the reader.

The routine `main` searches for suspects by matching the fingerprints found at the crime location with those stored in the database. The SELECT statement illustrates a bulk data

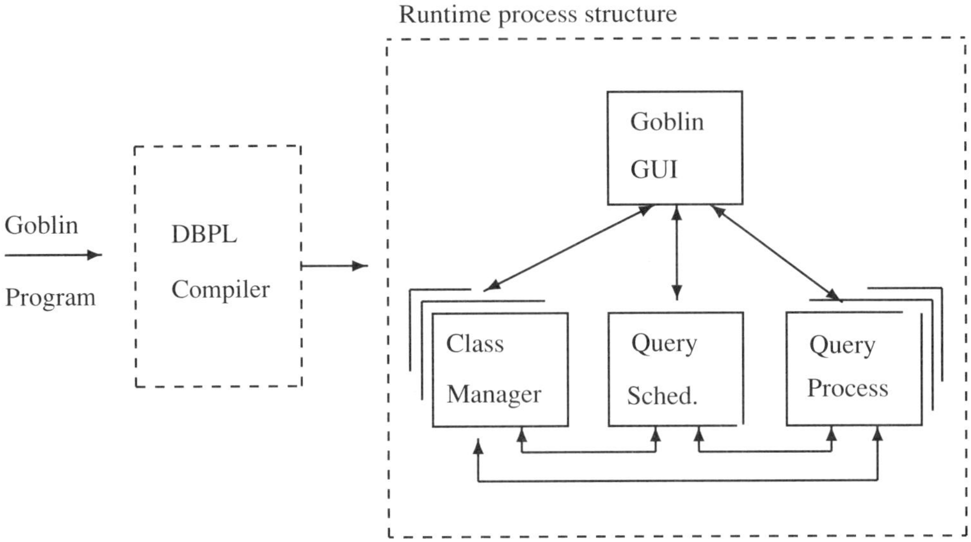

Figure 2: The Goblin compilation and runtime structure

operation, which applies the body to all candidates. Its syntax is derived from the SQL SELECT-FROM-WHERE construct. Since the order of evaluation is left to the system, the statement blocks can (potentially) be executed in parallel. In this example, however, the user is asked for confirmation on a subrange of matching values. This leads to (partial) serialization that requires efficient caching of intermediate results for confirmation (at the user workstation of the user) and dynamic allocation of processes to look-ahead for other candidates.

2.2 SYSTEM ARCHITECTURE

An overview of the Goblin system architecture is given in Figure 2. The heart of the system is a conditional term rewriter called GTR, which compiles Goblin programs into four kinds of C-programs [Kersten, 1992]. Object storage maintenance is handled by Class Manager programs, which are installed as server processes on each processor under the distributed operating system Amoeba or SUN/OS. These Class Managers cooperate to offer global object storage, which provides object persistency, replication and transaction management (See Section 7.1).

For each query (in a DBPL program), the compiler generates a Query Scheduler to control query execution and which aims at effective resource utilization through load balancing. Distributed query optimization in Goblin is for the greater part a run time issue. That is, after the logical query optimization phase, exploitation of parallel processing and load balancing are performed at run time by the query scheduler. The rationale is that in object-oriented systems most queries are encapsulated or used by parameterized methods. Their processing behavior is difficult, if not impossible, to predict sufficiently precise for good static query plan generation.

Furthermore, a Query Program is generated, which is installed as a query service on several processors in the pool. The Query Scheduler uses the Query Processors to solve parts of the query. The query evaluation at each Query Processor is not fixed at compile time, but depends on the availability of the data.

When the runtime process structure has been established, the user can activate the pre-compiled queries and the system automatically extracts the potential parallelism using its *dynamic query optimization* scheme. This scheme works as follows. Upon activation of a compiled query, the Query Scheduler selects the database portion that might contribute to the query result. It breaks them into smaller partitions, such that a partition combination for all operands mentioned in the query can be handled by a single Query Processor. Then, it instructs a (lightly) loaded Query Processor to cache a copy of the partition combination and to solve the query. The answer is cached at the query processor until it is requested by the user.

For selective query parameters a single query processor might be sufficient, while parameters that cover a large range lead to activation of as many query processors as effective to obtain maximal response time reduction. A detailed account on the query processing scheme employed and its performance figures are given in [Kersten et al., 1990; vdBerg et al., 1991; vdBerg and Kersten, 1992].

3 OBJECT STORAGE MANAGEMENT

In this section, we introduce the core of the object storage management problem. That is, the representation of the database schema, the storage and access structures for the database extension, and their mapping. A reformulation of this problem in terms of a function graph is given in Section 3.1 and an analysis of two different solutions to the storage problem is given in Sections 3.2 and 3.3. The Goblin approach is introduced in Section 3.4. Management of method invocations (transaction management) is beyond the scope of this paper.

3.1 STORAGE FUNCTIONS IN A OODBMS

The storage management problem to be solved by a DBMS can be described in abstract terms as finding a good implementation for three kinds of basic functions, namely: *schema-*, *path-*, and *storage-* functions. This problem is illustrated by Figure 3 using part of our example. The top of this figure illustrates the database schema in terms of the datamodel constructors, such as tuple construction ($\ominus$), set construction ($\otimes$), and atomic types. The latter includes the type OID to enable modelling sharing at the intentional level. The *schema* functions describe the relationships to be maintained and they form a basis for the semantics of query expressions. For, search expressions in the query language can be seen as composite applications of *schema* functions over (atomic) types.

For example, the function S_{Person}:OID $\rightarrow$ SET(OID) is a set-valued function, which maps the OID associated with a class into a set of OIDs that represent its extent. Similarly, schema functions S_{name}:OID $\rightarrow$ STR and $S_{address}$:OID $\rightarrow$ OID are tuple-valued functions and describe 1-1 mappings between a tuple OID and its attributes.[1]

[1]The liberal use of the notion of OID as a reference to any item at the schema level is not supported by all data models. Many reserve the concept OID to the name of a member of a class.

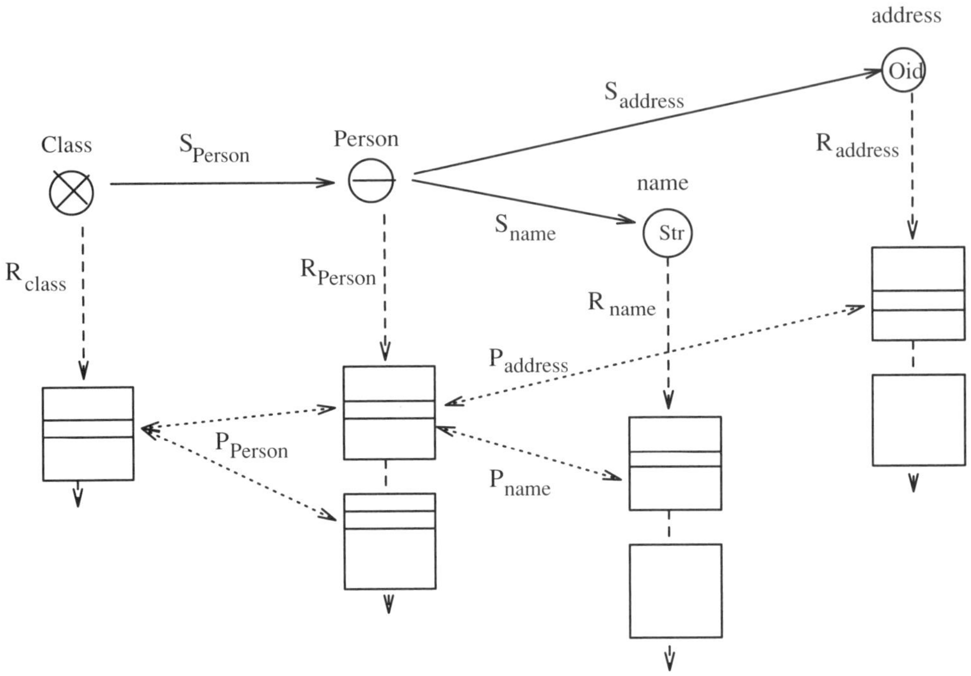

Figure 3: The basic DBMS functions.

At the implementation level, the graph is complemented by data structures and data access functions. The counterpart of the OID at the physical level is called the Physical Identifier (PID). Atomic values are mapped to their underlying representation directly. PIDs and values are often grouped into partitions for efficient storage management. The *schema* functions find their counterpart in *path* functions. In general, a walk through the schema graph is simulated by a walk through the implementation graph.

For example, in Figure 3 the basic data structure is a block of PIDs and values. The 1-1 and 1-Nary *path* functions are shown as dotted arrows. The function P_{name}:PID $\rightarrow$ STR and $P_{address}$: PID $\rightarrow$ PID relate a single tuple-valued object with its attribute values. The *path* function P_{Person} : PID $\rightarrow$ SET(PID) relates a class with the members of its extent.

The mapping between intentional and extensional layers is captured by *storage* functions. They relate the constructors, OIDs and values at the schema level to PIDs and values at the implementation level. This mapping involves the distribution of data over multiple partitions to improve disk, main-memory, and network-transport management. Furthermore, the distribution can be used to cluster PIDs and values to improve query processing. The partitioning function is commonly a hash- or range-based distribution.

For example, the function R_{class}: OID $\rightarrow$ PID maps the class name into its corresponding representation. Actually, the compiler maps the symbolic name into an OID first. Similarly, the functions R_{Person}, R_{name}, and $R_{address}$ are defined.

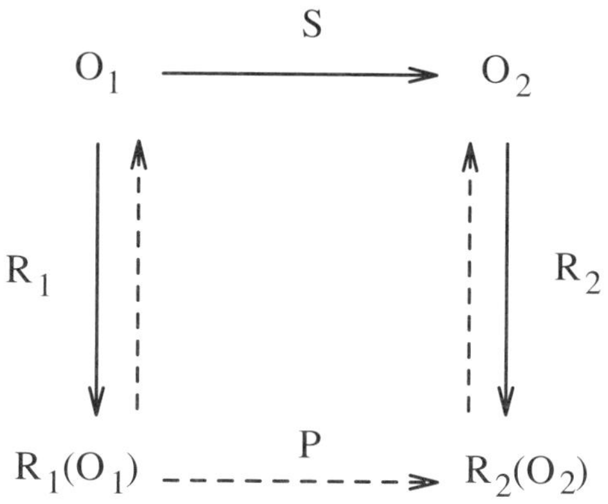

Figure 4: The constraints between schema, path and storage functions

A good OODBMS implementation provides a balanced solution to the representation of the two graphs and the implementation of the three functions. Furthermore, it should guarantee the following constraints:

Constraint 1 *Let* $o_1 \in$ OID *and* $o_2 \in$ ATOM $\bigcup$ OID *with corresponding storage functions* R_1, R_2 *and let* T *a tuple-valued schema function such that* $T(o_1) = o_2$ *then there exists a (composite) path function* F *such that* $F(R_1(o_1)) = R_2(o_2)$.

In essence this constraint states that given an tuple attribute, the related attribute values can be found through the path and storage functions and their inverse functions (See also Figure 4). A similar constraint can be formulated for sets, which enables traversal at the implementation level through set constructors.

Constraint 2 *Let* $o_1 \in$ OID *and* $o_i \in$ OID $\bigcup$ ATOM *with corresponding storage functions* R_1, R_2 *and* S *a set-valued schema function such that* $S(o_1) = \{o_i\}$ *then there exists a (composite) path relation* F *such that* $F(R_1(o_1)) = \{R_2(o_i)\}$.

The abstract object storage management problem sketched here is often hidden behind the implementation techniques chosen. In particular, the top-level is managed by the compiler or data-dictionary system and simplifying assumptions are made on the mapping from OID to PID. Therefore, we illustrate the concepts introduced so far with two well-known storage strategies before the Goblin solution is given.

3.2 N-ARY STORAGE MODEL APPROACH

The base line for all (OO)DBMSs is to efficiently represent flat and set-valued objects. Flat objects are of the form $(S, A_0, \ldots, A_k)$ where S is a surrogate or object identifier and A_i are the corresponding attribute values. A common implementation track is to map flat objects into record structures provided by the underlying implementation language, i.e. to use an n-ary storage model (NSM) [Khoshafian et al., 1987].

The implementation of set-valued objects require slightly more effort. It should include the design of index structures for fast access within a single bucket and clustering techniques to improve access to related portions of the database. To improve load balancing in a distributed environment, the set-valued objects are declustered over the processing pool.

In this approach there is a 1-1 mapping between the schema and physical representation. The *storage* functions are mostly handled at run time. Either the OID and PID are made identical to speed-up processing, i.e. a declustering function is used, or the mapping is administered in an (distributed) object table.

Moreover, subgraphs at the schema level are combined into one storage structure. In a NSM approach, the record is simply a cheap implementation for a group of similar 1-1 *path* functions. That is, the *storage* function implicitly defines the attribute storage (through record offsets). Incidental note that NF2 storage structures merely combine larger portions of the *path* functions into a single storage structure.

The prime advantages of a NSM are summarized as follows:

- *Reduced impedance mismatch.* The language impedance mismatch disappears when applications are written in the language of the underlying OODBMS, because objects in the database can be manipulated without expensive conversion cost (or pointer swizzling).
- *Storage savings.* NSM is perceived storage efficient, because the surrogate of attribute values are factored out at the physical level. Likewise, administrative data, such as class/attribute/type indicators, can be factored out too.
- *Implementation simplicity.* Implementation of a OODBMS can rely on the handling of record structures by the underlying compiler (C(++)). Alignment problems are automatically dealt with and the compiler will generate efficient code to (un) pack small attributes like bit-fields.

3.3 DECOMPOSED STORAGE MODEL APPROACH

Another way to implement flat objects is the Decomposed Storage Model (DSM), which breaks the object into a series of binary relationships. This approach has been partially studied in [Khoshafian et al., 1987]. They describe a query processing strategy for DSM and a preliminary implementation of the Wisconsin database shows that a DSM provides better performance for retrieval queries in a distributed setting (due to the smaller intermediate results and using join indices). The DSM is slower on single updates and deletions. The underlying cause is the number of additional page accesses to maintain the binary associations on disk.

The DSM approach corresponds more directly with the graph shown in Figure 3. Its surrogate combines OID and PID into a single concept; the *storage* function is the identity function. The partitions contain the association between a surrogate and a value (or another surrogate). Moreover, the *path* functions are represented by double join-indices, which support bi-directional access by join value.

A decomposed storage model has a number of advantages:

- *Attribute extensions.* It is much easier to add attributes to an aggregate type, because it does not require a complete storage reorganization.

- *Atomic type extensions.* A new atomic type is also added more easily, because it requires implementation of a data structure for a single data type (including the access functions).

- *Primary storage representation.* For each attribute we can independently decide on the best storage technique, e.g. fixed or variable sized records. When all attributes are stored together such decisions will strongly interact.

- *Storage adaptation.* Each attribute table can be adapted to their predominate use independently, i.e. reorganization and indexing becomes easier. If all attributes are stored physically adjacent this becomes more difficult.

3.4 GOBLIN STORAGE MODEL

The approach taken in Goblin is to pursue the DSM track further with a focus towards a main-memory implementation and a loosely coupled multi-processor. The rationale behind this choice stems from the disadvantage of fixing a single storage structure, to deal with aggregate types only, from the outset of a DBMS implementation. It means that extensibility at the lower system level is a priori sacrificed for initially good performance.

Rejection of the NSM approach is a direct consequence of its disadvantages (=advantages of DSM) and the feature of Goblin to permit users to add attributes to objects on an individual basis. Using the NSM approach would require continual database re-organization or an implementation that claims storage space for all possible attributes of an object from the outset.

The second reason is that the high maintenance and reconstruction cost for DSM do not apply to a main-memory system, because these extra costs are far less prohibitive than for disk based systems. We feel that a well-designed main-memory based DSM system should at least provide the performance of an NSM-based system. The reason is that at the lowest implementation level in NSM each attribute of a flat object can be represented by a single pointer and a (mostly) fixed offset. DSM merely requires a register file to denote the object components.

Furthermore, a DSM approach is more efficient in a distributed environment, where semi-join operations do not require expensive unpacking of an NSM storage structure.

Therefore, the Goblin storage management scheme is a DSM-like implementation of the three DBMS access functions combined with ADTs for the atomic types. The basis for this implementation is the administration of the *path* function definitions in, so-called Binary Association Tables. The *schema* functions are captured in a Class Administration Table, which describe a Goblin database schema. Finally, the *storage* functions are captured in a Redistribution Administration Table.

The Goblin storage management scheme supports different interpretation of OID and PID, which means that storage locations can be reclaimed. Moreover, we assume that all functions have their associated inverse functions implemented as well. This introduces a degree of freedom in choosing the appropriate representation for each function. Moreover, it permits alternative traversal of the object structure to located related information. The details of our storage management scheme are elaborated upon in the subsequent sections.

4 BINARY ASSOCIATION TABLES

The storage system of Goblin is based on *Binary Association Tables*, or BATs, which provide efficient implementations of binary relations. Flexibility is a key design issue in developing a core of BAT implementations. Their implementation should be optimized towards the operating system limitations and their role in query processing (i.e. persistency, concurrent use, version management). For example, the size of a BAT can be aligned with the OS capabilities to maximize throughput over the network or the granularity of the memory manager.

4.1 THE BAT INTERFACE

BATs are similar to arrays for which the PID is the subscript and the attribute type correspond with the element type. Unlike normal arrays, however, BATs also support access by content, which make them more like associative arrays. Their interface consists of six kinds of operations:

- *Creation, erasure, and destruction* of BATs.
- *Direct access by* PID. Given the PID the attribute value can be read and written, deleted, or it can be tested for emptiness.[2]
- *Access by attribute value.* For each attribute type we can define a search function for a particular value or a value range. They result in a "marking," a built-in BAT to represent presence/absence of PIDs. Complex searches can be modeled by combining the markings of individual simple search operations in various ways.
- *Iteration over BATs.* This allows the programmer to process the individual entries in a BAT. No particular order of processing is guaranteed and, in fact, some of the processing might be done in parallel.
- *Miscellaneous operations.* Upper software layers may wish to give hints and to asks for details, which are used to control BAT behavior. For example, extensive searching can be announced to prompt the BAT to optimize its internal organization for fast searching. Similarly, the user could enquire the BAT about its actual size.

BATs for the atomic types (INT, FLOAT, STR, and PID) are provided by Goblin kernel. This collection can be extended by the programmer providing both the operations for the typed values and the algorithms to maintain its bulk data operations. Though this is more work for the programmer, it also means simplified control over bulk data handling.

4.2 IMPLEMENTATION CONSIDERATIONS FOR BATS

Since BATs model binary associations, there are only a limited number of implementation strategies. Namely, a component of the association can be stored explicitly or implicitly. These leads to the following implementation schemes:

- (implicit, explicit), which is closest to an array-like implementation, where the location of a value is calculated from the PID;

[2]Note that we must know if an entry is empty or used and cannot simply say that unused entries contain garbage. Otherwise, search operations may fail to produce valid items.

- (explicit, implicit), which could be considered if the range contains a few values only organized in a search-tree to find the corresponding PIDs,;
- (implicit, implicit), which describe a pure functional association;
- (explicit, explicit), which is used to support a non-predominant access pattern.

Within each scheme there are ample opportunities to further optimize towards CPU processing or storage cost. For example, for sparse domain and range of an association an (explicit,explicit) scheme can be augmented with two search structures to obtain a fast retrieval and minimal storage. Alternatively, a replica of a BAT can be kept around for simplified transaction rollback.

4.3 ADAPTIVE REPRESENTATIONS

Goblin does not insist on a single storage method for a particular BAT. As long as two implementations provide the same interface, they can be interchanged freely. One of our main goals is to hide these alternative implementations behind the BAT interface description and to exploit the differences as best as possible without interference of the user. That is, Goblin adapts the implementation using statistics about BAT usage.

The adaptive algorithm lets the BAT automatically select among the internal representation that is best under the given circumstances. Therefore, each BAT implementation includes cost functions to help making decisions. In particular, the BAT programmer should supply storage-, search-, and transport- costs functions. Balancing the requirements is captured by a single adaptation routine, which is time-, query-, update-, or user- triggered. Once called, it compares the weighted cost of the current implementation against the benefits of an alternative representation. In needed, it will convert the BAT to its new storage structure. It may also decide to keep multiple incarnations around to satisfy conflicting usage patterns at the cost of additional update overhead.

5 SCHEMA GRAPH ADMINISTRATION

The *schema* functions are collected into Class Administration Tables. They describe the database schema and the structure relationships between objects. There are, broadly speaking, four implementation tracks:

- *Static definitions.* A static database definition can be compiled into the programs, i.e. the knowledge on *schema* functions is embedded in the program code. This results in fast programs at the cost of redundant administration storage. It is also highly inflexible, because the description of the data is kept separate from the data itself (e.g. in program header files). This means that changing the object structure requires program location and recompilation and it becomes difficult to write a generic program to process an arbitrary object.
- *Dynamic typing.* With dynamic typing all type information is kept with the data elements (e.g. Smalltalk). That is, make all *schema* functions explicit and use the *storage* function to keep the OID and PID together (or make them identical). The prime disadvantage is the storage overhead of type information with each data element. Moreover, it incurs processing overhead to repeatedly type check operations.

- *Factor out the type information for bulk data.* This corresponds to explicitly storing both *schema* and used to type-check operations, while the latter is used speed. for access to bulk data.

  This means losing some of the flexibility of dynamic typing, but also greatly reduces the storage and interpretation overhead. By "bulk" processing a high performance is attainable.

In Goblin we focus on the third approach, i.e. factoring out type information for bulk data only. Because operations on bulk data provides a good handle on distributed query processing. It amortizes the overhead of communication and query task scheduling over multiple instances.

5.1 FUNCTIONALITY PROVIDED BY CATS

In Goblin, we differentiate between objects contained by other objects and referenced objects. For instance, an object cannot contain itself as a subobject, but it can refer to itself. Similarly, an object cannot be contained by two separate objects, but it can be shared by any number of objects. Therefore, we choose to make all references explicit. As a consequence, the graph of *schema* functions becomes a tree of containment relationships.

The CAT storage level allows creation of such trees of any depth. The nodes of the tree are formed by constructors e.g. tuples or sets of subtrees. The leaves of the tree are atomic types and references. After a tree has been created, each node is extended with a BAT for storage of the database extent. Insertion of data involves walking through the graphs implied by the *path* functions, guided by the schema functions. After location of the insertion point, the *path*, *schema* and *storage* function definitions are updated. That is, the corresponding BATs are modified.

Likewise, selection over the database starts at a root PID in the database extent followed by composite *path* function traversal. Or a selection starts at a leaf and uses the inverse *path* functions to access the enclosing or sibling objects.

For example, we can express the function P_{name} using a combination of R^{-1}_{Person}:PID $\rightarrow$ OID, S_{name}:OID $\rightarrow$ OID, and R_{name}:OID $\rightarrow$ STR. The advantage is that the representation for each BAT can be optimized independently. Some, e.g. S_{name}, do not necessarily require additional storage.

In the current implementation of the CAT tree the leaf nodes represent atomic types. They contain a BAT of the appropriate type to store the data. Non-leaf nodes provide a few simple functions to the higher levels, such as:

- *Path expressions.* The ability to walk through the CAT tree by path expressions.
- *Implicit functions.* They provide a cheap way to map PID numbers from level parent nodes to their sibling nodes in the CAT tree. Thereby greatly reducing the storage requirements. For a tuple this mapping is simply the identity function - all attributes of the same tuple have the same subscript number in their BATs. But for a set constructor one incoming subscript number would be mapped onto multiple numbers, one for each set element.

New constructors require implementations of the *path* and *schema* functions. This makes it easy to add, for instance, tuples with optional attributes.

6 OBJECT STORAGE PARTITIONING

A *storage* function R maps the OIDs into PIDs at the physical level. Using a single BAT as a target for the *storage* function complicates distributed object management severely. Therefore, Goblin assumes that the range of R is a series of BATs and the mapping R:OID $\rightarrow$ PID is a hash- or range-based partitioning function. A user can extend their implementation to suit his needs, but his implementation should guarantee the constraints of Section 3.1 for the (inverse) *path* functions. Each individual BAT forms the unit for replication and distribution decisions. The *storage* functions are administered in the Redistribution Administration Table.

6.1 RAT INTERFACE

The functionality for the RAT interface is straightforward. The current implementation is focused on the features of novel distributed operating systems, such as in efficient management of shared (memory-mapped) files and cooperative responsibility in managing replicated files. Moreover, we assume basic OS facilities to implement transaction management on the (memory-mapped) file level.

The kind of functions provided by the RAT library are:

- *Change* the storage functions. This includes partitioning a BAT into a series of BATs, based on simple functions.
- *Access by PID(s)*. Translation functions of OIDs into PIDs and the BATs where they can be located.
- *Access by Value*. Translation of valued-based selections over a group of BATs using the partitioning information to reduce the search space.

6.2 IMPLEMENTATION CONSIDERATION FOR RATS

The partitioning layer is built on top of the BAT library. Partitioning can be based on fixed count or fixed size partitions. Fixed count partitioning stores a fixed number of objects in a BAT, but makes it variable in size. The prime advantage is quick translation of OID to PID. Alternatively, in fixed size partitioning the BATs have the same size, which facilitates memory management. Then localization of the objects in the (distributed) store becomes a look-up operation.

In Goblin we have opted for the fixed size partitioning, because BATs are the unit of transport and storage management. Unfortunately, the simple 1-1 correspondence between BATs storing related tuple attributes is lost, because each BAT contain a variable number of PIDs, depending on the size of the objects stored.

To support clustering and partitioning on (multiple) attribute values we introduce the term GID (Group Id). A group consists of zero or more BATs, with non-overlapping PID value ranges. The partitioning index can be organized as a B-tree or T-tree structure. If during an insertion a BAT overflow occurs, a new BAT is allocated and added to the group.

Before a tuple t with attributes $a_0, \cdots, a_n$ is inserted, its GID is determined using the partition functions on the partition attributes. The GID then becomes part of the OIDs assigned to each attribute.

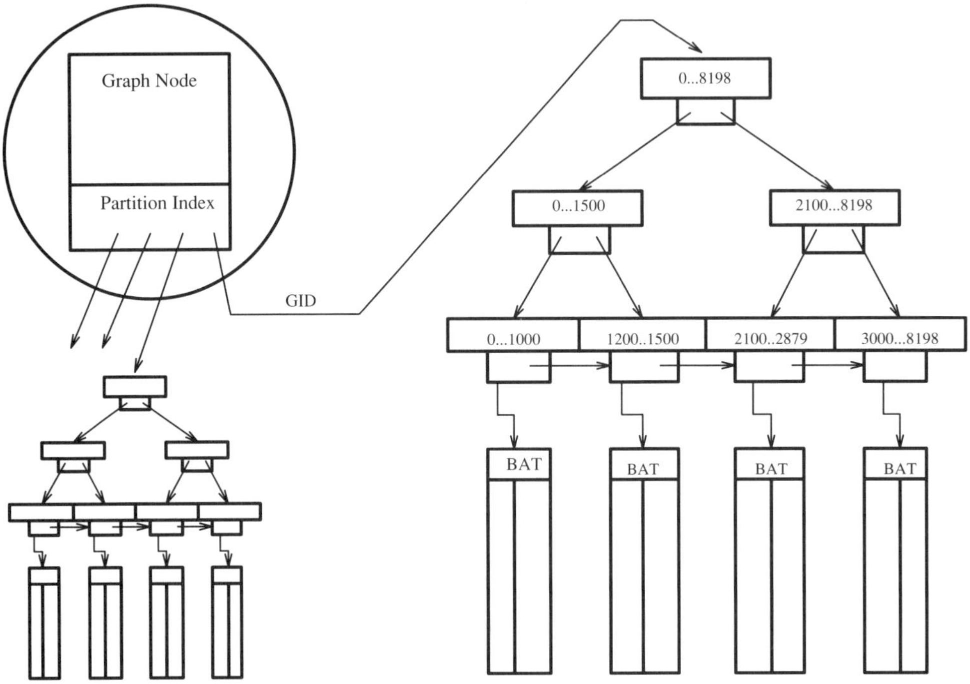

Figure 5: Graph data structure

As a result, the attributes of a tuple are always stored in the partition with the same GID. The BAT where the attribute value is stored can be found through the GID and the OID. The resulting data structure for a node in the schema graph is shown in Figure 5.

6.3 ADAPTIVE REPARTITIONING

The main design decision for the Goblin physical storage level is to make the storage structures adaptive to their usage. This idea results not only in the design of an adaptive scheme for the access structures and data representation within a single BAT, but also extends to repartitioning aspects.

Therefore, a RAT implementation includes a decision function to change the partitioning of PIDs over BATs. This function is triggered by collected statistics on their use. For example, when for query processing a certain partitioning is frequently requested, the RAT can decide to distribute the PIDs according to the partitioning. Whether this track proofs valuable is a research issue currently studied.

7 DISTRIBUTED OBJECT MANAGEMENT

The previous sections have been focussed on object and schema representation, partitioning and access structures. Object persistency, stability and consistency are not addressed by the BAT, CAT or RAT layers. For these issues we partly rely on the evolution of file systems for distributed operating systems. We believe that novel operating systems will offer transaction management primitives, use replication techniques to increase availability and stability, and perform load balancing for coarse grain objects (i.e. files). The Class Managers implement this functionality, as it is not yet offered by the current operating systems.

7.1 FUNCTIONALITY PROVIDED BY THE CLASS MANAGER

On each processor there is a CM process, which manages part of the database ensuring data persistency. If one of the processors comes up after system crash, it recovers its data using the replicas managed by the other CMs or stored on disk. The amount of replication is under the control of Goblin.

During query execution objects are continuously copied and transmitted between the CM processes on the network. Each CM process uses a significant amount of the processors memory to cache the temporary copies and to maintain replicas. It uses a cache replacement policy that favours frequently used objects in order to reduce this communication. As the Goblin QS has an overview of what data is required on each processor, the CM offers primitives to control its cache replacement policy to the QS.

The CM processes migrate or replicate objects to distribute the object references evenly, and to spread the storage for persistent objects over the available CM processes. Object migration and replication can not be controlled by the Query Scheduler, because this optimisation technique tries to improve the object availability and access time over all queries. The allocation information of objects is available, so that the Query Scheduler can allocate subqueries to a processor, which requires a minimal amount of data transport.

The CM offers a standard set of transaction management primitives, such as shared/exclusive read/write locks and two phase commits. The Goblin language semantics require a nested transaction management scheme, which can easily be built from these building blocks.

8 SUMMARY

In this paper we have given an overview of the Goblin DBMS with a focus on the design of its object storage management scheme. The novelty of our storage architecture lies in a strict separation of the basic DBMS access functions. The direct benefit of this approach is the degree of freedom introduced to change the underlying implementations on a selective basis. In particular, we are interested in algorithms for adaptive storage structures for main-memory object management and their performance.

Furthermore, our approach complements and extends the work on Decomposed Storage Model. We perceive this as the prime implementation track for a both flexible and efficient OODBMS in a distributed main-memory system architecture.

The current status of the implementation is as follows. The query processing scheme has been implemented under Amoeba using Intel 386 machines and under SUN/OS using network of SPARC stations. The target database and queries for this prototype where derived from the Wisconsin benchmark. Initial (efficient) implementations of the BAT, RAT and CAT exist. The Goblin compiler has been written using a combination of YACC/Lex and feed into our conditional term rewriter (a Prolog program). A full functional prototype is expected to be delivered around the summer of 1992.

Additional Goblin activities focus on database programming language support of advanced application areas [Kersten et al., 1990; Kersten, 1991]. Furthermore, the facets of database triggers have been surveyed in [vdVoort et al., 1991] and the results are currently converted into a design theory for active databases [Siebes and vd Voort, 1992].

Object Grouping in Eos

Olivier Gruber
INRIA, Rocquencourt
Projet Rodin
78153 Le Chesnay Cedex
France

Laurent Amsaleg
INRIA, Rocquencourt
Projet Rodin
78153 Le Chesnay Cedex
France

Abstract

Eos is an object-oriented programming environment for distributed systems. Leos, the language for Eos, provides transparency for both distribution and persistence. In this paper, we address the problem of object grouping transparency. Object grouping is the declustering of an object graph onto a number of nodes and the clustering of objects on disks. Transparency means minimal impact on the programming process. Eos grouping is transparent and user-driven. Eos proposes an innovative approach which provides Eos users with a finer control than existing systems. Furthermore, Eos grouping is dynamic without being stochastical. It copes automatically with evolutions of the object graph topology (i.e., added or removed links) as evolutive control from users. The grouping implementation is based on the garbage collection process and adds very little overhead.

1 INTRODUCTION

The Eos system [Gruber et al., 1992] is a persistent and distributed programming environment that strives for extensibility and transparency. The language of Eos, named Leos, is an object-oriented programming language, which is made generic through parameterized classes [Meyer, 1988]. Leos genericity makes Eos extensible [Carey et al., 1986a] by permitting add-on collection constructors like generic sets or arrays to be defined by Eos users. Hence, neither Leos nor Eos provide built-in collection constructors.

Leos upholds persistence transparency. Persistence is that property of objects to live for an arbitrary period of time. Persistence transparency is that property of programming languages to abstract persistence issues to programmers. In [Atkinson et al., 1983a] a model of persistence achieving full transparency through an extension of garbage collection was proposed. Any object persists as long as it is reachable from a root of persistence. The full range of persistence is then allowed to all objects independently of their type and instantiation. We will term this model of persistence *uniform persistence*.

Leos supplies distribution transparency. Distribution is that facility to use distributed systems. A distributed system is composed of multiple processors interconnected via a network. Each processor has its own local memory and communicates with others through messages. In Eos, we are concerned with small networks up to the size of a local area network. Distribution transparency is the property to invoke an object independently of its location. Transparent method shipping have been used by many systems for that purpose.

Both persistence and distribution transparencies shield programmers from the complexity of persistent and distributed programming. But this should not be at expense of performance. Combining these two transparencies, Eos provides a flat, virtual, and garbage collected object space. However, this view of an object space conflicts with the reality of computer architectures where object stores are paginated and distributed. In such environments, performance requirements translate into minimizing the costs of communications and disk accesses.

Object grouping might minimize the above costs. Object grouping includes both object declustering onto nodes and object clustering on disks. Object declustering is a partitioning of the object graph and a mapping of the resulting subgraphs onto nodes. Object clustering is the process of grouping objects on disks. Objects accessed together are grouped closely on disks so that they can be fetched with minimal latency and block transfers. Close means within the same I/O block, or in close blocks with respect to arm movements.

Object grouping enhances performance only if objects are grouped according to access patterns of computations. Access patterns of computations can be approximated by object aggregation since computations navigate through the object graph. This suggests clustering of parent (pointing-to) and child (pointed-to) objects together. In this approach, shared objects, i.e., child objects pointed-to from multiple parent objects, are a problem because they have to be ubiquitous to be clustered with each of their parents. Shared objects are usually the stumbling block of grouping mechanisms.

This paper presents object grouping in Eos. Object clustering in Eos is based on object aggregation and is fully transparent like Orion and O_2 systems [Kim et al., 1987; Kim et al., 1989; Benzaken and Delobel, 1991]. Eos clustering goes two steps further. On the one hand, Eos provides fine and deterministic user control in case of object sharing. On the other hand, this clustering model is extended to support object declustering which therefore benefits from the same full transparency and fine control.

Another prime contribution of Eos grouping is its dynamicity. The object store is able to reorganize itself to cope with evolutions of the graph or access patterns. Unlike existing systems which provide dynamic clustering, Eos is not based on a stochastical approach. Eos grouping dynamicity relies on the garbage collection process. Grouping adds very little overhead to garbage collection and none to user computations. Grouping is achieved in parallel with user computations, thereby Eos reorganizes itself without logical interruptions for its users.

This paper is structured as follows. Section 3 introduces object grouping in Eos from a policy point of view. Section 4 presents the underlying machinery behind dynamic grouping of objects. In particular, clustering algorithms are presented. Section 5 presents how garbage collection is the corner stone of our solution and ensures the performance of our dynamic scheme. Finally, we conclude in Section 6.

2 RELATED WORK

Most of the object-oriented systems base their clustering policy on object aggregation. In other words, an object A which references another object B, attracts B in its physical container. Physical containers are the basic storage units in which objects are grouped. The rationale for using object aggregation is that it approximates computation locality in object-oriented programming since computations navigate through the object graph.

However, object sharing limits the use of object aggregation as a basis for clustering. A shared object is an object which is referenced from multiple other objects, called its parent objects. Hence, a shared object is required to be clustering ubiquitous, i.e. to be clustered with each of its parents.

There are two families of answers to shared object ubiquity. Some systems (e.g., [Hornick and Zdonik, 1987; Haerder et al., 1987]) achieve ubiquity through a replication strategy which effectively cluster a copy of shared objects with each of their parents. If such systems benefit from perfect locality, they suffer from the overhead of the necessary protocol to keep replicas coherent. Other systems reject replication and *elect* instead one and only one parent that effectively clusters the shared object. Among systems that advocate election-based clustering, two schools of thought exist that differ based on who elects the clustering parent: those who advocate self-electing systems and those who rely on user hints.

Self-electing systems [Hudson and King, 1989; Tsangaris and Naughton, 1991; Tsangaris and Naughton, 1992; Stamos, 1984] all use statistics on which they base their decisions. The statistics maintained are about the frequency of reference dereferencing. These approaches have several prime advantages. In addition to achieving complete transparency with respect to both persistence and clustering issues, complete dynamicity is achieved as well. The clustering of objects is automatically adapted to evolutions of the object graph topology (added or removed links between objects) and also to evolutions of workload (access pattern evolutions). However, this dynamicity is potentially a severe drawback because clustering might never stabilize, yielding time-consuming reorganizations which leave little processing power for user computations. Finally, maintaining statistics may prove costly.

User-driven systems further divide into three categories. The first category [Carey et al., 1988; Bellosta-Tourtier et al., 1990; Black et al., 1987; Moss, 1989] provides persistent object containers like segments or nodes in which programmers explicitly cluster their objects. Therefore, these systems do not provide any form of transparency and will not be further discussed. The second category [Kim et al., 1987; Kim et al., 1989] upholds clustering transparency but neither declustering nor uniform persistence transparency. The Orion system is an example of this category. The last category of user-driven systems further provides uniform persistence as clustering transparency but lacks declustering transparency [Benzaken and Delobel, 1991].

The Orion system bases its clustering policy on labelling aggregation links between objects. A complex object is defined through the IS-PART-OF relationship, that is the notion that an object is a part of another object. Components of a complex objects are clustered together. Orion users define complex objects through a labelling of object references within class definitions. Possible labels are exclusive, shared, and weak [Kim et al., 1989]. Exclusive and shared labels express IS-PART-OF relationship, while weak labels express traditional object aggregation of object-oriented languages. Hence, complex objects are determined as, given a root instance, the transitive closure from that root object though exclusive and shared links.

The O_2 system is an example of this last category. The O_2 system bases its clustering policy on the concept of placement trees. Intuitively, the type structure of a class in the O_2 system may be represented as an infinite tree (in case of recursive types) [Abiteboul and Kannellakis, 1989]. A placement tree is any finite subtree extracted from this infinite tree. O_2 system users define a clustering strategy as a set of placement trees. Given a clustering strategy, each class in the system is the root of at most one placement tree. A placement tree for class c expresses the way in which components of an instances of c are to be clustered. In other words, a placement tree expresses the IS-PART-OF relationship between its root class c and the components of an instance of c.

Both Orion and O_2 achieve a quantum leap toward clustering transparency. But both approaches suffer from the same lack of control. Neither system permits its users to control the clustering of shared objects, i.e., shared objects are non-deterministically grouped with one of their parents. The problem originates from the usage of the IS-PART-OF semantics which is inherently too poor to cope with sharing. Indeed, when an object is shared, more than one parent may declare that shared object as a part of itself, leaving the run-time system electing which of those parents will effectively cluster the shared object. Moreover, none of them provides dynamic clustering. Finally, neither Orion nor O_2 uphold object declustering.

3 OBJECT GROUPING

This section presents object grouping in Eos from a policy point of view. We will first introduce Eos clustering policy and then move on to Eos' declustering policy.

3.1 OBJECT CLUSTERING

Eos' object model permits the definition of arbitrarily complex objects as aggregation of objects of arbitrary depth. An object is an instance of a class which has an identity. Identity is system-wide since Eos upholds an entirely flat object space, i.e. there are no user-visible notion of segments, pages, or any physical containers of any kind.

Classes form an inheritance tree, i.e. only simple inheritance is supported. A class has a number of attributes which can be base-types (integer, char, etc.) or object references. An object reference holds an object identity or *nil* which denotes a reference pointing to no object. Object references are typed with a class which restricts the possible objects pointed-to by this reference.

Two graphs can be defined from the above object model which are necessary to formalize the Eos clustering policy: object and class aggregation graph. The object aggregation graph is the traditional aggregation of objects using their identity.

The class aggregation graph (CAG) is a graph defined as follows. Given a set of classes, for each class X having attributes α_1 to α_n which are object references, respectively typed Y_1

to Y_n, the CAG includes the vertices $(X, Y_1, \ldots, Y_n)$ and edges from X to $(Y_1, \ldots, Y_n)$ labelled by α_1 to α_n. An example of classes and the corresponding CAG is depicted in Figure 1.

```
Class X {          Class Y {
  P  a;              P  c;
  Q  b;              X d;
};                 };

Class Z {
  Q  e;
}
```

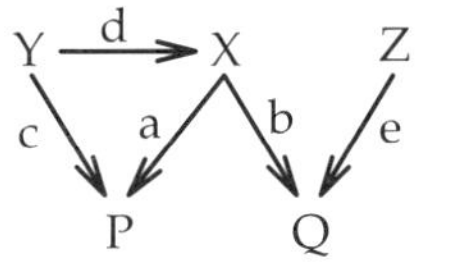

Class Aggregation Graph

Figure 1: Class Hierarchy and Class Aggregation Graph

Eos includes a global schema which manages the class and class hierarchy definitions as the CAG. Given a class hierarchy, Eos can deduce the CAG from the global schema and provide it to users as a simple extension to class definition. The traditional class definition is augmented with the list of parent classes. Parent classes are defined for a given class c as the set of classes c_i in the CAG for which an edge from c_i to c exist. Figure 2 shows the parent class lists extracted from our previous example of CAG and shows the corresponding syntactic extension of class definitions. Note that parent lists are automatically deduced from the inheritance hierarchy and class attributes, users do not have to type them in.

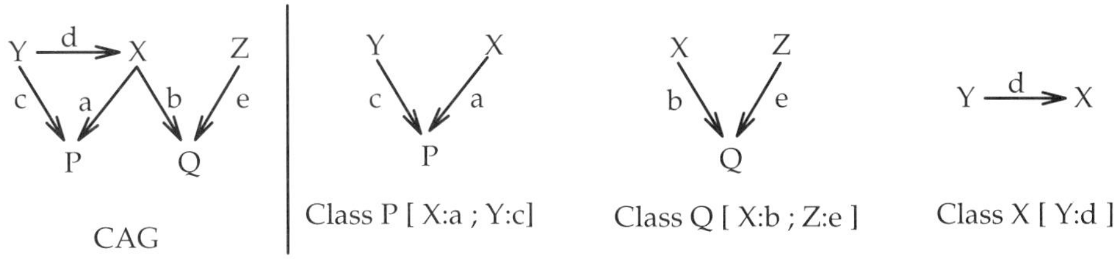

Figure 2: Parent Classes and Extended Class Definition

Now that we have defined the CAG, we can present how Eos users drive the Eos clustering mechanism to achieve the ubiquity of shared objects.

Eos users drive object clustering by non-strictly ordering the parent classes of potentially shared objects. Potentially shared objects are instances of classes that have more than one parent class. The non-strict ordering is supplied by Eos users by simply weighting parent classes in the class definition. Pondus weights represent the relevances of parent classes, i.e., their relative importance. Relevances must be understood as the importance of one access path with respect to others access paths leading to a shared object. The higher the relevance of a link, the more likely that the link will be walked through by computations. A shared object between instances of several classes will be clustered towards the instance of the most relevant class.

A possible weighting and the corresponding object clustering are shown Figure 3. Relevances control the clustering as follows. Between several links reaching a given object, the link with the highest relevance will force the object clustering. Thus, objects of class P shared between objects of classes X and Y, are clustered with instances of Y. Objects of class Q shared between objects of classes X and Z, are clustered with instances of Z.

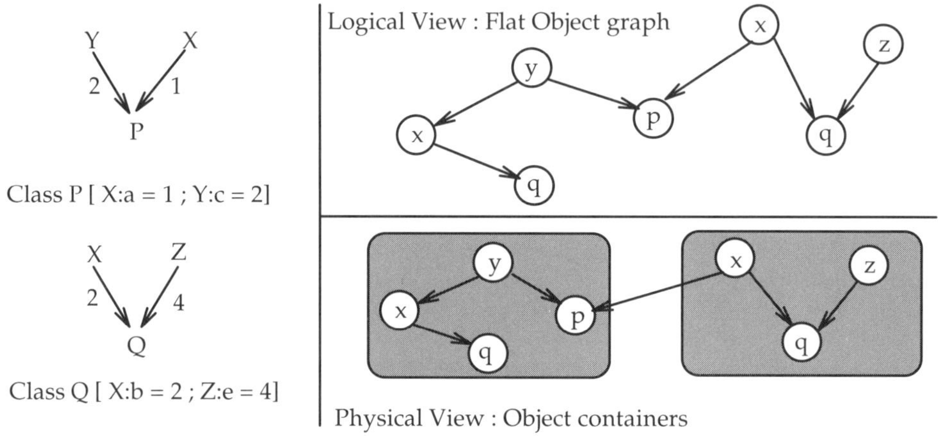

Figure 3: Class Relevances and Object Clustering

Note that setting relevances in a CAG is a local process which is achieved on a per class basis only. There is no global ordering of edges, but only a local ordering of parents for each single class. This approach is innovative because on the one hand the clustering decision is encapsulated within the shared object; on the other hand the decision is based on a non-strict ordering of parent classes. The non-strict ordering of parent classes is provided by Eos users and enables them to finely and deterministically control the clustering of shared objects. Encapsulating this user control within shared object classes enables the localization of the clustering decision within single classes instead of spreading it all over the class hierarchy.

3.2 OBJECT DECLUSTERING

Object declustering is the ability of partitioning the object graph into subgraphs and mapping them onto physical nodes. Declustering transparency is a two-fold problem. First, users should be provided with a simple and efficient way to partition their object graph into disjoint subgraphs. Second, mapping these objects subgraphs onto nodes should be as easy as possible.

An intuitive approach to graph partitioning is the following. Given a set of objects called rooted objects, a subgraph per rooted object can easily be determined as all objects reachable from that rooted object. However, those subgraphs are not disjoint because some objects might be reachable from more than one rooted object. Disjoint subgraphs can be produced if link relevances are used. Link relevances permit to keep only one link per object: the link with the highest relevance. Hence, the above transitive closure going through most relevant links only will yield disjoint subgraphs.

Consequently, the only two things needed to partition the object graph is a set of rooted objects and link relevances. Relevances are already provided for clustering purposes. The set of rooted objects is provided through a *rooted property*. This property can be set or removed at any time on any object. Each rooted object defines and identifies the subgraph of objects reachable through most relevant links. We will use the term *Rooted Object Graph* (ROG) to name these subgraphs.

ROGs have to be mapped onto nodes. For that purpose Eos provides the *anchoring call*. Any rooted object can be anchored at any time at any node. The anchoring node is specified via the identifier of the node. Nodes are logically designated in Eos through the use of a system table which hides physical nodes. Hence physical independence is achieved this way. A rooted object can be anchored at only one node at a given time. However, the anchoring can be dynamically changed. The consequence of this approach is that the entire ROG of a rooted object will be placed on the anchoring node.

One can point out that half transparency is supported with respect to declustering. Eos achieves the same degree of transparency with respect to partitioning as for clustering since a reachibility model is used. However, mapping subgraphs is explicit through the anchoring system call. Albeit anchoring hurts transparency, we believe it is necessary because mapping is highly application-dependent. For instance, applications that target high performance and those that target fault tolerance have converse mapping strategies [Bal et al., 1989].

4 GROUPING MACHINERY

Eos users are provided with an object-oriented language through which they build complex object graphs within a flat object space. These object graphs are reachable from a root of persistence that is nothing else than a naming service. These object graphs are managed within an object store which provides storage and identity regimes for objects.

The Eos store upholds both single-level store and single-level identity mechanism for efficiency. Single-level store means that the persistent object store is directly mapped into virtual spaces of users' computations [Bensoussan et al, 1972; Copeland et al., 1990]. This suggests the use of larger virtual spaces than today, like [Bakoglu et al., 1990; Shekita, 1991]. Single-level addressing means that virtual addresses are directly used to support object identity. In order to support object moves, a forwarding mechanism is used associated with a jump strategy [Fowler, 1985]. When an object moves, it leaves a forwarder in place which indicates its new location. When a user follows an object reference that points to a forwarder, a jump is made, i.e. the reference is updated to point to the new location of the object. The garbage collector finishes the jumps not yet done by users and reclaims forwarders now become unreachable.

Single-level store requires object clustering for best performance. A clustering mechanism suggests a notion of physical containers in which objects should be grouped. The rationale for clustering is to obtain a better locality of reference within those physical containers. Thereby, it reduces the negative effect on performance of small bandwidth and high latency of both disks and networks.

Physical containers in Eos are the *harbor* and the *pier* containers. The harbors aim at improving node locality. A harbor is the storage structure of a single ROG. Note that a harbor is always local to a single node, independent of whether the root is anchored or not. A node may contain multiple harbors. A harbor is itself divided in pier containers. A *pier* is a set of disk tracks. The rationale for piers is the following. First, they improve disk bandwidth since transfers take place on a track basis. Furthermore, global disk locality is ensured by clustering related tracks in close cylinders. The track relationship is given by the membership of tracks in piers and piers in harbors. Another purpose of piers is to provide a finer clustering of objects than harbors.

The purpose of this section is to describe the machinery that actually groups objects within the above physical containers. Eos users provide link relevances which are used by that machinery to group objects. Objects are grouped within physical containers according to the following rule: objects are grouped with their most relevant parent. In fact, there may be several most relevant parents since link relevances introduce a non-strict ordering only. In such a case, object grouping is nondeterministic between parents having the highest relevance. Note that this nondeterminism can be avoided if users provide strictly ordered relevances in the schema.

A grouping machinery based on most relevant parent semantics introduces several challenging issues. The first challenge is to achieve a fast clustered allocation. The second challenge is to support the dynamic nature of clustering, i.e., to cope with evolutions of both the object graph topology and evolutions of link relevances. Finally, internal fragmentation[1] should be kept low in presence of object reclustering and reclaimation. Each of these challenges are discussed respectively in the next three sections.

4.1 OBJECT ALLOCATION

The allocation scheme of objects has a goal and a constraint. The goal is to cluster objects correctly when they are instantiated. The constraint is the allocation speed. Previous works [Gautron, 1990; Bellosta-Tourtier et al., 1991] in object-oriented programming environments showed that linear allocation is the only satisfactory mechanism. Particularly, free-list management should be avoided.

In Eos, clustering objects at instanciation time means that objects should be allocated near their first parent. The earlier rule of most relevant parent indeed specializes into first parent upon allocation since there is no other parent. The first parent of an object is perfectly known in Leos since Leos adopts an object instantiation identical to the Eiffel object-oriented programming language [Meyer, 1988]. In Eiffel, all object references are typed by a class and respond to a create method which instantiates an object of the reference class. In other words, an object is instantiated through the first reference attribute pointing to it within its first parent.

Allocating objects "near" their first parent means in the same I/O granule, i.e., the same track. This is an ideal view, however, because tracks have a fixed size, and full tracks force objects to be allocated elsewhere. In such a case, an attempt is usually made to pack the track. If this fails, a place is searched somewhere up a hierarchy of containers. In Eos, this hierarchy would be the first parent track, then the pier containing that track, and finally the harbor containing that pier. Another possible strategy would be to use an overflow area where objects intended to go in full tracks are allocated. Both strategies are inherently slow and further produce poor locality as soon as overflows appear.

Eos approach is innovative. Eos adopts a slightly relaxed notion of *near*, near means in the same pier container instead of the same track. The difference is that a pier container is a set

[1]This should not be confused with the declustering or data-partitioning of a collection.

of tracks of a variable size and therefore never physically overflow. When a pier exhausts its free space, it simply allocates itself a new track. Thereby, allocating objects within the pier of their first parent is always possible. Consequently, a fast linear allocation can be used.

The above allocation scheme is fast but has a major drawback: uncontrolled pier sizes. Nothing prevents a pier to ever expand to accept new objects. However, grouping objects within larger containers than the physical I/O granule does not enhance performance. This suggests that pier size should be maintained as close as possible to a track size. Hence, piers larger than a track are said to be in a logical overflow state. In contrast to physical overflow, logical overflow does not forbid object allocation, and therefore linear allocation is possible. A logical overflow state simply indicates the necessity to reduce the pier size. For that, Eos adopts an asynchronous splitting strategy.

Splitting a pier in Eos is impacted by the single-level support of object identity. Objects, upon a move, must leave a forwarder in place which indicates their new location [Fowler, 1985; Copeland et al., 1990]. Hence, splitting can only be achieved through a copy-and-free approach. The overflowing pier, called the from-pier, is first split by copying its objects into new single-tracked piers, called to-piers. The split, by copying objects in to-piers, fills up the from-pier with forwarders. Later on, all these forwarders will be jumped and reclaimed by the garbage collector. Once empty, the from-pier will be freed.

A pier split works as follows. A pier has a set of pinned objects from which all objects within the pier are reachable. How pinned objects are determined will become clear shortly. The from-pier is recursively copied in a depth-first manner into to-piers. During this recursive process, the object graph is walked through most relevant links only. Single tracks of each to-pier is filled up to a *filling threshold* value which is a system generation parameter like loading factors for B_trees in database systems. When the unique track of to-piers reaches this threshold, another to-pier is allocated and the copying process resumes. The algorithm is given in Figure 4.

During the split of a pier, pinned objects are determined for each to-pier created. During the depth-first recursive copy, a copied object is pinned in its to-pier if its most relevant parent and itself are in two different to-piers. One can remark that all objects within a pier are reachable from pinned objects of that pier, at least just after the split. This property motivates the use of pinned objects to root the recursive copy of pier split.

However, there are is no guaranty that all objects still be reachable from pinned objects at some arbitrary time after the split. Indeed, due to removed links, some objects that were once reachable from pinned objects, might no longer be. Unreachable objects are left within the from-pier by the split algorithm, i.e., not copied in to-piers. These leftover objects will not prevent Eos from freeing the from-pier because Eos will detect these objects as misclustered and will recluster them in other piers as explained in the next section. Consequently, the from-pier will get once empty and will be freed.

Pier split and pinned objects introduce a recursion that need an initialization. The split algorithm uses pinned objects as a root and pinned objects are determined by the split. The initialization is at the creation of a harbor. Originally, a harbor is created with a single pier to support a ROG. The only pinned object of the very first pier of a harbor is the rooted object of a ROG for which that harbor is created.

```
object::scavenge(pier_t * to_pier)
{
  self->copy(to_pier);
  low_bound = first_child();
  current = low_bound ;
  while ( current != nil ) {
    scavenge(current);
    current = next_child(current);
    if ( to_pier->size() > optimum_value ) {
        // Pin all objects belonging to the cutset
        // as the pinned objects of the current to_pier.
        ...
        // Then allocate a new to_pier.
        to_pier = new pier_t;
    }
  }
}
```

Figure 4: Scavenge and Split Algorithm for Piers

An example of pier overflow is given in Figure 5. The figure shows three snapshots taken during the splitting process of a pier. The first snapshot represents a pier in overflow just before the beginning of the split. Note that object E is shared between B and C and should be grouped with C based on link relevances. The depth-first recursive copy will in fact ignore the link between B and E because it uses only the most relevant links, and therefore will yield the correct clustering. The second snapshot is taken just after the first to-pier reaches the filling threshold and the first object is copied into the new to-pier. This snapshot shows the result of the depth-first recursive copy of objects A, B, F and C as their forwarders left in their place. Note that C is pinned because its most relevant parent and itself are in two different piers. The third snapshot represents the two to-piers after the end of the split algorithm.

The split algorithm relies on a walk through most relevant links only, which is not difficult. As we presented earlier, link relevances are easily known from the class tags in objects by looking up the schema. Moreover, each object remembers the highest relevance of links pointing to it. Given the highest relevance, and knowing the relevance of the link we are walking through, we are able to tell whether we use a most relevant link or not.

4.2 DYNAMIC RECLUSTERING

Basically, mapping evolutions of the object graph, i.e., added or removed links, in evolutions of link relevances may make an object misclustered. An object is misclustered if itself and its most relevant parent are in two distinct piers. In order to preserve good clustering, a misclustered object should be dynamically slided to the pier of its most relevant parent.

Dynamic reclustering should be stable, i.e., objects having multiple parents with the same relevance should not be alternatively grouped with two or more parents, crossing a pier boundary back and forth. Recall that an object is said to be grouped with another object when it is in the same pier. Reclustering is made stable by enforcing the following rule.

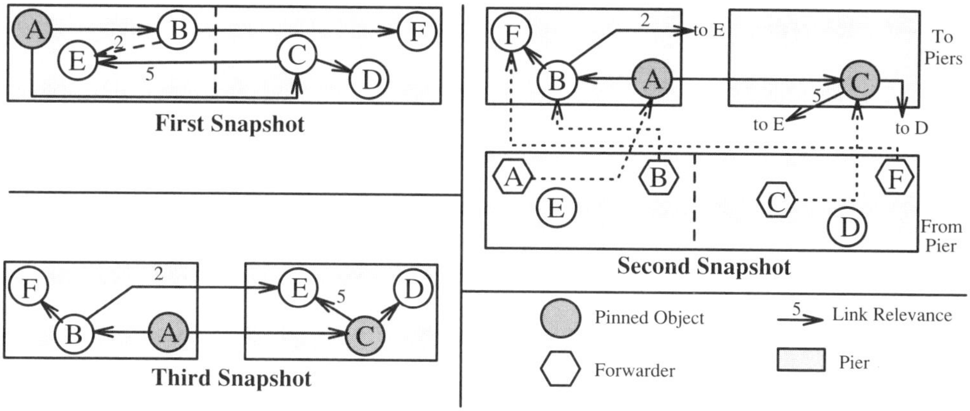

Figure 5: Pier Overflow

Rule: An object is reclustered if and only if it has a parent outside its current pier which has a strictly stronger relevance than parents inside.

Theoretically, objects can be reclustered one by one, but practically, we need to move as much misclustered objects as possible at once. Objects are detected as misclustered at the rate most relevant parents are dynamically checked for. The detection of most relevant parents is asynchronously done as a side-effect of garbage collection (see Section 5). Therefore, most relevant parent knowledge is actualized at a frequency which is too low to cope with an object-based move. Indeed, it would mean only one object slide at every garbage collection! Instead of moving a single object, we move its grape. The grape of an object is the graph of all objects, inside the same pier, reachable from that object through most relevant links.

An example is shown in Figure 6. The left hand side of the figure shows two piers before dynamic reclustering of objects. The dashed link between G and A depicts the removed that justified once the actual clustering. By now, the most relevant parent of A is F: A is misclustered. The reclustering mechanism will slide the A's grape of objects. The right hand side of the figure shows the result of this reclustering process. Note that the grape contains only reachable objects through most relevant links. For instance, D and E are not reclustered.

A special case has to be made with respect to dynamic grouping for the pinned objects of a pier. Clearly, most pinned objects will be considered misclustered since they are at the cutset between piers and likely without parents inside their current pier. However, they should not be moved towards their most relevant parent in order to preserve the effects of pier splits. Otherwise, dynamic reclustering would undo what pier splits have done. In a way, pinned objects of a pier define the pier content: the fact that pinned objects are not allowed to move forces their grape within their pier.

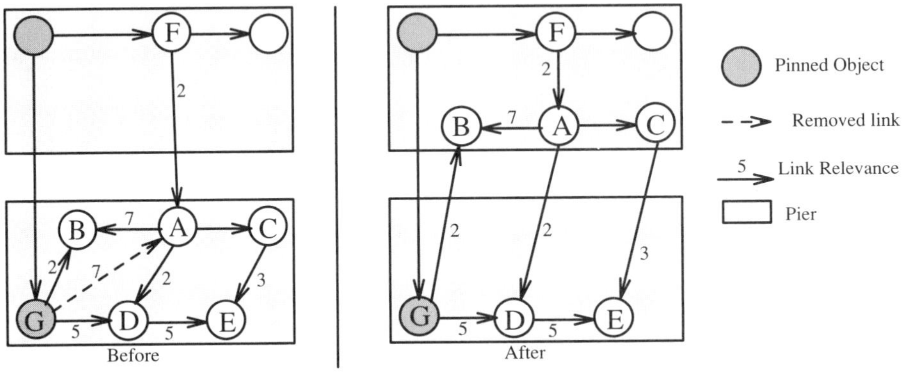

Figure 6: Dynamic Reclustering wrt. Link Relevance

4.3 PIER MERGE

Piers merge to reduce fragmentation. Fragmentation appears because of garbage, but also because of dynamic reclustering. Pier merge has one goal but also one constraint. The goal is to produce piers with sizes above a threshold that limit internal fragmentation. This threshold is a fraction of a track size which is specified as an Eos generation parameter. The constraint is that clustering should not degrade through pier merge.

Clearly, two piers cannot be merged based on size consideration only because there would be no enhancement of clustering. Even worse, totally unrelated objects might get clustered together. On the contrary, pier merges should and can enhance clustering.

The idea is to look at pier merges as a special case of dynamic reclustering. First of all, a pier is said to underflow when its size drops bellow the aforementioned threshold. When a pier underflows, its pinned objects are first unpinned, then all pier's objects are forced as misclustered. Therefore, dynamic reclustering will move them all towards their most relevant parent outside the pier. The pier is thereby emptied and then later freed once all forwarders it contains have been reclaimed.

An example is given in Figure 7. The pier containing A, B, C and D in the upper part underflows. Thus, pinned objects A and B are unpinned and their grape are reclustered. The result of the merge is presented in the lower part of the figure.

5 DYNAMIC GROUPING SUPPORT

Dynamic grouping of objects in Eos is based on most relevant parent semantic. The most relevant parents is an evolutionary semantic in presence of topological evolutions of the object graph or evolutions of link relevances in the schema. To grasp this dynamicity, Eos run-time has to have the knowledge of all parents of a given object and relevances of their links. Assuming parents of an object are known, relevances are easily obtained from the schema. The knowledge of parents is more complex to obtain.

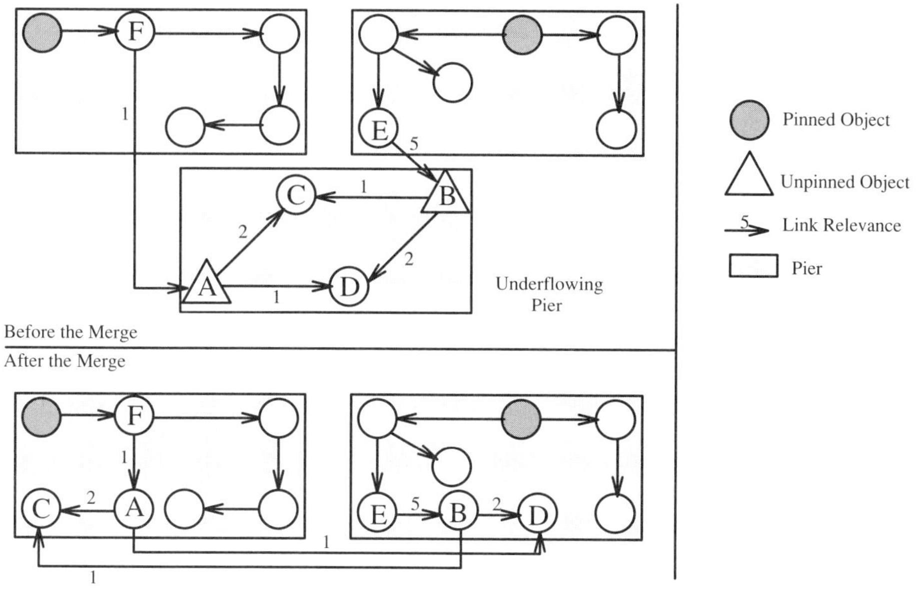

Figure 7: Pier Merge

Eos proposes an innovative approach to have that parent knowledge. The basic idea is that a scan-based garbage collector [Dijkstra et al., 1978] walks through the entire object graph and therefore sees all parents of objects. We point out that this parent knowledge may not be exact if mutators (user programs) run in parallel with the collector and therefore may change the graph topology. This section discusses the garbage collector support for object grouping.

Dynamic determination of most relevant parents is possible with very little space and time overhead added to the garbage collector already in place in Eos. Space overhead is simply that each object has to remember its current highest relevance, this is likely to be as small as a byte. Time overhead is, for each link traversed, to get the link relevance from the schema and to update the relevance maximum stored in the object if necessary. The schema accesses to have relevances of links are almost no overhead because the schema is in the single-level store, replicated at each node. Schema accesses are as fast as virtual memory accesses.

Most relevant parents are detected as follows. During its scan phase, the collector updates the maximum of relevances stored in objects, and builds the list of misclustered objects. Recall that misclustered objects have their most relevant parent outside their current pier. For better stability of object clustering in case of multiple most relevant parents with equal relevances, an object is considered misclustered only if it has a parent outside its current pier which has a strictly greater relevance than relevances of parents within its current pier.

Once most relevant parents are dynamically determined, there is no major difficulty to dynamic object grouping. Eos is able to move misclustered objects and their grapes towards their most relevant parents as explained earlier. However, Eos makes garbage collection the cornerstone of its dynamic object grouping and one may argue about the collector's own performance. The rest of this section provides the readers with sufficient insights on the garbage collection in Eos so that they can be convinced of its feasibility.

The garbage collection process has two phases: detection and reclamation. Both are traditionally glued, but they are achieved independently in Eos.

The detection of garbage is on-the-fly, incremental, and conservative. It is on-the-fly because mutators run concurrently with the collector [Dijkstra et al., 1978]. It is incremental because harbors are independently collected. It is conservative because each harbor maintains two tables of incoming and outgoing references so that local collections can be independent and without global synchronization [Ladin and Liskov, 1986; Hughes, 1985; Shapiro et al., 1990].

The global sketch is the following. Each harbor is insulated with respect to object composition by two tables. One table, called the Incoming Reference Table (IRT), keeps track of incoming references from the outside. Each entry is called a scion. The other table, called the Out-going Reference Table (ORT), maintains the outgoing references to objects in other harbors. Each entry is called a stub. For a given object O in harbor H which is externally referenced, there is a stub in ORTs of harbors having objects which reference object O and there is a corresponding scion for each stub in the IRT of harbor H. This is depicted in Figure 8.

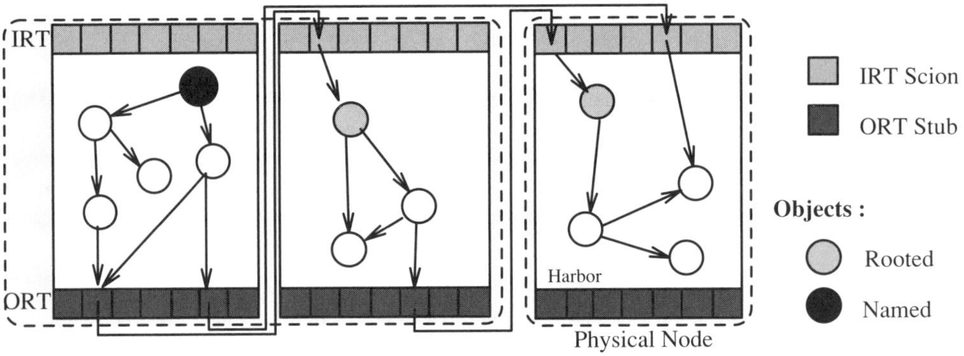

Figure 8: Harbor Isolation Through IRT and ORT Tables

Each harbor is locally and independently scanned. Local detections are conservative with respect to the IRT, detect local garbage, and therefore clean the ORT. When stubs disappear, the pointed-to IRTs are informed and corresponding scions are in turn removed. The local detections are independent, i.e., there is no global synchronism.

The reclaimation of garbage is separated from its detection. The detection process *detects* garbage and marks the objects as dead at a harbor granule. Then, an asynchronous process incrementally packs the store at a pier granule.

The rationale is that the store is persistent and therefore it is likely that large portions of the store are quite stable from one collection phase to another. In other words, only a fraction of the entire store need to be packed after a collection. An incremental approach to packing is able to benefit from that property while traditional collectors, mark-and-sweep or scavenging, systematically copies the entire store. Note that generational collectors are inherently unadapted to our approach since they are incompatible with a user-driven clustering.

6 CONCLUSION

Eos is a general-purpose programming environment for building applications that need persistence and distribution capabilities. Such applications are fragile with respect to locality. Locality suggests an adequate grouping of objects in order to improve performance. But object grouping is a major programming burden of most existing systems. In others that uphold transparency, users lack control. This paper presented the grouping model of Eos which has several major contributions.

The first contribution is a complete transparency while providing a fine and deterministic control. Transparency is obtained through the use of the schema for users to drive the grouping machinery. Fine control is permitted by using the richer semantics of aggregation link relevances than the traditional IS-PART-OF semantic which is too poor to cope with shared objects.

The second contribution is the complete dynamicity of object grouping without renouncing user control. Dynamicity is not stochastic but based on the most relevant parent semantics which is dynamic by definition. The machinery to support this dynamicity relies on garbage collection and adds very little overhead.

The third contribution is easy declustering of objects which permits easy load balancing. Partitioning the graph is as simple as setting a rooted property on some objects. Similarly, mapping is as simple as anchoring those rooted objects on nodes. Load balancing is easy because object rooting and anchoring is completely dynamic and can be changed during the normal operation of the Eos system.

The Eos solution to object grouping presented in this paper suggests an interesting research track. Eos upholds transparency and ease of object clustering but lacks tuning tools. We are currently looking at the use of statistics as a tuning feedback that would help Eos users in the difficult process of improving the overall system performance.

Acknowledgements

We thank the reviewers for their helpful comments. We are especially grateful to Patrick Valduriez for helping us clarifying this paper. We appreciate the fruitful discussions with Laurent Daynès and Eric Amiel. We also thank Véronique Benzaken for her help.

Object Management in SeeQFD

Kirk Kandt
Jet Propulsion Laboratory
4800 Oak Grove Drive
Pasadena, CA 91009
U.S.A.

Abstract

SeeQFD is a software system developed to support concurrent engineering. A key component of it is an object management system. The object management system supports object persistence, object distribution, and demand-based access. The object management system was developed in both LISP and C++. This paper describes these two implementations and compares it to other work. Various aspects of the systems are described. More specifically, the construction and translation of object addresses, garbage collection of objects, the software architecture, the services provided by it, and some of the system internals are discussed.

1 INTRODUCTION

There are many approaches to the development of quality products. One of these is Quality Function Deployment (QFD). The QFD methodology originated in 1972 at Mitsubishi's Kobe shipyard site [Hauser and Clausing, 1988]. It has proven to be very effective in reducing costs and improving product quality [Sullivan, 1986]. QFD does this by focusing and coordinating the skills of a project team so that it designs, manufactures, and markets consumer products better. The QFD methodology has been extended and a computer-based tool called SeeQFD has been developed to support the enhanced methodology.

SeeQFD must manage several design artifacts. The type of modeled artifacts can be extremely diverse; the artifacts can be hierarchical, in addition to forming more complex relationships. Because design efforts tend to occur in a distributed environment, whose proximity ranges from the very close to the extremely distant, the management and residence of this information must likewise be distributed. Furthermore, because the lifetime of a design spans multiple work sessions, design objects must be persistent. Since these designs can be extremely large, a mechanism for demand-based object access is needed. Consequently, the Object Management System (OMS) has been developed to support these needs. OMS provides the basic underlying representation and processing substrate for all information manipulated by SeeQFD.

OMS has been implemented using LISP and CLOS [Steele, 1990] during 1990-1991. LISP is a symbolic programming language and CLOS is its object-oriented language component. OMS runs on a variety of UNIX [Ritchie and Thompson, 1974] workstations. The maintenance and evaluation of the prototype is being done at Rockwell International. A delivery version is currently being implemented in C++ [Lippman, 1991] and is expected to be available to the public in early 1993.

The remainder of this paper is comprised of sections which describe the method for managing and reclaiming objects, the client-server architecture, a comparison between the two implementations, and a discussion of related systems. Thereafter, a summary of the research results and conclusions are presented.

2 OBJECT REPRESENTATION

Before proceeding, some basic terminology must be defined. An object is a unique member of a collection of storage structures which share a common set of features. In Common Lisp or C++ an object is an instance of a class. A persistent object is an object which exists until it is explicitly deleted. In other words, a persistent object has a lifetime which spans across multiple user log-in sessions or virtual memory images. Stated in another way, an object may have a short-term representation in the virtual memory of a process, but it has a long-term (or persistent) representation on a secondary device, such as a disk drive. A distributed representation of an object is when its description resides on multiple computers. Demand-based object access is when an object is read upon first access; until this time, only a reference to the object exists in the virtual memory of a process. Demand-based object access is a form of lazy evaluation [Turner, 1979].

These definitions help explain how data is represented and accessed in OMS, which is the subject of this section. Data is represented as objects in a two-level store. These objects may reside on multiple machines and are accessed on demand.

2.1 KEYED ACCESS

Data access in OMS is based on keys. A key is used to find a related piece of information. For example, in a database containing information about several people the first name of each individual can be used as a key to retrieve their age, sex, and other data. However, the problem with using the first name of a person is that several people may share the same name. This ambiguity demonstrates the importance of unique identification.

Consequently, OMS uses unique keys for object identification. Unique identification and keyed access were first explored in a knowledge-based management system called PIE [Goldstein and Bobrow, 1981]. Keyed access of objects in a knowledge base was later used by FSD [Balzer, 1985]. The result of these two efforts identified the following two facts — unique identification of objects requires a small amount of storage space and non-unique identification has the potential for storing different objects using the same key. In the latter case, a retrieval or matching operation based on a Unique IDentifier (UID) is not guaranteed to return the correct object.

A UID is used to save, match, and retrieve an object. Since these operations must be extremely fast, a simple scheme should be used, such as those based on machine address/counter and machine address/timestamp representations. The first representation is slightly slower since the counter must be written to disk each time a UID is allocated. The second representation, although faster, requires more storage. However, knowing when an object was originally created is sometimes useful and is often needed in database systems. Given these differences, the machine address/timestamp scheme was chosen for object access because of speed and practicality.

2.2 TWO-LEVEL MEMORY

OMS objects are maintained in a two-level store — virtual and secondary memories. This is an artifact of using a standard programming language. As a result, a method for preventing multiple copies of the same object within a client must be used as well as providing a mechanism for translating between the virtual and secondary memory representations.

2.2.1 Virtual Memory

The objects which are maintained by a client process are placed on a internal cache with keyed access based on the UID of an object. The purpose of the internal cache of a client is to insure that references to the same object use the identical storage structure contained in virtual memory. Without this caching mechanism, references to the same object would point to different objects although their contents would initially be the same. With this cache, an object is acquired by first determining if it has previously been restored from secondary memory and cached in virtual memory. If so, the object is acquired from the cache. Otherwise, the object is restored from secondary memory, cached, and then returned to the requesting process.

2.2.2 Secondary Memory

Objects that are represented on secondary memory are contained in databases. A database has several components, as shown in Figure 1. One component is a layer map. A layer map is a vector of pointers to each layer of the database. A layer represents a collection of objects. Newer layers represent those objects which have most recently changed. The primary purpose of layers is to restrict the number of objects that have to be inspected during garbage collection.

The second component of a database is the type registry. The type registry is a vector of elements which contain information about each type of object stored in a database. Each one of these elements contain two fields which represent the name of a type and the size of an instance of the type; the vector index is used to associate a numeric value with a type. This information is used to represent the type information of instances in a concise manner. It is also used to validate the contents of the database with that of an OMS server.

The third component of a database is the object registry. The object registry maintains an association between the UID of an object and its location within a database (i.e., a hash table). When an object must be restored, the object registry is consulted.

The fourth component of a database is the database registry. The database registry is a vector of database names which are allowed access to objects contained in a database. These database names are used during garbage collection operations to determine which databases may reference objects contained in it. Each time an object is saved in a database each external object that it references is determined and each host database of each external reference has its database registry updated to contain the database of the saved object.

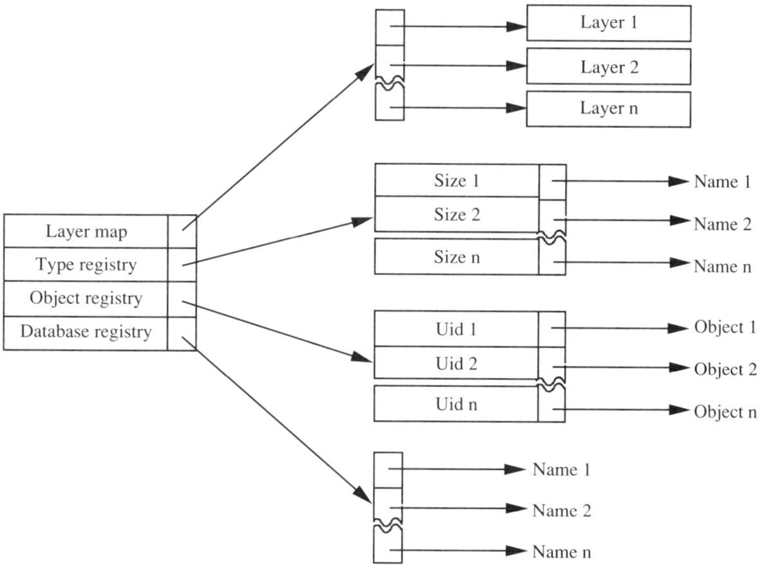

Figure 1: The structure of a database.

The remaining components of a database are the several layers. A layer is partitioned into several fields, as shown in Figure 2. One field indicates the size of the layer. Another one indicates the next memory location where an object can be stored; this field is meaningless unless it is the last (or outermost) layer. The third field represents the amount of garbage that is contained in a layer. The ratio of the first and third fields are used to determine when a layer should be compacted.

The fourth field of a layer contains the address of the first reclaimed block of data (i.e., garbage). Each data block which contains garbage has two useful fields. The first field contains the type identifier of the block, which can be used to determine its size, and the second field contains the address of the next free block. If this address is 0 then the last free block has been found.

The fifth field contains the time when the last scavenge was performed. The primary purpose of this is to determine if unchanged objects may need to be written from virtual memory of a process to secondary storage. This is needed because an object can have no references to it within any secondary memory representation although there may be one or more to it in a virtual memory representation. This timestamp is used to quickly determine if a scavenge has been performed since the last time the object was written. If so, it may have to be written again since it could have been deleted during the scavenge.

The sixth field is an external reference registry. Each UID of an object, which is external to a database layer but referenced by an object contained in it, is represented in sorted order using a tree data structure. This registry is used to improve the performance of garbage collection operations.

The remainder of a layer is populated by the objects stored in it. These objects are written from virtual memory to secondary memory and read from secondary memory into virtual memory.

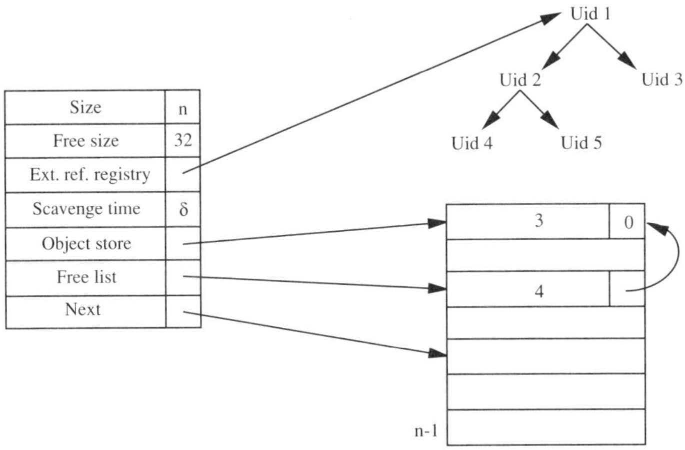

Figure 2: The structure of a layer.

3 OBJECT READ AND WRITE

The process of reading and writing an object is somewhat complex, at least more so than one would think. The algorithms to perform these two actions are now described.

When a read is performed, the UID and host database are already known. Based on this information, an attempt to derive the object from the internal cache is attempted. If the object is found then it is returned. Otherwise, the address of the object on secondary memory is derived from the object registry of the database. The object is then read into the virtual memory of the OMS server machine, which then provides it to the client. It also caches it for faster retrieval by other clients. If the type registry for the database has not yet been read by the client then it is read and cached in the virtual memory of the client. Then the client uses the type registry to cast the object to the proper type. Finally, this object is cached in virtual memory and returned.

The write process is slightly different. All objects are written as one update. There are two modes — checkpoint and cleanup. The checkpoint mode will write each changed object to secondary memory. The cleanup mode will do the same thing but it also will write out any unchanged objects that might have been erroneously garbage collected from secondary storage.

The following actions occur in the checkpoint mode. First, it is determined if the object was previously stored in the last layer. If so, it is simply written back to its previous storage location. The only change is that the storage area occupied by the object has different contents. If, however, it was stored in a inner layer then several things must occur. First, the previous storage area has to be placed on the garbage list of its layer. Second, the field keeping track of the amount of garbage has to be incremented for that layer. Third, if required, this layer may need to be compacted. Fourth, the object is given a new storage area and written to it. Fifth, the next free location of the outermost layer is updated. Finally, the object registry is updated to reflect the new location of the object.

In the cleanup mode the same things happen but some unchanged objects may have to be written too. Therefore, each object still registered in the object registry of the database that contains it is determined. If the object is still registered then nothing happens. But if it is not then it is written back to its database. When this occurs the object is allocated new storage in the database, the free pointer is updated, and the object registry is updated to point to the new location.

One last issue concerns what happens when an object has previously been updated by another client. The current solution is a simple one. Each time an object is written its write time is compared to the write time of the object in secondary memory. If it is the same then no update has been performed since it was last read. In this case, the object is written. However, if this is not the case then another client updated the object. When this occurs, the user is simply asked if the update should be continued, thus overwriting a prior update made by someone else.

4 GARBAGE COLLECTION

In many applications objects are dynamically allocated when needed. These objects are used for some period of time and are later reclaimed when they are no longer used. The process of reclaiming storage space occupied by unused objects is called garbage collection. There are three primary types of garbage collectors: stop-and-copy [Baker, 1978], concurrent [Steele, 1975], and generation-scavenging [Ungar, 1984].

A stop-and copy collector partitions memory into two regions called the from-space and the to-space. During the execution of a program objects reside in the to-space. When the to-space is exhausted processing halts. At this time the identities of the two spaces are flipped (i.e., from-space is now the to-space and vice versa). The root-objects of the from-space are copied into the to-space. Objects of the to-space are searched for pointers to the from-space. When an external pointer is found the referenced object is copied from the from-space to the to-space. It, in turn, is checked for external objects which causes this process to repeat. A forwarding pointer of each object copied from the from-space to the to-space is left so that other references will be updated correctly. This process copies all referenced objects from one space to the other. Everything not copied is garbage and the result is that the whole from-space can now be reclaimed.

The disadvantages of this type of garbage collection are two-fold. First, this scheme requires roughly twice the available memory of what is used. In a large database this storage requirement is impractical. Second, the simple act of stopping normal processing to reclaim storage in a large database can cause excessive delays in normal operations. This is also impractical! In contrast, the remaining two methods quickly reclaim storage.

The concurrent garbage collector is similar to the stop-and-copy version. The major difference is that the application does not have to stop running when storage is being reclaimed. It simply does not allow the application access to pointers in from-space and thus the application cannot distinguish that a collection is incomplete. The disadvantage of this is that this type of collector also requires a significant amount of memory to operate.

The generation-scavenging garbage collection technique, on the other hand, does not require a large storage overhead. In addition, since only small subsets of an entire database are garbage collected this technique is the preferable choice. The way that it works is as follows. First observe that most objects become garbage soon after being allocated. Older objects, on the other hand, tend to be reclaimed much less frequently. Generation-scavenging collectors capitalize on these facts by partitioning memory into multiple regions. These regions are normally called generations but in this paper they are called layers. These layers are temporally ordered. Each one can be independently garbage collected and the older ones are garbage collected much less frequently than the newer ones.

When a new object is created it is written to the most recently created (the outermost) layer. After surviving several scavenges it is moved to the next older layer. This process is repeated until the oldest objects migrate to the innermost (or oldest) layer.

To scavenge layers independently, the collector must be able to determine which objects in a layer are externally referenced. These external references can come from any layer of another database or from older layers of the same database. Since there tends to be few references from older generations of a database to newer ones or between databases, the overhead for managing the external references is low. These external references are captured by the external reference registry. Finally, when a layer is scavenged all younger layers are scavenged too.

The two choices considered for scavenging a layer were based on reference count and marking algorithms. The reference count strategy was quickly eliminated for two reasons. First, either the assignment operator of the base programming language would have to be modified or each assignment operation would have to be augmented by another procedure call that would update the reference count. Neither of these solutions were reasonable or practical. Second, because the memory model is a two-level store there is no way to maintain a consistent representation of the reference count of an object on both virtual and secondary memory.[1] Consequently, a marking and gathering scheme was used.

The marking and gathering scheme works as follows. Each UID and address of each object of a layer not already garbage collected (i.e., not contained on the free list) is collected. This is done by collecting the objects contained in the root object registry[2] and all objects referenced by them and their progeny. Then all external references of each layer of each database on the database registry are collected. These combined references are then used to mark used objects. Figure 3 shows an example of a database whose used objects have been marked; shaded areas indicate marked items. At this point all unmarked objects are garbage

[1]It also has been claimed that the reference count strategy is unsuitable because cyclic storage structures cannot be reclaimed [Dickman, 1992]; several others also concur with this statement (e.g., [Schorr and Waite, 1967]). Consequently, a hybrid policy normally using reference counts but periodically activating a marking strategy to reclaim acyclic structures has been advocated [Weizenbaum, 1969; Dickman, 1992]. However, [Standish, 1980] shows that cycles can be reclaimed although it is generally unthinkable to do so since the worst case behavior is $O(M \cdot 2^M)$, where M is the size of memory.

[2]For clarity, this attribute of a database was not previously described. It simply contains all root objects of a database. Its format is identical to the object registry of a database.

and are added to the free list of unused objects. Compaction is only performed when the ratio of garbage object storage space to used object storage space exceeds a specified threshold. When this occurs each object contained in the layer has its location updated in the object registry and root object registry. Afterwards, the free list is empty and the next field points to the beginning of the unused space at the end of the layer.

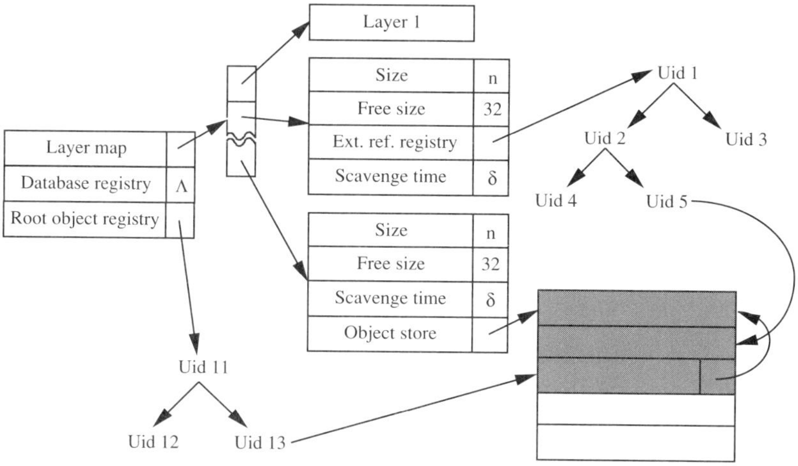

Figure 3: The state of the database after marking.

The one limitation to this scheme is that it may require concurrent write access to several databases, and possibly several host machines, before a garbage collection can be completed. However, this limitation can be eliminated by using a more complicated algorithm based on remembering partial states and updating them during database updates. The benefits of the current scheme are extremely fast reclamation of memory albeit with some slow-down during object write.

5 CLIENT-SERVER ARCHITECTURE

The manipulation of an object can only be done through an OMS server. An OMS server is the unique process residing on a machine which handles all its database requests. The kinds of requests are openDatabase, gcDatabase, closeDatabase, allocateType, allocateId, getObject, putObject, and remObject. The openDatabase service readies a database for input and output by a client. The gcDatabase service reclaims any unused space in a database and possibly compacts one or more layers. The closeDatabase service prevents a database from being written or read by a client. The allocateType service allocates a new data type to a client. The allocateId service returns to the client the next available UID for the server. The getObject service returns to the client the object corresponding to a requested UID. The putObject service writes an object to a database. The remObject service deletes an object from a database. Finally, an OMS client is a process which requests a service from an OMS server.

An OMS server is started by using the following UNIX command syntax (denoted using regular expressions).

```
oms {-c} {-t} {-v integer} &
```

 The -c option specifies whether objects should be cached by the server. If caching is enabled then when a client tries to satisfy a request the server first examines the cache. Only upon failure does the server retrieve an object from the database. The -v option is only meaningful when the -c option is given. The -v option specifies that the cache should be validated periodically (i.e., every integer minutes). The -t option specifies that the OMS server also allocates type information; only one OMS server in a network can do this.

5.1 INTERNAL CACHING

The purpose of the internal cache for the server is to improve the access time for objects. The cache is organized as a hash table. The hash key is computed from the UID of each object stored in the hash table.

5.2 TRANSACTION PROCESSING

The approach used by OMS to permit atomic updates is to shadow the object space [Traiger, 1982]. More specifically, the persistent store is maintained as a layered hash file (i.e., a file-based hash table). The hash file is composed of two key areas: the object indexes and several object stores. The object indexes are composed as a collection of key/value pairs. The key is always a UID and the value is two file addresses of the beginning of the old and new object locations.[3] During a transaction all object updates are written to unused areas of the object store of the file. During this process, all key/value pair updates are performed with respect to the object index which is not current. If all of them are completed then the object index is made the current one. In addition, the object index which is now the old one is updated. Once this has finished then both object indexes are identical and this is indicated in the header of the hash file. If the atomic transaction should fail, then the current index will still be as it was prior to the aborted transaction. However, the other object index will not be the same and will have to be rewritten.

6 CLASSES AND BEHAVIORS

There are two primitive classes in OMS — OMSDatabase and OMSBaseObject. A OMS-Database corresponds to a collection of persistent objects. These objects can be read from it or written to it. The key functions and methods which operate on a database are described below.

void openDatabase(String filename, int maxEntries) Open a database. Filename is the name of the database. MaxEntries is the maximum number of entries which can be stored in the database before it must be expanded. The newly created database is returned.

void OMSDatabase::dump() Dump all objects of a database to secondary storage.

[3]Earlier you were told that the value was one address just so you could understand the basic data representation scheme without the added complexity required to ensure the integrity of the object stores.

void OMSDatabase::close() Close a database. As a side effect all streams associated with a database are closed.

Boolean OMSDatabase::validate() Insure that the objects in the virtual memory of a process are consistent with the current versions of their associated databases.

In an application some objects are temporary but others may need to be saved. These objects are called saveable objects and are defined by the OMSBaseObject class. Saveable objects which are actually saved are said to be persistent. Persistent objects are maintained from one session to another. Temporary objects, on the other hand, have a lifetime of only one session. If a saveable object is not made persistent at the end of a session it is equivalent to a temporary object. Thus, the three categories of objects, in terms of saveability, are never persistent (temporary), potentially persistent (saveable), and persistent.

A saveable object has four key attributes — a UID, a proper name, a change indicator, and a persistence indicator. A UID distinguishes one persistent object from the many. A UID for a persistent object is generated by OMS when the object is created. Thereafter, it always has this same UID. A proper name provides a means for accessing an object in an unambiguous context. If a saveable object has been given a proper name then it is used as the print representation. The change indicator represents if a object has been modified since it was last read. Finally, the persistence indicator represents if a object is persistent or not. The key functions and methods which manipulate objects are described below.

void OMSBaseObject::dump() Print a representation of an OMSBaseObject object so that when the representation is read the object will be correctly reconstructed. This is the method that must be changed to perform additional computations during object restoration.

OMSBaseClass* restoreObject(String filename, Uid uid) Restore the object whose unique identifier is uid and has been written to a database. Filename must be a database that has been opened by the openDatabase function.

7 LISP VERSUS C++

The development of the LISP version of OMS was much easier than the C++ version. The reasons for this are based on the inherent generality of LISP. Specifically, LISP provides the following features:

1. LISP objects contain type information. If an object is asked for its type, the object can return it. In C++, this is not the case. The only reason objects in C++ can respond to messages is because each object contains a pointer to a table of methods which can operate on the object.
2. LISP functions (unless compiled) and computational forms are represented as linked lists. LISP provides a function, called `eval`, which allows a linked list to be executed (interpreted) as a program. C++ provides no such capability.
3. The LISP function to create a new object is called `make- instance`. It accepts an argument which specifies the type of object to be created. This argument can be a variable which may be dynamically bound. Thus, the type of object to be created is determined at run-time, not at compile time, and can produce a different type of object each time it is called. In C++, the corresponding function is called `new`. Its argument

is a literal and each execution of a unique `new` statement cannot produce different types of objects; it must always produce the same type of object.

Persistent objects in LISP are represented textually. For example, a person named John whose age is 15 is represented on secondary storage as shown below.

```
(make-instance 'person :name "John" :age 15)
```

This computational form is written to a disk by sending a dump message to the object. To create the object in LISP, the file pointer is positioned at the beginning of the form, a read statement is issued to read the form, and then `eval` is called to evaluate (or execute) the form. For example, the statement `(eval (read))` will result in an object being created representing John.

Now examine what must occur to read and write an object in C++. Type information does not exist in C++, so it must be faked. There may be several ways of doing this, but assume that we maintain a 1:1 correspondence between each class of objects and a integer value. Then, for each object this value must be written to disk followed by some representation of the member values of the object.

This creates two problems. First, the encoding of type information must be properly managed. Only one process can allocate type identifiers among all processes using the OMS. However, a database which is ported to another OMS environment may have a different assignment of type names to type numbers. The result of this is that each time a database object is read its type must be made consistent with the OMS environment. Second, a single, non- extensible read routine must be written for each type of object. In LISP, the provided read function can read any type of object.

Instead of using the idea of maintaining a correspondence between data types and some other range of values, a language could be created for describing objects and a translator written for it. The translator would produce objects from descriptions written in this language. The problem with this strategy is that the interpretation process would dramatically slow data access and require the development of a translator, which is no small task. In other words, what you would have achieved by doing this is what LISP already provides!

Another problem with the C++ implementation is that each time a new class of objects is created new code must be added to the software system and recompiled. There are several methods for easing this process but they are all more difficult than the LISP method. The result of all this is that the generality of LISP made the development of OMS much easier, but at a cost in efficiency. The C++ implementation, on the other hand, is much faster, but suffers in terms of extensibility and data management issues.

8 RELATED WORK

8.1 PS-algol

There are several approaches to managing persistent objects. These usually are based on either special-purpose hardware [Smith and Welland, 1992], a operating system [Dearle et al., 1992; Madany and Campbell, 1992], or a programming language [Gruber et al., 1992]. PS-algol [Atkinson et al., 1983a; Atkinson et al., 1983b; Atkinson et al., 1983a; Atkinson and Morrison, 1985; Cockshott et al., 1984], for example, is based on a special-purpose programming language. It tends to be very similar to OMS even though the constraints placed on the design of the two systems are different, as are the adopted implementation strategies.

PS-algol was developed to overcome two perceived weaknesses associated with the existing technology: programming languages and database management systems (DBMSs), which provided two different views of data. First, converting data between these two representations is inefficient in terms of both computer and human resources. Programs are larger and run slower, and these larger programs require more time to write. Second, the data type protection of information provided by the programming language often does not survive the translation into a DBMS. OMS, on the other hand, was developed to support object persistence for a specific application. It did not attempt to improve the state-of- the-art, it only meant to provide a solution for a particular problem.

Since OMS was developed to support a specific application no attempt was made to provide a unified mechanism for handling data at the language level. PS-Algol, because it was a research project, did take this approach. In addition, this was also a practical choice since they had access to the source code and knowledge of the internals. This was not the case for the OMS development effort and such an attempt would not have been practical given the near-term delivery schedule. Now that these differences have been identified the similarities, which are many, can be discussed.

The Persistent Object Management System (POMS) of PS-algol uses an addressing scheme very similar to OMS. POMS maintains two separate heaps, one on disk and one in the virtual memory of a computer. The disk-based heap is called a database. Each heap uses a different type of address. The first type of address is called a Persistent IDentifier (PID) and describes where an object resides on disk. The second type of address is simply a virtual address; these are called local addresses. When a program commits, objects are copied from the local heap to the persistent heap. When this occurs each local address is converted to a PID. The conversion between addresses is aided by the Persistent IDentifier to Local Address Map (PIDLAM). The PIDLAM is implemented by two hash tables which maintain PID/LA and LA/PID key/value pairs. Finally, objects are only brought in on demand when a PID is dereferenced.

Similarly, OMS uses two types of address — UIDs and virtual addresses. A UID, although computed differently, is essentially the same thing as a PID. The one notable difference is that a UID is guaranteed to be unique; no two objects in the world will have the same UID. Furthermore, like POMS, there is a hashtable that contains mappings from UIDs to virtual addresses. However, the inverse is not true. A UID is associated with each object and is only needed when writing objects back to the persistent storage medium. Finally, objects are only read into the virtual memory when a UID is dereferenced.

The manner that both systems use to handle transactions is based on the notion of shadowing. The primary difference is that OMS works in a distributed environment and must have a server process which controls access to a persistent store.

The method that OMS uses to handle type information was described in the last section. POMS does not use this scheme because it causes databases to be non-portable. The type code, or trademark, is specific to the machine the object resides on. OMS, however, does have a procedure for importing and exporting objects. POMS uses the better method of maintaining a pointer to a string corresponding to the class name. This strategy, although better, is not a viable one in a C++ implementation; if it were, it would have been used in OMS.

OMS makes no attempt at localizing objects. This is because of two facts: aggregate objects in SeeQFD tend to form tree-like structures, which are inherently non-local; and linked lists and other types of sequences in SeeQFD tend not to be composed of the same type of objects. Because of the object allocation strategy which is used sequence items are, quite by accident, assigned sequential addresses. POMS, on the other hand, assumes that lists are made of like objects and attempts to put like objects in the same blocks and tries to allocate adjacent items of a linked list to the same block.

8.2 Thor

Thor [Liskov et al., 1993] is a object-oriented DBMS which operates in heterogeneous computing environments. Thor is language-independent and permits access to objects via path names, navigation, and queries. A object can refer to other objects and thus form complex structures such as object graphs and trees. Access to objects occur within atomic transactions which guarantee database consistency. To reduce the workload of database servers objects are cached by the clients. When starting a new session, a client can specify the initial setup which loads the cache of a client with useful objects. Thor also uses (or intends to use) a prefetching strategy. Although it is not explicitly discussed, this implies that object clustering [Gruber and Amsaleg, 1993] is also performed. In addition, it is not clear if a distributed garbage collection scheme is operational although it is stated that a generational scheme is being investigated.

OMS is similar to Thor in some ways and different in many others. OMS is dependent on the host language, whereas Thor is not. OMS uses the class hierarchy and associated class methods of the host language to define the storage structures, inheritance mechanisms, and behaviors of object instances. It augments the host language with several special-purpose methods which provide persistence to objects and permit reliable object reading and writing. Thor, on the other hand, provides a language-independent type system which allows data to be shared among applications written in different programming languages. Access to objects in OMS is only available via UIDs; Thor provides several access mechanisms normally found in DBMSs. Both systems allow objects to refer to other objects. Both systems also access objects within atomic transactions.[4] Both systems use caching schemes. Likewise, the initial setup for both systems can be specified. In OMS, a save set is specified, which is generally a list of root objects of an engineering document. Finally, it appears that both systems use a generational garbage collection scheme.

A major difference between OMS and Thor (and other systems too) is that OMS does not use a prefetching strategy, nor does it use a clustering scheme. Prefetching is based on the notion that when one object is accessed there is a high probability that related objects will be accessed shortly thereafter. For example, consider a typical query — list all employees whose salary is above $60,000 and whose age is greater than 50. In this case when fetching the first employee it makes since to fetch several others too, especially if they are clustered together so that only one disk read operation is performed. In OMS this type of access is not likely. Since access is performed strictly interactively and non-procedurally there is only one predictive basis for determining what may be accessed next, which is to load all objects

[4]The details of how OMS performs transaction processing have not been described although it is based on techniques described in [Moss, 1985].

which are referenced by an accessed object. The problem with this is that many objects will be loaded into virtual memory which may never be accessed. This was exactly what was being avoided by using a demand-based access mechanism. Since design documents are extremely large the virtual memory could become cluttered with unused data very rapidly.

8.3 Bellerophon

Bellerophon [Dickman, 1992] keeps multiple versions of objects with rollback and historic query capabilities. OMS could keep multiple versions but it does not. As new versions of an object are created the older ones are placed on the free list of a layer (i.e., collected for later reuse via first-fit allocation). Since the first two words are overwritten to link free blocks together the old versions are essentially deleted. So before and after an atomic transaction only one version of each object exists but during an atomic transaction two versions may exist simultaneously — the version which existed before the transaction and the new one which will exist after the transaction.

9 SUMMARY AND CONCLUSIONS

Realizing object persistence can be done in several ways, but the most practical method in C++ and Common Lisp is to use a file-based approach. The two most common of these are indexed file access methods and DBMSs. The first approach is more efficient in terms of both speed and storage utilization although the second approach is more general. Although a DBMS permits more flexibility an indexed file access method was chosen to represent SeeQFD objects because of computational efficiency. Later on, more capabilities can be added to OMS as needed.

The method used by OMS to maintain persistent objects is based on one or more hashfiles. A hashfile is analogous to a hash table, but instead of residing in virtual memory it is maintained as a file. A key is used to retrieve or store an associated value into a file-based hash table (i.e., a hashfile). A key is a UID and its associated value is a representation of a persistent object.

During restoration, this representation is read, which produces the original object. Conceptually, that is what you can think. In reality, persistent objects are restored from a hashfile into virtual memory when they are first accessed. References to them are maintained until that time. Thus, object hierarchies are built incrementally and only when necessary, which has several benefits.

There are several characteristics that persistent objects have. First, if two persistent objects reference a common persistent object they will still share it after restoration. This, however, does not apply for objects which have no persistence. For example, if two persistent objects have attributes whose values are the same string then these attributes will not share the same string after restoration. Second, cycles and mutual reference among persistent objects do not pose a problem for OMS. Third, an object of one database can reference a object of another database.

These capabilities provided by OMS have been sufficient to support concurrent engineering activities which use the SeeQFD methodology and software tool in business environments. It is anticipated that further work will extend OMS. The most logical choice is to provide a domain-specific query facility.

Acknowledgments

OMS has benefitted from my discussions with Bill Pardee, Bruce Seely, and Pete Tinker. I wish to thank Elmain Martinez and Bill Pardee for useful comments on earlier drafts of this work. This research was partially supported by Rockwell International Science Center. UNIX is a registered trademark of AT&T Bell Laboratories. SeeQFD is a registered trademark of Rockwell International.

PART 3
DISTRIBUTION AND QUERY PROCESSING

Issues in Distribution Design of Object-Oriented Databases

Kamalakar Karlapalem
Georgia Institute of Technology
College of Computing
Atlanta GA 30332-0280
U.S.A.

Shamkant B. Navathe
Georgia Institute of Technology
College of Computing
Atlanta GA 30332-0280
U.S.A.

Magdi M.A. Morsi
Georgia Institute of Technology
College of Computing
Atlanta GA 30332-0280
U.S.A.

Abstract

Design of distributed databases enhances the performance of the applications in two ways: by reducing the amount of irrelevant data accessed by the applications and by reducing the amount of data transferred in processing the applications. This is done by fragmenting the class of objects (fragmentation scheme) and by allocating these fragments (allocation scheme) to various sites respectively. The distribution design consists of a fragmentation and an allocation scheme. The semantics of the processing done by the application, structural and behavioral properties of the database governs the distribution design for an object oriented database. In order to come up with a good distribution design we need to have a good understanding of the issues involved in distribution design. This paper evaluates some general characteristics of the distributed object oriented database systems pertinent to the distribution design problem and presents the complexity of the problem, issues involved and some possible approaches for designing the fragmentation and allocation algorithms.

1 INTRODUCTION

In any distributed database there are two main factors that affect the performance of the applications: first, I/O operations, and second, data transfer plus data communication. In case of distributed object-oriented databases, as the behavioral and the structural aspects are encapsulated within the objects, the communication delay depends upon both the number of messages and number of bytes of data that is transferred between nodes while processing an application defined by a set of method invocations. There are two ways by which the performance of the applications can be improved.

Fragmentation. is the process of clustering relevant data accessed by an application into a class. This reduces the amount of irrelevant data accessed, thus reducing the number of disk I/O's. The result of the fragmentation process is a fragmentation scheme. For object-oriented data models, the clustering of a class may apply both to the set of instance variables and the set of objects that belong to the class.

Allocation. is the process of placing the fragments generated by the fragmentation scheme at the sites of the distributed database systems so as to minimize the data transfer cost and the number of messages to execute the set of given applications. The result of an allocation process is an allocation scheme.

The fragmentation and allocation scheme define the distribution design for a distributed database [Ceri et al., 1983]. Distribution design is going to be one of the major research problems whose solution will enhance the performance of the distributed databases [Özsu and Valduriez, 1991a]. Conventionally, both fragmentation and allocation schemes have applied to data and not to the transactions that process data. However, for Object-Oriented databases fragmentation deals with a partitioning of objects and methods (i.e. encapsulating the methods of a class to its fragments). The allocation of methods to sites becomes an additional decision problem (see discussion of the types of transparency in Section 2.3.)

The algorithms for allocation must allocate the fragments defined by the fragmentation scheme. In case there is only one node and only one method,[1] then the problem of allocation does not arise and the fragmentation process consists of clustering all the instance variables and objects accessed by the method into a class-fragment and storing it so that the method does not access any irrelevant data. But if there is more than one method that accesses a set of objects, then the problem of fragmentation becomes complicated as two methods can access an overlapping set of instance variables and a common subset of objects. In relational databases, transactions are not an integral part of the database. They occur externally with some known frequencies. In an object-oriented database, the methods which cause the database processing to occur are an integral part of the database. The fragmentation problem reduces to an optimization problem of fragmenting a set of objects into a set of class-fragments so as to minimize the amount of irrelevant data accessed by the methods.

Now consider the case wherein all these methods reside at different sites. We need to consider allocating these fragments near the methods so as to reduce the total number of messages between the sites and the amount of data transferred between the sites. Again

[1] Here we use the term method in its broadest sense in that it accesses a set of objects and instance variables of a class. A method is considered to be an application accessing the object-oriented database.

this is an optimization problem whose solution gives an allocation scheme stating which fragments have to be placed at which sites. We have thus described very briefly the simplest case of distribution design problem (with an analogy for relational databases wherein the objects are the tuples of the relation and the methods are transactions accessing the relations).

In relational databases, it is very easy to conceptualize a distributed database by means of relations and its fragmentation scheme, but for an object-oriented database with its complex objects and class hierarchies, it is difficult to conceptualize the distributed object-oriented database. In object-oriented database systems, the database state consists of a set of objects. Each object represents a state and a set of methods for accessing and manipulating its state (encapsulation). An object state is a set of values for its instance variables which are described in the object's home class. These instance variables are classified as value-based instance variables and object-based instance variables. The value-based instance variables are atomic values which exist as a part of the state of an object. However, the object-based instance variables may exist independent of any other objects. That is, the object-based values are references to other objects (through object identity). The object-oriented databases support encapsulation wherein the methods and instance variables are encapsulated within the objects. Also, as there is no standard object-oriented data model, or a well established architecture for an object-oriented database system, it is not possible to present a general solution to this problem of distribution design of an object-oriented database.

In this paper, we first present the issues that effect the distribution design for an object-oriented distributed database. Later, we propose some solutions and issues for the distribution design problem for an object-oriented database based on our model and assumptions.

2 ISSUES AFFECTING DISTRIBUTION DESIGN

In this section we describe the different aspects of a distributed object oriented database system that are critical to the distribution design process. The distributed object-oriented database system that we are considering in this paper is basically a set of nodes connected by a network, with each node having an object-oriented database system; there is no distributed shared memory.

2.1 DATA MODEL

The data model defines the core concepts provided to the users to conceptualize the data and the processing requirements of their applications. The data requirements are described by the structural components of the data model and the behavioral requirements are described by the methods. In some data models, like ER or relational, only structural components can be described. But in case of object-oriented data model, both the structural and behavioral requirements of an application can be defined. An object is defined to represent an encapsulation of instance variables defining a state, and methods for manipulating it. A set of objects having the same properties are grouped into a class. The instance variables and the methods of a class together define its properties. The classes are organized into a class hierarchy by using the specialization property (IS-A relationship). The more characteristics or features that the data model provides to the user, the more complicated the fragmentation problem.

In the relational data model the fragmentation problem is defined in terms of horizontal and vertical fragmentation. But in the case of object-oriented data model with class hierarchies and inheritance of instance variables from a superclass, and multiple inheritance from several superclasses, it is not trivial to define what exactly is a fragment. Moreover, the domain of an instance variable may be any class, including value-based instance variables (those whose domain is integer, character, etc). Thus there is a hierarchy which arises from the aggregation relationship between classes and its instance variables. This hierarchy, known as *class-composition hierarchy* is orthogonal to the class hierarchy [Kim, 1990]. The aspect of how the multiple inheritance is handled will play a significant role in fragmentation design. Each mechanism like full forced inheritance will impose additional constraints on the fragmentation scheme.

Some of the interesting data model issues that affect the distribution design are:

- How do full or partial inheritance schemes affect the fragmentation algorithms?
- How does the overriding of methods in the subclasses of a given method affect the fragmentation scheme?, or
- What kind of fragments would be defined in the presence methods accessing multiple objects in a class hierarchy or multiple instance variables spanning a class- composition hierarchy?

2.2 METHOD INVOCATION

Methods are used to conceptualize and specify the processing requirements of the applications. Typically, methods are encapsulated within the framework of an object along with its instance variables. As the same method can be applicable to more than one object of the class, for the reusability of the code, the methods are attached to the classes. Methods are also classified based on the type of instance variables accessed. A method invocation that accesses only value-based instance variables is called a *primitive method*. A *non-primitive method*, on the other hand, may access value-based instance variables as well as object-based instance variables. An object-based instance variable is one that is defined with another class as its domain. Also, methods are classified by their effect on the object state. A method invocation that has a side effect on its object state is called a *transformation method*. A method that does not have any side effect is called an *access method*. The values of an instance variable of an object state can be computed dynamically.

The invocation of methods in an object-oriented database requires the creation of a main memory computational object. The management of these computational objects is the responsibility of the object manager. In order to efficiently support method invocation, the object manager may fetch the accessed objects as well as the referenced objects through object-based instance variables. The support for object caching requires accessing the referenced objects and interpretating its state in order to get the object identity of the referenced objects. In addition, the database schema has to maintain additional information about the instance variables referenced by a method implementation. This information is captured as *implementation dependencies*. The computation of the relevant instance variables for a method invocation are computed only once for all objects.

The way that methods are invoked plays a major role in allocating objects. In case of a relational system, the transactions are independent of the relations and can be invoked from any node, and the distributed transaction manager would generate the optimal execution plan for the transaction. In case of an object-oriented database system, there is a tight coupling between objects and methods; a method may access an object in any one of the following ways:

Remote procedure call. The method can reference a set of objects, which the object manager determines to be residing in a remote site and then will invoke a remote procedure to access the objects, do some computation and return the results. This would require sending a message for invoking the remote procedure and the results are transferred by the remote procedure to the invoking site.

Prefetching and caching. Caching is keeping in the main memory representation of objects after being modified. Prefetching is fetching of the objects that may be accessed by a method. This may not require the construction of the main memory representation of the object.

The support for prefetching of related objects for method invocation can be achieved using two mechanisms; *clustering* and *indexing*. In the first mechanism, the object storage unit contains not only its instance variable values but also those of referenced objects. In the second mechanism, a path *index* is maintained for the referenced objects which eliminates the need for the interpretation of the object state in order to identify the relevant objects.

In an object-oriented system the above mechanisms may be used for accessing objects by invoking methods depending on the semantics of the methods (i.e., the type of operations being done on the objects accessed by the methods). Any algorithm that is used for developing the allocation scheme for allocating objects to the sites must take into consideration the different strategies for method invocation. Just as the query processing strategies affect the allocation strategies of fragments in distributed relational databases [Apers, 1988], the method invocation strategies will affect the allocation strategies of fragments in distributed object-oriented database system. What further complicates the allocation problem is that the methods themselves can reside on any site. This implies that an application invoking a method does not know if the method is resident locally or at a remote site. This kind of transparency can be supported by the object catalog of the distributed object- oriented database system.

2.3 TYPES OF TRANSPARENCY

The system architecture defines the components of the object-oriented database system and how they are interrelated. In this paper we are considering only a homogeneous distributed object-oriented database system. The distributed database environment consists of a set of sites with each site having an object-oriented database system with a similar data model, method invocation strategies, object manager, etc. The major aspect that affects the distribution design is the type of location transparency that is provided by the system architecture.

Object transparency. The location of the objects is transparent to the methods accessing it. The method just requests a set of object references and the request goes through to the object catalog to figure out the location of the object and fetches the requisite objects for the method. When object transparency is only provided and the location of the methods is fixed, an object catalog needs to be designed that maintains and manages the location of the methods. Any change in the location of the method will have to be immediately propagated to the object catalog. Moreover, as methods invoke other methods, if for each method invocation the object catalog has to be queried then the process of executing a method becomes costly. A tradeoff would be to hard-wire the location of the methods in the method that invokes them. This is costly only if there is a frequent change in method location. Though this reduces the complexity of the allocation problem (by just considering only the allocation of objects), it increases the complexity of the method management and maintenance.

Object and method transparency. In an object-oriented database system there is a tight coupling between the objects and methods; a true distributed object-oriented database system would provide both object and method transparency. This would mean that when a method is invoked by the user, the object catalog decides the location of the method and invokes it. The object catalog maintains and manages the location of the methods and the objects. But in this case the sites from which the methods are requested will be fixed and the problem of the distribution design can be stated as *"Given that the following methods are requested from these sites, and that these methods access these sets of objects, generate an optimal fragmentation scheme that clusters the objects into fragments and optimally allocate these fragments and methods to the sites."*

Thus we have presented how the problem of distribution design is affected by the level of location transparency that is supported by the underlying system architecture. It does not matter whether one operates under a client-server architecture, or tightly coupled one with each object-oriented database system having the capability of being a coordinator for supporting distributed applications.

2.4 TRANSACTION MANAGEMENT

In order to efficiently support concurrent access to the underlying database, the effect of the transaction management has to be addressed. The transaction management component of the system includes the support for a concurrency control mechanism, a recovery manager, and a commit protocol. However, these components are inter-related. An added complexity of the transaction management is the need to support long duration transactions. The long duration transactions may consist of several subtransactions and unlike traditional business transactions may be active for hours or even days.

The inclusion of behavioral components (procedural methods) define how objects are accessed. Understanding the semantics of the behavioral components may enable the user to achieve a higher degree of concurrency within an object. This can be achieved by providing the user with a set of tools to customize their own concurrency control mechanism. These transaction management issues will be useful in evaluating the distribution designs.

From the above discussion it is clear that the problem of generating an optimal distribution design is multi-faceted and that many issues need to be taken into consideration. In order to develop algorithms for distribution design of distributed object-oriented databases, the designer needs to pin down the above characteristics of the system. We shall now present an example of a distributed object-oriented database system and develop some preliminary ideas towards fragmentation and allocation algorithms.

3 A DISTRIBUTED OBJECT-ORIENTED DATABASE ENVIRONMENT

The main aspect of an object-oriented database environment is the data model. In the next subsection we shall present the core data model along with the abstract model of its storage manager.

3.1 AN OBJECT-ORIENTED DATA MODEL

In this subsection, we describe the core concepts of object-oriented data models with which our object-oriented data model is consistent. The adopted data model maintains its implementation components as well as user-defined classes as a part of the overall schema definitions. We use the term *object* to represent an encapsulation of instance variables containing a state, and methods for manipulating it. *Classes* are used to describe object types, as defined by their instance variables and methods. The *properties* of a class connote its instance variables and methods. Objects communicate via *messages*. The *domain* of an instance variable is the set of values it might have from its class type, which is called the *domain class*.

Inheritance is a mechanism used for defining specialization relationships between classes. Given a property V applicable to a number of classes, we define the *origin* of V as the most generalized class where V is locally defined. *Multiple inheritance* allows a class to inherit properties from several superclasses. If a property is inherited from more than one superclass that has a single origin, only one property is included in the class definition.

We use the notion of *full forced inheritance* (*FFI*). Under *FFI*, even if there is a naming conflict among inherited properties, all of these properties must be inherited and none should be rejected. To resolve the naming conflict, the property name is prefixed with the name of the class in which it is locally defined.

The ISA relationship captures the relationship between a class and its superclass and is represented in a class hierarchy. Because of multiple inheritance, the resulting structure is not just a hierarchy, but a single rooted DAG (lattice). The database schema consists of a class hierarchy along with the set of locally defined properties of each class.

Subclasses are allowed to restrict the domain of an inherited instance variable. The domain of an instance variable inherited from multiple superclasses is restricted to the intersection of the instance variable domains.

The *scope* of a class C contains all objects that are visible through C which consist of all objects of type C as well as those of the subclasses of C. The *direct scope* of a class C contains all objects in the scope of C which are not in the scope of any subclass of C.

The object model adopted separates the schema components from the objects storage. Also, the object state is stored independent from the class to which they belong. That is, the home class of an object contains the description of the set of instance variables as an ordered set. An object state is stored as a contiguous sequence of bytes. The object identifier is stored as the first instance variable in each object state. The object catalog associates each object identifier with its home class, and its physical storage. Also, the object label is maintained in the object catalog. The object label is a unique label (string) for external referencing of the object. These relationships are depicted in Figure 1.

Structural class schema

Class_id	Attri_1 : Domain_1	Attri_2 : Domain_2	. . . . .	Attri_n : Domain_n

Object catalog

Obj_id	Class_id	Physical_Location	Object_label	Other infromation

Object state

Obj_id	Off_1	Off_2	. . . .	Off_m	Val_1	Val_2	. . . .	Val_m

Figure 1: Object storage model

In Figure 1, the values maintained in the object state can be either an atomic value or an object identifier. The object catalog also maintains additional information about other properties such as *access* and *existence* constraints. The *existence* dependencies are defined on the object references. An object X may have one of the following three types of existence dependencies with respect to another object:

Reference dependent. Object X is reference dependent on object Y if there exists an instance variable Z in Y that has the reference (object identity) of X as its value. That is, X cannot be deleted because Z is referencing it. Supporting reference dependence implies keeping a count of the references to X.

Exclusive Dependent. Object X is exclusive dependent on a set of objects S if each object in S has an exclusive reference to X as a value for an instance variable. In this case, X can be deleted only if its set of exclusive references is an empty set. Supporting exclusive dependence requires maintenance of back references from X to the objects in the set S.

Independent. Object X is independent of an object Y that references it via an instance variable. This implies that X can exist even when Y is deleted or Y no longer references X and X can be deleted freely.

Example 1 A database schema, shown in Figure 2 contains three classes: *Auto*, *Person*, and *Company*. The instance variables of the *Person* class include *drive* whose domain class is *Auto* which is reference dependent on *Person* `P_1`. Also, the *Company* class has an *owns* instance variable whose domain class is *Auto* that is exclusive dependent. In the database state, the object `P_1` in the scope of the *Person* class references the object `A_1` through the *drive* instance variable. Also, the `C_1` object in the scope of the *Company* class references the `A_2` object through the *owns* instance variable. The `A_1` and `A_2` objects in the scope of the *Auto* class have two different existency constraints. They imply that auto `A_1` cannot be deleted as long as person `P_1` exists because `P_1` is referencing it. Similarly, `A_2` can exist only as long as some company owns it. □

Since an object may be referenced by several objects (shared) that may lead to conflicting existence dependencies, our model supports precedence among the dependencies to resolve

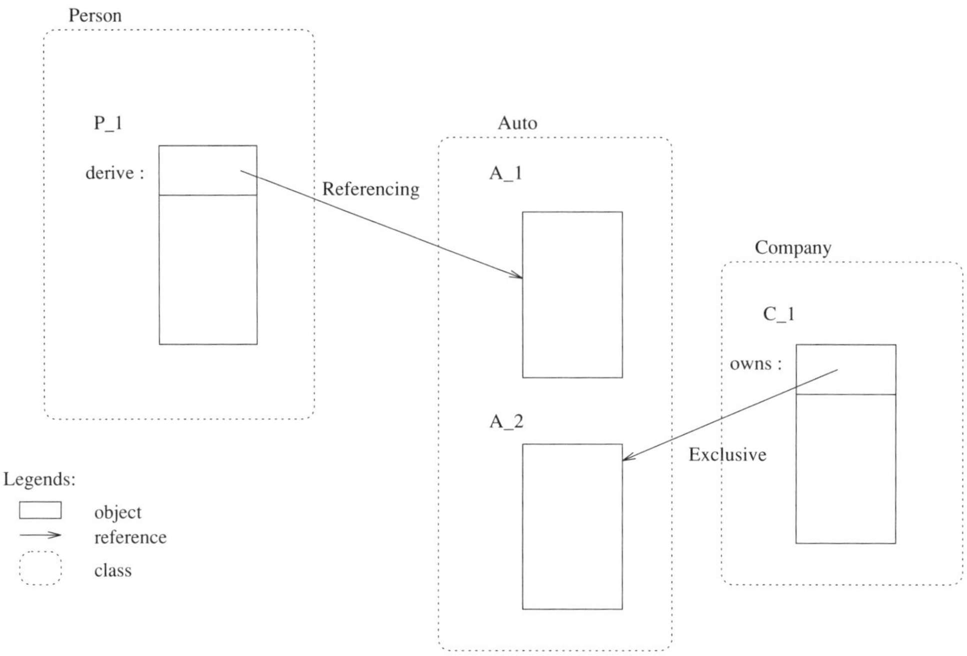

Figure 2: An example of existence dependency

this conflict. The order of these dependencies is *independent*, *reference*, and *exclusive*. In order to support these constraints, the object catalog maintains the total number of references, the set of referencing objects (for exclusive dependency), and the number of reference dependencies. Consider the following example.

Example 2 In the example database schema shown in Figure 3, A database state may have an object `P_2` in the scope of the *Person* class that references the object `A_3` through the *drive* instance variable. Also, the `C_2` object in the scope of the *Company* class references the `A_3` object through the *owns* instance variable. The `A_3` object in the scope of the *Auto* class has two different existency constraints, namely exclusive and reference dependencies. In applying the default precedence order, the reference dependency prevails over exclusive and the object `A_3` is maintained as having reference dependency. However, the system will maintain the set of exclusive dependent objects. `A_3` cannot be deleted as long as there is a person `P_2` or a company `C_2` that references it. □

The *access constraints* describe the sharing of the referenced objects. The access constraints restrict accesses to referenced objects. The type of restrictions include *shared*, *nonshared*, and *restricted*. The *shared* objects may be referenced by any other objects. The *nonshared* objects may not be referenced by any other objects. *Restricted* access enables the user to control which other objects may reference an object-based instance variable. The type of restrictions may be either set of classes or more specifically a set of instance variables of other classes. *Unlike the existence dependencies, the* access *constraints are enforced and cannot be relaxed. That is, a nonshared object cannot be referenced by other objects.*

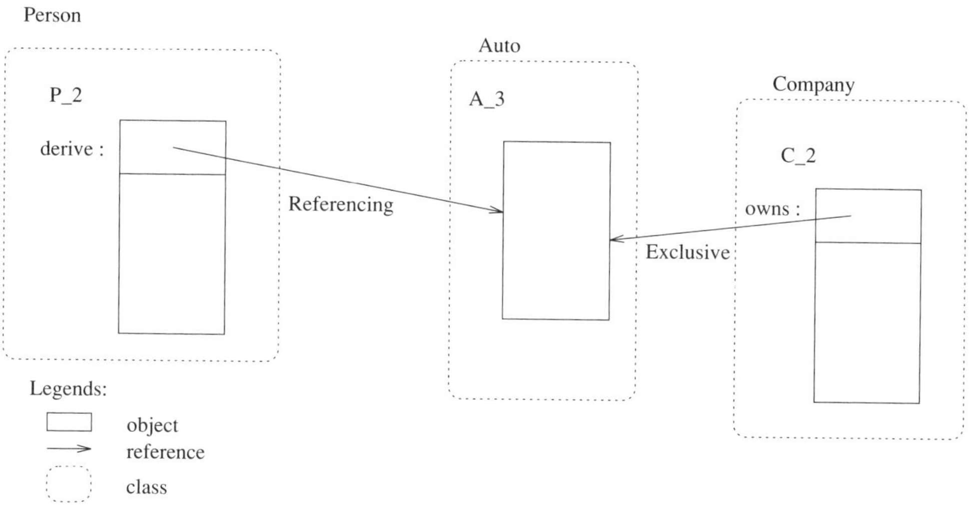

Figure 3: An example of mixing identity

Whereas the *existence* dependencies describe the lifetime of an object and its relationship to other object referencing it, the *access* constraints describe which objects might reference an object. The following table describes the different combinations of existence and access constraints.

		Existence constrains		
		independent	referencing	exclusive
Access constraints	shared	valid	valid	valid*
	restricted	valid	valid	valid
	nonshared	valid	valid	valid

(*) Shared only by an enumerated set of objects.

Figure 4: The valid combination of existence and access constraints

The most restricted reference is the *exclusive* existence and *nonshared* access constraints. The objects of this type are similar to value-based instance variables. That is, they cannot exist independent of the referencing object and cannot be directly accessed manipulated. The *independently* existing and *shared* objects are the least constrained objects. That is, they can be referenced and manipulated directly with the least constraint. The valid existence and access constraints are described in Figure 4. The *independent* and *nonshared* references to an object may result in objects being in the database which cannot be referenced by at most one object. The *referencing* and *nonshared* references to object may result in garbage collecting objects if they are no longer referenced by other objects.

4 DISTRIBUTION DESIGN STRATEGIES

In this section, we shall first describe the two possible approaches for generating fragmentation schemes, issues in allocating fragments, and then propose two alternatives for the type of support to be provided by the object-oriented database system for maintaining the distribution design.

A fragmentation scheme consists of a set of fragments. A given class of objects can be fragmented either vertically or horizontally by generating vertical class-fragments and horizontal class- fragments respectively.

The direct extension of a class is a set of objects that have their home class as that class. The structural definition of the schema of a class consists of set of instance variables. That is, it is those set of instance variables and objects whose home class (or origin) is that class. This implies that none of the instance variables or objects of the subclasses rooted at this class are included in this set.

Given a class C, its structural definition consists of set of instance variables I = $\{i_1, i_2, \ldots, i_n\}$, and its direct extension consists of set of objects O = $\{o_1, o_2, \ldots, o_m\}$.

A vertical class-fragment of a class C is defined by the *nonempty proper subset* of the instance variables I of its direct extension. All vertical class-fragments V of a class C have the same set of objects O in their direct extension as class C. Given M as the set of methods having their origin as class C and that V is a vertical class-fragment of class C, we partition M to M_c and M_v where all methods in M_v access a *non-empty subset of instance variables* defining the vertical class-fragment V, and M_c consists of methods that access instance variables of more than one vertical class-fragment. A class can have many vertical class-fragments.

A horizontal class-fragment of a class C is defined by the *nonempty proper subset* of the object O of its direct extension. All horizontal class-fragments H of a class C have same set of instance variables I in their structural definition as class C. As for vertical class- fragments above, the set of methods M accessing the class C is partitioned to M_c and M_h where all methods in M_h access a non-empty subset of objects in the defining the horizontal class-fragment, and M_c consists of methods that access more than one horizontal class-fragment.

Example 3 In the schema shown in Figure 5 the structural definition of the class `Minivan` consists of instance variables `Id, Capacity, HorsePower,` and `Num Passengers`. Therefore, the subset of instance variables `{Id, HorsePower, Num Passengers}` forms a vertical class-fragment of the class `Minivan`. The direct extension of the class `Minivan` is the set of objects `{o1, o2, o3, o4, o5, o6, o7}`, thus any subset of these objects say, `{o2, o5, o6}` forms a horizontal class-fragment. □

In general, a method that accesses a nonempty proper subsets of instance variables and objects from the structural definition and i direct extension of a class C respectively defines a mixed class- fragment.

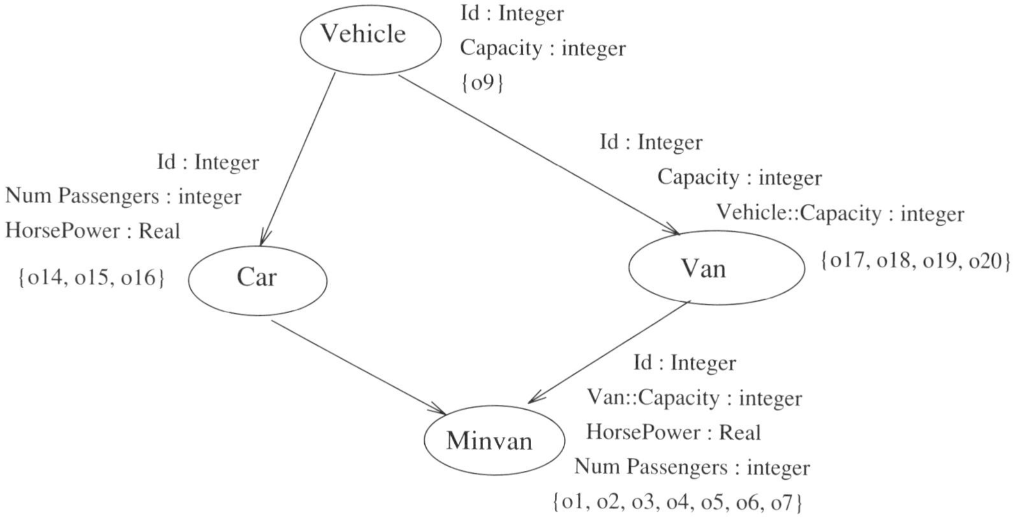

Figure 5: An Example Schema of a Class

4.1 FRAGMENTATION ALGORITHMS

In this subsection, we shall develop some preliminary ideas for designing fragmentation algorithms for distribution design. The distribution design as mentioned earlier consists of a fragmentation scheme and an allocation scheme. A fragmentation scheme consists of a vertical and a horizontal or a mixed fragmentation scheme. In order to design good algorithms for fragmentation scheme we need to understand the processing requirements in terms of which objects and which instance variables of the objects are being accessed by the methods. This leads to a classification of the methods. A method that does not invoke any other method is known as a **simple method**; otherwise it is known as a **complex method**.

A method accesses a set of instance variables of a set of objects. Also a method can invoke a set of methods that access a set of objects. Thus an application can be considered as an invocation of a set of methods each of which access a set of instance variables of a set of objects. The set of objects being accessed by a method can be characterized by a set of predicates on the instance variables of the objects being accessed.

We present a two level approach for generating the algorithms for the fragmentation scheme.

1. The case where a set of simple methods are considered that access a set of value-based instance variables of the objects of a class.
2. The case where a set of complex methods are considered that access a set of instance variables of the objects.

4.1.1 Simple Methods Accessing Value-based Instance Variables

A simple method M accesses a set of Instance Variables I of the objects based on a set of predicates P. Therefore a simple method can be characterized as M(I, P).

Thus an instance variable of a set of objects of a class can be accessed by a method, and a method can access many instance variables of the set of objects of a class. These primitive methods can be invoked from various sites at different frequencies. This will provide us with instance variable usage matrix (IVUM) by the methods for the instance variables of a class. This is similar to the attribute usage matrix proposed in [Navathe et al., 1984] for the vertical partitioning algorithms. From this matrix we can generate the instance variable affinity matrix (IVAM) on which we can run the algorithm proposed in [Navathe and Ra, 1989] to partition the class into a set of vertical class fragments. Similarly, we can use the predicate usage and affinity matrices as given in [Navathe et al., 1990] to come up with a set of horizontal class fragments.

4.1.2 Complex Methods Accessing Value-based Instance Variables

The major problem with the above approach is that the fragmentation algorithms developed in [Navathe et al., 1990] work only on flat structures like relations and not on class hierarchies. Also most of the applications invoke complex methods. Note that we consider a **complex method** as being synonymous with an application. Thus a complex method accesses a set of objects and instance variables, unlike the standard notion of a method accessing a single object. In this scenario it becomes very difficult to define the instance variables accessed by methods. Thus we are currently working on a generalized approach that works on the methods and the objects that it accesses, meaning that we define O(M) as the set of objects that a method M accesses. We can define I(M) as the set of instance variables of the objects accessed by the method M. There is a two part approach that will be used to fragment the objects to generate the set of vertical and horizontal class fragments.

Object-class relationship. From the set O(M) we determine the home classes of the objects accessed. This would require classifying the set of objects accessed O(M) into sets of set of objects O_1, O_2,O_3, ..., O_n, such that each set of objects O_i belong to exactly one class C_i. Similarly, we can classify the set of instance variables I(M) accessed by the method into subsets I_1, I_2,I_3, ..., I_n, such that each subset of instance variables I_i belong to exactly one class C_i. Note that if a method accesses an instance variable of an object, then it accesses the object and vice versa. Hence if a method accesses instance variables of a class it accesses the objects of the class and vice versa.

Fragmentation. Now we have a relatively flat structure (a class hierarchy) such that a set of objects and instance variables of these objects are accessed by methods. We have $(O_i, I_i), i = 1, 2, \ldots, n$, to denote the set of objects and their instance variables being accessed from a class C_i by a method. Each (O_i,I_i) defines the mixed class-fragment of class C accessed by a method m_i. It can also be considered as the method m_i's view of class C. Therefore, we can use the concepts developed in [Pernul et al., 1991] of fragmenting the relations based on overlapping views, and extend them to fragment the classes of the object-oriented database based on the overlapping sets of objects and instance variables of a class being accessed by the methods.

The pair (O_i,I_i), $i = 1, 2, \ldots, n$ denote the set of objects and their instance variables being accessed from a class C_i. We will term it a *Method-Based View* (MBV) of a class. Since each class is accessed by many methods, we have for a class C a method m_k accessing a view (O_k, I_k), $k = 1, 2, \ldots, m$, of class C. These sets of MBV's (O_k, I_k) may be overlapping by having common sets of instance variables or objects. Now we can evaluate the overlapping MBV's (O_k,I_k) for each class C to generate the class-fragments. This is a viable approach that generates a set of candidate fragments of the class which groups the set of objects and their instance variables frequently accessed by most methods into a class-fragment. This choice is logical in that the methods that access this class-fragment access the least amount of irrelevant data. This is possible because each class-fragment is generated by intersecting the sets of set of objects and/or instance variables of a class accessed by the methods. The approach has been used in organizing relations by fragmenting them based on overlapping views [Pernul et al., 1991].

4.1.3 Constraints Imposed On Fragmentation Algorithms

The above set of proposed algorithms assume that the objects and instance variables of a class can be clustered based on their affinity in terms of common use by one or more methods. But in order to efficiently maintain the consistency of the database, it will be necessary to consider the access constraints on the objects. These constraints are imposed on the horizontal fragmentation algorithms.

1. Objects of a class that have *nonshared access* can be clustered in any manner as the fragmentation algorithms decide. This is because these objects are not referenced by any other objects.
2. Consider objects O of a class that have *restricted access*; that is, they are referenced by a restricted set of objects R, via object-based instance variables. Then whenever these restricted set of objects R are accessed, the set of objects O may also be accessed. Therefore, by clustering the objects O and R we may enhance the performance of methods as all the relevant objects are accessed at the same time. Horizontally fragmenting the home class of objects R will involve corresponding derived horizontal fragmentation (see [Ceri and Navathe, 1983] for definition of this concept) of the home class of objects O. This is because objects in R refer to objects in O.
3. For those set of objects O of a class that have *shared access*, that is, they can be referenced by any other object as an object-based instance variable, then we cannot limit the objects that can reference these objects O. Therefore we cannot consider the aspect of derived fragmentation. But we can consider one special case: to cluster all the objects in O referenced through a shared access by an object of another class as a horizontal class-fragment.
4. In case of non-primitive methods (i.e., those that access object-based instance variables) we may need to cluster all the objects having all the instance variables rooted at the object-based instance variable in the class-composition hierarchy into a horizontal-class fragment. This is because a method that accesses an object-based instance variable will access all the objects that are referenced by this instance variable. These objects may themselves have object-based instance variables thus forming a class-composition hierarchy which would govern further clustering.
5. Due to encapsulation, the methods will use parameters to access the objects of a class. In order to derive the horizontal class-fragments we need to analyze the parameter values being frequently used.

4.2 ALLOCATION ALGORITHMS

The fragments defined by the fragmentation scheme need to be allocated to the sites of the distributed object-oriented database environment. If the location of the methods is not predecided then the methods also need to be allocated. This is essentially true in case when the methods invoke other methods. This dependency between the methods needs to be considered when allocating them. Following are the characteristics of the allocation problem:

1. The basic aim of allocation of fragments and methods is to reduce the data transfer and communication between the sites. This is done by allocating the methods and objects they access at sites that are most frequently invoked. But as complex methods invoke other methods depending upon the application processing semantics, that invocation sequence is to be considered while generating an allocation scheme.
2. The restricted and shared type of access to objects may require the objects to be replicated at those sites where they are referenced.
3. If the location of the methods is fixed then the fragments will be allocated at sites based on the type of processing being done on the objects accessed. If a complex object is accessed and then modified frequently, then it would be advantageous to have all of its component objects at the same site.
4. The class composition hierarchy defines a relationship between the instance variables of two classes and forms the basis for defining complex objects. If the complex object is accessed often from a site then the whole object may need to be allocated at that site, even though there may be methods accessing parts of the complex object from other sites.
5. The type of inheritance mechanism used will constrain the classes that need to be grouped together for allocation. If full forced inheritance is used then all the super classes from which an instance variable inherits a value may need to be allocated at the site that instance variable is allocated.
6. The problem of allocation of objects is complicated by the presence of different versions of objects and their access from various sites. It is not clear as to how this issue can be handled.

The problem of allocation has not yet been satisfactorily solved in case of distributed relational database and with further complications of the object-oriented database environment it seems to be even more difficult.

4.3 SYSTEM SUPPORT FOR MANAGING DISTRIBUTION DESIGNS

The support for a distributed object-oriented database system has been addressed in a client server architecture in several projects, namely Orion-2 [Kim et al., 1990], GTE DOM, [Manola, 1988; Manola, 1989], Workstation-Server architecture [De Witt et al., 1990]. In the client server architecture, the clients do not store any information about the database state or the schema components. The client caches updated objects locally. However, the caching policy of the client site has not been addressed in Orion-2. In Orion-2, the transaction management component also resides on the server site. The major problem with this architecture is the contention on the server site and the single site failure. The objective of this architecture is to increase the availability of the objects locally and providing partial support in case of communication failure and node failures. In this section, we address the architectural issues needed to support location and fragmentation transparencies.

The architecture of the system includes the object catalog, schema manager, and objects. The object catalog includes information about the object reference type such as the *existence* dependency and *access* constraints. The object state does not include any structural information (home class) or physical locations of its value-based instance variables. This information is contained in the object catalog. We are considering two alternatives by which the distributed object-oriented system can manage and maintain object fragmentation. That is, the relationship between the partial object state and its references. The first alternative relies on storing additional information about the object fragmentation in the object catalog. This would result in increasing the size of the object catalog entries. This overhead may be reduced by maintaining this structural information separately. The second alternative is based on modifying the class hierarchy by using the schema-evolution operations (like delete, modify, add) on the classes based on the fragmentation policy used.

The second issue has to do with the support for location transparency. That is, the user should be able to access both locally stored objects or remotely stored objects in the same manner. In order to support this type of transparency, the object catalog should include additional information about the location and the schema of remotely stored object fragments. However, this information may not be complete or up-to-date due to object migration.

5 RELATED WORK

We draw upon the work done in relational databases for developing efficient algorithms for generating the fragmentation and allocation schemes. To the best of our knowledge, no work is done in fragmentation and allocation algorithms for distributed object-oriented databases. The major reason for this is that the it is a very complicated problem, as illustrated in the Section 2. There has been work done at GTE Labs in design and development of Distributed Object Management [Manola, 1988; Manola, 1989; Manola et al., 1992]. But this effort has been towards intergrating data and knowledge from heterogeneous information sources, and not towards using DOM for enhancing performance of applications in homogeneous environment. The work done at TI [Wells and Blakeley, 1993] describes the mechanisms to support distribution and persistence in object-oriented databases. In this paper, we do not relate to any distributed object oriented database system but to the general concepts of distributed object management that affect the distribution design.

Data fragmentation is performed during the design of a distributed database to improve the performance of the transactions. In order to improve transaction processing performance, fragments must be "closely matched" to the requirements of the transactions. In the design of a multi-site distributed database, fragments are allocated, and possibly replicated at the various sites.

Two ways to partition a relation are well recognized: vertical partitioning and horizontal partitioning [Ceri and Pelagatti, 1984]. *Vertical partitioning* is the process of subdividing the attribute set of the relation into subsets, wherein each of these subsets form a vertical fragment. This is equivalent to projecting a subset of attributes from the relation. *Horizontal partitioning* is the process of subdividing the tuples of a relation into subsets, each of which forms a horizontal fragment. This is equivalent to selecting a set of tuples of the relation based on some condition. There had been large body of work done in developing algorithms for vertical partitioning [Hoffer and Severance, 1975; Navathe et al., 1984; Cornell and Yu, 1987; Chu and Ieong, 1991; Chu, 1992, Muthuraj et al., 1993], and for horizontal fragmentation [Ceri et al., 1982; Ceri and Navathe, 1983; Shin and Irani, 1991], but there was no methodology in existence that guided the designers in using these algorithms. Moreover, applying one before the other introduces certain biases and restrictions that limit the applicability of these techniques. This prompted further work in this area which led to the distributed database design tool project D^3T (funded by NSF) at University of Florida [Navathe and Ra, 1989; Navathe et al., 1990], which was predicated on the concept of mixed fragmentation generated by simultaneously applying both vertical and horizontal fragmentation algorithms. Mixed fragmentation gives rise to a set of mixed fragments which need to be allocated to the sites of the distributed database environment. A related piece of work for mixed fragmentation is based on the overlapping views [Pernul et al., 1991]. A set of related methods can be used to define as a view accessing a set of objects in an object-oriented database as we haved done above. The main objective for allocating the fragments is to reduce the data transfer cost while processing the transactions or the applications. There had been a fair amount of work done [Apers, 1988; Ceri et al., 1983] in developing algorithms for generating the allocation scheme.

We plan on porting the extensible object-oriented database system [Morsi et al., 1991; Morsi et al., 1992] on Clouds distributed operating system [Bernabeu-Auban et al., 1988; Bernabeu-Auban et al., 1989] and evaluating the algorithms for the distribution design.

6 CONCLUSIONS

In this paper we address the issues involved in distribution design of the object-oriented databases. There is no doubt that a good distribution design enhances the performance of applications based on object-oriented database. But there are a number of issues and tradeoffs that need to be addressed before developing a good distribution design. In order to address these issues we need a good understanding of the data model on which the object-oriented database is based, the method invocation strategies, level of transparency being provided, inheritance schemes, application processing semantics, etc. But the most important aspect of the distribution design is *understanding the processing semantics* of the applications accessing the object-oriented database. The processing semantics refer to the objects and instance variables accessed, and processing done once they are accessed. The tight coupling of structural and behavior aspects (i.e. class with methods) through encapsulation of objects makes it difficult to understand the processing semantics of the applications. The problem is not simple and their solution would enable the designers to design object-oriented databases that efficiently support applications.

In this paper we have not provided detailed solutions but have enumerated the issues that need to be considered in order to design algorithms that generate a good distribution design.

Issues in Distributed Object Assembly

David Maier
Oregon Graduate Institute
Department of Computer Science & Eng.
19600 NW von Neumann Dr.
Beaverton, OR 97006–1999
USA

Goetz Graefe*
University of Colorado
Department of Computer Science
Boulder, CO 80309–0430
U.S.A.

Len Shapiro
Portland State University
Department of Computer Science
Portland, OR 97207–0751
U.S.A

Scott Daniels
Tom Keller
Bennet Vance
Oregon Graduate Institute
Department of Computer Science & Eng.
19600 NW von Neumann Dr.
Beaverton, OR 97006–1999
U.S.A.

Abstract

One of the most significant challenges of query processing in object-oriented databases is avoiding "pointer chasing on disk." The Revelation project, which is investigating query processing in object bases, has developed an "assembly" operator to address this problem. This assembly operator is designed to improve processing of bulk data types such as sets in object bases. We have shown good results with this operator in centralized query processing, and this paper presents our initial thinking on what the major issues are for supporting assembly in a distributed environment. We assume a common schema, and pay particular attention to distributed systems performing as a single database. We describe assembly, indicate the problem areas for distributing the operator, and define three categories of query processing strategies for distributed assembly. Potential

*Current address: Department of Computer Science, Portland State University, Portland, OR 97207-0751, U.S.A.

problems and advantages for each category of solution are described, and the possibility of selecting mixed strategies is considered.

1 INTRODUCTION

The Revelation project has been investigating query processing techniques in object-oriented database systems. To the greatest extent possible, we want to adopt bulk-processing technology, as used in relational systems, for query evaluation in Revelation . However, unlike relational systems, our collection elements are not always uniform flat records. Complex values for object state, and references to other objects, mean that we need to assemble several fragments of objects' states into an "object complex" in order to process a collection element (for example, to execute a method being used as a selection predicate or a mapping operator over a collection of objects). Naively accessing object fragments as demanded by method computations can produce unacceptable performance penalties, since the pieces of object representation needed by a method are not guaranteed to be contiguous on disk. When the object complexes to be assembled span multiple sites in a distributed database, the overhead of naive assembly is even greater, given the added costs of network communication and remote procedure calls.

In the framework of centralized processing of object queries, we have designed and tested an "object assembly" operator. It takes a template describing the required portions of objects in a collection needed for a particular processing step, and efficiently assembles the necessary parts of those objects into memory. It does so by reordering fragment access to exploit such things as physical location of objects, sharing of subobjects, clustering and selectivity hints, and useful data already present in database buffers.

The Revelation prototype query processor is using the Volcano query evaluation software [Graefe, 1990a]. The Volcano software has the capability of running in parallel and distributed environments, and we plan to expand the Revelation query processor to function in such environments in the future. However, we are not certain of the best approach to extending object assembly to distributed databases.

This paper sets forth our initial thinking on what the major issues are for distributed assembly. We do not pretend to have the final answer here. We are certain, however, that assembly operators are an important tool in object management, and that in many cases the objects to be assembled will be distributed over a network.

The paper begins with an overview of the Revelation query processing strategy and architecture. It then provides more detail on the iterator model that Volcano uses for query evaluation and the assembly operator, which is a particular iterator added to Volcano to support object query processing. After introducing a little notation, we consider some of the decisions we face in extending Revelation to the distributed case. These include strategies for assembly and management of logical versus physical pointers.

2 THE REVELATION STRATEGY

We believe that four concepts are crucial for the performance of object-oriented database systems. First, collection-oriented processing allows leveraging expensive operations, e.g., disk seeks. Second, retrieval and in-memory assembly of object structures are frequently used operations, therefore a determinant of performance. Third, query optimization and access planning, proven to be a cornerstone of relational systems performance, will gain even more importance for semantically richer queries and complex data. Fourth, parallel processing techniques can be exploited more easily if the underlying processing paradigm uses collections that can be partitioned, rather than single object instances.

We concentrate here on collection-oriented processing to improve object retrieval and assembly—a combination of the first two concepts. Our main contribution to date is the *assembly* operator, implemented on top of the Volcano query processing system. The assembly operator was designed to retrieve and assemble object structures in a manner that outperforms *naive* (*object-at-a-time*) object assembly, using physical and logical information such as object clustering and the degree of subobject sharing. In addition, the assembly operator is able to retrieve objects selectively, based on arbitrary selection predicates. Object assembly is closely related to the pointer-based join methods of relational database systems. Assembly resembles a functional join, linking objects based on inter-object references. An early pointer-based join optimization, join indices [Valduriez, 1987], maintained a pre-computed join by storing pointers to pairs of joining records. More recently, pointer-based joins [Carey et al., 1990; Haas et al., 1990; Shekita and Carey, 1990] use either explicitly stored pointers or system-maintained pointers. We, however, do not require collections of objects to be confined to distinct disk files or that object references contain a physical component (only that there be a mapping from object reference to physical location). Also, our operator supports assembly orders not realized by any current pointer-based join algorithm.

3 REVELATION ARCHITECTURE

Revelation concentrates much of its effort on efficient support of user-defined database types, an important kind of extensibility. In Revelation, new data types are created from previously defined types and the type constructors provided by the system. Base types provided by Revelation are Boolean, Integer and String. There are currently three type constructors: Sequence, Tuple and Protocol, the last of which defines an abstract data type. The facility to define new data types allows the database system to model a wide range of applications, and user-defined types may be used anywhere that system-defined types are accepted. Perhaps most important, however, is that protocol types are abstract and encapsulated. These features provide an expressive data model along with logical data independence and reusability.

To meet the goals of the Revelation project, we have developed the software architecture shown in Figure 1. User queries and definitions of new types and their behavior are presented to the system in the Revelation language. Definitions of new types of objects and their behavior are formatted and stored by the Schema Manager. A Revelation schema consists of protocols, implementations and a name space. Protocols describe the interface to database objects in terms of the operations that may legally be performed on them. Implementations are composed of representations and methods. A representation physically describes the internal state of an object; methods encode the operations on the objects. Representations are constructed from system-supplied types, system-supplied type constructors and other user-defined data types. Methods are written in the Revelation programming language [Daniels, 1990]. The final part of the schema is the persistent roots. Revelation queries are expressed at the top level as a single message being sent to a root object, possibly with other named values passed as arguments.

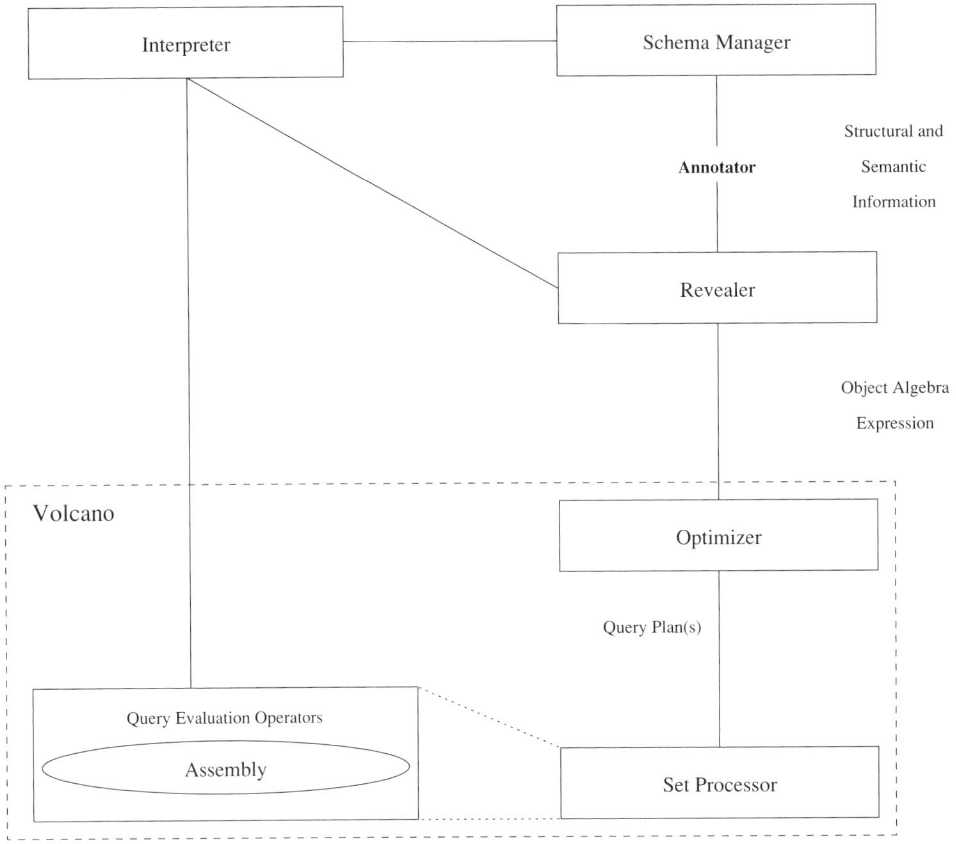

Figure 1: Revelation Architecture

Once a query is parsed, it is passed to the Revealer. The purpose of the Revealer is to break the encapsulation barrier to create the choices necessary for effective query optimization. The Revealer gathers query processing information both directly from the objects and from the Schema Manager (by calling the Annotator, the Schema Manager's interface.) The Annotator makes inferences on behalf of the Revealer based upon Schema Manager information.

The output from the Revealer, and thus the input to the optimizer, is an object algebra expression [Vance, 1992]. An object algebra expression is composed of nodes that are part of the object algebra, control constructs, and "black boxes" (unrevealed messages). An object algebra expression may have other query information attached, such as the structural description of objects involved in the query, statistics and possibly behavioral descriptions other than the object algebra expression. The Revelation Optimizer, which we are building using the Volcano optimizer generator [Graefe and McKenna, 1991], will produce an optimized query plan from some or all of the information provided by the Revealer.

Finally, the query is evaluated by the bulk-processor, built upon the Volcano query execution library. Parallel execution is also available in Volcano [Graefe, 1990b] and used to increase query processing performance. Pieces of the query that could not be revealed into the algebra require the query evaluator to call the Interpreter at runtime.

An alternative way to produce an operational system is by adding a storage system for the system-supplied types and functions for the Schema Manager and Interpreter. While addressing modeling needs for modern applications, such a system would not meet performance requirements. For example, naive execution of methods result in object-at-a-time access, when physical considerations could make an alternate access plan more efficient. Following the lead of relational database management systems, we translate queries into equivalent object algebra expressions. Once available, the object algebra expression of the query can be optimized and subsequently executed.

4 THE VOLCANO ITERATOR MODEL

The Volcano query execution library is based on a uniform interface between operations implemented as iterators. Since this interface is used for all algorithms, we use the terms "operator" and "iterator" interchangeably. The uniform iterator interface requires that each operator be implemented by three functions, called *open*, *next*, and *close*, and that each operator obtain its input items by calling the *next* function of (one of) its input iterators. This interface permits arbitrarily complex query evaluation plans to be executed very efficiently, because data items never need wait between operators and because operator synchronization and communication is as fast as one procedure call-return pair per data item. The definition of what constitutes a data item is unspecified in Volcano: for relational query processing, an item might be a tuple or record, while in object-oriented query processing, it might be an object identifier, an object's state, or a fragment of an object. The interpretation of the structure, value, and semantics of data items is also left open, and is imported into Volcano operators by means of *support functions*. For example, a call to the *next* procedure of Volcano's *filter* iterator invokes the *next* procedure of the filter's input until a data item satisfies the *predicate* support function provided to the filter operator. The filter then forwards the data item to the caller of its *next* procedure.

Two innovative operators included in the Volcano system are the *exchange* operator for parallel processing and the *assembly* operator for use in the Revelation object-oriented database project. The assembly operator is based on the realization that query processing in object bases frequently requires materialization of a number of objects in memory and that naive pointer chasing ("goto's on disk") is extremely inefficient. This point has been made repeatedly both in the relational world in connection with unclustered indices and in the object-oriented database world in connection with object assembly or materialization in memory. Thus, instead of following one reference at a time, our object assembly operator maintains a collection of unresolved references to object components on disk and resolves them in an order determined by their location and other factors [Keller et al., 1991].

Volcano's exchange iterator can be inserted between any two iterators in order to provide for parallel and distributed query processing. It uses the standard iterator interface; thus, neither producer nor consumer operators require any change when combined with an exchange iterator in a query evaluation plan. The exchange iterator provides two services essential for parallel processing, namely inter-process pipelines and partitioning. For pipelining between processes, the exchange operator "lives" in both the producer and the consumer processes. In the producer process, it drives its input operator as fast as possible and inserts data items into either shared-memory queues or distributed-memory messages; in the consumer process, it receives data items via queues or messages and passes them to its consumer operator, one item for each invocation of the *next* procedure. Flow control is used to keep producers from running too far ahead of consumers. For parallel processing based on partitioning, the exchange operator provides partitioning in single-producer-multiple-consumer and multiple-producer-multiple-consumer relationships as well as merging (ordered or unordered) in multiple-producer-single-consumer and multiple-producer-multiple-consumer relationships.

For parallel and distributed object assembly, this model of parallel processing is insufficient. The critical assumption in the present model is that data flows only upward in the query evaluation plan, from the leaves (scan algorithms) to the root, and that each process executes all its operators completely for each data item received without horizontal communication or synchronization with other processes executing the same operators. For most collection-based query processing algorithms, such as those for intersection, relational join, and selection, this assumption is realistic and justified; however, transitive closure computations and object assembly are notable exceptions. Consider two processes assembling a set of two objects, i.e., two instantiations of the assembly operator executing the same logical operation. In order to exploit parallel processing capabilities, each process should assemble one object. However, if the two objects share a subcomponent, the two processes will have to communicate about when the component (or the page containing it) is fetched from disk and (for shared-memory systems) where the component is located in memory.

We are planning on modifying Volcano's exchange operator to permit communication, synchronization, and data exchange among multiple parallel instantiations as in the example above. We hope to implement parallel algorithms requiring communication among their parallel or distributed instances with the same ease as algorithms without such communication requirements.

5 TERMINOLOGY

An object of a protocol type is a data structure encapsulated with the set of operations that act on that data structure. The encapsulation provides assurances that all access to the data structure occurs through the interface, thus isolating the data structure from the rest of the software environment. In some object-oriented languages, the data structure is a tuple, with the elements of the tuple being referred to as "instance variables." In Revelation, and some other object-oriented database systems such as O_2 [Deux et al., 1991], the part of the representation within the encapsulation envelope can actually be a complex value, consisting of nested tuple and collection structures. This complex value can be accessed and modified directly only by the object's methods. We refer to this complex value as the *local state* of the object. The physical implementation of the complex value is not assumed to be a contiguous chunk of secondary storage. Rather, a complex value can be implemented as several physical records (or whatever the minimal units of physical addressability are called). We call the records that make up the local state of an object *object fragments*. The local state of an object may contain embedded references to other objects in the form of object identifiers (OIDs). We refer to an object's local state plus all the other objects reachable (transitively) by OIDs in the local state as the *global state* of the object. In general, a method has access to global state of an object: to the local state via data structure accessors, and to the global state via message sends. In executing a particular method on an object, it is unlikely that the entirety of its global state is needed. Indeed, the global state of an object could be the whole database. It is more likely that some fragments of the local state of the object are needed, along with fragments of the global state. We refer to this collection of related fragments as an *object complex*. Our Revealer attempts to develop templates describing the object complexes needed for different operations, and the Optimizer decides when to insert assembly operators to assemble collections of object complexes before their use.

As an example of these concepts, consider a library database with `Book` objects. The local state of a `Book` object might be a tuple with values for title, author, copyright date and so forth. The `author` field might itself be a tuple of first, middle and last name. The top-level tuple might also have fields that hold references to other objects, such as a `Publisher` object, an `Accession` object, and a `CatalogInfo` object. The local state of a `CatalogInfo` object might contain a structured value for the call number, another structured value for the location (floor, aisle, stack), references to three `CatalogCard` objects (author, subject and title cards), and a reference to a `Division` object to whose collection the book belongs (rare books, reference desk, and so forth). Figure 2 diagrams this situation. The dotted boxes represent the encapsulation boundary around the local state of a single object. Thin arrows represent connections between fragments composing the local state; thick arrows represent OIDs leading to other objects. The global state of a `Book` object includes its local state, plus the `Publisher`, `Accession` and `CatalogInfo` objects it references, their local states, the objects those local states reference, and so on.

Consider a query to find all `Books` in a set by author Anita Smith in the rare books division published by a foreign publishing house. This query could use an object complex consisting of the top-level tuple and the `author` subtuple of the local state of each book, that fragment of the local state of the `Publisher` object needed to get the address and the country value within that, the top-level tuple of the local state of the referenced `CatalogInfo` object, and the top-level local state of the `Division` object for that `CatalogInfo` object.

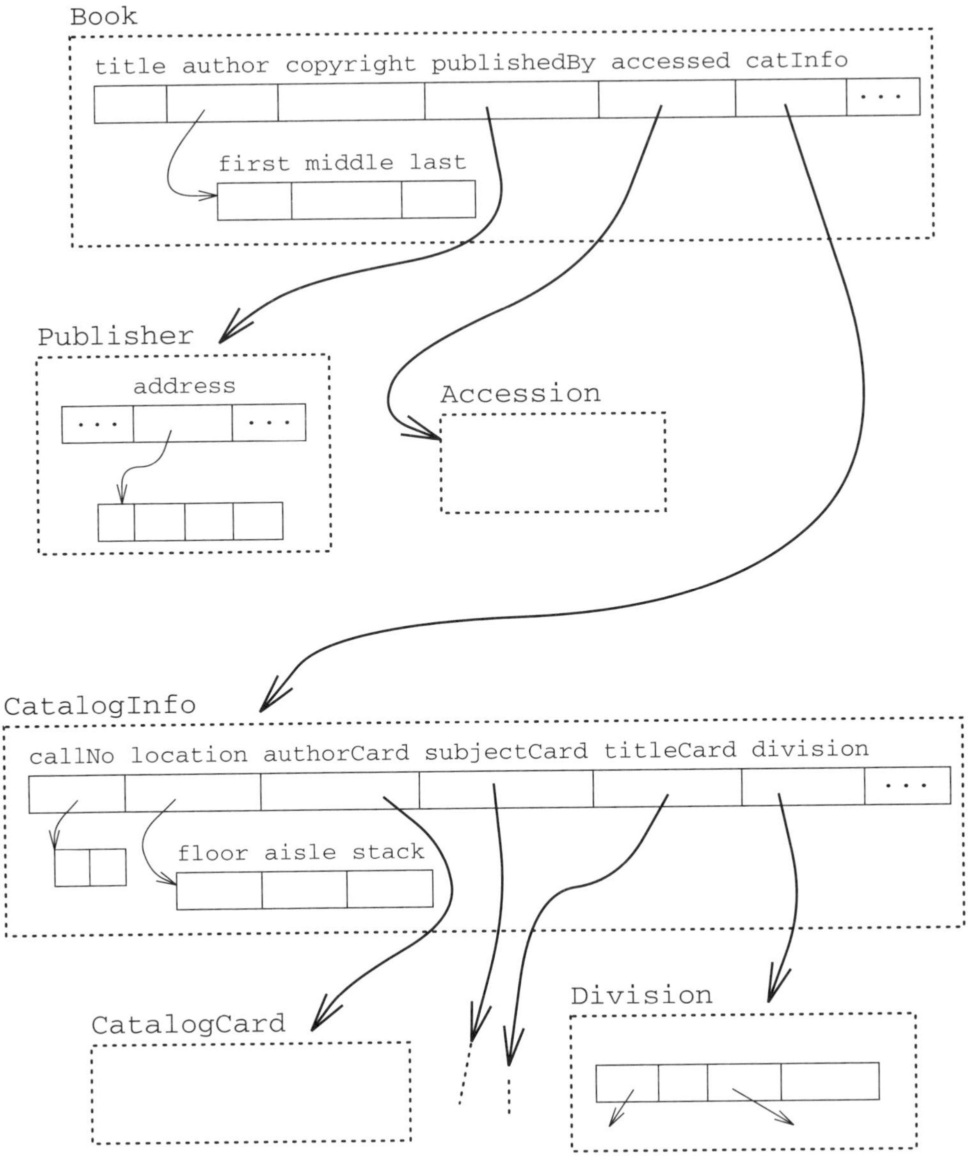

Figure 2: Local and Global State of a Complex Value

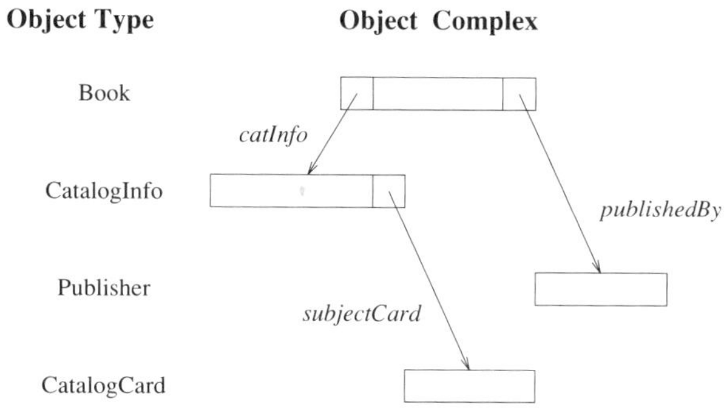

Figure 3: Sample Object Complex

6 OBJECT ASSEMBLY

The purpose of the assembly operator is to efficiently translate a collection of object complexes from their disk representations to a readily traversable memory representation. Note that we do not restrict the implementation of inter-object references in an object complex, nor do inter-object references imply ownership as in *composite objects*. (For example, many `Books` can reference the same `Publisher` object.) However, *intra*-object references are unique. To achieve efficiently traversable memory-resident object complexes, all relevant object and fragment references are changed to memory pointers. This "pointer-swizzling" process results in a structure that can be scanned without the need to consult an OID-to-memory-address mapping table. Instead, object-complex scanning is reduced to following memory pointers. Figure 3 illustrates an object complex where each box is the root fragment of an object and each intra- and inter-object reference is shown as a directed edge. This particular figure should be interpreted as a **`Book`** and its **`Publisher`**, and a portion of its catalog information (**`CatalogInfo`**)—in particular, the portion that describes the book's subject catalog entry (the **`CatalogCard`** in the `subjectCard` field). The assembly operator has the ability to find and resolve multiple, possibly shared, object references contained within the objects it receives. In order to do so efficiently, the operator uses physical, structural and statistical information. Instead of working on a single object complex, the assembly operator works on a window, of size W, of partial object complexes. As soon as any one of these object complexes becomes fully assembled and is passed up the query tree, the operator adds another to the window. We refer to this interleaved activity as a *delayed* or *sliding assembly operator*. Using a window of object complexes increases the pool size of unresolved references and results in more options, leading to a greater expected effect on efficiency. One cost of using the sliding assembly operator is the need for enough buffer space to hold W partially assembled objects.

Consider a small example using three object complexes structured like the one shown in Figure 3. Suppose that the assembly operator is using a window size of 2. Figure 4 illustrates a possible sequence of assembly stages. In the figure, italics represent *references* to object fragments. For example, *A2* represents a reference to fragment A2.

Assembly begins by filling the window with references to the first two object complexes. Figure 4a shows the starting condition. The assembly operator begins with a choice of two references to resolve. After resolving *A1*, and fetching the required fragment of the object,

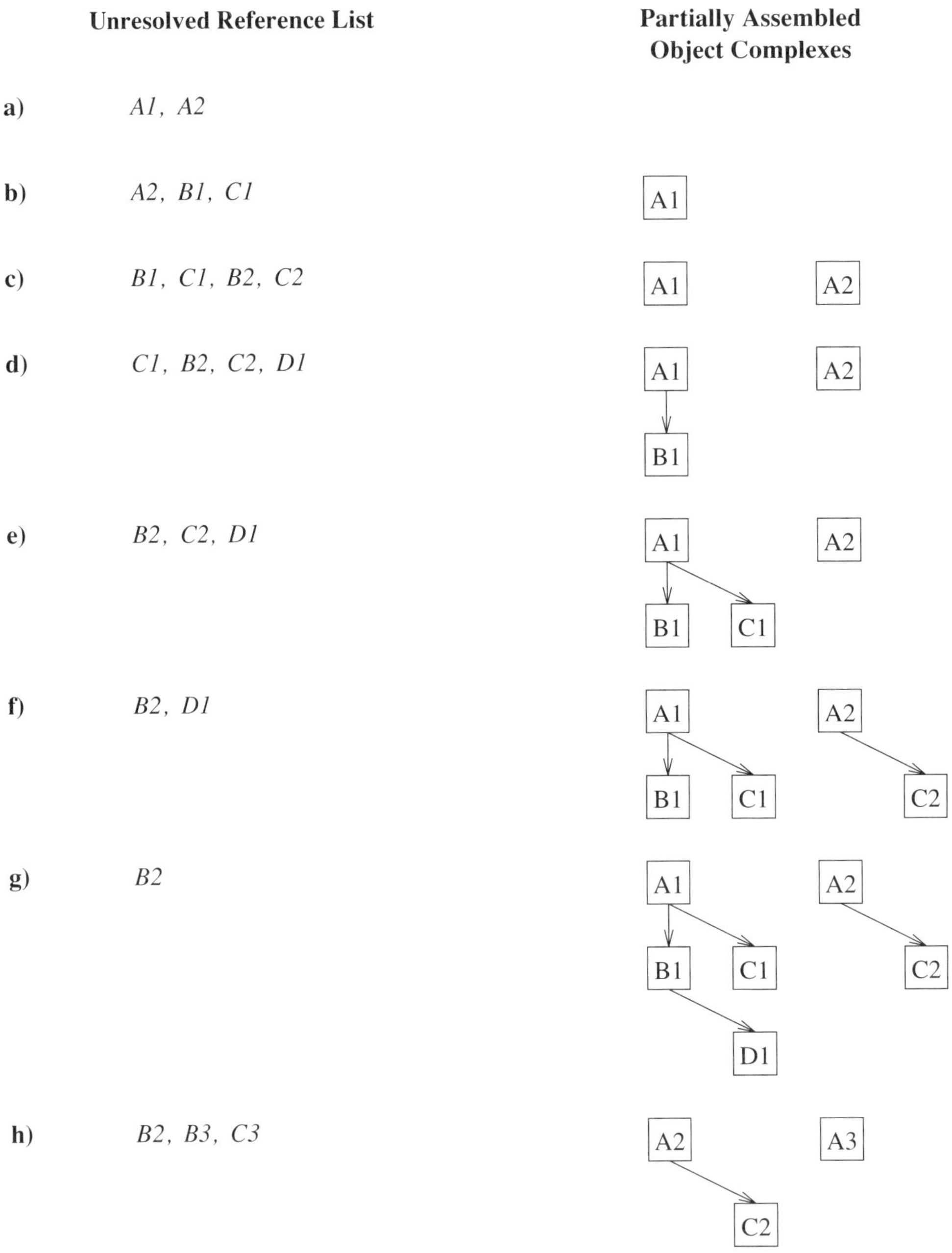

Figure 4: Sliding Assembly Operator Example

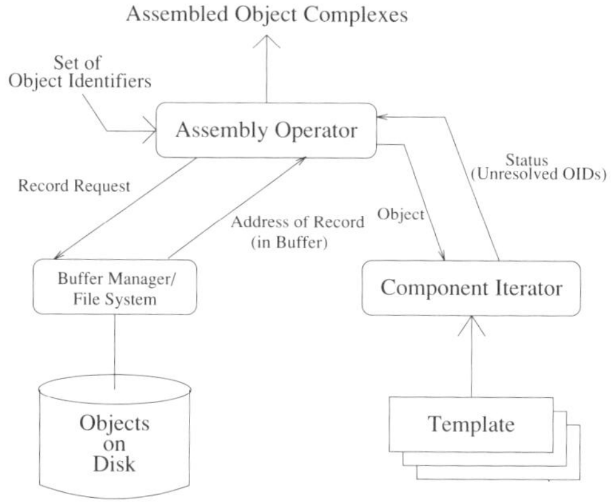

Figure 5: Assembly Operator Architecture

two new unresolved references, *B1* and *C1*, are added to the list. The new state is shown in Figure 4b. Next, reference *A2* is resolved (4c), resulting in references *B2* and *C2* being placed on the list. Figure 4d is the result of resolving *B1*, which places unresolved reference *D1* on the list. After *C1*, *C2* and *D1* are resolved (4g), the first object complex is fully assembled. In order to keep the window full, after the first object complex is passed to the caller of the *next* procedure of the assembly operator, a new reference is added to the list (4h).

The example depicts one order that results in the *A1* object complex being assembled first. There are, however, many other scheduling orders. At each step in Figure 4, an unresolved reference must be chosen. Ideally, the reference that reduces disk head movement and overall assembly time will be chosen. For example, *C2* may have been chosen from the list in Figure 4e because it was fetched when *C1* was fetched. The scheduling order is only restricted by the need to fetch objects top-down. (We are considering use of auxiliary access structures for bottom-up object assembly.)

In the previous discussion and example of the assembly operator, there was no mention of how the operator determines what part of an object complex to assemble, when assembly is complete or how to find unresolved references within a newly retrieved object fragment. Such information is specific to each query and is type and structure dependent. In our design, these tasks are the responsibility of the *component iterator*, a companion routine to the assembly operator.

Figure 5 shows the detailed architecture of the assembly operator and the component iterator. The component iterator uses structural and statistical information contained in a *template* to control the assembly operator. An assembly template resembles a tree similar to the representation of an object complex as shown in Figure 3. In addition to structural information, the template is annotated with statistical information. Currently the statistical information consists of predicate selectivity and the degree of sharing between objects.

As currently implemented, multiple assembly operators in a single query plan conflict in their disk access behavior, since their disk accesses are interleaved. We can avoid this interference with "build-ahead": when an assembly operator gets a *next* request, it builds, say, ten object complexes and returns one. The next nine *next* requests require no disk reads. This strategy requires no change to the Volcano operator model.

7 ASSUMPTIONS

In considering assembly of object complexes in a distributed object base, we anticipate that most objects will have the entirety of their local state at a single site. For example, we would not have the top-level tuple of a `Book` object at one site, and the `author` subtuple at another site (though we might replicate the whole `Book` object at more than one site). However, the global state of an object might indeed be distributed. Perhaps `Book` objects are distributed over divisional computers, but all the `Accession` objects they access are on a separate machine in the Purchasing and Donations department. Thus the assembly of object complexes can involve more than one site. The only exception to local state not being partitioned that we consider is collection objects, the "bulk types" of the system, where there is the potential for distributing data and computation by spreading large instances of these types across the various processors. This distribution provides a way to involve multiple sites in processing a query. If, for example, collections are distributed by hashing the object identifiers of the collection members to site identities, then each collection can be considered to be the union of the (smaller) collections on the various sites. Subproblems such as intersection, union, and selection all can proceed independently in the separate databases, reducing the amount of work necessary at any one site. In the library example, we might have one object, `Holdings`, that is a set of all `Book`s the library owns. The local state of `Holdings` is a set value of `Book` references. That local state might be partitioned across divisional machines, based on where the book is housed.

There are a few other assumptions we make in our analyses. One is about the nature of the distributed database we are working in. Using the taxonomy of [Özsu and Valduriez, 1991b], we are considering databases where the *autonomy* is integrated or tightly-federated, the *distribution* can be single or multi-site and there is little *heterogeneity* (at least among the data management components). In particular, we are assuming a common object schema across sites, and in some cases common physical representation of objects. A case of special interest to us is data distribution among multiple processors and disks on a parallel machine running as a single database system.

In this setting, it makes sense to think about two variations on assembly. One is where all the assembled object complexes are needed at a single, central site. The other is where the results of assembly are partitioned across multiple sites, say in anticipation of a subsequent processing step. In this paper we concentrate on distributed assembly for central-site results since distributed multi-site assembly behaves like a number of simultaneous single-site assemblies.

A final assumption is that objects are identified with logical object identifiers (LOIDs) that do not in general convey physical location information. The LOIDs must therefore be keys to some kind of object-locator table in order to retrieve the object. However, we assume that fragments composing the local state of an object are identified with physical identifiers (PIDs) for efficiency.

8 STRATEGIES FOR DISTRIBUTED ASSEMBLY

In choosing query processing strategies for distributed Revelation, we must decide how much processing can be done at remote sites before results are sent to the central site. We first discuss three possible categories of distributed query processing strategies and the advantages of each. The first category is essentially a centralized query processing strategy: ship all data to the central site for processing there. The second category is analogous to what most commercial relational database systems use: minimal processing at remote sites, typically just select, or in our case, assemble local state. The third category is the most ambitious and includes complex operations, e.g., join or complete assembly of remote objects, at remote sites, with only the final results sent to the central site.

8.1 CATEGORY I

Category I query processing strategies require all data to be shipped, unprocessed, to the central site for processing. The advantages of Category I strategies are similar to those for the relational case: simplicity of implementation. The query optimizer for this category is similar to the optimizer for the non-distributed case, except that the cost estimate for retrieval is greater. Query processing is identical.

8.2 CATEGORY II

Category II consists of strategies that perform, where possible, selects and local assembly at a remote site. For example, suppose object O at the central site includes references to objects $A1$, $A2$, $A3$, ... satisfying a condition, and $A1$, $A2$, $A3$, ... are at a single remote site S. Query processing strategies in Category II would first select objects at S satisfying the condition. Suppose $A1$ is one such. Then these strategies allow assembling $A1$ to include all parts of the object complex available at S. When $A1$ is assembled as fully as possible at S, it is shipped to the central site.

There are at least two variations here. One is to assemble objects up to the boundary of the local state. Another is to assemble those fragments of global state that are reachable on the same site.

Category II strategies have the advantage of simplicity of control: everything is managed from the central site, with messages only between the central site and remote sites; there are no messages from one remote site to another. The latter can significantly complicate the control structure, locking mechanisms, and crash recovery. Furthermore, increased message overhead makes processing less efficient.

Most commercial vendors of relational databases have developed their distributed systems using Category II strategies [Kelley, 1991]. Although one can define distributed object assembly examples for which Category II is quite inefficient, it is our belief that, as in the relational model, essentially all real distributed object assembly queries can be processed efficiently by strategies in Category II.

8.3 CATEGORY III

Category III strategies ignore remote site boundaries. They perform arbitrary operations at remote sites and ship arbitrary data between remote sites. In our example above, $A1$ will be fully assembled at *S* before it is shipped to the central site. Category III also includes strategies in which *A1* travels to another remote site while it is assembled. An example of this strategy is for one site to assemble complex *A1* until it contains no more local references, then to send it to the site having the most outstanding references in the partially assembled complex. Of course the optimizer must decide whether such a strategy is optimal.

As in the relational case, Category I strategies produce the most processing load on the central site, Category III strategies the least. It is not clear that the Category III strategies are optimal. For example, if the remote sites are quite slow, and communication is fast, it may pay to ship all data to the central site unprocessed. An implementation of a distributed object-oriented database may include strategies of one category or more than one category.

8.4 ILLUSTRATION OF CATEGORIES

We consider an example to illustrate the difference in these three strategies. Suppose we need to assemble object complexes for `Book` objects that involve local state from a `Book` object, and the associated `Accession` and `CatalogInfo` objects. Assume the answer site for the query is Site *GC* (General Circulation Division), but some of the `Books` are at Site *RB* (Rare Books Division). Assume the `CatalogInfo` object for each `Book` is at the site of that book, and that all `Accession` objects are at Site *PD* (Purchasing and Donations).

Under the Category I strategy, Site *GC* would make requests for `Book` objects from Site *RB*. When *GC* receives a `Book` object from *RB*, it can then request the appropriate `CatalogInfo` object from *RB* and `Accession` object from Site *PD*.

With Category II strategies, Site *RB* would deliver back partial object complexes consisting of the needed `Book` and `CatalogInfo` state. Site *GC* would then go to Site *PD* for an `Accession` object to complete the object complex.

With the third strategy, Site *RB* could assemble a `Book` and `CatalogInfo` fragments, and get the appropriate `Accession` object directly from Site *PD*, then return the complete object complex to *GC*. Alternatively, *RB* could send `Book–CatalogInfo` partial complexes to Site *PD*, which would add the `Accession` object and forward the completed complex to Site *GC*.

8.5 FURTHER ISSUES

8.5.1 Data Transfer

One issue we are considering is what should be shipped from remote to central sites: the page on which each object resides, just the object, or a batch of several objects? Similar issues are discussed in [Franklin and Carey, 1993].

When an object is requested from a remote site, the first option is to ship the entire page on which the object resides. This option makes the most sense when objects are appropriately clustered, so that future requests for similar objects can be satisfied locally. However, it is impractical with strategies in Category II or III above.

Another option is to ship just the object requested. This option is simplest, but may result in many small objects being shipped, encountering significant message overhead.

A final option is to batch object requests, e.g., request not one book but several at a time. This approach allows batching of objects but avoids the complexity of moving pages. This option is facilitated by the exchange buffering mechanism of Volcano and it is this option which we intend to pursue in distributed Revelation .

8.5.2 Logical Object Identity Translation

Another set of choices we consider are related to translation of LOIDs and PIDs, as well as tracking of the location of objects, fragments and object complexes.

So far we have assumed that object references are logical (LOIDs) but that fragment references within local state can be physical (PIDs). This assumption is consistent with having an object table per site that translates each object LOID to the PID of its root fragment. Which LOIDs should be in this table?

The first choice is to have only LOIDs of local objects in the object table. But local objects may have references to remote objects. One solution is to ensure that remote references include the remote site of the object in the LOID. Then the remote LOIDs can be sent to the proper site for resolving. However, having LOIDs include site information prohibits site migration of objects. Other problems with this approach are discussed below. Another choice is to include in the object table LOIDs of all objects in the system at every site. This choice is probably prohibitively expensive. A third choice is to include LOIDs of local objects and of those remote objects that are referenced locally. This alternative is likely to be hard to manage.

In evaluating these choices for the object table, we must keep in mind that in Category I an object may be shipped to the central site unassembled. The unassembled object may have PIDs or LOIDs for the remote site. Even in Category II, objects arriving at the central site may include LOIDs of objects at remote sites. These are additional reasons that the problem of remote IDs will be important in distributed Revelation .

Another approach to this problem is to have remote sites translate the PIDs or LOIDs before sending them to another site, perhaps adding enough information that the central site can interpret them. This approach makes more sense for Category I, since in that case there will be more remote references involved. On the other hand, many LOIDs sent will never be accessed, so it may not make sense to "pre-translate" them. (A related issue is how object complexes can be "swizzled" remotely yet contain proper local memory addresses.)

However, for Category II strategies, it often makes sense for the remote site to selectively provide LOID translations. If the remote site is made aware that the partial object complex it provides is going to be augmented with object state from other sites, it can provide translations of LOIDs leading to those other objects. For example, suppose Site *GC* is assembling object complexes involving a `Book`, `Accession` and `CatalogInfo` object, using a Category II strategy. A request for a partial object complex from Site *RB* will bring back state from the `Book` and `CatalogInfo` object. If Site *RB* is told, however, that Site *GC* will also be assembling the `Accession` object from Site *PD*, then *RB* can supply the translation from its local LOID for the `Accession` to the LOID for Site *PD*. Supplying this information saves Site *GC* a later communication with *RB*.

There are actually a couple of variations on locally caching the translation of LOIDs of resident foreign objects. One is to only keep track of the translation for LOIDs explicitly requested. However, if object requests bring back physical units that also contain unrequested objects, one could cache the LOID translations for those objects as well, if the remote site provided them. In fact, it has been suggested that duplicating relevant portions of the object table in physical storage segments might be a useful performance enhancement in any case in the centralized database world [DeWitt, 1991]. With such a scheme, a physical transfer automatically provides LOID translation information for all objects in the physical unit.

We mentioned having the receiving site track the foreign objects it currently buffers, along with LOID translation information to locate them. Is it useful for the sending site to try to keep track of what objects the receiving site currently holds? For example, imagine the sending site, using a Category II or III strategy, is assembling `Book–Publisher` object complexes and shipping them to the central site. Since many `Books` might reference the same `Publisher` object, if the sending site kept track of what `Publisher` objects it has sent, there might be some savings in not repeatedly sending the same `Publisher` object. Our initial feeling is that object tracking of this form is not worthwhile. Without a lot of additional communication, it is not possible for the sending site to know if the receiving site has retained a previously sent object. Furthermore, the cost of resending a component object is likely to be small. For example, if the same `Publisher` appears in multiple object complexes, that object probably remains in the sending site's memory buffers. Thus, the only cost in resending it is lengthening a message. On the other end, the receiving site can easily discard the object (or containing physical unit) if it is already present.

8.6 EFFECT ON ASSEMBLY OPERATOR

This section briefly discusses the effect of the previous issues on the implementation of the distributed assembly operator. For Category I strategies, the central site contains a single assembly operator. Logically, the central assembly operator treats each site from which objects must be retrieved as a device. Thus, depending on the method chosen for sending object requests and getting their results, the assembly operator extracts object references and distributes the requests. At each site, a "slave" assembly operator would only retrieve object fragments from disk, not doing any actual assembly. With a Category I strategy, the central assembly operator would carry most of the workload. The central assembly operator would be required to choose a window size sufficiently large to make requests from "slave" sites efficient. That is, one would want to have a window large enough so that there are likely to be multiple unresolved references to a given remote site, which can be batched together in a single request.

Category II strategies distribute the work of assembling object complexes to multiple sites, results are shipped only to the central site. Under these strategies, as much work as possible should be distributed to other sites. This implies the central assembly operator should request large batches of object complexes. However, the ability to do so at one remote site may depend on receiving results from other sites. For example, requests from the central query site, *GC*, for `Book–CatalogInfo` partial object complexes are sent to Site *RB*. The number of requests to Site *PD* depends on getting results from *RB*. Even more challenging is ensuring that the central assembly operator is kept busy. If it has too few object complexes in its window, it may sit idle waiting for requests to remote sites to be filled. It needs a sufficient number of object complexes in progress to mask the latency in communication with other sites, hence should have freedom in choosing its window size.

Category III strategies differ from Category II strategies in the lack of a central controlling assembly operator. Although a final destination site is possible, intermediate results (partial object complexes) are shipped between sites, not to a central site. These strategies require each assembly operator to make requests to other sites for partial object complexes.

In strategies from Categories II and III, the policy that must be determined is shipping of requests (and receiving their results). Ignoring the format of data being shipped and LOID translation, Categories II and III require flow control of requests and results between local assembly operators. Efficient local-site assembly depends on a large window of unresolved references. For sites that are assembling a large portion of the object complex (i.e., many objects reside on that site), each incoming request will result in a large number of local unresolved references. Sites that contain only a single object that belongs to an object complex will only have a single unresolved local reference generated from each non-local request. We venture that window size for local assembly operators must vary proportionately to the fraction of object complex contained at any site.

9 FUTURE WORK

First we will work on solutions to the problems above, both implementation issues (re-designing exchange and other operators) and conceptual issues (who is responsible for translations of LOIDs, etc.). Next we plan to move on to a complete design of distributed Revelation, and then to implementation. As in centralized Revelation, our goal will be to show that the sophisticated algorithms we have described (e.g., windowing), and their distributed counterparts, will perform better than naive versions of distributed assembly. For the longer term, we hope to generalize the central-site-answer model to support answers at multiple sites.

Acknowledgements

This research was supported in part by NSF Grants IRI-8920642 and IRI-9012618; by DARPA Order No. 8230 under contract DAAB-07-91-C-Q518; and by research grants from the Oregon Advanced Computing Institute, Intel Supercomputer Systems, ADP, and Sequent Computers.

Fine Grained Object Migration

Jean Dollimore
Queen Mary and Westfield College
Department of Computer Science
Mile End Road, London E1 4NS
U.K.

Claudio Nascimento
Queen Mary and Westfield College
Department of Computer Science
Mile End Road, London E1 4NS
U.K.

Wang Xu
Queen Mary and Westfield College
Department of Computer science
Mile End Road, London E1 4NS
U.K.

Abstract

This paper discusses the migration of fine grained objects in a distributed object-oriented system in a context in which people use workstations on a local area network to share information and to communicate with one another. The paper introduces an abstract model for distributed objects that move from one object context to another, taking sufficient pre-requisites with them. This is followed by a description of mechanisms for deep and shallow migration with eager and lazy variants. We argue that deep migration allows programmers to specify precisely the collection of objects to be migrated. The lazy variant of deep migration improves its performance. We propose that in the case of shared objects replication is preferable to migration. We conclude with a discussion of issues relating

1 INTRODUCTION

This paper discusses the issues relating to fine grained object migration in a distributed object-oriented environment. To move an object, both state and operations must be moved — this is our smallest unit of migration. However, most objects refer directly or indirectly to a set of other objects. We also allow for larger units of migration consisting of such sets of objects. An important issue related to migration of sets of objects is how to decide how many of them should be subjected to the move.

A set of objects may be subjected to an eager form of migration in which the entire set is moved all together to its destination. For example, from a persistent object store to a user object context. When an object is moved to the location of its invoker or to a user's workstation it is hard to predict whether it will eventually invoke many other objects in the set of objects which it references. The eager migration may not be the best policy in all situations. An alternative is a lazy form of migration in which each object is moved on demand only when it is referenced from the destination.

1.1 OUR PROTOTYPE ENVIRONMENT

We are building a prototype of a distributed object-oriented environment which is based on Brouhaha — a local implementation of Smalltalk-80 [Miranda, 1987]. We chose to base our distributed object system on Smalltalk because our primary motivation is to be able to make use of the system for constructing distributed applications for use by several people. Object-oriented programming in general and the Smalltalk environment in particular are very effective for application development. We therefore felt that distributed Smalltalk was a promising approach to the construction of distributed applications.

Our prototype system applies a two level naming scheme in which objects are accessed from outside their object context by means of globally unique identifiers. A transparent remote invocation mechanism is also implemented in our system [Dollimore et al., 1990].

2 A MODEL FOR MOBILE OBJECTS

In this section we describe our distributed object model. The four main aspects of the model are objects, object activities, object contexts and object mobility.

2.1 OBJECTS, ACTIVITIES, AND OBJECT CONTEXTS

An object encapsulates a set of private states and a set of operations that manipulate or observe the state of the object. In general, an object's set of states is completely protected and hidden from all other objects. Each state may represent either a value or the identifier of another object. The only way a state can be examined or modified is by sending a message which invokes one of the object's operations.

We use the term *object activity* to refer to a chain of related executions of operations in a set of objects. All the current executions of operations comprise object activities which implement the required application functions.

Object activities take place within object contexts. Certain things in an object context influence the effect of the execution of the operations of the objects involved in an activity. These include: the class hierarchy; the shared variables; the object naming scheme; the object memory; and the object activity.

Objects are located in an object memory associated with an object context. A distributed garbage collector co-operates with the local garbage collectors to reclaim the local memory space taken by objects which cannot be reached from the local root.

An object has four activity control states:

- *ready* - the object is ready to receive a message and is not part of any activity;
- *active* - the object is executing an operation and is therefore involved in an activity;
- *waiting* - the object is waiting for a reply after invoking an operation in another object and is still involved in an activity;
- *suspended* - the object is temporarily unable to be invoked.

The activity control states are independent of the object's internal state.

2.2 OBJECT MIGRATION

Object migration means moving an object from one object context to another object context which is usually physically located on another machine. In our model, objects cannot migrate whilst they are currently involved in an object activity (Some systems such as Emerald [Jul et al., 1988] allow objects to migrate whilst they are involved in activities).

An object in an active or waiting state must not be migrated, otherwise its activity will be broken. Objects in the ready state can be migrated by first switching them into the suspended state. This prevents the object from taking part in any activity during the migration. After the object has settled in the destination object context, it is switched to a ready state to allow it to continue to participate in activities. The object migration process must be atomic in the sense that the entire set of object states and operations must be preserved across the migration.

It is important that the source and the destination contexts are compatible in the sense of allowing the object to be active. If the operations of an object refer to shared variables then it requires access to shared objects as well as its operations in order to be active. We refer to all the objects required by an active object as its pre-requisites [Shapiro et al., 1989a] — they include its class and superclasses and all the objects referenced by shared variables in its operations.

In some cases, pre-requisite objects may need to be migrated prior to migrating an object in order to establish a compatible object context in the destination for the migrated object. For example, a class object may be needed before an instance object can be migrated and activated in the destination object context if the class is new to it.

2.3 MIGRATING AN OBJECT

The migration of a single object is done in two main steps: the first involves the shipping of the object from source to destination [Vegdahl, 1986]. Shipping an object means that a copy of the original object is activated at the destination after having installed any necessary pre-requisite objects. The second step involves the creation of a proxy (for the copy) at the source to replace the original object. The proxy is given the same local object identifier as the original object [Decouchant, 1986].

To achieve atomic migration of the states of an object, we must prevent it from executing any of its operations. To achieve this, we replace the object by a blocking-proxy object that is responsible for blocking all invocation messages during the first stage of migration. Thus migration requires all the following steps

- A blocking-proxy is created for the object to be migrated
- The blocking-proxy replaces the object (the object is now unable to receive messages).
- The object is packed and transmitted to the destination.
- Any necessary pre-requisite objects are migrated.
- The object is unpacked (including the creation of any necessary proxies) and activated at the destination.
- A proxy to the migrated object is created at the source.
- This proxy replaces the blocking-proxy (the migrated object can now receive messages).
- Eventually, the original object and the blocking-proxy at the source are garbage collected.

We use the term *composite object* to refer to any object whose state contains object identifiers of other objects. In general a composite object may refer directly or indirectly to a set of objects and this object structure takes the form of a graph. A crucial issue when migrating composite objects is deciding how much of the graph to move.

When migrating a composite object it is possible to either move the entire graph of the object (deep migration) or just the object itself, with the consequent creation of proxies at the destination (shallow migration). A third possibility is to move a certain portion of the graph, for example the first and second layers. This idea is based on the practical notion that an object will generally access its directly referenced objects, before (if ever) accessing the subsequent layers of the graph. We call this layered migration. With these three types of migration, users can then choose the one that best suits the needs of their application.

2.4 REPLICATION OF CLASSES AND OTHER SHARED OBJECTS

Classes and other shared variables can be accessed by some or all of the objects within an object context. Consider a situation in which an object that shares pre-requisites with other objects needs to migrate: the pre-requisites will be required in both object contexts. Therefore, replication of the pre-requisites is generally preferable to migration. Some classes and shared variables can be defined as immutable and may be freely replicated in every object context.

2.5 LAZY MIGRATION: THE USE OF DEMANDERS

To improve the performance of object migration, a mechanism called demanding is used. Migrating an object's graph on demand means that only the referenced object is initially migrated, thereby saving on the time needed to pack the whole object's graph and unpack it at the destination. Also, parts of the graph may never be used at the destination.

At the destination, a demander is created for each referenced object at the source. Demanders are similar to proxies but, upon receiving a message, instead of forwarding it to the remote object, the demander queues the message and requests the remote object to migrate and replace the demander. Then, the object executes the message.

2.6 MIGRATION OF CLASSES

We discuss three different approaches to the migration of classes. In the first approach, source code is migrated. In the other approaches, compiled classes are migrated. Compiled operations are represented by bytecodes in Smalltalk.

In the first approach a copy of the source code of a class is migrated and then re-compiled at the destination. When an operation is re-compiled, its references to classes and other shared objects will be re-associated with the corresponding objects in the destination context. If such objects are not available, a compilation error will occur. We have also observed that the time required to compile a class is not acceptable as an overhead for migration.

In the second approach a class is migrated in the same way as any other object. This is the approach which we currently use. Our approach is to use eager deep migration to migrate a class-object.

We are currently investigating a third approach which exploits a form of lazy migration. Our idea is to migrate the source code of the class definition including the names of the operations, but without their compiled operations; to compile it at the destination and then to bind it to the compiled operations through eager demanders - a variant of demanders that request eager migration. This scheme has the following advantages over the second:

- initial packing and unpacking overheads of the composite class-object are reduced;
- compilation of a class template is fast and the metaclass is automatically created.

We are still experimenting with this approach and have not yet achieved conclusive results.

3 CONCLUSIONS

We have designed an abstract model for object migration, which clearly distinguishes between objects and object activities. This model enabled us to define what to migrate and when to migrate it, thereby simplifying the design for object migration.

Deep migration provides programmers with the ability to select the groups of objects they want to migrate. Lazy migration is well suited for a context in which composite objects are commonly used. Lazy migration is based on the concept of object demanders, which provide location transparency — the invoker is not aware either that the invoked object is remote or that it migrates.

As a result of this work, we have a running prototype built on our distributed version of Smalltalk, which allows clients to migrate objects between different Smalltalk images.

PART 4
TRANSACTION PROCESSING AND CONCURRENCY CONTROL

Long-Lived Concurrent Activities

Bruce Martin*
Hewlett Packard Laboratories
1501 Page Mill Road
Palo Alto, CA 94304
U.S.A.

Claus H. Pedersen
Hewlett Packard Laboratories
Filton Road, Stoke Gifford
Bristol BS12 6QZ
England

Abstract

Transactions provide programmers with execution guarantees that simplify the task of implementing concurrent activities. However, the traditional transaction model does not apply to long-lived concurrent activities. We present five examples of such activities. For each example we argue why the traditional transaction model does not apply to the activity. Through the examples we explain how the traditional transaction model can be extended to support the long-lived concurrent activities. We identify a dichotomy of extensions: three that preserve transaction isolation and one that isolates cooperation. The first three extensions provide transaction guarantees more flexibly by capturing application semantics and structure. The last extension allows localized cooperation between a group of transactions.

1 INTRODUCTION

Traditional database transactions [Gray, 1979] are effective for controlling short, concurrent accesses to databases with strict consistency requirements. The model provides a fixed set of guarantees that make it simple to implement concurrent applications that share data.

The traditional transaction model does not apply equally well to concurrent activities of longer duration. We will verify this claim by presenting five examples: shared desk top, concurrent make, concurrently moving and editing a large document, concurrently updating software and arranging meeting rooms.

*Current address: SunSoft, Inc. 2550 Garcia Avenue, Mountain View, CA 94043, U.S.A.

Transaction guarantees dramatically simplify the programming of concurrent applications because they isolate reasoning about failures and concurrency. Rather than abandoning transaction notions, they should be extended to support long-lived concurrent activities.

Through the examples we explain how the traditional transaction model can be extended to support the long-lived concurrent activities. We identify a dichotomy of extensions: three that preserve transaction isolation and one that isolates cooperation. The first three extensions provide transaction guarantees more flexibly by capturing application semantics and structure. The last extension allows localized cooperation between a group of transactions.

To set the framework for the examples, we give an overview of the traditional transaction model. This is followed by the presentation of the examples. For each example we discuss why the traditional transaction model does not apply and explain how it can be extended in order to apply to the example. Finally, we summarize the presented extensions and relate several extended transaction models proposed in the literature to them.

None of the proposed extended transaction models are able to support all of the examples. We believe the examples can serve as benchmarks for extended transaction models.

2 TRADITIONAL TRANSACTIONS

A transaction consists of a sequence of basic steps, usually called *actions*. Actions read and write data items in the database. The system ensures that a transaction is *failure atomic* and that any interleaving of actions from competing transactions is *serializable*. That is, the system guarantees that a transaction executes to completion or not at all and the effect on the database of the interleaved actions is the same as the effect of *some* serial execution of the transactions. The changes that a transaction makes to the data items are made *permanent* if the transaction *commits* or are discarded if the transaction *aborts*.

The traditional transaction model is based on the assumption that a transaction is correct; it maps the database from one consistent state to another. For example, with a database with a consistency constraint that no employee makes more than his boss, a transaction that gives an employee a raise and the boss an equal or greater one is considered correct.

Since the database management system ensures that concurrent transactions do not interfere with each other and that partial effects of a transaction are not seen, the programmer's task is simplified. He must only ensure that the transaction maps the database from one consistent state to another.

Traditional transactions are programmed in isolation. A transaction does not know the identity of other transactions, nor their relative order of execution; any serialization of concurrent transactions is considered correct.

To provide serializability and failure atomicity, the traditional transaction model considers low-level access to shared data. An *ordering dependency* occurs between two transactions if one reads a data item and the other then writes it, if one writes it and the other then reads it or if they both write it. A concurrency control algorithm provides *read-write serializability* if it ensures that dependencies between a set of transactions are acyclic.

Simple algorithms implementing the transaction notions of read-write serializability, failure atomicity and permanence have been developed and execute efficiently for commercial data processing applications. The two-phase locking algorithm [Eswaran et al., 1976] associates read and write locks with each data item. A transaction must possess a read lock to read the value of a data item and a write lock to update the value of a data item. To ensure read-write serializability, transactions must manipulate locks in two phases. A transaction must request all locks before releasing any locks. If another transaction holds a write lock on a data item, other transactions requesting locks must wait for the transaction to release the write lock. *Strict* two-phase locking ensures failure atomicity by requiring a transaction to update copies of data items and to hold all locks until it either commits or aborts. If the transaction aborts, the updated copies are discarded. If the transaction commits, the copies become the new values for the data.

Optimistic concurrency control algorithms [Kung and Robinson, 1981] let a set of concurrent transactions access shared data and then abort transactions if the resulting schedule is non-serializable.

The transaction guarantees of failure atomicity and serializability are valuable for simplifying the task of programming, especially in a distributed environment. However, a transaction is not a general enough mechanism; its properties are specifically defined to meet the requirements of data processing. We now demonstrate through examples how the traditional model fails and derive requirements for extending transactions.

3 SHARED DESK TOP

The desk top metaphor, used widely in office automation environments, gives the user the illusion of directly manipulating a set of objects by moving them around and organizing them in folders. The interface system interprets the user's gestures and passes them on to the applications as more meaningful events.

The desk top metaphor naturally extends to distributed environments where the objects presented may be shared. Users can view and manipulate shared objects. An object contained in a folder can be moved to another folder by "selecting it" from the source folder in which it resides and "dropping" it on the destination folder where the user wants it. The object must be deregistered with the source folder and registered with the destination folder.

```
src-folder->deregister(obj)
dest-folder->register(obj)
```

Either both or neither of the updates must happen. Otherwise, the involved objects may be left in an inconsistent state. An object may, for example, become unreachable if a failure occurs right after `src-folder->deregister(obj)` is completed.

Consider two users, John and Dean, who are both viewing the objects on Dean's desk top. John accesses the objects on Dean's computer via a slow wide area network and Dean works locally. John moves a document from one folder to another. Dean concurrently moves a different document between the same two folders.

3.1 TRADITIONAL TRANSACTIONS

Traditional transactions fail to provide appropriate concurrency control. Assume the interleaving in Figure 1.

This interleaving yields the desired effect; both documents are moved from the source to the destination folders. Furthermore, it is a highly desirable interleaving because Dean

T_{John}: `src-folder->deregister(doc-one)`
T_{Dean}: `src-folder->deregister(doc-two)`
T_{Dean}: `dest-folder->register(doc-two)`
T_{John}: `dest-folder->register(doc-one)`

Figure 1: A correct interleaving that is not read-write serializable

can proceed without waiting for John. Otherwise, Dean could experience the same poor response times that John does, although Dean is operating locally.

Although this interleaving is correct, it is not read-write serializable because `register` and `deregister` operations would be considered writes. A cycle is established when T_{John} executes `dest-folder->register(doc-one)`.

In the case of strict two-phase locking the two transaction would be forced to execute serially.

3.2 EXTENDED TRANSACTIONS

An extended transaction model that captures application semantics can consider the interleaving from Figure 1 to be correct.

Semantic-based concurrency control

Two operations O_1 and O_2 *commute* [Weihl, 1988] if the effect of executing O_1 followed by O_2 is the same as executing O_2 followed by O_1. Since the commutativity information is application specific, it must be provided by the programmer.

The example illustrates the need of semantic information for judging whether an interleaving is correct or not. Two `register` operation on the same folder commute if the objects being registered are different. So do two `deregister` operations on the same folder.

Commutativity of the operations implies that the interleaving in Figure 1 above is serializable. It is semantically equivalent to executing T_{John} to completion and then executing T_{Dean}. It is also equivalent to the opposite order.

4 CONCURRENT MAKE

This example is based on the Unix make facility. The example is inspired by [Shrivastava and Wheater, 1990] but differs as it emphasizes the need for semantic-based concurrency control.

Make is a Unix utility program that can be used for maintaining consistency between interdependent files. An entry in a make file specifies a target file, a command and a set of prerequisite files on which the target file depends. Given a make file and a target file, make recursively makes the prerequisite files. Then, if any of the prerequisite files are newer than the target file, it executes the command associated with the target file.

Consider the make file in Figure 2. The target file `foo` has `shared1.o` and `shared2.o` as prerequisite files. Make recursively ensures that the prerequisite files are consistent and the time of last update is then read for `foo`, `shared1.o` and `shared2.o`. If any

```
foo       : shared1.o shared2.o ...
              cc -o foo shared1.o shared2.o ...

bar       : shared1.o shared2.o ...
              cc -o bar shared1.o shared2.o ...

shared1.o: shared1.c
              cc -c shared1.c

shared2.o: shared2.c
              cc -c shared2.c
                 ⋮
```

Figure 2: A make file

of the prerequisite files are newer than `foo`, the command "`cc -o foo shared1.o shared2.o ...`" is executed to re-establish consistency of `foo`.

A user executes make by specifying a target file to be made consistent. When make is executed in isolation it has the following properties:

- If no failures occur, it guarantees that the specified target file and the closure of its prerequisite files are consistent after the execution of make.
- In case of a failure, partial results are preserved. For example, if a compilation fails the results of previous compilations are preserved.

The performance of software configuration can be enhanced by compiling different modules in parallel. Since software configuration is often a time-consuming task, this could be a substantial gain for large software projects.

However, unwanted effects can occur if several makes are invoked concurrently. Assuming the make file from Figure 2, consider two programmers who concurrently execute `make foo` and `make bar` after `shared1.c` has been changed. The interleaving illustrated in Figure 3 below could take place if concurrency is not controlled. It leaves `foo` inconsistent because `shared1.o` will be newer than `foo`. If `make foo` were executed again, it would find this inconsistency and redo work that in fact has already been done twice.

In general, the entire execution of make must be serializable. Otherwise, it is not possible to argue that prerequisite files are mutually consistent when the command to ensure the consistency of a target file executes. For example, it is not possible to guarantee that `shared1.o` and `shared2.o` are mutually consistent when "`cc -o foo shared1.o shared2.o ...`" is executed.

4.1 TRADITIONAL TRANSACTIONS

Traditional transactions guarantee failure atomicity for the entire transaction. This is not appropriate for this example. Using the make file from Figure 2 as an example, it is undesirable to lose the effects of previously executed compilations if a failure occurs.

T_{foo} : read last modified time of `shared1.c` and `shared1.o`
T_{bar} : read last modified time of `shared1.c` and `shared1.o`
T_{foo} : `cc -c shared1.c`
T_{foo} : read last modified time of `shared2.c` and `shared2.o`
T_{foo} : read last modified time of `foo`, `shared1.o` and `shared2.o`
T_{foo} : `cc -o foo shared1.o shared2.o` ...
T_{bar} : `cc -c shared1.c`
T_{foo} : read last modified time of `shared2.c` and `shared2.o`
T_{bar} : read last modified time of `bar`, `shared1.o` and `shared2.o`
T_{bar} : `cc -o bar shared1.o shared2.o` ...

Figure 3: Incorrect interleaving due to uncontrolled concurrency

The interleaving illustrated in Figure 4 would not be considered correct with read-write serializability. It is considered incorrect because it contains a cycle of read and write operations. T_{bar} writes `shared1.o` before T_{foo} reads it but T_{bar} reads `shared2.o` after T_{foo} writes it.

T_{bar} : read last modified time of `shared1.c` and `shared1.o`
T_{bar} : `cc -c shared1.c`
T_{foo} : read last modified time of `shared1.c` and `shared1.o`
T_{foo} : read last modified time of `shared2.c` and `shared2.o`
T_{foo} : `cc -c shared2.c`
T_{bar} : read last modified time of `shared2.c` and `shared2.o`
T_{bar} : read last modified time of `bar`, `shared1.o` and `shared2.o`
T_{bar} : `cc -o bar shared1.o shared2.o` ...
T_{foo} : read last modified time of `foo`, `shared1.o` and `shared2.o`
T_{foo} : `cc -o foo shared1.o shared2.o` ...

Figure 4: A meaningful interleaving that is incorrect with read-write serializability

The effect of the interleaving in figure 4 is equivalent to executing T_{bar} followed by T_{foo}, but it is still considered incorrect. The requirements of read-write serializability restrict concurrency unnecessarily.

We further note that strict two-phase locking would not allow any concurrency because the shared files would be locked throughout the entire execution of make.

4.2 EXTENDED TRANSACTIONS

An extended transaction model must meet the following requirements in order to support concurrent executions of make.

Separate boundaries of transaction guarantees

Traditional transactions provide the same boundaries for failure atomicity and serializability.

In this example the boundary required for failure atomicity is different from the one required for serializability. We only require the command that updates a target file to be failure atomic but we require serializability over the entire make.

Referring to Figure 2, we want serializability over the entire `make foo` command, but we only want failure atomicity over the individual commands that compile and link object files.

Semantic-based concurrency control

After make has recursively ensured the consistency of the prerequisite files, it executes the `make-consistent` operation on the target file. The `make-consistent` operation

1) reads the last modified time of the target file and its prerequisite files and then
2) executes the associated command if any prerequisite file is newer than the target file.

Two `make-consistent` operations on the same target file commute. Figure 5 restates the interleaving from Figure 4 in terms of `make-consistent` operations.

T_{bar} : `make-consistent shared1.o`
T_{foo} : `make-consistent shared1.o`
T_{foo} : `make-consistent shared2.o`
T_{bar} : `make-consistent shared2.o`
T_{bar} : `make-consistent bar`
T_{foo} : `make-consistent foo`

Figure 5: The interleaving from Figure 4 in terms of `make-consistent` operations

The schedule in Figure 5 is not cyclic because the `make-consistent` operations commute.

5 MOVING AND EDITING A LARGE DOCUMENT

Consider a distributed object system in which a user may move documents from one location to another. A user may decide to move a document from one location to another to improve the performance of accessing the document or to manage the use of secondary storage. Suppose the document is large and it takes several hours to complete the move over a wide-area network. It would be desirable to allow a user to also edit the document while it is being moved. Similarly, an edit session takes an arbitrarily long period of time; it is desirable to allow the move to proceed concurrently while the document is being edited.

Program code accesses the document by supplying an object identifier (OID) for it. An OID uniquely identifies an object independent of its location.

We assume that the system is described in terms of objects. To make the example concrete, we give the interfaces to the objects involved in the move and edit.

The interface to the document is:

```
interface document {
      move(location)
      edit()
  }
```

The document is a composed of a set of paragraph objects, that is, it is a nested object [Martin, 1987; Martin, 1988a]. The interface to a paragraph is

```
interface paragraph {
      move(location)
      edit()
  }
```

Each paragraph and the document itself are identified by OIDs. The state of a paragraph object is simple text. The state of the document is the ordered set of OIDs of the paragraphs in the document.

Although OIDs are location independent for application programs, the message delivery system must maintain a mapping between OIDs and locations. OIDs in the system are bound to a particular location using a shared location object, referred to as the `map`. When a message is sent to an object, the message delivery system obtains the binding from the map.[1] If an OID has previously been bound to a location, the state of the object at the old location is effectively lost after binding the OID to a new location. The object then resides at the new location and messages will be delivered to the new location.

The interface to the `map` is via two functions:

```
void WRITE_loc(OID,location)
location READ_loc(OID)
```

The document object stores the OIDs of the contained paragraph objects in a `block`. Similarly, a paragraph object uses a block to store text. The location values returned by the `map` are meaningful identifiers of blocks. A block is at a fixed location and has the functional interface:

```
READ(location, buffer)
WRITE(location, buffer)
```

The `READ` operation transfers the block's state to the buffer. The `WRITE` operation assigns the state of the block to be that of the buffer.

Figure 6 gives a graphical representation of the document and the map.

5.1 MOVING THE DOCUMENT

To move a paragraph, the location of the text is found using `READ_loc`, the text is read from the block, the `map` is updated with the new location using `WRITE_loc` and the text is written at the new location.

The move of a single paragraph must be failure atomic, i.e. we want the read of the text, the update of the location map and the write of the text to happen or none of them to happen. We do not want the location of the paragraph to be set to the new location without writing the text to the new location.

[1] Logically, there is a *single* map. For efficiency and availability, it may be replicated with appropriate algorithms for maintaining the replicas consistent.

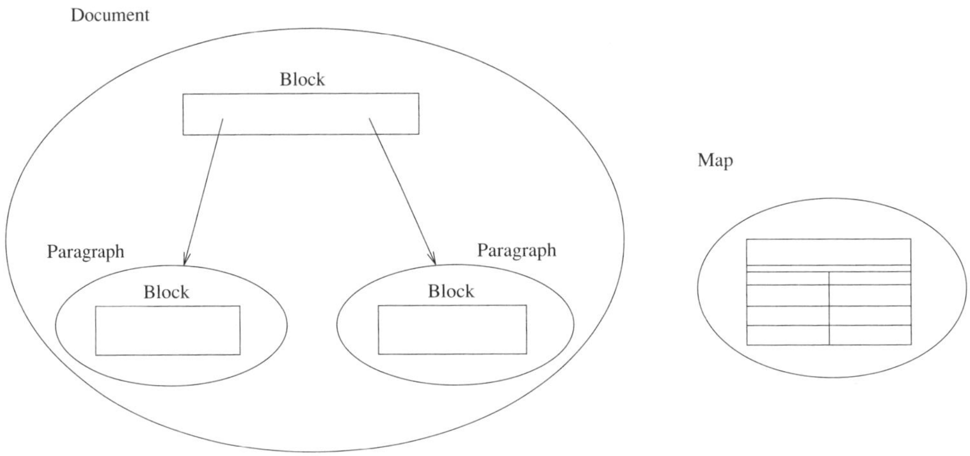

Figure 6: The document and its components

Moving the document implies moving the block storing the OIDs of the contained paragraphs and executing the move operation on each of the contained paragraphs.

The document `move` operation should also be failure atomic, that is, it should move all of the paragraphs or none of them.

5.2 EDITING THE DOCUMENT

While the document is being moved, users would like to be able to edit it. Waiting several hours until the move completes is unacceptable. An editing session consists of editing a sequence of paragraph objects. The user identifies the paragraph being edited by positioning the cursor on the textual representation of it on the screen. When the user moves the cursor to the screen representation of the paragraph, the editor reads the text of the paragraph and accepts the user's updates. When the user moves the cursor off the screen representation of the paragraph, the editor writes the updated text of the paragraph.

The edit operation on a paragraph guarantees that the updates will all happen or none of them will happen. If a failure occurs, at most the updates to a single paragraph will be lost. The edit operation on the document makes no failure atomicity guarantees. It does, however, guarantee that updates to the document will be serialized with other concurrent edits and concurrent moves.

5.3 TRADITIONAL TRANSACTIONS

We now consider using traditional read-write transactions and discuss the inadequacies of the approach. We assume T_{move}, a transaction that moves the document and T_{edit}, a transaction that edits the document. Since these are traditional transactions, they are described as sequences of `READ` and `WRITE` operations of blocks and the `map`. The higher level semantics of the `edit` and `move` operations on the paragraphs and the documents are not apparent.

Consider the T_{move} transaction given in Figure 7. T_{move} (1) obtains the location of the block storing the OIDs of the contained paragraphs of the document, (2) reads that location into a local array of OIDS called `mpgraphs`, (3) sets the new location of the document, and (4) writes the local array of paragraph OIDS at the new location.

Then, for each paragraph *i*, T_{move} (5) reads the location of paragraph *i* using the OID stored in the `mpgraphs` array, (6) reads the paragraph's text stored in the block, (7) writes the new location for paragraph *i*,[2] and (8) writes the text buffer to the new location.

```
transaction move(oid,nloc)
    1) mloc = READ_loc(oid)
    2) READ(mloc, mpgraphs)
    3) WRITE_loc(oid,nloc)
    4) WRITE(nloc,mpgraphs)

       for (i=0; i<no_paragraphs; i++) {
          5) mloc = READ_loc(mpgraphs[i])
          6) READ(mloc, mtext)
          7) WRITE_loc(mpgraphs[i], f(nloc,i))
          8) WRITE(f(nloc,i),mtext)
       }
end_transaction
```

Figure 7: Traditional transaction to move the document

Similarly, for each paragraph *i*, identified by the user, the traditional transaction T_{edit} does the sequence of `READ` and `WRITE` operations given in Figure 8.

```
1)  eloc = READ_loc(epgraphs[i])
2)  READ(eloc, textbuffer)
3)  update textbuffer until user moves the cursor
4)  eloc = READ_loc(epgraphs[i])
5)  WRITE(eloc, textbuffer)
```

Figure 8: Edit of a paragraph *i*: part of the transaction to edit the document

T_{edit} (1) reads the location of paragraph *i*, (2) reads that location into a local buffer of text, (3) updates the textbuffer until the user moves the cursor outside the paragraph, (4) reads the location of the paragraph, and (5) writes the text to the block at that location. Note that the `edit` operation of a single paragraph is arbitrarily long in duration because it involves the user.

The need for concurrency control

Concurrent access to the paragraphs and the location object must be controlled or inconsistencies can result. Figure 9 gives an interleaving of steps 5-8 of Figure 7 and steps 1-5

[2] Note that `f(nloc,i)` in steps 7 and 8, is a function whose value is a location of paragraph *i*, given the location of the document containing paragraph i.

of Figure 8. This interleaving is incorrect. The user's updates to paragraph i are lost. The system should prohibit such interleavings from happening.

T_{edit} : `eloc = READ_loc(epgraphs[i])`
T_{edit} : `READ(eloc, textbuffer)`
T_{move}: `mloc = READ_loc(mpgraphs[i])`
T_{move}: `READ(mloc, mtext)`
T_{edit} : `eloc = READ_loc(epgraphs[i])`
T_{edit} : `WRITE(eloc, textbuffer)`
T_{move}: `WRITE_loc(mpgraphs[i], f(nloc,i))`
T_{move}: `WRITE(f(nloc,i),mtext)`

Figure 9: An incorrect interleaving: the user's updates are lost.

Read-write serializability

On the other hand, traditional read-write serializability is too strict. The interleaving of

T_{edit} : `eloc = READ_loc(epgraphs[i])`
T_{edit} : `READ(eloc, textbuffer)`
T_{move} : `mloc = READ_loc(mpgraphs[i])`
T_{move} : `READ(mloc, mtext)`
T_{move} : `WRITE_loc(mpgraphs[i], f(nloc,i))`
T_{move} : `WRITE(f(nloc,i),mtext)`
T_{edit} : `eloc = READ_loc(epgraphs[i])`
T_{edit} : `WRITE(eloc, textbuffer)`

Figure 10: A correct, but "cyclic" interleaving

Figure 10 is considered incorrect in the traditional transaction model because it is not read-write serializable. T_{move} writes paragraph i in T_{move} : `WRITE(f(nloc,i),mtext)` after T_{edit} reads it in T_{edit} : `READ(eloc,textbuffer)` but before T_{edit} writes it in T_{edit} : `WRITE(eloc,textbuffer)`. The interleaving is semantically correct. We know that the move did not update the state of the paragraph, it only read it and wrote it to transfer it to another location. Furthermore, this interleaving is highly desirable because the move operation on paragraph i executes while the user edits paragraph i.

We note that in a strict two-phase locking [Eswaran et al., 1976] environment, other activities would be prohibited from accessing the document while it is being moved. They would be blocked waiting for the *move* to commit or abort. Assuming the message delivery system accesses the `map` via `READ_loc` when sending all messages, the situation is even worse with two-phase locking. All concurrent activities in the system are blocked while the document is being moved since the `map` remains locked. A traditional, two-phase locking transaction is clearly not the solution.

5.4 EXTENDED TRANSACTIONS

To preserve isolation, a distributed object system supporting concurrent execution of edit and move of the large document needs the following characteristics.

Semantic-based concurrency control

By introducing return-value commutativity semantics [Weihl, 1988], the interleaving in Figure 10 can be considered correct. T_{edit}: `READ` and T_{move}: `WRITE` of the same block commute because they read and write the same value. No ordering dependency is established and thus the interleaving is not considered cyclic.

Further semantics can be utilized in the system to limit order dependencies between concurrent activities. The `READ_loc(x)` and `WRITE_loc(y, loc)` operations on the `map` commute if $x \neq y$. By utilizing these simple semantics, order dependencies are not established between the move and every concurrent activity that sends messages.

Layers of abstraction

The use of semantics at a single layer of abstraction is not enough. Even when considering the return-value commutativity semantics of read and write, the interleaving of Figure 11 is still considered cyclic if we do not consider the semantics of the paragraph object. We can argue the correctness of the interleaving in Figure 11 by using semantics at multiple levels.

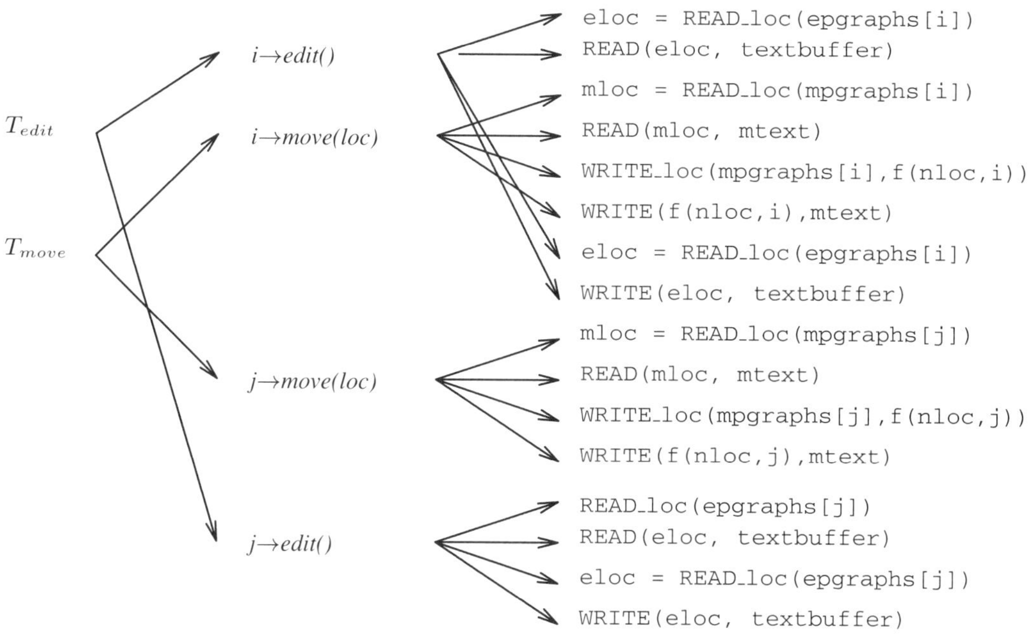

Figure 11: Another correct, but "cyclic" interleaving

Note that moving and editing paragraph *i* are commutative operations. Executed in either order, the result is a moved and edited paragraph. This fact allows multi-level schedulers to ignore order dependencies established at the `block` level. However the order dependencies of the suboperations of commutative operations cannot form cycles. For example, even though order dependencies between $i\rightarrow$ $edit()$ and $i\rightarrow$ $move()$ can be ignored, they cannot be interleaved as in Figure 9.

We might be tempted to schedule only at the level of the paragraphs. If so, the move and edit operations of paragraph i execute serially. This would be inadequate because it would not allow the move of the document to proceed while paragraph i was being edited. Interleaving the suboperations of the move and edit of a paragraph is required because the user's updates are part of the paragraph edit operation. Scheduling using semantics at multiple levels of abstraction is required to concurrently edit and move the document.

Separate boundaries of transaction guarantees

Traditional transactions provide the same boundaries of guarantees for serializability, failure atomicity and permanence of effect. This is too inflexible for the example. The move requires serializability and failure atomicity for the entire document. On the other hand, the editor requires that updates to a single paragraph are failure atomic but not the updates to the entire document. The edit of the document must be serialized with concurrent edits and moves.

6 CONCURRENTLY UPDATING SOFTWARE

Consider a Computer-Aided-Software-Engineering (CASE) environment. The environment supports multiple programmers designing, coding and testing software systems. Central to the CASE environment is a global database maintaining all of the software artifacts. The database stores the interface and implementation(s) of a procedure as separate objects.

The CASE database maintains the global consistency requirement that an interface matches all the implementations of it and all calls to it. That is, the parameter and return value types defined by the interface are consistent in the implementations of the interface and calls to the interface in other implementations. Thus for example, a programmer that is going to change the definition of the *foo* interface must also consistently change any objects that call and implement *foo*.

Consider a programmer Bill. Bill decides to change the *foo* interface, named `foo-interface`. He must also change the implementation of *foo*, named `foo-impl` and the single call to *foo* in the *bar* implementation, `bar-impl`.

Independently, another programmer, Dave, decides to update the *bar* interface, named `bar-interface`. Besides `bar-interface`, Dave must also change `bar-impl` and the single call to *bar* in the *foo* implementation, `foo-impl`.

Bill and Dave want to minimize any lost work due to failures or inconsistencies. Since the updates that Bill is making take a relatively long period of time, Dave does not want to wait until Bill finishes. Similarly, Dave does not want to wait until Bill finishes. They want to work concurrently, even if they must cooperate to maintain global consistency.

Notice that Bill and Dave are both concurrently updating `foo-impl` and `bar-impl`. The CASE system needs to control this in some fashion or inconsistent updates can result. For example, if Bill and Dave are allowed to update `bar-impl` and `foo-impl` in an uncontrolled fashion, the CASE database may contain Bill's `bar-impl` without the changes Dave made to it to be consistent with the new definition of `foo-interface`.

6.1 TRADITIONAL TRANSACTIONS

The traditional transaction model is inappropriate. Failure atomicity implies that in the presence of a failure, all updates made by Bill and Dave will be lost. Bill and Dave have no ability to participate in failure recovery. Furthermore, in a traditional environment, no real-time guarantees are made. Just guaranteeing that the updates will eventually be made or never be made is insufficient. Bill and Dave prefer to cooperate in order to meet real time constraints.

We explain these observations further in terms of a pessimistic, two-phase locking environment. In such an environment, the following interleaving is possible:

> Bill write locks and updates `foo-interface`
> Dave write locks and begins updating `bar-interface`
> Bill write locks and updates `foo-impl`
> Bill write locks and updates `bar-impl`
> Bill commits `foo-interface, foo-impl, bar-impl`
> Dave write locks and updates `bar-impl`
> Dave write locks and updates `foo-impl`

This interleaving is undesirable. Dave waits a long time for Bill to commit before he works on `bar-impl`.

An even more undesirable interleaving could happen:

> Bill write locks and updates `foo-interface`
> Bill write locks and begins updating `foo-impl`
> Dave write locks and updates `bar-interface`
> Dave write locks and begins updating `bar-impl`
> Dave blocks waiting for the write lock `foo-impl`
> Bill blocks waiting for the write lock `bar-impl`

Poor Bill and Dave have deadlocked. Each need objects held by the other. In a traditional transaction environment, this deadlock would be detected and the work of either Bill or Dave would be aborted. This is unacceptable. Neither Bill nor Dave want to lose work.

Optimistic concurrency control is also inappropriate. Optimistic concurrency control validates the resulting interleaving at commit time and aborts transactions as needed so that the resulting interleaving is serializable. Again, this is unacceptable. Neither Bill nor Dave want to lose work.

6.2 EXTENDED TRANSACTIONS

An obvious solution is for Bill and Dave to cooperate in changing `foo-impl` and `bar-impl`. Their cooperation can be isolated from other concurrent activities. We use the term *cooperative atomicity* to describe isolated cooperation.

Cooperative atomicity
Bill and Dave's activities cannot be serialized with respect to each other. The effects on the interface and implementation objects are not necessarily the same as if Bill had performed his updates and then Dave had performed his updates, or vice versa. For

example, Dave's partial changes to `bar-interface` may influence Bill's changes to `foo-impl`.

Bill and Dave need to share a set of objects and coordinate their updates to them. On the other hand, Bill and Dave's cooperative activity can be viewed as a single atomic activity by other concurrent activities. They can be serialized with respect to Bill and Dave's cooperative activity.

We note that just as it was unacceptable for Bill and Dave's activities to be isolated from each other, it may be unacceptable for another activity to be isolated from Bill and Dave's cooperative activity. If Bill and Dave agree, the activity can become part of their cooperation. However, as the cooperative activity grows, coordinating the cooperation becomes more complex.

Bill and Dave's cooperation establishes termination dependencies. Neither can unilaterally commit or abort the changes to the software. Similarly, if Bill should decide to restore a set of objects to some previous state, he must cooperate with Dave.

Bill and Dave both began their tasks of changing `foo-interface` and `bar-interface` independently, that is without knowing of each others' activities. There must be some mechanism for them to learn about each other and their need to cooperate.

7 ARRANGING MEETING ROOMS

Consider two individuals, William and Daniel, trying to book rooms for meetings starting at the same time. We will illustrate how humans naturally solve the occurring conflicts by breaking organizational guidelines, but in an isolated manner.

The organization has two meeting rooms. A big meeting room, Extravagant, seats 25 people. It has several facilities for meetings, including a 35mm slide projector and an electronic white board. The organization also has a smaller room, Humble, that only seats eight people and is equipped with the most basic facilities.

Several of the pieces of equipment in Extravagant are mobile. For the ease of administration, organizational guidelines state that this equipment will be available in Extravagant. This avoids a separate booking scheme for these resources and avoids having to move them in an out of a separate storage room every time they are used. Thus, individuals who are arranging either large meetings or meetings needing sophisticated equipment book Extravagant.

Daniel is arranging a meeting involving 18 people. For the purpose of this meeting Daniel has booked Extravagant. This meeting will have several presentations using many of the facilities of the room, but not the 35mm projector.

William is arranging a meeting of four people starting at the same time. He has a set of 35mm slides he wants to show and would therefore like to use Extravagant. But Daniel has already booked it.

7.1 TRADITIONAL TRANSACTIONS

It is not possible to model the situation with traditional transactions. Both William and Daniel require Extravagant at the same time. William needs it to get the projector and Daniel to get enough seats. With the traditional transaction model, the two meetings cannot take place at the same time. One of the meetings will have to be cancelled.

7.2 EXTENDED TRANSACTIONS

This problem is easily solved if William and Daniel cooperate. William contacts Daniel and requests to borrow the projector so that he can hold the meeting in Humble. Their decision to also use Humble and temporarily move the projector can be considered in isolation from other concurrent activities. This is another example of cooperative atomicity.

Cooperative atomicity

Their two meetings can be considered to be one atomic event that can be serialized with respect to other concurrent activities. However, William and Daniel's meetings cannot be serialized with respect to each other. They cooperate by moving the projector from Extravagant to Humble and back again.

To ensure other concurrent activities do not observe Extravagant without the projector, Daniel cannot finish his meeting before William has moved it back. Similarly, Daniel cannot unilaterally decide to cancel the meeting. William would be left without the projector. Daniel would have to notify William so he can transfer the booking.

Again, we note that the cooperation was unplanned. The two activities needed to learn about each other in order to establish cooperation.

8 SUMMARY OF EXTENSIONS

Using the five examples of long-lived concurrent activities, we demonstrated the inadequacies of the traditional transaction model. From the examples we identified a dichotomy of extensions: three that preserve transaction isolation and one that isolates cooperation.

8.1 PRESERVING ISOLATION

By preserving isolation, it remains easy to program concurrent activities. The first three preserve transaction isolation by capturing application semantics and abstractions and by providing flexible boundaries of transaction guarantees.

Semantic-based concurrency control

Commutativity allows programmers to provide information about correct ordering of operations on an object. This semantic information allows interleavings that would be considered incorrect with read-write serializability to be considered correct. Concurrent activities can be programmed in isolation, that is without considering interleavings of other concurrent activities. The shared desk top, the make and the move examples all illustrated the need for semantic-based concurrency control.

Layers of abstraction

By considering the layers of abstraction of a concurrent activity, low level ordering dependencies can be ignored when higher level operations commute. This allows a class of concurrent activities to execute concurrently for long periods of time and still be programmed in isolation. The move and edit example demonstrated the need to consider layers of abstraction. The low level ordering dependencies of read and write operations of a block could be ignored at the paragraph level because the move and edit operations of a paragraph commute.

Separate boundaries of transaction guarantees

Providing the same boundary for failure atomicity and serializability is inflexible. Programmers should be able to specify different boundaries for each. The make and move examples illustrated the need for this extension. The make example required failure atomicity for a single command but serializability over the execution of make. Similarly, the edit operation on the document required failure atomicity for a single paragraph but serializable with respect to other edit and move operations.

8.2 ISOLATING COOPERATION

In general, concurrent activities cooperate when they explicitly exchange partial results in order to achieve their goals. The CASE and the meeting room examples, however, required a more restricted form of cooperation which we denoted as cooperative atomicity.

Cooperative atomicity

A group of concurrent activities cooperate atomically when they isolate their cooperation from other concurrent activities. Internally, the cooperating activities can be viewed as a *concurrent program* in which the activities themselves are involved in synchronizing their access to shared data. Externally, other concurrent activities view the group as a single action and are scheduled with respect to the group as a whole. The generality and pitfalls of concurrent programming are localized to the concurrent activities participating in the group.

Cooperating concurrent activities cannot unilaterally terminate since the activities cooperate in maintaining global consistency. The CASE and meeting examples illustrated this. Daniel could not finish his meeting before William returned the projector. Furthermore, Daniel could not cancel his meeting without notifying William.

Similarly, cooperating concurrent activities must cooperate if one is going to restore some objects to prior states. For example, if Dave were to undo his updates to `foo-impl`, it could affect Bill's later updates `foo-impl`.

Note that the concurrent activities which cooperate may have to be determined dynamically. That is, statically specifying the group is not powerful enough. In the CASE example, Bill did not know the identity of Dave *a priori*. It was during their activities that they decided to cooperate. The meeting room example illustrated the same requirement of unplanned cooperation.

9 RELATED WORK

The extensions presented in this paper are related to extended transaction models proposed in the literature. Although none of the models supports all of the examples, we have shown how some of the concepts introduced by the models together support long-lived concurrent activities. We will now briefly discuss how these models relate to the presented extensions.

Commutativity of operations is described in [Weihl, 1988]. *Typed locks* [Schwarz and Spector, 1984] embody the use of commutativity in a two-phase locking environment. Commutativity was used in the shared desk top, make and move examples. Commutativity is important for supporting long-lived concurrent activities because it allows apparent ordering dependencies to be eliminated.

The use of semantics is not limited to concurrency control. In [Badrinath and Ramamritham, 1987], the authors introduce *recoverability* as an expanded use of semantics in transaction management beyond commutativity. Recoverability limits abort dependencies between transactions. All commutative operations are recoverable but not all recoverable actions are commutative. For example, *push(X) and* push(Y) on a shared stack do not commute but they are recoverable. If transaction T_i executes *push(X)* and T_j executes *push(Y)* and then later T_i aborts, T_j need not be aborted as well. Without the use of stack semantics, T_j would also have to be aborted since it observed intermediate results of T_i. Although our examples do not illustrate the need for recoverability, it is important for supporting long-lived concurrent activities because it allows apparent abort dependencies to be eliminated.

In [Martin, 1987; Martin, 1988a] a model of *nested objects* is presented. The model allows programmers to specify the algorithm implementing an operation in isolation. It requires programmers to specify commutativity relations for each type of object at multiple levels of abstraction. However, the reasoning is localized to considering pairs of operations on a single type. The correctness notion of the model incorporates the commutativity relations at multiple levels of abstraction. The nested object model characterizes the concurrency control requirements of the move and edit example presented in Section 5 but does not address its failure atomicity requirements. Nested objects are important for supporting long-lived concurrent activities because ordering dependencies established in the implementations of commutative operations can be systematically ignored.

The *saga* model [Garcia-Molina and Salem, 1987] is a refinement of the model proposed in [Garcia-Molina, 1983]. A *saga* consists of a number of transactions and corresponding compensating actions. It is assumed that the transactions can be interleaved in any way with other transactions. If a failure occurs, compensating actions will be executed to compensate for the effects of the transactions that have executed. Sagas separate the boundaries of serializability and failure atomicity. The unit of serializability is the individual transaction and the unit of failure atomicity is the entire saga. The unit of failure atomicity always encloses the unit of serializability.

Glued actions [Shrivastava and Wheater, 1990] separates the boundaries of transaction guarantees. A set of glued actions is serializable while each individual action is failure atomic. In the event of a failure, only the effects of the currently executing action are undone. As opposed to sagas, the unit of serializability always encloses the unit of failure atomicity.

Split-transactions [Pu et al., 1988] enable a transaction to split into two new transactions that will be serializable with respect to each other. The split operation associates subsets of the data with each of the new transactions. It can be used to define a boundary of failure atomicity relative to a subset of data. This occurs when a split partitions the data into two disjoint subsets. After the split, one of the transactions commits a subset and the other continues. The *join* operator introduced along with the split allows two independent transactions to become one and share uncommitted data. One of the transactions identifies the other and performs the join. Sequences of split and join can partly support the CASE example. Bill and Dave can exchange uncommitted data by joining and then splitting their activities. However, one could commit or abort the other's changes without his consensus.

Transaction groups [Skarra and Zdonik, 1989] provide a notion similar to cooperative atomicity. A transaction group (TG) consists of a set of *cooperating transactions* but is viewed as an atomic event outside the TG. A cooperating transaction can itself be a TG.

Local correctness notions can be defined for a TG through *semantic patterns* and *conflicts*. Semantic patterns declaratively define the required interleavings of the cooperating transactions within a TG. Similarly, *conflicts* define illegal interleavings. The model enables transactions to cooperate without forcing the programmer to deal with the full generality of concurrent programming. Like commutativity relations, patterns and conflicts are declarations about interleavings. Unlike commutativity, a programmer specifying patterns and conflicts must consider multiple types and instances of objects.

Finally, as a framework for characterizing the models in more detail we recommend [Chrysanthis and Ramamritham, 1990]. We found it useful, especially for describing termination dependencies.

10 CONCLUSION

Implementing long-lived concurrent activities is complicated without high level support. The guarantees provided by the traditional transaction model are valuable because they isolate reasoning about concurrent activities. We believe that these guarantees should be provided as widely as possible. We demonstrated the need for four extensions to the traditional transaction model. Together these extensions support the long-lived concurrent activities presented here. Three of the extensions preserve the guarantees and isolation of the traditional transaction model. The three extensions are semantic-based concurrency control, layers of abstraction and separate boundaries for transaction guarantees.

Some activities are inherently cooperative. Serializability is not a valid correctness notion for such activities. It may be impossible for the activities to produce effects that could have been obtained through serial execution of the activities. We identified cooperative atomicity as an extension that supports cooperation.

Cooperative atomicity is the encapsulation of a group of concurrent activities whose effects can be viewed as single atomic event. The group as a whole is serialized with respect to other atomic events. Cooperative atomicity implies that termination and restoration dependencies are established between cooperating activities.

We have not defined how cooperating activities synchronize with each other. We consider that to be a problem that is closely related to concurrent programming and recommend looking to the programming language community for appropriate solutions.

Cooperative atomicity is an acceptance of the need for programmers to explicitly handle concurrency in long-lived concurrent activities. We believe it is a necessary, but not very desirable, solution. The example of moving and editing a large document illustrated that the isolation provided by execution guarantees from traditional transactions can be pushed very far before it is necessary to resort to cooperative atomicity.

An Activity/Transaction Model for a Distributed Multi-Service System

Umeshwar Dayal*
Hewlett-Packard Laboratories
1501 Page Mill Road, Mail Stop 3U-4
Palo Alto, CA 94304
U.S.A.

Abstract

Complex enterprises support heterogeneous, distributed, multi-service computing environments. Many activities in these enterprises are of long duration and consist of multiple steps that require different services and that may involve interaction with multiple individuals. Concurrent activities have to be synchronized and made reliable against failures. Current technology provides only transactions as atomic execution units. However, enforcing the strict concurrency and failure atomicity properties of transactions is difficult and expensive in a heterogeneous, distributed multi-service environment. Also, activities typically have weaker requirements than transactions. This paper gives an overview of an Activity/Transaction Model that introduces activities as execution units in addition to transactions, and defines the semantics of activities. The model supports concurrent execution of steps, communication among steps, and rich failure semantics, including compensation, exception handling, and roll forward.

1 INTRODUCTION

Typically, business computing environments consist of a number of *services*, each of which automates some business function or collection of functions (e.g., order entry, inventory, accounting, billing). Many of these services may use resource managers such as file systems

*This work was done while the author was at DEC Cambridge Research Laboratory, Cambridge, MA. Joint work with Mei Hsu, DEC Activity Management Group, Mountain View, CA; and Rivka Ladin, DEC Cambridge Research Laboratory, Cambridge, MA.

or database management systems to store and access the data they need. In a large enterprise, each service may be implemented by one or more servers on different hardware and software platforms interconnected by a network. Each service may be encapsulated as an object, whose interface specifies the functions offered by the service, and whose implementation describes how the functions are realized (perhaps by invoking the functions of other services, executing application programs, or interacting with users). Client applications interact with a service by invoking the functions specified at its interface.

Currently, these services represent isolated islands of automation. However, as the enterprise becomes more integrated, complex applications are developed to automate business processes that need to span several of these services. These applications typically consist of many steps, which may be of long duration, may require one or more services from the heterogeneous, distributed multi-service environment, and may involve interaction with multiple individuals and multiple organizational units of the enterprise. We call such applications *long running activities* (LRAs). An example of an LRA is making travel arrangements to attend a conference: this activity is initiated by an employee filling out a travel request; the request is passed to the employee's manager for budget approval, and to the security department for clearance; then it is passed to accounting for generating a registration cheque, and issuing a cash advance; and from there to the travel coordinator to make flight, hotel, and car reservations. Other examples of LRAs include purchase order processing, service request processing, claims processing, patient tracking, planning and scheduling, controlling scientific experiments or simulations, and manufacturing processes.

Organizing and managing LRAs in a distributed, multi-service environment poses several problems. The flow of control and data between the steps of an LRA has to be specified and orchestrated. Because the steps may access shared data resources, they need to be synchronized among themselves and with the steps of other concurrently executing LRAs. Steps or servers may fail; LRAs must be made reliable against such failures.

In Section 2, we describe the limitations of current technology for dealing with LRAs. In Section 3, we give an overview of our approach, including highlights of our Activity/Transaction Model for LRAs. (For details, the reader is referred to [Dayal et al., 1990a; Dayal et al., 1991].) Then, in Section 4, we compare our model with related work.

2 INADEQUACY OF TRANSACTIONS

Current technology for building robust applications that access shared data resources is confined to the use of *transactions*, which are guaranteed to be *atomic* (either all of a transaction's effects are visible, or none are), *serializable* (the interleaved execution of transactions is equivalent to a serial execution), and *permanent* (effects of committed transactions are never rolled back).

Treating an entire LRA as a single transaction is expensive or impossible in a multi-service environment. It may lead to excessive lock conflicts, severely limiting concurrency, and delaying short transactions. When several distributed servers are involved, guaranteeing atomicity requires expensive two-phase commit processing, and requires that all servers be operational simultaneously. The problems are exacerbated in a heterogeneous environment, because servers with disparate concurrency control protocols have to be coordinated, and some of the servers may be incapable of participating in commit processing (because internal transaction states such as *prepare_to_commit* are unobservable).

LRAs usually have weaker concurrency and failure atomicity requirements than transactions. In the travel arrangements example, it may be acceptable to release locks on budget records after the manager's approval step, and before the accounting or reservation steps. Also, when a step (e.g., reserving a hotel) fails, it is usually undesirable to roll the LRA all the way back to the beginning, thus losing several hours or days of work.[1]

Alternatively, each step of an LRA may be modelled as a transaction. However, in most transaction processing (TP) systems, the control flow among the steps is embedded in the application programs, and this renders it difficult to change or understand. Also, there is no system support for failure handling over the entire LRA. Some TP systems do provide chaining primitives or a task definition language for specifying flows; however, even these do not support failure semantics over a flow.

Furthermore, transactions are typically used to make a single user application robust, whereas LRAs require the integration of multiple applications (services) involving multiple users.

3 OVERVIEW OF OUR APPROACH

In our approach, *activities* are treated explicitly as units of execution. An activity consists of multiple steps (called *actions*), each of which is an activity or a transaction. Actions may be nested to arbitrary levels (with the proviso that activities may not be nested within transactions), and may execute sequentially or concurrently. Control and data flow within an action is specified statically via a predefined *script*; but may also be dynamically modified through *rules* whose execution is triggered by events. Actually, actions are organized in *classes*, and each class has a script that defines the actions nested within it, their execution scopes, and the control and data flow among them. Each action may include requests for one or more services (essentially, the invocation of functions defined for the service objects). The script language includes constructs for sequential and parallel execution, iteration, and branching; and supports the passing of data between actions. In addition, Event-Condition-Action rules ([Dayal et al., 1988a; Dayal et al., 1990b]) may be used to modify the flow: when the event specified in the rule is detected, the specified condition is evaluated; if the condition is satisfied, then the corresponding action is triggered (as a nested action of the activity).

The program creating an activity is returned a *handle* for the activity. The handle may be used to query the *status* and *history* of the activity, or to *abort* the activity.

The execution of activities and nested actions is governed by the Activity/Transaction Model (ATM), which is based on an extended nested transaction model.

In the conventional nested transaction model of [Moss, 1985], transactions can be nested within other transactions, forming a transaction tree. A child transaction has access to the data locked by its parent; it is atomic with respect to its parent and its siblings; it is serializable with its siblings; and it becomes permanent only if its parent does. A parent commits only after all its children have terminated.

[1] Several research efforts (e.g., [Breitbart et al., 1990a]) are aimed at developing protocols for guaranteeing concurrency and failure atomicity of *global* transactions in heterogeneous, multidatabase systems. Such protocols are inefficient, and usually unnecessary: we believe that, in many cases, the applications are better modelled as LRAs rather than as transactions.

In the extended nested transaction model (described in [Hsu et al., 1988]), a nested transaction may execute in a different scope from its parent (who created it), depending on the *mode* specified for it. Three modes are supported. The *immediate* mode corresponds exactly to the conventional nested transaction, where the execution scope is the parent. In the *deferred* mode, a child transaction is executed in the scope of the top transaction (i.e., the root of the transaction tree), rather than in its parent's scope (i.e., the child transaction executes after the normal operations of the top transaction have finished). In the *decoupled* mode, the child transaction is executed as a separate top transaction. Optionally, in the decoupled mode, a *causality* constraint can be imposed, which specifies that the child transaction can commit only if the parent (creator) commits, and the child follows the parent in the serialization order. The deferred mode is useful for checking integrity constraints (e.g., travel_budget_balance > 0) or for propagating updates to derived data. The decoupled mode with causality is useful for chaining related actions that do not have to execute in a single transaction (e.g., schedule_ meetings can execute in a separate transaction that is causally dependent on reserve_flights, so that if the latter aborts, it will abort too). The decoupled mode without causality is useful for independent actions (e.g., order_tourist_brochures is independent of reserve_flights).

ATM extends this model further to include activities. Activities differ from transactions in that the child of an activity can commit independently of its parent, and the children of an activity are not required to be serializable. However, as with nested transactions, a child action has access to its parent activity's data, and a parent activity can commmit only after all its children terminate.

Aborting an activity results in aborting all its active children. However, committed children have to be compensated for. The model allows compensation actions to be specified with each action in the script.

Not all actions may be compensatable (e.g., mailing a cheque). It is undesirable to allow the effects of non-compensatable actions to become visible (permanent) until some ancestor activity commits. To get this behaviour, an action may be defined as *critical*, which means that its effects do not become permanent until its first non-critical ancestor commits. (For example, the action to mail a registration cheque may not be committed until the entire travel arrangements activity commits.)

Extensive exception handling is supported, the goal being to avoid (unless necessary) aborting an activity if an action within it fails. One or more exception handlers are associated with each action, and are invoked by the action's parent if the action fails. If the exception handler terminates successfully, then the parent can continue (thus the activity makes forward progress). Otherwise, the parent starts an alternate execution path or itself aborts and passes the exception up the action tree. The desired behaviour is encoded in the parent action's script or is dynamically invoked via rules.

The execution of rules is also governed by ATM. The condition and action parts of rules are evaluated inside nested actions with execution scopes specified in the rules.

ATM is appropriate for building reliable applications in multi-service environments because it reduces the need to coordinate the execution of concurrency control and commit protocols over heterogeneous resource managers. For each service requested, a nested action can be started. Most transactions can execute purely locally. The effect of non-fatal failures can be localized, and the whole activity can continue to make forward progress. Only if the extra atomicity guarantees are required, is it necessary to execute a distributed transaction across multiple resource managers.

4 RELATED WORK

Early workflow models that were developed mostly for office or business procedures include some notion of tasks, with workflow among tasks specified by triggers or augmented Petri nets. However, these models were not transactional, and hence did not address the problems of shared data access and failure recovery.

Transactions support shared data access and failure recovery, but we have argued that the conventional transaction model is too strict for LRAs, and too expensive to support in a heterogeneous, distributed environment.

Several other extended transaction models for LRAs have been proposed in the literature: sagas [Garcia-Molina and Salem, 1987], migrating transactions [Klein and Reuter, 1988], contracts [Reuter, 1989], multi-transaction activities [Garcia-Molina et al., 1990], flexible transactions [Elmagarmid et al., 1990], open transactions [Weikum and Schek, 1992], and the Reliable Flow Manager activity model [Hsu et al., 1991]. While these models are similar in spirit to ATM, there are some differences. Some are based on flat transactions. ATM is based on nested transactions, so the activity definer has flexibility in specifying intra- and inter-step parallelism. Most of the other models support only two levels of nesting: activities and transactions. ATM supports arbitrarily nested subactivities. Also, ATM has rich failure semantics, supporting rollback with compensation, rollforward, and alternate execution paths. Typically, the other models support only fixed control flow and a rigid compensation policy. ATM allows both static specification of flows and dynamic modification through rules. None of these other models have rules. The DOM transaction model of [Buchmann et al., 1992] is very similar to ATM: it is based on extended nested transactions and allows arbitarily nested activities, it supports compensation and alternate execution paths, and it allows rules to dynamically determine workflow. However, it does not have the concept of activity classes with static scripts; flows are specified only via rules. We believe that ATM's combination of classes, scripts, and rules is a powerful organizational device: complex activity classes can be built up from simpler ones; classes may inherit scripts from other classes; and rules provide flexibility in specifying constraints or responses to unanticipated situations.

Generalized transaction frameworks such as ACTA [Chrysanthis and Ramamritham, 1991] and ES [Klein, 1991] define a small number of primitive dependencies among execution units from which different transaction models can be synthesized. These frameworks could be used to define the semantics of ATM (similar to the way in which the semantics of DOM have been specified using ACTA), and could form the basis for an implementation of transactions in a heterogeneous distributed system over which ATM could be layered.

In Search of Acceptability Criteria: Database Consistency Requirements and Transaction Correctness Properties

Krithi Ramamritham
University of Massachusetts
Department of Computer Science
Amherst, MA 01003
U.S.A.

Panos K. Chrysanthis
University of Pittsburgh
Department of Computer Science
Pittsburgh, PA 15260
U.S.A.

Abstract

Whereas serializability captures *database consistency requirements* and *transaction correctness properties* via a single notion, recent research has attempted to come up with correctness criteria that view these two types of requirements independently. In this paper, we develop a taxonomy of various *correctness criteria* that focus on database consistency requirements and transaction correctness properties from the viewpoint of *what* the different dimensions of these two are. This taxonomy allows us to categorize correctness criteria that have been proposed in the literature. To help in this categorization, we have applied a uniform specification technique, based on ACTA, to express the various criteria. Such a categorization helps shed light on the similarities and differences between different criteria and to place them in perspective.

1 INTRODUCTION

Database consistency requirements capture correctness from the perspective of objects in the database – as transactions perform operations on the objects. On the other hand, *transaction correctness properties* capture correctness from the perspective of the structure and behavior of transactions. That is, they deal, for example, with the results of transactions and the interactions between transactions. Serializability [Eswaran et al., 1976] captures database consistency requirements and transaction correctness properties via a single notion: (1) The state of the database at the end of a set of concurrent transactions is the same as the one resulting from some serial execution of the same set of transactions; (2) The results of transactions and the interactions among the set of transactions are the same as the results and interactions, had the transactions executed one after another in this serial order. As applications using databases become more complex, the *correctness criteria* that are *acceptable* to the application become more complex and hence harder to capture using a single correctness notion.

Recent research has attempted to come up with correctness criteria, or *acceptability criteria*, that view these two types of requirements independently. An early example is nested transactions [Moss, 1985], in which the database consistency requirements are captured by requiring the serializability of independent (sub)transactions; additional transaction structural properties specify the correctness of subtransactions of individual nested transactions. The search for more flexible correctness requirements is further motivated by the introduction of other transaction models that extend the traditional atomic transaction model. (See [Elmagarmid, 1991] for a description of some of the *extended transaction models*.) These extensions came about because the atomic transaction model in conjunction with serializability is found to be very constraining when applied in advanced applications such as design databases that function in distributed, cooperative, and heterogeneous environments.

Proposed correctness criteria range from the standard serializability notion to eventual consistency [Sheth and Rusinkiewicz, 1990]. Quasi-serializability [Du and Elmagarmid, 1989], predicatewise serializability [Korth and Speegle, 1988], etc., are points that lie within this range. *Eventual consistency* can be viewed as a "catch-all" term with different connotations: For example, requiring consistency "at a specific real-time," "within some time" or "after a certain amount of change to some data," or enforcing consistency "after a certain value of the data is reached," etc. Whereas serializability and its relaxations are, in general, application and transaction model independent criteria, eventual consistency, as the examples above show, are application and transaction model specific. It is not difficult to see that these relaxed correctness requirements are useful within a single database as well as in multi-database environments.

Whereas serializability works under the simple assumption that individual transactions maintain the consistency of the database, proposed correctness criteria require more from the transaction developers. In particular, a transaction may have to be aware of the functionality of other transactions, especially in a cooperative environment. This makes transaction development as well as management more difficult. Our goal in this paper is to understand the conceptual similarities and differences between different correctness criteria without getting into the practical implications of adopting them.

So, in this paper we examine database consistency constraints and transaction correctness properties from the viewpoint of *what* the different dimensions of these two types of correctness are. This taxonomy allows us to categorize existing proposals thereby shedding some light on the similarities and differences between the proposals and to place them in perspective. The categorization also helps us determine whether or not a correctness notion is transaction model specific or application specific. We will see that even though some of the correctness notions were motivated by specific transaction models or specific applications, they have broader applicability.

To help in this categorization, we apply a uniform specification technique to express the various correctness criteria that have been proposed. The technique is based on the ACTA formalism [Chrysanthis and Ramamritham 1990; Chrysanthis and Ramamritham, 1991] which heretofore has been used for the specification of and for reasoning about extended transactions. One of the key ingredients of ACTA is the idea of constraining the occurrence of *significant events* associated with transactions, *Begin*, *Abort*, and *Split*, for example. These constraints are expressed in terms of necessary and sufficient conditions for events to occur. These, in turn, relate to the ordering of events and the validity of relevant conditions. Such constraints can also facilitate the specification of database consistency requirements and transaction correctness properties. The ACTA formalism is introduced in Section 3.

The rest of the paper is structured as follows: Subsection 2.1 provides a taxonomy of database consistency requirements while 2.2 provides a taxonomy of transaction correctness properties. A specification of existing proposals as well as their categorization (based on the taxonomy) is the subject of Section 4. Section 5 concludes the paper with some discussions of the next step in this work.

2 A TAXONOMY OF CORRECTNESS CRITERIA

We study different dimensions of the two aspects of correctness, namely, consistency of database state and correctness of transactions, in order to develop a taxonomy of correctness criteria. For concreteness, we give examples as the taxonomy is developed.

2.1 DATABASE CONSISTENCY REQUIREMENTS

Database consistency requirements can be examined with respect to two issues with further divisions of each as discussed below.

- *Consistency Unit:*
  - *Complete Database*:
    All the objects in the database have to be consistent locally as well as mutually consistent, i.e., they should satisfy all the database integrity constraints typically specified in the form of predicates on the state of the objects. Semantics of the objects can be taken into account to improve concurrent access to the objects while maintaining consistency [Chrysanthis et al., 1991].
    Example: Traditional serializability (SR) applied to atomic transactions [Bernstein et al., 1987].
  - *Subsets of the objects in the database*:
    * *Location-independent subsets*:
      The database is viewed as being made up of subsets of objects. The subsets are not necessarily disjoint and are specified as part of the database definition. Each object in the database is expected to be consistent locally but mutual consistency is required only for objects that are within the same subset.
      Example: Setwise serializability (SSR) applied to *compound transactions* [Sha, 1985] and Predicatewise serializability (PSR) applied to cooperative transactions [Korth et al., 1988].
    * *Location-dependent subsets*:
      Each subset corresponds to one of the sites of a (distributed heterogeneous) database. In addition to mutual consistency among objects in a subset (i.e., site), consistency among subsets is also required depending on which parts of a database are accessed by a transaction.

Example: Quasi-serializability (QSR) [Du and Elmagarmid, 1989] and its generalization [Mehrotra et al., 1991] applied to distributed transactions.

- *Individual Objects*:
  Each object in the database is expected to be consistent locally.
  Example: Linearizability [Herlihy and Wing, 1987] applied to objects accessed by concurrent *processes*.

- *Consistency Maintenance:*
  This is related to the issues of *when* a consistency requirement is expected to hold and *how* consistency is restored if it does not hold.
  - *When is a consistency requirement expected to hold?*
    - *At activity boundaries*: (An activity denotes a unit of work)
      - *When an operation completes*:
        When an operation on an object completes, the necessary consistency specifications must hold.
        Example: Concurrent processes accessing shared objects.
      - *When a set of operations completes*:
        When a set of operations performed by a transaction completes, the necessary consistency is expected to hold.
        Example: Semantic atomicity [Garcia-Molina, 1983] and multilevel atomicity [Lynch, 1983]
      - *When a transaction completes*:
        Consistency is expected to hold upon a transaction's completion.
        Example: Atomic transactions.
      - *When a set of transactions completes*:
        Consistency is expected to hold not when individual transactions complete but when a set of transactions completes.
        Example: Cooperative transactions [Korth and Speegle, 1988], sagas [Garcia-Molina and Salem, 1987].
    - *At specific points of time*:
      Consistency is required only at/after specific points in time. This is an example of *temporal consistency* [Sheth and Rusinkiewicz, 1990].
      Example: A bank account is expected to be made consistent, with respect to the debits and credits that occur on a given day, upon closing of business.
    - *At specific states*:
      Objects may be required to be mutually consistent only when a certain number of updates have been made to one of the objects or a state satisfying a certain predicate is reached.
      Example: A centralized database of a department store chain may require updates only upon the completion of 100 sales at a particular store. Such requirements are referred to as *spatial consistency* in [Sheth and Rusinkiewicz, 1990].
  - *If a consistency requirement does not hold at a point it is supposed to, how is it restored?*
    - *Impossible*:
      This applies when the consistency requirement must hold at activity boundaries. The activity is allowed to complete only if the requirement holds, i.e., completion is delayed until consistency holds. If an activity cannot complete successfully while maintaining consistency, it is aborted or compensated.

Example: SR, PSR, QSR, and cooperative serializability (CoSR), applied to atomic, nested, and distributed transactions.

∗ *Consistency is restored in a deferred manner*:
This typically applies when consistency is expected in certain states or at certain times. When it is applied to consistency that is expected at an activity boundary, the activity is allowed to complete and restoration is begun subsequently.

· *Eventually*:
Consistency between objects must be restored eventually.
Example: If mutual consistency is required between two objects and one is changed by a transaction, another can be *triggered* to make changes in the other object.

· *By a certain time*:
A deadline may be imposed on the time by which consistency is restored.
Example: In real-time systems, the state of the controlled environment should be reflected in the internal state of the controlling system within a certain time so that appropriate and timely control can be exercised.

2.2 TRANSACTION CORRECTNESS PROPERTIES

As was mentioned in the introduction, serializability suffices as a correctness criterion for traditional atomic transactions since once *individual transactions are guaranteed to take one consistent database state to another consistent state*, serializability guarantees that a set of concurrent transactions when started in a consistent state take the database to another consistent state. So the only transaction correctness property of interest is: Each transaction when executed by itself must maintain database consistency. From this it follows that, under serializability, the output of a transaction reflects a consistent database state. However, more elaborate correctness properties have been proposed in the context of additional application requirements and newer transaction models. These transaction correctness properties can be discussed with respect to three criteria:

- *Correctness of transaction results*:
  - *Absolute*:
    The output of transactions must reflect a consistent database state.
    Example: SR applied to atomic transactions, QSR applied to distributed transactions.
  - *Relative*:
    Outputs of a transaction are considered correct even if they do not reflect a consistent state of the object, as long as they are within a certain bound of the result that corresponds to the consistent state.
    Example: Epsilon-serializability (ESR) [Pu and Leff, 1991] applied to epsilon-transactions, approximate query processing [Hou et al., 1989].
- *Correctness of transaction structure*:
  Correctness depends on the (structural) relationship between transactions. This is typically specified in terms of prescribed and/or proscribed *commit, abort, begin*, and other types of dependencies [Chrysanthis and Ramamritham, 1991] between transactions. Since structural properties are governed by a particular transaction model, the specifications of the model express these requirements.

Example: Sagas [Garcia-Molina and Salem, 1987], multi-level serializability [Korth and Speegle, 1990].

- *Correctness of data access related transaction behavior*:
  Transactions are required to perform operations on objects in a certain manner to be considered correct. That is, these requirements are constraints on the history of concurrent operations.

  Example: To satisfy serializability, conflict relationship between transactions – as they access data concurrently – must be acyclic. Patterns [Skarra, 1991] are more application specific correctness requirements that reflect the (semantics of) usage of the object.

- *Correctness of temporal behavior of transactions*:
  Transactions have start time and completion time (deadline) constraints.

  Example: Transactions in real-time systems.

The taxonomy just presented shows how the various correctness requirements can be viewed from the perspectives of database consistency and transaction correctness. It is perhaps clear that, from a database application designer's perspective, what is required is to specify which leaves of the taxonomy correspond to his/her application and then provide additional specifications required by the individual leaves. For instance, if correctness depends on transactions' structural properties, additional specifications will be needed to specify what these properties are. For example, if transactions in an application behave according to the nested transaction model, an axiomatic specification of the nested transaction model [Chrysanthis and Ramamritham 1991] will supplement the identification of the fact that transactions have structure related correctness requirements.

We revisit the correctness notions in Section 4.1 where serializability related correctness notions are formally specified and categorized along the different dimensions of the taxonomy. Sections 4.2 and 4.3 deal with the formal specification of more general correctness criteria that are not directly related to serializability but deal, for example, with transaction structure and behavior, specific states of objects, or specific times.

3 A QUICK INTRODUCTION TO THE ACTA FORMALISM

ACTA is a first-order logic based formalism. As mentioned earlier, the idea of significant events underlies ACTA's specifications. Section 3.1 discusses these events. Specifications involve constraints on the occurrence of individual significant events as well as on the history of occurrence of these events. Hence the notion of history and the necessary and sufficient conditions for the occurrence of significant events are introduced in Section 3.2. Finally, Section 3.3 shows how sharing of objects leads to transaction inter-relationships which in turn induces certain dependencies between concurrent transactions.

3.1 SIGNIFICANT EVENTS ASSOCIATED WITH TRANSACTIONS

During the course of their execution, transactions invoke operations on objects. Also, they invoke transaction management primitives. For example, atomic transactions are associated with three transaction management primitives: *Begin, Commit* and *Abort*. The specific primitives and their semantics depend on the specifics of a transaction model [Chrysanthis and Ramamritham, 1991]. For instance, whereas the *Commit* by an atomic transaction implies that it is terminating successfully and that all of its effects on the objects should be made permanent in the database, the *Commit* of a subtransaction of a nested transaction implies that all of its effects on the objects should be made persistent and visible with respect to its parent and sibling subtransactions. Other transaction management primitives include *Spawn*, found in the nested transaction model [Moss, 1985], *Split*, found in the split transaction model [Pu et al., 1988], and *Join*, a transaction termination event also found in the split transaction model.

Definition 1 Invocation of a transaction management primitive is termed a *significant event*. A transaction model defines the significant events that transactions adhering to that model can invoke.

The set of events invoked by a transaction t is a partial order with ordering relation $<_t$ where $<_t$ denotes the temporal order in which the related events occur.

$ts(\epsilon)$ gives the time of occurrence of event ϵ according to a globally synchronized clock.[1] Clearly, $ts(\beta)$ will be larger than $ts(\alpha)$ if α appears earlier in the partial order. Further, no two significant events *that relate to the same transaction* can occur with the same ts value.

3.2 HISTORY, PROJECTION OF THE HISTORY, AND CONSTRAINTS ON EVENT OCCURRENCES

The concurrent execution of a set of transactions T is represented by the *history* [Bernstein et al., 1987] of the events invoked by the transactions in the set T and indicates the (partial) order in which these events occur. The partial order of the operations in a history is consistent with the partial order of the events of each individual transaction t in T.

The *projection* of a history H is a subhistory that satisfies a given criterion. For instance,

- The projection of a history H with respect to a specific transaction t yields a subhistory with just the events invoked by t. This is denoted by H_t.
- The projection of a history H with respect to a specific time interval [i, j] yields the subhistory with the the events which occurred between i and j (inclusive) and is denoted by $H^{[i,j]}$.

  When i = system initiation time, we drop the first element of the pair. Thus $H^j = H^{[system\_init\_time,j]}$ denotes all the events that occur until time j.

Consistency requirements imposed on concurrent transactions executing on a database can be expressed in terms of the properties of the resulting histories.

The occurrence of an event in a history can be constrained in one of three ways: (1) An event ϵ can be constrained to occur *only after* another event ϵ'; (2) An event ϵ can occur *only if* a condition c is true; and (3) a condition c can *require* the occurrence of an event ϵ.

Definition 2 The predicate $\epsilon \rightarrow \epsilon'$ is true if event ϵ *precedes* event ϵ' in history H. It is false, otherwise. (Thus, $\epsilon \rightarrow \epsilon'$ implies that $\epsilon \in H$ and $\epsilon' \in H$.)

---

[1] This is obviously an abstraction – the effects of realizing this by a set of closely synchronized clocks on individual nodes in a distributed system will not be discussed here.

Definition 3 $(\epsilon \in H) \Rightarrow Condition_H$, where $\Rightarrow$ denotes *implication*, specifies that the event ϵ can belong to history H *only if* $Condition_H$ is satisfied. In other words, $Condition_H$ is *necessary* for ϵ to be in H. $Condition_H$ is a predicate involving the events in H.

Consider $(\epsilon' \in H) \Rightarrow (\epsilon \rightarrow \epsilon')$. This states that the event ϵ' can belong to the history H *only if* event ϵ occurs before ϵ'.

Definition 4 $Condition_H \Rightarrow (\epsilon \in H)$ specifies that if $Condition_H$ holds, ϵ should be in the history H. In other words, $Condition_H$ is *sufficient* for ϵ to be in H.

We now describe some common types of constraints.

1. $(Commit_{t_j} \in H) \Rightarrow ((Commit_{t_i} \in H) \Rightarrow (Commit_{t_i} \rightarrow Commit_{t_j}))$. This says that if both transactions t_i and t_j commit then the commitment of t_i precedes the commitment of t_j. This **Commit-Dependency** is indicated by $(t_j\ \mathcal{CD}\ t_i)$. In general, $((Commit_{t_j} \in H) \Rightarrow condition)$ specifies that $condition$ should hold for t_j to commit.
2. $(Abort_{t_i} \in H) \Rightarrow (Abort_{t_j} \in H)$ i.e., if t_i aborts then t_j aborts, states the **Abort-Dependency** of t_j on t_i $(t_j\ \mathcal{AD}\ t_i)$. In general, $(condition \Rightarrow (Abort_{t_j} \in H))$ specifies that if $condition$ holds t_j aborts.
3. $(Begin_{t_j} \in H) \Rightarrow (Begin_{t_i} \rightarrow Begin_{t_j})$ states that transaction t_j cannot begin executing until transaction t_i has begun.

3.3 OBJECTS, OPERATIONS, AND CONFLICTS

A transaction accesses and manipulates the objects in the database by invoking operations specific to individual objects. It is assumed that an operation always produces an output (return value), that is, it has an outcome (condition code) or a result. The result of an operation on an object depends on the current state of the object. For a given state s of an object, we use $return(s, p)$ to denote the output produced by operation p, and $state(s, p)$ to denote the state produced after the execution of p.

Definition 5 Invocation of an operation on an object is termed an *object event*. The type of an object defines the object events that pertain to it. We use $p_t[ob]$ to denote the object event corresponding to the invocation of the operation p on object ob by transaction t. Object events are also part of the history H.

Definition 6 Let $H^{(ob)}$ denote the projection of the history with respect to the operations on ob. Two operations p and q *conflict* in a state produced by $H^{(ob)}$, denoted by *conflict*$(H^{(ob)}, p, q)$, iff

$$\begin{array}{rcl} (state(H^{(ob)} \circ p,\ q) & \neq & state(H^{(ob)} \circ q,\ p)) \quad \vee \\ (return(H^{(ob)},\ q) & \neq & (return(H^{(ob)} \circ p,\ q)) \ \vee \\ (return(H^{(ob)},\ p) & \neq & (return(H^{(ob)} \circ q,\ p)) \end{array}$$

Two operations that do not conflict are *compatible*.

($\circ$ denotes functional composition; $H \circ p$ appends p to history H.) Thus, two operations conflict if their effects on the state of an object are not independent of their execution order (first clause) or their return values are not independent of their execution order (second and third clauses). From now on, we drop the first parameter of conflict, namely, $H^{(ob)}$.

4 SPECIFICATION AND CATEGORIZATION OF CORRECTNESS CRITERIA

In this section, we study various database consistency requirements and transaction correctness properties that have been proposed and place them in perspective, given the taxonomy of the previous section. *Broadly speaking*, Section 4.1 deals with transaction model and application independent correctness criteria (even though, as we will see, those who proposed them may have had a specific transaction model or application in mind), Section 4.2 discusses transaction model dependent but application independent criteria, and Section 4.3 examines transaction and application dependent consistency requirements. (For a complete axiomatic semantics of the various extended transaction models, the reader is referred to [Chrysanthis and Ramamritham, 1991].)

4.1 TRANSACTION AND APPLICATION INDEPENDENT CRITERIA

In general, transaction and application independent correctness criteria are extensions to serializability. In this section, we first specify some of these extensions using the formalism described in the previous section and then use the specifications to show how the different extensions relate to each other. All of these criteria are based on the notion of *conflicts* and their preservation in equivalent histories. Thus, we do not discuss correctness criteria such as *view serializability* [Yannakakis, 1984] that are not as easy to realize.

Definition 7 Let $\mathcal{R}$ be a binary relation on a set of transactions T, $t_i, t_k \in T$, $t_i \neq t_k$. $\mathcal{R}^*$ is the transitive-closure of $\mathcal{R}$; i.e.,
$(t_i\ \mathcal{R}^*\ t_k)$ if $[(t_i\ \mathcal{R}\ t_k) \vee \exists t_j \in T\ ((t_i\ \mathcal{R}\ t_j) \wedge (t_j\ \mathcal{R}^*\ t_k))]$.

4.1.1 Serializability

In traditional databases, serializability and, in particular, *conflict serializability*, is the well-accepted criterion for concurrency control.

Let $\mathcal{C}$ be a binary relation on transactions in T.

Let H be the history of events relating to committed transactions in T.

Definition 8 $\forall\, t_i, t_j \in T, t_i \neq t_j$,
$(t_i\ \mathcal{C}\ t_j)$ if
$\exists ob\ \exists p, q\ (conflict(p_{t_i}[ob], q_{t_j}[ob]) \wedge (p_{t_i}[ob] \rightarrow q_{t_j}[ob]))$.

Definition 9 H is *(conflict) serializable* iff
$\forall t \in T, \neg(t\ \mathcal{C}^*\ t)$.

To illustrate the practical implications of these definitions, note that the $\mathcal{C}$ relation captures the fact that two transactions have invoked conflicting operations on the same object and the order in which they have invoked the conflicting operations. Consequently, the $\mathcal{C}$ relation captures direct conflicts between transactions in a history as well as their serialization order. The fact that a serialization order is acyclic is stated by requiring that there be no cycles in the $\mathcal{C}$ relation.

Note also that the above definitions do not involve any significant events. This reflects the fact that serializability per se does not constrain the occurrence of any significant event, e.g., a *Commit* event to happen only after another *Commit* event. (If the $\mathcal{C}$ relationship between transactions is acyclic, transactions in H can commit in any order.) That is, the *commit order* of transactions is not necessarily the same as their serialization order and hence, the commit order cannot be used to induce the serialization order. However, a commit order induced by a $\mathcal{C}$ relation is consistent with the serialization order. For example, consider the case of *rigorous histories* [Breitbart, et al., 1991] such as the ones produced by the strict two-phase locking protocol [Eswaran et al., 1976]. In this case, if transactions t_i and t_j have a $\mathcal{C}$ relationship, i.e., they have invoked conflicting operations, a commit dependency [Chrysanthis and Ramamritham, 1991] forms between t_i and t_j. (Conflicting operations may also produce abort dependencies between the invoking transactions; but an abort dependency implies a commit dependency.) By requiring that the $\mathcal{C}$ relation be acyclic, commit dependencies must also be acyclic. By inducing a commit dependency between every pair of transactions invoking conflict operations, the commit order specified by the commit dependencies is the same as the serialization order.

With respect to the taxonomy of Section 2, for serializability, the consistency unit is the complete database, and consistency is required at transaction boundaries. Absolute correctness of transaction results is expected. Atomic transactions and top-level transactions of nested transactions, for example, behave according to the serializability correctness criterion.

The semantics of the operations on the objects (for example, see [Badrinath and Ramamritham, 1990; Herlihy and Wing, 1987; O'Neil, 1986]) can be used to define the *conflict* relationship between operations. Furthermore, different *degrees* of consistency [Gray et al., 1976] can be ensured by ignoring some of the conflicts. The resulting inconsistencies can be accommodated in applications that can cope with such inconsistencies or when these are masked by the structuring of the objects used by the applications. The former is the case in [Gray et al., 1976] and with ESR [Pu and Leff, 1991] (see [Ramamritham and Pu, 1992] for a formal characterization of ESR). The latter is the case with abstract serializability – used in the context of multi-level transactions [Beeri et al., 1989; Moss, et al., 1986; Martin, 1988b; Badrinath and Ramamritham, 1990].

4.1.2 Predicatewise Serializability

Predicatewise serializability has been proposed in [Korth et al., 1988; Korth and Speegle, 1988] as the correctness criterion for concurrency control in databases in which consistency constraints are in a conjunctive normal form. In such cases, consistency constraints can be maintained by requiring serializability only with respect to objects which relate to a disjunctive clause.

Let $P = (P_1 \wedge P_2 \ldots \wedge P_n)$ be the database consistency constraint. Suppose the disjunctive clause P_k relates to objects in $D_k \subseteq DB$, where DB is the database.

$\forall k \in \{1 \ \ldots \ n\}$, let $\mathcal{C}_k$ be a binary relation on transactions in T.

Let H be the history of events relating to committed transactions in T.

Definition 10 $\forall k \in \{1 \ldots n\}, \forall\, t_i, t_j \in T,\ t_i \neq t_j,$
$(t_i\, \mathcal{C}_k\, t_j)$, if
$\exists ob \in D_k\ \exists p, q\ (\mathit{conflict}(p_{t_i}[ob], q_{t_j}[ob]) \wedge (p_{t_i}[ob] \rightarrow q_{t_j}[ob]))$.

Definition 11 H is *predicatewise serializable* iff
$\forall t \in T\ \forall D_k\ 1 \leq k \leq n\ \neg(t\, \mathcal{C}_k^*\, t)$

In [Sha, 1985], each D_k is said to be an *atomic data set*. With respect to the taxonomy, for predicatewise serializability, an atomic data set [Sha, 1985] forms a consistency unit and consistency is required at transaction boundaries. Absolute correctness of transaction results is expected. Compound transactions [Sha, 1985] behave according to the predicatewise serializability correctness criterion.

4.1.3 Cooperative Serializability

We define *cooperative serializability* (CoSR) with respect to a set of transactions which maintain some consistency properties. Transactions form cooperative transaction sets. A cooperative transaction set could be formed by the components of an extended transaction or transactions collaborating over some objects while maintaining the consistency of the objects. In such cases, consistency can be maintained if other transactions which do not belong to the set are serialized with respect to all the transactions in the set. In other words, a set of cooperative transactions becomes the unit of concurrency with respect to serializability.

Let T_c be a set of cooperative transactions, $T_c \subseteq T$.

Let $\mathcal{C}_c$ be a binary relation on transactions in T.

Let H be the history of events relating to committed transactions in T.

Definition 12 $\forall\, t_i,\ t_j,\ t_k\ \in\ T, t_i \neq t_j, t_i \neq t_k, t_j \neq t_k\ \forall T_c \subseteq T$
$(t_i\, \mathcal{C}_c\, t_j)$, if
$\exists ob\ \exists p, q\ ((t_i \notin T_c, t_j \notin T_c\ (\mathit{conflict}(p_{t_i}[ob], q_{t_j}[ob]) \wedge (p_{t_i}[ob] \rightarrow q_{t_j}[ob]))) \vee$
$(t_i \notin T_c, t_j \in T_c, t_k \in T_c\ (\mathit{conflict}(p_{t_i}[ob], q_{t_k}[ob]) \wedge (p_{t_i}[ob] \rightarrow q_{t_k}[ob]))) \vee$
$(t_i \in T_c, t_j \notin T_c, t_k \in T_c\ (\mathit{conflict}(p_{t_k}[ob], q_{t_j}[ob]) \wedge (p_{t_k}[ob] \rightarrow q_{t_j}[ob])))))$

In this definition, the first clause expresses how a dependency between two transactions which do not belong to the same set is directly established when they invoke conflicting operations on a shared object. This is similar to the clause in the classical definition of (conflict) serializability. The other two clauses reflect the fact that when a transaction establishes a dependency with another transaction, the same dependency is established between all the transactions in their corresponding cooperative transactions sets. These clauses can be viewed as expressions of the development of dependencies between transaction sets.

Definition 13 H is *cooperative serializable* iff
$\forall t \in T\ \neg(t\, \mathcal{C}_c^*\, t)$

With respect to the taxonomy of the previous section, for cooperative serializability, the consistency unit is the complete database, consistency is required when an ordinary transaction (not a member of a T_c) completes or a set of cooperating transactions complete. Absolute correctness of transaction results is expected. The correctness requirement expressed informally in [Martin and Pedersen, 1992] corresponds to CoSR.

4.1.4 Quasi-serializability

Quasi-serializability (QSR) has been proposed in [Du and Elmagarmid, 1989] as a correctness criterion for maintaining transaction consistency in multidatabases, e.g., heterogeneous distributed databases. In these systems, transactions can either execute on a single site (called *local* transactions), or can execute on multiple sites (called *global* transactions).

In QSR, the correctness of the execution of a set of global and local transactions is based on the notion of a *quasi-serial history* which, unlike a serial history, specifies that only global transactions are executed serially. A history is *quasi-serial* if (1) all local histories are (conflict) serializable, and (2) there exists a total order of all global transactions g_m and g_n where g_m precedes g_n in the order and all g_m's operations precede g_n's operations in all local histories in which they both appear. A quasi-serializable history is equivalent to a quasi-serial history.

Let G be the set of global transactions and g_n^i be a (sub)transaction of a global transaction g_n ($g_n \in G$) executing all the operations of g_n on site i.[2]

Let T_i be the set of transactions, both local transactions and global (sub)transactions, executing on site i. $T = (\cup_i T_i)$.

Let H be the history of events relating to committed transactions in T.

Let $\mathcal{R}$ be a binary relation on a set of global transactions G.

Definition 14 $\forall\, g_m,\ g_n \in G, g_m \neq g_n,$

$$
\begin{array}{l}
(g_m\ \mathcal{R}\ g_n), \text{ if} \\
\quad \exists k, g_m^k, g_n^k\ \ (g_m^k\ \mathcal{C}\ g_n^k) \vee \exists p, t_0 = g_m^k, t_p = g_n^k\ \forall i, 0 \leq i \leq p-2 \\
\qquad \exists ob\ \exists p, q\ ((\mathit{conflict}(p_{t_i}[ob], q_{t_{i+1}}[ob]) \wedge (p_{t_i}[ob] \rightarrow q_{t_{i+1}}[ob])) \wedge \\
\qquad \exists ob'\ \exists p', q'\ (\mathit{conflict}(p'_{t_{i+1}}[ob'], q'_{t_{i+2}}[ob']) \wedge (p'_{t_{i+1}}[ob'] \rightarrow q'_{t_{i+2}}[ob'])) \wedge \\
\qquad\qquad (q_{t_{i+1}}[ob] \rightarrow p'_{t_{i+1}}[ob']))
\end{array}
$$

where $\mathcal{C}$ is the binary relation defined in Definition 8.

The $\mathcal{C}$ relation captures the fact that two global transactions *directly conflict* in a local history when they invoke conflicting operations on a share object. Two global transactions might also *indirectly conflict* in a local history even if they don't access any share objects. Indirect conflicts are introduced by other transactions that directly conflict with each other and with the global transactions. These, indirect conflicts between two transactions, particularly those introduced by local transactions, are captured by the second clause of the definition of $\mathcal{R}$. Note that this clause, and consequently $\mathcal{R}$, is not equivalent to the transitive-closure of $\mathcal{C}$ which does not place any restriction on the execution ordering of the conflicting operations, but $\mathcal{R} \subset C^*$.

Definition 15 H is *quasi-serializable* iff

1. $\forall i\ \forall t \in T_i\ \neg(t\ \mathcal{C}^*\ t)$, and

[2] That is, at most one (sub)transaction of a global transaction can execute on a particular site.

2. $\forall g \in G \neg(g \mathcal{R}^* g)$

It should be pointed that since the $\mathcal{R}$ relation captures both direct and indirect conflicts between two global transactions in a history, the serializable execution of global transactions is in terms of both direct and indirect conflicts. Indirect conflicts between local transactions induced by conflicts of global transactions that execute on multiple sites are not captured by either clause, the reason being that QSR assumes no data dependency across sites.

With respect to the taxonomy of the previous section, for Quasi serializability, (site-based) subsets of the database objects form the consistency units (i.e., objects in each site form a subset) and consistency should hold when a transaction completes. Absolute correctness of transactions' results is expected. quasi-serializability has been proposed in the context of distributed (multi-database) transactions.

4.1.5 Relationship between different Serializability-based Correctness Criteria

Thus far in this section, we have specified four serializability-based correctness criteria using the ACTA formalism and classified them with respect to our taxonomy in Section 2. Here, we will use the formal definitions of the various criteria to relate them to each other.

According to predicatewise serializability, each D_k is associated with a $\mathcal{C}_k$ and hence conflicting transactions can be serialized differently with respect to different D_k. This is contrary to serializability which permits only a single system-wide serialization order involving conflicting transactions based on $\mathcal{C}$. However, if D_k is the complete database, then $\mathcal{C} = \mathcal{C}_k$, and consequently, predicatewise serializability is equivalent to serializability.

In the case of cooperative serializability, transactions in different cooperative transaction sets may be related by the $\mathcal{C}_c$ relation (individual transactions not belonging to any cooperative set can be viewed as singleton cooperative transaction sets). Hence, if each cooperative transaction set has just one member, then $\mathcal{C}_c = \mathcal{C}$ and, in this case, cooperative serializability is equivalent to serializability.

In the case of quasi-serializability, there are two distinct conditions under which QSR is equivalent to serializability. These correspond to the situations in which one of the two clauses of the definition of QSR is trivially true: (1) In the absence of global transactions, transactions in T_i are serialized based only on $\mathcal{C}$. (2) In the absence of local transactions, transactions in T_i are serialized based only on $\mathcal{R}$, i.e., here $\mathcal{R} = C$. Indirect conflicts due to local transactions are not possible whereas indirect conflicts due to global transactions are considered by $\mathcal{C}^*$.

Finally, we would like to point out that these different correctness criteria can be combined and/or adopted within a single database. For instance, it is easy to picture how cooperative serializability can be used in conjunction with predicatewise serializability and how cooperative serializability can be used in conjunction with even quasi-serializability.

For such combinations of correctness criteria, their specification can be derived from the specification of the individual correctness criteria. As an example, let us examine one way that cooperative serializability can be combined with quasi-serializability in order to support a multidatabase system in which component databases allow local transactions to form cooperative groups. In this case, according to cooperative serializability, global (sub)transactions as well as other local transactions that do not belong to a cooperative set, are serialized with respect to all the transactions in the set. The formal definition of this combined criterion is derived from the definition of QSR [Definitions 14 and 15] by replacing the binary relation $\mathcal{C}$ with a binary relation similar to $\mathcal{C}_c$ defined in the context of CoSR. Specifically:

Let T_i be the set of transactions, both local transactions and global (sub)transactions, executing on site i. $T = (\cup_i T_i)$.

Let T_{c_i} be a set of local cooperative transactions on site i, $T_{c_i} \subseteq T_i$.

Let $\mathcal{C}_{c_i}$ be a binary relation on transactions in T_i.

Let H be the history of events relating to transactions in T.

Definition 16 $\forall\, t_i,\, t_j,\, t_k\, \in\, T_i, t_i \neq t_j, t_i \neq t_k, t_j \neq t_k\; \forall T_{c_i}$
$(t_i\, \mathcal{C}_{c_i}\, t_j)$, if
$\exists ob\, \exists p, q$
$((t_i \notin T_{c_i}, t_j \notin T_{c_i}\; (\mathit{conflict}(p_{t_i}[ob], q_{t_j}[ob]) \wedge (p_{t_i}[ob] \rightarrow q_{t_j}[ob]))) \vee$
$(t_i \notin T_{c_i}, t_j \in T_{c_i}, t_k \in T_{c_i}\; (\mathit{conflict}(p_{t_i}[ob], q_{t_k}[ob]) \wedge (p_{t_i}[ob] \rightarrow q_{t_k}[ob]))) \vee$
$(t_i \in T_{c_i}, t_j \notin T_{c_i}, t_k \in T_{c_i}\; (\mathit{conflict}(p_{t_k}[ob], q_{t_j}[ob]) \wedge (p_{t_k}[ob] \rightarrow q_{t_j}[ob]))))$

Definition 17 H is *local cooperative quasi-serializable* iff

1. $\forall i\, \forall t \in T_i\, \neg(t\, \mathcal{C}^*_{c_i}\, t)$, and
2. $\forall g \in G\, \neg(g\, \mathcal{R}^*\, g)$

4.2 TRANSACTION MODEL DEPENDENT AND APPLICATION INDEPENDENT CRITERIA

Transaction model dependent but application independent correctness criteria are typically related to the structure of transactions that conform to a particular model. (Note that specific transaction models may be more suited to specific applications.) As was mentioned earlier, different transaction models produce different transaction structures where the structure of an extended transaction defines its component transactions and the relationships between them. Dependencies can express these relationships and thus, can specify the links in the structure. For example, in hierarchically-structured nested transactions, the parent/child relationship is established at the time the child is *spawned*. This is expressed by a child transaction t_c establishing a weak-abort dependency (defined below) on its parent t_p $((t_c\ \mathcal{WD}\ t_p))$ and by a parent establishing a commit dependency on its child $((t_p\ \mathcal{CD}\ t_c))$. The weak-abort dependency guarantees the abortion of an uncommitted child if its parent aborts whereas the commit dependency prevents a child from committing after its parent has committed.

In [Chrysanthis and Ramamritham, 1991] and [Chrysanthis and Ramamritham, 1992] we gave axiomatic definitions of different transaction models in terms of dependencies that occur between transactions that conform to a particular model. So we now formally specify some of the dependencies that can occur in addition to the **Commit Dependency**, **Abort Dependency**, and **Begin Dependency** specified in Section 3.2.

Let t_i and t_j be two transactions and H be a finite history which contains all the events pertaining to t_i and t_j.

Weak-Abort Dependency $(t_j\ \mathcal{WD}\ t_i)$: if t_i aborts and t_j has not yet committed, then t_j aborts. In other words, if t_j commits and t_i aborts then the commitment of t_j precedes the abortion of t_i in a history; i.e., $(Abort_{t_i} \in H) \Rightarrow (\neg(Commit_{t_j} \rightarrow Abort_{t_i}) \Rightarrow (Abort_{t_j} \in H))$.

Strong-Commit Dependency $(t_j\ \mathcal{SCD}\ t_i)$: if transaction t_i commits then t_j commits; i.e., $(Commit_{t_i} \in H) \Rightarrow (Commit_{t_j} \in H)$.

Termination Dependency $(t_j\ \mathcal{TD}\ t_i)$: t_j cannot commit or abort until t_i either commits or aborts; i.e., $(\epsilon' \in H) \Rightarrow (\epsilon \rightarrow \epsilon')$ where $\epsilon \in \{Commit_{t_i}, Abort_{t_i}\}$, and $\epsilon' \in \{Commit_{t_j}, Abort_{t_j}\}$.

Exclusion Dependency $(t_j\ \mathcal{ED}\ t_i)$: if t_i commits and t_j has begun executing, then t_j aborts (both t_i and t_j cannot commit); i.e., $(Commit_{t_i} \in H) \Rightarrow ((Begin_{t_j} \in H) \Rightarrow (Abort_{t_j} \in H))$.

Force-Commit-on-Abort Dependency $(t_j\ \mathcal{CAD}\ t_i)$: if t_i aborts, t_j commits; i.e., $(Abort_{t_i} \in H) \Rightarrow (Commit_{t_j} \in H)$.

Serial Dependency $(t_j\ \mathcal{SD}\ t_i)$: transaction t_j cannot begin executing until t_i either commits or aborts; i.e., $(Begin_{t_j} \in H) \Rightarrow (\epsilon \rightarrow Begin_{t_j})$ where $\epsilon \in \{Commit_{t_i}, Abort_{t_i}\}$.

Begin-on-Commit Dependency $(t_j\ \mathcal{BCD}\ t_i)$: transaction t_j cannot begin executing until t_i commits; i.e., $(Begin_{t_j} \in H) \Rightarrow (Commit_{t_i} \rightarrow Begin_{t_j})$.

Begin-on-Abort Dependency $(t_j\ \mathcal{BAD}\ t_i)$: transaction t_j cannot begin executing until t_i aborts; i.e., $(Begin_{t_j} \in H) \Rightarrow (Abort_{t_i} \rightarrow Begin_{t_j})$.

Weak-begin-on-Commit Dependency $(t_j\ \mathcal{WCD}\ t_i)$: if t_i commits, t_j can begin executing after t_i commits; i.e., $(Begin_{t_j} \in H) \Rightarrow ((Commit_{t_i} \in H) \Rightarrow (Commit_{t_i} \rightarrow Begin_{t_j}))$.

Let us look at further examples of structure-related transaction correctness properties. In the transaction model proposed in [Buchmann et al., 1990; Buchmann et al., 1992; Garcia-Molina et al., 1991] a parent can commit only if its *vital* children commit, i.e., a parent transaction has an abort dependency on its *vital* children t_v $(t_p\ \mathcal{AD}\ t_v)$. Child transactions may also have different dependencies with their parents if the transaction model supports various spawning or coupling modes [Dayal et al., 1990a]. Sibling transactions may also be interrelated in several ways. For example, components of a *saga* [Garcia-Molina and Salem, 1987] can be paired according to a compensated-for/compensating relationship [Korth et al., 1990a]. Relations between a compensated-for and compensating transactions as well as those between them and the saga can be specified via begin-on-commit dependency $\mathcal{BCD}$, begin-on-abort dependency $\mathcal{BAD}$, force-commit-on-abort dependency $\mathcal{CAD}$ and strong-commit dependency $\mathcal{SCD}$ [Chrysanthis and Ramamritham, 1992]. In a similar fashion, dependencies that occur in the presence of alternative transactions and contingency transactions [Buchmann, et al., 1992] can also be specified [Chrysanthis and Ramamritham, 1992].

With respect to the taxonomy, an application that uses an extended transaction model will have correctness requirements related to transactions' structure where these requirements are specified via axioms that express the dependencies that are formed when transactions execute according to the given model.

4.3 TRANSACTION AND APPLICATION DEPENDENT CRITERIA

We now focus on the required *behavior* of a transaction and hence on the requirements imposed by the application that employs that specific transaction. We distinguish between two types of behavior related properties:

1. Those that relate to constraints on a transaction's access to objects. Some of these are mandated by the concurrency properties of the objects. For instance, as discussed in Section 4.1, serializability demands acyclic $\mathcal{C}$ relationships. Here we will discuss additional access requirements.
2. Those that relate to properties that deal with its other behavioral properties, such as, *when* a transaction can/must begin and *when* it can/must end. Spatial and temporal requirements are related to this type.

We elaborate upon the first type through an example. Consider a *page* object with the standard $read$ and $write$ operations, where read and write operations conflict. A read's return-value is dependent on a previous write, whereas a write's return-value is independent of a read or another write. In addition, consider transactions which have the ability to reconcile potential read-write conflicts: When a transaction t_i reads a page x and another transaction t_j subsequently writes x, t_i and t_j can commit in any order. However, if t_j commits before t_i commits, t_i must reread x in order to commit. This is captured by the following requirement:

$$(read_{t_i}[x] \rightarrow write_{t_j}[x]) \Rightarrow ((Commit_{t_j} \rightarrow Commit_{t_i}) \Rightarrow (Commit_{t_j} \rightarrow read_{t_i}[x]))).$$

In this example, t_i has to reread the page x when, subsequent to the first read, the page is written and committed by t_j. In general, t_i may need to invoke an operation on the same or a different object. For instance, instead of x, t_i may have to read a *scratch-pad* object which t_i and t_j use to determine and reconcile potential conflicts. In general, the specification of correct transaction behavior can include the specification of operations that need to be controlled to produce correct histories as well as the specification of operations that *have* to occur in correct histories. These correspond to *conflicts* and *patterns* in [Skarra, 1991].

Let us now turn to other behavioral specifications, for example, those that concern the beginning and termination of transactions. Consider the following simple requirement which states that if $condition$ is true then transaction t_j must begin:

$$condition \Rightarrow (Begin_{t_j} \in H)$$

$condition$ can depend on the occurrence of an event, on the state of the database, and on time. As we will see, the above requirement can be used for the flexible enforcement of consistency, to trigger the propagation of changes, to react to consistency violations, and to notify changes. Thus, the above specification can be considered to be a specification for the automatic triggering of situation-dependent actions, e.g., for expressing the rules that govern the triggering of actions in an active database [Dittrich and Dayal, 1991].

Suppose $condition$ is related to the occurrence of some significant event within a transaction t_i. In this case, the additional structural relationships (for instance, the different *coupling modes* [Dayal et al., 1990a]) between t_i and t_j can be specified via the dependencies discussed in Section 4.2.

 If $condition$ relates to the state of the database, what we have is related to *spatial consistency* discussed in [Sheth and Rusinkiewicz, 1990]. For instance, consider the following $condition$: "One hundred sales have occurred at this store since the master database at the store's headquarters was last updated."

If $condition$ relates to time, for instance, if $condition$ is "$time > 8pm$", we have a *temporal consistency* requirement.

Now let us consider situations where *constraints* are placed on the beginning of transactions. For example, a transaction t_i to compute daily interest can start after midnight but only after the day's withdrawals and deposits have been reflected in the account (say by a transaction t_j). This can be specified as

$$(ts(Begin_{t_i}) \geq 12am) \wedge (t_i \; \mathcal{BCD} \; t_j).$$

This is an example where a transaction has a time-based start-dependency as well as a begin-on-commit dependency on another transaction.

Let us consider another example. If a deposit is made by time x then the transaction that reflects it in the account should not be started until time y. This is specified by

$$((Commit_{t_i} \in H) \wedge (ts(Commit_{t_i}) < x)) \Rightarrow ((Begin_{t_j} \in H) \Rightarrow (ts(Begin_{t_j}) > y)).$$

Through several examples, we now consider requirements and constraints associated with the termination of transactions.

Sometimes, we may want to specify that some specific change of state (by one transaction) triggers [Dayal et al., 1990a] another transaction (that perhaps fixes the inconsistency resulting from the first transaction). Clearly, this type of constraint is related to deferred consistency restoration. This can occur, for example, if we had two versions of a database, one which was complete and another (at perhaps a different site) which only contained data required at that site. The two are not required to be consistent at all times but changes done to the complete database are required to percolate to the other within a specified delay. If the changes should be reflected within d units of time, we have the following "temporal commit dependency":

$$((Commit_{t_i} \in H) \wedge (ts(Commit_{t_i}) = t)) \Rightarrow (Commit_{t_j} \in H^{t+d}).$$

This says that if t_i commits at time t, t_j should commit *by* time $t + d$. For another example, consider the following:

$$(temperature \geq threshold \wedge time = t) \Rightarrow (Commit_{t_j} \in H^{t+function(temperature)})$$

Here t_j could be a transaction that opens a valve to pass more coolant into the reactor whose temperature is above *threshold*. The length of time available to complete this transaction is a function of the current temperature. This is a form of triggered transaction but with specific time constraints imposed on its completion [Korth et al., 1990b]. Such time constrained activities occur in real-time databases [Ramamritham, 1993].

In some situations, it may be desirable to specify an interval $[l, u]$ such that t_j does not commit before l (the lower bound) but definitely commits before u (the upper bound). For example, consider deposits into a bank account. During the day, if a deposit is made before 3pm, it is just "logged" into a file but is reflected in the appropriate account between 10pm and 4am that night. Such constraints take the form

$$((Commit_{t_i} \in H) \wedge (ts(Commit_{t_i}) < t)) \Rightarrow (Commit_{t_j} \in H^{[l,u]})$$

The above conditions imposed on the initiation and termination of transactions can be viewed as generalizations of the preconditions and postconditions associated with specific transactions [Korth and Speegle, 1988].

For a final example of behavior related specifications, consider the situation in which it may be desirable to prevent a transaction t_i from aborting after a time t. This corresponds to the assumption that a transaction is implicitly committed if it has not aborted by a certain time [Rusinkiewicz et al., 1990]. For example, no bets can be canceled after a race is started and a lottery ticket cannot be refunded after a given time.

$$(Abort_{t_i} \notin H^t) \Rightarrow (Commit_{t_i} \in H^{t+1})$$

Other examples of behavior related requirements appear in [Ramamritham et al., 1991].

5 CONCLUSIONS

In this paper, we have examined different types of acceptability criteria and have attempted to provide a taxonomy with respect to *database consistency requirements* and *transaction correctness properties*. Given space limitations, we could examine, in detail, only a subset of the proposals that have been made to capture the correctness properties applicable to extended transaction models as well as those demanded by the newer database applications.

We have approached the problem of categorizing the different proposals by formally specifying them using the framework of ACTA. This allows us to clearly see where one proposal differs from another and what its relationship with serializability is.

We believe this taxonomy to be a good starting point in our endeavor to classify proposed correctness criteria and to compare and contrast them. It can be viewed as a common framework with respect to which one can study where a new correctness criterion fits and how it relates to existing criteria. In this regard, we expect the taxonomy to evolve as better understanding is gained about the correctness needs of emerging database applications.

Let us now examine some of the other implications of this work. In the context of a multidatabase system, the specifications of database consistency and transaction correctness can be viewed as requirements on the coordinator of the blackboxes [Breitbart et al., 1990b] that control individual databases. We would like to apply the reasoning capabilities of the ACTA formalism to study the properties of mechanisms, such as in [Sheth et al., 1991], for maintaining relaxed correctness properties of interdependent data. In the same context, we would like to investigate ways in which the ACTA primitives themselves can be used as part of these mechanisms [Rusinkiewicz et al., 1991; Sheth et al., 1992]. Similarly, in the context of active databases, we can see how the semantics of the rules that govern the triggering of actions can be formally specified. In addition, the relationships between the triggering action and the triggered action can also be expressed precisely using dependencies. Just as we were able to reason about extended transactions using ACTA [Chrysanthis and Ramamritham, 1991], we see the formalization of different aspects of active databases as the starting point for addressing issues, such as, reasoning about the consequences of rule firings, changes to rules, and coupling modes.

Commutativity Based Concurrency Control and Recovery for Multiversion Objects

Tatsuo Nakajima*
Carnegie Mellon University
School of Computer Science
Pittsburgh, PA 15213
U.S.A.

Abstract

Atomic objects have suitable properties to realize reliable distributed computing. Using semantic information of atomic objects can make reliable distributed computing highly concurrent. This paper describes a commutativity-based concurrency control algorithm in a multiversion object for highly concurrent distributed computing. Weihl proposed two concurrency control algorithms based on a commutativity relation: forward commutativity and backward commutativity. However, these commutativity relations are not subsets of each other, so that one cannot say which algorithm is better. The advantage of the algorithms depends on application programs. Moreover, each algorithm requires a different recovery algorithm and a different implementation of an object.

Using multiversion objects makes it possible to combine the two algorithms because multiversion objects enable atomic actions to access both committed states and current states of objects at the same time. We call our commutativity relation a *general commutativity relation*. The two commutativity relations are not subsets of each other, but a general commutativity relation includes both commutativity relations completely. This means that a general commutativity relation can achieve a higher degree of concurrency.

*Current address: Japan Advanced Institute of Science and Technology, 15 Asahidai, Tatsunokuchi, Ishikawa, 923-12, Japan.

1 INTRODUCTION

Designing and understanding highly concurrent reliable distributed systems can be very complicated. The major complexities arise from asynchrony inherent in distributed computing with regard to message delivery and unexpected behavior of processors. Distributed systems must be designed to function correctly even if it is possible for messages to be lost, for messages to arrive out of order, or for some processors to fail. An atomic action is a useful tool to hide the complexities by failures and concurrency [Bernstein et al., 1987; Eswaran et al., 1976; Gray, 1981; Spector and Schwarz, 1983]. Unfortunately, the atomic action may limit the degree of concurrency in systems due to the strong restrictions it imposes [Franaszek and Robinson, 1985].

Atomic objects, which combine object model and atomicity, were developed to achieve reliable and modular distributed computing. Atomic objects have the following merits over non-object based atomic actions:

- If all objects satisfy a same local atomicity property [Weihl, 1989a], all actions are atomic.
- Semantic information can be independently extracted from each object to enhance the degree of concurrency [Allchin and McKendry, 1983; Herlihy, 1986; Ng, 1989; Weihl, 1988].

The two merits are closely connected with each other. Using non-object based atomic actions, it is difficult to extract semantic information from applications because it is required that programmers consider the interaction among all atomic actions. Atomic objects enable all applications to be atomic only if every object is ensured to be atomic. Each object can extract its semantic information independently to relax serializability constraints. Since atomic objects can realize atomic actions in a modular way, they make the structure of highly concurrent reliable distributed applications much clearer.

Several researchers studied on concurrency control algorithms using semantic information of applications [Garcia-Molina, 1983; Korth, 1983]. A commutativity-based concurrency control algorithm is very attractive because we can reason about a commutativity relation from the specification of an object. Weihl proposed two commutativity-based concurrency control algorithms: forward commutativity and backward commutativity [Weihl, 1988]. Neither commutativity relation includes the other; so we cannot say which algorithm is better in all situations. The advantage of these algorithms depends on application programs. Moreover each algorithm requires a different recovery algorithm and a different implementation of an object.

Multiversion objects enable us to combine the two concurrency control algorithms. Forward commutativity uses latest committed states of objects to determine a conflict relation, and backward commutativity uses current states of objects. Using multiversion objects makes it possible to combine the two algorithms because multiversion objects enable atomic actions to access both latest committed states and current states of objects at the same time. We call our commutativity relation the *general commutativity relation*. The two commutativity relations are not subsets of each other, but a general commutativity relation includes both commutativity relations completely. This means that a general commutativity relation can provide a higher degree of concurrency than the two traditional algorithms. However, traditional implementations of objects which use only one state for each object cannot allow us to use a general commutativity relation. Using multiple versions provided by multiversion objects enables us to use a general commutativity relation.

In Section 2, we describe the properties of atomic actions and the use of semantic information in atomic objects. Section 3 shows a model for atomic objects. In Section 4, we define commutativity relations and present a concurrency control and a recovery algorithm for multiversion objects in Section 5. In Section 6, we discuss about the cost of our algorithm and give some discussions in Section 7. Section 8 presents related work.

2 ATOMIC OBJECTS

In this section, we give a brief overview of the properties of atomic actions and the use of semantic information in atomic objects.

2.1 ATOMIC ACTIONS AND ATOMIC OBJECTS

Atomic actions hide concurrency and failures in systems from users so that they make reasoning about the behavior of programs easy. Atomic actions have the following three properties.

- Serializability
- Recoverability
- Correctness

Serializability ensures that concurrent executions of atomic actions are equivalent to their serial executions. Recoverability ensures that the effect of an atomic action can be undone if the atomic action cannot continue to be executed due to site failures or user's interrupts. When atomic actions are terminated normally and confirmed to be consistent with other atomic actions, they are committed. On the other hand, if they are terminated abnormally or confirmed to be inconsistent with other atomic actions, they are aborted and all effects of their executions are undone. The correctness ensures that entire computation satisfies to be correct when each application is correct.

Object model is adopted in many distributed systems as the method of decomposing systems into small modules. In distributed systems, the autonomy of objects is important so that concurrent object model becomes very attractive [Yonezawa and Tokoro, 1987]. Atomic objects combine both concurrent object model and atomic actions which are very nice tools for reasoning about distributed computing.

2.2 USING SEMANTIC INFORMATION

Atomic objects have many nice properties for application programmers. However, we sometimes give up using them due to the limitation of the degree of concurrency. We can consider two approaches to relax its very strong restriction. The first approach is to relax serializability properties. In this approach, we create a specification which ensures the correctness of all applications. The specification should be rewritten whenever task sets are changed. The cost of rewriting the specification becomes very expensive if the task sets are changed frequently. The second approach is to exploit the semantic information of objects in concurrency control algorithms. Each object decides its own concurrency control algorithm using the semantic information of objects, but the object should be ensured to be atomic. We adopt the second approach to design our concurrency control algorithm because we consider that modularity introduced by serializability is very important in distributed systems.

To use semantic information, we can consider the following two approaches.

- Extracting semantic information from the specifications of objects.
- Extracting semantic information from the histories of objects.

There are several methods to use semantic information of objects. We use a commutativity relation in our concurrency control algorithm because a commutativity relation can be easily introduced from the specifications of objects. The second approach uses the semantic information of histories of objects. Multiversion concurrency control algorithms [Bernstein et al., 1987] use multiple versions of states of objects as semantic information to enhance the degree of concurrency. However, multiversion concurrency control algorithms use only committed versions, not uncommitted versions. Our algorithm uses uncommitted multiple versions as semantic information to enhance the degree of concurrency.

2.3 SERIALIZABILITY CRITERIA

The definition of the correctness for distributed applications is different from the correctness for parallel applications. In parallel applications, programmers can ensure the correctness of entire computation in systems. In distributed applications, however, each application may be programmed and executed by different users. Thus, each programmer can ensure the correctness of only his own applications. Also, the execution of applications may be impossible by the crash of machines and networks.

Serializability is a powerful tool because entire computation is ensured to be correct whenever each application is correct even if applications are executed concurrently and part of a system crashes. Also, we do not need to be aware of the existence of other applications, thus serializability can ensure the modular behavior of computation. Modularity is important in a distributed environment because we cannot assume to know all applications in advance.

In object-oriented systems, serializability should ensure that entire computation is correct if each object is correct. The properties was first proposed in [Weihl, 1989a]. He proposed three properties to satisfy serializability in object-oriented systems. When each object uses the concurrency control and recovery algorithm which satisfies the same local atomicity property, entire computation becomes serializable. In other words, each object can use a different algorithm which satisfies the same local atomicity property, enabling each object to select a suitable algorithm using its semantic information.

2.4 SERIALIZABILITY USING SPECIFICATION

By considering the behavior of computation at the specification level, the detailed behavior at the implementation level is hidden and we can focus on the essential properties of programs. Moreover, specifications can present the explicit semantic information which cannot be extracted from an actual implementation easily. However, in traditional programming languages, essential and non-essential states cannot be classified in the syntax of programs. The fact makes it difficult to use semantic information of objects in the implementation level. Then, our approach uses specifications instead of actual programs to extract semantic information.

Objects may be specified serially [Guttag, 1980] or concurrently [Lamport, 1983]. A serial specification is used when objects are executed sequentially and a concurrent specification is used when objects are accessed by concurrent activities. In distributed computing, concurrency is inherent, which is why we need to use concurrent specifications. Because concurrent specifications are very complex, it is difficult for users to use them and the verification using the specification is complex. Atomic objects enable us to use a serial specification to show the correctness of applications because the executions of atomic actions are equivalent to a serial execution.

Moreover, when we discuss the correctness of atomic objects, we need not consider the histories of aborted atomic actions, because aborted atomic actions do not affect the states of objects. Then, we can use a serial specification to show the correctness of atomic objects, because concurrency and failures are hidden in the specification level. In this paper, we use a serial specification similar to the specification proposed in [Liskov and Weihl, 1986].

3 MODEL

Basic abstractions for computation in atomic action are histories and objects. An object is a basic container of data. Each object has a type, which defines a set of possible states and a set of methods that provide means to create and manipulate the object. Computation is modeled as the interactions among objects, and a set of events is represented as a history. Events represent the interaction among objects, and a set of events is represented as a history. In this section, we discuss a specification and a history for atomic objects. We also define atomicity using the definition of histories.

3.1 OBJECTS AND SPECIFICATIONS

We can regard an object as an automaton and methods of objects as state transition functions. The automaton M for an object is expressed as $< state, s_0, op, \delta >$, where the universe of *state* is possibly infinite, s_0 is a set of initial states, *op* is a state transition function and δ is a state transition $\delta : state \times op \rightarrow state$ for the automaton. We define a sequence of *op* as op^*. State transition functions are a triple of a method name, argument names, and a return value. The transition is represented as [Method Name: Argument List/Return Value].

Next, we discuss how to deal with the specification of methods, using a counter object as an example. A counter object has two methods (*increment*, and *decrement*) and three state transition functions: [increment/ok], [decrement/ok], and [decrement/no]. The automata for a counter object is shown below.

$$
\begin{aligned}
& state \in \text{positive integer} \\
& s_0 = 0 \\
& op = \{[increment/ok], [decrement/ok], [decrement/no]\} \\
& \delta = \{[increment/ok](s) = s + 1, [decrement/ok](s) = s - 1, \\
& \qquad [decrement/no](s) = s\}
\end{aligned}
$$

We define δ^*: $state \times op^* \rightarrow 2^{state}$ (where 2^{state} denotes the power set of states) when the *op* modifies a state nondeterministically.

A specification for each method in a serial specification (simply specification) has a precondition which must be satisfied before executing methods and a postcondition which must be satisfied after methods have been executed. The specification for an object is represented below.

Object objectName
    State [*set of states*]
    Transition [*set of transition functions*]
    [function/return]
        REQUIRES (*set of preconditions*)
        ENSURES (*set of postconditions*)

In the specification, *objectName* is the name of the object which the specification expresses. *State* is a set of some states in specification and *Transition* is a set of pairs consisting of a method call and a return from a method, which means a transition of state caused by executing a method. Also, *REQUIRES* is a set of preconditions for the method and *ENSURES* is a set of postconditions for the method. If a transition is represented as $< s_1$ *op* $s_2 >$, s_1 must satisfy a precondition and s_2 must satisfy a postcondition.

3.2 HISTORY

Computation of atomic objects is modeled as a history, which is a finite sequence of events because of the absence of failures and concurrency. An event is a state transition function to change the state of an object. Let us call an event *e* and the state of an object *s*, Then, $s_{new} = e(s_{old})$ means that *e* changes an old state to a new state. In our model, events are classified into four types: a request, a reply, a commit, and an abort event. A request event is generated when receiving a message from other objects and a reply event is generated when replying to the message. Also, a commit event is generated when an atomic action is terminated normally, and sends commit messages to all objects which have been accessed. An abort event is generated when the atomic action is terminated abnormally. The order in which events are generated is represented by a concatenation operator •. Consider two events e_1 and e_2 are generated in the order e_1, e_2. Using a concatenation operator, the history of these events is represented as $e_1 \bullet e_2$.

When events $e_1 \cdots e_n$ occur in that order, the history is represented as $H = e_1 \bullet \cdots \bullet e_n$. Also, the current state of a system is represented as $H(s) = e_n(\cdots(e_1(s)))$ because histories are considered to be the concatenation of events which are the state transition functions. An event is considered as a history which is constructed from only one event. Thus, $H_1 \bullet H_2$ can be defined as a concatenation of events which appends all events in H_2 after the events in H_1. We define Λ as a history which has no event. Then, $H \bullet \Lambda = \Lambda \bullet H = H$ is satisfied.

Let us denote an atomic action as *a* and an object as *o*, Then, $H|a$ is a subhistory including all events of atomic action *a*, and $H|o$ is a subhistory including all events of object *o*. The states of atomic actions can be classified as *committed*, *aborted*, and *active*. We introduce three functions: *committed(H)*, *aborted(H)*, and *active(H)* in order to extract atomic actions in each state. The functions lead to the subhistories, $H|committed(H)$, $H|aborted(H)$, and $H|active(H)$; each history is constructed by the atomic action of that state. A history is a useful tool to reason about a distributed computation. We assume that atomic actions do not contain concurrency to simplify our discussion. Then $H|a$ does not include concurrent events, and all events is the history can be ordered sequentially.

The histories of atomic objects which satisfy our assumption must be *well-formed.* $H|a$ is well-formed if it satisfies the following conditions.

Definition 1 ***Well-Formed History***

- *The atomic action a must wait for generating a reply event after the corresponding request event, and an object which can generate a reply event for a must have a corresponding request event. In addition, a request event and a corresponding reply event must involve the same object.*
- *The atomic action a can generate a commit or an abort event in H, but not both; i.e., $committed(H) \cap aborted(H) = \phi$.*
- *The atomic action a cannot generate a commit event if it is waiting to generate a reply event, and cannot generate any request event after it generates a commit event.*

□

The assumption which simplifies the correctness ensures that $H|o$ is a *sequential history*. A *sequential history* has no event generated by other atomic actions between a request event and the corresponding reply event. This means that there is no concurrency in objects. We define a *sound history* as one whose $H|a$ is a well-formed history and $H|o$ is a sequential history. In our discussion, concurrency control algorithms and recovery algorithms should generate sound histories.

3.3 CONFLICT AND ATOMICITY

We define an atomic history using the notion of commutativity. Intuitively, two methods which have a commutativity relation can be executed in any order. If two methods in an object have no commutativity relation, however, we say that the methods have a conflict relation. The conflicting method should be controlled by, for example, blocking the execution of atomic actions. Below, we define a conflict relation, a serial history, and an atomic history. A commutativity relation is defined in the next section.

Definition 2 ***Conflict Relation*** *Let us define m_i as a method of an object and a_i as an atomic action. When a_1 executes m_1, a_2 executes m_2, and m_1 and m_2 do not have a commutativity relation, a_2 conflicts with a_1. The conflict relation between the two atomic actions is represented as $a_1 < a_2$. All events of a_2 conflicting with a_1 are executed after the conflicting event of a_1.* □

Defining a conflict relation in each object is the most important task of constructing atomic objects. We represent the conflict relation in object O as *ConflictRelation(O)*. *ConflictRelation(O)* is a binary relation on methods in object O. In commutativity-based concurrency control, all conflict relations should be symmetric.

Definition 3 ***Serial History*** *Serial history is a history in which the atomic actions are executed in a serial order. If the atomic actions $a_1, \cdots, a_n$ are executed in the order $a_1 \cdots a_n$, the serial history is represented as $H|a_1 \bullet \cdots \bullet H|a_n$.* □

Definition 4 ***Equivalence of Histories*** *Let each atomic action be represented as a_i, and two histories be represented as H_1 and H_2. If $\forall i : H_1|a_i = H_2|a_i$, H_1 is said to be equivalent to H_2.* □

The executions of atomic actions have to be equivalent to a serial history. We call the history which satisfies atomicity an *atomic history*. An atomic history can be defined as follows:

Definition 5 ***Atomic History*** *Let S be a serial history and H be a sound history generated by atomic actions a_i. If $\forall i : S|a_i = H|a_i$ is satisfied, H is called an atomic history.* □

All conflict relations in atomic histories should be consistent with serial histories. If $a_i < a_j$ appears in an atomic history, $a_i < a_j$ must be found in an equivalent serial history.

4 COMMUTATIVITY RELATION

In this section, we present forward commutativity and backward commutativity relations introduced by Weihl. Next, we propose a new commutativity relation: *general commutativity*.

4.1 TWO COMMUTATIVITY RELATIONS

One of the approaches to introduce the semantic information of objects in concurrency control algorithms is to use commutativity relations as conflict relations. Weihl proposed two types of commutativity relations [Weihl, 1988]: forward commutativity and backward commutativity. These commutativity relations are defined between state transition functions each of which is a pair of a method name and a return value (denoted as $[M_i/R_i]$).

Definition 6 ***Forward Commutativity Relation***
Two methods $[M_1/R_1]$ and $[M_2/R_2]$ are said to forward commute if and only if

$$\forall s : [M_1/R_1](s) \neq \perp \wedge [M_2/R_2]([M_1/R_1](s)) \neq \perp \\ \wedge [M_1/R_1]([M_2/R_2(s)]) = [M_2/R_2]([M_1/R_1(s)])$$

where $\perp$ indicates the function is undefined. □

Definition 7 ***Backward Commutativity Relation***
Two methods $[M_1/R_1]$ and $[M_2/R_2]$ are said to backward commute if and only if

$$\forall s : [M_1/R_1]([M_2/R_2(s)]) = [M_2/R_2]([M_1/R_1(s)]).$$

□

Let us consider a banking object as an example. The object has four methods: *Withdraw*, *Deposit*, *Post*, *Balance*. *Withdraw* is a method for withdrawing money from the account, *Deposit* is a method for depositing to the account, *Balance* is a method for checking the remaining money in the account, and *Post* is a method for adding an interest on an account. For example, *Post(5)* adds 5% interest on the account. We present the specification of the banking account below.

	withdraw/ok	withdraw/no	deposit/ok	balance/r	post/ok
withdraw/ok		×	×	×	×
withdraw/no	×		×		
deposit/ok	×	×		×	×
balance/r	×		×		×
post/ok	×		×	×	×

× indicates that the method for the given row and column does not have a backward commutativity relation.

Table 1: A Backward Commutate Relation of a Banking Account Object

	withdraw/ok	withdraw/no	deposit/ok	balance/r	post/ok
withdraw/ok	×			×	×
withdraw/no			×		
deposit/ok		×		×	×
balance/r	×		×		×
post/ok	×		×	×	×

× indicates that the method for the given row and column does not have a forward commutativity relation.

Table 2: A Forward Commutativity Relation of a Banking Account Object

Object BankAccount
State [s]
  [Withdraw: a/ok]
    REQUIRES ($s \geq a$)
    ENSURES ($s = s - a$)
  [Withdraw: a/no]
    REQUIRES ($s < a$)
  [Deposit: a/ok]
    REQUIRES ($s \geq 0$)
    ENSURES ($s = s + a$)
  [Balance/a]
    REQUIRES ($s \geq 0$)
  [Post: a]
    ENSURES ($s = s \times (1 + a)$)

The two commutativity relations of the banking object are shown in Tables 1 and 2.

4.2 GENERAL COMMUTATIVITY RELATION

The commutativity relations described in the previous section are not subsets of each other. Combining the two may provide a higher degree of concurrency, but this is impossible in traditional implementations of atomic objects. This is because forward commutativity requires the committed states of objects to check a conflict relation while backward commutativity requires the current states of objects. Traditional implementations cannot use

	withdraw/ok	withdraw/no	deposit/ok	balance/r	post/ok
withdraw/ok				×	×
withdraw/no			×		
deposit/ok		×		×	×
balance/r	×		×		×
post/ok	×		×	×	×

× indicates that the method for the given row and column does not have a general commutativity relation.

Table 3: A General Commutativity Relation of a Banking Account Object

both states at the same time so that they do not allow checking both commutativity relations at the same time. Multiversion objects enable atomic actions to access both committed states and current states of objects at the same time. The two commutativity relations can be combined in multiversion objects.

A commutativity relation that combines the two commutativity relations, called *general commutativity relation*, can be defined as follows:

Definition 8 ***General Commutativity Relation*** *Let forward commutativity relation for object o be FC(o), and backward commutativity relation be BC(o). General commutativity relation GC(o) is defined as* $GC(o) = FC(o) \cup BC(o)$. □

We present the commutativity relation using a general commutativity relation of a bank account object in Table 3.

4.3 RELATION BETWEEN TWO ALGORITHMS

As mentioned before, forward commutativity and backward commutativity relations are not subsets of each other. Weihl discusses the impact of recovery on concurrency control [Weihl, 1989b], concluding that each concurrency control algorithm requires a different recovery algorithm. The right combination of concurrency control algorithms and recovery algorithms can generate atomic histories. For example, forward commutativity requires an intention list algorithm for recovery while backward commutativity requires an undo log algorithm. The problem is that different recovery algorithms need different implementations of objects. However, implementing the two recovery algorithms in one system is very difficult. Multiversion objects solve the problem because we can use the same recovery algorithm for both commutativity relations.

5 MULTIVERSION OBJECTS

In multiversion objects, each object consists of several versions. Whenever a method is executed, a new version is created. The merits of multiversion objects are the followings:

- Uncommitted versions of multiversion objects can be used as history information to enhance the degree of concurrency.
- Committed versions of multiversion objects can be used to enhance the degree of concurrency of read-only atomic actions.

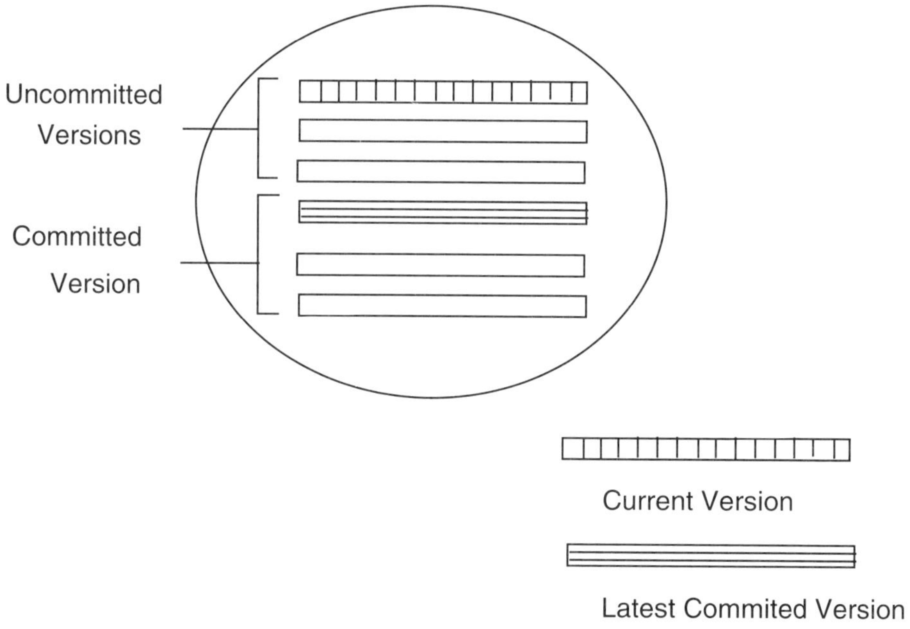

Figure 1: Structure of Multiversion Object

Multiversion concurrency control algorithms [Bernstein et al., 1987] exploit the second merit to enhance the degree of concurrency, but our algorithm exploits the first approach in a concurrency control algorithm. In this paper, we focus only on the first issue.

5.1 STATES OF OBJECTS AND UNDO OPERATION

First, we define the states of objects in multiversion objects and undo operations used in recovery algorithm.

Definition 9 ***States of Objects*** *Each object keeps all versions created by atomic actions, ordered according to their creation. Thus, an object consists of a sequence of versions. We classify the versions into two categories: one is a committed version and another is uncommitted version. Committed versions are those created by committed atomic actions and uncommitted versions are those created by uncommitted atomic actions. The top version of uncommitted versions is called a current version. Also, the top version of committed versions is called a latest committed version. We represent the current versions of object* o *as* $CV(o)$, *and the latest committed version as* $LCV(o)$. □

We show a multiversion object in Figure 1.

Definition 10 ***Undo Operation*** *Consider two methods* m_1 *and* m_2, *and their state transition functions* $op_1 = [m_1/r_1]$ *and* $op_2 = [m_2/r_2]$. *If* $op_1(F(op_2(s))) = F(s)$ *is always satisfied for any* s *and* F, *method* m_2 *is called an undo operation of* m_1. □

Undo operations are important to use in a commutativity relation as described later.

5.2 COMMUTATIVITY RELATION AND MULTIVERSION OBJECTS

Each version of atomic actions keeps a pair of a method name and a return value corresponding to the versions. When using forward commutativity, the execution of a method requires LCV(o), which is used to calculate a return value. We call a pair of a method name and a return value a *current pair*. Forward commutativity is determined using a current pair. Backward commutativity uses CV(o) instead of LCV(o). This means that the two commutativity relations require different states of objects. If we like to use both commutativity relations at the same time, objects must provide both CV(o) and LCV(o). This is the reason why we cannot use a general commutativity relation for traditional atomic objects. In the traditional implementation of atomic objects, a method in an object accesses only one version either CV(o) or LCV(o). However, multiversion objects enable the execution of methods that use both versions of objects as the semantic information of histories of atomic actions. Thus, multiversion objects enable us to use the general commutativity relation.

5.3 CONCURRENCY CONTROL AND RECOVERY

In this section, we describe a concurrency control and a recovery algorithm for multiversion objects.

First, we describe a concurrency control algorithm. The concurrency control algorithm of object o executes the following sequences in each object.

Algorithm 1 ***Concurrency Control Algorithm***

1. *Create a new version NV(o) using CV(o).*
2. *Calculate a return value using CV(o) and check for backward commutativity using the [method name, calculated return value] pair.*
3. *Skip the next step if the executed method has backward commutativity with other methods which were executed previously.*
4. *Calculate a return value using LCV(o) and check for forward commutativity using the [method name, calculated return value] pair.*
5. *Discard NV(o) and re-execute the algorithm from the Step 1 if the method does not have both forward and backward commutativity.*
6. *Let NV(o) become new CV(o).*

Second, we describe a recovery algorithm. The recovery algorithm for multiversion object o executes the following sequences:

Algorithm 2 ***Recovery Algorithm***

1. *Search the version created by an aborted atomic action.*
2. *If the version searched in Step 1 is a current version, CV(o), discard the version, and make a previous version be CV(o), and skip all of the following steps.*
3. *If the version is not CV(o), execute the undo operation of the method executed by an aborted atomic action in object o.*

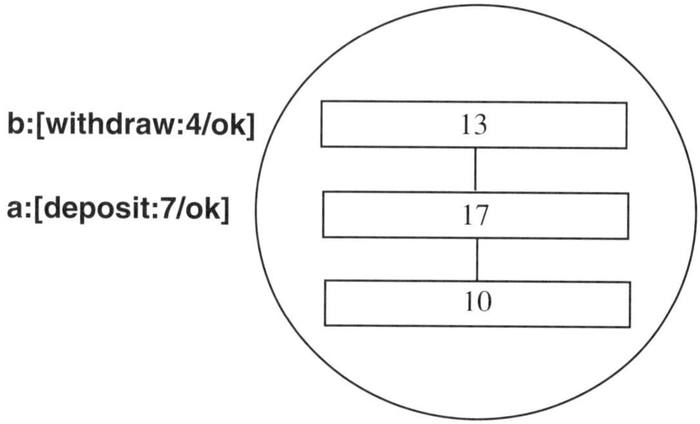

Figure 2: Bank Account Object

4. *Make the version created by the execution of the undo operation be the new current version CV(o).*

It is sometimes difficult to define an undo operation. However, if we cannot define an undo operation, we cannot use any of the commutativity relations. Let us reconsider the bank account example. The latest committed version of the bank account object is 10 and there is no uncommitted version. Two methods [deposit: 7/ok] and [withdraw: 4/ok] are executed in that order by atomic actions a and b. The versions 17 and 13 are created in the order of the execution of the atomic actions as shown in Figure 2. When atomic action a is aborted, we cannot recover the consistent state of the object because the current state of the object includes the effect of atomic action a. The execution of method [withdraw: 4/ok] should be suspended until a is committed unless we can use undo operation of [deposit: 7/ok]. If we can use the undo operation, we can recover the object by executing [withdraw: 7/ok] and creating the new version 6 where the undo operation of [deposit 7:/ok] is [withdraw: 7/ok]. Thus, undo operations are important to enhance the degree of concurrency in our algorithm.

6 COST OF OUR ALGORITHM

We first consider the cost of our concurrency control algorithm. The cost is divided into the cost of creating a new version and the cost of validating general commutativity. The creation of a new version becomes more expensive as the size of an object becomes bigger. In this case, we need to allocate memory space for the new version, copy the content of the previous version to the new version and change the content of the new version by executing the method. The cost of creating and copying a version is higher if the size of the object becomes larger. We can solve the problem using a copy-on-write technique, where we need to allocate and copy only those pages which the method actually modifies. Also, we can reduce the cost of caching the old version recycle the version for a new version. However for other recovery algorithms such as an intention logging protocol and an undo logging protocol, a redo log or an undo log is created for undoing the effect of atomic actions. The creation of a redo log and an undo log incurs the cost of creating logs and copying the states of objects to logs. Thus, the creation cost of versions is almost same as an undo logging protocol.

Next, we consider the computational cost of checking for the general commutativity relation. In the algorithm, if a method does not have backward commutativity with previous methods, it needs to be executed twice: once for checking backward commutativity and a second time for checking forward commutativity. However, shared memory multiprocessor systems are becoming common, and if we can check the two commutativity relations simultaneously, we may improve the response time to be almost the same as traditional algorithms.

The cost of our recovery algorithm is divided into two cases: the first case is discarding a version and the second case is executing an undo operation. In the first case, we need to deallocate the memory for an aborted version. The cost is cheaper than the recovery cost of a traditional undo logging protocol. In the second case, an undo operation should be executed for undoing the effect of atomic actions. The cost of the second case is the same as the cost of an undo logging algorithm. Thus, the recovery cost is cheaper than an undo logging protocol.

Another cost is the storage cost for multiversion objects. In the algorithm, all versions of active atomic actions are kept. Thus, if there are n atomic actions, n versions are created. However, our algorithm does not require the use of committed versions except the latest ones. Thus, we could keep only the latest committed versions and discard all other committed versions.

7 DISCUSSION

In this section, we discuss two issues. The first issue is the interaction between concurrency control and recovery and the second issue is the selection of concurrency control algorithms.

7.1 INTERACTION BETWEEN CONCURRENCY CONTROL AND RECOVERY

Weihl points out that the interaction between concurrency control and recovery is a subtle problem [Weihl, 1989b]. However, in multiversion objects, concurrency control and recovery algorithms can be selected independently. As described in Section 5, forward commutativity uses LCV for validating a commutativity relation, and backward commutativity uses CV. We can separate a conflict relation from a concurrency control algorithm because a conflict relation can be used in any concurrency control algorithm. For example, Herlihy shows that serial dependency can be used in either two-phase locking, timestamping, or optimistic protocol [Herlihy, 1986; Herlihy, 1987]. We can do the same. All conflict relations are validated using LCV or CV. Validating a conflict relation does not require a special recovery algorithm, but requires special states of objects. Thus, Weihl's conclusion that the correct combinations of concurrency control and recovery algorithms generate atomic histories is replaced by our conclusion that the correct combinations of conflict relations and state management strategies generate atomic histories. Multiversion objects allow the use of all states to validate conflict relations so that the best commutativity relation can be chosen for each object.

7.2 SELECTION OF ALGORITHMS

Several concurrency control algorithms such as traditional read/write locking, simple commutativity relation, forward/backward commutativity, or general commutativity relation can be used for the same atomic objects. Each object may dynamically select one of the algorithms because each algorithm has a different cost and a different degree of concurrency.

We need a systematic approach to change the algorithms. If an object requires a high degree of concurrency, sophisticated algorithms such as general commutativity is better. In the case where we cannot be allowed to use such an expensive algorithm, we may use cheaper algorithms which have weaker constraints. Such a framework promises the flexible execution of atomic objects and satisfies the requirement of future applications.

If some concurrency control algorithms are very similar to others, we may use the compositional framework of the algorithm in [Nakajima and Tokuda, 1992]. Complex concurrency control algorithms can be created by the composition of several small algorithms such as commutativity-based concurrency control and real-time concurrency control algorithms. We can create the best concurrency control algorithm from existing algorithms. The framework should be introduced from the specification of applications. To achieve the requirements, the implementation of concurrency control should be separated into mechanism parts and policy parts. Policy parts consist of the composition of algorithms. Complex algorithms such as commutativity-based real-time concurrency controls are created by the composition of several simple algorithms. The framework makes it easy to create complex concurrency control algorithms. The interface between policy and mechanism parts and between policies are important to create good framework.

8 RELATED WORK

Various concurrency control algorithms based on a locking protocol and a timestamping protocol for databases are described in [Bernstein et al., 1987]. Initial work in atomic actions left data uninterpreted, or viewed operations as simple reads and writes. For example, in Argus [Liskov et al., 1987] synchronization is achieved using two-phase locking. For built-in atomic data types, the operations are still considered in terms of reads and writes. Argus also provides user-defined atomic types which allow more concurrency by using the semantic information of the operations but requires complex implementations for application programmers.

Recently, a number of researchers have considered placing more structure on the data accessed by atomic actions, and have shown how this structure can be used to permit more concurrency. In [Allchin and McKendry, 1983], different levels of locking using more semantic information is provided. The choice of the level of locking is left to the programmer. Furthermore, the specifications concerning the compatibility of the operations have to be given by the user. We feel that the designer of an object needs to only specify the semantics of methods; their compatibility ought to be determined from the specification. In [Schwartz, 1984], synchronization of shared abstract data types is done by type specific locking. The compatibility of operations is determined by considering all the type-specific dependencies. Also, a commutativity relation can be led from the specifications [Weihl, 1988].

Several concurrency control algorithms that exploit semantic information of objects are proposed by Herlihy [Herlihy, 1986]. The algorithms use serial dependency as a conflict relation. Serial dependency is defined by using the validation of a serialization order. Serial dependency is an asymmetric relation unlike a commutativity relation. In serial dependency, if two methods can return the same results in any possible serialization order, a method has a serial dependency with previous methods executed by active atomic actions in the same object. A concurrency control algorithm determines to delay or refuse the execution of methods. This approach offers a high degree of concurrency, but it is difficult to extract serial dependency from the specification. Moreover it is difficult to use asymmetric conflict relations because in pessimistic algorithms we do not know the serialization order of active atomic actions in advance. Asymmetric conflict relations may increase the degree of concurrency, but these relations are more suitable for timestamping algorithms or optimistic protocols. In these, whenever conflicts between methods are checked, the serialization order is already known. We cannot exploit an asymmetric relation if we use a locking-based protocols. Thus, commutativity-based concurrency control is more suitable for a pessimistic approach.

In optimistic protocols [Kung and Robinson, 1981; Herlihy, 1986], the execution of methods is not delayed or refused during the execution of methods. The conflict relations are checked at commit time. When an atomic action is committed, the atomic actions which have inconsistent conflict relations are aborted. Optimistic protocols are suitable when conflicts are rare.

While many theories has been developed for concurrency control, these have been less theoretical analysis of recovery algorithms. Most studies treat concurrency control and recovery algorithms separately. Concurrency control assumes that recovery algorithms work correctly. Unfortunately, concurrency control and recovery algorithms interact in subtle ways. For example, a correct recovery algorithm, such as the undo logging algorithm, does not work with a concurrency control based on forward commutativity, and an intention list algorithm does not work with one based on backward commutativity [Weihl, 1989b]. For example, let us use undo logging. Consider atomic actions a and b which modify the same entry of object o. Suppose a modifies o first, saving the initial value of o to be restored when a aborts. When b modifies o, it saves the value written by a. Now suppose b commits and then a aborts. The value saved by a will be restored, thus restoring o to its initial value and erasing both updates. The recovery algorithms have subtle impacts on concurrency control algorithms, so we must consider a concurrency control algorithm and a recovery algorithm together.

Traditional algorithms for atomic objects use only one state of an object for both concurrency control and recovery. The algorithms limit the degree of concurrency because the history information of active atomic actions cannot be used. Other approaches use the sequence of events instead of states of objects. The approaches are useful to prove the correctness of the algorithm, but an efficient implementation is difficult to manage the events. Our algorithm uses a set of states of objects, so efficient implementation is possible, and can enhance the degree of concurrency.

Recently, Ng proposed *history objects* [Ng, 1989]. History objects achieve atomicity by considering serialization orders for active atomic actions. We cannot determine the serialization orders of active atomic actions in advance. He classifies the methods as observer methods and mutator methods. An observer method returns some values reflecting the state of an object. A mutator method modifies the state of an object. A concurrency control algorithm requires the following constraints:

- The execution of an observer method must not be invalidated by mutator methods executed by other active atomic actions.
- The execution of a mutator method must not invalidate observer methods executed by other active atomic actions.

He shows that atomicity is satisfied if the above constraints is ensured.

9 CONCLUSION

In this paper, we discuss a concurrency control algorithm and a recovery algorithm for multiversion objects. Our algorithm enables us to combine both forward commutativity and backward commutativity so that we can enhance the degree of concurrency.

In our algorithm, we use the following two types of semantic information to enhance the degree of concurrency.

- Semantic information of the specifications of objects.
- Semantic information of the histories of objects.

Traditional algorithms consider only the first semantic information, but our algorithm uses both semantic information in a concurrency control algorithm and improves the degree of concurrency.

Acknowledgement

We would like to express our appreciation to Prof. Mario Tokoro for his helpful comments and discussions.

Composite Events in a Distributed Object-Oriented Database

H.V. Jagadish
AT&T Bell Laboratories
600 Mountain Ave.
Murray Hill, NJ 07974
U.S.A.

Oded Shmueli *
AT&T Bell Laboratories
600 Mountain Ave.
Murray Hill, NJ 07974
U.S.A.

Abstract

Active database systems require facilities to specify triggers that are fired when composite events, specified in terms of other (basic) events, occur. These events may be detected within the object or remotely at some other object. We define a formal model for a set of communicating objects. and a formal model for composite events. With these models we study the interaction between the two, define a notion of correctness and show how to achieve it. Finally, we study the interaction of composite events with the traditional concept of transaction.

1 INTRODUCTION

Of late, there has been a surge of interest in active databases [Dayal et al., 1988; Dayal et al., 1991; Beeri and Milo, 1991; Silberschatz et al., 1991; Gehani and Jagadish, 1991; Lohman et al., 1991; Stonebraker and Kemnitz, 1991]. In an active database, a trigger fires when an event of interest happens and some condition is satisfied. Most efforts have focussed on the trigger firing mechanism and the execution of the triggered action. However, recent work [Dayal et al., 1991; Chakravarthy and Mishra, 1991; Gehani et al., 1992a; Gehani et al., 1992b], has recognized the importance of event specification. Of special interest is the specification of *composite* events, which are constructed from (simpler) basic events.

We consider a database system comprising a collection of objects. Basic events are database operations of interest such as the update of an attribute or the execution of a method in

*Current address is Department of Computer Science, Technion, Haifa, Israel 32000.

an object, the commit of a transaction, etc. All basic events occurring in a (centralized) database can be collected in an ordered set (in the order of occurrence), called the *system history*. Each object, conceptually, maintains a projection of the system history called the *object history* containing events of interest to this object. Composite events are specified as predicates on object histories. Triggers are predicates on histories together with a procedure to be executed when the predicate becomes true. When the system is distributed, it contains a number of sites each having a set of objects. (In this paper, we assume that no individual object is itself distributed to more than one site).

We introduce a definition of a "correct execution" in a distributed system and provide techniques for attaining such a correct execution. These techniques synchronize the posting order of events at the various sites. They resemble methods for synchronizing distributed transactions [Bernstein and Goodman, 1981].

We then introduce the traditional concept of transaction into the model. We show that if each transaction independently maintains correctness then the system as a whole maintains correctness. With transactions, we may also admit synchronization methods for events that work by aborting transactions that fail to obtain correct intra-transaction executions.

The notion of composite events is introduced in Section 2, and a model for expressing composite events is defined. Some distributed event specification examples are presented in Section 3, and the need for distributed composite events in an object-oriented active database is motivated. In Section 4, the formal model for distributed objects is introduced. Basically, it provides a software architecture specification for an object base with triggers. In Section 5 we introduce distributed protocols for attaining correct executions. These bear resemblance to protocols for ensuring serializability. In Section 6 we introduce transactions into the model. We show how a particular scheduling of transactions operations achieves correct overall system executions. We conclude in Section 7 with a list of open problems.

2 EVENTS

An "event" is a happening of interest. Events, including composite events, happen instantaneously at specific points in time. In object-oriented databases, for example, events are related to object manipulation actions such as creation, deletion, and update or access by an object method (member function). The events can be specified to happen just prior to or just after the above actions. In addition, events can be associated with transactions and specified to happen immediately after a transaction begins, immediately before a transaction attempts to commit, immediately after a transaction commits, immediately before a transaction aborts, and immediately after a transaction aborts. Events can also be associated with time, for example, clock ticks, and the recording of the passage of a day, an hour, a second, or some other time unit.

Event specification must start with a set of *basic* events, such as the ones mentioned above, which are supported by the database system. *Primitive* events[1] are basic events optionally qualified by a *mask*, which is a predicate used to hide or "mask" the occurrence of an event. For instance, the event "before a large withdrawal" can be composed using the basic event ''before execution of the method withdrawal" and qualifying it with the mask "withdrawal amount > 1000". We shall use primitive events as the basis of our discussion of composite

[1]Primitive events are referred to as *logical* events in [Gehani et al., 1992a].

event specification. We assume that primitive events are mutually exclusive and that their number is finite.

2.1 EVENT OCCURRENCES AND EVENT HISTORIES

An *event occurrence* (informally referred to as an event) is a tuple of the form *(primitive event, event-identifier)*. Event-identifiers (eids) are used to define a total ordering, denoted by $<$, on event occurrences. An example of an event identifier is a time-stamp specifying the time at which the primitive event occurred.

An *event history*, or simply a *history*, is a finite set of event occurrences in which no two event occurrences have the same event identifier. When this set is empty, the history is called the *null* history. The event occurrences in a history are sometimes referred to as *points*. An event occurrence e_1 takes place after (before) an event occurrence e_2 if the eid of e_1 is larger (smaller) than the eid of e_2. Two event occurrences e_1 and e_2 refer to the same event occurrence if their eids are identical.

2.2 EVENT EXPRESSIONS

An *event expression* E, which specifies a primitive or composite event, is a mapping from (domain) histories to (range) histories:

E: *histories* $\rightarrow$ *histories*

The result of applying an event expression to a history h is itself a history which contains the event occurrences of h at which the events specified by E take place. These intuitive notions are formalized below.

Let E be an event expression. $E[h]$ denotes the application of E to history h. It is always the case that $E[h] \subseteq h$. We say that E *takes place* at event e in h iff $e \in E[h]$. An event occurrence $e \in h$ *satisfies* expression E iff $e \in E[h]$; E is said to be *satisfied* by e.

An *event expression* is formed using primitive events and the operators (connectives) described below. An event expression can be `NULL`, any primitive event `a`, or an expression formed using the operators `&&` (and), `!` (not), `relative`, and `relative+`. The semantics of event expressions are defined as follows (E and F are used to denote event expressions):

- $E[null] = null$ for any event E, where $null$ is the empty history.
- `NULL` $[h] = null$.
- `a`$[h]$, where `a` is a primitive event, is the maximal subset of h composed of event occurrences of the form $(a,\ eid)$.
- $(E$ `&&` $F)[h] = h_1 \cap h_2$ where $h_1 = E[h]$ and $h_2 = F[h]$.
- $(!E)[h] = (h - E[h])$.
- `relative(`E`,`F`)`$[h]$ are the event occurrences in h at which F is satisfied assuming that the history started immediately following *some* event occurrence in h at which E takes place.

  Formally, `relative(`E`,`F`)`$[h]$ is defined as follows. Let $E^i[h]$ be the ith event occurrences in $E[h]$; let h_i be obtained from h by deleting all event occurrences whose eids are less than or equal to the eid of $E^i[h]$. Then relative(E,F) $[h] = \cup_i F[h_i]$, where i ranges from 1 to the cardinality of E $[h]$.

- relative+(E)$[h]$ $= \cup_{i=0}^{\infty} relative^i(E)[h]$ where relative$^0(E) = E$ and relative$^i(E) = relative(relative^{i-1}(E),\ E)$.

Regular expressions are widely used for specifying sequences. The above event expression language has the same expressive power as regular expressions [Gehani et al., 1992a].[2] Another widely used mechanism is temporal logic with its many variants. In particular, two such variants, QPLTL and SOLLO, have the same capabilities as regular expressions in specifying languages over Σ^+ [Emerson 1990].

It can be shown that the operators &&, !, relative, and relative+ constitute a minimal operator set; reducing it will make the expressive power less than that of regular expressions.

2.3 MORE OPERATORS FOR EVENT EXPRESSIONS

We present some additional operators (connectives) that make composite events easier to specify. These operators do not add to the expressive power provided by the operators introduced in the previous section.

Let h denote a non-null history, and E, F, and E_i denote event expressions. The new operators are

- E || F = !(!E && !F).
- any denotes the disjunction of all the primitive events
- prior(E, F) specifies that an event F that takes place after an event E has taken place. E and F may overlap. Formally, prior(E, F) = relative(E, any) && F.
- prior(E_1,..., E_m) specifies occurrences, in order, of the events E_1, E_2,..., E_m. prior(E_1,..., E_m) = prior((prior(E_1,..., E_{m-1})), E_m).
- sequence(E_1,..., E_m) specifies immediately successive occurrences of the events E_1, E_2, ..., E_m:
  - sequence(E_1,..., E_m) = sequence(sequence(E_1,..., E_{m-1}), E_m).
  - sequence(E_1, E_2) = relative(E_1,!(relative(any,any))) && E_2.
    The first operand of the conjunction specifies the first event following event E_1. The second operand specifies that the event specified by the complete event expression must satisfy E_2.
- first identifies the first event in a history.
  first = !relative(any,any).
- (E|F)$[h]$ = $F[E[h]]$; i.e., F applied to the history produced by E on h. Operator | is called *pipe*, with obvious similarity to the UNIX[3] operator.

---

[2] In [Gehani et al., 1992a] the operator $\vee$ is used instead of the operator && but the proof is similar.
[3] UNIX is a trademark of USL.

- $(<n>\ E)$ specifies the nth occurrence of event E. Formally, $(<n>\ E) = ((E|\texttt{seq}(any_1,\ any_2, \ldots,\ any_n))|\ \texttt{first})$, where each any_i is simply any.
- $(\texttt{every}<n>E)$ specifies the nth, $2n^{th}, \ldots,$ occurrences of event E. Formally, $(\texttt{every}<n>E) = (E|\texttt{relative+}(<n>\ any))$.
- $(F/E)[h] = F[h']$ where h' is $null$ if $E[h] = null$ and otherwise h' is the history obtained from h by eliminating all the event occurrences before and including $(<1>E)[h]$. Formally, $F/E = \texttt{relative}((\texttt{!prior}(E,\ any)\ \texttt{\&\&}\ E), F)$, equivalently, $F/E = \texttt{relative}((E|\texttt{first}), F)$.
- Suppose that E takes place m times in h. $F\ \ /\texttt{+}\ \ E\ \ [h] = \cup_{i=1}^{m} F[\,h'_i]$. h'_i, $1 \leq i < m-1$, is obtained from h by eliminating all event occurrences before and including event $(<i>E)[h]$ and all event occurrences including and following $(<i+1>E)[h]$. h'_m is obtained from h by eliminating all event occurrences before and including event $(<m>E)[h]$.

  E is used to delimit sub-histories of h, where the "delimiters" are event occurrences at which E takes place. F is applied to each such sub-history, and the results of these applications are combined (unioned) to form a single history.
- $\texttt{firstAfter}(E_1, E_2, F)[h]$specifies events E_2 that take place relative to the last preceding occurrence of E_1 without an intervening occurrence of F relative to the same E_1. Formally,

  $\texttt{firstAfter}(E_1, E_2, F) = (E_2\ \texttt{\&\&}\ \texttt{!prior}(F,\ any))\ /\texttt{+}\ E_1$.
- $\texttt{before}(E) = \texttt{prior}(E,\ any)$.
- $\texttt{happened}(E) = E\ ||\ \texttt{prior}(E,\ any)$.
- $\texttt{prefix}(E)\ [h]$ is satisfied by each event occurrence e such that there exists a history h' identical to h up to event occurrence e, and E is satisfied in h' at some event occurrence following e. In other words, $\texttt{prefix}(E)$ is recognized at each event occurrence as long as a possibility exists that an E event will be recognized eventually. This operator is normally used in the form $\texttt{!prefix}(E)$, which occurs as soon as we can be sure that E cannot occur.
- $E * T$ is a series of zero or more E events followed by a T event. $E * T = T\ \texttt{\&\&}\ \texttt{!prior}(!E,\ T)$.

In addition to the operators described above, there may be composite event sub-expressions that are used repeatedly in particular applications. Such sub-expressions may be defined, named and then used in building up larger expressions.

2.4 EXAMPLES

2.4.1 Event Expressions

- All occurrences of an event `a`: `a`
- The $5 - th$ occurrence of `deposit`: `(<5>deposit)`
- `deposit` followed immediately by `withdraw`:
  `sequence(deposit, withdraw)`

- `deposit` followed eventually by `withdraw`:
  `prior(deposit, withdraw)`
- `deposit` followed eventually by `withdraw` with no intervening `interest`:
  `relative(deposit, !before(interest)) && withdraw`
- Event expression that is satisfied when an `E` occurs provided there is no "non-`E`" event before it. We are essentially recognizing a series of `E` events:
  `E && !prior(!E, E)`

2.4.2 Discount Rate Cut

The United State Federal Reserve Board raises and lowers a key interest rate, called the discount rate, to control inflation and economic growth. Three or more successive discount rate cuts (`D`) without an intervening discount rate increase (`I`) is a rare phenomenon and is of interest to the financial community. Many other events can occur, for example, the prime rate may be cut and the stock market can crash, but these events do not interest us here. Our problem is to write an event expression that is satisfied by such cuts in the discount rate.

We will now give an event expression that specifies a composite event satisfied when three or more successive discount rate cut events `D` take place without an intervening rate increase event `I`. We specify this composite event in steps. First, the event expression

```
prior(I, D)
```

specifies `D` events that are preceded by an `I` event. Expression

```
!prior(I, D)
```

specifies all events except the occurrences of `D` that are preceded by `I`. Expression

```
!prior(I, D) && D
```

specifies `D` events that are not preceded by an `I` event.

The expression

```
relative(D, !prior(I, D) && D)
```

specifies a `D` event followed eventually by another `D` event with no intervening `I` events. This expression gives us a pair of `D` events with no intervening `I` events. Note that in this case, the `relative` operator is used to look at the history starting after a `D` event.

Finally, the event that we are interested in can be specified as

```
relative (relative (D, !prior(I, D) && D),
!prior(I, D) && D)
```

The outermost `relative` finds another `D` without a preceding `I` giving us three `D` events without an intervening `I` event.

Using the pipe operator, we can write the composite event for the three successive discount rate cuts simply as

```
(I || D) | sequence(D, D, D)
```

3 DISTRIBUTED COMPOSITE EVENTS

In terms of efficiency of implementation, it is desirable for an object only to take cognizance of events local to it. With this point of view, the initial design for Ode permitted only intra-object constraints and triggers [Gehani and Jagadish, 1991]. However, it soon became evident that facilities to express inter-object constraints declaratively would be highly desirable, and in [Jagadish and Qian, 1992] techniques are presented to map inter-object constraints into sets of equivalent intra-object constraints. In the case of general triggers with composite events, such mapping ideas may be applied, and indeed could form the basis for implementation. However, the direct expression of triggers after mapping all composite events to be local can be quite inelegant and not a desired form for users to write, as we shall argue with the help of the following example.

Let there be classes `Employee` and `Division`, the relevant parts of whose definition are shown below:

```
class Employee {
   persistent Division *works_in ;
   ...
   Boolean   ask_for_raise() ;
}

class Division {
   int earnings ;
   ...
}
```

Now suppose an employee would like to execute the function `ask_for_raise()` whenever her division posts earnings larger than some specified `threshold`, twice in a row. How do we do this? A basic event occurs at a Division object when its `earnings` attribute is updated. The occurrence of this event can be masked by checking whether the new value of earnings is larger than `threshold`. A complementary event is defined when this mask predicate is not satisfied. A composite event can be defined as a `sequence` of two occurrences of the masked basic event, with no intervening occurrences of the complementary event.

In the definitions of which objects do we place the triggers? The basic event of interest is an update to a `Division` object, but if we specify a trigger with class `Division`, we have several problems: firstly, we may not have an easy way of getting from a division to all its employees; secondly, not all employee objects may wish to activate this trigger; thirdly, even the employees who do activate it may choose different `threshold` values above which they consider earnings to be good enough to ask for a raise.

The alternative is to define the trigger with the employee object. Now there is a need for this trigger to be informed of events at the relevant division object. If we permit only local events, then updates to the division earnings attribute must cause a local trigger to fire in the division object, with this trigger causing new local events to happen at all the interested employee objects. It is unsatisfactory for such a technique to be programmed explicitly by the user since redundant events and triggers have to be defined merely to satisfy the requirement of locality. Furthermore, the problem of determining the affected employees remains, unless the division object maintains such an attribute explicitly.

Even worse, one could obtain incorrect executions in a distributed system. Consider, for instance, three objects O_1, O_2, and O_3 at three different sites. O_2 has defined a trigger that fires when event e_1 occurs at O_1. This trigger action sometimes causes event e_2 to occur at O_2. Finally O_3 has defined a trigger that fires when it observes, locally via processing messages, the event sequence e_1 followed by e_2. Now suppose e_1 occurs at O_1. Consequent local events are sent to O_2 and O_3. Suppose the O_2 local event happens quickly. This could cause an e_2 to occur, and a consequent local event to be sent to O_3, with this arriving at O_3 *before* the notification of e_1 arrives. Thus the trigger at O_3 may not fire even though it should have.

Errors of the sort mentioned above are difficult, if not impossible, to avoid if the user is restricted to local events. At the very least, intricate nested distributed sub-transaction models will be required. The alternative approach, followed in this paper, is to permit explicit use of non-local events in trigger specifications. For instance, in the example above, an `Employee` object could be interested in the non-local event

```
works_in->(after update) && (works_in->earnings > threshold)
```

The first part specifies an update event to the `Division` object representing the division the employee works for, the second part is a mask checking whether the earnings justify a raise request.

The trigger compilation system will identify these non-local events specified, and create a list of objects that have to be notified whenever an event occurs. This list is transparent to the user, and its incremental maintenance could itself involve some rule processing on updates. There is nothing conceptually difficult about this, and for the purposes of this paper, we assume that such a list can be created and maintained. Then, the hard question is how to ensure that non-local event occurrences are recorded consistently by objects that could be at different sites in a distributed system. This is the problem addressed in the rest of this paper.

4 MODEL

4.1 A CENTRALIZED SYSTEM: OBJECTS, TRIGGERS, AND DISTRIBUTORS

There is an alphabet, which may be infinite, of events $ES = e_1, \ldots,$. A *centralized system* contains:

- A set S of *objects* (described below).
- A *distributor* which is a software module in charge of event communication. The distributor sends and receives *messages*.

An active *object* (conceptually) includes the following two parts: (1) the *standard part*, containing data members, member functions, object identifier, and other "standard" object features; and (2) the *active part* containing the following:

- A set of *triggers* (described below).
- A set of *relevant event* which is a subset of ES.

- An *event processor*, a software module in charge of communicating with the distributor and determining trigger firing.

The *object state* is (1) the set of component-value pairs associated with each object component in either of the parts, and (2) the point of control of the computation (program counter). The *object standard state* is the set of component-value pairs associated with each standard part data member.

An object's *event history* is the sequence of events, in the order they were *posted* to the object, i.e. processed by its event processor. We shall also refer to this as an *object history*. A *trigger* is a specification of basic or composite events, formally it is a predicate, called the *trigger predicate* on the object's event history, together with a *trigger body* which is a procedure, this procedure may contain calls upon member functions.

An object can be in one of two states: *active* or *idle*. Objects are generally idle. Objects perform actions upon receiving an *interrupt*. An idle object becomes active upon being interrupted. An interrupt is caused by one of the following:

- An internal object event is detected.
- A message arrives from the distributor.

An interrupt is processed by the event processor as follows:

- An internal event e: The object enters the idle state. A message m is sent to the distributor with this event as its content. Eventually, the distributor will send a message m_1 back to the object notifying it of the same event. Once this message m_1 is completely processed (see next list item), execution will resume from after the interrupt point. Prior to receiving message m_1 it is possible for the object to receive other messages that may result in trigger firing and state modifications.
- A distributor message: Let e be the reported message event. First the object enters a non-interruptible state. e is appended to the object's event history; this operation is called *event posting*. All active triggers t are checked as follows. The history is checked against t's predicate. In case t's predicate is satisfied, t is said to *fire*. Let $t_1, \ldots, t_k$ be the triggers that fired.
  The object enters an interruptible state. In some non-specified order, one at a time until total completion (i.e. a *halt* instruction), each t_i, $1 \leq i \leq k$, body is executed. Upon completion of this execution, processing is complete and control returns to the point prior to the interrupt introducing e. This point can be within a method computation, within (an interrupted) trigger processing or the idle state. Note that while executing a trigger body, new interrupts may occur, and new triggers fired and executed, prior to continuing the execution of *this* and other trigger bodies which fired at e.

The distributor performs the following steps repeatedly:

- All messages arriving at the distributor are collected into a set of *pending distributor messages*. The distributor examines the set of pending distributor messages. If this set is non-empty, it chooses one of the messages to process and deletes it from the set of pending messages. (Some notion of fairness may be imposed but this is orthogonal to the model.)
- Let a message containing event $e \in ES$ be chosen, the distributor sends a message containing e to *all* objects such that e is in their relevant event set.

We make the following assumptions concerning message communication:

- All messages arrive at their destinations.
- Messages from the distributor to an object arrive in the order they are sent.
- Messages from an object to the distributor arrive in the order they are sent.
- No assumptions are made concerning relative arrival order from/to different objects to/from the distributor.

Method invocation in objects is done through the event mechanism as follows. When an object O_1 wishes to execute a member function at another object O_2, it (conceptually) detects a local event f_{start}. This event is then posted to object O_2, and causes the execution of a "trigger body" which is nothing but the desired member function. Once O_2 completes execution of the member function invoked, it detects a local event f_{end}. This event is posted back to object O_1, and causes a trigger to fire that causes object O_1 to resume execution from the point following the method invocation.[4] We may assume that each invocation is associated with a unique f_{start} and f_{end}.

The above mechanism for executing simple method invocations may seem baroque. It is presented here to show that the notion of events and triggers is quite powerful and can capture even fundamental procedural control mechanisms such as method invocation. Moreover, the correctness arguments in the rest of the paper rely upon objects not communicating except through event notifications. As such, even if member function invocations are implemented in the traditional way, the f_{start} and f_{end} events are required.

The *centralized system history* is the sequence of events contained in messages processed by the distributor, in the order the distributor chose them.

The above describes how a set of objects interact dynamically. The distributor ensures that each object's event history is a sub-sequence of the system history. At any point in time an object's event history is a prefix of the system history restricted to events in the object's relevant event set. The "outside world" may be modeled by a single object that generates the messages coming from outside; the initial state of the system has only this object as active.

4.2 A DISTRIBUTED SYSTEM: OBJECTS, TRIGGERS AND DISTRIBUTORS

A *distributed system* is composed of a finite set of *sites*. Each site is a centralized system as described above except that the distributors operate differently. The distributors at various sites cooperate to achieve a "correct" execution. The nature of the cooperation depends on the notion of correctness required. So, upon receiving a message, a distributor may record it and/or forward it to other distributors or objects. The distributor may also perform computations to decide how to treat a message.

An *augmented object history* is an object history in which each event is marked with three *labels*:

- Locality label: either *local* or *non-local*, indicating whether the event was detected at this object.

[4] This is similar to the "wait on condition" facility in most monitors.

- Trigger label: the set of all triggers that fired upon posting at this object; this set may be empty.
- State label: an object standard state, indicating the values of all standard object components at the time the event message interrupt is received from the distributor.

We assume the existence of a global clock, such that between any two adjacent *clock ticks* t_i and t_{i+1} an object can perform exactly one of the following:

- Nothing.
- Do some computation in its standard part, possibly changing its standard object state, and possibly detecting a local event. Make no computation in its active part.
- Do some computation in its active part but not in its standard part.

So, between clock ticks an object is either idle or active, but this activity must be confined to either its standard state or its active part. A *system execution*, E, is the sequence $E(t)$ for each point t in time, where $E(t)$ is the set of augmented object histories in the system at point t.

Definition 1 S-Correctness

Let D be a distributed system. An *initialization* of D by a total order H on a set of events S, is done by assigning to each object O in D an augmented object history, composed of the events in S which are in the relevant event set of O, in their order of appearance in H. With each such event there are associated labels.

A system execution $SX = E_D(0)\ E_D(1) \ldots$ for D such that $E_D(0)$ is some initialization of D, is *s-correct* iff there exists a total order T on the events appearing in SX such that for all times t, for all objects O,

1. O's event history, as derived from its augmented object history in $E_D(t)$, is a restriction of a prefix of T to events in the relevant event set of O.
2. The augmented history of O at $t-1$ is a prefix of its augmented history at t, where $t > 0$.

System D is *s-correct* if all system executions for D are s-correct.

Intuitively, s-correctness implies that all objects "behave" as though they were part of a centralized system. (We assume that the objects are programmed so that any centralized system execution is considered correct.) We shall make this precise below. Note that no demand of "progress" is made on D, i.e. a system that simply does nothing is s-correct. We may assume that D is required to make progress although we omit the precise definition of this concept.

Example: Consider 4 sites A, B, C and D, each having a single object, O_A, O_B, O_C and O_D, respectively. Objects O_A and O_B generate events a and b, respectively, which are in the relevant event set of O_C and O_D. Suppose a takes place at O_A and b at O_B. It is possible that the message arrival order will be $a\ b$ at O_C and $b\ a$ at O_D. However, in a total order on events, the order will be either $a\ b$ or $b\ a$. So, without synchronization, s-correctness may not be achieved. □

Theorem 1
In an s-correct execution of a system D, all objects go through the same augmented histories as in some centralized system execution.

Proof: We present the proof only for finite executions.

Let SX be a finite s-correct execution in a distributed system D. Let $T = e_1, \ldots, e_n$ be the total order on events, whose existence is ensured by SX being s-correct. We now construct a centralized system C and an execution for C in which all objects go through the same augmented histories as in SX.

Consider $e_1, \ldots, e_n$ in order. We have the following inductive hypothesis when receiving e_i at the centralized distributor of C.

- $e_1, \ldots, e_{i-1}$ have already been posted to objects in C having these events in their relevant event set and is the same order as in SX.
- For all objects O, for all events e_k in $e_1, \ldots, e_{i-1}$, the posting of e_k at O, if any, took place in the centralized system C at the same object state as in the distributed system.
- No events other than $e_1, \ldots, e_{i-1}$ have been posted to any object.

There are two cases to consider:

- Event e_i has *not* already been detected in C.
  - Let O_j be the object detecting e_i. Advance, in the centralized system C, O_j's state to its state s in SX when detecting e_i. If any local event other than e_i is detected, send it to C's distributor but do not yet accept it at C's distributor.
    Claim
    The above-mentioned advancement is possible.
    Proof: By the induction hypotheses, in the centralized system C the local computation of each object O is exactly the same as it was in SX up to posting e' which is the latest event preceding e_i which is in O_j's interest set (or the initial state if this is the first posting at O_j). The idea is to follow exactly the computation performed by O_j in SX, starting from the state s' O_j was in SX when posting e'. We claim that in D, the computation from s' to s was not interrupted by an event message arrival. Suppose, for the sake of contradiction, that such a message e_h has interrupted, then e_h would appear in O_j's event history, and therefore in T as well, after e' and before e_i, but no such e_h exists by definition of e'. This proves the claim.
  - So, we can advance O_j's state to s and detect e_i, and send it to C's distributor. Let the distributor process it by sending it to all objects with e_i in the relevant event set. These messages are not yet accepted by these objects.
  - Now advance O_j's state to state s'' in which O_j is interrupted with e_i. By an argument similar to the claim above, advancement is possible as O_j was not interrupted in SX by any other event message prior to e_i.
  - If there exists an object O_k, $k \neq j$, which has e_i in its relevant event set do the following. Advance, in C, O_k's state to its state s in SX when detecting e_i. If any local event is detected, send it to C's distributor but do not yet accept it at C's distributor. Advancement is possible by the same argument as in the above claim.
    So, we can advance the state to s and accept e_i at s.

- Event e_i has already been detected in C. Accept e_i by C's distributor. It is possible that e_i has already been detected since the order of detection and that of posting of events in D's objects are not necessarily the same when these events are detected at different sites.
  For all objects O_j, which have e_i in their relevant event set do the following. Advance, in C, O_j's state to its state s in SX when detecting e_i. If any local event is detected, send it to C's distributor but do not yet accept it at C's distributor. Advancement is possible by the same argument as in the above claim.

Observe that in advancing states we also mimic the computation of SX as far as trigger body execution is concerned. For all objects posting e_i, the posting in C is done at the same object standard state as it was done in the distributed system. Furthermore, events are posted at each object in C in the same order as in the distributed system. Thus, the only additional event posted to objects is e_i and the inductive hypothesis holds.

The base case is true when execution begins by definition of initialization. Hence the theorem is proved by induction. □

Corollary 1
In an s-correct execution of a system D, all objects go through the same sequence of standard object states as in some centralized system execution. □

5 DISTRIBUTOR PROTOCOLS IN A DISTRIBUTED OBJECT SYSTEM

5.1 ATTAINING S-CORRECTNESS

Here are three straightforward ways of ensuring s-correctness:

1. *Central site method.* All events are sent by local distributors to a central site distributor, this distributor defines a global history. The central site distributor, in turn, sends messages back to the local distributors residing in sites with objects having this event in their relevant events set. The local distributors then send these events to objects. Assume that messages arrive in the order sent. An event is *global* if it is in the relevant events sets of two objects belonging to different sites. Then, for all global events, each distributor defines projections out of the central site system history, and the system is s-correct.
2. *Events as transactions* (locking). Sending a message to a distributor is viewed as a write operation. Each event is viewed as a transaction that writes into all distributors that reside in sites having the event in their relevant events sets. A standard concurrency control algorithm, such as two-phase locking is used to synchronize transactions. In case of abort of an event (transaction), it is re-issued.
3. *Events as transactions* (timestamps). Here each site maintains a counter of *timestamp numbers*. (A timestamp is a pair of <counter number, site identifier>; the second component is needed to resolve ties.) When an event is sent to distributors at other sites, the current timestamp is attached to this event, and the timestamp counter is incremented. A local distributor collects events from all sites that may send events in relevant events sets of objects in the site. Assume that messages arrive in the order sent.

A local distributor sends an event message to objects in its site only once it can make sure that *no site* will later on send it a message with a lower timestamp in the future. To prevent starving for an event message that never arrives, if a site has not sent a message to an interested site for a certain pre-set time interval, a dummy event message with the current timestamp is sent to the interested site. Every so often, sites exchange messages containing their current counter. A site updates its counter to the maximum counter it learns about. This scheme is essentially the conservative timestamp method as described in [Bernstein and Goodman, 1981]. Then, all distributors define projections out of the global history, made out of events in timestamp order, and the system is s-correct.

In the first and third case, a unique ordering of events is globally enforced. In the second case a partial ordering is imposed such that there exists a global event ordering consistent with the order of events in each object.

5.2 CONFLICT

While s-correctness ensures that a distributed system behaves as though it is centralized, obtaining s-correctness as described above may be costly. Here, we relax the requirement of s-correctness based on a notion of *conflict* between events.

Definition 2 Distinguished

Event p is *distinguished at* O if one of the following holds:

- Event p is detected at O, OR
- There is a trigger in O that may fire on posting p.

Definition 3 Valid Triggering Augmented History

History H is *a valid triggering augmented history* for an object O if H is an augmented history for O and the trigger label of each event is the set of triggers of O whose trigger predicates are satisfied at that event.
Given a sequence of events at the object and the trigger predicates defined on it, one can determine the events at which triggers should fire.
Intuitively, valid triggering guarantees that triggers do indeed fire at these points and at none other.

Definition 4 Valid State Augmented History

H is *a valid state augmented history* for an object O if H is an augmented history for O and the state label of each event e is a possible standard state for O to be in, given the sequence of events, trigger firings and states preceding e.
Intuitively, valid state isolates the proper sequence of states given the sequence of events, trigger firings and states at the object. The key observation here is that events that are not distinguished do not have any immediate direct effect on the execution, and hence the object state. Therefore, only distinguished events need be considered for changing objects' standard states.

Definition 5 Valid Augmented History

H is *a valid augmented history* for an object O if H is a valid triggering and a valid state augmented history for O and the locality label of each event e is correct.
Intuitively, an augmented history for O is valid if it is feasible as far as O is concerned. In general having an augmented history being valid at each object is not sufficient for ensuring that each augmented history is part of a feasible global system execution.

Definition 6 Conflict

Events p and q *conflict at O* if one of the following holds:

- Both p and q are distinguished at O, OR
- There exists a valid triggering augmented history H for O of the form:
  $e_1[local_1, trigger_1, state_1], \ldots,$
  $e_i[local_i, trigger_i, state_i],\ e_{i+1}[local_{i+1}, trigger_{i+1}, state_{i+1}], \ldots$
  such that $\{e_i, e_{i+1}\} = \{p, q\}$ and the following augmented history, obtained by exchanging the event e_i with the event e_{i+1} (along with their labels and introducing some new states), and keeping the rest of H identical, is *not* a valid triggering augmented history:
  $e_1[local_1, trigger_1, state_1], \ldots,$
  $e_{i+1}[local_{i+1}, trigger_{i+1}, state'_{i+1}],\ e_i[local_i, trigger_i, state'_i], \ldots$
  Above, $state'_i$ and $state'_{i+1}$ are some states, they do not influence valid triggering which is only concerned with the sequence of events and the trigger predicates holding at each event.

Definition 7 Valid Exchange

A *valid exchange*, is the exchanging in an execution SX, at time t, in the augmented history of object O, of the order of two adjacent non-conflicting (at O) events e_i and e_{i+1}. Formally, exchange the sub-sequence

$e_i[local_i, trigger_i, state_i],\ \ e_{i+1}[local_{i+1}, trigger_{i+1}, state_{i+1}]$

with the sub-sequence

$e_{i+1}[local_{i+1}, trigger_{i+1}, state'_{i+1}],\ \ e_i[local_i, trigger_i, state'_i]$

If e_{i+1} is not distinguished, then $state'_{i+1}$ and $state'_i$ both equal $state_i$. If e_{i+1} is distinguished, then $state'_{i+1}$ and $state'_i$ both equal $state_{i+1}$.

Let D be a distributed system in which each site has a local site distributor and the site distributors exchange messages, where the assumptions about sending and receiving messages are satisfied.

Proposition 1
Let SX be an execution history in D and O an object in D. Perform a valid exchange of events e_i, at standard state s_i, and e_{i+1}, at standard state s_{i+1}, in each augmented history of O in SX that contains these e_i and e_{i+1} events, to obtain SX'. For each object O, for $SX'(t)$ at each point t in time:

- The augmented history for O in $SX'(t)$ is valid. In particular, there exists a computation of O consistent with SX' (i.e. locally to O SX' agrees with a feasible computation), and
- in $SX'(t)$, O goes through the same sequence of object standard states as in $SX(t)$, the history before the modification.

Proof: There are two cases to consider:

- e_{i+1} is not distinguished. Consider an augmented history H on which the exchange is performed. Then e_{i+1} is not local to O and also there is never a trigger firing at O upon posting e_{i+1}. So, had it arrived earlier, at state s_i, it would simply be posted and there would be no standard state change because of that. Then, e_i can still arrive at state s_i by simply not advancing the computation on the standard part of O. By the second condition in the definition of conflict, the resulting augmented history is valid triggering as e_i and e_{i+1} do not conflict. As locality labels are properly exchanged, the resulting augmented history H' is valid. Observe that O goes through the same sequence of standard states in H and in H'.
- e_{i+1} is distinguished. The basic idea is that since e_i is not a local event, we can change its posting time without affecting the validity at O. Consider an augmented history H on which the exchange is performed. This means that e_i is not distinguished, so e_i is not local and O never fires a trigger upon posting e_i. The change in H makes both e_i and e_{i+1} take place at standard state s_{i+1}. This state sequence is possible if e_i arrives after e_{i+1} arrived, trigger firings in lieu of posting e_{i+1} took place, O entered an interruptible state, but no trigger body execution (if any) or returning to the point of interruption, have taken place yet. By the second condition in the definition of conflict, the resulting augmented history is valid triggering as e_i and e_{i+1} do not conflict. As locality labels are properly exchanged, the resulting augmented history H' is valid. Observe that O goes through the same sequence of standard states in H and in H'.

In both cases (1) and (2), there exists a computation of O consistent with SX', that is SX' agrees with a feasible computation as far as O, locally, is concerned. □

Definition 8 Conflict Equivalence

Two augmented object histories at an object are said to be *conflict equivalent* (or simply *equivalent*) iff one can be obtained from the other via a sequence of valid exchanges.

Equivalent augmented object histories maintain the same relative order for each pair of conflicting events. In other words, each of the equivalent histories is a topological sort of the partial order imposed by conflicting pairs of events in which a precedes b if a occurs before b and a and b conflict.

Definition 9 Computationally Correct

A system execution $SX = E_D(0)\ E_D(1)\dots$ for D such that $E_D(0)$ is some initialization of D, is *computationally correct* iff there exists a total order T on the events appearing in SX such that for all times t, for all objects O,

1. O's event history, as derived from its augmented object history in $E_D(t)$, is `conflict equivalent` to a restriction of a prefix of T to events in the relevant events set of O.

2. The augmented history of O at $t-1$ is a prefix of its augmented history at t, where $t > 0$.

System D is *computationally correct* if all system executions for D are computationally correct.

Intuitively, we have relaxed s-correctness here by allowing the history at each object to be permuted without affecting the ordering of conflicting events. Informally, such a permutation is acceptable since the relative order of non-conflicting events "does not affect" the execution of the system.

Theorem 2
Let SX be a computationally correct execution for D. In SX all objects go through the same sequence of object standard states as in some centralized system execution.

Proof: We present the proof only for finite executions.

- Let $T = e_1, \ldots, e_n$ be the total ordering on events in SX. SX can be transformed into SX', by valid exchanges within objects' histories, so that in each augmented object history in SX', the order of events is the same as their relative order in T.

- By Proposition 1, each augmented object history in SX' is valid and in SX' each object goes through the same sequence of object standard states as in SX. Therefore, SX' is a hypothetical s-correct execution history in which the total order is T. Intuitively, SX' is hypothetical since although from the point of view of each object SX' "makes local sense" it is not clear whether SX' "makes global sense". So, we still need to prove that SX' is a possible execution history for some centralized system.

- The proof is essentially that of Theorem 1. The proof of Theorem 1 relies on two features of the execution SX treated in that proof:

  - There is a total order T such that in SX, for each object, the order of events is consistent with T.

  - In SX, for each point in time, for each object O, the augmented object history is valid (locally for O).

  These two features are also present in SX'. So, we can construct a centralized system execution as in the proof of Theorem 1 in which all objects go through the same sequence of standard object states as in SX', and hence also as in SX. □

Definition 10 Conflict Graph

Define an undirected graph G_D, called the event *conflict graph* whose node-set is ES, the alphabet of events. An (undirected) edge connects nodes q and p if q and p conflict at some object in the system. Divide graph G_D into its connected components. A connected component of an undirected graph $G = (V, E)$ is a maximal subset of V such that for all nodes $u, v \in V$, there exists a path in G between u and v [Aho et al., 1985]. Let $D_1, \ldots, D_k$ be the nodes, respectively, in each of the k components.

Definition 11 Independent Serialization

A set of events E is *independently serialized* in a system D if for all executions SX for D there exists a total order T on the events in SX which are in E, such that for all times t, for all objects O, the events in E, which are in the relevant event set of O, occur in O's augmented object history at t in the same order they appear in T.

Practically, to independently serialize a set of events E in a system D, we may use any of the methods for obtaining s-correctness on the events in E.

Theorem 3
Let G_D and $D_1, \ldots, D_k$ be as in the definition of conflict graph. If in an execution each set D_i of events is independently serialized, the resulting execution is computationally correct.

Proof: To show computational correctness we need to show a total order for all events in the execution, we do this in two stages. First, we define an arbitrary total order, $D_1, \ldots, D_k$, on the connected components. Second, consider the augmented object history of an object O. Since adjacent events from different connected components do not conflict, we can perform a series of valid exchanges to obtain an equivalent augmented object history in which all events of component D_1 precede all those of component D_2, which precede all those of component D_3, etc. Events that belong in the same connected component are independently serialized, so that their relative order is the same in all objects. So, we obtain a total order for *all* events in the resulting equivalent execution. □

All distinguished events of an object O are in the same connected component so they all conflict with one another. If O has no distinguished events then it might as well not be interrupted by event messages as they do not affect its behavior. If O has in its relevant events set distinguished events, say all in connected component D_1, and some other events, say from D_2, then those from D_2 have no effect on O's behavior and they might as well not interrupt O at all. So, intuitively, the above Theorem simply says that if the system can be divided into multiple disjoint pieces that do not interact, one can serialize each disjoint piece independently.

5.3 SITES AND CONFLICTS

The graph G_D is overly conservative. Consider the following three sites, three objects system:

`prior(`a`,`b`)` in object O_1 at site 1.
`prior(`b`,`c`)` in object O_2 at site 2.
`prior(`c`,`d`)` in object O_3 at site 3.

Assume that a and b are detected at site 1, c at site 2 and d at site 3. G_D is $a - b - c - d$ and is connected.

The synchronization suggested by Theorem 3 will require a single global distributor. However, local site distributors suffice, and there is no need for additional synchronization, in order to obtain s-correct executions (or computationally correct ones). In any execution controlled only by site distributors, we can easily obtain a total order consistent with the objects histories.

Finally, consider the following modification to the previous system:

`prior(`a,b`)` in object O_1 at site 1.
`prior(`b,c`)` in object O_2 at site 2.
`prior(`c,a`)` in object O_3 at site 3.

Assume that a is detected at site 1, b at site 2 and c at site 3. Here, relying on only local distributors may lead to executions which are not computationally correct. For example, O_1 may record a_1 followed by b_1, O_2 may record b_1 followed by c_1 and O_3 may record a_1 followed by c_1. There is no total order such that each object history is conflict equivalent to a projection of that total order. For example, a_1, b_1, c_1 agrees with $a_1 b_1$ and $b_1 c_1$ but not with $c_1 a_1$.

This example suggests that G_D should be modified to reflect *site information* and in particular cycles that span more than one site as in the last example.

6 TRANSACTIONS

Suppose now that all operations on objects are done within the context of transactions. In particular, the distributor actions, sending messages and receiving them, are all done as part of transactions. Conceptually, in a centralized system, each transaction is equipped with its own distributor. (Since all distributor actions are performed as part of the respective transactions, serialization of transactions will automatically provide the necessary coordination between transaction-specific distributors). When the transaction operates in a distributed system, it will have one distributor per site in which it is active. Sending a message is implemented by writing into a data structure within an object (or a distributor), receiving a message is done by reading (and perhaps writing) these data structures. Within a transaction, this reading and writing of data structures may be controlled using semaphores, monitors, or other methods: the coordination is left unspecified. Assume that the granularity of data at which concurrency control is applied is an entire object.

For instance, in a lock-based implementation, the above means that transactions employ *object level locking*. Thus, sending a message to an object requires locking it, as a write to the object is performed. This may lead to conflicts among transactions, and may result in deadlocks and abortion of transactions. When a transaction aborts all objects it accessed are brought to their state prior to being locked by the transaction. A transaction may terminate and commit only once all messages produced while it executed have been processed completely (this also implies that all procedures activated upon trigger firing have halted).

For technical reasons, assume that all updates to objects are done to a "scratch copy" which becomes the new object atomically upon commit. This implies that when we look at objects at any point in time we see only the *committed state of the system*, i.e., those values produced by committed transactions.

Theorem 4
Consider a distributed transaction based system D such that each transaction, if run separately, generates a computationally correct execution. At any point t in time, the committed state of the system is such that it is identical to the state of a computationally correct system that processes only the committed transactions.

Proof: Let all the committed transactions in the system since it started executing till time t be $T_1, \ldots, T_n$. The use of scratch copies and standard transaction processing ensure that there is a global serialization for all transactions. W.l.o.g., let the order be $T_1, \ldots, T_n$. In this serialization, the sequence of values produced for each object is identical to those that could have been produced in a computationally correct system processing the transactions one at a time in the order $T_1, \ldots, T_n$. □

Once the notion of transactions is available, one can rely upon the possibility of a transaction abort, to implement "optimistic" techniques for ensuring correctness, along the lines of optimistic concurrency control presented in [Kung and Robinson, 1981]. The idea is that no checking need be imposed on the recording of events, or upon any consequent trigger firings, while the transaction is active. When a transaction attempts to commit, the recording of events at the various sites must be certified as correct.

A simple certification procedure is as follows. Each site determines a set of partial orders such that for each partial order, for each total order consistent with that partial order, each object in the site can have the same augmented local history. A certification is done by checking that there is a total order such that, for all sites, it is consistent with at least one partial order supplied by the site. Observe that the simplest set of partial orders supplied by a site could be the singleton containing the total order established by the site's distributor. Also, the certification can be done incrementally, i.e., in parallel with the actual computation.

A more practical refinement of the above idea is to perform checks on event recording while the transaction is executing, on some selective basis. For instance, if two events from different sources arrive at some site very close together in time, then there is a possibility these could have arrived at another site in the opposite order, and a check is performed immediately to determine if this is indeed the case. Thus the loss of compute effort on account of abortion can be limited in return for some extra coordination effort while the transaction is running. Final certification of correctness is still required.

7 CONCLUSIONS

In this paper we define a formal model of a set of communicating objects. We consider centralized and distributed environments. We formally define the components of such a system: objects containing event processors and triggers, distributors for serializing event ordering, and messages for event notifications.

We define the notions of *s-correctness* and *computational correctness*. We prove that an s-correct execution is identical to some execution in a centralized system. We show that a computationally correct execution has the same observable effects as some execution in a centralized system (though some intermediate states that it passes through may be different).

We explain how s-correct executions may be obtained in a distributed environment. We also show how computationally correct executions can be obtained with lower overhead, with the help of the notion of a *conflict graph*.

We study the interaction of composite events with the traditional concept of transactions. We show how the use of transactions with object level locking can be used to obtain s-correctness. We also observe that with transactions present we can employ optimistic schemes, which may fail, to obtain s-correct executions.

Many interesting topics are left for future research.

- The concept of conflict between events can be refined. It may be overly conservative as presented. While in traditional concurrency control operations either conflict or do not conflict regardless of their usage, event order matters if it can affect some predicate, so it is a relativized notion of conflict. New synchronization methods can be developed based on this refined definition.
- As noted, we can regard events as transactions and synchronize them as ordinary transactions (or sub-transactions, when we deal with a transaction based system). This leads to a uniform treatment of transactions and events and simplicity in implementation. However, due to their simplicity, being a one operation transaction, this may be an overkill, especially when there are numerous events. So, the relative merits of the various mechanisms need be evaluated.
- It has been suggested that events have *parameters*, possibly representing the state of the system at the time at which they occurred. The use of parameters appears to restrict severely the flexibility available for coordination between sites in a distributed system. This issue requires further study.

In summary, we believe that the notions of event histories and composite events are crucial to active object-oriented databases of the future. In this paper we have taken the first steps towards designing a correct distributed system of this type.

Acknowledgement

Thanks to Inderpal Mumick for several illuminating discussions.

PART 5
OPERATING SYSTEM SUPPORT

Operating System Support for Cooperation in Distributed OODBs

Dinesh C. Kulkarni
University of Notre Dame
Computer Science and Engineering
Notre Dame, IN 46556
U.S.A.

Arindam Banerji
University of Notre Dame
Computer Science and Engineering
Notre Dame, IN 46556
U.S.A.

David L. Cohn
University of Notre Dame
Computer Science and Engineering
Notre Dame, IN 46556
U.S.A.

Abstract

While languages directly address the needs of distributed object-oriented databases, operating systems do not. Operating systems offer abstractions that are closely related to hardware and inadequate for close cooperation at the application level. This mismatch can be addressed by viewing an operating system as a mapping from the application domain to system resources. A new model of OODB applications as abstract directed graphs lends structure to this mapping. Experience with the ARCADE data abstractions, which essentially realize the passive portion of this model, clearly indicates the value of encapsulation, meta-data and even meta-computing. It has lead to the proposed π object architecture as an overall solution to the mapping problem. π is based on the generalized object model and supports meta-computation through manipulation of event-based interfaces. Its goal is to present an application-based interface which effectively utilizes hardware resources.

1 THE CASE FOR OPERATING SYSTEM SUPPORT

In any distributed application, threads of execution on disjoint processors must be able to cooperate. With proper operating system support, this cooperation can be both efficient and effective. Efficiency requires that the cooperation entail minimum overhead and effectiveness demands ease of use for the application programmer. These are most readily achieved when the operating system support is closely matched to the needs of the application. Therefore, this paper examines the requirements of distributed object-oriented database applications and details the kind of support they need. It notes that support from currently available languages and traditional operating systems is insufficient. It presents a flexible graph model that captures the programmer's view of the problem and maps this model onto a computational reality.

First, we must consider the needs of an OODB in a distributed environment. Not only must cooperation extend across machine boundaries, it must also cross the boundaries of languages, architectures and operating systems. For example, an interactive image management system written in Smalltalk running on a personal computer may have to deal with an image store on a mainframe containing images generated by a C++ program on a UNIX-based workstation. More interestingly, a CAD circuit simulator may want to distribute the simulation among available workstations. The distribution might also be adaptive to account for changing workstation load and availability. The CAD system could use one machine as a front end for rendering, a separate set of compute servers and a totally different system for storage. In these cases, the application would be crossing many boundaries. If the operating system paradigms do not hide these boundaries, they can significantly impede writing the application.

1.1 CURRENTLY AVAILABLE SUPPORT

Most operating system support for cooperation is based on hardware models. Classically, resource cooperation has been in the form of arbitrated access to physical devices and files. The exported interfaces are designed to appear as though only one entity is using the resource. The limited operating system support for data cooperation is typically based on either physical or *virtual* shared memory. Again, the interface hides the sharing and, with virtual shared memory, any distribution. Operating systems offer computational cooperation through IPC and communication primitives. IPC is based on the *process* model and the communication tools try to mimic a hardware channel. In general, then, the virtual machine approach continues to dominate available operating system paradigms.

Object-oriented languages also offer cooperation capabilities. However, rather than presenting a hardware-based model, they try to match the problem domain. By providing application-oriented solutions, they significantly ease the programmer's burden. Normally, they do a fine job of supporting data cooperation but say little about resource cooperation. To the extent that they address computational cooperation, they limit it to single applications. Rarely do they offer a mechanism to go *between* applications [Bloom and Zdonik, 1987]. Finally, since each language defines its own world, it can be extremely difficult to cooperate between elements written in different languages.

Thus, classic operating systems and languages fall short of providing the necessary cooperation tools. Such tools must allow effective resource utilization but must also be responsive to the application needs. They must be both generic and specific.

1.2 WHY CHANGE THE OPERATING SYSTEM ?

One might ask why we propose placing these cooperation tools at the operating system level instead of making them part of the language environment. The answer is twofold: they *can* be and they *should* be. They can be because they are generic. They are based on a model that can be applied both to OODB problems and to a broad range of other situations. They should be to improve performance. Although they use high-level abstractions, their efficient implementation requires full control of hardware resources.

Procedural languages like C and FORTRAN will continue to coexist with their object-oriented counterparts for some time. Hence, their needs cannot be overlooked in supporting object technology. Therefore, we begin by proposing a generic programming model.

2 A PROGRAMMING MODEL FOR OODB APPLICATIONS

We contend that OODB applications can be effectively modeled as *dynamic directed graphs*. The nodes of the graph represent *objects* and the arcs are *relationships* between the objects. The objects can be active, passive or both; and there are a variety of relationship options. The arcs may be object references, activation protocols, delegation targets and so forth. The graph is dynamic since new nodes can be created, old ones can be purged and relationships can be changed. The approach is best explained with an example.

2.1 A VLSI CAD EXAMPLE

Consider the VLSI circuit simulator example described in [Brockman and Director, 1992]. The goal is to evaluate the performance of a particular VLSI circuit that has been laid out by some design tool. The circuit includes devices whose characteristics have been determined, and it is to be driven by some test input. Thus, the simulator object has references to four passive objects: a netlist indicating circuit topology; the device model parameters; a test pattern of stimuli, and the resulting circuit performance. The simulator uses the first three as inputs to produce the fourth as output. The resulting model, including other links to the data objects, is shown in Figure 1.

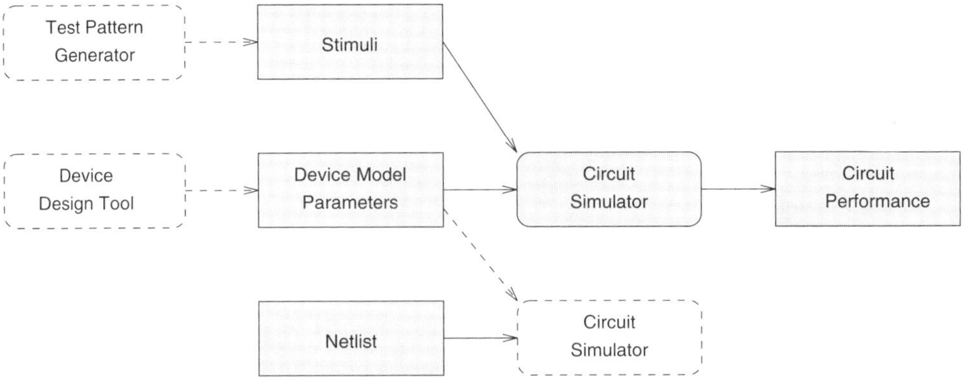

Figure 1: A Graph Model for a VLSI Circuit Simulator

The input data objects are persistent since they are the output of other tools. Once the simulation is run, the result object should also become persistent. However, it cannot stand alone. It must retain reference links to the three input objects so users can know how it was generated. Thus, the saved object looks like that in Figure 2. It is interesting that the same type of graph model describes the passive persistent object and the active computation.

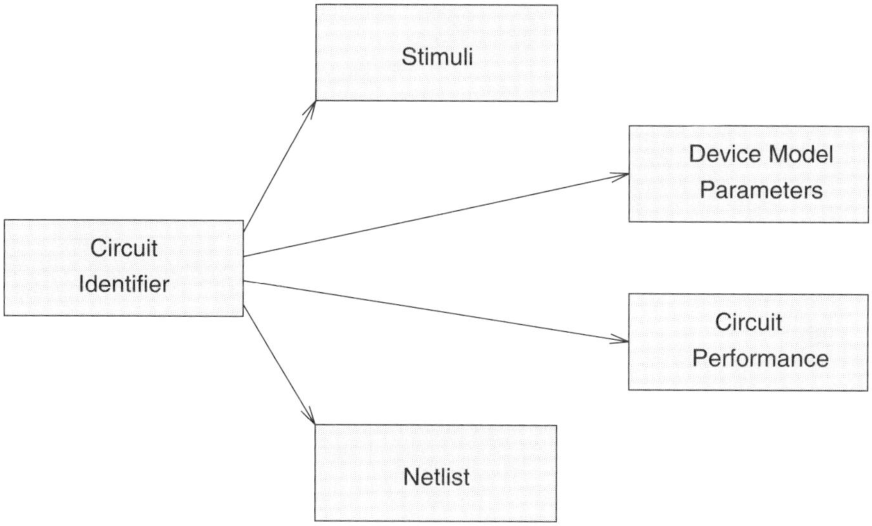

Figure 2: A Persistent Data Object

2.2 MODELING PASSIVE OBJECTS

A data object can also be modeled as a directed graph. For example, the CAD model of a robot could have a set of data objects containing the descriptions of its parts and a set of *links*, that tie these data objects together. The links represent the "is composed of" relationship, so that the arm "is composed of" a hinge and a gripper and so on.

The decomposition of data into these two components is universal, regardless of the application domain. However, the relative mix of data objects and reference objects depends on the application. Thus, a matrix computation would require far fewer references than a sophisticated VLSI CAD schematic tool.

2.3 MODELING PROCEDURAL PROGRAMS

The graph model even applies to classic procedural programming. In its simplest form, a procedural program is a piece of code that manipulates data. The code is linked to the data in some way, with different links to different parts of the data.

If we introduce a *code object* to contain the code, we can apply the graph model. A snapshot of the program would have nodes representing the code object and the data objects and arcs modeling reference objects. Nodes and arcs are first class objects and can be uniquely identified. In addition, subgraphs can also be considered to be accountable entities.

For more complex applications, the graph becomes more complex. In particular, the links represent a variety of relationships. If there are multiple processes, there will be multiple code units with their corresponding nodes. Links between code units would represent computational cooperation paths, and joint access of data objects would depict data sharing. If there were multiple threads in a process, this would be treated as metadata about the code object. Indeed, the code object would include all state information about the running process.

2.4 EVENTS

So far, we have only a static model. However, as an application progresses, its graph evolves. Thus, the topology of the graph can be dynamic. The progress of the application and changes in the graph model are triggered and influenced by *events*. Events occur both within and outside the boundaries of the application. Function calls, interrupts and messages from other objects are just some examples of events. An event is generated by a state change within a node which is exported by that node. Another node handles the event after being notified along a link from the generating node. Thus, event management deals with the generation, notification and handling of events.

2.5 BOUNDARIES

The reference links in the graph may cross a variety of boundaries. Links between active entities may represent cooperation between machines. A data object may have been created by a C++ tool and may be currently accessed by one written in CLOS. A currently-used data object may have been created by a now-deceased program. Numeric data may have been created on a big-endian machine and may be in use by a process on a little-endian machine. Thus, the boundaries can be between machines, languages, time and representation conventions.

While heterogeneity and interoperability are essential to run an application, they only confuse the programmer. He or she should see a clean model of objects and relationships. Clearly, there must be metadata to a support boundary crossing, but it should not be the concern of the programmer. Some lower-level tool, typically the operating system, must take care of the details.

The job of system software is to map the abstract application model onto a computational reality. A language gives the programmer the tools to express the application, and the run-time environment and the operating system control the resources that realize the model. Figure 3 shows the relationship between the graph model and the resources. It does not, however, depict the events which make the model dynamic. Events cause state changes in both the operating system and the application.

The mapping should hide a variety of changes in the computational reality. For example, new hardware technology may alter the tradeoff between computation and communication. Therefore, the mapping of the application model to the hardware cannot be fixed; it must allow evolution, perhaps even in fundamental ways.

Finally, the cooperation supported by the model should be *flexible* enough to accommodate the needs of a broad range of applications. For example, the coherency needs of different applications may vary; some cooperating entities require that atomicity be maintained while

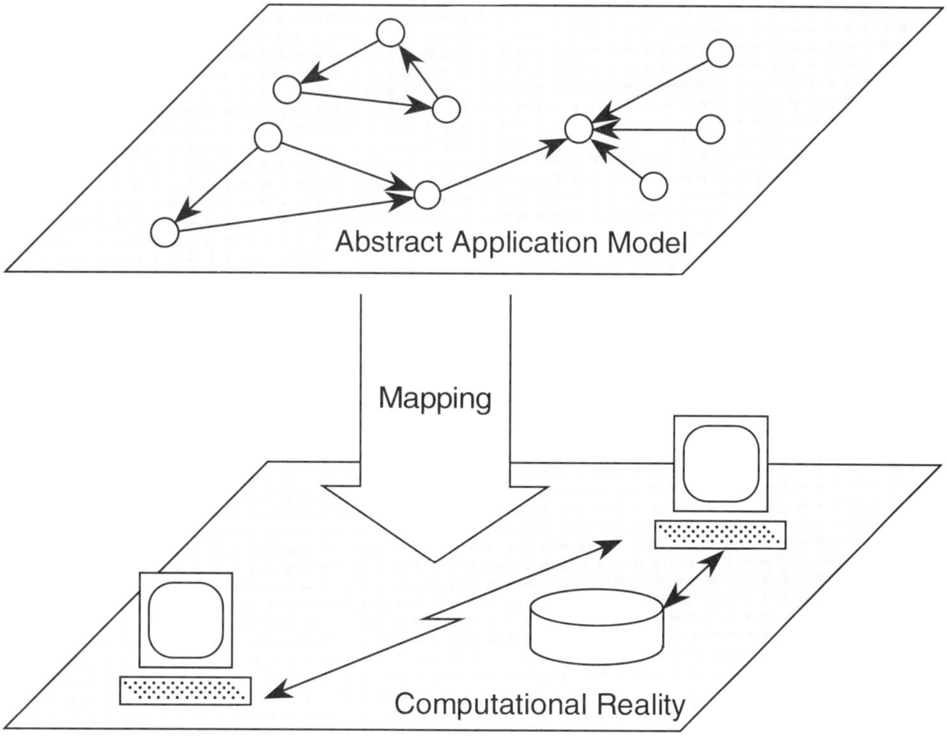

Figure 3: Mapping from Abstract Model to Computational Reality

others relax coherency constraints for better performance. Thus, programmers should be able to convey these needs to the underlying system.

3 LEARNING FROM AN EXAMPLE

We can learn what a proper application model must do by studying an important object-oriented database example.

3.1 EXAMINING THE EXAMPLE

Consider a typical VLSI CAD environment where various tools perform related tasks like circuit simulation, fabrication process simulation and layout. As noted, the relationships between the tools and their components can be modeled as a graph. The tools' resource requirements are dynamic and vary significantly. A circuit simulator using sophisticated device models is compute-intensive, while a layout tool interacts heavily with the persistent object repository and with the console. Further, the resources could be distributed; the persistent object repository may be on a server while the layout tool is running on a workstation. Interconnected workstations may be used to speed up a time-consuming logic simulation applications.

Data is generally an important corporate asset and its consistency and longevity must be guaranteed. Also, the transfer of data from and to persistent storage is a critical performance factor. The same applies to data movement between cache and main-memory in workstations and local and remote memory for distributed shared memory.

The cooperation pattern among tools also show great diversity. Sometimes it is sufficient to feed the results of one tool to the input of another. For example, the device design tool output could be input directly to the circuit simulator. Closer cooperation may be required between the router and the placement tool. A design rule checker or a constraint verifying tool may demand still more fine-grained cooperation. Thus, some tool cooperation may be satisfied with pipes, some may require RPC and some may benefit from shared memory.

The implementation issues related to address space boundaries and machine boundaries complicate cooperation and hamper utilization of available resources. Existing means, such as those available in UNIX, are non-uniform because they make boundaries visible. For example, data can be easily shared within a UNIX process's address space, while sharing it between address spaces or especially between machines is a different story.

Integration of VLSI CAD tools is a complicated problem. It has been pointed out [Brockman and Director, 1992] that tools rarely provide abstract interfaces on which to build a unified cooperation framework. Thus, events generated by one tool, such as method invocations or exceptions, may not have matching handlers in other tools. The mismatch could be the lack of a method handler, a type mismatch or incompatible method semantics.

3.2 THE MESSAGE FOR OPERATING SYSTEM DESIGNERS

There is a clear message for operating system designers in this problem: appropriate support for cooperation and management of resources and events is required. Some of the issues that need to be addressed in this context are:

- Applications and their components have differing and dynamic resource requirements. These resources include computation, storage and communication.
- Data could be anywhere in the storage hierarchy: cache, local or remote memory or even persistent storage. The hierarchy must be utilized effectively and, since data is a critical asset, provisions must be made for persistence.
- Applications use a variety of cooperation patterns that have different optimizations. Simple applications should access a standard interface without regard to implementation; others may provide hints to improve performance.
- Environments are heterogeneous. Cooperation should not be impeded by differences in machine architectures, languages or the base operating systems.
- Interfaces are critical for cooperation and component integration. They must integrate event management and should allow seamless resource utilization.

Implementations of an early version of the graph model have demonstrated the value of basing resource control on application-oriented abstractions. This partial model does not include a fully worked out event abstraction, but it does offer an effective graph model for data.

4 ARCADE - A PARTIAL MODEL IMPLEMENTATION

A passive subset of the general graph model has been implemented as the *ARCADE data model*. ARCADE [Delaney, 1989] is a set of high-level, data-oriented abstractions which offers ease of use, power and efficiency. It was designed to support closely cooperating distributed applications in both shared-memory multiprocessors and distributed memory interconnections. The basic data-oriented abstractions define a high-level model of data, much like that presented by programming languages. It has been implemented in several ways and we have found it easy to add support for distribution, persistence and other features.

4.1 DATA UNITS AND DATA UNIT LINKS

The principal ARCADE abstraction is the *data unit*, a typed data object with programmer-defined structure. The structure is specified when a process creates a data unit and can include common data types as well as *data unit links*. A data unit link is a generalized pointer, and its target is another data unit. Thus, data units and data unit links are the nodes and arcs of a graph. In a simplistic implementation, a data unit could be a record or structure and a data unit link could be a pointer. However, since they are defined as abstractions, a variety of implementations are possible and the links can model various relationships.

Although basically simple, the data unit is a rich abstraction. It is mobile; one process can send a data unit as a message to another. Using the known structure, the contents of a data unit are automatically translated when it is moved between heterogeneous machines. Thus, data units are a good basis for RPC. Unlike pointers, the data unit link abstraction can span machine boundaries. The implementation provides remote dereferencing, even for data units previously created by deceased tasks. ARCADE extends the concept of *moving* data units to allow *sharing*. Underlying support moves a replica of the data unit and maintains coherency. In this way, a shared data unit becomes a region of distributed shared memory. Data unit *locks*, modeled after database locks, allow applications to control coherency.

Data units and data unit links clearly demonstrate the inherent power of high-level abstractions. The abstractions say nothing about distribution, but data units can move between machines and data unit links can span machine boundaries. A range of *coherency protocols*, using locks, hints and access patterns, can be made available [Nitzberg and Lo, 1991]. Since data units exist independently of any process, a *persistence* structure can be added on top of them. As they are updated, a hidden record of *versions* can be kept to allow rollback when needed. Indeed, a full *nested transaction* structure has been built for data units. This abstract view of data and relationships has been used to model language-level facilities in both procedural and object-oriented languages.

4.2 THE IMPORTANCE OF METADATA

These high-level abstractions derive their power and flexibility from the use of *metadata*, information about data. This includes information on structure, replicas and coherency. Ancillary properties typically increase the pool of metadata which is normally protected from user processes. Separate parts of the metadata may be maintained by different components of an implementation. For example, the kernel implementing data units may maintain the metadata related to coherency while a server task manages that concerning persistence.

Saving metadata allows the structure of composite data objects to be preserved. Indeed, metadata is the basis for implementing persistent store management. Similarly, if an underlying system knows the layout of data object instances, it can provide interoperability between languages which use different layouts.

Since the ARCADE data model is a high-level abstraction, there are many implementation options. The next section describes several that are matched to various hardware platforms and operating systems and demonstrates the ability of the data unit paradigm to support higher-level functionality such as nested transactions and language-level entities.

5 USING THE ARCADE DATA MODEL

This section summarizes several ARCADE implementations and explains how they have been used as building blocks for higher-level abstractions. It describes a nested transaction support system which uses persistent data units and shows how data units can be used to create a dynamic distributed data structure. It ends with a description of models for language-level distributed objects.

5.1 DATA UNIT IMPLEMENTATIONS

The ARCADE *service provider* actually implements the abstractions and has several different realizations. Data unit and data unit link support has been used as the basis for micro-kernels on both 80x86-based IBM PS/2s and an IBM System/370 machine, and has been added to Mach, OS/2 and VM/CMS [Cohn et al., 1992]. These implementations interoperate, illustrating that cooperation across a wide range of platforms is feasible, and that implementation is straight-forward. The high-level view avoids assumptions about the underlying platform and its conciseness creates a RISC-like effect in software implementations.

In each implementation, the service provider is custodian of the metadata which supports the basic data model. It also maintains client information to ensure location-independent cooperation. It seamlessly interacts with other service providers to support the movement and sharing of data and the activation and synchronization of process-like entities. While the structure of the service providers varies drastically, the exported data model interface remains the same.

5.2 PERSISTENCE

The basic ARCADE data model includes mobility and coherence, but it does not explicitly include persistence. However, we have extended the model and added persistence as an *ancillary property*. A persistent data unit is created normally and then shared with a *persistence server*. Using data links, this means that a persistent object can have arbitrary structure and can span machine boundaries. When it is stored, the persistence server preserves the full data structure. Thus, the burden of "flattening" has been lifted from applications.

The persistence server knows the full *structure* of composite objects; both the overall linkage topology and the structural types of the component data units. Hence it can support run-time structural type checking for flexible and type-safe binding. Unlike in Napier [Morrison et al., 1990], the persistence server is not involved in name-equivalence checking for type safety since that is a language-specific issue.

5.3 NESTED TRANSACTIONS

A nested transaction system can guarantee reliability by making changes to related persistent objects atomic. *Atomicity*, like persistence, can be added as an ancillary property to data units. A nested transaction system has been implemented on top of the 80x86 micro-kernel realization as a set of service tasks [Kulkarni, 1991; Kulkarni et al., 1992]. These tasks manage a new type of lock on behalf of client tasks and ensure recoverability by cooperating with the persistence server. The basic locks provide *coherency* among replicas of a data unit; the new locks ensure serializability, and hence *consistency*. However, these details are transparent to the application. It views an atomic data unit simply as an enhancement of the basic abstraction.

From a developer's perspective, the creation of the nested transaction subsystem was facilitated by the data model. The basic data abstraction is uniformly used by a transaction manager for interaction with peer transaction managers on other machines, with the local persistent store manager and with clients. Ancillary persistence is used for exporting the even richer property of atomicity. Compared to the early version of Camelot [Bloch, 1989] library, a transaction support component for Mach which had comparable functionality, the nested transaction subsystem required less development time and programming effort.

5.4 A SAMPLE APPLICATION - DISTRIBUTED TREE

As an example of the use of the basic model and the ancillary properties, consider a group of processes that share a tree data structure [Cohn et al., 1991]. The nodes of the tree are data objects and each process may read or write any object. The *grain of coherency* is the data object; that is, there may be a single writer or multiple readers for each node. Thus, the nodes can be implemented as data units and the arcs as data unit links. The goal is to distribute the work among multiple processors and maximize concurrency.

Each process is given access to the root of the tree and can search the tree by following data unit links. At each step, if the target of a data unit link is not replicated locally, a copy is created automatically. Coherency is obtained through the use of locks and is guaranteed by the implementation. Since each link points to a single data unit, the traversal of the tree always gives the same data object at each step, regardless of the location of the task performing the traversal. At any stage during the execution, the application can decide to make a subtree (or the entire tree) persistent simply by invoking the persistence service and handing over the root of the subtree to the server. Thus, the user has full control over granularity, distribution and persistence.

5.5 MELDING THE MODEL AND LANGUAGES

Naturally, programmers see the ARCADE data model through the filter of a high-level language. Data units and data unit links have proven to be effective building blocks for abstract data types in object-oriented languages and for structural types in procedural languages. They support data objects and a generalization supports instantiations of active objects. Moreover, distribution can be added to the run-time environment of languages like C++ by using class libraries that support data units and data unit links. Data units and data unit links are encapsulated abstractions and are therefore an excellent basis for mobile objects. This subsection describes two ARCADE-based language implementations, one using objects and the other essentially procedural.

5.5.1 Object-oriented Extension of C

An object-oriented extension of C was created which uses the encapsulation and mobility of data units to provide language-level objects with methods and data [Bryden, 1989]. It provides five basic messaging primitives:

TELL sends a simple message from client to server without any reply.
ASK implements a synchronous method invocation with reply similar to RPC.
SUBMIT is an asynchronous ASK where the client collects results later.
REPLY is used by the server to return results for ASK and SUBMIT.
FORWARD can be used for inheritance through delegation.

Since all the links in a message object are independent of the context of the task, delegation can be effected without additional support for marshalling. This project showed that the data unit abstraction could support encapsulated objects. Code sharing was achieved using the underlying basis of the ARCADE task abstraction.

The data unit link abstraction can be generalized to support static inheritance as in languages like C++ to refer to both data as well as code. Such *executable links*, along with normal data unit links, can provide the efficiencies static inheritance guarantees. Thus, ARCADE services can extend the power of traditional languages and their implementations.

5.5.2 ABC - Adding Distribution to C

ARCADE-Based C or ABC [Banerji, 1990], offers the data unit and data unit link abstractions in the context of normal C semantics. For example, a data unit can be declared essentially as a normal structure:

```
du_struct tag_s
{
int x;
char* y;
}*eg;
```

This data unit has one entry that is an integer and one that is a data unit link pointing to a data unit which contains characters. To instantiate this data unit, instead of a normal `malloc()`, the programmer uses:

```
eg = (du_struct tag_s *) abc_alloc (typeof(du_struct tag_s));
```

where `typeof()` has replaced `sizeof()`. In a similar way, a C programmer can deal with concurrency through synchronous and asynchronous function calls.

RPC is a valuable cooperation mechanism because it is a simple extension of the familiar procedure call. Likewise, in ABC, shared data is treated as a specialization of global variables. Thus, structured distributed shared memory and asynchronous activations can have a natural place in existing languages.

5.6 OBJECT MODEL EXTENSIONS

Similar extensions could be made to run-time support for traditional object-oriented languages like C++. For example, class constructors could use ARCADE's version of new() and delete(), effectively allowing the ARCADE service provider to manage the object instances. The base classes of `data unit` and `data unit link` could be used to implement remote operations, asynchronous activations, distributed shared object instances and persistent objects.

The implementation of various distributed object models can be facilitated by the ARCADE data management services. For example, object *fragments* and their relationships could be realized as data units and data unit links. Then, the language implementor could choose between message passing and distributed shared memory to manipulate fragment instances [Makpangou et al., 1991a]. The *FORWARD* primitive mirrors the proxies [Shapiro, 1986] necessary to communicate between different fragments. More importantly, the ARCADE data model would naturally include object identification with data unit links. Links provide the functionality of Bellerophon references [Dickman, 1993b] and can be used to implements surrogates as in Thor [Liskov et al., 1993].

5.7 THE VALUE OF MOBILITY AND STRUCTURE

Run-time systems for distributed languages must support remote activations and track migrating tasks. However, migrating an ARCADE task is transparent and finding them is automatic. In fact, a task management system [Tracey, 1991] has been written for the 80x86 micro-kernel implementation which places tasks on idle machines and moves them in response to changes in local load. Languages such as Emerald [Black et al., 1987], implement remote activations through data object mobility. ARCADE's data units are easily replicated across machine boundaries which reduces the communication burden for invoking Emerald-like methods. Emerald does not assume a coherence control subsystem so only immutable data objects can be replicated. Thus, the ARCADE model would be an ideal substrate for Emerald and similar languages.

Structurally-typed data objects facilitate several kinds of interoperability. The uniform availability of type information allows run-time type checking for flexible client-server binding. Mercury [Liskov, 1991] uses RPC to offer similar support between components written in different languages. However, with data units, heterogeneous components can share data for closer cooperation. They even allow cross-language interaction between procedural and object-oriented languages.

6 THE LESSONS OF ARCADE

Although ARCADE offers only a partial realization of the graph model, it provides valuable insight on the approach. This section summarizes these lessons.

- *Abstractions should match the needs of languages.* The mismatch between classic hardware-based abstractions and applications affects both performance and ease of use. We have found that distributed shared data is a much better model than distributed shared memory.
- *Metadata is critical.* It provides much of the power of the abstractions by adding meaning to the data. The ability to manipulate this metadata would add a new dimension to the model.
- *Multiple*, even seemingly redundant, cooperation models are needed. Different situations require different tools and choice is important for supporting a variety of applications. With choice, the stage is set for eventually adding adaptation.
- *High-level abstractions enable heterogeneous interoperation.* Abstractions which span machine, operating system and architectural boundaries allow the programmer to focus on application problems. Heterogeneous interoperation is inhibited by the virtual machine model of operating systems.
- *A flexible graph model is a powerful basis.* It can model the application and can evolve as relationships change. ARCADE used it for passive data objects and it can be extended to active objects and behavioral changes.
- *Implementation choices should be available.* Focus should be on functionality and the abstraction service interface should be implementation-independent. The implementation can then evolve without changing the abstractions. Different situations can have different implementations and cooperation between realizations will identify the value of the model.

7 π: VISION AND FOUNDATIONS

Using the lessons from ARCADE and a careful analysis of OODB application requirements, we propose π, a new mapping from the problem domain to the computational reality. π has a uniform object architecture for its constituent objects and those in its application model. The structure of these objects and their interaction defines π.

π objects have explicit interfaces and support identification of objects. Each object has an interface describing its behavior and may have a second interface for metacomputing to alter its behavior or implementation. The *application interface* encapsulates the behavioral description and the *system interface* the metacomputational. An application developer can use these interfaces directly and can extend them through interface inheritance. He or she builds an application through inheritance by gluing interfaces or by augmenting them.

7.1 THE APPLICATION INTERFACE

The application interface of a π object is based on the *generalized object model*. First, an operation request can have parameters which may identify objects. Second, method selection may ultimately be based on these parameters and on the operation itself. Thus, method selection is done by the system, rather than by the requesting object [Soley, 1990]. The combination of metacomputing and the generalized object model provides a powerful tool for customizing the operatin g environment.

The application interface specifies both the *incoming* events handled by the object and the *outgoing* events generated by the object. Such events may include method invocations, exceptions and interrupts. The interface defines the type of any accompanying data and any constraints on the data or the event.

Consider, for example, the incoming event specification in the application interface of a data unit object for the MOVE invocation. It would contain the name *MOVE* and the types of the invocation parameters. These include the target of the move, the data unit to move, a return code, etc. In addition, if MOVE has additional requirements for a successful invocation, they are specified as constraints. For example, the target machine may have to be reachable over a secure communication channel.

The use of the generalized object model allows fine-grained control over the implementation of the interface. In the MOVE example, suppose the transfer could use either a connection-based or a datagram service. An application's MOVE invocation could become either a MOVE_CONNECTION or a MOVE_DATAGRAM incoming event for the data unit object.

When we say that a π object *supports* an interface, we mean that it meets the following three conditions:

- All outgoing events that the object generates are specified in the interface. There may be events that it does not generate.
- The object provides handlers for all events specified in the interface. It may have handlers for additional events.
- The type of the data accompanying events, both incoming and outgoing, must match those declared in the interface.

An object's application interface may actually have multiple *views*, each being a subset of the actual interface. A given client object will only see one particular view of a server object [Shilling and Sweeney, 1989]. This approach is similar to views in relational databases. If a client object may change its view, then a method to do so needs to be part of the view.

7.2 EVENTS

The event abstraction in π has six main components:

- Generator - the object that *causes* the event.
- Event name - *identification* of the event within some scope.
- Type - *declaration* of the arguments and the context of the event.
- Constraints - *restrictions* on the arguments or the event itself.
- Notification mechanism - *connection* between the generator and the handler(s).
- Handler - one or more objects that receive the notification.

Generator and event name are straightforward concepts. For an exception event, the type can indicate what contextual information is need to handle the exception. Constraints that specify atomicity or security can be requested by the generator. The type, name and constraints constitute the *signature* of an event. The balance of the event abstraction, the generator, notification mechanism and handler, together with information on a particular instance of the event make up the *trace* of the event.

The system uses the event signature to be sure that the generator's outgoing event is consistent with the handler's incoming event. Interestingly, the signature does *not* specify the handler. Thus, π decouples the generator from the handler and allows dynamic redirection of an event. If the signatures are compatible, one handler can be replaced with another that provides greater functionality. Indeed, several handlers can be notified of a given event. Some or all of them may even be unknown to the event generator and different notification mechanisms may be used. This decoupling is a generalization of incremental linking and dynamic server binding. This decoupling is important for component engineering [Sullivan and Notkin, 1991]. However, π always requires type conformity and constraint satisfaction.

7.3 THE APMI HIERARCHY

In addition to changing its view, a client object may be allowed to *tune* a server object. For example, a MOVE client may ask that it be allowed to continue running while the transfer is in process or that it block until the transfer has finished. Also, it may ask for connection-based or datagram-based communication. It may even specify communication parameters such as time-out value and packet size. Methods for this tuning could be provided as part of the application interface.

π recommends a conceptual structure for behavioral tuning called the *APMI hierarchy*. At the highest level of the hierarchy are the *abstractions* that define the basic functions of an object. The next level includes the *policies* that refine the abstractions without changing their interface. Various *mechanisms* can be used to realize a given policy. Finally, *implementations* are the tools that actually cause the functions to take place. This APMI hierarchy can be demonstrated with the help of an example of distributed shared data.

Distributed shared data with coherency requirements simulates physically shared data. The basic concept is an abstraction which allows allocation, read/write manipulation and destruction. There are a range of policies for maintaining coherency of the shared data [Nitzberg and Lo, 1991]. Some applications require strict coherency while others can tolerate stale data and prefer an update-on-demand policy. The mechanisms for realizing these policies include explicit locks and the page-fault mechanism. Finally, each mechanism could select an implementation based on the tradeoff of simplicity vs performance. The APMI hierarchy allows a client to alter the semantics of the methods. In each case, a method involving one level can affect the semantics of the higher level.

7.4 THE SYSTEM INTERFACE

Major changes to the functionality of an object are available through the system interface. These changes can affect essentially anything about the object. For example, an object could be made multithreaded to run on multiple processors. A passive object may be moved, cached or archived as resources permit. The potential changes are fundamental and alter the mapping from the abstractions onto the resources. The mapping can even be dynamic, taking into account changes in object needs and resource availability. This kind of change is called *metacomputing* or in certain cases, *reflection* [Maes, 1987; Yokote et al., 1991].

Two critical events specified in the system interface are the *constructors* and *destructors* of the object. When an object is instantiated, its constructor is activated. The constructor *reifies* certain properties of the object. That is, properties that are normally implicit or abstract are made explicit or concrete. These include inheritance, storage used, representation, events handled and current location as meta-objects. Depending upon the nature of the object, the constructor creates either the entire object or a proxy as a front end to the main object [Shapiro, 1986]. In either case, reification is performed for entities that can be broadly categorized into two groups: *structural* entities and *computational* entities.

Structural entities reify properties that are *internal* to the nature of the object, such as its representation, the storage used, its name and entities encapsulated within it. Computational entities reify properties and operations that are *external* to the object, such as events handled, its protection domain and its dynamic inheritance structure. The system interface allows the user to manipulate both the behavior and the implementation of these entities.

Allowing changes to both internal and external properties provides a flexible and dynamic run-time environment. Objects may change the interfaces of other objects. The evolution of an interface is handled in much the same way as a *version-set* [Skarra and Zdonik, 1986]. That is, multiple versions exist and are seen by different clients. Thus, if one client changes an interface, others may continue to use the old interface.

Suppose an application program changes the interface to the file-system object. How does this affect the other file-system clients? If they are to use the new interface, they must know of it. Classically, this would require a global knowledge base which is contrary to the philosophy of open systems [Kahn and Miller, 1988]. Instead, π reifies change-management. The initiator of an interface could maintain a list of *acquaintances* [Agha, 1987], which are other objects that may be using the same interface. The initiator's change meta-object could notify its peers in each of the acquaintances when a change occurs. They may, in turn, use the new version of the interface and continue to propagate the change. This change propagation mechanism requires no global information.

Currently, a prototype implementation of the π architecture is being developed.

8 RELATED WORK

Research in distributed systems has produced several distributed cooperation mechanisms, ranging from RPC to distributed shared memory. DSM [Nitzberg and Lo, 1991] is typically too low-level for distributed OODBs, since its page-based view does not match the language-level view of data. Its most significant shortcoming is the lack of a general reference abstraction to truly support transparent distribution.

The goals of OMG's Common Object Request Broker Architecture (CORBA) [OMG, 1991] are close to those of π and it is a significant step in satisfying the needs of applications. It makes a substantial contribution to interoperability and provides a high-level view for developing and integrating applications. However, it is limited to the classical object model and lacks an explicit view of resources.

IBM's System Object Model [IBM, 1991], available for OS/2 2.0, addresses the need for metacomputing. It does so through reification of a class as a *class object* which is treated as an instance of the metaclass. It also provides flexible method resolution mechanisms to accommodate different languages. It does not, however, explicitly address dynamic resource availability or distribution.

Muse [Yokote et al., 1991] is the first attempt to use reflection to tailor operating systems. It uses metaobjects to reify the execution environment of an object. It represents a major step towards the goal of maximum flexibility, even though it apparently does not have a clearly defined notion of flexible and safe event handling.

9 CONCLUSIONS

Our experience with ARCADE and π convinces us that operating system abstractions should match those of high-level languages. Such an approach relieves the programmer from the burden of solving non-application domain problems. On the surface, this might appear to reduce the expressive power of the abstractions. However, if the abstractions support metacomputing, applications actually have fine-grained control over interfaces and implementations.

The use of the directed graph metaphor can shorten the development cycle. Since the operating system directly supports manipulation of the realizations of graph components, a developer can use the appropriate level of granularity. Thus, he or she could deal with components of large granularity during prototyping. Later, while fine tuning, the APMI hierarchy allows optimization of individual objects. Reification and metacomputation allow control over the mapping of a graph onto resources. A flexible implementation can change the mapping at compile-time, startup-time or even run-time using the metacomputational interfaces of the system software.

Acknowledgements

We would like to thank Michael Casey, Paul Greenawalt and John Saldanha for their comments and criticism. This work was supported by a grant from the IBM Corporation.

The Bellerophon Project: A Scalable Object-Support Architecture Suitable for a Large OODBMS?

Peter Dickman*
University of Cambridge
Computer Laboratory
Cambridge
U.K.

Abstract

The needs of large distributed object-oriented databases are considered and compared with the facilities provided by the Bellerophon scalable distributed object-support architecture. It is shown that the object model and related object management mechanisms are, in fact, well suited to the needs of a large OODBMS and could provide efficient, albeit incomplete, low-level support for such systems. Key features of the architecture that are of interest are the light-weight explicit references and the structured object tables. The garbage collection strategy, which involves a hybrid algorithm built around weighted reference counts, is briefly discussed.

1 INTRODUCTION

The Bellerophon project [Dickman, 1992] was an investigation into scalable mechanisms to support object management in distributed systems. An explicit decision made at the outset of that work specifically excluded the demands of distributed databases from consideration, beyond acknowledging the distinction between persistent and transient objects. In this paper the needs of large distributed object-oriented databases are considered and compared with

*Currently at INESC, Lisbon, Portugal under an ERCIM fellowship. Permanent address after September 1993: University of Glasgow, Department of Computing Science, Glasgow G12 8QQ, Scotland.

the facilities provided by the Bellerophon scalable distributed object-support architecture. It is shown that the object model and related object management mechanisms are, in fact, well suited to the needs of a large OODBMS and could provide efficient, albeit incomplete, low-level support for such systems.

The paper is divided into four main parts. Section 2 introduces the key features of the architecture that are of interest. The motivation for the various concepts, as well as many of the details and special cases, have been omitted from this presentation in the interest of brevity, however all of the significant concepts are covered. A brief survey of some of the system-level issues that arise when developing an OODBMS is then presented in Section 3. Section 4 relates the two earlier sections to each other, demonstrating the main result of this paper: that a scalable object-support layer founded on light-weight explicit references is well-suited to the task of supporting a large OODBMS. Proposals for future work and a brief survey of related material are presented in Section 5. It must be made clear, however, that no attempt has been made to construct an OODBMS over the Bellerophon emulators; indeed the object- support layer itself is incomplete. This paper addresses the abstract question of how much of the required support for an OODBMS can (and should?) be provided by a general-purpose object-support layer.

2 THE BELLEROPHON MODEL

The Bellerophon architecture defines two main views: the external view details the model presented to an overlying programming language run-time system and hence to applications; the internal view describes the manner in which this can be implemented, in terms of non-scalable object and message-passing primitives provided by an OS kernel.

2.1 THE EXTERNAL VIEW

The Bellerophon object model supports two main concepts, references and the objects they refer to. Objects have identity, so two references can be compared to see if they indicate the same object, but objects do not have visible identifiers.[1] Objects hold references as well as other state (bit-patterns) and have associated methods for manipulating the encapsulated, hidden, state and references. The only way in which an object may be indicated is by means of a reference, and these provide location, access and address transparency [Herbert, 1989], to use ANSA [APM, 1989] terminology. That is, given a reference it is not possible for the application to deduce on which machine the object resides, nor how invocations are passed from the reference to the object. One consequence of this is that all invocations may, potentially, be remote and hence may fail due to network and other problems.

2.1.1 References

All references in the model are explicit. Transforming a reference into a value of another type is permissible, however casting of values into references is utterly forbidden. A form of name-server permits human comprehensible names to be associated with references. The

[1] In fact all remotely referenced objects have an associated globally unique identifier, however this is used only for reference similarity testing and to recover from certain failures. These internal identifiers are not visible in the external object model presented by Bellerophon; a similarity test is explicitly supported so that these identifiers can be hidden.

references so held act as roots for garbage collection purposes and such entries are retained until explicitly deleted.

2.1.2 Distribution and Variant References

In general, the distributed system appears to be a single widely distributed pool of objects only a part of which is known to an application. Explicit knowledge of particular locations (processors) is normally not available to the application; there are circumstances, however, in which such an approach is undesirable. Each distinguishable location therefore has an associated (conceptually) immovable object and variant references may be used to ensure that an object remains at the desired location.

A colocator reference behaves exactly as a normal reference in every respect bar one. Normally, marshalling of a reference, as an argument in a remote invocation or during object migration, leads to the construction of data structures embodying a remote pointer, permitting the connection between the reference and its target to be maintained. When a colocator is marshalled, however, the indicated object (if local) is also marshalled; that is, the indicated object is migrated. To ensure that an object is not migrated it suffices to embed within it a colocator indicating a local unmarshallable object; this ensures that any attempt to migrate the object will fail. Colocators are also used to ensure that objects which must remain together for performance reasons, or to simplify the failure semantics of the application, do so.

Contralocator references are duals to colocators, as any attempt to unmarshal a contralocator at the same processor as the object it indicates will fail. Thus placing mutual contralocators in two separate objects, or two replicas of some replicated object, will ensure that they remain apart. This is particularly useful when managing replicated objects in a system which load balances. The contralocators ensure that the load balancer cannot accidentally migrate all replicas of an object to a single location, which then becomes a potential single point of failure.

Finally, objects may have persistence markers associated with them. These markers may not be unmarshalled at an object pool unless that pool guarantees the required level of support.[2] Again, as in the case of contralocators, migration failures are used to ensure that constraints are maintained.

2.2 THE INTERNAL VIEW

The internal model of the system is, obviously, rather more complex. Each *processing element* is connected to one or more networks that are internal to an establishment. These internal networks are called EINs (Establishment Internal Networks) to distinguish them from the Common Carrier Networks (CCN) which connect establishments. Establishments are connected to one or more CCNs by special gateway machines.

A processing element contains a single *object pool* and an *interface* for each of the EINs to which it is connected. These interfaces consist of an *entry table* and an *exit table* or *proxy list*. The entry table slots contain pointers to objects in the pool. The exit table slots contain pointers to *proxy objects*. Objects contain references, which are local pointers to

[2] The prototype implementation simply used a single bit to indicate whether or not the pool was (notionally) stable across transient faults and whether or not an object required such stability.

other objects in the same pool or to local proxy objects. The proxy objects themselves contain a network address and an entry table index (slot number), they point to an entry table slot in another machine (processing element or gateway) on the same EIN and act as remote pointers.

Each proxy object is referred to by an arbitrary number of local objects and exactly one exit table slot in precisely one interface exit table. Normal objects are indicated by at most one entry table slot in each interface entry table, as well as by an arbitrary number of other local objects. It is unusual, but possible, for an entry table slot to indicate a proxy object.

Each processing element also includes an *object table*, this contains pointers to every local object and, perhaps, some proxies (where an object has recently migrated away leaving a proxy in its place). Provided that enumeration of all objects is possible (for garbage collection purposes), the structure of this table is essentially irrelevant. The preferred approach is, therefore, to structure the object table as a set of class tables; that is, the object pointers are collected together by class. Insertions into the class tables are performed on object creation and unmarshalling.

Figure 1 shows a Bellerophon processing element, including two EIN interfaces and an I/O interface (not discussed in this paper). Gateway machines have a similar structure except that only proxy objects occupy the object pools.

An external-view reference is constructed from internal-view references (local pointers), proxy objects and entry table slots; usually just consisting of a single local pointer. This approach has the advantage of provided scalable references whilst ensuring that the labels used within networks, interfaces and object pools are carefully confined to manageable parts of the total system.

2.2.1 Migration and Remote References

Objects may migrate between object pools, and such migrations leave a proxy object behind, so that a chain of pointers exists to the object. Entry table slots that indicate a local object which is being migrated away are modified to become forwarding pointers. Messages sent to these are returned to the originator with the new address of the object; this permits rapid updating of the proxy object and elimination of the indirection steps and associated third-party dependencies.

Passing a reference to a remote machine involves the updating (or creation) of the entry table slot corresponding to the referenced object, as well as the construction of a proxy object at the remote node. Subsequent copying of a remote reference will, however, require only the construction of a proxy object at the recipient. Entry table slots and proxy objects use a highly optimised form of weighted reference count [Dickman, 1993a] that always permits the copying of the proxy contents. Thus no third party dependencies are introduced by reference copying (unlike mechanisms such as [Piquer, 1991; Shapiro, 1993]).

In more complex cases, involving multiple EINs or establishments, short chains may arise where a reference is passed through a gateway or from one EIN to another. Gateways are required to provide stable storage, however, and establishments with multiple EIN networks are assumed to be rare, so few problems arise in practice.

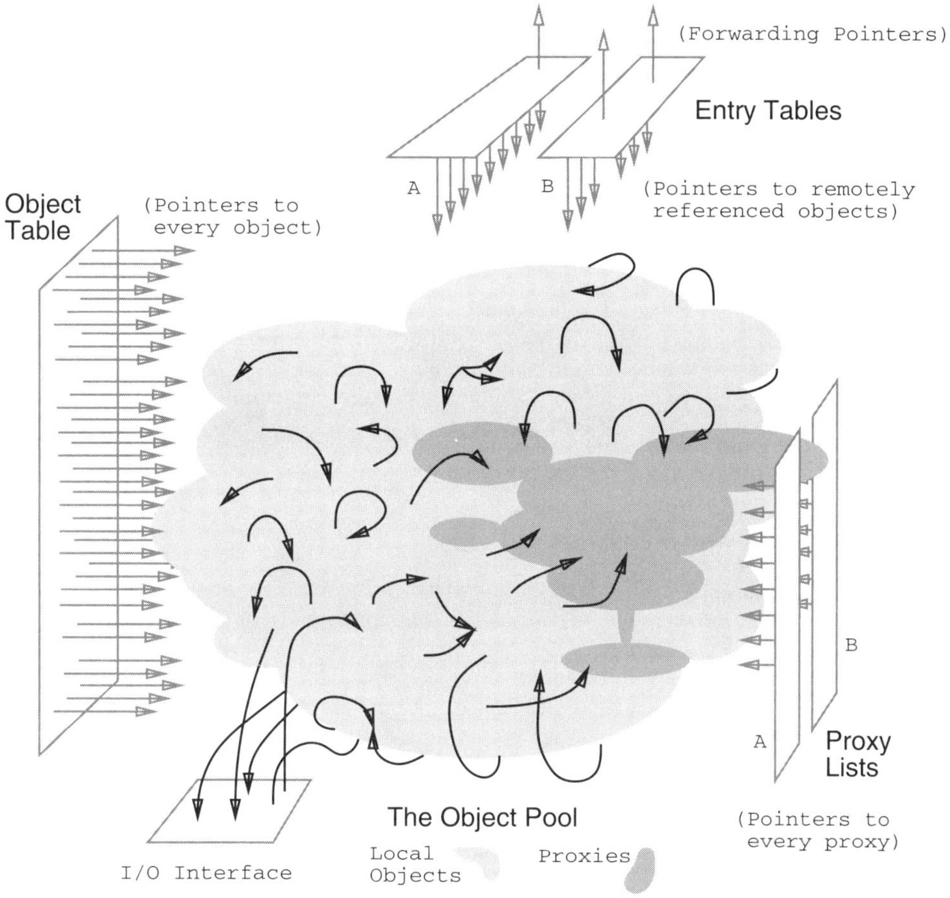

Figure 1: A stylised Bellerophon processing element

2.2.2 Invocation, Fallback Searches and Equality Testing

The standard invocation mechanism involves the forwarding of messages along the pointer chain until the target object is reached (usually in a single step), with a corresponding chain of stack-frame-like structures being generated to ensure that the results of the invocation can be passed back to the originator. If a forwarding pointer is encountered the message is returned one step along the chain and the pointer corrected to indicate the new location.

In the rare cases in which a non-trivial chain of pointers exists, and is disrupted by a machine failure, a fallback mechanism exists. The chain of pointers leading to an object must pass through an entry table slot either in a gateway or, more likely, the object's current host processor. This permits Emerald-style searching to be used. Every remotely referenced object is given a hidden, globally unique, identifier; this is copied into all proxy objects and entry table slots associated with the object. Thus searching of entry tables permits the object to be found provided that it is not resident on a failed machine.

Similarity testing of references (that is, equality testing of objects) is performed as a purely local operation; using the identifiers held in proxy objects where necessary.

2.2.3 Object Granularity and Variant Reference Tags

The granularity assumption in Bellerophon is that objects are at least a significant fraction of the size of a page of memory. This has the immediate consequence of permitting an efficient implementation in which each object is aligned on a longword boundary, freeing the bottom two bits of the local pointers for use as indicators for the special references. If, further, alignment is on 16 byte boundaries an additional two bits become available for use by the local garbage collector.

2.3 MANAGEMENT ISSUES

In a complex system many management problems arise which can only be poorly resolved by the application programmer. It is therefore desirable that such problems be addressed in the lowest appropriate level of the architecture.

The two key management features of the Bellerophon architecture are the support for garbage collection and load balancing. The object-model supported over Bellerophon is only weakly specified, to ensure that as wide a variety of object languages as possible can be supported. Demanding, however, that all references are explicit, and that every object supports operations enumerating the embedded references, offers the possibility of system level garbage detection. Although limited to single establishments, a novel approach to load balancing, based on information provided by local garbage collectors, was also investigated. The important features of the approach are described in [Dickman, 1991].

Other issues, such as security and network management, are addressed in [Dickman, 1993a] but only garbage collection is discussed further here.

2.3.1 Garbage Collection

The principal advances made in the Bellerophon project were in the area of garbage collection, including a multi-layered hybrid algorithm, the key component of which was an optimised weighted reference counting mechanism [Dickman, 1993a]. distributed garbage.

Local garbage collectors used the entry table slots as supplementary root sets and eliminated unreachable proxy objects, thereby generating background messages to the indicated entry table slots, which might cause reclamation of those slots. The weighted reference counting mechanism, which is essentially a low-cost extension of the marshalling and unmarshalling of references, ensured that entry table slots were not reclaimed whilst matching proxy objects existed. This approach, like all mechanisms based on reference counts, cannot detect cyclic garbage and was therefore supplemented with an essentially arbitrary complete GC algorithm (a distributed mark and sweep algorithm was used in the prototype), which was used infrequently to eliminate cyclic distributed garbage. This relies on the entry and exit tables at gateways to restrict the collection to single establishments (or single projects spanning a few establishments). Two techniques were provided for handling cycles that crossed establishment and project boundaries. One, based on timestamps, was potentially unsafe and could, in extremely unlikely circumstances, lead to the collection of non-garbage. The alternate approach was simply to migrate those objects that had been inactive for a considerable length of time, and which might lie in large cyclic structures, to some form of secondary (or even off-line) storage.

2.4 SUMMARY

The Bellerophon architecture provides a rich and powerful programming model constructed over an efficient and effective base layer, using only facilities of the sort found in non-scalable object-support kernels. The main feature that permits this scalable approach is the use of lightweight explicit references. These references, combined with an approach to naming that ensures that the required naming domains are limited in size, are the source of the power of this model.

In Section 4 many of the requirements of a large OODBMS will be shown to correspond well with the facilities described above.

3 SYSTEM-LEVEL REQUIREMENTS OF AN OODBMS

Before discussing the support required for an OODBMS it is essential that the sense in which that term is being used is clarified. Throughout this paper the term OODBMS is used to indicate a persistent object store together with an application program which supports both modifications to the contents of that store and queries on the contents. That is, some form of transaction mechanism is integrated with a query language and facilities for modification of the information in the persistent data repository.

The information stored in the OODBMS will be structured. It will consist of encapsulated objects containing state: bit-patterns and references to other objects. Associated with each object will be a collection of methods, representing the behaviour of the object and through which all interactions with the state of that object must occur. These methods will permit both modification of the object state and complex structured queries on the object. The OODBMS is thus fully object-oriented in the sense of the introduction to [Dittrich, 1988]. Furthermore, it is assumed that the application and query processing system is object-based, i.e., implemented in an object language. The detailed model of invocation or message-passing is not specified, beyond assuming that a transaction mechanism ensures that consistency is maintained.

3.1 PERSISTENT OBJECTS AND TRANSACTIONS

Persistent objects are clearly essential in an OODBMS, that is some form of persistent store for objects is needed, together with references to these persistent entities and a transaction based mechanism for manipulating them. Research into persistent stores has been underway for many years, [Atkinson et al., 1982; Rosenberg and Koch, 1990; Dearle et al., 1991], and discussion of the main issues is omitted from this paper.

3.2 ROLLBACK, GC AND HISTORIC QUERIES

As rollbacks may occur, due to aborted transactions, it is essential that objects are not discarded until it is certain that no rollback will lead to them being used again. It is thus the case that garbage collection of the persistent store would require knowledge of any objects affected by transactions in progress. In practice, however, any important database is likely to require audit trails of some form and it is therefore assumed here that temporal queries on the data base are supported. That is, queries of the state of the data base at some specified historic time are permitted. Such an assumption requires that all of the objects in the persistent store be retained.

This approach would also require that, when the state of an object changes, two versions of the object arise: an old immutable form and the new modified object to which further modifications may be made. These must be distinguished by some form of temporal discriminator and both forms would have to be reachable through existing references.

An object would, therefore, actually consist of a set of persistent versions, all but one of which would be immutable. In addition there would be various uncommitted (transient) children of that modifiable object, generated by ongoing transactions. Garbage collection of the persistent store would not, then, be required; however migration of older versions of objects to slower or off-line stores would be essential if the system were not to become full. This view of an object database as a collection of versions with a linearised subset of committed instances was heavily influenced by [Moss, 1991].

Timestamps would also be required, in such an approach, to discriminate between elements of an object version set. As logical or vector clocks [Mattern, 1988] are of little value in a query description language, 'real-world' clocks should be used, controlled by one of the known clock synchronisation algorithms (e.g., [Mills, 1988]).

3.3 EVOLUTION OF CLASSES

Not only must versioning of instances be provided, so that historic queries may be answered, but in addition versions of classes may be required. Schema evolution systems, and the like, remain a research topic. Extensive searching and rewriting of objects and references might be required to solve the problem of modifying objects to match an evolved class descriptor. The advent of reflective systems [Yokote et al., 1989] may, however, provide simple interfaces through which such changes could be managed. This paper addresses such issues only in so far as they can be solved using class indices: lists of all instances of a class.

3.4 RECONSTRUCTIBLE INDICES AND TRANSIENT OBJECTS

In addition to the objects held in the persistent store there are two other categories of object that must be considered. To optimise searching and query processing in general it would be of great value to have a variety of indices available. An index is, essentially, a (possibly structured) collection of references enumerating the objects which satisfy some predicate. In particular, an index could be reconstructed from the persistent store contents, if necessary, and hence could be long-lived but non- persistent. A simple example would be a list of all instances of some class. Such index objects are not part of the persistent store proper, rather they are internal state of the query processing subsystem intended to optimise searches. An index could either be updated to ensure that they consistently reflect the contents of the database, or timestamped to indicate the most recent point at which they were known to be consistent. Garbage collection of the indices may not be necessary: a large number of index objects might be generated, so some form of explicit management of them, perhaps based on an LRU cache, would be essential. It is crucial, however, that the indices themselves do not refer to garbage objects.

Finally, during query processing and modification of the persistent store contents a variety of transient objects will be generated. It is these objects which absolutely must be garbage collected, since otherwise they will rapidly accumulate and overwhelm the system. The transient objects would also have to be referenced, and a uniform mechanism for referencing all objects simplifies the task of making a transient object persistent.

3.5 SUMMARY

A number of topics that arise in the development of a large OODBMS have briefly been presented. Several of the facilities mentioned cannot adequately be supported by the current Bellerophon model, whilst others fit extremely well into the architecture. In the next section the limits and advantages of the model, as a support layer for an OODBMS, are considered.

4 SCALABLE SUPPORT FOR AN OODBMS

There are two principal omissions from the Bellerophon architecture that would have to be rectified before an OODBMS could be constructed over it. The invocation model does not address the issue of transactions, and the persistence markers do not, of themselves, constitute a Persistent Object Store (POS).

All transaction mechanisms are built from message passing primitives; it is, therefore, clear that a transaction layer could be provided over Bellerophon. Such an approach has certain drawbacks, however, since the transaction is a key concept and would not be visible within Bellerophon. Consider the case, for example, of transient objects that arise in the context of a single transaction, or a single set of nested transactions, and which are never shared with other, unrelated, queries or database updates. Clearly the garbage collection of such objects could be achieved simply by labelling the transients with some form of transaction identifier and eliminating those which are not reachable from the persistent store at the time the enclosing transaction completes (aborts or commits). Of course this glosses over the difficulty of determining which transients are reachable from the persistent store (and hence should also be promoted to persistent status) and, indeed, of locating all transients associated with some transaction. It does however hint at the optimisations that could be exploited were the transaction to be a fully supported Bellerophon concept.

Conversely, beyond ensuring that persistent objects (as opposed to transient copies of persistent objects) never migrate to non-persistent object pools it is not clear that much is to be gained in fully integrating the POS into the Bellerophon architecture. Obviously to build such a system special marshalling routines and updating primitives would be required, however these do not influence the work of the garbage collector or load balancer. It follows that separate but linked POS and Bellerophon implementation would be perfectly adequate, and the model of references and persistent markers suffices in such an approach.

Whereas the lightweight references make the copying of immutable objects straightforward and efficient, some care is required when considering true replication of mutable objects. Clearly, transactions and point-to-point message passing or invocation protocols can be used to support replicated objects, however such an approach may be somewhat inefficient. Replicated objects might be of interest in an OODBMS and would then best be implemented as an additional layer relying on the use of contralocators and any available low-level multicast protocols (e.g., [Peterson et al., 1989; Birman and Joseph, 1987]). Note that it is not intended that Bellerophon bar the use of such lower-level mechanisms, except where they directly contradict the assumptions of the architecture. Thus, provided that the appropriate marshalling and unmarshalling primitives are provided, a multicast protocol can be incorporated into the architecture with only minor complications (the one significant difficulty lies in the use of weighted reference counts when the degree of a multicast is not accurately known).

Finally, there is no assumption explicitly in the Bellerophon architecture that any form of synchronised clocks are available. However, such a mechanism is needed in many applications and low- level algorithms (the SCMP message passing algorithm for example) and it is therefore not unreasonable to assume that any implementation of the architecture will be able to offer sufficiently high quality timestamps to the OODBMS.

Having considered the shortcomings of the model, the remainder of this section details some aspects of Bellerophon which are well-suited to supporting an OODBMS.

4.1 LIGHTWEIGHT REFERENCES

Assuming that unique object identifiers were 128 bits (16 bytes) long, and ignoring security-related components of the data structures (which are not discussed in this paper), the size of the components in the Bellerophon architecture can be considered. If local pointers are 4 bytes long (which is adequate, at present, even if the object pool is a disk pack and associated drivers), a proxy object would occupy 28 bytes whilst an entry table slot would require 24 bytes. The marshalled form of a reference would be 23 bytes long. Thus the space overhead on reference passing is under 50% of the size of an identifier, whilst using 4 byte local pointers rather than 16 byte identifiers would constitute a space saving if, on average, each locally known remote object is referenced a little more than twice. The CPU overheads of this approach are also reasonable: for example, the implementation described in [Dickman, 1993a] requires at most 10 machine instructions to marshal the weight for a weighted reference.

These low-cost, uniform references ensure that complex reference-rich structures can be efficiently supported. This is of advantage both within the structured information held in the repository and in the database application layer. Constructing additional indices is somewhat eased by having cheap and easily copied references. Furthermore, the transient objects involved in query handling will pass many references to persistent objects as arguments and results; the overhead involved in this is also reduced by the use of small references within the object pools.

4.2 THE CLASS-STRUCTURED OBJECT TABLE

It is postulated that most practical indices are either lists of all objects belonging to some class or type, or a subset of such a list. The local object table contains references to a superset (some of its referents may be proxies for objects which recently migrated away from this pool) of the local objects belonging to each class. Thus, implicit in the object table is a complete set of local class indices.

Care must, however, be exercised, as the object table includes references to all objects, including garbage objects. Permitting the application unrestricted access to this table would, therefore, either introduce significant semantic confusion concerning the rôle of the garbage collector, or simply make all objects permanently accessible, including the transients generated during query processing. To avoid this problem it is therefore necessary to distinguish between references to persistent and non-persistent objects in the object table. As historic queries are supported, no persistent objects are ever garbage collected; conversely, transient objects should be known to the transaction that generated them but not elsewhere.[3] Appropriate class indices can thus be supported provided that transaction commits lead to the insertion of all objects reachable from the persistent store into that store, together with the marking of the relevant entries in the object table. A class index then consists of those references held in the class-specific component of the object table that are marked as persistent, together with any non-garbage transients from this class that are currently available to the transaction. Determining the appropriate set of transients is non-trivial, requiring as it does a GC-like search from the registers and any modified objects, however the search can be significantly constrained by the transaction-specific knowledge that is available. Furthermore, it is postulated that, in practice, class indices will generally be used without transients of that class having been constructed.

A full class index would, unfortunately, require the reading of the local class indices at every component of the system, but these local class indices do provide a reasonable starting point.

Whereas a class is a combination of an interface and an implementation, a type refers solely to an interface, that is a set of method signatures. A local type index could be constructed by collecting together pointers to all of the local class indices which support the desired interface precisely. Including, in addition, pointers to indices for all subtypes (that is, all types in which the set of signatures is a superset of the method signature set for the type in question) provides complete local indices for each type. Again, however, care must be taken over (non)accessible transients and generating a full index for some type in a large system could be very costly. Furthermore, efficiently combining indices that contained duplicated references to replicated objects would require that the references be sortable. Thus an ordering primitive, to supplement the similarity test on references, would be required.

[3]This point is directly related to the requirement noted at the start of this section, concerning the association of transients with a transaction for garbage collection purposes.

It is clear that, in practice, global searches in extremely large systems are not desirable and geographical constraints, based on establishments, would appear to be essential. Although the Melampus project [Cabrera et al., 1990], for example, would have in principle permitted such searches, in practice they are unlikely to be feasible. Optimising searches based on class and type does appear to be a valuable aid to large-scale searching, however, and the preferred structuring of the object table is of considerable assistance in this regard.

4.3 GARBAGE COLLECTION

If the persistent object store is to be garbage collected (that is, if the historic queries approach described above is not taken), then some form of distributed garbage collection algorithm will be required. A hybrid collector supplemented by a means of recovering almost all acyclic garbage very efficiently, offers significant advantages in this area. More importantly, the effective garbage collection of transient objects will be fundamental to the database application and the Bellerophon GC model is well suited to this problem.

5 RELATED AND FUTURE WORK

A number of investigations of distributed object support layers have been performed or are underway, [Borghoff, 1992] catalogues many of these. For example, the COOL-2 layer [Lea et al., 1991], being constructed over the Chorus Microkernel, is a follow-on project from COOL (the Chorus Object-Oriented Layer) [Habert et al., 1990]. COOL has many features in common with the Bellerophon model, in particular both assume that objects have 'medium' granularity. Also related to this is the Soul object-support operating system kernel [Shapiro, 1991], being developed at Project SOR. Soul includes a form of light-weight reference which is somewhat similar in aim to that described above, although the implementation is rather different. Integrated with this form of reference is an acyclic garbage collection protocol based on robust reference lists rather than reference counts [Shapiro, 1993]. The Soul references incur a higher overhead, particularly in terms of space usage and the background processing required for garbage collection, but all (as against almost all) acyclic garbage is recovered. Soul is designed to correctly and efficiently handle duplicated messages, which are the only significant problem for weighted reference counting approaches Both the Soul references and weighted reference counted messages can tolerate lost and reordered messages. In addition to the original work on weighted reference counts [Watson and Watson, 1987; Bevan, 1987], later extended by [Corporaal et al., 1990], a variant of reference counting that is effective, but incurs third party dependencies, has been proposed in [Piquer, 1991].

The location model, that is the chains of pointers approach, used both in this paper and in Soul are derived from the Emerald model, itself based on [Fowler, 1986]. This is in sharp contrast to models such as that proposed by ANSA [Herbert, 1989] and the OMG [Soley, 1990] in which some form of trader or directory service is used to generate references.

There are several substantial similarities between the Bellerophon architecture and the system model of the Thor OODBMS described in the preceding paper. Both use an Emerald-like location mechanism based on chain-following, although the Thor surrogates are immutable, unlike proxies, and chain shortening only occurs as a side-effect of garbage collection. This distinction reflects the differing assumptions concerning object mobility made by the two projects. The stronger emphasis on fault-tolerance, and the concomitant avoidance of third-party dependencies, in Bellerophon is also a reflection of different underlying assumptions. The Thor system assumes a pool of highly-available servers, with a separate collection of potentially faulty user processors on which computation occurs using copies of objects. In the Bellerophon model only gateways (and some background servers) are assumed to be completely controlled by the system administrators, all other machines are assumed to be vulnerable to failure. A further, possibly superficial, similarity is that both of these systems were prototyped using strongly-typed distributed programming languages from the CLU family. Thor was built using Argus [Liskov, 1988], while the Bellerophon emulators were implemented in CCLU, a CLU [Liskov et al., 1981] extension with concurrency primitives, fine-grained locking [Cooper and Hamilton, 1985] and an inbuilt RPC mechanism [Hamilton, 1984], but no support for transactions.

Although the Bellerophon project is temporarily in abeyance, further work will be undertaken on it. This will involve a new implementation as well as investigations of the integration of reference management with replicated objects and multicast protocols. The area of load balancing also requires more study and significant applications must be constructed over the support layer to permit further evaluation of the concepts and techniques. An obvious candidate application would be a large, distributed OODBMS system.

6 CONCLUSIONS

The light-weight explicit references offer significant advantages to an OODBMS, and these gains would be increased if garbage collection of the persistent object store were also required. Since additional local copies of references, and additional remote references to some local object, are easily and cheaply constructed the widespread use of references is encouraged. This has advantages in terms of distributing activity in the system, reducing the overheads of concurrent query processing and index replication.

Class and type based searching are also well supported and it is postulated that these provide the fundamental basis on which most queries will be founded. The lack of visible object identifiers, using instead references (implemented as local pointers), provides both a space saving and a conceptually cleaner approach. The explicit provision of reference similarity testing provides the key facility for which identifiers would normally be required.

The sole conclusion that can reasonably be drawn, in this paper, is that the Bellerophon architecture appears well suited to supporting a large OODBMS, but that it lacks certain essential features. In particular the issue of transactions and transient objects must be addressed if an effective support layer is to be provided. Integrating transactions into the model appears to offer the possibility of optimisations that would not be feasible with a separately layered implementation.

Acknowledgments

The work described here was carried out at the University of Cambridge Computer Laboratory and partially funded by the UK Science and Engineering Research Council. This paper was written while the author was funded by the European Research Consortium in Informatics and Mathematics (ERCIM) and attached to Projet SOR, INRIA Rocquencourt, France and the Comandos group at INESC Lisbon, Portugal. Thanks are due to the workshop participants, in particular Malcolm Atkinson, for their insightful comments on this paper.

Operating System Support for Distributed and Persistent Objects

Marc Shapiro
INRIA Projet SOR
B.P. 105 Rocquencourt
78153 Le Chesnay Cedex
France

Abstract

This position paper is intended as a very terse introduction to the operating system work, in the area of distributed and persistent objects, of the SOR group at INRIA Rocquencourt (France). For more detail you are referred to the bibliography; many of the references are available by anonymous FTP on ftp.inria.fr.

1 INTRODUCTION

Object-based systems are of ever increasing importance, but are not well supported by existing operating systems. Our project, "Systèmes d'Objets Répartis" (Distributed Object-Support Systems) studies efficient OS support [Shapiro, 1991] for implementing, identifying, invoking, migrating, and storing objects. In such a system, the main technical issue is distributed sharing of objects. Different implementations are possible, e.g., centralized data and processing; partial or complete replication, with associated consistency problems; or partitioning. The above are all abstractly *fragmented objects*.

We have previously developed two systems: SOS and COOL. Our current objectives are:

- efficient object-support mechanisms including kernel support [Shapiro, 1991], and flexible references supporting garbage collection [Shapiro et al., 1992],
- support for fragmented objects and distributed abstractions [Makpangou et al., 1991b].

2 PREVIOUS WORK

The SOS system [Shapiro et al., 1989b] supports both fragmented and local objects, object migration, persistent objects [Shapiro et al., 1989a], dynamic linking [Gautron and Shapiro, 1987] and arbitrarily complex user-defined objects (written in C++ or FOG). A very simple object model based on "prerequisites" and "reinitializers" allows a language-specific run-time to maintain type safety.

SOS system services are FOs. They include: a distributed object manager, a user-centered name service, a storage service [Shapiro et al., 1989a], and a communication service.

COOL (a joint project with Chorus-systèmes for SEPT) is also an efficient object-support OS [Habert et al., 1990]. The object manager is implemented as a kernel server above the Chorus micro-kernel. COOL was developed specifically for the SEPT "Cidre" application of intelligent circulating documents.

3 FRAGMENTED OBJECTS

"Fragmented Objects" (FOs) [Makpangou et al., 1992] are a key concept for structuring distributed systems as objects. The abstract view of a FO is a single, shared object; its distribution is hidden to clients. In the concrete view, the FO designer controls the distribution of data and function and of the communication between its fragments.

FO programming is eased by using the FOG language [Gourhant and Shapiro, 1990], an extension of C++, and by BOAR, a toolbox of predefined FOs.

BOAR [Makpangou et al., 1991a] is a library of pre-defined, universally-useful distributed abstractions. BOAR provides the designer of a distributed service with pre-defined FO types, encapsulating various implementations of commonly used abstractions, necessary for structuring distributed applications.

4 SOUL

Our new project Soul [Shapiro, 1991] is in *high performance support for objects*. This project (which is co-ordinated with Chorus-systèmes' COOL-2 project) comprises the following items:

- Kernel abstractions for object support: a uniform interface to all kernel resources; grouping any number of resources into a single resource; upcall hooks for managing objects according to high-level semantics.
- High-performance, primitive mechanisms adapted to object-oriented applications and subsystems: system-supported, garbage-collected references that can be stored or sent in messages; simple, efficient cross-context invocation.

To support naming, binding and location, we propose lightweight, fine-grain *references*, the OS equivalent of pointers. A reference is a sequence of *links* bound into a *chain*. An individual link contains a few bytes of opaque data and a a few assembly instructions that interpret the data.

To ease the management of distributed and/or persistent shared data, references [Shapiro et al., 1992] support distributed garbage collection [Shapiro et al., 1990]. The GC protocol is a conservative, fault-tolerant variant of reference counting, augmented to deal with cyclic garbage.

A straightforward presentation protocol is used to pass references, with no message, system call, or kernel overhead. Occasionally, longer-than-necessary chains will form. These are short-circuited in a lazy fashion by the binding and location protocol.

5 KITLOG

A number of services require a history of events, e.g. fault tolerance and debugging. To support these, we have designed and implemented a generic, object-based logging service called Kitlog [Ruffin, 1992]. Kitlog supports multiple logical logs, multiplexed and replicated across multiple physical devices. Kitlog is based on the "stacked objects" technology, which enables an application to configure its own logical logs to its needs, without paying the price of services it does not use. We are currently implementing a log-structured file system on top of Kitlog.

PART 6
INTEROPERABILITY

An Approach to Interoperable Object Models

Frank Manola
GTE Laboratories Incorporated
40 Sylvan Road, MS 62
Waltham, MA 02254
U.S.A.

Sandra Heiler
GTE Laboratories Incorporated
40 Sylvan Road, MS 62
Waltham, MA 02254
U.S.A.

Abstract

This paper describes the concept of a "reduced instruction set" or "RISC" object model, based on work on the formal foundations of object models, and related sources. The model would consist of a few basic, but in combination very powerful, facilities to allow features found in conventional object models to be defined as combinations of the basic facilities. The intent is to provide a common framework for understanding heterogeneous object models, by allowing their semantics to be defined in terms of a single set of concepts. This framework can then be the basis for understanding differences among object models, for defining mappings between different object models, or for defining new, application-specific models.

1 INTRODUCTION

Future information processing environments will consist of a vast network of *heterogeneous*, *autonomous*, and *distributed* (HAD) computing resources (hardware, programs, and data). There is increasing agreement that modeling such a system as a distributed collection of objects provides the appropriate framework for integrating HAD resources, in both distributed computing and telecommunications environments. This is illustrated by the number of standards activities related to HAD systems, including communications, distributed systems, database, and programming language standards, that are moving toward adopting, or have already adopted, an object-oriented approach [Fong et al., 1991]. These activities include not only those of official standards bodies, such as ANSI, but also those of industry consortia, such as the Object Management Group (OMG). The use of an object-oriented approach in integrating heterogeneous and autonomous components is also a characteristic of recent developments in personal computer application integration software, such as Object Linking and Embedding (OLE) in Microsoft Windows, and interapplication communication (IAC) facilities in the latest Apple Macintosh operating system.

The *distributed object management* technology required to support HAD systems continues trends in object-oriented programming, distributed system models, application integration environments, and database systems, with the goal of allowing the resources available in a distributed network to be treated as a commonly-accessible collection of objects which can be combined in arbitrary ways to provide new information processing capabilities. These objects can range in granularity from entire systems to individual application objects (text strings, images, etc.). [Manola et al., 1992] describes general aspects of this technology in more detail.

A number of proposals for generic Distributed Object Management System (DOMS) architectures have been developed, for example, the Common Object Request Broker Architecture (CORBA) defined by the OMG [OMG, 1991]. A typical feature of such architectures is the use of a *common object model* to provide a shared set of abstractions understood and supported by all components. This is similar to the use of a common global *data* model in a heterogeneous DBMS, except that in a DOMS an *object* model is required to model the diverse behavior provided by the objects in the system. General acceptance (or standardization) of the object model and interfaces of such an architecture would facilitate independent development of interoperable objects and supporting software in a DOMS environment (which is, e.g., the goal of the OMG in specifying and promoting such an architecture).

A number of candidates exist that could serve as the common object model, including models developed explicitly for this purpose. While interoperability may be achieved by the universal adoption of one of these models, it is possible (even likely!) that no one model will achieve universal adoption. In this case, the next best situation would be for there to be straightforward (not necessarily easy!) mappings between the features of the various object models used in the network. Achieving this is complicated by the existence of various features that extend the basic notion of an object as an *independent* unit of computation, able to respond autonomously to messages directed to it. Examples of such features include attributes (or properties) defined at object interfaces, class-based object implementations, separate model constructs representing object relationships [Albano et al., 1991] or various *kinds* of relationships (e.g., containment) [Fong et al., 1991], and generic functions. (Note that we do not question the *utility* of these features in various circumstances, we only question the need for them to be considered as *primitives*.)

To address this problem, we suggest defining what might be termed a "reduced instruction set" or "RISC" object model, based on work on the formal foundations of object models, e.g., [Beeri, 1990; Danforth and Tomlinson, 1988; Agrawal, 1991], and related sources. The model would consist of a few basic, but in combination very powerful, facilities to allow features such as those mentioned above to be defined as combinations of the basic facilities. A familiar example of this idea is the way in which an attribute can be defined in terms of a pair of get and set operations. More complex examples are the use of rules to define the semantics of various object relationships [Dayal et al., 1990], or to define the semantics of delegation and inheritance [Aksit and Tripathi, 1988]. We propose extending this idea to include all parts of an object model definition.

The intent is to provide a common framework for understanding heterogeneous object models, by allowing their semantics to be defined in terms of a single set of concepts. This framework can then be the basis for understanding differences among object models, for defining mappings between different object models, or even for defining new, application-specific models. Work on such a framework, and on comparing and defining mappings between specific object models, is part of the standards activity recommended in [Fong et al., 1991], and may become part of the work program of the new ANSI X3H7 Object Information Management technical committee. At the same time, a RISC model could provide the basis for improving the flexibility with which existing components (procedural and data), treated as objects, could be combined into new objects at higher levels of abstraction, by providing model concepts equally applicable to objects of arbitrary granularity. This is an important issue in a HAD environment, which must deal with both "legacy" code and data, which may exist as fairly large aggregates, as well as new objects constructed from them.

The rest of this paper briefly motivates and describes some of the potential components of a RISC object model.

2 POTENTIAL RISC OBJECT MODEL COMPONENTS

The basic approach to the RISC object model involves incorporating, at the *"object"* level, constructs that are *representation*- or *meta*-level constructs in other object models. The model would include explicit primitives for describing the basic components of objects in any object model, specifically methods (procedural or computational objects), state, object identifiers, and interfaces, together with other necessary primitives to allow object representations (including classes) and types to be definable in the object model itself. The model would also include explicit primitives for modeling messages (invocation requests), invoking methods, and representing expressions.

The inclusion of explicit metalevel objects, and the ability to specify their behavior (including defining specializations), would provide the basis of a programmable object model, such as that provided by the CLOS metaobject protocol [Kiczales et al., 1991]. Explicit messages are necessary in a distributed system, and their presence would also allow aspects of less traditional models, such as Linda [Carriero and Gelernter, 1989] or rule/logic-based models, to be modeled more directly. The inclusion of method objects would also allow representation of existing programs as objects, and would also be the basis for defining dispatching mechanisms tailored to specific requirements (method or function objects play an important role in the models described in [Beeri, 1990; Heiler and Zdonik, 1990; Zhu and Maier, 1989], among others).

Conventional class-based models include built-in mechanisms for dispatching (often involving traversal of an inheritance hierarchy). However, these mechanisms differ considerably among models (compare, e.g., dispatching in Smalltalk and CLOS). Moreover, in a HAD system dispatching (resolution) could be a much more complex process, requiring selection of methods on the basis of node availability, system load, and other factors, and might also be application-, object-, or model-dependent. It should be possible to define complex dispatching or delegation mechanisms in terms of a simple method invocation mechanism plus, for example, additional methods that could be hidden from ordinary object clients using a flexible interface definition mechanism (see below). The integration of conventional methods and multi-methods in [Chambers, 1992], and the mechanisms used to describe method invocation in [Beeri, 1990], illustrate related ideas.

The model would also include general mechanisms for constructing objects (including objects representing methods and identifiers). Constructors such as the tuples and sets found in many object models are basic. However, a general construction mechanism should, for example, be able to describe the states of objects resulting from the various forms of inheritance, e.g., `tuple[stuff in superclass + stuff in subclass]`,without introducing numerous special cases. More complex composition mechanisms can be based on object algebra/functional composition techniques, particularly in the case of method objects [Beeri, 1990]. This depends on being able to compose or otherwise manipulate RISC model objects, such as method objects, that represent *pieces* of objects in conventional object models. Note that object construction is not quite the same as a view mechanism, since, in the former, the new objects are not *derived* from intact base objects as in a view, but instead have distinct identity, and thus may diverge from the base objects. The construction mechanism should be able to construct both ordinary object abstractions and complex procedural objects such as generic functions.

The model would also include a general mechanism for defining object interfaces, i.e., a generalized view mechanism. This is necessary in modeling the different forms of object interfaces found in various object models (including both multiple interfaces visible to ordinary clients and differences in visibility of object internals to methods, sub- and superclasses, etc.), as well as providing the basis for object database views and inter-model mappings. The model must also deal explicitly with the scoping (name space) issues introduced by the mechanism. A number of papers have (correctly) justified the need for multiple object interfaces tailored to specific requirements (e.g., [APM, 1989; Richardson and Schwartz, 1991]), and variations on extended view mechanisms have appeared in, e.g., [Aksit and Tripathi, 1988; Heiler and Zdonik, 1990; Shilling and Sweeney, 1989] in both database and non-database contexts. Moreover, the browser of [Hebel and Johnson, 1990] essentially illustrates how a generic function can be considered as a view over the set of messages and objects implementing a multiple-dispatching mechanism (or, potentially, vice-versa). View definitions also require the mechanisms provided for object construction (e.g., the use of object algebras in defining database views). Derived objects in views require derived identifiers, which can be provided by, e.g., using the concept of identifier constructor functions from object logics such as [Kifer and Lausen, 1989] (in the case of view objects, these functions become part of the view definition, and the view definition essentially becomes part of the derived object identifier).

The ability to directly manipulate interface specifications provides the basis of the ability to describe the many variants of object type systems, since types can be modeled as descriptions of (predicates over) interface specifications. A number of such type system variants are described in [Danforth and Tomlinson, 1988; Manola et al., 1992]. The ability to describe the type systems of different object models is critical in using the RISC model to address certain interoperability problems. Object logics such as [Kifer and Lausen, 1989] illustrate the mixture of first- and second-order capabilities that may be required to describe variations of both *objects* and *object types* within the same framework.

Other important aspects of object models would also be definable in terms of RISC model primitives. For example, query algebras could be defined as polymorphic operators defined for specified aggregate objects (e.g., sets or tuples) that are useful in query processing [Beeri, 1990; Manola and Dayal, 1990]. Also, inclusion of a primitive event concept (including such events as invocation of object operations and transaction control operations such as "commit"), and compositions of such events, would provide the basis of a connection between the RISC model and similar (in some respects) approaches, such as ACTA [Ramamritham and Chrysanthis, 1993] and the TSME of [Georgakopoulos et al., 1992], for describing different *transaction* models in terms of a few basic primitives.

It should be noted that the proposed model is intended in some cases to be *descriptive* only. Systems implemented using their own object models will not make all the details describable in the RISC model actually visible or programmable in the RISC model. However, the "basic-ness" of the RISC features does not necessarily mean that a direct implementation of it (assuming one were to exist) would impose onerous run-time overhead (although this would have to be tested), since it might well be possible to "compile away" much of the apparent overhead involved in defining conventional facilities in more basic terms.

As this section indicates, we believe that much of the technology required for a RISC object model already exists in various forms. However, it needs to be pulled together in a clean way.

A Canonical Model for the Interoperability Among Object-Oriented and Relational Databases

Malú Castellanos
Universitat Politècnica de Catalunya
Departament de Llenguatges i
Sistemes Informàtics
Barcelona, Spain

Fèlix Saltor
Universitat Politècnica de Catalunya
Departament de Llenguatges i
Sistemes Informàtics
Barcelona, Spain

Manuel García-Solaco
Universitat Politècnica de Catalunya
Departament de Llenguatges i
Sistemes Informàtics
Barcelona, Spain

Abstract

In the interoperability context, autonomous pre-existing databases are federated at some degree in order to share their data. The growing importance that the interoperability among object-oriented and relational databases is gaining, makes essential the development of adequate data models that serve as canonical models for the federation. The canonical model constitutes the basic building block for methodologies and tools for the detection of interdatabase semantic relationships that is required to access the federation in an integrated way. This paper presents one such canonical model and points out its usage for coupling relational and object-oriented databases thru a semantic enrichment process.

1 INTRODUCTION-MOTIVATION

Relational and object-oriented (O-O) approaches are the two paradigms that have gained wider acceptance in the database field during the last years. Databases based on these paradigms will proliferate and the need to access them in an integrated way will arise as a natural consequence. Several architectures have been proposed for this purpose [Sheth and

Larson, 1990], where the databases are tightly or loosely coupled in a federation. In any of them, the semantic relationships that exist among the databases must be identified for the integrated access to the federation. This is a critical task complicated by the semantic heterogeneities that exist among these databases and the lack of an exact understanding of the meaning of their contents. As a first step to solve this problem, data models and methodologies based on these models must be developed. This is the aim of the BLOOM project whose data model is described in Section 2. The methodology includes a semantic enrichment step for upgrading the semantic level of the local schemas in order to facilitate the detection of the interdatabase relationships, as well as to couple relational and object-oriented databases as discussed in Section 3. The final result of the project will be a tool that semi-automatizes the overall process and can serve as a testbed for experimenting with it.

2 AN OVERVIEW OF THE BLOOM MODEL

2.1 CONSTITUENTS OF THE MODEL

BLOOM [Castellanos et al., 1991] is a semantic extension of an object-oriented model which complies with the essential features of suitability of canonical data models for interoperable databases reported in [Saltor et al., 1991]. The main constituents of the model are objects, types, classes and semantic abstractions.

Objects represent real world objects and are instances of ADTs manipulated by means of their interface. Object identity is mantained by the system. We distinguish primitive objects, considered elementary and provided by the system, from derived objects whose type is user defined deriving it from other types.

Types describe the structure and behaviour of their object instances, according to the ADT concepts. Types are arranged in a type semi-lattice which reflects the subtype relationship "is_a". Inclusion semantics is used for subtyping and multiple inheritance is supported. An object may be an instance of more than one type where each one of them provides a certain view on the object.

A class is a set of objects (members) associated with a type. There may be more than one class of a type. An object may be member of multiple classes and/or instance of multiple types. A subclass relationship between two classes is a combination of the subtype relationship among their types and the subset relationship among their extents.

Semantic Abstractions: the description of the structure entails the description of the relationships which are characterized by the abstractions that they represent:

- Classification/instantiation
- Four kinds of specialization: complementary, disjoint, alternative and general
- Three kinds of aggregation: simple, collection and association

The operational functionality models the dynamic properties which can range from the specification of insertion and deletion constraints to the modeling of operations. These constraints used to maintain the integrity of the semantic database, are embodied in the metaclasses that specify the behavioural interpretation of the semantics of the model. There are inherent constraints for each abstraction (Section 2.3 and 2.4), as well as inherent constraints for different kinds of specific existence dependencies (Section 2.2).

Metaclasses are a useful mechanism for adapting the model to different contexts by extending it with new metaclasses and for specifying not only the behaviour of their class instances, but also that of the instances of their instances as in [Klas et al., 1990].

2.2 EXISTENCE DEPENDENCIES

Strict existence dependencies. As its name suggests, the existence of the dependent object strictly depends on the existence of the one on which it depends, called dependor here. These dependencies can reflect a situation where an object cannot exist in the real world independently of another one, or else an interest dependency where the dependent continues to exist but it is not of interest anymore.

The insertion constraint linked to this concept makes sure that the dependent object cannot be created if the object upon which it depends has not been created before. With respect to the deletion constraint, this can have two different implications: in one case the deletion of the dependor object entails the deletion of the dependent object, this corresponds to the *Propagate_Strict_Dependency* case, and in the other case, called *Block_Strict_Dependency*, the deletion of the dependor simply cannot be made if there are objects dependent on it. Each one of these dependencies can be classified as *exclusive*, *shared* or *all* according to the number of instances of the dependor object type on which an object depends.

Relaxed existence dependencies. As its name suggests, it is a relaxed version of the strict dependency. The idea is that the dependent object cannot be created if the object on which it depends doesn't exist, but once it is created, its existence turns out to be independent of it. Therefore, its implications are only with respect to insertion, since the deletion of the dependor has no impact on the dependent. *Exclusive_*, *Shared_* and *All_Relaxed_Dependency* are distinguished here.

2.3 THE GENERALIZATION/SPECIALIZATION DIMENSION

All semantic models capture the notion of generalization/specialization but in BLOOM we go one step further by distinguishing different types of specialization in order to express yet more semantics: *Disjoint_*, *Complementary_*, *Alternative_* and *General_Specialization*.

As in any other object-oriented model, two kinds of insertion are distinguished: "new" and "add". Their semantics are specified in the insert constraints of the metaclass corresponding to the generalization/specialization abstraction. The "new" operation on a subclass implies an insert on the superclass as well. In contrast, the "add" operation on a subclass implies an insert on the superclass only if it didn't exist there previously.

For deletion, we also distinguish two kinds, one called "kill" that makes the object disappear definitively from the object base, propagating its deletion to its super and subclasses. The other one called "remove", only removes the object from the class indicated and from its subclasses.

According to the type of specialization, these constraints are further refined as follows:

- **Disjoint specialization**: The specialization subclasses are disjoint, that is, each object of the superclass belongs at most to one subclass. The only implication that this

- **Complementary specialization**: In this case the subclasses are complementary and overlapping, that is, each object of the superclass belongs at least to one subclass. Then, when we make "add" or "new" in the superclass, this insertion must be propagated to at least one subclass (system prompts for it). In contrast when there is a delete in a subclass and the object belongs to only one of the complementary subclasses, then either the deletion is blocked or else it is propagated to the superclass. This leads to two kinds of complementary specialization: the *Blocks_* and the *Propagates_Complementary_Specialization*.
- **Alternative Specialization**: In this case, the subclasses are complementary and disjoint, that is, each object belongs to one and only one subclass. The "add" or "new" operations on a superclass has the same effect as in the complementary specialization, but when the insertion is on a subclass, we must check that the object doesn't exist in a sibling subclass. The deletion of a subclass can be blocked or propagated giving rise to the *Blocks_* and *Propagates_Alternative_Specialization*.
- **General Specialization**: This type of generalization has no restrictions and no further implications.

2.4 THE AGGREGATION DIMENSION

Aggregation [Smith and Smith, 1977] in general, is the abstraction by which several objects are aggregated into a new, complex object. In BLOOM we distinguish three types of aggregation according to the different semantics found in the real world, one simple and two complex: *Simple_, Collection_* and *Associaton_Aggregation*

Simple aggregation. Objects $O_i, \ldots, O_n$ are *simple_aggregated* to another object O_j, just to model a property of it. In the real world, O_j is not the result of the aggregation of $O_i, \ldots, O_n$, which constitute merely its properties of interest in the universe of discourse. In this sense, aggregation provides a means for specifying the attributes of an object type. This is called "reference" by some authors and "weak reference" in [Kim et al., 1989].

Attributes can be primitive or derived depending on their types, single-valued (by default) or multi-valued (*set_of*), *obligatory* or not (by default). A dependency may exist between an object and another one *simple_aggregated* to it. The kind of this dependency can be any one of those explained before and must be specified thru the corresponding construct.

Collection Aggregation. Contrasting with the previous one, an object type O_i that is *collection_aggregated* to another type O_j, is not only a simple multi-valued property of O_j, but it is precisely this property what gives rise to O_j. This abstraction permits treatment of a collection of objects as another object. This concept, more commonly known by cover aggregation, was introduced by [Hammer and McLeod, 1981] who simply called it "aggregate". In turn, the *simple_aggregation* concept is used to specify the properties of the collection.

The behaviour of this abstraction is given by the *shared_strict_dependency* because the existence of the aggregate object strictly depends on the existence of the collection of objects that constitute it. Two kinds of collection aggregation are distinguished: *blocks_collection* and *propagate_collection*, depending on whether the deletion of the last member of the collection is blocked or entails the deletion of the aggregate object.

Association aggregation. The aggregate object is formed by associating one (or more) object instances of the types involved in the association. The associated objects are not simply properties of the aggregate one, but it is their association that gives rise to it. The aggregate object, in turn, has its own properties specified by the *simple_aggregation* abstraction explained before.

The behaviour of this abstraction is given by the composition of the different kinds of *strict_dependency* linked to the relationship between each component and the aggregate object. Two different situations can arise. One where the aggregate object cannot exist if any of its components objects doesn't exist. The other situation is similar but here it is possible to delete a component object as long as it is not the last object of one of the associated types.

2.5 OTHER FEATURES OF BLOOM

Next we comment some characteristics related to the semantic relativism of our model. BLOOM provides a set of integration operators including discriminated operators [García-Solaco and Saltor, 1991; Saltor et al., 1992] like the discriminated generalization, to support multiple semantics in a federated schema, and to overcome schematic discrepancies by transforming metadata into data and vice versa. Besides downward inheritance, BLOOM also includes upward inheritance as in [Schrefl and Neuhold, 1988], by which global types obtained from the integration of local ones inherit the structure and behaviour of these last ones. This facilitates the task of defining federated schemas.

3 COUPLING OF RELATIONAL AND OBJECT-ORIENTED DATABASES

The BLOOM model has been conceived in the context of database interoperability and it eases the task of coupling relational and object-oriented databases. In [Castellanos and Saltor, 1991] we have described how the semantic level of relational schemas is upgraded through a semantic enrichment process based on inclusion dependencies in their whole generality. There, we can contrast the poor expressiveness of the relational model against the richness of BLOOM.

Since BLOOM is an object-oriented model, the conversion from database schemas expressed in other object-oriented models to the richer set of abstractions of BLOOM results less complicated. Object-oriented models incorporate much more semantics than the relational one; at least every object-oriented model includes specialization and the set and tuple constructors. Furthermore, semantic integrity constraints are encapsulated inside the definition of the object type and they can be directly analyzed to obtain the necessary to identify the corresponding BLOOM abstractions.

Once object-oriented and relational schemas have been converted to rich BLOOM schemas, they can be effectively coupled by our schema integration methodology. Integration of database schemas involves a comparison task that searches for the semantic relationships that exist among them. The complexity resulting from the excessive number of comparisons that have to be performed, is due to the fact that the search is not guided at all. Each object in one schema must be compared with every object in the other schema, and these comparisons are in turn decomposed in comparisons between their attributes. In contrast, in our approach [García-Solaco et al., 1992] the complexity is reduced because the search is guided by the structures of the generalization and aggregation semi-lattices that conform the BLOOM schemas. Many non meaningful comparisons are eliminated and the most promising ones are identified. A systematic procedure for analyzing the structures in a meaningful way is given. The strength of the technique stems from the formal and precise semantics of BLOOM.

4 CONCLUSIONS

A model captures the semantics of the universe of discourse by means of the abstractions it supports in the generalization/specialization and aggregation dimensions, and how these abstractions are structured. Because BLOOM is based on a rich set of semantic concepts, which distinguish different kinds of dependencies, specializations and aggregations, it can capture more semantics than most existing models. This allows the definition of object bases with type structures which are really expressive.

As stated in Section 3, in the context of interoperability we need a canonical model rich enough to capture the semantics already expressed in the local schemas and the one captured by the enrichment process. Furthermore, we need an adequate model by means of which object-oriented and relational databases can be coupled. BLOOM has been designed for this purpose. Its practical significance in the semantic enrichment, detection of interdatabase semantic relationships and conformation phases of the integration process make of BLOOM the key component of our approach.

Acknowledgements

This research was partially supported by the Spanish PRONTIC program, project TIC89/0303.

Integrating Distributed Data Sources Using Federated Objects

Henry R. Tirri*
Purdue University
Department of Computer Sciences
West Lafayette, IN 47907
U.S.A.

Jagannathan Srinivasan†
Purdue University
Department of Computer Sciences
West Lafayette, IN 47907
U.S.A.

Bharat Bhargava
Purdue University
Department of Computer Sciences
West Lafayette, IN 47907
U.S.A.

Abstract

We address the problem of integrating heterogeneous data sources for collaborative environments such as groupware systems. Pre-existing related distributed data is modeled by a *composite* object, where each data source is treated as a fragment of the composite object. We define a collection of methods which allow manipulation of the related distributed data in a controlled and consistent manner. The composite object created in this manner is referred to as *federated object* , and it provides a pragmatic approach to data integration. Our approach is different from the approach of integrating heterogeneous database systems, as we do not require each data source to have full database system capabilities. For the collaborative application environments the data sources can be simple files, application generated binary files, or commercial data servers. The federated objects are suitable building blocks for computer-supported-cooperative work (CSCW) applications, where the type of collaboration is dynamic in nature. In this paper, we discuss the general properties of federated objects, present implementation

*On leave from Department of Computer Science, University of Helsinki, Finland.
†Current Address: Digital Database Systems, Nashua, NH 03062, USA.

principles for the required mappings, and show how federated objects can be used to implement a simple report writer application that needs to access several distributed data sources. A fully developed federated object mechanism relies on a "toolkit" approach, where federated objects are constructed from existing data sources using a C++ class library, which provides the mechanisms needed for access and manipulation of a wide variety of data sources.

1 INTRODUCTION

Over the past five years, attention to collaborative computing has increased dramatically. Collaborative computing uses networking, communications, concurrent processing, and windowing environments. Colab project [Foster and Tatar, 1988] introduced the notion of seamlessness between individual and group work, that is, the merging of group tools with individual tools. However, developing a self-contained and wholly integrated environment over a variety of computer systems that support both individual and cooperative work, has proven to be a difficult task. One of the important issues to be addressed is how existing (individually owned) data sources can be integrated without violating their normal use, i.e., individually owned data can be shared among several cooperating users in a flexible manner.

Several approaches have been used for integrating existing data to allow access and updates in a controlled and consistent manner. The research efforts in building federated database systems [Sheth and Larson, 1990; Ahmed et al., 1991b; Gupta, 1989] focus on integrating heterogeneous database systems by providing a software layer on top of the database systems. However, these attempts assume existence of a full capability database system at each of the sites. In the collaborative environment there are many cases where data is managed in an ad-hoc manner and only minimal services are provided to the user. For example, data may exist in regular files and a collection of programs may be used to manipulate the data, in which case the set of possible operations are "hardwired" into the individual programs.

To deal with data having a wide variety of access capabilities, ranging from a minimal access (say through a collection of programs) to access via a full database system with support for transactions, we propose an object-oriented approach for *loose* integration through special "data integration" objects. Our approach is similar to the approach adopted by Distributed Object Management Systems such as DOM [Buchmann et al., 1992]. However, our main goal is data integration, not the general integration of applications and our target environment is characterized with frequently changing collaborative needs that prohibit development of complex mechanisms. Also in our case, providing a high degree of autonomy in manipulation of individual data sources is more a rule than an exception; the owners of individual data sources are willing to share their data as long as it does not interfere with their primary activities.

We propose integrating related distributed heterogeneous data by a *composite object* [Kim et al., 1989], where the data residing on each site is viewed as a *fragment* of the composite object. A set of *methods* is defined to manipulate these fragments collectively as a single entity in a consistent and controlled manner. Such a *fragmented composite object*, referred to as *federated* object, allows loose integration of data residing on multiple sites. The federated object is created in a *bottom-up* fashion as opposed to *top-down* creation of composite objects in distributed homogeneous database systems [Bhargava et al., 1992].

Data integration through federated objects is aimed for collaborative applications, i.e., groupware, which require *dynamic grouping* of data according to individual user's (or group's) needs. On the other hand, owing to the nature of collaboration, the original data sources can still be accessed and manipulated by the individual users, and an essential requirement of such an integration environment is that the individual user should not be disturbed by the sharing mechanism as too much interference would reduce the willingness of the individual to participate in the collaborative activity.

An example of such a collaborative activity is preparing a project report that involves access to several independently manipulated data sources such as text files, files containing figures in various formats, speadsheet generated files containing budget information, etc. In each of these cases, the individual users should be able to access the data sources they own directly even after the integration, without being affected by the collaboration level activities. For example, accounting users should not be hindered in entering new cost information to the speadsheet files just because the editor of the project document has already placed an earlier version of the data in the document. Our federated object approach allows application programmers to use various data sources without requiring the original individual users to conform to the use of the new group application, or its interface, a fact that reduces the resistance to share data in a collaborative environment.

In the CSCW literature many competing models of group activities have been proposed. However, regardless of the model used a set of basic operations for data sharing have to be supported: retrieval, update, mutual exclusion, etc. Such primitive operations form a "core" of data sharing functionalities in any CSCW software platform. Thus for our purposes the choice of the exact model of cooperation is not important.

We have adopted a pragmatic approach for integrating data sources. This is based on the observation that the existing heterogeneity is not only due to the various representation formats, but is also due to the different operational capabilities supported by the sources. We adopt a "bottom-up" strategy, that is, we assume the existence of data sources with certain representation formats (e.g., ASCII text, postscript, or binary files) as well as standard capabilities (e.g., an SQL interface) which cannot be changed. Our federated object mechanism encapsulates such dimensions of heterogeneity to allow flexible application programming. We are especially interested in environments where the integration needs are dynamic: the set of data sources involved in a collaboration changes frequently. An example of such a collaborative activity is a short-term project documentation, at the end of which the integration of the various "source parts" of the report becomes obsolete. This is in contrast to the traditional database integration (homogeneous or heterogeneous), where the configuration of the set of participating databases is usually stable.

In Section 2 we outline the federated object architecture. Section 3 presents how federated objects can be manipulated as well as discussing interesting properties of such objects. Section 4 describes the implementation of a simple report writer application using the notion of federated object. We conclude in Section 5 and outline the planned future work.

2 FEDERATED OBJECT SYSTEM ARCHITECTURE

Layered system architectures result in clean and open systems. Unfortunately having many layers imposes a heavy penalty on the system performance. For practical purposes, the federated object system architecture has only two layers: the Data Source layer and the

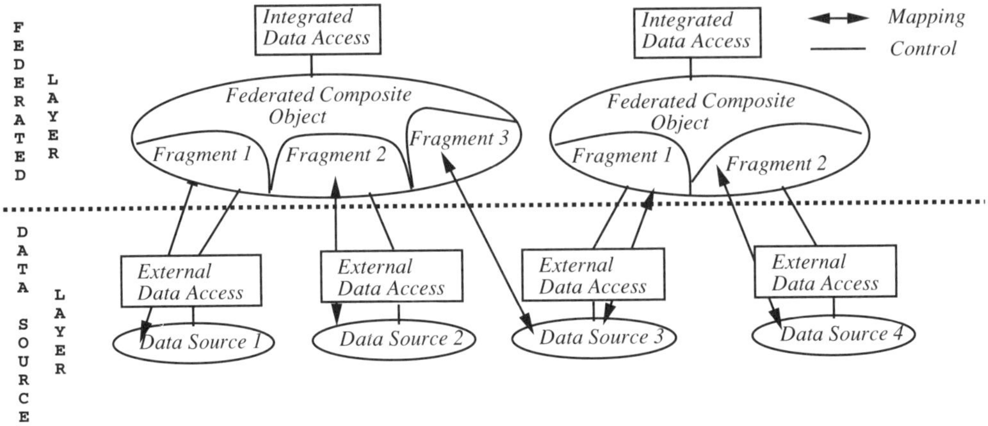

Figure 1: Federated Object Architecture

Federated layer. As the primary goal is to provide a tool for short-term data integration (e.g., for a temporary cooperative work in preparing a report), the complex support beyond these two levels is usually not required. Thus, the system does not support hierarchical federated objects. The federated object system architecture is illustrated in Figure 1. We identify the following components:

- one or more data sources that allow external data access (Data Source Layer),
- one or more Federated Objects (FO[1]) that can share data sources via fragments (Federated Layer), and
- mappings between the FO fragments and the data sources.

In general, the data sources (files, databases, etc.) can be accessed independently by other users without requiring all the accesses to be performed through the FO-interface. This is typical of applications where the owners of the data source are willing to allow access to their data as long as it does not affect their primary activities. Later we discuss the enhancements to this scheme, where users by accepting the use of a given filter (tightly-coupled cooperation) can improve the performance characteristics of the federated access.

2.1 DATA SOURCES AND ACCESS CAPABILITIES

Federated object allows integration of data sources with a wide range of access capabilities. In principle, these data sources can be classified into two categories:

1. *Passive data sources.* Ordinary files with read/write (blind write) capabilities fall into this category. A limited set of operations are supported, and the data sources lack communication support. Examples of such passive data sources are ASCII text files, program generated binary files, etc. For such data sources only read and/or write

[1]The abbreviation FO is also used in [Makpangou et al., 1992] to denote fragmented (active) object. However, these fragmented objects model distributed applications.

operations are allowed, and all the processing support is handled at the federated level. These operations can involve the entire file or a selected part of the file.

2. *Data servers.* This category contains data sources with a range of access capabilities as provided by the corresponding data server. On one end, the data server can provide a query language interface to access and manipulate data stored in a database. Note that the data source need not encompass the entire database. For example, in relational database systems, a data source can be one or several relations. Also on the other end, the data server may provide only read access to the data it manages.

For a meaningful integration, at least access capability must be allowed on the data sources, whereas the update capability is optional. Sometimes, only the update capabilities are meaningful, but for simplicity we assume that for those data sources we also have access capabilities.

2.2 FEDERATED OBJECT STRUCTURE

A federated object is composed from the following type of data members (see Figure 2):

- *Fragment.* One fragment per data source is created. The fragment can be either *embedded* in the federated object or can *reside elsewhere.*
  - Embedded fragments improve performance as the translated data is maintained as part of the federated object. However, mutual consistency between embedded fragment and corresponding data source has to be maintained. The decision to use embedded fragments depends on the expected access frequency for the data source as well as the consistency requirements. For example, if a data source is frequently accessed and rarely updated, having an embedded fragment will reduce the communication and translation overhead. Similarly, if the application can work with older versions of the data even when there are external (individual user) updates, the embedded fragments will be useful. For example, older versions of a customer data can be used in the design phase without sacrificing a meaningful end result.
  - Non-embedded fragments are useful for the data sources that are infrequently accessed. Also, the non-embedded fragments allow interfacing with database systems. Often, an interface is needed for the entire database and the data to be accessed is not known in advance.

  Note that the retrieved data can be cached even for non-embedded objects (similar to caching of results of procedure attributes in POSTGRES [Rowe and Stonebraker, 1987]. However, for clarity of the presentation we do not consider supporting caching of non-embedded fragments.

- *Subobject and simple data value.* This data member contains data common to one or more data sources. For example, the subobject may contain *aggregate* values generated from one or more fragment values.

The federated object constructed from different data sources are accessed and manipulated by a collection of *methods*. The methods can access more than one fragment of the federated object and hence can be used to capture *implicit* dependencies between different data sources.

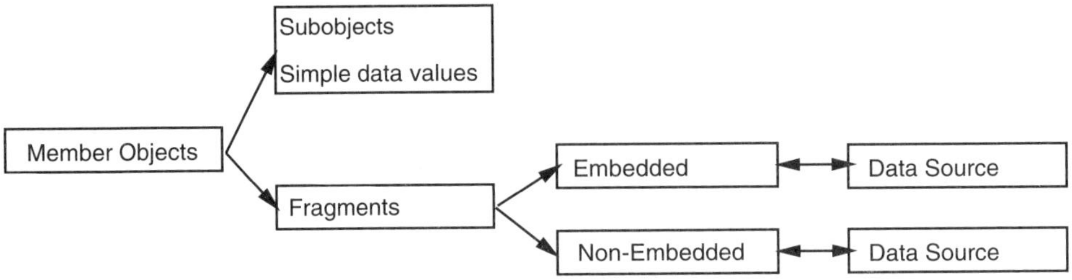

Figure 2: Components of a Federated Object

2.3 MAPPINGS

In many cases the original data has to be transformed to be in a suitable format for the federated object manipulation. These transformations may prune the data, e.g., remove control characters for display, or may augment the data by adding special formatting strings to ease the integration task. An example of latter is to augment an ASCII format relation (resulting from a query) with format characters in order to generate a table that can be included in a LaTex [Lamport, 1986] document. Thus, for each data source two translation routines need to be defined between the data source and the corresponding federated object fragment:

1. `fragment_to_data` routine maps federated object fragment to the data source.
2. `data_to_fragment` routine maps a data source to corresponding fragment.

These translation routines are defined as methods for the federated objects. Unlike other methods, these methods can update at most one fragment. This keeps the mechanisms simple and avoids the complex issues raised by the distributed updates. However, the method can access and update any number of subobjects and data values. Naturally the reverse mapping `data_to_fragment` need not be defined if the corresponding data source is only read and never updated. Also, in the case of `fragment_to_data` mapping problems analogous to view update problem can exist. In such situations the method code has to resolve the ambiguity.

3 MANIPULATING FEDERATED OBJECTS

The creation of a federated object itself is done through the execution of constructor methods. Additional methods can be defined for accessing and manipulating the federated object. In the following we illustrate the capabilities of such methods and how they should be designed.

3.1 RESTRICTING MAPPINGS FOR CREATING FEDERATED OBJECTS

As discussed earlier, for each data source a `data_to_fragment` translation method has to be defined. In our case such a translation method can update exactly one fragment object, although there is no restriction on the subobjects and data values it updates. In addition we restrict the translation method not to be able to access (read) any part of the federated object. The mapping from data to the fragment performs a *blind write* on the federated object in question. This restriction on mappings simplifies the creation of federated object as different fragments can be generated from the data sources in an arbitrary order. Specifically, let m_i and m_j be two translate methods that generate fragments from data source i and j respectively. The federated object FO will reach the same state for the two execution sequences, namely, m_i followed by m_j and m_j followed by m_i. In other words, the execution of translation methods is commutative.

3.2 ACCESSING FEDERATED OBJECTS VIA METHODS

The methods defined for federated object can be classified as follows:

- Methods that read parts of the federated object.
- Methods that update parts of the federated object.
- Methods that read as well as update parts of the federated object.

The advantage of using the first two types of methods is that the required system overhead is much less than for the last type. Thus the last type of methods should not be used unless they are really needed.

Methods accessing parts of federated objects. For pure read methods there are two cases:

- The methods access fragments only, not subobjects or common data values. It is sufficient to ensure that the accessed fragments are up to date. This check can be done by maintaining a bit vector, with one bit per data source. The bit is set whenever a data source has been updated, but the corresponding update is not propagated to the federated object at this time. The propagation is delayed until the fragment is really accessed. At the access time, a simple *and* operation on the bit vector can be employed to determine if the fragment being accessed is out of date with respect to the corresponding data source. If so, the corresponding constructor method is executed to regenerate the fragment and update the common subobjects and data values. The advantage of this approach is that if a data source is updated several times between accesses, only one propagation effort is needed. This reduces both communication cost and blocking delays.
- The method accesses the common subobjects and/or data values. In general, we do not know the data sources on which the subobject being accessed depends. In such a case the bit vector containing data source up-to-date information is examined. If it is non-zero, that is at least one data source has more recent data, the constructor methods are executed for corresponding data sources to bring the federated object to an up-to-date state.

The above strict scheme will result in bringing the entire federated object up to date before accessing the common subobjects and data values. Often, it may be enough to allow a demand driven update mechanism where a method accessing common subobjects and data values can avoid bringing the federated object up to date, especially if the subobject and data values accessed do not depend on the underlying data source that has changed. To support such a scheme the user is required to define the dependency of the method on the corresponding data sources.

For example, if a method m depends only on data sources ds_1 and ds_3, that is,

$$m : ds_1, ds_3$$

then prior to execution of the method m, only the updates corresponding to data sources ds_1 and ds_3 need to be propagated. Such explicit dependency specifications give additional flexibility to our system, if such dependencies are not known or they are too difficult to be analyzed, the above strict scheme can be followed.

Method updating fragments. Due to the natural semantics of federated objects, the members of such an object are related. There usually are dependencies between a subobject and a fragment. Updating a fragment may involve updating one or more subobjects. Such dependencies can be *implicitly* captured in method definitions. Since a fragment is always updated by a method, the method can be defined to update other related subobjects to bring the entire federated object into a consistent state. Note that in general there could also be dependencies between two fragments. Such dependencies are harder to capture; especially creating fragment from the data source can no longer be done independently in arbitrary order.

Method updating fragments can cause inconsistency as the equivalent updates have to be propagated to corresponding data sources. Since the data sources are autonomous and can be independently updated, in general the update propagation may not always succeed. The problem of providing multi-fragment update methods is in general as difficult as the update problem in heterogeneous multidatabases [Sheth and Larson, 1990]. Thus we only support methods that update at most one fragment.

3.3 PROPERTIES OF FEDERATED OBJECTS

Embedded Fragment Mutual Consistency. If a fragment is embedded in a federated object, then mutual consistency between the fragment and corresponding data source needs to be maintained. The mechanism has to address two types of updates:

- *Updates on Embedded Fragment*: The update has to be propagated to corresponding data source. For a simple data source such as a file the data source is overwritten (*blind-write*) after generating the equivalent file using the `fragment_to_data` method. If the underlying data source is controlled by a data server, then an appropriate update request is sent e.g., in SQL.
- *Updates on Data Source*: Similarly updates have to be propagated to the corresponding fragment. Two schemes are possible:
  1. *Instantaneous Update*: The user performing the update invokes an additional method (defined for federated object), which regenerates the fragment and any other associated subobjects and data values.
  2. *Demand Driven Update*: The update on the data source only causes updating the timestamp associated with the data source. Almost all types of data source have such timestamp information indicating when they were last updated (e.g, file header information, database version information). Now when the corresponding fragment is accessed first time after the data source update, the timestamp of fragment is compared with that of the data source. If there is a mismatch, a method is invoked to regenerate the fragment and related subobjects and data values.

Non-Embedded Fragments. The non-embedded fragments can be implemented through methods that retrieve data from the corresponding data source. For example, a method could simply be a query in a relational database system. Here there are no consistency problems as a fragment is derived on demand and is automatically up to date. This corresponds to the view mechanism in databases [Elmasri and Navathe, 1989]. Updates on non-embedded fragments are done by submitting an appropriate update request to the corresponding data server. For improving performance, the data retrieved through the method can be cached. In that case, one has to deal with the problem of cache getting out of date due to updates on the underlying data source. Such cache consistency issues are clearly related to the notion of quasi-copies and many of the mechanisms discussed in [Alonso et al., 1990] can be applied.

Atomic Execution of Methods. When a method updates a fragment the update needs to be propagated to the corresponding data source. If a method manipulates more that one fragment, the atomic execution of method is more complex. Specifically there are two cases:

- All the manipulated fragments are embedded. In this case the updates can be performed. However, the equivalent updates on the corresponding data sources need to be propagated.
- One or more fragments are pointers, i.e., data sources are either servers or nonresident files. In this case the updates on the corresponding data sources can fail. For such a case a set of methods that implement transaction support (e.g., commitment, isolation) is needed. For an example of such a mechanism see [Tirri et al., 1991].

4 BUILDING APPLICATIONS USING FEDERATED OBJECTS

Applications can be built using the notion of federated objects. To reduce the effort involved in building applications, a collection of C++ [Margaret and Stroustrup, 1990] classes (system classes) is provided. These classes support the basic mechanisms required for the access and manipulation of various (standard) types of data sources. In this section, we describe these system classes, outline the steps involved in building an application, and present the process layout of the application built in this manner.

4.1 FEDERATED OBJECT SYSTEM CLASSES

For each type of data source a separate class is defined. All federated object system classes are prefixed with `Fo` to distinguish them from the user-defined classes. Figure 3 shows the system class inheritance hierarchy. All classes inherit from the system class `Fo_Data_Source`. This class contains attributes and methods common to all data sources as shown below. For example, the method `get_timestamp` obtains the timestamp of the last update performed on the data source. The timestamp information is used to determine if a fragment data is out of date.

```
class Fo_Data_Source{
int    ds_id;                    // data source id
char *ds_name;                   // uniquely identifies the source
char *ds_site;                   // host site name
```

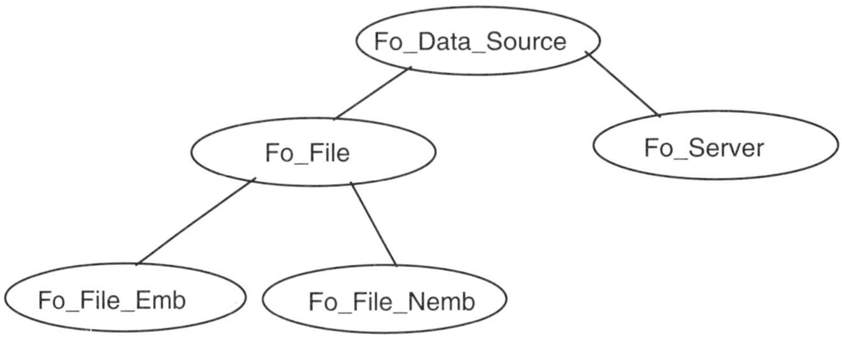

Figure 3: Federated Object System Class Hierarchy

```
int  ds_is_readonly;           // 1 means readonly else updatable
long ds_timestamp;             // when the data was last modified
int  ds_is_opened;             // 1 means data source has been opene
virtual long get_timestamp();  // obtains timestamp of last update
};
```

The method code for the system classes is divided into two files:

1. *Client code*: The client code contains the method stubs which are linked with the application program.
2. *Server code*: The server code contains the detailed implementation of the methods. These methods are invoked via Sun[2] Remote Procedure Call (RPC) [Sun, 1988] mechanism from the application.

4.2 WRITING AN APPLICATION

The applications are written in C++ programming language. The application writer composes a federated object from the desired data sources. The steps involved are as follows:

1. Identify the set of data sources that need to be integrated.
2. Define the federated object structure:
   (a) Define subobjects and data values
   (b) For each data source define the fragment structure. If the data source is of type `Fo_File` then this involves deciding if the fragment will be embedded or non-embedded and respective structure definition. If the data source is of type `Fo_Server` then by default the fragment is of non-embedded type.
3. Define two translation methods per data source. If no translation is required then the *identity* function is used as the translation method.
4. Define a set of methods to manipulate the federated object. These methods can potentially invoke any of the methods defined in the classes of the included data sources.

[2] Sun is a registered trademark of Sun Microsystems, Incorporated.

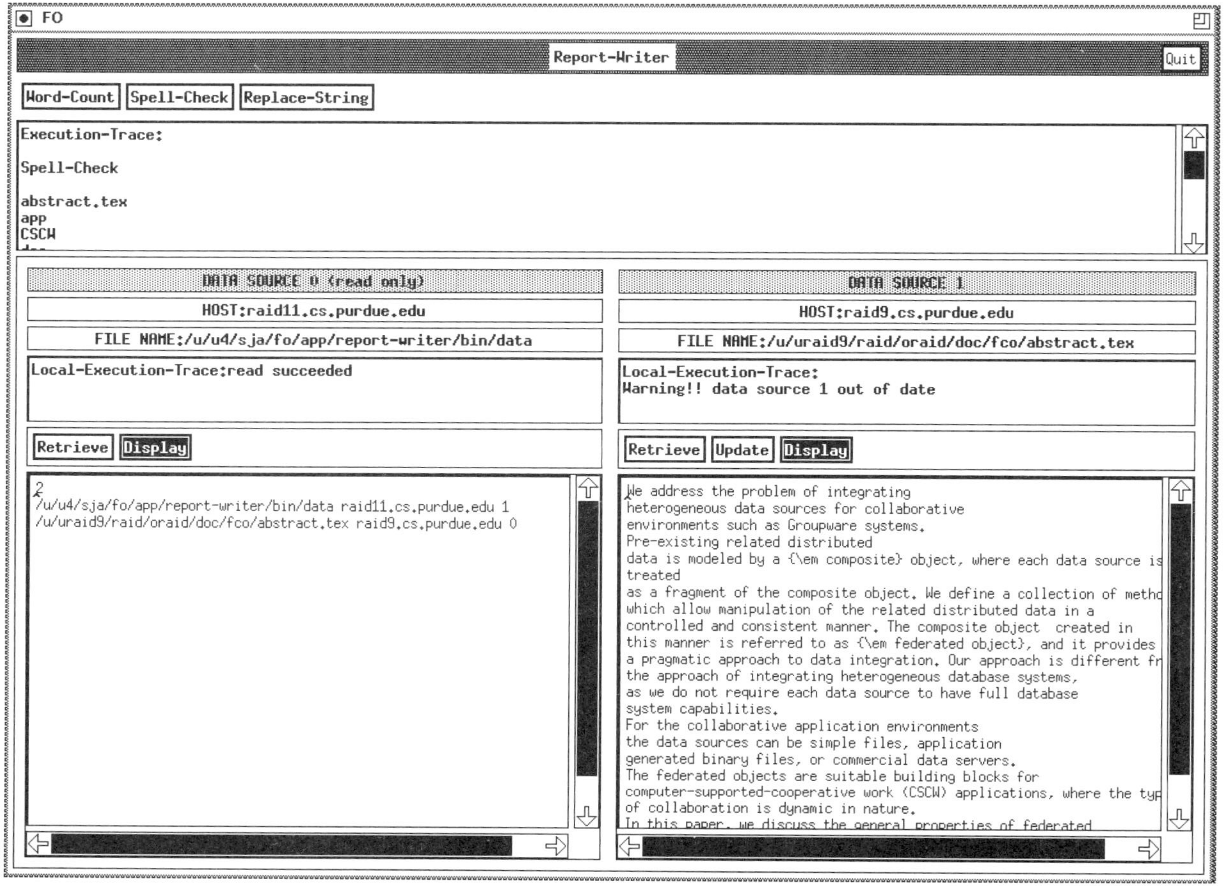

Figure 4: The Report-Writer application with two data sources

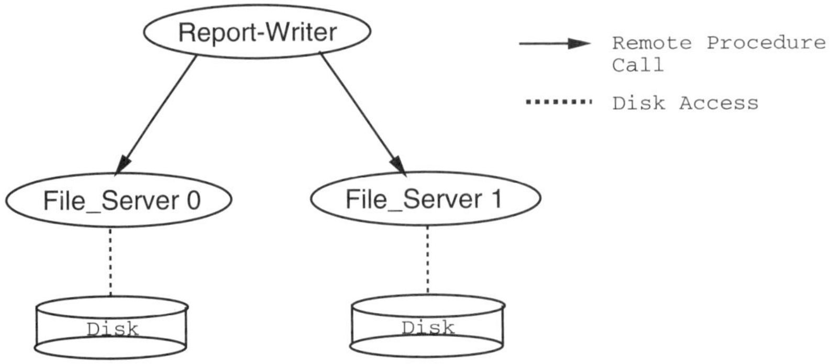

Figure 5: Process Layout for the Report-Writer application

Example 1 A Simple Report-Writer Application To illustrate the design, let us consider a *Report-Writer* application. The application uses multiple data sources (files) to form a report. We built the application using X [Scheifler and Gettys, 1983] windows. Figure 4.2 shows the Report-Writer with access to two data sources. The data source is specified by giving a triple: (site, pathname, isreadonly). Each of the included data sources is displayed in a separate window. User can retrieve and update data sources by clicking the *Retrieve* and *Update* buttons. After retrieving the data user can click on *Display* button to view the data. The retrieve, update, and display operations (methods) apply on individual data sources. User can directly edit the corresponding display window and can save the edited buffer by clicking on the update button. If the data source is *readonly* then updates are disallowed (e.g. data source 0 in Figure 4.2).

There are three common methods *Word-Count*, *Spell-Check*, and *Replace-String*, which collectively apply on all the data sources. Clicking on the Word-Count displays a count of lines, words and characters (similar to `wc` command in UNIX[3]) of the entire report. Clicking on the Spell-Check displays spelling errors in the entire report (similar to `spell` command in UNIX). Clicking on the Replace-String opens a window where user can specify a string and its replacement. The replacement operation is performed on all the data sources. All generated messages are displayed in the *Execution-Trace* window. In addition, each data source has a *Local-Execution-Trace* window that displays messages (if any) generated by the execution of the local methods on the fragment. For example, the Local-Execution-Trace window for data source 1 displays the warning message generated when its *Display* button is clicked.

The application uses `Fo_File` system class, and is compiled and linked with the client module for the `Fo_File` system class.

4.3 PROCESS LAYOUT

Invoking the application results in creation of one *application process* and several *server processes* (one per data source). For example, the execution of Report-Writer results in three processes as shown in Figure 5. The application accesses and updates the underlying data

[3]UNIX is a trademark of AT&T Bell Laboratories.

sources through the associated server process. As mentioned before Sun RPC mechanism is used for executing the methods of the server process.

The server processes for the data sources are created on demand. That is, when an application needs to retrieve or update a data source, the corresponding server process is created. However, the process does not terminate on the completion of the method execution. Instead, once created the server process remains active as long as the application process is active. When the application process exits, the server processes associated with its data sources are terminated.

For data sources shared by multiple applications, one server per application is created. Thus each application has its own set of servers. The system classes do not provide any mechanism for controlling updates on a data source by multiple servers. However, when a fragment is accessed, the timestamp information is used to determine if the fragment contains most up to date data. If there are updates more recent than the timestamp, then a warning is generated. User can then re-read the fragment through the associated server process and update the timestamp information.

If a fragment is updated (for example through the update button) then before performing the update the timestamp information for the corresponding data source is obtained. If the underlying data source is not same as the copy on which user performed updates, a special error window is displayed. This window allows user to either abort or continue with the update operation.

4.4 DISCUSSION

The above Report-Writer application was built using the federated object approach. Currently, the application is written in C as the related X-window code and library uses C. It runs on a network of Sun workstations under UNIX operating system.

The building of an application, even such a simple one, demonstrates the feasibility and usefulness of this approach. In future we will be rewriting the application in C++. We also plan to complete the implementation of *Fo_Server* system class and use that to build an application which requires sharing of both passive data (such as files) as well as data servers (database relations).

5 CONCLUSIONS AND FUTURE WORK

We have presented a pragmatic approach for building applications that require access to multiple heterogeneous and distributed data sources. The two characteristic features of this approach are: (1) data sources are not required to have full database system capabilities, and (2) the object-oriented approach is used for access and manipulation of the data sources. In this approach, building an application involves constructing a composite object (called federated object) from the desired set of data sources. Each data source is viewed as a fragment of the composite object. Methods can be defined to operate on both individual fragments as well as the entire composite object.

For each different type of possible data sources, a separate C++ class is defined which specifies the structure as well as the operations. A weaker mechanism for consistency between fragment and corresponding data sources is provided through the methods defined in the class corresponding to the data source. This weaker notion of consistency is desirable for applications such as those used for CSCW. Since the mechanism is built into the classes defined for data sources, they can always be replaced by adding code for stronger notion of consistency, if so desired.

Our initial experience of building a simple report writer application has demonstrated the feasibility of this approach. In future, we plan to extend the report writer application to involve access to both passive data (such as files) as well as access to data through a data server (e.g a database management system). An advantage of this approach is that it is evolutionary. After building a standard core library, enhancements to the mechanisms can be done quickly.

Acknowledgements

This research is supported in part by a grant from AIRMICS and UNISYS.

Integrating Independently Developed Classes

Svein Erik Bratsberg
University of Trondheim
Department of Computer Systems and Telematics
N-7034 Trondheim
Norway

Abstract

We address the problem of integrating classes that are developed independently. We propose to factorise the intensional and extensional dimensions of classes and let them be organised in separate hierarchies. Class integration becomes the problem of integrating extent graphs, and to describe relations between the properties of the classes to be integrated. Our approach may be seen as extending class hierarchies towards the semantics of views, making them more suited for class integration.

1 INTRODUCTION

A part of the problem of distributed object management, is to be able to integrate classes that are developed independently, either within the same or from distinct class hierarchies.

The most common approach to class integration is to use views (ViewSystem [Kaul et al., 1990] is an excellent example). Here, an integrating view is defined as a query towards classes in existing class hierarchies. The views often exist only for the purpose of integrating classes, and have behaviour different from ordinary classes. Our approach is to loosen up traditional class hierarchies by separating the extensional and intensional dimensions of classes, and let them exist in separate hierarchies. This allows a class to have a semantics similar to views, and the problem of class integration becomes a subset of the problem of evolving class hierarchies.

In our approach class integration becomes the problem of connecting extent graphs and describing the relations between the properties of the classes to be integrated. We treat both cases where the classes to be integrated exist in the same class hierarchy and where they do not. This latter case requires the capability of managing external (user-defined) identities. We start by introducing the integration framework, including connecting extent graphs and integration of objects and properties. Then, we show how our approach relate to object-oriented views.

2 INTEGRATION FRAMEWORK

2.1 OBJECT MODEL

Objects and *values* are the basic bricks of our object model. Objects are uniquely defined by (proxy) *object identifiers* (OIDs) (identities are further discussed in Section 3.1). An *intent* is a description of the implementation and the interface of objects, and is similar to a class in C++. An intent has a set of *properties*, which we divide into *public*, which are visible and accessible to clients of the intent, and *private* which are encapsulated. A *property* is either an *attribute* or an *operation*. We allow for both attributes and operations to be public. The rationale for this is that both operations and attributes may be implementation, and both may naturally be parts of the observable interface of an object.

Intents may be organised in inheritance hierarchies, *intent hierarchies*. Here, an intent can be defined to inherit (through *inheritance links*) from several other intents. An *intent hierarchy* is a directed acyclic graph (DAG), where the vertices correspond to intents and the edges correspond to inheritance links. The semantics of an inheritance link is *copying*, i.e. an intent behaves equally if the properties are defined locally or inherited.

An *extent* is a named set of objects. There is an one-to-one and onto mapping from intents to extents. An intent–extent pair will be called a *class*. An *extent propagation link* is a directed connection between two extents. An object existing in the extent at the tail of the link, will also exist in the extent at the head of the link. An *extent graph* is a directed graph where the vertices correspond to extents and the edges correspond to extent propagations. An object existing in one extent will be transitively propagated to all other reachable extents. We distinguish between the *creation* of an object (generating OIDs) in an extent and the *insertion* of an object into an extent.

2.2 CLASS INTEGRATION

Our approach to class integration is built around the extent graphs. Integration is done by connecting two extent graphs by proper extent propagations. Integration may or may not cause new classes to appear.

Extent graph integration is the creation of new extents (possibly none) and extent propagations to the extent graphs D_1 and D_2, resulting in a new extent graph D_I, such that D_1 and D_2 are directed subgraphs of D_I. A *class integration* is an extent graph integration with with N (≥ 0) new extents, and the definition of N corresponding intents (possibly by inheriting from existing intents).

Intent hierarchies are directed acyclic graphs (DAGs), while extent graphs are general directed graphs. Thus, an extent graph and its corresponding intent graph do not have to be isomorphic. The intent hierarchy indicates partly the creation order of the classes, while the extent graph does not. The reason for us to separate the extent dimension from the traditional class hierarchy, is that the intent hierarchy has inherent constraints like non-cyclicity and that it only can be extended downwards. This makes it very dependent on *when* the abstraction is discovered. Extent graphs do not have the non-cyclicity constraint and are much more independent with respect to when the abstraction is discovered.

We will now show some integration situations that might appear within the extent graph notion when two classes C_1 and C_2 are going to be integrated.

1. *Generalisation*: This means creating a generalisation class (C_G) of two classes (C_1 and C_2) representing the union of the extents.
2. *Role generalisation*: This is a generalisation of different "roles" (C_1 and C_2) of the same objects into one class C_R. This is similar to the (normal) generalisation, but requires the capability of "joining fragments" of an object. Related to views, generalisation will be accomplished by the union operator, and role generalisation by the join operator.
3. *Specialisation*: This is a situation where the integration of the two classes (C_1 and C_2) gives the need for creating a specialisation class (C_S).
4. *Intermediate abstraction*: There is a missing intermediate class (C_I) between the two classes (C_1 and C_2).
5. *Connecting specialisations/generalisations*: The two classes (C_1 and C_2) are generalisation/specialisation of each other, and no new class needs to be created.
6. *Connecting variants*: The two classes (C_1 and C_2) are variants of each other, and need to connect their extents.

3 PROPERTY INTEGRATION

3.1 OBJECT/IDENTITY INTEGRATION

As in [Kent, 1991a], we will distinguish between *real world* and *proxy* objects. Real-world objects are the conceptual objects that are modelled in the database by proxy objects. Two proxy objects may represent the same real world object. These objects are then said to be *real-world identical*. If these proxy objects also are identical database objects, they are said to be *proxy identical*. A (unique) *proxy identity* is assigned upon object creation, while we will assume that real-world identities may be handled (i.e. compared) through user-supplied functions. Sometimes, such a function may be inferred from other properties of the objects, like employee number or social security number, but often one has to rely on explicit enumerations [Kent, 1991a].

Two classes to be integrated may or may not exist in the same extent graph prior to the integration. If the two classes are existing in distinct extent graphs, objects of these two classes cannot be proxy identical. In Section 4 we will present parts of a query algebra that has operators both for the real-world and proxy identity cases.

3.2 ATTRIBUTE INTEGRATION

Extent propagation ensures that an object is a member of several classes. The properties associated with an object in two classes that are connected by an extent propagation link, are often partly overlapping. This overlap is described using *attribute consistency relations (ACR)*. Consider two classes C_1 and C_2 that are connected by an extent propagation link, and having attributes a_1 through a_n and b_1 through b_m, respectively. Attribute consistency relations exist in two categories:

- **Derivable relation**: $(x_1, \ldots, x_k) = \mu\,(y_1, \ldots, y_p)$
  Attributes x_1 through $x_k \in \{a_1, \ldots, a_n\}$ are derivable from attributes y_1 through $y_p \in \{b_1, \ldots, b_m\}$ using the attribute mapping μ. If μ is complete and has an inverse, we may facilitate shared representation for the two sets of attributes.
- **Non-derivable relation**: $(x_1, \ldots, x_k) = \phi\,(y_1, \ldots, y_p)$
  Attributes x_1 through $x_k \in \{a_1, \ldots, a_n\}$ are dependent on all attributes y_1 to $y_p \in \{b_1, \ldots, b_m\}$, but it is not possible to derive them.

Given a non-derivable ACR, $(x_1, \ldots, x_k) = \phi\,(y_1, \ldots, y_p)$, where a client attempts to update one of the attributes y_1 through y_p. The following different policies are possible:

1. Insert *null values* in the non-derivable attributes x_1 through x_k, meaning that their values are not known. The correct values for the x's will be inserted manually when they are known.
2. Deny updates to y_1 through y_p, because we do not have an "updatable dependency" [Larson et al., 1989].

We may also allow inconsistencies to appear by omitting to specify dependencies, which gives the responsibility for maintaining the dependencies to the clients.

ACRs will be implemented by shared representation and mappings, or by separate representation and *operation consistency relations (OCRs)*, which may be seen as special cases of database triggers. OCRs may also be seen as alternatives to ACRs, where it is a large discrepancy between the attributes to be integrated, but the operations are quite similar. We provide for both *lazy* and *eager* consistency maintenance by the support of two timing models for OCRs.

4 OBJECT-ORIENTED VIEWS

Our understanding of objects, classes, and class hierarchies resembles very much object-oriented views, which often are defined as a type (corresponding to our intent) and a query (representing the extent). Our objects may reside in many classes having overlapping properties, which means that the problem of maintaining consistent objects resembles the problem of maintaining consistent views.

In [Bratsberg, 1992] we have outlined a realisation of our approach to class evolution by using object-oriented views. Our views include intents, operation consistency relations, and extents defined using an "objectified" version of the relational query algebra. This algebra has identity-preserving operators, i.e. the output objects have the same identities as the input objects. The operators are working on proxy identifiers, e.g. the join criterion is equal object identifiers. To support class integration, we need to extend this to real-world identities. We will give some examples of these extensions:

- *Real-world object join*: $S_1 \bowtie_{\Im} S_2$
  This is similar to the proxy object join, but the join criterion is a user-supplied function $\Im$ that evaluates if two objects are real-world identical. It is the $\Im$-function which

decides what should be the identity of the objects in the result. Generally, it may the proxy identity of the object in S_1, S_2, or a newly generated identity.

- *Real-world set operators*: Like the join operator, the set operators have their real-world counterparts: *union* ($\cup_{\Im}$), *intersection* ($\cap_{\Im}$), and difference ($-_{\Im}$).

5 CONCLUSIONS AND FURTHER WORK

By separating between the intensional and extensional dimensions of classes, we were able to extend the semantics of classes towards the semantics of views, which made classes more suited for integration (because the relationships between our classes are richer than in traditional class hierarchies). This class integration approach is a part of a work on general class evolution [Bratsberg, 1992]. One basic assumption here is the extent graph. With this assumption, we are not able to handle database integration cases where it is larger discrepancy in the modelling, e.g. aggregate integration [Kaul et al., 1990], and meta-object/ ordinary object integration [Kent, 1991a].

Object-oriented classes may be complex. In this paper, we assume all extent definitions to be done manually based on the integrator's understanding of the classes. We would like to give the integrator some help in understanding the semantics of classes [Sheth, 1991], and to be able to use this to define extent propagations and property consistency relations between the classes to be integrated.

An Approach to Behavior Sharing in Federated Database Systems

Doug Fang
University of Southern California
Computer Science Department
Los Angeles, CA 90089
U.S.A.

Joachim Hammer
University of Southern California
Computer Science Department
Los Angeles, CA 90089
U.S.A.

Dennis McLeod
University of Southern California
Computer Science Department
Los Angeles, CA 90089
U.S.A.

Abstract

An approach and mechanism to support the sharing of behavior among the component database systems in a federation is described. In the context of a functional object-based database model, a technique to support inter-component behavior as well as inter-component information unit sharing is presented. An experimental implementation of the behavior sharing mechanism and algorithms is examined, and its practical utility and effectiveness are assessed. This work is couched in the framework of the Remote-Exchange research project and experimental system.

1 INTRODUCTION

A principal goal of the current Remote-Exchange research project at USC is to provide a comprehensive mechanism for the transparent sharing of objects among autonomous components in a federation of database systems. In addition to the sharing of instance and type objects [Fang and McLeod,1992], behavior sharing constitutes the third aspect of intercomponent information exchange that is currently under investigation. In this paper, we provide an overview of our underlying theory of behavior sharing in federated database systems. We specifically present an overview of the possible behavior sharing patterns, using examples from our experimental prototype system based on the Omega [Ghandeharizadeh et al., 1991] and Iris [Fishman et al., 1987] object-based database management systems. We address the essential problems that are associated with each sharing situation and describe our mechanism to support sharing as implemented in our experimental prototype system.

1.1 RELATED RESEARCH

At the top level, there are two distinct aspects of behavior sharing: (1) the remote execution of behavioral objects, and (2) the location of the actual information units upon which behavioral objects operate. Research in the area of distributed programming languages has of course addressed issues of the remote execution of behavioral objects (which may also be termed operations, methods, or functions) [Liskov, 1988; Strom and Yemini, 1985]. The primary concern of this work is with the programming of the functions themselves, e.g., language constructs, communication primitives for sending and receiving data, etc. The location of data used by these functions is directly coded into the methods themselves.

Work in the area of database systems, on the other hand, predominantly focuses on the manipulation of information units; this is related to the second main aspect of behavior sharing. Research on object-oriented database systems has approached the problem of supporting behavior in the database itself [Atkinson et al., 1989; Fishman et al., 1987; Kim et al., 1990; Lecluse et al., 1988; Maier et al., 1986]. When these systems are extended to a distributed environment, it is the location of the (persistent) data that determines the location of the remote execution of the functions [Fishman et al., 1987; Kim et al., 1990; Maier et al., 1986]. In the Remote-Exchange approach, functions are implemented without explicit knowledge of where they will be executed or where the data will reside.

1.2 A FUNCTIONAL OBJECT-BASED CONTEXT FOR BEHAVIOR

The conceptual database model considered in this research draws upon the essentials of functional database models, such as those proposed in Daplex [Shipman, 1981], Iris [Fishman et al., 1987], and Omega [Ghandeharizadeh et al., 1991]. Our functionally object-based model contains features common to most semantic [Afsarmanesh and McLeod, 1989; Hull and King, 1987] and object-oriented database models [Atkinson et al., 1989], such as GemStone [Maier et al., 1986], O_2 [Lecluse et al., 1988], and Orion [Kim et al., 1987]. In particular, the model supports complex objects (aggregation), type membership (classification), subtype to supertype relationships (generalization), inheritance of functions (attributes) from supertype to subtypes, run-time binding of functions (method override), and user-definable functions (methods).

In this model, functions are used to represent inter-object relationships (attributes), queries (derived data), and operations (methods). Three types of functions can thus be distinguished:

- *Stored Functions*: A stored function records data as primitive facts in the database. Stored functions can be updated.

- *Derived functions*: A derived function is defined by a data manipulation language (DML) expression. The value of a derived function cannot always be updated directly.

- *Computed functions*: A computed function (sometimes termed a foreign function) is defined by a procedure written in some programming language. The value of a computed function cannot be directly updated.

For the purposes of this paper, derived and computed functions are treated uniformly, and will be termed "computed functions" herein.

2 THE SHARING OF BEHAVIOR

Let us assume the existence of a function $\mathcal{F}$, which can be shared among components of a federation; without loss of generality, assume $\mathcal{F}$ takes as input the argument a.[1] The argument type can be a literal (i.e., **Integer**, **String**, ...) or a user-defined type such as **Research-Papers**, for example. Sharing takes place on a component-pairwise basis, meaning that $\mathcal{F}$ is exported by a component $C1$ and imported by a component $C2$. The importing component is called the *local database*, while the exporting component is called the *remote database*. There are several ways components $C1$ and $C2$ can share the service provided by $\mathcal{F}$, depending upon the location where $\mathcal{F}$ executes and upon where its input argument a resides (i.e., there are two degrees of freedom). At this level of abstraction there are four distinct *function-argument* combinations:

- local function - local argument
- local function - remote argument
- remote function - local argument
- remote function - remote argument

Upon closer analysis we can note that it is also necessary to differentiate between stored functions and computed functions. At this (finer) level of granularity, we can now distinguish between a total of eight different sharing scenarios,[2] as presented in Figure 1.

In this table of Figure 1, "Local" refers to the domain of the local database while "Remote" refers to the domain of the remote database. Local objects are those that belong to the local database, while remote objects belong to the remote database.

It is important to note that a principal goal of our approach is to provide a mechanism for behavior sharing that makes the location of a function and its argument transparent to the user. The details of how this transparency can be achieved are more fully described in Section 3, but we will briefly highlight the process here. In particular, we note that the state of a remote object (i.e., its functional values) always resides in the remote database, but when the object is imported to a local database, a surrogate is created for it in the local component. The creation of such surrogates is necessary in order to refer to remote objects using local database system tools without modification [Fang et al., 1991]. Since these surrogates are created locally, the local system is able to interpret and manipulate remote objects as usual, for example, when using them as arguments in local function calls. However, when retrieving the actual state of a remote object, the use of surrogates alone is not sufficient. Our approach exploits the extensible nature of our object-based database

[1] Since the argument can be a complex unit of information, this is not a limitation; multiple arguments can be handled by an obvious extension of our approach.

[2] We now have three degrees of freedom.

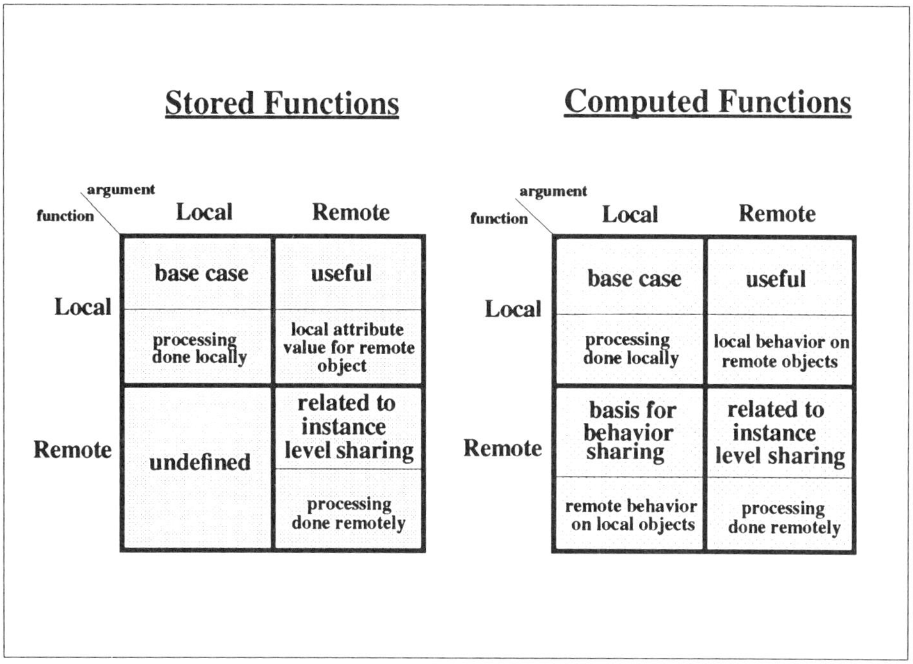

Figure 1: Eight different situations for sharing of behavior

model by rewriting the functions encapsulating surrogate objects as computed functions. These higher-level computed functions serve as place holders, and retrieve the results of applying the function on the remote component where the object is actually stored.

Given the above observations, it is now possible to consider each of the behavior sharing situations summarized in Figure 1. We first focus on stored functions, and then turn our attention to computed functions.

2.1 STORED FUNCTIONS

As a framework for analysis, consider the scenario of two collaborating researchers: Researcher-A and Researcher-B maintain separate databases of journal and conference publications. Figure 2 specifies the meta-data (conceptual schemas) for two example components.[3] Let Researcher-A denote the local component and Researcher-B denote the remote component.

The four situations for the sharing of stored functions among components can be analyzed as follows:

1. *Local function - Local object*
   This is what we term the *base case*. Both objects, the stored function $\mathcal{F}$ and its

[3] In order to keep the signature of each function as short as possible, we have omitted the input argument whenever it is obvious; the result type, on the other hand, is always explicitly shown.

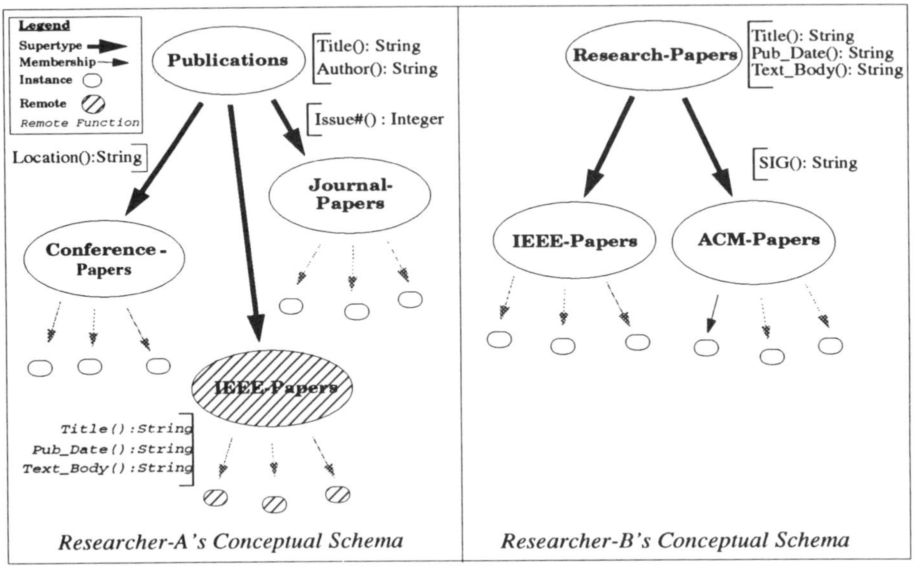

Figure 2: Two component databases

argument a, reside in the local component and can be executed as usual without any additional mechanisms.

2. *Local function - Remote object*
In this case, $\mathcal{F}$ is a local stored function that is applied to remote argument a. For example, Researcher-A's $Author()$ function can be applied to the **IEEE-Papers** that have been imported from Researcher-B. As previously mentioned, surrogates are created in Researcher-A's database for each remote object. These surrogates are collected in a newly created subtype of **Publications** called **IEEE-Papers**. All local functions, for example the functions defined on **Publications** in Figure 2), operate normally on the surrogates (i.e., the instances of **IEEE-Papers**). In the case of local functions that do not have counterparts in the remote component (e.g., $Author()$), new function values can be created locally for each imported instance. As a result, each imported object also has local state in Researcher A's database and can be altered by Researcher-A without affecting the original object in Researcher-B's database. The three functions $Title()$, $Pub\_Date()$, and $Text\_Body()$ that are shown next to Researcher-A's **IEEE-Papers** in Figure 2) are actually remote functions defined in Researcher-B's schema; these have been included in Researcher-A's database for completeness. Exact details of how these functions are created and invoked are presented in Section 3. Provided that Researcher-A has created new values for $Author()$ for each of the imported **IEEE-Papers**, s/he might pose the following OSQL query in this context:

```
select Author(PAPERS)
for each IEEE-Papers PAPERS
```

3. *Remote function - Local object*
This situation is somewhat meaningless, since stored functions only have a meaning in

the local context of the component in which they were initially created. For example, suppose that Researcher-A, who does not have the $Pub\_Date()$ function defined in his/her schema, wants to see the publication date of all his/her **Conference-Papers**. Researcher-A would first need to create a new function and then populate it with the appropriate values, rather than being able to use Researcher-B's $Pub\_Date()$ function. However, when looking at this situation from Researcher-B's point of view, one can argue that this case is merely the mirror image of the second case (Local function - Remote object). Rather than executing Researcher-B's function remotely in Researcher-A's database, one can integrate Researcher-A's **Conference-Papers** into Researcher-B's schema (create a new subtype, **Conference-Papers**, of **Research-Papers** and populate it with Researcher-A's **Conference-Papers**) and execute the $Pub\_Date()$ function locally.

4. *Remote function - Remote object*
This case serves as the basis for *instance level sharing*. All remote objects of interest to a component, say Researcher-A, must already be imported into the local database using surrogates. Each time a remote object is referenced, the surrogate "points" to the remote object and the desired functional value is fetched using a remote procedure call to the other component (see Section 3). In this situation (see Figure 2), Researcher-A might pose the following OSQL query against his/her schema:

```
select Pub_Date(PAPERS)
for each IEEE-Papers PAPERS
```

In order to find the $Pub\_Date()$ of all remote **IEEE-Papers**, surrogates for each of these papers are used to locate the remote papers. For each remote paper, the publication date is determined using the remote $Pub\_Date()$ function and the result of this function is returned to the local database.

2.2 COMPUTED FUNCTIONS

In order to consider sharing for computed functions, consider again the example of two collaborating researchers. Figure 3 shows the two example component databases as before, but with additional (computed) functions: **DviView()**, a dvi format previewer, **PostView()**, a postscript previewer. The four situations for the sharing of computed functions among components can be analyzed as follows:

1. *Local function - Local object*
As in the case of stored functions, this is the base case. Computed function $\mathcal{F}$ as well as its argument a resides in the local component and the execution is local (e.g., **latex(Text_Body(**a**)))**.

2. *Local function - Remote object*
This situation can be reduced to the base case described in case 1. For example, if Researcher-A wants to view one of Researcher-B's papers, s/he will run $latex$ on the $Text\_Body()$ of the surrogate for that paper, say *inst*, and apply $DviView()$ to the result (e.g., **DviView(latex(Text_Body(***inst***))))**.

3. *Remote function - Local object*
This is the reverse of the previous case: the function executes remotely and the input argument is supplied from the local database. For example, Researcher-A may desire

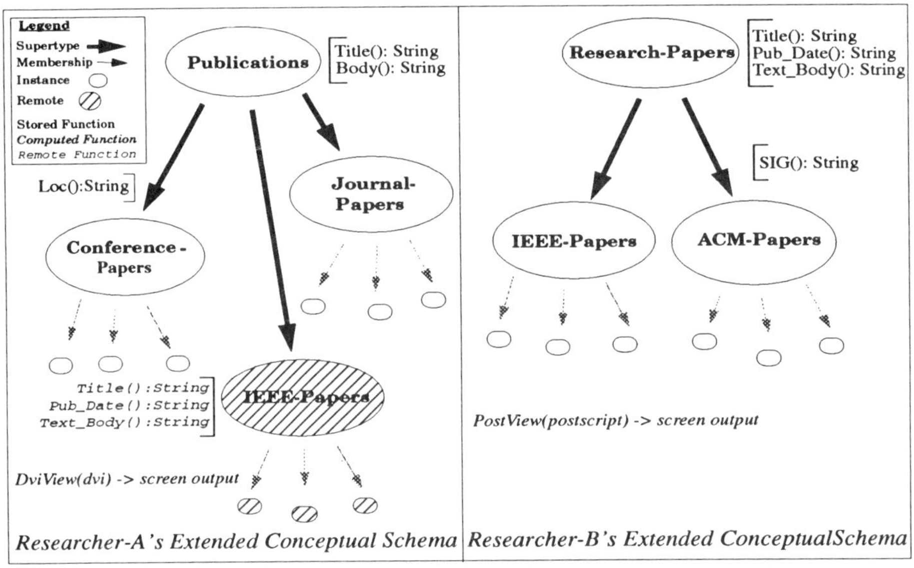

Figure 3: Two component databases with extended functionality

to view postscript text but does not have a postscript previewer in his/her own local database. In this case, s/he will invoke Researcher-B's $PostView()$ function remotely through a previously created handle in his/her own database and supply it with a local argument. In effect, the remote database is providing a non-local "service". Intuitively, from Researcher-A's perspective, this is what "sharing of behavior" corresponds to.

4. *Remote function - Remote object*
   This situation is similar to the first case (Local function - Local object) in that both the state of the object and execution of the function are in the same component. For example, Researcher-A views one of Researcher-B's **IEEE-Papers** using Researcher-B's original $PostView()$ function. Compared to the first case (Local function - Local object) where no sharing takes place and execution occurs locally, in this case all the processing is done on the remote site. In order to invoke a remote computed function using remote arguments from within the local component, surrogates for the remote objects must be created locally. These surrogates enable the local component to access the actual state of desired objects which reside with the remote component. This procedure is similar to instance level sharing (see Section 3.2) where surrogates for shared instances are created locally in order to provide access to the actual state of each instance in the remote component.

In the examples above, the functions being shared have returned a literal type (e.g., the $Author()$ function returns a **String**). However, functions with signatures involving abstract (user-defined) types can also be shared. In this case, both the input and output argument types must be defined locally; if they are not, their meta-data must be imported beforehand. The location of the result argument is determined by the location where the function executes.

2.3 OBSERVATIONS ON THE PRACTICAL USE OF BEHAVIOR SHARING

With the above analysis and framework in place, it is now possible to make some observations on the practical utility of the behavior sharing capabilities supported by our mechanism. In the above analysis of behavior sharing, we stressed the separation of the location where the function executes from the location where the data resides. However, from a user's perspective, this separation of function execution and argument location is completely transparent.

Our analysis of eight different sharing patterns can be reduced to two "most interesting" cases: (1) executing an imported function on a local argument, and (2) executing a local function on an imported (shared) argument. The first case involves the reuse of a previously defined function in a different environment. This "reuse of function" is a principal reason why components would want to share behavior. The second case can be described as extending the "characteristics" of a remote object while at the same time respecting the autonomy of the originating site. That is, the importer can customize the remote object according to his local conceptual schema. These local attributes are managed entirely by the local component avoiding any unnecessary modification to the originating (remote) component.

In both cases above, the user is not aware of the environment in which a shared function executes, and need not worry about where the state of an imported object actually resides. Instead, components are able to freely browse the meta-data and behavior that have been made available (i.e., exported) by others in the federation in order to select the services that they would like to share[4] (i.e., import).

3 EXPERIMENTAL PROTOTYPE IMPLEMENTATION

An experimental implementation of our behavior sharing mechanism has been designed and built using our Remote-Exchange testbed consisting of a federation of Omega and Iris database components [Fang and McLeod, 1992]. In what follows, we describe the essential aspects of this testbed, and examine critical implementation issues we faced in our experiments.

3.1 OBJECT SHARING IN THE REMOTE EXCHANGE TESTBED

In the current Remote-Exchange testbed, we have implemented the seamless (transparent) importation of objects from remote databases. In our functional object-based model, objects can be instances, functions or types. The various functional sharing patterns described above can be examined in the context of instance and function level sharing.

Conceptually, in instance level sharing, a remote instance object is imported directly into a local type. This remote instance behaves in the same manner as a local instance object from the user's perspective. However, the actual state of the remote instance exists in the remote component database; retrieval of any state of the remote object is done by accessing

[4]Our discussion has in a sense assumed that there are no access restrictions in place that would further complicate the sharing process. An investigation of behavior-based authorization in object-based databases is the subject of a related research project at USC.

the remote database transparently. Hence, access to remote instance objects corresponds to the Remote function - Remote object situations described above.[5]

The importation of a function object corresponds to the sharing of behavior. Intuitively, when an instance object is imported, only data is being shared. On the other hand, importing a behavioral object gives the importer access to services not provided by his/her local system. This corresponds to the Remote function - Local object situations described above.

The only remaining useful situation described, which is not covered directly by instance or function level sharing, is the important case of Local function - Remote object. Among other things it allows users to add additional state to remote objects without modification of the exporting database, thereby preserving the autonomy of the exporter. This ability to create local state for remote objects is achieved automatically from the way we implement instance level sharing and is analogous to simple local database access.

3.2 INSTANCE LEVEL SHARING IMPLEMENTATION

Our mechanism for importing instance level objects follows three steps:

1. Create local surrogates for remote objects.
2. Create computed functions for retrieving data from remote components.
3. Overwrite functions defined on surrogates to use (or refer to) the newly created computed functions in step 2.

The local surrogate serves as a local handle for accessing a remote instance. By using the surrogate, differences between remote representations of objects, e.g., object identifiers (OIDs) can be masked out (made transparent). Since the state of the remote object exists externally, computed functions for accessing that state must be created. These computed functions use the Remote Procedure Call (RPC) paradigm [Birrell and Nelson, 1984] for accessing the remote component. Finally, in order to have the surrogates use the remote functions, any existing functions defined on the surrogate must be overridden to use the RPC defined functions. This is implemented by dynamically binding functions to objects.

In terms of the collaborating researchers, we can envision a scenario where Researcher-B wants to import instances of another remote type **IEEE-Papers** into his/her local schema using the above approach. This is depicted in Figure 4. Surrogates are created as instances of both a local type (i.e., Researcher-B's **IEEE-Papers**) and a remote type called **R-IEEE-Papers** in Figure 4. The purpose of the new surrogate type is to override the local functions that surrogates inherit from the local type to which they belong. By additionally creating the surrogate as a member of this surrogate type, the functions that the surrogate instance originally inherited are overridden. The two thin dotted arrows from **R-IEEE-Papers** ("R" for remote) and **IEEE-Papers** to the surrogate instance serve to indicate that surrogate instances (i.e., remote instances) of **IEEE-Papers** are created as members of both **IEEE-Papers** and **R-IEEE-Papers**. Thus these (remote) instances inherit functions multiply from both **R-IEEE-Papers** and **IEEE-Papers**; any duplicately named function from the two types is overridden by the function defined for **R-IEEE-Papers**. The functions defined on **R-IEEE-Papers** are computed functions, which make RPC requests to the remote component database and retrieve the values of functions on remote instances.

[5]Note that this does not depend upon whether the function is stored or computed.

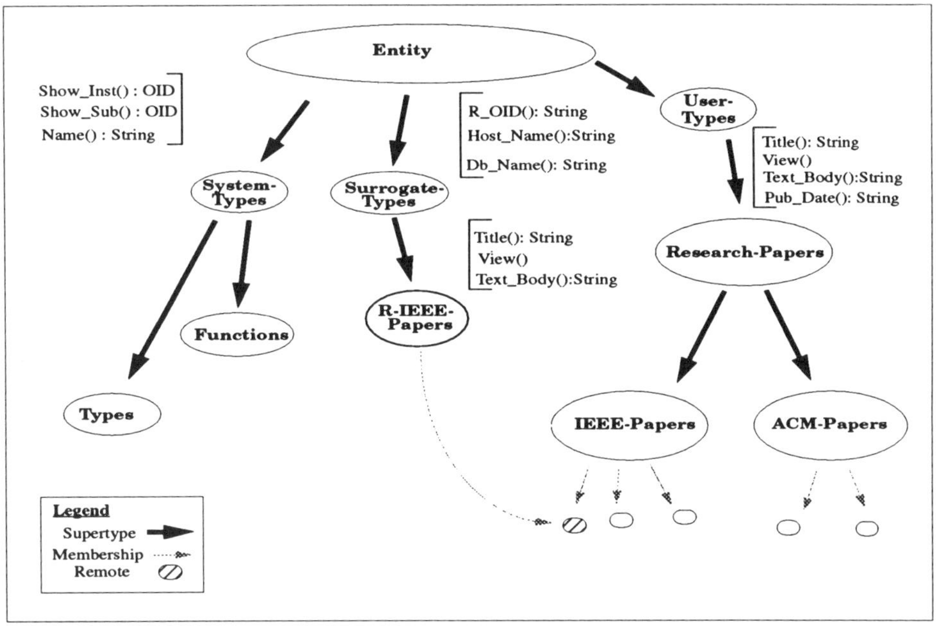

Figure 4: Sharing instance objects

3.3 FUNCTION LEVEL SHARING IMPLEMENTATION

As in instance level sharing, meta-information containing the location (e.g., remote OID and remote component name) of the remote function object being imported must be stored locally. However, by contrast with the case for instance level sharing, this meta-information is associated directly with the function being imported. In instance level sharing, the meta-information is indirectly kept for remote functions such as *Title()* and *View()* via the surrogate instance object (see Figure 4). Thus, in our implementation we distinguish between two kinds of "remote" functions: those implicitly defined through instance level importation and those directly imported through function level importation. Figure 5 shows our mechanism for incorporating meta-information for function level importation. We exploit the fact that meta-information is also represented using our functional object-based model. Imported functions are created as instances of the type **Remote-Functions** and can thus store and access the additional location meta-information required to execute the imported function.

Figure 5 depicts a slightly different sharing pattern from Figure 4. In this scenario, the *View()* function is imported from some remote component. In addition, **R-IEEE-Papers** no longer supplies a *View()* function. Hence both the remote and local instances of **IEEE-Papers** use the same imported *View()* function for displaying research papers. This is evident in Figure 5 by the absence of the *View()* function from the type **R-IEEE-Papers** and the addition of a new (italicized) *View()* function defined on **Research-Papers**.[6]

[6]The italicized font is used to indicate that the *View()* function is imported and no longer local.

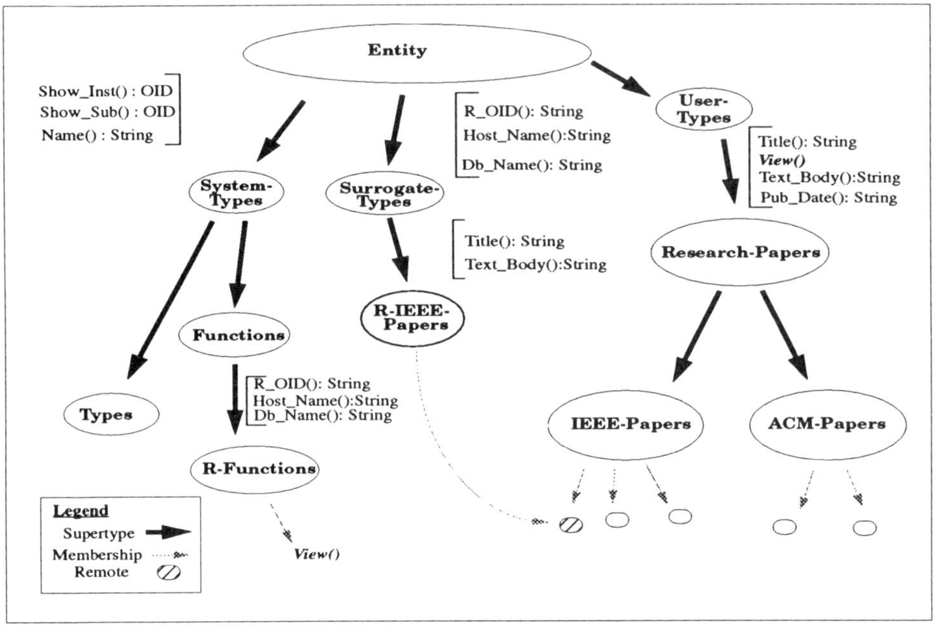

Figure 5: Sharing function objects

In order to explain how the *View()* function works, we must first explain how our implementation addresses the issue of side-effects. By side-effect we really mean two things: (1) any kind of implicit input other than the input argument that is necessary to compute the result, and (2) any modifications to the state of the database where the function executes other than to the input argument. For functions whose arguments are literals, this simply requires that the function being imported computes its result value solely based on its input argument without modifying any database state. Functions whose input argument is non-literal pose additional difficulties. In this case, the input argument is the OID of an instance. The problem then lies in determining what information a computed function accesses in order to compute its results. Strictly applying our definition of side-effects would restrict computed functions on non-literals to solely accessing and then manipulating the input OID. But realistically, a computed function must be able to access some state of the instance corresponding to the OID when computing its result. In our implementation, we take the position that the only state that a computed function can access are those functions that serve to encapsulate that object. In other words, the only state the computed function will possibly access are those functions that are defined on the types of which the instance is a member. In the case of the *View()* computed function, these functions are *Title()*, *Text_Body()*, and *Pub_Date()*.

Having determined what information a computed function on a non-literal type can access, a problem arises when trying to execute such a function remotely on a local object. The problem occurs when supplying local arguments to a remote computed function. Although we know the computed function is limited to only accessing the functions that encapsulate the instance, we do not know exactly which ones it does need. Even if we pass all the possible values the computed function can access, the computed function must be written in such a way as to retrieve these arguments from the remote component and not the local one. This would be undesirable and contrary to our goal of relieving the computed function writer of needing to know where the data on which it operates is located.

The best approach to this problem in our autonomous environment is to allow computed function writers to define functions without concern as to whether the function is to be exported. Thus, in our implementation, whenever a remotely executing computed function needs state from the local component, it performs a callback to the local component to retrieve that state. For the instance level sharing described in Section 3.2, the local component simply runs as a client and makes RPC requests to the exporter running as a server. However, for function level sharing, when the callback mechanism is used, the local component must in addition run as a server to accept the callback requests. Computed functions can be written using any programming language that can be compiled to re-entrant object code. This object code is then dynamically linked into the database management system kernel when the computed function is accessed. In our prototype using the Omega database management system, a computed function accesses the local component through *Omega_eval()*, which has two parameters: an argument and the function that is to be applied to the argument.

We can now consider how the callback mechanism works transparently and how it allows a computed function to be written uniformly without regard as to whether that function is to be exported. Consider again the example using the *View()* computed function. Suppose that the imported *View()* function retrieves the *Text_Body()* of an instance (say in latex format), computes the dvi formatted version, and displays the formatted version through a dvi previewer (say xdvi). When the user of the local component invokes the *View()* function on a local object, the *View()* function is passed the local OID of a **Research-Papers** instance. The *View()* on the remote server makes a call to *Omega_eval()* to retrieve the *Text_Body()*, *Omega_eval()* recognizes that the OID passed in as its argument is not local and performs a callback to the server of the local component that invoked the *View()* function. Since the local server recognizes the OID as a local OID, it performs the request and passes back the *Text_Body()* to the remote server which can than complete its computation and display the results on the local database monitor.

4 CONCLUSIONS AND FUTURE DIRECTIONS

In this paper, we have presented an approach and mechanism to support the sharing of behavior among the component database systems in a federation. We considered the various situations for supporting the sharing of behavior. An experimental implementation of the behavior sharing mechanism using the Remote-Exchange experimental testbed was examined.

In our approach, we have considered the importance of decoupling the location of (persistent) data and the location of the execution of methods that operate on it. Traditional approaches inextricably link the location of the data and the execution of the operation. An area of research that has not been considered in this paper involves local component updates of objects at a remote component. Other research efforts specifically address the issues in this area [Breitbart et al., 1990a]. However, our approach allows the local component to create local (e.g., stored) functions on remote objects. This has the overall benefit of allowing the local component to create local state for remote objects that completely conform to the local system's mechanism for updates.

The focus of our experimental prototype implementation has been mainly on instance level sharing and behavior sharing of functions. We have found these sharing patterns to be very natural and easy to use in our environment. We are currently further investigating abstract (complex) object sharing, and are proceeding to more substantially quantify the performance efficiency of our mechanisms.

Acknowledgements

This research was supported in part by IMAR and NSF grant ECD-8717322, and in part by NSF grant IRI-9021028. The authors would like to acknowledge the valuable comments of Shahram Ghandeharizadeh of USC, as well as those of the workshop participants.

Supporting Local Autonomy in a Distributed Object-Oriented Database

Biju J. Kalathil
University of Illinois
Department of Computer Science
1304 W. Springfield Ave.
Urbana, IL 61801
U.S.A.

Geneva G. Belford
University of Illinois
Department of Computer Science
1304 W. Springfield Ave.
Urbana, IL 61801
U.S.A.

Abstract

In this paper we propose a new model of distributed object-oriented databases where data that are shared between the individual databases are instances of class versions in *globally accessible class version trees*. Central to this model is a new concept called *federated collections*, which are collections of objects of the same class that may be distributed across a number of databases in one or more sites. The administrator of each database that participates in a federated collection may create a new version of a globally available class and adopt it for the local component of a federated collection. *Class version mapping* and *federated queries* support seamless querying of federated collections.

1 INTRODUCTION

A federated database system is a distributed database system where the individual databases have local autonomy. [Sheth and Larson, 1990] classifies *local autonomy* into four types - *design autonomy* which implies that a database in the federation can choose whatever data model, implementation of the data model, or schema that fits its needs; *communication autonomy* through which an individual database can decide who else in the federation it will communicate with; *execution autonomy* which means that the federation does not interfere with the local operations nor is any knowledge of the federation needed for performing local operations; and *association autonomy* which implies that the the local database can decide how much of its data and functionality it will share with the others in the federation. Work on federated database systems has focussed on integrating pre-existing databases [Sheth and Larson, 1990; Litwin et al., 1990]. In this paper we propose a new model of distributed object-oriented databases where the individual databases can take a given schema and adapt it to their individual needs, but still be able to share data and functionality with the rest of the distributed system. We thus address a gap between classical federated databases (which integrate independently developed schema) and classical distributed databases (where all databases have to adhere to the same schema). Central to this model is a new concept, the *federated collection*, which we describe below.

A *federated collection* (FC) is a collection of objects of the same class that may be distributed across a number of databases in one or more sites. Each participating database in a federated collection contains only its part of the federated collection, called a component of the FC, and the data objects are typically not replicated. In this sense a federated collection is analogous to a nonreplicated horizontally-fragmented relation in a distributed relational database management system. Any database administrator in the distributed system may create a federated collection and export it together with the schema for the class of objects it contains. The exporter of the federated collection specifies the group of databases that can participate in the federated collection. A database specified in the participant list has to explicitly import the federated collection to become a participant. The class definition for member objects of a federated collection is globally available and the database administrator (DBA) of a participating database is free to create a new version of the class and adopt it for the local component of the FC.

Federated queries (section 6) provide for transparent access to distributed data. Differences in schema across different databases are handled in two ways, depending on the query and the extent of the differences in the schema. If the query involves only messages provided by the class of objects in the federated collection, and the signatures of the messages are the same across the different databases, then the system executes the appropriate version of the method for each participating database in the FC. If the signatures of the messages are different across databases, then the class version mappings (Section 5) are used to translate messages from one version of the class to another. If the query involves data members of objects in the FC, and versions of the class differ in their data structure, again class version mappings are used for converting objects from one version to another.

In the next section we present a motivating example which can be modeled naturally using federated collections. In Section 4 we describe the architecture of a testbed system we are building to experiment with the functionality of federated collections, namely the FEDerated COllections TeStbed (FEDCOTS). Class version mapping, the distinguishing feature of the system, is discussed in Section 5. Querying of federated collections is described in Section 6. We describe the current status of the project and conclude the paper in Section 7.

2 A MOTIVATING EXAMPLE

We describe in this section a university administration application, managing student academic information for the various colleges in the university, like Engineering, Medicine, Graduate College, Liberal Arts & Sciences (LAS) etc. The various colleges have different degree offerings, degree and admission requirements and policies. Ideally each individual college would like the schema of their student information database to be customized to their needs both in their data fields (attributes) and also in their functionality (methods).

However the various colleges need to have limited access to other colleges' databases in a manner they are familiar with. Also, the University Administration Office needs to have uniform access to databases at the various colleges.

Figure 1 shows three schemas that would be ideal for three colleges in the federation. We note that the graduate college needs different data fields in its schema, like "GRE" and "GMAT" scores in place of the "ACT" and "SAT" scores in the LAS College database. Also constraints on data fields "Year" and "Degree Objective" have changed. The two schemas differ also in their methods. For example, determining whether a student is in good standing in the Graduate College needs to be done differently from that for the LAS College. The University Administration Office may need to run queries on all the databases in a uniform fashion to check if students are in good standing. Each college may allow authorized personnel from other colleges to access some of its information, but deny access to some other information like Grade Point Average (GPA) of students. The colleges may allow selected users like the University Administration Office to read more of its data than it allows other colleges, but still deny write access to most of its data.

The FEDCOTS system will provide the functionality to support such an application very naturally.

3 CLASS VERSIONING VERSUS SUBCLASSING

Can we use subclassing in the place of class versioning for the purpose of adapting a schema to the needs of an individual database? In other words in our university administration example, can the university administration office put out a generic student class, and the other colleges subclass it to create las_student, grad_student, med_student and so on for their local schemas? We argue below that class versioning is indeed better suited for our model than subclassing.

Subclassing is a class evolution paradigm where divergence takes place primarily through addition. In the standard model of inheritance, all attributes of a superclass have to be inherited by its subclasses. Also one cannot change the domain or constraints on inherited attributes. Partial inheritance of messages and changing the message signatures and their corresponding methods are allowed, however. The standard model of inheritance supports a restricted model of evolution where subclasses are specializations of their superclasses. A superclass abstracts out the common properties of its subclasses. The relationship between a class and its superclass is characterized as an is_a relationship.

In a federated system, to support local design autonomy, we need to allow the local databases to make arbitrary changes to a class definition, including dropping attributes and changing definitions of existing attributes. In other words, we need to support an is_a_variant relationship between classes (versions of classes).

Even if the semantics of inheritance were extended to allow such arbitrary changes to a class, we would still need class versioning to support *schema evolution*. The adaptation of a class to the needs of an individual database is not a one time affair, it is an ongoing process. Any schema that is being used by a database in the federation needs to be made available for use to the rest of the federation to enhance data and functionality sharing. Hence, when one of the databases using the globally available schema decides to evolve the schema, it cannot do so by overwriting the existing schema, but rather by creating a new version of it.

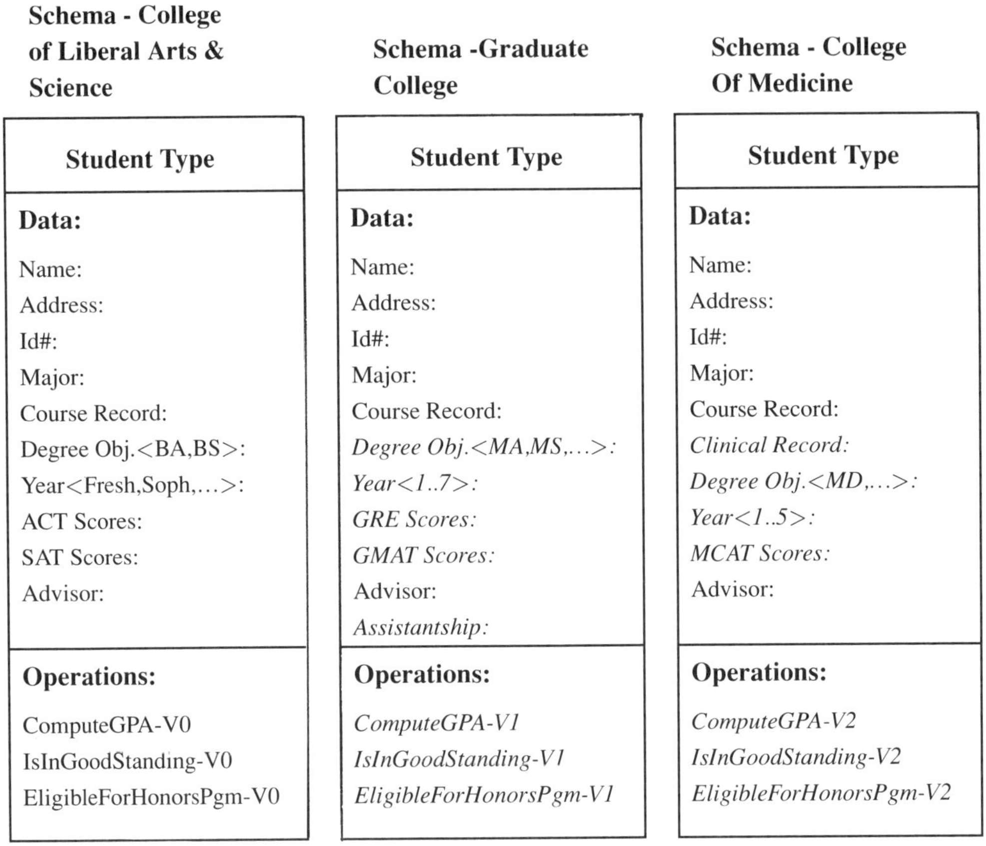

Figure 1: Database schemas needed for three colleges in an university

It is obvious that subclassing is not an appropriate solution for this problem as it will result in the cluttering of the class hierarchy.

4 ARCHITECTURE OF THE FEDCOTS SYSTEM

The FEDCOTS (FEDerated COllections TeStbed) system may consist of one or more sites, with each site containing one or more databases. A database may participate in one or more federated collections and each federated collection could have components in one or more databases in the same or different sites. A federated collection server (FCS) process residing at each site in the federated system manages federated collections and globally shared class version trees. It provides the federated querying and class version mapping functionalities of the system.

5 CLASS VERSION MAPPING

FEDCOTS provides two messages[1] **define-map-instance** and **define-map-messages** which can be sent to class versions for mapping to and from other class versions of the same class. The message **define-map-instance** is sent to a source class version or a target class version to specify how an instance of the target version can be constructed from an instance of the source version:

(**define-map-instance** *<SourceClassVersion>* | *<TargetClassVersion>*
  :to *<TargetClassVersion>* | **:from** *<SourceClassVersion>*
  :map *<ListOfAttributeMapSpec>*)

An *<AttributeMapSpec>* specifies how an attribute of an instance of *<TargetClassVersion>* is to be constructed:

(**:target-attribute** *<TargetAttributeName>*
  :constructor *<AttributeConstructorExpression>*)

An *<AttributeConstructorExpression>* returns an object in the domain of the target attribute, and may involve one or more attributes in the source class version and/or global variables and functions.

The message **define-map-messages** is send to a class version (target or source) to specify how messages of the target class version can be constructed from messages of the source class version:

(**define-map-messages** *<SourceClassVersion>* | *<TargetClassVersion>*
  :to *<TargetClassVersion>* | :from *<SourceClassVersion>*
  :map*<ListOfMessageMapSpec>*)

A *<MessageMapSpec>* is specified as:

(**:target-message** *<TargetMessageName>*
[**:source-message** *<SourceMessageName>]*
[**:map** *<ListOfParameterMapSpec>*])

A *<ParameterMapSpec>* specifies how a parameter of the target message can be constructed from one or more parameters of the source message.

6 FEDERATED QUERIES

To select instances of a federated collection, an **fselect** message is sent to the collection object:

(**fselect** *<FederatedCollection>*
  :where *<WhereExpression>*
  [**:database-group***<DatabaseGroup>*])

[1] We have adopted a subset of the programming-language interface described in [Kim, 1990] and have extended it further to support federated collections.

The *<WhereExpression>* is a boolean-valued expression involving instance variables of objects and/or messages to the objects in the collection. A transient collection of objects that satisfy the *<WhereExpression>* is returned. The **:database-group** argument specifies the subset of the FC components on which the query will be performed.

To run an arbitrary query expression on a federated collection, an **fquery** message is sent to the collection:

(fquery *<FederatedCollection>*
[**:where** *<WhereExpression>]*
:query *<QueryExpression>*
[**:database-group***<DatabaseGroup>*])

The **fquery** message returns a transient collection of objects returned by the *<QueryExpression>* when applied on objects in the receiver collection that satisfy the *<WhereExpression>*.

7 CONCLUSIONS

The FEDCOTS project is currently in its design phase. Of the four types of autonomy (Section 1), it will support three types fully – communication, execution and association. With regard to design autonomy, it will allow a database to adopt any schema, but will restrict all databases to the same database model and implementation. We shall shortly begin the implementation of the testbed system and subsequent development of example applications to help us investigate further the functionality of federated collections.

Object Algebra and Views for Multi-Objectbases

Marc H. Scholl*
University of Ulm
Department of Computer Science
D–W–7900 Ulm
Germany

Hans-J. Schek
ETH Zürich
Department of Computer Science
CH–8092 Zürich
Switzerland

Markus Tresch*
University of Ulm
Department of Computer Science
D–W–7900 Ulm
Germany

Abstract

This paper addresses the problem of defining views that span several objectbases. Views are expressed in terms of an object algebra. We are interested in the degrees of coupling and in the degrees of integrity maintained through multi-objectbase views. A key issue is the problem of global object identity. Each local system has its private object identifiers (OIDs) to represent objects. Globally, however, we need other mechanisms to uniquely refer to objects. We propose a technique that is based on the definition of (updatable) views: Queries to other objectbases are used as a referencing mechanism. The mechanism is useful as a formal basis for (partial or complete) schema integration in multi-objectbase systems.

1 INTRODUCTION

Object-orientation is supposed to offer advantages in the context of multi-database systems. The advanced modeling capabilities of object models provide generalizations and the possibility to include computations (in the form of methods) in schema definitions. This

*Work done while at Department of Computer Science, ETH Zürich.

surely facilitates the interoperability of heterogeneous data or object bases as far as schema integration is concerned [Kaul et al., 1990; Saltor et al., 1991]. Object query languages and algebras for objectbases re-introduce generic, general-purpose functionality to object management, similar to relational algebra [Straube and Özsu, 1990; Shaw and Zdonik, 1989; Kim, 1989; Cluet et al., 1990; Bancilhon et al., 1989].

Supporting views by allowing any query expression to serve as the definition of derived object collections (view classes) is the next logical step. We have been working on object preserving views in order to have a simple means for supporting updates. Object identity is the main feature used for it. Separation of types and classes helps to distinguish projection kinds of views from selection views [Scholl and Schek, 1990; Scholl et al., 1991]

A further step is the application of the object algebra and of views for tasks which span several objectbases. Again we want to preserve the advantages of state-of-the-art commercial systems which already allow us to query and update several databases within one application/transaction (see for example ORACLE). But actually we want more support for integrity preserving updates in such a multi-objectbase scenario: instead of explicitly having to update related data in different local objectbases, we want a (partially) integrated global schema, such that the multi-objectbase system can automatically maintain inter-objectbase constraints. Further, we want to overcome the limitations of relational systems (with respect to view updates) and we do not want to lose the higher degree of integrity supported in OODBMS by the notion of objects, their types, classes and distinction between values and objects. Notice that we are not aiming at fully integrated global databases. Rather we want a flexible way to partially integrate existing databases while retaining their local autonomy.

The purpose of this paper is to extend the view definition mechanism that is already offered by the COOL language to serve as the formal basis for schema integration in multi-objectbase systems. We can apply the object algebra, which has been defined for a single objectbase so far, without major changes to multiple objectbases. In order to show this, the main questions that have to be answered are the following:

1. What is the minimal degree of object schema integration in order to link several objectbases by algebra expressions? What kind of views can be used?
2. How do we define, cope with, and maintain the integrity that two objects from different objectbases are "identical" in the sense that they represent the same 'real-world' object?
3. Is there a way to obtain a spectrum of different degrees of integration of local objectbases; and what are the impacts on integrity maintenance during updates?

A lot of work has been devoted to the problem of schema integration (see [Batini et al., 1986] for a survey); relatively few of them consider integration of existing objects, that is, populated objectbases. Exceptions are the Multibase project [Landers and Rosenberg, 1982] and Pegasus [Ahmed et al., 1991b; Krishnamurthy et al., 1991]. These attack similar problems. However, Multibase is retrieval-only, and for Pegasus, we did not see precise definitions and maintenance of multi-objectbase identity, yet. Kent introduced a separation of real world entity objects vs. proxy objects [Kent, 1991a]. The latter ones represent entities in different objectbases. The next closest work we are aware of is that of Neuhold/Schrefl et al. [Schrefl, 1988; Neuhold and Schrefl, 1988; Kaul et al., 1990; Geller et al., 1991]. We will compare our approach with their work in more detail below.

Our approach differs from Pegasus and also from Schrefl/Neuhold in that we define (global) object id in terms of algebraic (extend) views. We show that, with a small revision of the notion of object identity, we can define views over multi-objectbases, that unify the proxy objects in different local objectbases, if they represent the same real-world entity.

The structure of the paper is as follows: Section 2 motivates the importance of views and subschemas in multi-objectbases and gives a summary of the COOL object algebra and its view definition mechanism. In Section 3 we describe how the algebra can define links between objects from different objectbases. A specialized linking mechanism is used in Section 4 to unify objects across multiple objectbases. The problem of update propagation is discussed in Section 5.

2 SCHEMAS AND VIEWS IN MULTI-OBJECTBASES

2.1 SCHEMA ARCHITECTURE OF MULTI-OBJECTBASES

Multi-objectbases are built up of several components – local objectbases (LOBs) –, each of which has the structure of its objects described by a local schema. The composite schema gives the structure of the global objectbase (GOB). Figure 1 shows this architecture, which is a part of the five-level schema architecture for federated database systems (DBS) proposed in [Sheth and Larson, 1990]. Throughout this paper, we concentrate on homogeneous multi-objectbases. That is, we separate the issue of data model transformation from the rest, and assume that all schemas are already transformed into a uniform data model.

Views (virtual classes) and subschemas (collections of classes and views) play an important role within multi-objectbases [Motro, 1987; Abiteboul and Bonner, 1991]. For an LOB, the local schema can be tailored by adding local views to better meet external requirements (external schema). Afterwards, a subpart of the local schema (export schema) can be exported for use in the multi-objectbase system. In a GOB, views and subschemas can again be used to tailor the composite schema. In addition, the creation of views and subschemas that span several LOBs can be utilized as a formal basis for global integrity maintenance during updates, that is, to achieve a higher degree of integration.

The goal of the global schema is to allow queries and updates that involve several LOBs. The power of global transactions, in particular that of global updates, critically depends on the degree of integration of local schemas into a global schema. The tighter the integration is, the more powerful can integrity maintenance be. We distinguish the following levels of integration:

Level 0 is the weakest level, where no integration of the LOB schemas is performed at all. Global transaction management allows us to query and update several LOBs within a single transaction. Each operation is explicitly directed to one LOB, it is not possible to address objects from multiple LOBs in one statement of the query language.

Level 1 has the local schemas *composed*. Again, this is not yet a real integration. Simply the local schemas are put side-by-side, such that the name spaces of the local schemas are merged. Now, queries/updates can be performed on multiple LOBs (because the names of the classes and views are known to each other). However, as we will see later, objects are strictly separated.

Level 2 finally supports real integration. Proxy objects from multiple LOBs must have been identified to represent the same entity object from the real world. Parts of the

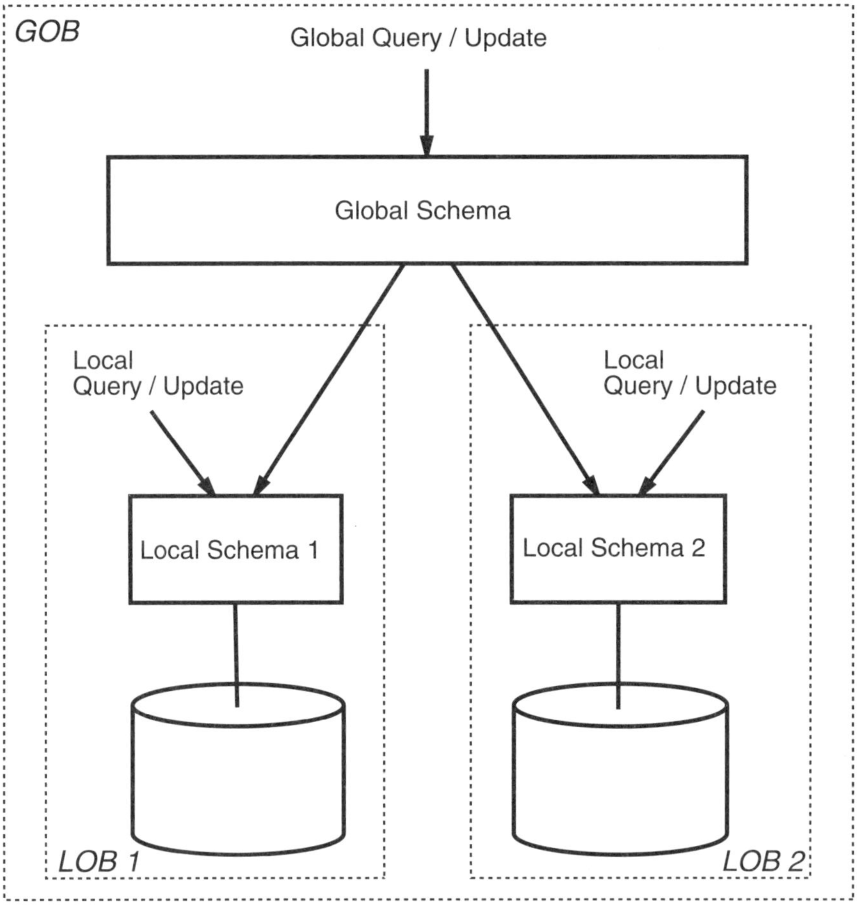

Figure 1: Schemas and Operations in Multi-Objectbase

local schemas are unified as well. Now, real inter-objectbase queries/updates are possible. Updates propagate through multiple LOBs.

Our approach is to start using an object algebra in Level 1 to define the necessary parts to achieve Level 2. As a representative, we use the object model COCOON with the COOL language that is sketched below. However, this is just a representative to illustrate the basic principles. The global observations are valid for other models as well.

2.2 AN OBJECT MODEL AND ALGEBRA

Throughout this paper we use COCOON as the underlying object-oriented data model [Scholl et al., 1992; Scholl and Schek, 1990]. Example 1 illustrates a definition of three COCOON databases, serving as the running example.

Example 1 Shown here is a case study of a possible multi-objectbase situation in a factory that produces screws and nails. The factory has several departments, each of which uses its own autonomous database (see Figure 2).

The design department is responsible for the design of new screws and nails. It works with the database *DesignDB* (or *DDB*, for short). The production department established a database called *ProductionDB* (or *PDB*) for information required for producing parts at the production branches. It also holds information about suppliers of raw materials. Finally, the sales department keeps in the *SalesDB* (or *SDB*) information on available articles and the company's customers.

```
define database DesignDB as
        define type item isa object = dno, matn: integer ,
                                      weight: kilo ;
        define type nail isa item = size: integer ;
        define type screw isa item = thread: string ;
        define class Items: item ;
        define class Nails: nail ;
        define class Screws: screw ;
end ;

define database ProductionDB as
    define type part isa object = cno, cplan: integer ,
                prodin: branch inverse produces ;
    define type branch isa object = bname, bstreet, bcity: string ,
                produces: set of part inverse prodin ;
    define type material isa object = mno: integer ,
                weight: pound ,
                supplby: supplier inverse supplies ;
    define type supplier isa object = sname, sstreet, scity: string ,
                supplies: set of material inverse supplby ;
    define class Parts: part ;
    define class Branches: branch ;
    define class Materials: material ;
    define class Suppliers: supplier ;
end ;
```

define database ***SalesDB as***
define type *article* ***isa object*** **=** *ano, price:* **integer ,**
weight: kilo ,
boughtby: ***set of customer inverse bought ;***
define type *customer* ***isa object*** **=** *cname, cstreet, ccity:* **string ,**
bought: ***set of article inverse boughtby ;***
define class ***Articles: article ;***
define class ***Customers: customer ;***
end *;*

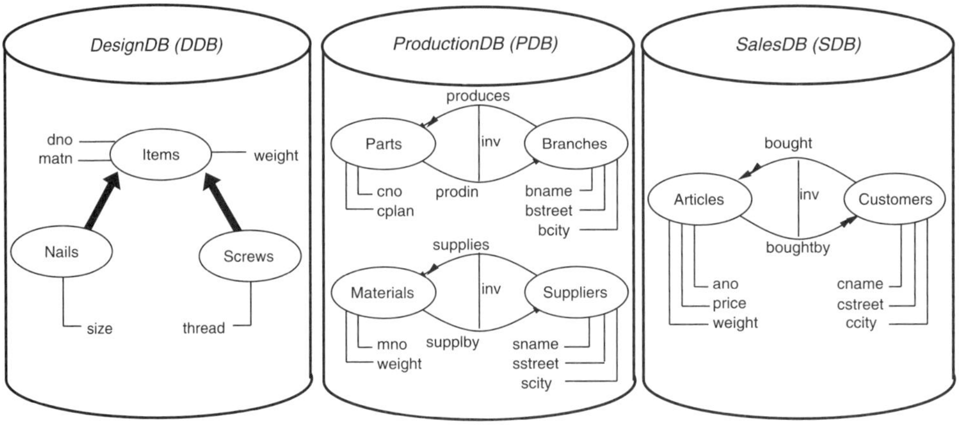

Figure 2: Multi-objectbase scenario for the running example

COCOON is an object-function model with the basic constituents *objects, functions, types, classes*, and *views*:

Objects are instances of abstract types, specified by their interface operations. *Data* are instances of concrete types (e.g., numbers, strings) or constructed types, such as sets.

Functions are either retrieval functions or update methods. They are described by their name and signature (that is, domain and range types). Functions may be set-valued.

Types are described by their name and the set of functions that are applicable to their instances. Types are arranged in a *subtype hierarchy*, where subtypes inherit functions from their supertypes. Objects are "instances of" types, possibly of more than one type at the same time ("multiple instantiation"). The top element of the type lattice is the most general type **object**. Therefore, all instances of any type in the database are also instance of **object**. The bottom element is the type **bottom**.

The language is strongly typed, in the sense that we support full static type checking. We can make use of type names as (type) predicates to check whether an object o is instance of a specific type T or not; e.g. *employee(p)* checks whether person p is of type employee.

Classes are typed collections of objects ("type extents"). Classes are arranged in a *subclass hierarchy* that is defined by the set inclusion between the sets of objects they represent. Objects are "members of" classes, possibly more than one at a time ("multiple class membership"). Particularly, superclasses contain all members of their subclasses. The top element class is called **Objects**. All objects in the database are member of this class.

For each object class, its *membertype* is an associated type, and its *extent* denotes a set of objects of that type. An important additional feature distinguishes our model from others: class predicates. These are usually found in knowledge representation (classification) languages such as KL-ONE [Brachman and Schmolze, 1985; Borgida et al., 1989]. Our classes may be constrained by a predicate that must be satisfied by all members of the class. We distinguish two cases: class predicates may be only necessary or necessary and sufficient conditions.

We use a *set-oriented* query language similar to relational algebra, where the inputs and outputs of the operations are *sets* of objects. Hence, query operators can be applied to extents of classes, set-valued function results, and query results. The algebra has an object-preserving semantics, in the sense that queries return (some of) the input objects. This semantics for queries allows the application of methods and generic update operations to results of a query, since these contain base objects.

View definitions introduce new (virtual) classes, whose extent is defined by the query. For views defined by each of the basic COOL operators, we describe what the membertype and extent is, and how these are positioned in the type and class hierarchies. For ease of presentation, assume that all views are defined over base classes. In general, views may also be defined over other views, or by composite queries (see [Scholl et al., 1991] for a detailed exposition).

Selection (**define view** V **as select** $[P](C)$). The view class V is a subclass of the base class C, with the same membertype as C. Notice, that we now have two classes, V and C, of that type. The extent is the subset of C-members satisfying predicate P.

Projection (**define view** V **as project** $[f_1, \ldots, f_n](C)$). The view class V is a superclass of C: The membertype, of V is a supertype of the original (less functions are defined, only those listed in the projection), the extent of V is the same as that of C.

Extend (**define view** V **as extend** $[f_i := < expr_i >, \ldots](C)$). Projection eliminates functions, extend defines new derived ones. $< expr_i >$ can be any legal arithmetic, boolean, or set-expression. The view V is a subclass of C: their extents are the same and the membertype of V is a subtype of C's (all the old functions plus the new ones are defined).

Set operations (e.g., **define view** V **as** $C1$ **union** $C2$). As the extent of classes are sets of objects, we can perform set operations as usual. With a polymorphic type system, we need no restrictions on operand types of set operations (ultimately, they are all instances of type **object**). The result type, however, depends on the input types: a union view is a common superclass of its base classes, where the membertype is the lowest common supertype (in the type lattice) of the input types. Difference views are subclasses of their base class with the same membertype; finally, an intersection view is a common subclass with a member type that is the greatest common subtype of the input types.

Generic update operations. Beyond type-specific update operations (i.e. methods), COOL provides a collection of generic update operators to facilitate set-oriented processing. First, there is a set-iterator for updates, **update**$[m](< set - expr >)$, that takes as argument a set of objects and an operation, m, to be performed on all elements. The other generic update operators are **insert** and **delete** for creation and destruction of objects, **add** and **remove** for including and excluding existing objects into/from sets (in contrast to **insert** and **delete**, **add** and **remove** have no effect on the existence of the objects), and **set** to assign return values to functions.

3 ESTABLISHING LINKS BETWEEN OBJECTBASES

In this section, we present a first approach to the interaction of objectbases that places only minimal requirements on the degree of schema integration between participating objectbases. First, the schemas are "composed", which basically just imports the names of schema elements from local objectbases. Second, we show that the COOL query language can be used to define inter-objectbase links by means of query expressions. This allows us to combine information from several sources (LOBs) into a global schema.

3.1 SCHEMA COMPOSITION

The least requirement that has to be imposed on two objectbases, in order to be used jointly, is that they make known to each other the names of their schema elements. That is, in the case of our object model, they have to export the names of their functions, types, and classes. For this purpose, we provide a *schema composition statement*, that lists the names of the participating objectbases. In contrast to schema integration, schema composition just makes names globally available, without really establishing any connection between the composed parts.

Example 2 Suppose we want to work on the design and production objectbases in a global application. We define a composite schema by the following COOL statement:

define schema ***CompositeDB as***
  import ***DDB;***
  import ***PDB;***
end;

A graphical representation of the composite schema is given in Figure 3.

We use the following naming conventions: names of local schema components are suffixed by "@" and the name of the local schema, for example, the class *Items* in the *DDB* has as globally unique name "*Items@DDB*", and similarly for types and functions. As a shorthand, when using generic names such as LOB_i, we often write, for instance, "$object_i$" instead of "$object@LOB_i$".

In general, the composition of (local) objectbases LOB_i yields a global objectbase (GOB) where the two parts of the global schema, the type and class hierarchies, are combined in the following trivial way:

- The global type hierarchy consists of a new top element "*object@GOB*" that is the common supertype of the top elements of all component type hierarchies, $object_i$. Also, a new bottom element "*bottom@GOB*" is introduced as common subtype of the local bottom types. No other subtype relationships are established by schema composition. Therefore, the global schema is "integrated" at the very top level. No instance of "*object@GOB*" is instance of more than one component type $object_i$.

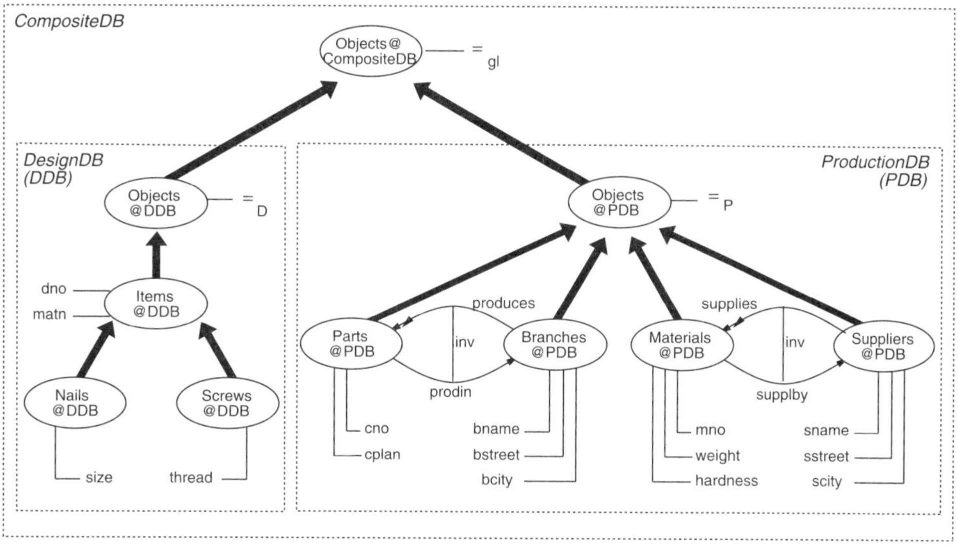

Figure 3: Composition of *DDB* and *PDB*

- The global class hierarchy has a new top element "*Objects@GOB*", which is common superclass of the local top classes, $Objects_i$. The extent of "*Objects@GOB*" is partitioned into disjoint subsets $Objects_i$.

As a consequence, no two objects in "*Objects@GOB*" can be the same (identical), unless they originate from the same local objectbase, LOB_i, and are identical in LOB_i (cf. Figure 3).

Definition 1 ***Global Identity*** *Formally, the global object identity predicate '$=_{gl}$' on the new (global) type* object@GOB *is defined as:*

$$
\begin{aligned}
=_{gl} &\quad:\quad object@GOB \times object@GOB \rightarrow boolean \\
=_{gl}(o_1, o_2) &\quad=\quad \exists i : object_i(o_1) \wedge object_i(o_2) \wedge o_1 =_i o_2
\end{aligned}
$$

In essence, with this first global schema we have not yet performed any "real" integration, but we do have a common basis for queries over composed schemas: a global parser can be provided with the (disjoint) union of names of schema elements from the component objectbases.

Despite the above basic assumption that schema composition just places the two (or more) participating schemas "side-by-side", notice that we do assume that the underlying *basic data types* (such as integer, boolean, string, ...) are unified.[1] Therefore, the global schema contains only one of each of these basic types. Hence, we can already compare the primitive data values contained in all component objectbases. This is a necessary prerequisite, since otherwise we could not even define the global identity predicate above (the unified base type **boolean** is used in the definition).

[1]Conversion from one representation to another one are automatically provided.

It is beyond the scope of this paper to prove that the object algebra defined on the component objectbases is now well defined also on the composed objectbase. In order to prove this, we need to represent the global meta objects in terms of the local ones, see also later.

3.2 INTER-OBJECTBASE QUERIES

Once we have composed two (or more) local objectbases into a global schema, we are ready for formulating queries that span objectbases, that is, involve arguments from more than one LOB. In this subsection we analyze the possibilities and limitations of such inter-objectbase queries under the assumptions of the basic composition defined above. The analysis follows the structure of the COOL language, that is, we look at each COOL operator in turn.

3.2.1 Connecting LOBs via Extend Operations

The extend operator of COOL allows us to define new, derived functions. The derivation is by a COOL query. As a result, the new function is available on the result type and is executed whenever it is used later. In the context of composite schemas, we can use **extend** to establish inter-OB links: suppose we apply an extend operation to a class from LOB_1 defining a derived function by a query on LOB_2.

Example 3 In *CompositeDB*, let us define the following link from the *PDB* to the *SDB*: for each part we want to see the names of potential local customers, that is, the names of customers in the city where the part is being produced.

$$\begin{array}{l} extend\ [\ plcn := extract\ [cname] \\ \qquad\qquad (select[ccity(c) = bcity(prodin(p))](c : Customers))\ ] \\ \quad (p : Parts) \end{array}$$

The extend operation defines a new function *plcn* (for potential local customer names) by an external query: Parts is a class in the *PDB*, whereas Customers is one in the *SDB*. Notice this query is perfectly valid since the right-hand side of the function definition is executed in *SDB*: before that, however, '$bcity(prodin(p))$' is replaced by a constant, its function value from *PDB*. The selection predicate passes type checking, because basic data types (string, in the example) are unified by the composition of schemas.

The general principle behind this example is that in order for LOB_i objects to refer to objects or values from foreign (i.e., other) objectbases LO_j, we use queries on LOB_j to retrieve the information from the foreign LOB. Such queries are used from within LOB_i, that is, they can be "parameterized" with values from LOB_i. In our example above, the only parameter was the city address of the branch where the part is produced, $bcity(prodin(p))$.

Using queries as the external referencing mechanism seems very natural, since this is the way how all operations on any objectbase are expressed. The extend operator further lets us predefine query expressions as derived functions, such that later on we only have to call this function by its name. Since the function is executed once per reference to its name (at least conceptually), there are no problems with "dangling" references due to changes in the foreign objectbase. For example, if customers change their address in *SDB*, no action is required in *PDB*, the reference is always up-to-date upon use.

3.2.2 Unary COOL Operators: Select, Project, Pick

All of the unary COOL operators take as (initial) argument a single class name, and return as result a (set of) object(s) from that input class. So essentially, they all operate *within one LOB*. All functions that can be used in selection predicates or in projection lists have to be defined on the member type of the input, so they have to stem from the same component schema (LOB).

Any attempt to use functions from another LOB_j in an operation on LOB_i would be rejected at compile-time by the type checker because of type incompatibilities. Remember that the type hierarchies have been "connected" only on the very top, and two objects from different objectbases are different because of our equality definition so far.

Example 4 The type incompatibilities between the component schemas can be seen in the following selection predicate, which would be rejected (at compile time) by the type checker:

$select\ [\ i \in select[\ldots](Parts)\ ]\ (\ i : Items\ )$

Since the type of the inner selection is "set of parts" and the type of i is item, and because item and part are not related to each other, this selection predicate will not pass type checking.
However, we can retrieve data values from another component objectbase and use it inside a selection predicate, as shown in the next query:

$select\ [\ dno(i) = cno(pick(select[\ldots](Parts)))\ ]\ (\ i : Items\ )$

This query passes the type checker, for basic types, namely integers in this example, have been unified by schema composition. Therefore, we can compare the numbers of parts and the numbers of items.

Later we will provide the necessary means to compare not only data values, but also objects from different LOBs (Section 4).

3.2.3 Assignments

For the same reasons as above, no assignments "across" LOBs pass the type checker yet, since variables defined in a local type system of LOB_i are incompatible with any types from another type system LOB_j, if $i \neq j$.

3.2.4 Binary COOL Operators: Union, Intersection, Difference

The binary operators of COOL are the set operators. The definition of these is basically the mathematical definition, so they all rely on the equality (i.e., identity) predicate. Therefore, set operations applied to two arguments from different LOBs can be permitted, but since no two objects from distinct LOBs are identical, the result is always obtained in a trivial way: for the union, it is the disjoint union, for difference the result is always the first argument, and for intersection the result is always empty. On arguments from one LOB, of course, the operations work as usual (cf. Definition 1).

This defines the effect of the set operations on the collection aspect, that is, the extent of the result. For the intentional aspect, the result type, we know [Scholl and Schek, 1990] that difference results in the type of the first argument, union in a common supertype, and intersection in a common subtype. Because the component type systems of the LOBs have not been integrated yet, there are no common functions among the argument types, so the result type of a union is "*object@GOB*" and the result type of an intersection is "*bottom@GOB*". Section 4 presents techniques that allow for more useful applications of unions and intersections spanning LOBs.

3.2.5 Inter-Objectbase Views

We have seen above that the extend operation of COOL (or any similar mechanism in other object database language) can be used to define "relationships" between objects from different local objectbases, once their schemas have been composed. While schema composition is only a very rudimentary first step towards the integration of multiple OBs, the **extend** mechanism can be used to more closely couple the objects from the different sources. By using this mechanism in view definitions [Scholl et al., 1991; Scholl and Schek, 1990], we can enrich the global schema.

Example 5 If the interconnection of parts and the names of their potential local customers is not only relevant for one application program but is used in a few of them, we would want to make the new derived function a part of the global schema by the following extended schema definition:

define schema ***CompositeDB2 as***
  import ***SDB;***
  import ***PDB;***
  define view *Parts'* **as extend** [*plcn* := …] (*Parts*);
end;

As the view definition is included in the schema definition, any user accessing schema *CompositeDB2* can use the class *Parts'* and the *plcn* function defined there.

4 UNIFYING VIEWS OVER OBJECTBASES

In the previous section, we have shown how the extend operator of COOL can be used to establish links between objectbases. No particular semantics were given to such links, they have been defined by arbitrary queries. Now we turn to the problem of identifying objects from multiple OBs.

The first subsection (4.1) addresses the problem in general and demonstrates a solution based upon inter-objectbase links. Subsection 4.2 applies the technique to schema objects, that is, objects representing types, functions, or classes, for example. In doing so, we show how (real) schema integration can be supported. The last of the subsections (4.3) combines the results and shows the full power of objectbase integration obtained by our approach.

4.1 UNIFYING OBJECTS

Since LOBs have been used independently of each other, one real world ("entity") object may be represented by different ("proxy") objects in different LOBs [Kent, 1991a]. The fundamental assumption of object-oriented models, namely that one real world object is represented by exactly one database object is no longer true. Consequently, the fundamental concept of "object identity" found in objectbases needs revision. Within one OB, identity is based on object identifiers (OIDs).[2] Two objects are identical if they have been created by the same object creation event (that is, if they have the same internal OID).

Now that we consider several local objectbases, we need an additional notion: we say that two (local, or proxy) objects are *the same*, iff they represent the same real world (or entity) object. Notice that two proxy objects from two different LOBs are in general *not identical*, even if they are *the same*.[3] Following Kent, an *entity object* occurs in the real world, a *proxy object* is an LOB-specific representation of (some aspects of) an entity object. *Entity (or global) identity* unifies proxy objects, iff they represent the *same* entity object. *Proxy (or local) object identity* is defined only with respect to one LOB; in this LOB, it is the usual notion of object identity found in (single) objectbases, namely the one based on internal OIDs.

In the following, we deal with the "same" or global object identity problem in two steps: first, we define the *unification* of proxies, i.e., we discuss how to find out what the "same" object in another LOB is; second, we devise a way to re-establish a notion of global (entity) object identity.

4.1.1 Finding the Same Object in other LOBs

Within one objectbase, the referencing mechanism is typically based on the internal OIDs. These have been introduced to uniquely refer to objects, especially in the case of sharing. From the outside of an objectbase, however, OIDs are not available (or at least, should not be available). Other means for the specification of the "object(s) of interest" are therefore needed. Every objectbase system provides some form of query language (that might just be C^{++}-Code or an SQL-style language), which can be used to retrieve objects. Obviously, the query language of an LOB is a good (if not the only) choice for a referencing mechanism across LOBs.

Therefore, our approach to the first step, the *unification* of different proxy objects from different local OBs, is to use the inter-objectbase linking mechanism of COOL's extend operator. Given a proxy object o_i in some LOB_i, the information we are after is: what is the proxy object o_j, if any, in some other LOB_j that represents the same entity object in the real world? An extend operation can establish a link to some object(s) in that other LOB_j, all we need is a query expression that determines what the "*same*" object in that other objectbase is. We have to use the standard mechanisms offered by LOB_j to select objects of interest: an appropriate selection predicate. Notice that, due to the complex structure of the schema of LOB_j, we may use simple properties (atomic values associated to LOB_j-objects) as well as complex context conditions (such as properties of other LOB_j-objects related to them via object-valued functions).

For example, if two LOBs contain classes of persons, we might assume that two person proxies from the two LOBs represent the same real person if they agree on the name and birthdate properties (atomic valued functions defined of the corresponding types in both LOB schemas). Alternatively, as an example of a more complex condition using context information, we could assume that names and birthdates as well as those of spouses and

[2] There is also a notion of equality between objects, this is based on properties associated with the objects. One can even distinguish several kinds of equality, such as shallow, deep, n-deep [Shaw and Zdonik, 1989]. As a result, two objects can be equal but still not identical.

[3] Even if two proxy objects from two LOBs happen to have the same internal OID, this does not mean anything!

children (if any) have to agree. In the latter case, we made the assumption that both LOBs carry the necessary information and that we have already found out that this is the case (see also Section 4.2).

4.1.2 Global (Entity) Identity

Formally, we require that for any two types from different LOBs, T_i from LOB_i and S_j from LOB_j, the instances of which shall be unified, we are given a query expression that determines, for a given T_i-object o_i, what the corresponding S_j-object is (if any), and vice versa. This query expression is used to define a derived function $same_{T_i,S_j}$ from T_i to S_j and its inverse, $same_{S_j,T_i}$. Obviously, these query expressions are application dependent and can, in general, not be derived automatically.

Given the definition of some of these same-functions, we can now extend the definition of global object identity (cf. Definition 1 and Figure 3) to account for these user-defined same-functions (see also "merge conditions" in [Dayal, 1983]).

Definition 2 ***Global Identity – Revised*** *The global (entity) object identity predicate '$=_{gl}$' on the global type* object@GOB *is defined as:*

$$\begin{aligned} =_{gl} \quad &: \quad object@GOB \times object@GOB \rightarrow boolean \\ =_{gl}(o_1, o_2) \quad &= \quad (\exists i : object_i(o_1) \wedge object_i(o_2) \wedge o_1 =_i o_2) \\ & \quad\quad \vee (\exists i, j : \exists T_i, S_j : \exists same_{T_i,S_j} : \\ & \quad\quad\quad\quad object_i(o_1) \wedge object_j(o_2) \wedge o_2 =_j same_{T_i,S_j}(o_1)) \end{aligned}$$

If we use this notion of object identity throughout the object algebra, that is, in selection predicates and in all set operations (as the criterion for duplicate detection, for example), then we have a global notion of object identity which is a generalization of (proxy) object identity as supported by each local objectbase: two objects are the same, if they stem from the same LOB and are identical in it, or if they have been defined (by the user) to be the same in a same-predicate.

4.1.3 Examples

In our example multi-objectbase application, there are plenty of opportunities to define a global notion of identity.

Example 6 All LOBs, *DDB*, *PDB*, and *SDB* contain some information about the parts that are being designed, produced, and sold by the company. Let us assume that an analysis of the local schemas has found out that *Items@DDB*, *Parts@PDB*, and *Articles@SDB* all represent the same real world entity objects. Notice that the correspondence need not be total in the sense that all items of the DDB are necessarily present as articles in the SDB as well, but some of them surely are, and vice versa.

For simplicity reasons, let us further assume that *dno, cno, ano* are actually all represented in the same way and that they agree for the same real world objects. In this simple case, we can define some of the same-functions as follows:

$$\begin{aligned} & extend\ [same_{part,item} := pick(select[cno(p) =_D dno(i)](i : Items))] \\ & \quad\quad (p : Parts); \end{aligned}$$

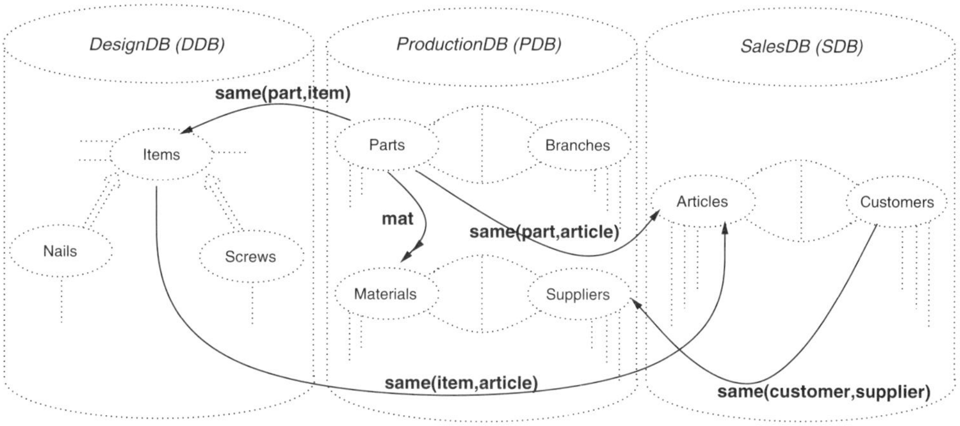

Figure 4: Multi-objectbase scenario extended with derived functions

$$extend\ [same_{part,article} := pick(select[cno(p) =_S ano(a)](a : Articles))]\ (p : Parts);$$

$$extend\ [same_{item,article} := pick(select[dno(i) =_S ano(a)](a : Articles))]\ (i : Items);$$

The other three same-functions are defined analogously. Notice, that same-functions define an equivalence relationship and are therefore transitive. In addition to each same-function, the inverse is defined automatically. See Figure 4 for an illustration. For the sake of readability, we left out the full specification of global names (e.g., *Parts* instead of *Parts@PDB*) since local names are globally unique. Further note that "$=_D$" stands for local (proxy) object identity within *DesignDB*, and so on.

A more complex condition for global identification may involve path expressions in either of the LOBs. Example 8 shows such a case. In order to prepare for it, and to show another interesting case, namely one where we define an LOB-internal link based upon inter-OB links, we give a further example before that.

Example 7 The following statement defines a derived function within *PDB* that uses information from the *DDB*: For each part, we want to know the raw material used for its production. This information is not explicitly represented in *PDB*, but it can be obtained from the *DDB*, where materials are recorded for all items (see Figure 4).

$$extend\ [mat := select[mno(m) = matn(same_{part,item}(p))](m : Materials)]\ (p : Parts)$$

Using this newly derived function, we can proceed to the complex case, where objects from the LOBs are unified using their context.

Example 8 Obviously, two of our local objectbases contain information about other companies: *Suppliers@PDB* and *Customers@SDB*. Typically, some of our supplier companies may well purchase some of our products. Therefore, we may have some pairs of proxies in the two classes that actually represent the same entity.

Let us assume the following: if a supplier s and a customer c agree on their names (*sname* and *cname*, respectively), and if the customer has not bought any of the articles produced from the raw materials supplied by the supplier, we conclude that they are the same. We do not make use of the address information contained in either of the LOBs, since order and delivery addresses of the other companies usually disagree. Notice that the identification predicate actually involves our third database, namely by reference to the mat function defined above.

We define the same-function from *Customers@SDB* to *Suppliers@PDB* as

$$\begin{aligned}&extend\ [same_{customer,supplier} := pick(\\&\quad select\ [select\ [sname(supplby(mat(same_{article,part}(a)))) = cname(c)]\\&\quad\quad\quad (a : bought(c)) = \emptyset \wedge cname(c) = sname(s)]\\&\quad\quad (s : Suppliers))]\\&\quad (c : Customers)\end{aligned}$$

Notice that, even though we use object-valued functions in the path expression, the final comparisons are again between data values, so we do not need to subscribe the equality signs '=' in the selection predicate (see Figure 4 again).

The last example showed that criteria for unifying (proxy) objects from different LOBs can be based on quite involved query expressions. Conceptually, however, there is no other way to refer to foreign objects than by a query.

4.2 SCHEMA INTEGRATION

We have presented a mechanism to unify (proxy) objects in different LOBs. We now concentrate on schema integration, that is to find out, what the common parts in the local schemas are, and to define a correspondence among them [Civelek et al., 1989; Spaccapietra et al., 1992].

We can consider Example 1, where *Items*, *Parts*, and *Articles* have a number function defined on it. Although they are named different, their semantics may be the same. Moreover, three functions with name *weight* are defined in the multi-objectbase. The weight of *Items* has the same semantics as the weight of *Articles* (synonyms). Nevertheless, one is given in kilo and one in pound. Yet another weight is the one of *Materials*. Though having the same name, its semantics are different: here it means the specific weight of raw materials (homonym).

4.2.1 The global Meta Schema

In Section 3, when introducing schema composition, we said that the effect is to create a new "*object@GOB*" and "*bottom@GOB*" type, as well as a new "*objects@GOB*" class. Also, we assumed that the basic data types (integer, etc.) are unified. Actually, more than this happens when two (or more) local schemas are composed. As all LOB schemas contain a meta schema that is structured in the same way [Tresch and Scholl, 1992], also these meta types and meta classes are combined.

To be precise, each LOB contains three meta types (*type, function, class*), and three meta classes (*Types, Functions, Classes*), respectively. Schema composition creates a global meta schema, with new types "*type@GOB*", "*function@GOB*", and "*class@GOB*", as well as the new classes "*Types@GOB*", "*Functions@GOB*", and "*Classes@GOB*". Thus, the

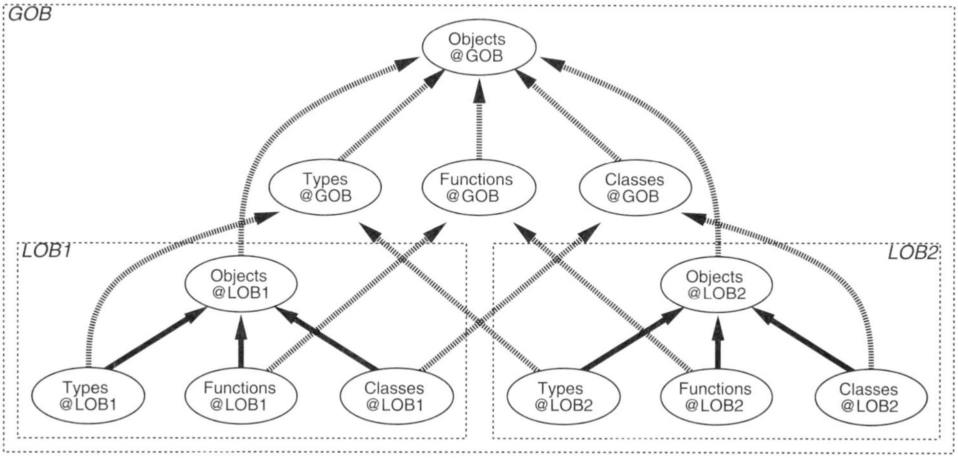

Figure 5: The Global Meta Schema

meta schema of the GOB has the same structure as that of each LOB. In addition to this, schema composition makes the local meta types and classes subtypes/subclasses of their global counterparts (cf. Figure 5). Thus, the global meta objects are the union of the local meta objects, representing local meta types and classes ($\ldots @LOB_i$), plus the meta objects representing the newly created global meta types and classes ($\ldots @GOB$).

Furthermore, meta functions are unified during the composition process, e.g. in LOB_1, there is a meta function *super_types(t)* finding all supertypes of type t. This function is automatically unified with the *super_types* function of LOB_2, and so on.

4.2.2 Unifying Meta Objects

The next step in schema integration (after schema composition that combines the meta schemas) is to define correspondences among functions of different LOBs. We make use of the fact that every function is represented by a meta object. In Figure 5, these function objects are kept in the meta classes *Functions@LOB*$_i$.

Integrating functions from *LOB*$_i$ and *LOB*$_j$ is now straightforward: we unify the objects that represent the functions in the meta schema, by defining a *same*-function from the meta type *function@LOB*$_i$ to the meta type *function@LOB*$_j$.

Example 9 To unify the functions *dno* with *ano* and *weight* with *weight* between *DDB* and *SDB* the following *same*-function is defined on the meta schema of *DDB*:

$$\begin{array}{l} extend\ [\ same_{\ function@DDB, function@SDB} := pick(\\ \qquad\qquad select\ [\ (name(f) = \text{“dno”} \wedge name(g) = \text{“ano”}) \vee \\ \qquad\qquad\qquad (name(f) = \text{“weight”} \wedge name(g) = \text{“weight”}) \\ \qquad\qquad\quad]\ (g : Functions@SDB))\ ] \\ \quad (\ f : Functions@DDB\ ) \end{array}$$

For each further correspondence of functions, the selection predicate must be extended with another name-equality term.

This is the way to integrate homogeneous functions from different databases. If there are structural or semantic inhomogeneities, these must be resolved before. Examples include different types for currency values or units of measure in general (here we need conversion functions), functions that have different names in different LOBs despite carrying the same semantics (here we need renaming), functions with the same names but different semantics (again, we need renaming), and so forth.

Renaming can easily be realized in COOL with the extend operator: we define a new derived function (with the new name) that takes exactly the value of the old function. Also, conversion functions can be expressed using the extend operator, since we can apply arbitrary computations in the definition of derived functions.

Example 10 Consider the inhomogeneities between the different *weight* functions. They are resolved with the following redefinitions:

$$extend\ [\ weight\_kilo := weight(i), weight\_pound := weight(i) * 2.2046\ ]\ (\ i : Items\ );$$

$$extend\ [\ weight\_kilo := weight(a) * 0.453, weight\_pound := weight(a)\ ]\ (\ a : Articles\ );$$

$$extend\ [\ spec\_weight := weight(m)\ ]\ (\ m : Materials\ );$$

Notice that, in general, derived functions can not be updated. In many cases, however, it is quite obvious how to propagate such updates. In the case of conversion functions as shown above, we can expect that the system automatically determines *inverse* functions (e.g. *pound_to_kilo* vs. *kilo_to_pound*). Consequently, these functions can be updated. More generally, we allow the definition of update methods "*set_f*" for each function *f* that will be used when assigning values to *f* in generic update statement.

4.3 INTEGRATION OF OBJECTBASES

We now have defined all prerequisites for tight objectbase integration: On the object level, we showed how to find the "same" object in other LOBs and introduced a notion of global identity based on the *same*-functions. On the schema level, we discussed integration of functions as a unification of meta objects.

Example 11 We stated in Example 6 that all LOBs, *DDB, PDB, SDB* contain information about the same real world entities, namely nails and screws. We can now integrate the three objectbases, for example by defining an intersection view *Elements* over multiple object-bases: On the object level, we unify *Items, Parts,* and *Articles* if they have equal numbers (*dno* = *cno* = *ano*). On the schema level, we integrate the number functions (renaming it to *eno*) and the weight functions (resolving semantic inhomogeneities).

```
define schema ElementsDB as
        import DDB, PDB, SDB;
[1]     define view Items'@DDB as
[1a]                extend [ same_item,part(i):= ...,
[1b]                         same_item,article(i):= ...,
[1c]                         eno:= dno(i),
[1d]                         weight_kilo:= weight(i),
```

```
[1e]                     weight_pound:= weight(i) * 2.2046 ]
                    ( i:Items@DDB );
[2]   define view Parts'@PDB as
[2a]             extend [ same_{part,item}(p):= ...,
[2b]                      same_{part,article}(p):= ...,
[2c]                      eno:= cno(p),
[2d]                      mat:= select [ ...]
                    ( m:Materials@PDB ) ] ( p:Parts@PDB );
[3]   define view Materials'@PDB as
[3a]             extend [ spec_weight:= weight(m) ]
                    ( m:Materials@PDB );
[4]   define view Articles'@SDB as
[4a]             extend [ same_{article,item}(a):= ...,
[4b]                      same_{article,part}(a):= ...,
[4c]                      eno:= ano(a),
[4d]                      weight_kilo:= weight(a) * 0.453,
[4e]                      weight_pound:= weight(a) ]
                    ( a:Articles@SDB );
[5]   define view Functions'@DDB as
                 extend [ same_{function@DDB,function@PDB}(f):= ...,
                          same_{function@DDB,function@SDB}(f):= ...]
                    ( f:Functions@DDB );
[6]   define view Functions'@PDB as
                 extend [ same_{function@PDB,function@SDB}(f):= ...,
                          same_{function@PDB,function@DDB}(f):= ...]
                    ( f:Functions@PDB );
[7]   define view Functions'@SDB as
                 extend [ same_{function@SDB,function@DDB}(f):= ...,
                          same_{function@SDB,function@PDB}(f):= ...]
                    ( f:Functions@SDB );
[8]   define view Elements as Items'@DDB intersect Parts'@PDB
                          intersect Articles'@SDB ;
end ;
```

The method of database integration by finding corresponding properties and proxy objects was investigated by Neuhold and Schrefl [Schrefl, 1988; Neuhold and Schrefl, 1988] as well. They introduce for each kind of semantic relationship between objects a new special type of generalization class: data-type-generalization, role-generalization, history-generalization, counterpart-generalization, category-generalization. Object coloring is used to decide from which local database the objects in the generalization class originate and message forwarding is presented to overcome semantically inhomogeneous representations.

Our approach makes exclusive use of an algebraic object views, using the **extend** operator to establish links between objectbases, in order to find the same object in other LOBs and to resolve semantics inhomogeneities. All LOBs are strongly typed systems, such that static type checking of objects is possible.

Consider Example 11: extensions $(1ab, 2ab, 4ab)$ define the *same* functions to unify proxy objects. This is similar the Schrefl's "object-correspondence-rules" in the generalization classes. The derived functions $(1c, 2c, 4c)$ rename the different number functions to *eno*, and $(1de, 4de)$ resolve semantic inhomogeneities between the *weight* functions, such that "pounds" are translated to "kilos" and vice versa. To avoid confusion, "specific weight" gets a new name $(3a)$. To perform this, Schrefl introduces "data-type-generalization" classes with the possibility the define "transformation methods". Once all inhomogeneities are resolved, we are ready to define the *same* functions $(5, 6, 7)$ on the meta level to unify the functions *eno, weight_kilo, weight_pound* from all LOBS. Schrefl's generalizations achieve the same by introducing "corresponding relationships/attributes". Our approach needs no special generalization mechanism to define a unifying view of these databases, i.e. to create an intersection view (8) over several databases.

5 PROPAGATION OF UPDATES

A critical issue in multi-database systems is the propagation of updates , particularly when admitting local transactions. In fact, the view mechanism that we propose offers a big advantage in that respect: since all COOL views are updatable, we will see that a basic update propagation across multiple LOBs comes for free.

5.1 INTER-OBJECTBASE LINKS

If we establish links between different LOBs via extend views, that is, by means of query expressions against the foreign (referenced) objectbase, all updates that happen within the foreign objectbase are automatically reflected in the referencing LOB. No special care has to taken. Whether the referenced objects change some of their properties (including "relationships" to other objects) or whether they are removed or new ones are created within the foreign OB, all these changes are visible from within referencing LOBs, since they all use query expressions that are evaluated upon each reference.

Symmetrically, we can even update foreign objects (in the referenced LOB_i) from within transactions on LOB_j: like with all **extend**-views, the objects obtained from the application of the derived function can be updated (using the update statements available in LOB_i in our case).

Example 12 In our running example we could, for instance, have a function lc, returning for each supplier of PDB its local customers of SDB. Assuming that $s0$ is one particular supplier, we can modify the names of its local customers as follows.

update [cname:="New Yorker"] (lc(s0))

5.2 UNIFIED OBJECTS

If we have unified (proxy) objects in different LOBs, we would expect that a global delete operation will actually delete all proxies in all LOBs. In fact, since updates on union views are propagated to all base classes [Scholl et al., 1991], this is exactly what will happen. Conversely, if individual proxy objects are deleted by autonomous local transactions, only the local proxy is removed, but other proxies representing the same entity object may still be present in other LOBs. Again, this is what we would expect if we permit autonomous updates to LOBs that are not executed under the control of a global integrity monitor.

Technically, this effect is automatically achieved by the fact that the **delete** operation is actually derived from COOL's **lose** operation that dynamically changes the type of an object: in each LOB_i, **delete**(o) is defined as **lose**[$object_i$](o) [Laasch and Scholl, 1992; Scholl et al., 1992]. Therefore, since in the global context $object_i$ is not the root of the type lattice, only the local proxy, but not all the other proxies (if any) are removed.

Example 13 Consider the deletion of a part object in the first case locally on the production objectbase *PDB*, and in the second case globally on the integrated objectbase. The global schema includes the same functions between parts, items, and articles, and the global superclass "Elements". The effect of the deletion depends on the target objectbase to which it is applied:

- A *local* execution against *PDB* removes the part (proxy object) with the given construction number from the production objectbase.

  delete (**select** [cno=123456789] (Parts))

  However, no propagation into the other two objectbases is implied, since local execution does not even know about the existence of these.

- A *global* execution on the other hand means that *all proxies* in all participating LOBs are removed, since a global delete 'knows' about potential proxies in the other LOBs that represent the same entity.

  delete (**select** [eno=123456789] (Elements))

  In case we had no globally integrated schema that unified the three classes, we would have had to issue three separate delete operations, one per LOB.

6 CONCLUSION

We presented an approach towards the stepwise integration of (populated) objectbases into a multi-objectbase system. The basic mechanisms that we described allow for the following steps:

(i) Schema composition makes the names of schema elements (such as types, classes, and functions) known across local objectbases. As a result, transaction against a composite schema can issue queries and updates on classes from different LOBs. We can define *inter-objectbase links* by defining new, derived functions across LOBs using the **extend** operator. Without any further means, however, only basic values (such as strings or numbers) can be 'transferred' between LOBs.

(ii) "Same" functions can be used to unify proxy objects from different LOBs that represent the same real world entity object. This accounts for the fact that different LOBs have created their own representations independently.

(iii) A global notion of object identity can be defined based upon these "same" functions. It is important to notice that this global notion of object identity is essentially based on values.

(iv) The mechanism of same functions can be used on the meta level in order to unify schema elements from different LOBs. This provides a sound formal basis for what is generally known as "schema integration". Once correspondences between local schemas have been detected, we provide a way of unifying them.

The advantage of our approach is that it uses almost exclusively the expressive power of a query language, together with a view definition facility. The only extension that we added is the global object identity predicate. Given that an objectbase system allows for the redefinition of all generic functions, this does not even require to change anything in the implementation of local systems.

Because our views are updatable, this approach is also a starting point for multi-objectbase updates. This distinguishes our approach from [Landers and Rosenberg, 1982], for example. However, to provide full updatability, we need further work, e.g., on the derivation of inverse functions for extend views.

While from a conceptual point of view our approach looks simple and clean, we have to spend more effort on the implementation issues. Particularly an efficient, but overridable, implementation of the identity test seems to require further investigations. Till now, comparing OIDs is typically hardcoded into the implementation of local OBMSs. As we have seen, the (global) identity test now depends on user-defined *same*-functions. Therefore, we need efficient support by indexes or some other form of replicated information.

Declarative Definition of Object-Oriented Multidatabase Mappings

Jan Chomicki*
Kansas State University
Dept. of Computing and Information Sciences
Manhattan, KS 66506-2302
USA

Witold Litwin†
Hewlett-Packard Labs
1501 Page Mill Rd.
Palo Alto, CA 94061
USA

Abstract

We propose a language for declarative specification of mappings between different object-oriented multidatabases. The language is based on OSQL, the query language of the IRIS object-oriented database management system. We also outline the operational semantics of our language.

1 INTRODUCTION

Declarative definition of multidatabase mappings is one of the central problems of multidatabase interoperability. For object-oriented database systems (OODBS), one may need to map types (classes) in one database into types in another database, or functions into functions, or objects into objects. In the presence of schematic discrepancies [Krishnamurthy et al., 1991], one may further need to map objects (instances) into types or vice versa, or types into functions, etc. Because of the autonomy of different databases, one kind of data elements in one database may need to be mapped into the same or a different kind of data elements in another database.

We propose a language in which object-oriented multidatabase mappings can be defined in a declarative way using a small set of constructs. Those constructs make possible the definition of various kinds of derived data, namely *derived objects*, *derived types*, and *derived functions*. In particular, we introduce the notions of *object*, *type* and *function*

*Work performed while visiting HP Labs, Palo Alto, California.
†On leave from Université de Paris - Dauphine.

schemas that are suitable for dealing with schematic discrepancies, in effect providing "higher-order" features without using a higher-order language. We base our language on the OSQL query language and its dialects [Fishman et al., 1991; Annevelink, 1991; Ahmed et al., 1991a], to which we will collectively refer as OSQL. As a result, we obtain a generalization of OSQL suitable for multidatabase interoperability. Other declarative object-oriented languages, e.g., the query language of O_2 [Bancilhon et al., 1992], could be similarly extended.

A derived type may contain existing objects selected from another type using a derivation expression (a query). Alternatively, it may contain distinct instances of an *object schema* (also called *derived objects*), i.e., objects with distinct OIDs, derived from other data elements using a derivation expression. A single declaration of an *object schema* defines a family of derived objects, one object for each combination of parameter values. Similarly, a type (resp. function) schema defines a family of OSQL derived types (resp. functions).

We address only the issues of interoperability of semantically heterogeneous object-oriented databases with a common data model. How to define mappings between heterogeneous object-oriented models (or from heterogenous object-oriented models into a common one) is an open problem. Mapping relational to object-oriented databases has been addressed elsewhere [Ahmed et al., 1991a]. In [Kim and Seo, 1991], a comprehensive framework for classifying different kinds of heterogeneity arising in the relational data model was presented. Finally, we ignore here the implementation issues related to the physical distribution of the interoperable databases.

Multidatabase mappings can also be expressed in a sufficiently powerful higher-order logic programming language [Kifer et at., 1990; Barsalou and Gangopadhyay, 1992]. However, efficient implementation techniques for such languages do not yet exist. The authors of [Kifer et at., 1990; Barsalou and Gangopadhyay, 1992] suggest that their languages should be translated into Prolog, but Prolog, with the concomitant termination and efficiency problems, is far from being accepted as a database query language. In contrast, as we propose an extension to an *existing* query language, our approach should be more readily implementable.

Multidatabase mappings can also be expressed procedurally [Kent, 1991b]. In the presence of schematic discrepancies, however, the procedural approach leads to a much less transparent database schema resulting from the mapping. The procedural approach relies also on the underlying trigger mechanism which may be in conflict with the autonomy of different databases.

In Section 2, we survey OSQL and its dialects, and discuss the issues of semantic heterogeneity for OSQL databases. We introduce object and type schemas in Section 3, and function schemas in Section 4. In Section 5, we discuss the placement of derived types in an inheritance hierarchy and the problem of non-monotonic inheritance (overriding). In Section 6, we discuss the evaluation of queries. We summarize related work in Section 7. Section 8 concludes the paper.

2 OSQL AND ITS DIALECTS

2.1 OSQL

OSQL is a declarative query language in which queries are formulated using a functional notation. An OSQL database has two distinct parts: schema and state. A schema consists of type and function definitions, and subtype hierarchy, where the OSQL notion of *type* corresponds to the notion of *class* in most object-oriented database systems. A state consists of type extensions and function values.

An object (instance of a type) may be *literal* or *surrogate*. A literal object may be *atomic* (integer, real, string,...) or *aggregate* (set, bag, tuple, list). The extensions of user types consist of surrogate objects. To simplify the terminology, we will use the term *value* for *atomic literal object* and *object* for *user-defined surrogate object*, although one should note that all database elements (even types and functions) in OSQL are objects. A user type is explicitly created using the `CREATE TYPE` command. A type can be a subtype of other types, giving rise to a subtype/supertype hierarchy. If an object belongs to the extension of a type, it also belongs to the extensions of all the supertypes of this type.

A type extension is populated using the `CREATE` *Type* command (where *Type* is a user type) which creates an object and makes it a member of the extension of *Type*. At the time of object creation, values of various functions on this object may be provided. An object can be made a member of the extension of any type using the `ADD TYPE` command. Each type T gives rise to a unary predicate T that is true of every object belonging to the extension of T.

Functions can have any number of argument and result types. Function values for particular arguments are defined either explicitly (*stored functions*) or implicitly using an OSQL query (*derived functions*). A type inherits all the functions defined on its supertypes (*monotonic inheritance*), but it can also redefine some of them (*non-monotonic inheritance* or overriding).

The following is an OSQL example consisting of a user type definition (together with two stored function definitions), a derived function definition and an object creation command that creates two objects.

```
CREATE TYPE Employee SUBTYPE OF Person FUNCTIONS (
      Name String,
      Subordinates {Employee})

CREATE FUNCTION Boss (Employee e) →Employee b AS
      SELECT b
      FOR EACH Employee b
      WHERE e IN Subordinates(b)

CREATE Employee FUNCTIONS (Name, Subordinates)
      :boria ('Boris Yeltsin',{:sasza, :wania})
      :misza ('Mikhail Gorbachev',{})
```

HOSQL [Ahmed et al., 1991a] is an extension of OSQL to the heterogeneous multidatabase environment. It supports multidatabase queries to databases having OSQL-like schemas and a procedural mapping of schemas in other data models, e.g., relational, into HOSQL schemes. HOSQL also permits using database names as prefixes to type or function names in queries to solve name conflicts between autonomous databases. Finally, HOSQL allows the specification of subtype/supertype relationships and the inheritance of functions between types in different databases.

OSQL/IPL [Annevelink, 1991], adds to OSQL the capability to use derived functions written in a variant of the Scheme programming language.

2.2 MULTIDATABASE MAPPINGS

In the multidatabase environment, it is often necessary to use multiple object-oriented databases together. For instance, there may be a type `Employee` in `DB1` and another type `Senior` in `DB2` consisting of all the objects from `Employee` that correspond to employees over 65 years old. Furthermore, schematic discrepancies may need to be resolved, e.g., one might need to view the values of a derived function in `DB1` as types in `DB2`. For example, in `DB1`, the position of an employee may be represented using a function `Position` that maps `Employee` objects to position names. On the other hand, in `DB2`, the type `Employee` may be partitioned into subtypes corresponding to different positions, e.g., `Secretary` or `Manager`.

Consequently, the definition of multidatabase mappings requires richer notions of type and function than those available in OSQL and its dialects. In the context of relational databases, it was postulated [Krishnamurthy et al., 1991] that multidatabase mappings involving schematic discrepancies should be formulated in a higher-order logical language. This approach was further pursued and applied to the case of mappings involving multiple data models [Barsalou and Gangopadhyay, 1992]. In our approach, "higher-order" features are obtained without using a higher-order language.

Multidatabase mappings can be categorized along several different dimensions. They can be classified as *explicit* (defined as a set of tuples) or *implicit* (defined using a query expression), partial or total, 1:1 or 1:n or m:n. Of special interest to us is the classification stating which elements of one database are related through the mapping to which elements of the other database. We distinguish the following kinds of database elements: value, object, type and function. Accordingly, there are 16 kinds of mappings written as X$\mapsto$Y where X,Y$\in$ {Value,Object,Type,Function}, for example Value$\mapsto$Type.

Our goal is to specify mappings declaratively. We mostly consider 1:1 and n:1 mappings, conjecturing that other cases can be dealt with using the set (bag) construct of OSQL. Similarly, a mapping involving aggregate objects can be defined using OSQL, once the mappings for the components of those objects have been defined.

At present, only some of the above 16 kinds of mappings can be expressed declaratively in OSQL. Side-effect-free OSQL functions are unable to construct new objects, types or functions, and are therefore limited to representing Value$\mapsto$Value, Object$\mapsto$Value, Type$\mapsto$Value and Function$\mapsto$Value mappings. The last two kinds of mappings can be represented only by accessing the meta-information about the database. The remaining 12 kinds of mappings can be defined in OSQL procedurally. One should use functions whose bodies contain explicit commands to create new objects, types or functions. However, the names of the constructed types or functions are then built on-the-fly and are hidden in the programs that implement the mappings. Therefore, there is no explicit database schema for the data collection resulting from the mapping. This makes the use of this data, e.g., for querying, difficult.

Another problem with the procedural approach is the reliance on the underlying trigger mechanism that is necessary to adjust mappings in the presence of object creations ("mapping faults" [Kent, 1991b]) and deletions.[1] Such a mechanism seems to be in conflict with the *autonomy* of different databases. For instance, one would need procedures to monitor insertions and deletions to `Employee` in order to keep the extension of `Senior` consistent with its definition. These problems do not arise in our approach.

We will show now how our extensions to OSQL allow the declarative specification of multidatabase mappings. Table 1 sums up various concepts that we discuss.

Mapping	*Concept*
Object$\mapsto$Value, Value$\mapsto$Value	Derived functions (OSQL)
Type$\mapsto$Value, Function$\mapsto$Value	Derived functions (OSQL) with meta-types
Value$\mapsto$Object, Object$\mapsto$Object	Object schemas
Type$\mapsto$Object, Function$\mapsto$Object	Object schemas with meta-types
Value$\mapsto$Type, Object$\mapsto$Type	Type schemas
Type$\mapsto$Type	Type schemas with meta-types
Value$\mapsto$Function, Object$\mapsto$Function	Function schemas
Function$\mapsto$Function	Function schemas with meta-types
Function$\mapsto$Type, Type$\mapsto$Function	Type and function schemas with meta-types

Table 1: Summary of concepts

3 DERIVED TYPES

We distinguish several different cases: types defined by a membership condition, type schemas, types defined using object schemas and meta-types.

3.1 TYPES DEFINED BY A MEMBERSHIP CONDITION

Any result of a query can be made into a derived type, provided the result consists of surrogate objects. This is consistent with the philosophy of OSQL where user-defined types also consist of surrogate objects.

The syntax for a definition of such a type is very simple:

```
CREATE TYPE Type AS
      Query
```

The syntax of *Query* is that of an OSQL query. A variety of derived types can then be defined, especially subtypes and type unions. For instance, consider the need for mapping

[1] As indicated in [Kent, 1991b], the proper handling of object deletions in this context is very much an open problem.

the type Employee in a database DB1 into a more specific type Senior in another database DB2. The corresponding declaration is:

```
CONNECT DB2
CREATE TYPE Senior AS
      SELECT e
      FOR EACH DB1.Employee e
      WHERE DB1.Age(e)>65
```

This definition may be seen as an explicit 1:1 mapping consisting of a pair of types (DB1.Employee, DB2.Senior). Also, this definition implicitly maps the extension of DB1.Employee into the extension of DB2.Senior. The latter mapping is actually an identity mapping which is partial because the Employee objects of age less or equal to 65 will not be mapped to anything.

In the above definition, the prefix DB2 (before Senior) is omitted, as the connection to DB2 is in force. Since name conflict is not our primary concern, we will omit database names and CONNECT statements for simplicity. We will come back to these issues in Section 5.

In OSQL, at present the only way to define the discussed mapping would be to define Senior as a type and populate it initially using the ADD TYPE statement, selecting all senior employees from Employee. Then, one would need to monitor the changes to the extension of Employee, and update the extension of Senior accordingly.

Similarly, we can define in our framework another subtype SpouseAlsoEmployed:

```
CREATE TYPE SpouseAlsoEmployed AS
      SELECT e1
      FOR EACH Employee e1, Employee e2
      WHERE Spouse(e1)=e2
```

This definition is more complex as it involves a selection, self-join, and projection. Furthermore, as OSQL provides a union operator, *type unions* can be defined, for example:

```
CREATE TYPE Student AS
      SELECT s
      FOR EACH Graduate s
      UNION
      SELECT s
      FOR EACH Undergraduate s
```

This is an example of n:1 mapping between types. The corresponding mapping between the extensions of Graduate, Undergraduate and Student is a total (every graduate or undergraduate is a student) identity mapping.

Summing up, one can declare explicit Type$\mapsto$Type mappings, using derived types defined by a membership condition. Moreover, such mappings can be maintained without requiring procedures for adjustments when type extensions change.

3.2 TYPE SCHEMAS

We now allow the type definition to contain parameters, so that a single declaration can define multiple types. Each individual type corresponds to a combination of parameter values.

The corresponding syntax for a type schema definition is as follows:

```
CREATE TYPE Type[Parameters] AS
        Query
```

The *Query* can contain the parameters appearing in *Parameters*. One can view a type schema as being named by the term *Type*[*Parameters*]. [2] For every substitution that replaces *Parameters* by objects or values of appropriate types, we obtain a derived type, called an *instance type*.[3] This process is called the *instantiation* of the type schema. Instance types may be thought of as named by *ground terms* (terms without parameters). There may be infinitely many instance types if one of the parameters is drawn from an infinite domain, e.g., integers. This creates new issues for query evaluation that we address in Section 6. Type schemas are not types (they don't have extensions consisting of objects), but instance types are.

Example 1 Assume that in a database the function `Pos` maps an element of `Employee` into the corresponding position: manager, secretary, etc. Another database models this universe differently, as a family of subtypes consisting of all employees holding the same position. The corresponding mapping from the first database to the second can be expressed as follows:

```
CREATE TYPE EmpPos[String p] AS
        SELECT e
        FOR EACH Employee e
        WHERE Pos(e)=p.
```

For example, the instance type `EmpPos['secretary']` is the subtype of `Employee` consisting of secretaries.

The above definition is an example of an implicit 1:1 Value↦Type mapping that maps a string `p` to the type `EmpPos[p]` (an instance type of `EmpPos[String]`). The corresponding mappings of type extensions are partial identity mappings.

Example 2 Consider that `EmpDept[Dept]` is a type schema defining subtypes of `Employee` belonging to individual departments and `Contractor[Dept]` is a type schema defining subtypes of `Contractor` hired by individual departments.

One can map these type schemas into that of the set of people paid by a given department:

---

[2] We use square brackets to distinguish terms naming type and function schemas from function applications.

[3] *Instance* is used here in the logic programming sense (instance of a *term*), not in the object-oriented programming sense (instance of a *type*).

```
CREATE TYPE Compensated[Dept d] AS
      SELECT e
      FOR EACH EmpDept[d] e
      UNION
      SELECT e
      FOR EACH Contractor[d] e.
```

Using type schemas, we can formulate implicit Object↦Type and Value↦Type mappings. To express implicit Type↦Type and Function↦Type mappings, function schemas (Section 4) and meta-types (Subsection 3.4) are necessary.

Moreover, meta-types in conjunction with type schemas make possible the definition of mappings that achieve the effect of dynamically adjusting the type hierarchy (this type of mapping is not properly captured by our classification).

Example 3 Assume the following type hierarchy: `Paid` and `Unpaid` are subtypes of `Employee`. We have also a type schema `Emp[Bank]` whose instance types consist of all employees of a given bank. An instance type `Emp[b]` is a subtype of `Paid` if `b` is a solvent bank and a subtype of `Unpaid` if `b` is an unsolvent bank.

Creating types `Paid` and `Unpaid` makes perfect sense, because we may want to define functions applicable only to one of them (for example, unemployment compensation will be paid only to the members of `Unpaid`).

We have to be careful about how those types are populated. Initially, we just have `Employee`. The instances of the type schema `Emp[Bank]` are subtypes of `Employee`. Now `Paid` is the *union* of those instance types `Emp[b]` that correspond to solvent banks. `Unpaid` is defined similarly. Moreover, a given instance type `Emp[b]` is a subtype of either `Paid` or `Unpaid` depending on the status of the corresponding bank `b`.

This can be expressed as follows:

```
CREATE TYPE Paid AS
      SELECT e
      FOR EACH Bank b, Emp[b] e
      WHERE solvent(b)
```

3.3 OBJECT SCHEMAS

So far, we have only considered types whose extensions are obtained from extensions of other types. New objects could not be created. However, objects can also be implicitly defined using the same philosophy. We call such objects *derived objects*. Using derived objects, for example, values can be mapped to objects in a declarative way. Derived objects are defined using *object schemas*.

The existence of derived objects is predicated on the existence of appropriate values or objects in the database. The syntax for the definition of an object schema is as follows:

CREATE *Type*[*Parameters*] PROPERTIES (*Functions*) AS
      Query

The semantics is that for every distinct tuple in the value of *Query*, there is a distinct object of type *Type*.[4] The PROPERTIES clause is optional, but when present means that all the functions in *Functions* are automatically defined. Each such function takes as an argument an object of type *Type* and returns the result equal to the appropriate component of the tuple out of which the object was formed. This is similar to creating multiple objects using a single CREATE *Type* command in OSQL. The only difference is that the population of *Type* may vary in time depending on the value of the *Query*.

Example 4 We adopt here the stock market example from [Krishnamurthy et al., 1991]. The stock information is represented as a stored OSQL function:

```
CREATE FUNCTION Stock(Date d, String c) → Price p.
```

The second argument of this function is a string representing the name of a company.

Suppose we want to create a new type Company and an object of type Company for every company name that appears as an argument in the Stock stored function. Such an object should also have a property Name equal to the company name. We specify this application as follows (the type Company is created implicitly):

```
CREATE Company[String c] PROPERTIES (Name) AS
      SELECT DISTINCT c
      FOR EACH Date d, Price p
      WHERE Stock(d,c)=p.
```

Suppose now that the Stock function is not defined for any arguments. Then there are no objects of type Company. Assume now that through appropriate updates, we obtain:

```
Stock(06/05/95,'IBM') = $10
Stock(06/06/95,'IBM') = $8
Stock(06/06/95,'HP') = $15.
```

Now there are two objects of type Company: one with Name equal to 'IBM', the other – to 'HP'. The first has the object identifier equal to the Skolem term Company['IBM'], the second – to Company['HP'].

Object schemas are used to represent implicit Value↦Object (see the example above), Object↦Object, Type↦Object (an example is given later) and Function↦Object domain mappings. The last two kinds of mappings require the presence of type and function schemas, and meta-types.

3.4 META-TYPES

Meta-types consist of types or functions. It is convenient to assume two built-in meta-types: Type and Function containing all types (resp. functions) in the database.[5] Type schemas do not belong to Type, but instance types do. Similarly, function schemas (Section 4) do

[4] The OIDs of derived objects may be viewed as *Skolem terms* [Maier, 1986; Kifer and Wu, 1989]. In [Abiteboul and Bonner, 1991], several possible ways of constructing and maintaining OIDs of derived objects are discussed.

[5] Type and Function will of course be different for different databases.

not belong to Function, but instance functions do. So actually Type and Function may contain infinitely many elements. Type and Function are populated indirectly using the definitions of types, functions, type schemas and function schemas.

Example 5 Suppose we want to construct the inverse to the mapping described in Example 1. Thus, we are going to create NewEmp, the union of all the instance types of the type EmpPos[String] (this is an example of a union of an infinite number of types):

```
CREATE TYPE NewEmp AS
      SELECT e
      FOR EACH Type EmpPos[p]
      WHERE EmpPos[p](e).
```

The function NewPos that computes the position of a given employee in NewEmp is defined as follows:

```
CREATE FUNCTION NewPos :  NewEmp e → Position p AS
      SELECT p
      FOR EACH Type EmpPos[p]
      WHERE EmpPos[p](e).
```

Using meta-types together with type and function schemas, we can represent implicit Type↦Value mappings (as above) and also Type↦Type, Function↦Value, Function↦Type and Type↦Function mappings. In conjunction with derived objects, implicit Type↦Object and Function↦Object mappings can also be represented, as seen in the following example.

Example 6 As in the previous example, we start from a type schema EmpPos[p]. Assume p is a string and we want to create new objects of type PositionObject corresponding to instance types of EmpPos[String]. We write:

```
CREATE PositionObject[String p] PROPERTIES (Name) AS
      SELECT p
      FOR EACH Type EmpPos[p]
```

4 DERIVED FUNCTIONS

Derived functions are present in OSQL, so we deal here only with *function schemas*. The syntax of a function schema definition is as follows:

CREATE FUNCTION *Function*[*Parameters*] : *Arguments* → *Result* AS
Query

All the parts of the function schema definition are the same as in an OSQL function definition, except for the function name that has parameters which can appear in *Query*. A function schema with given values of *Parameters* is just an OSQL function (called an *instance function*), named by a ground term.

Example 7 For the OSQL function Stock defined in Example 4, we create a function schema that is parameterized by the name of the company:

```
CREATE FUNCTION StockComp[String c] :  Date d → Price p AS
      SELECT p
      FOR EACH Price p
      WHERE p=Stock(d,c).
```

The instance functions of this function could be, for example, `StockComp['IBM']` or `StockComp['HP']`.

The above is an example of a Value↦Function mapping. Object↦Function mappings are constructed similarly.

We show now an example of a query that is expressible only if function schemas are present.

Example 8 Assume that we have separate functions for every company: `IBMStock`, `HPStock` etc. For each such function, we can define a function schema with a parameter that is a constant (this function has just one instance function). For example:

```
CREATE FUNCTION StockComp['IBM']: Date d → Price p AS
      IBMStock(d).
```

Now, we can ask "higher-order" queries like "which stocks have ever gone above $200?" as follows:

```
SELECT c
FOR EACH String c, Function StockComp[c], Date d
WHERE StockComp[c](d)>$200
```

As indicated earlier in this section, function schemas, used together with other constructs introduced so far, complete the framework necessary for representing all 16 kinds of mappings under consideration (Section 2). Moreover, we can now model *integrator* functions [Ahmed et al., 1991a] as follows.

Example 9 Consider the type schema `EmpPos[Position]` and the function schema `SalPos[Position]` which is a position-specific way of computing the salary of an employee. A function that integrates those functions and computes the salary of every employee in `Emp` is defined as follows:

```
CREATE FUNCTION Salary (Emp e) → Integer AS
      SELECT SalPos[p](e)
      FOR EACH Type EmpPos[p], Function SalPos[p]
      WHERE EmpPos[p](e)
```

If we are concerned that such function may return multiple results which need to be reconciled, `Salary` may be used within a *reconciliation* function.

5 SUBTYPING AND INHERITANCE

5.1 SUBTYPE HIERARCHY

Establishing subtype relationship between derived types and other types (derived or not) is not an easy task. In OSQL, a subtype hierarchy is finite and static (to change it, explicit

CREATE TYPE commands have to be issued). In our approach, there may be infinitely many types (instances of type schemas). Moreover, a subtype hierarchy may depend on the database state (see Example 3). Therefore, we will have to live without an explicit subtype hierarchy. To what degree can we have an implicit one?

A subtype hierarchy is necessary for the proper handling of inheritance. We should be able to determine whether a given function is applicable to a given combination of argument values (monotonic inheritance). If more than one function with the same signature is applicable, then the one with the "most specific" signature has to be selected (non-monotonic inheritance). The first task can, however, be accomplished without consulting an explicit subtype hierarchy. It is enough to perform a number of type membership checks, namely check whether each argument value is of the appropriate type. Derived types are defined using queries, thus type membership checks can be performed using query evaluation.

Non-monotonic inheritance is much more difficult. In some specific cases though, a subtype relationship can be readily established. For Example, every instance type EmpPos[p] (Example 1) is a subtype of Employee. In [Abiteboul and Bonner, 1991], some general rules for establishing subtype relationships are given, although without considering type schemas. But the problem of providing a *complete* set of such rules and the *decidability* of subtype relationships in the presence of derived types are still open. To appreciate how difficult it is to establish subtype relationships, consider the following derived type definitions:

```
CREATE TYPE T1 AS
      SELECT e
      FOR EACH T e
      WHERE C1(e)

CREATE TYPE T2 AS
      SELECT e
      FOR EACH T e
      WHERE C1(e) AND C2(e)
```

In this example, T2 indirectly becomes a subtype of T1. But to establish that fact, we have to infer that the second WHERE condition implies the first, a task that is computationally difficult in general. Moreover, one can not infer subtype relationships just on the basis of derived type definitions, as subtype relationships can depend on the database state. In Example 3, Emp[b] is a subtype of Paid if b is a solvent bank.

In our approach, subtype relationships between derived types have to be explicitly provided by the user as *subtype declarations*. Of course, such relationships can be partially computed using rules, as in [Abiteboul and Bonner, 1991]. Subtype declarations are used to resolve overloaded function names. If there is no sufficient subtype information to resolve an overloaded function name at run-time, an error is generated, similarly to the case of multiple-inheritance conflicts.

It is the responsibility of the user to ensure that subtype declarations are consistent with the definitions of derived types. Possibly some tools may be created that provide the user with a partial assistance in this task (which also appears computationally hard). However, providing subtype declarations when subtype relationships depend on the database state requires a richer language than the one we are currently considering.

5.2 INHERITANCE ACROSS DATABASES

So far we have considered mappings of different types and functions in separation. But in reality types and functions are intimately related: types serve as arguments and results of functions. Moreover, functions are used to defined derived types.

Consider a multidatabase mapping from DB1 to DB2 that introduces a derived type Senior:

```
CONNECT DB2
CREATE TYPE Senior
      SUBTYPE OF DB1.Employee AS
      SELECT e
      FOR EACH DB1.Employee e
      WHERE DB1.Age(e)>65
```

Let us consider now what is involved in such a mapping. Clearly, the extension of DB2.Senior is defined to be a subset of the extension of DB1.Employee consisting of employees satisfying a condition. But mapping the objects alone is not enough: we need to have functions in DB2 defined on DB2.Senior to represent the information about senior employees.

Our approach here is to provide appropriate subtype declarations. The type DB2.Senior is declared to be a subtype of DB1.Employee. Consequently, the functions defined on DB1.Employee, for example Salary, can also be applied to DB2.Senior. It may be the case that a function f defined on DB1.Employee is subsequently redefined in a subtype S of DB1.Employee. Then if a DB2.Senior object e is in the extension of S, the latter definition will be used to evaluate $f(e)$.

An alternative approach would be to assume no inheritance between different databases. This would be rather inconvenient: type and function definitions from DB1 would have to be replicated in DB2 and appropriate mappings between them set up.

For example, to deal with employee salaries in the example above, we would need to define a new function in DB2 (the notation is simplified):

```
CREATE FUNCTION Salary (Senior e) → Decimal AS
      DB1.Salary(e)
```

If we want to map a function defined in DB1 into another function in DB2, we have to make sure that the argument and result types of the former are mapped to the right types in DB2 (this is called *type coherence* in [Abiteboul and Bonner, 1991]).

6 OPERATIONAL SEMANTICS

We outline here the operational semantics of derived types and functions. First, we discuss a basic repertoire of operations necessary to implement derived types and functions. Next, we discuss top-down evaluation of derived types and functions.

6.1 BASIC OPERATIONS

The following operations should be supported (in addition to the operations already provided for OSQL):

- *type or function schema instantiation*: obtaining a single derived type (function) from the corresponding schema and given parameter values.
- *membership test* in a derived type or an instance type. This is used to check whether a given object is of the given type.
- *instance enumeration* of all instances of a given type or function schema. This is required whenever the meta-type `Type` (or `Function`) appears as the range of a term in the `FOR EACH` part of an OSQL query (see Examples 5 and 6).

Schema instantiation consists of textual replacement of parameter occurrences in the schema definition by the corresponding parameter values. As a result, a type (or function) definition is obtained which is very much like an OSQL type (resp. function) except for the fact that some types or functions in it may be named by ground terms. Notice that schema instantiation is done at run-time, not at compile-time, because the set of instances of a given (type or function) schema may depend on the database state.

Given an object and a derived type or an instance type, we can check *type membership* by evaluating the appropriate type definition (which is just a query) and checking whether the object is an element of the result. This will work as long as the extension of the type is finite (the type should be *safe*). Determining type safety is a further research issue. Let us just mention that as long as derived types are built from user types using `SELECT` and `UNION`, they will be safe because user types are finite. Only if infinite literal types, e.g., `Integer`, are used in a `SELECT` list, the resulting derived types may be unsafe. Alternatively, we could develop special-purpose routines that check whether an object belongs to the result of a query by substituting the object into the query definition and evaluating the resulting definition.

Instance enumeration is by far the most difficult of the above three operations. It is implemented by *matching* a possibly non-ground term against the entire, possibly infinite, type hierarchy.

Example 10 Consider the following definition from Example 5:

```
CREATE TYPE NewEmp AS
      SELECT e
      FOR EACH Type EmpPos[p]
      WHERE EmpPos[p](e).
```

To enumerate the instance types of the type schema `EmpPos[String]`, the term `EmpPos[p]` is matched against the type hierarchy to obtain the values for `p`. However, the schema `EmpPos[String]` has infinitely many instances, thus there are infinitely many possible values for `p`.

So, if a type schema is to be used for instance enumeration, it should have finitely many instances. In this example, this may be achieved by the introduction of another type `Position`:

```
CREATE TYPE Position AS
      SELECT p
      FOR EACH Employee e
      WHERE Pos(e)=p
```

and the redefinition of the type schema `EmpPos[String]` to `EmpPos[Position]`:

```
CREATE TYPE EmpPos[Position p] AS
      SELECT e
      FOR EACH Employee e
      WHERE Pos(e)=p.
```

In the case, however, where such redefinition is impossible (if, for example, `EmpPos[String]` is defined in a different autonomous database), the definition of `NewEmp` will not lead to infinite enumeration only if the query processor recognizes the fact that the `WHERE` condition in this definition makes it possible to limit the attention to instance types with *non-empty extensions*. In this example, there is only a finite number of such instance types.

Sometimes there is not enough information in the query to allow the query processor to make this type of inference. In the definition from Example 6:

```
CREATE PositionObject[String p] PROPERTIES (Name) AS
      SELECT p
      FOR EACH Type EmpPos[p]
```

a new derived object should be constructed for every instance of `EmpPos[String]` and the enumeration of those objects is clearly infinite. If we intend, however, to construct new objects only for those instance types that have non-empty extensions, another definition should be given:

```
CREATE PositionObject[String p] PROPERTIES (Name) AS
      SELECT p
      FOR EACH Type EmpPos[p], NewEmp e
      WHERE EmpPos[p](e)
```

where `NewEmp` is the type defined earlier.

Moreover, some type schemas have infinitely many instances with non-empty extensions, for example the following type schema:

```
CREATE TYPE YoungerThan[Integer k] AS
      SELECT e
      FOR EACH Employee e
      WHERE Age(e)<k.
```

Type schemas with infinitely many non-empty instances can not be used where instance enumeration is required. Nevertheless, they can still be used elsewhere in queries.

6.2 TOP-DOWN EVALUATION

We claim that both the evaluation of derived functions and the computation of the extensions of derived types can be handled with only small extensions to the top-down model used in OSQL, *provided the type and function schemas are completely instantiated during the evaluation.* This requirement translates into several syntactic restrictions on the occurrences and definitions of type and function schemas.

Consider a derived function that is defined by a `SELECT` expression. The evaluation of this function consists of the following steps:

1. establishing whether this particular function should be selected for application to the given arguments (checking the validity of arguments and overload resolution).
2. establishing the ranges for the variables (`FOR EACH`). The order of range declarations matters.
3. evaluating the query using the condition (`WHERE`) to select appropriate values.
4. computing the result (the `SELECT` list).

Checking the validity of a function invocation can be accomplished by testing membership of the arguments in the corresponding types (determined from the function signature). This can be done, as shown earlier in this section. If more than one function is applicable, the most "specific" function should be selected, as shown in Section 5. For this process to be possible, the signature should consist of fixed types, either OSQL types or instances of type schemas. A type schema can not appear in the signature, because at the time of function invocation, there is not enough information to determine which instance of such a schema should be selected.

In the second step, an appropriate function definition has already been selected. Can a type schema be used as a range for a variable? If all the parameters of such a type are among the arguments of the function invocation or have been bound by earlier range declarations (the order is important), the type schema is fully instantiated and there is no problem (see Example 3). However, in other cases there is not enough information to uniquely identify the range.

In the evaluation of the query (third step) and the computation of the result (fourth step), a type schema has to be already fully instantiated, as those steps can not instantiate it.

The second and the third step should sometimes be interleaved in order to avoid enumerating infinitely many instance types (see Example 10 and the discussion that follows).

Function schemas can be safely used in the definitions of other derived functions or in queries if at the time of evaluation their parameters are fully instantiated.

7 RELATED WORK

Some of the concepts behind derived types and functions go back to late 1970s. The notions of type defined by a *membership condition* and *type union* were already present in SDM [Hammer and Mcleod, 1981]. To our knowledge, these proposals have never been implemented. The concept of *derived object* was introduced by Maier [Maier, 1986] and was subsequently refined in [Kifer and Wu, 1989; Hull and Yoshikawa, 1990; Abiteboul and

Bonner, 1991]. *Type schemas* (called *parameterized classes*) were mentioned in [Abiteboul and Bonner, 1991] without, however, any study of their properties. This is not surprising because the authors relate the semantics of their language to that of IQL [Abiteboul and Kanellakis, 1989] in which only databases with a fixed number of classes are allowed. In particular, the notion of *instance type* was not explored. *Meta-types* are present in every object-orientedDBMS, but usually contain only a finite number of stored user types or functions, not infinitely many instance types or functions. We are not aware of any mention of *function schemas*, although they are a natural analogue of type schemas. Moreover, none of the above works deals with the operational semantics of type and function schemas. In [Abiteboul and Bonner, 1991], the operational semantics of derived objects is discussed.

Previous OSQL extensions, HOSQL [Ahmed et al., 1991a] and OSQL/IPL, adopt a procedural approach to domain mapping. Such an approach suffers from a number of problems, as indicated in Section 2. To remedy those, Kent proposed some declarative constructs: *derived subtypes* (types defined by a membership condition) and *covered types* (essentially type unions) [Kent, 1991b]. Most mappings (particularly those involving schematic discrepancies) are, however, still specified procedurally in his approach. In our approach, the new language constructs are sufficiently expressive to formulate a large class of domain mappings in a completely declarative way.

Our goal was to extend OSQL to support multidatabase mappings. As shown in [Barsalou and Gangopadhyay, 1992], second-order logic can also be used for this purpose. That approach is similar in spirit to F-Logic [Kifer and Wu, 1989; Kifer et at., 1990], a very general second-order logic programming language. In this logic, some of our mappings also can be elegantly expressed.

Consider the definition of the type schema `EmpPos[String]` (Subsection 3.2). In F-Logic, we can express it as follows:

```
E : pos(P) ← E : emp[pos→P].
```

The inverse mapping can be equally easily specified by reversing the arrow.

It remains to be seen which approach to multidatabase mappings, one based on logic or one based on a single data model, will be more practical. One may observe, however, that the latter has an advantage of keeping as the kernel the data model that various database users are already accustomed to. Using a logic language to express a mapping between different OSQL databases would require providing two-way translations between this language and OSQL. On the other hand, using logic is considerably more general as it makes possible the mapping between different data models [Barsalou and Gangopadhyay, 1992].

A recent proposal [Kifer et al., 1992] applies the ideas of F-logic to an object-oriented SQL-like language. This paper contains many interesting ideas like various notions of query typing, but does not deal with the issues of type and function schemas.

Recent work on views in object-oriented databases is presented in [Schrefl and Neuhold, 1988; Tanaka et al., 1988; Kaul et al., 1990; Heiler and Zdonik, 1990; Bertino, 1992].

8 CONCLUSIONS AND FURTHER WORK

We have extended OSQL with constructs making possible a declarative specification of a broad class of object-oriented multidatabase mappings. Using our constructs, schematic discrepancies can be resolved. We summarize the relationships between various kinds of mappings and the supporting concepts in Table 1. We have also outlined the corresponding operational semantics.

This work opens up a lot of interesting problems, e.g., inference of subtype relationships between derived types, safety (finiteness of extensions) of derived types, or enumeration of instance types of type schemas. It is also challenging to characterize more precisely the class of mappings that can be expressed in our framework. Finally, one should extend this work to the problem of interoperability between heterogenous object-oriented languages.

Acknowledgments

Discussions with Bill Kent helped to shape these ideas, as well as comments from Ravi Krishnamurthy and Jurgen Annevelink.

Distribution of Schemata in H-PCTE

Udo Kelter
Fern Universität Hagen
Praktische Informatik V
Fachbereich Informatik
Postfach 940, D-5800 Hagen
Germany

Abstract

H-PCTE is a distributed structurally object-oriented database system in which schemata are also distributed. The conceptual schema is split into modules which can be stored at different sites. An application accesses the object base via an external schema; an external schema is constructed from one or several accessible schema modules. The external schema enables application programs to designate types using textual names and restricts access to the object base on the level of types.

1 BACKGROUND

Two important traditional achievements of database systems are *data independence* of applications and *access controls*. Both problem areas are typically addressed by external schemata or views. This paper sketches the concept of external schemata in H-PCTE, a distributed, structurally object-oriented DBSs which has been designed to be a basis of software development environments. We will use the term *object management system* (*OMS*) to refer to such database management systems and the term *object base* to refer to the database managed by the OMS.

H-PCTE is a high-performance, main-memory-oriented version of PCTE. PCTE is the first internationally standardized OMS [ECMA, 1990; ECMA, 1991]. The basic features of the data model of H-PCTE are complex objects, relationships, attributes, typing, and multiple inheritance. A relationship consists of two directed, mutually reverse *links*. Each outgoing link of an object has a unique key. A *pathname* is a sequence of such keys. Objects are accessed by navigating along links.

The basic features of the distribution model of H-PCTE are: (1) the object base is partitioned into segments which may be stored at different sites; (2) segmentation and location are transparent to applications; (3) individual objects can be moved between segments.

We assume that it is fairly probable that single workstations which are part of an OMS installation are unreachable (e.g. portable workstations), even for relatively long periods; therefore, some segments may be inaccessible. A very important design goal is therefore to remain *resilient against the inaccessibility of segments*. It should be possible to perform sensible work on a site with the segments accessible from this site. A special case of this is the autonomous operation of an isolated workstation. It must also be possible to install (or develop) new software development tools when only a subset of all segments is accessible. Since tools typically use private data types, their installation will require to extend or modify the conceptual schema and the external schemata. As a result,

- the conceptual schema and the external schemata must be managed in such a way that they *can evolve independently at different sites*;
- a single site may only know a *part* of the conceptual schema;
- a *centrally* administrated conceptual schema is unacceptable.

2 THE METABASE

The metabase is a set of objects which *represent* the conceptual and external schemata. It is organized in three layers (Figure 1). The highest layer contains the root of the metabase, which is reachable under a fixed pathname. This root has a number of component objects of type *schema definition set* (SDS). Each SDS has a unique name. SDSs are "modules" from which external schemata can be built. Each SDS has a number of component objects which represent types, e.g. object types, link types or attributes. Each type has a system-wide unique surrogate and may have a *local name* in the SDS.

A number of details of type definitions, e.g. the fact that an attribute is applied to an object type, or that a link type is an admissible outgoing link type of an object type, and so on, are represented by *links* with appropriate keys between the objects which represent the involved types (shown as dotted lines in the figure). Further details of the type definitions are represented as *attributes* of the objects or links.

Different SDSs can be stored in different segments and thus on different sites. Locally accessible SDSs can be independently modified. SDSs support in addition the *grouping of related type definitions*. An SDS will typically contain the definitions related to one particular application. SDSs can share components, that is a type can be contained in several SDSs.

Initially, a process has an empty external schema, that is, the process does not see anything. A new external schema of a process can be constructed at any time by invoking the operation which creates a new external schema for the calling process. The new external schema is *defined in terms of SDSs*, namely as a *sequence* of SDSs. The new external schema is then constructed from the types contained in the specified SDSs. Only these SDSs (and their type objects) need to be accessible. All relevant information is then *cached* in the descriptor of the process (no further accesses to the metabase are required). A process will normally include only a subset of all SDSs in its external schema. The advantage of this is that only

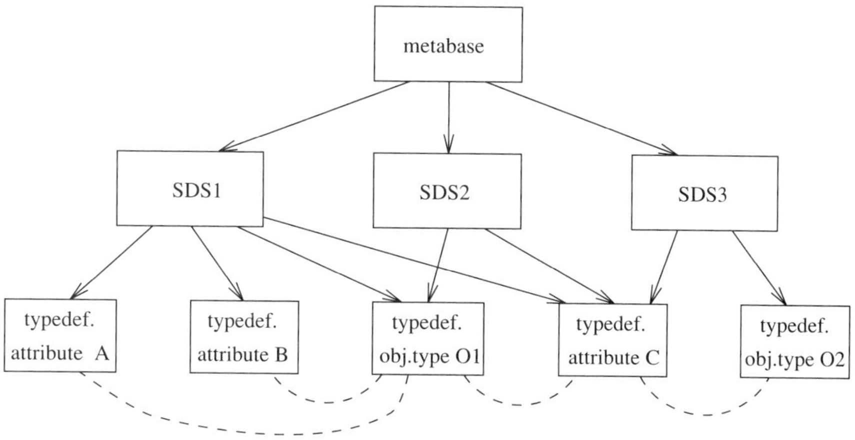

Figure 1: Metabase Structure

those types are made visible which are actually needed for the current application, not all types which the user is allowed to see.

3 EXTERNAL NAMES

H-PCTE gives applications a certain degree of independence from the object base schema through external names of types. An application will typically use a set of application-specific types. H-PCTE operations which, e.g., access an attribute instance have a parameter which specifies the attribute using an attribute designator. The problem is that such designators appear as constants in the *source program* of the application (which is not normally available to the user of the application), and that the application-specific types will have different type surrogates in different H-PCTE installations. Therefore, types are designated in H-PCTE operations by *external names*, i.e. strings, which are mapped onto type surrogates.

When an external schema is set, each visible type, if it has a local name in an SDS, gets the following initial external names: (1) the local name and (2) the SDS name followed by '-' and the local name; the latter names are globally unique.

The translation of the external names into internal identifiers is a non-negligible overhead in the case of "small" operations. H-PCTE has therefore operations which enable applications to pre-translate external names into *type handles*. Details of this are described in [Kelter, 1992a].

4 ACCESS CONTROLS

The second purpose of external schemata are access controls . H-PCTE offers discretionary access controls (DAC), which are means of restricting access to data granules on the basis of the identity of **subjects** and/or groups to which the subjects belong. H-PCTE distinguishes two *orthogonal* levels (or dimensions) of DAC: access can be restricted independently on the basis of individual object instances, i.e. on the *instance level*, and on the basis of types, i.e. on the *type level*. The overall effect of these levels is roughly the same as the effect of a selection and a projection which form a view in relational database systems (here, we regard an object as a tuple of a relation):

- the rights on instances restrict access to certain objects / tuples. In views, this is achieved by means of a selection. H-PCTE uses object-specific access control lists (ACLs) for this purpose.
- the rights on types restrict, for example, access to certain attributes of objects or links. In views, this is achieved by means of a projection. H-PCTE uses ACLs on the type-level, too. Roughly speaking, a type level ACL contains the complete information about the rights of all subjects on a particular type. It is stored at the object or link which represents this type (or part of a type definition).

Details of the instance-level and type-level access controls can be found in [Kelter, 1990; Kelter, 1992b], respectively. A number of features apply to both levels: the use of ACLs allows access rights to be administrated and checked in partitioned networks. The administration of rights is based on the concepts of owners. Arbitrarily many subjects can have rights on a granule of access control. Subgroup structures are directly supported. Access can be denied explicitly (the access logic is three-valued). External schemata in H-PCTE address only the type-level, since the H-PCTE data model is navigational. In the rest of this section, we will give a somewhat simplified description of the type-level DAC.

Type Definition Units. Type definition units are "granules of protection" on the type-level, that is they are units of information about types for which rights can be controlled independently. Each type definition unit is represented as an object or link in the metabase. Examples are:

- an individual object type, link type, or attribute
- an object type including all subtypes
- the fact that an attribute is applied to an object/link type

Each type definition unit has associated operations: an object or link of a given type can be created or deleted, an attribute can be read or written etc.; *access modes* are sensible groups of such operations.

The State. The type-level ACLs are actually an implementation of the *state of the object base with regard to type-level DAC*. More formally, this state is a mapping

$$tard : S \times T \times M \rightarrow V$$

with S being the set of subjects, T being the set of type definition units, M being the set of access modes, and V being the set of access values. Examples of access values are "granted", "denied" and "undefined". The mapping $tard$ can also be regarded as a set of quadruples (s, t, m, v), s being a subject, t being a type definition unit, m a mode, and v being a value which indicates whether s is to be allowed to access instances of t using operations in m. Such a quadruple is called a *type-level access right determination* (*TARD* for short). The object base contains, for each triple (s, t, m), exactly one TARD(s, t, m, v)

with $v = tard(s, t, m)$. The type-level ACL of a type definition unit represents thus *the set of all TARDs for this particular type definition unit.*

Type-Rights of a Process. TARDs determine access rights for *all* subjects known in an installation. A process in H-PCTE however, acts only on behalf of certain "active" subjects; two examples are the user who started this process and an explicitly activated user group. Only TARDs of active subjects are relevant for the type rights of a process. Formally, the type-rights of a process are a predicate

$$has\_type\_right : T \times M \rightarrow Boolean$$

with T and M as defined above. When an external schema is set, the TARDs of all *active* subjects are "added" according to the following formula:
has_type_right(t,m) := true if

- there is an active TARD $(s, t, m, \text{“}granted''\text{)}$
- there is *no* active TARD $(s, t, m, \text{“}denied''\text{)}$

If *has_type_right(t,m) = true* for a process, then we say that the process *has the m-right on t.*

Visibility and Ownership. There are two access modes with a specific meaning: if a process does not have the "existence" right on a type definition unit *t*, it does not know of *t* at all. If *t* is an object type or link type then this process cannot "see" instances of this type. If a process has the "owner" right on a type definition unit *t* then is can modify the ACL of *t*.

BIBLIOGRAPHY

S. Abiteboul and A. Bonner. (1991) Objects and views. In *Proceedings of ACM SIGMOD International Conference on Management of Data*, pages 238–247.

S. Abiteboul and P. Kannellakis. (1989) Object identity as a query language primitive. In *Proceedings of ACM SIGMOD International Conference on Management of Data*, pages 159–173.

H. Afsarmanesh and D McLeod. (1989) The 3DIS: An extensible, object-oriented information management environment. *ACM Transactions on Office Information Systems*, 7(4): 339–377.

G. Agha. (1987) *Actors: A model of concurrent computation in distributed systems.* Cambridge, MA: MIT Press.

R. Agrawal, editor. (1991) *Bulletin of the IEEE Technical Committee on Data Engineering*, 14(2) (special issue on foundations of object-oriented database systems).

R. Agrawal, M. Carey, and M. Livny. (1987) Concurrency control performance modeling: Alternatives and implications. *ACM Transactions on Database Systems*, 12(4): 609–654.

R. Ahmed, P. D. Smedt, W. Kent, M. Ketabchi, W. Litwin, A. Rafii, and M.-C. Shan. (1991a) Pegasus: A system for seamless integration of heterogenous information sources. In *Digest of papers – IEEE COMPCON*, pages 128–135.

R. Ahmed, P. D. Smedt, W. Du, W. Kent, M. A. Ketabchi, W. A. Litwin, A. Rafii, and M. Shan. (1991b) The Pegasus heterogeneous multidatabase system. *Computer*, 24(12): 19–27.

V. Aho, E. Hopcroft, and J.D. Ullman. (1985) *Data structures and algorithms.* Reading, MA: Addison-Wesley.

M. Aksit and A. Tripathi. (1988) Data abstraction mechanisms in Sina/st. In *Proceedings of OOPSLA'88 Conference*, pages 267–275.

A. Albano, G. Ghelli, and R. Orsini. (1991) A relationship mechanism for a strongly typed object-oriented database programming language. In *Proceedings of the 17th International Conference on Very Large Data Bases*. San Mateo, CA: Morgan Kaufmann, pages 565–575.

A. Albano and R. Morrison, editors. (1993) *Proceedings of the Fifth International Workshop on Persistent Object Systems. Design, Implementation and Use*, Berlin: Springer-Verlag.

J.E. Allchin and M.S. McKendry. (1983) Synchronization and recovery of actions. In *Proceedings of the 2nd ACM Symposium on Principles of Distributed Computing*, pages 31–44.

R. Alonso, D. Barbara, and H. Garcia-Molina. (1990) Data caching issues in an information retrieval system. *ACM Transactions on Database Systems*, 15(3): 359–384.

J. Annevelink. (1991) Database programming languages: A functional approach. In *Proceedings of the ACM SIGMOD International Conference on Management of Data*, pages 318–327.

APM. (1989) *The ANSA reference manual*, Cambridge, U.K.: Architecture Projects Management Limited.

M. Aoshima, Y. Izumida, A. Makinouchi, F. Suzuki, and Y. Yamane. (1990) The C-based database programming language Jasmine/C. In *Proceedings of the 16th International Conference on Very Large Data Bases*. San Mateo, CA: Morgan Kaufmann, pages 539–551.

P.M.G. Apers. (1988) Data allocation in distributed database systems. *ACM Transactions on Database Systems*, 13(3): 263–304.

P.M.G. Apers, C. A. van den Berg, J. Flokstra, P.W.P.J. Grefen, M.L. Kersten, and A.N. Wilschut. (1992) PRISMA/DB: A parallel, main-memory relational DBMS. *IEEE Transactions on Knowledge and Data Engineering*, 4(6): 541–554.

M.P. Atkinson. (1978) Programming languages and databases. In *Proceedings of the 4th International Conference on Very Large Data Bases*. San Mateo, CA: Morgan Kaufmann, pages 408–419.

M.P. Atkinson. (1989) Questioning persistent types. In [R. Hull et al., 1989], pages 2–24.

M. Atkinson. (1993) Persistent foundations for scalable multi-paradigmal systems. In this volume.

M.P. Atkinson and O.P. Buneman. (1987) Types and persistence in database programming languages. *ACM Computing Surveys*, 19(2): 105–190.

M.P. Atkinson and R. Morrison. (1985) Procedures as persistent data objects. *ACM Transactions on Programming Languages and Systems*, 4(7): 539–559.

M.P. Atkinson and R. Morrison. (1987) Polymorphic names, types, constancy and magic in a type secure persistent object store. In R. Carrick and R.L. Cooper, editors, *Proceedings of the Second International Workshop on Persistent Object Systems*, pages 1–12.

M.P. Atkinson, K.J. Chisholm, and W.P. Cockshott. (1982) PS-Algol: An algol with a persistent heap. *ACM SIGPLAN Notices*, 17(7): 24–31.

M. Atkinson, P. Bailey, K. Chisholm, P. Cockshott, and R. Morrison. (1983a) An approach to persistent programming. *The Computer Journal*, 26(4): 360–365.

M.P. Atkinson, K.J. Chisholm, and W.P. Cockshott. (1983b) CMS—A chunk management system. *Software — Practice and Experience*, 13(3): 273–285. 401

M.P. Atkinson, K.J. Chisholm, W.P. Cockshott, and R.M. Marshall. (1983c) Algorithms for a persistent heap. *Software — Practice and Experience*, 13(3): 259–272.

M.P. Atkinson, O.P. Buneman, and R. Morrison. (1988) Binding and type checking in database programming languages. *The Computer Journal*, 31(2): 99–109.

M. Atkinson, F. Bancilhon, D.J. DeWitt, K. Dittrich, D. Maier and S. Zdonik. (1989) The object-oriented database system manifesto. In *Proceedings of the 1st International Conference on Deductive and Object-Oriented Databases*, pages 40–57.

M.P. Atkinson and A. England. (1990) Towards new architectures for distributed autonomous database applications. In [Rosenberg and Keedy, 1990], pages 356–377.

M.P. Atkinson, C. Lécluse, P.C. Philbrow, and P. Richard. (1991) Design issues in a map language. In [Kanellakis and Schmidt, 1991], pages 20–32.

B.R. Badrinath and K. Ramamritham. (1987) Semantic-based concurrency control: Beyond commutativity. In *Proceedings of the 4th International Conference on Data Engineering*, pages 132–140.

B.R. Badrinath and K. Ramamritham. (1990) Performance evaluation of semantics-based multilevel concurrency control protocols. In *Proceedings of the ACM SIGMOD International Conference on Management of Data*, pages 163–172.

H. Baker. (1978) List processing in real time on a serial computer. *Communications of the ACM*, 21(4): 280–294.

H. Bakoglu et al. (1990) The IBM RISC System/6000 processor: Hardware overview. *IBM Journal of Research and Development*, 34(1): 12–22.

R. Balzer. (1985) A 15 year perspective on automatic programming, *IEEE Transactions on Software Engineering*, SE-11(11): 1257–1268.

H. Bal, J. Steiner, and A. Tanenbaum. (1989) Programming languages for distributed computing systems. *ACM Computing Surveys*, 21(3): 261–322.

F. Bancilhon, S. Cluet, and C. Delobel. (1989) A query language for the O_2 object-oriented database system. In [Hull et al., 1989], pages 122–138.

F. Bancilhon, C. Delobel, and P. Kanellakis, editors. (1992) *Building an object-oriented database system —The Story of O_2*. San Mateo, CA: Morgan Kaufmann, 1992.

A. Banerji. (1990) *A new programming model for distributed applications.* MS Thesis, Department of Computer Science, University of Notre Dame.

T. Barsalou and D. Gangopadhyay. (1992) M(DM): An open framework for interoperation of multimodel multidatabase systems. In *Proceedings of the 8th International Conference on Data Engineering*, pages 218–227.

C. Batini, M. Lenzerini, and S.B. Navathe. (1986) A comparative analysis of methodologies for database schema integration. *ACM Computing Surveys*, 18(4): 323–364.

C. Beeri. (1990) A formal approach to object oriented databases. *Data & Knowledge Engineering*, 5:353–382.

C. Beeri and T. Milo. (1991) A model for active object oriented database. In *Proceedings of the 17th International Conference on Very Large Data Bases*. San Mateo, CA: Morgan Kaufmann, pages 337–349.

C. Beeri, P.A. Bernstein, and N. Goodman. (1989) A model for concurrency in nested transaction systems. *Journal of the ACM*, 36(2): 230–269.

D.E. Bell and L.J. LaPadula. (1975) Secure computer systems: Unified exposition & Multics interpretation. Technical Report MTIS AD-A023588, MITRE Corporation.

M. Bellew, M. Hsu, and V. Tam. (1990) Update propagation in distributed memory hierarchy. In *Proceedings of the 6th International Conference on Data Engineering*, pages 521–528.

M.J. Bellosta-Tourtier, A. Bessede, C. Darrieumerlou, O. Gruber, P. Pucheral, H. Steffen, and J.M. Thévenin. (1990) GEODE : Concepts and facilities. In *Journées Bases de Données Avancées, Montpellier*, pages 375–396.

M.J. Bellosta-Tourtier, F. Viallet, and P. Valduriez. (1991) Design considerations for OMNIS, an object management interface system. In *Proceedings of the TOOLS'91 International Conference*, pages 87–99.

A. Bensoussan, C. Clingen, and R. Daley. (1972) The Multics virtual memory: Concepts and design. *Communications of the ACM*, 15(5): 308–318.

V. Benzaken and C. Delobel. (1991) Enhancing performance in a persistent object store: Clustering strategies in O_2. In [Dearle et al., 1991] pages 403–412.

C.A. vd Berg and M.L. Kersten. (1991) Engineering a MMDBMS. *CWI Quarterly*, 4(2).

C.A. vd Berg and M.L. Kersten. (1992) An analysis of a dynamic query optimization scheme for different data distributions. In J.C. Freytag, D. Maier, and G. Vossen editors, *Query Processing for Advanced Database Systems*, San Mateo, CA: Morgan Kaufmann.

C.A. vd Berg, M.L. Kersten and S. Shair-Ali. (1991) Dynamic Query Processing. Technical Report CS-R9112, CWI, Amsterdam.

J. Bernabeu-Auban, P. Hutto, M. Khalidi, M. Ahmed, W. Appelbe, P. Dasgupta, R. LeBlanc, and R. Ramachandra. (1988) Clouds — A distributed object-based operating system architecture and kernel implementation. In *Proceedings of the European UNIX Systems User Group Autumn (EUUG)*, pages .

J. Bernabeu-Auban, P. Hutto, M. Khalidi, M. Ahmed, W. Appelbe, P. Dasgupta, R. LeBlanc, and R. Ramachandra. (1989) The architecture of Ra: A kernel for Clouds. In *Proceedings of the 23rd Hawaii International Conference on System Science*, Volume II, pages 936–945.

P.A. Bernstein and N. Goodman. (1981) Concurrency control in distributed database systems. *ACM Computing Surveys*, 13(2): 185–221.

P. Bernstein, V. Hadzilacos and N. Goodman. (1987) *Concurrency control and recovery in database systems*. Reading, MA: Addison Wesley.

E. Bertino. (1992) A view mechanism for object-oriented databases. In *Proceedings of the International Conference on Extending Database Technology*, pages 136–151.

E. Bertino and W. Kim. (1989) Indexing techniques for queries on nested objects. *IEEE Transactions on Knowledge and Data Engineering*, 1(2): 196–214.

D. Bevan. (1987) Distributed garbage collection using reference counting. In *Proceedings of the PARLE'87 Conference, Vol.II*, pages 176–187.

B. Bhargava, S. Browne, and J. Srinivasan. (1992) Composite object replication in distributed database systems. In *Proceedings of the International Conference on Information Systems and Management of Data*, page .

K. Birman and T. Joseph. (1987) Reliable communication in the presence of failures. *ACM Transactions on Computer Systems*, 5(1): 47–76.

A. Birrell and B. Nelson. (1984) Implementing remote procedure calls. *ACM Transactions on Computer Systems*, 2(1): 39–59.

A. Black, N. Hutchinson, E. Jul, H. Levy, and L. Carter. (1987) Distribution and abstract types in Emerald. *IEEE Transactions on Software Engineering*, 13(1): 65–76.

J. Bloch. (1989) The Camelot library: A C language extension for programming a general purpose distributed transaction system. In *Proceedings of the 9th International Conference on Distributed Computing*, pages 172–180.

T. Bloom and S. Zdonik. (1987) Issues in the design of object-oriented database programming languages. In *Proceedings of the OOPSLA '87 Conference*, pages 441–451.

H. Boral, W. Alexander, L. Clay, G. Copeland, S. Danforth, M. Franklin, B. Hart, M. Smith, and P. Valduriez. (1990) Prototyping Bubba: A highly parallel database system. *IEEE Transactions on Knowledge and Data Engineering*, 2(1):4–24.

A. Borgida, R.J. Brachman, D.L. McGuinness, and L.A. Resnick. (1989) CLASSIC: A structural data model for objects. In *Proceedings of the ACM SIGMOD Conference on Management of Data*, pages 58–67.

U.M. Borghoff. (1992) *Catalogue of distributed file operating systems*. New York, NY: Springer-Verlag.

R. J. Brachman and J. G. Schmolze. (1985) An overview of the KL-ONE knowledge representation system. *Cognitive Science*, 9: .

S. E. Bratsberg. (1992) Unified class evolution by object-oriented views. In *Proceedings of the 11th International Conference on the Entity-Relationship Approach*, pages 423–439.

S.E. Bratsberg. (1993) Integrating independently developed classes. In this volume.

Y. Breitbart, D. Georgakopoulos, M. Rusinkiewicz, and A. Silberschatz. (1991) On rigorous transaction scheduling. *IEEE Transactions on Software Engineering*, 17(9): 954–960.

Y. Breibart, A. Silberschatz, and G. Thompson. (1990a) Reliable transaction management in a multidatabase system. In *Proceedings of the ACM SIGMOD International Conference on Management of Data*, pages 215–224.

Y. Breitbart, et al. (1990b) Final report of the workshop on multidatabases and semantic interoperability.

J. Brockman and S. Director. (1992) A schema-based approach to CAD task management, In T. Ryan and F. Rammig, editors, *Electronic Design Automation Frameworks*, Elsevier/North Holland (to appear).

A.L. Brown. (1988) *Persistent object stores.* PhD thesis, Department of Computational Science, University of St. Andrews.

A.L. Brown, A. Dearle, R. Morrison, D. Munro, and J. Rosenberg. (1990) A layered persistent architecture for Napier88. In [Rosenberg and Keedy, 1990], pages 155–172.

A.L. Brown, G. Mainetto, F. Matthes, R. Mueller, and D.J. McNally. (1992) An open system architecture for a persistent object store. In *Proceedings of the 25th Hawaii International Conference on System Sciences*, pages 766–776.

A.L. Brown and J. Rosenberg. (1990) Persistent object stores: An implementation technique. In [Dearle et al., 1991], pages 199–214.

T. Bryden. (1989) *C Language support for object-oriented programming in ARCADE.* MS Thesis, Department of Computer Science, University of Notre Dame.

A. Buchmann, M. Hornick, E. Markatos, and C. Chronaki. (1990) Specification of a transaction mechanism for a distributed active object system. In *Proceedings of the OOPSLA/ECOOP '90 Workshop on Transactions and Objects*, pages 1–9.

A. Buchmann, M. T. Özsu, M. Hornick, D. Georgakopoulos, and F.A. Manola. (1992) A transaction model for active distributed object systems. In [Elmagarmid, 1992], pages 123–158.

L.F. Cabrera, L. Haas, J. Richardson, P. Schwartz, and J. Stamos. (1990) The Melampus project: Toward an omniscient computing system. Technical Report RJ 7515, IBM Almaden Research Centre.

L.P. Cabrera and E. Jul, editors. (1992) *Proceedings of the 2nd International Workshop on Object Orientation in Operating Systems*, IEEE Computer Society.

L. Cardelli. (1990) The Quest language and system (tracking draft). Technical report, DEC Systems Research Center, Palo Alto, CA: DEC.

L. Cardelli and P. Wegner. (1985) On understanding types, data abstraction and polymorphism. *ACM Computing Surveys*, 17(4): 471–523.

L. Cardelli, J.E. Donahue, L. Glassman, M. Jordan, W. Kalsow, and G. Nelson. (1989) Modula-3 report (revised). Technical Report 52, DEC Systems Research Centre, Palo Alto, CA: DEC.

M. Carey and M. Livny. (1991) Conflict detection tradeoffs for replicated data. In *ACM Transactions on Database Systems.*, 16(4): 703–746.

M. Carey, D. DeWitt, J. Richarson, and E. Shekita. (1986a) Object and file management in the EXODUS extensible database system. In *Proceedings of the 12th International Conference on Very Large Data Bases.* San Mateo, CA: Morgan Kaufmann, pages 397–410.

M.J. Carey, D.J. DeWitt, D. Frank, G. Graefe, M. Muralikrishna, J.E. Richardson, and E.J. Shekita (1986b) The architecture of the EXODUS extensible DBMS. In *Proceedings of the International Workshop on Object-Oriented Database Systems*, pages 52–65.

M. Carey, D. DeWitt, and S. Vandenberg. (1988) A data model and query language for EXODUS. In *Proceedings of ACM SIGMOD International Conference on Management of Data*, pages 413–423.

M.J. Carey, E. Shekita, G. Lapis, B. Lindsay and J. McPherson. (1990) An incremental join attachment for Starburst. In *Proceedings of the 16th International Conference on Very Large Data Bases*. San Mateo, CA: Morgan Kaufmann, pages 662–673.

M. Carey, M. Franklin, M. Livny, and E. Shekita. (1991) Data caching tradeoffs in client-server DBMS architectures. In *Proceedings of the International ACM SIGMOD Conference in Management of Data*, pages 357–366.

N. Carriero and D. Gelernter. (1989) Linda in context. *Communications of the ACM*, 32(4): 444–458.

J. Carter, J. Bennett, and W. Zwaenepoel. (1991) Implementation and performance of Munin. In *Proceedings of the 13th ACM Symposium on Operating System Principles*, pages 152–164.

G. Castagna, G. Ghelli, and G. Longo. (1992) A calculus for overloaded functions with subtyping. In *Proceedings of the ACM Conference on LISP and Functional Programming-LFP*, pages .

M. Castellanos and F. Saltor. (1991) Semantic enrichment of database schemas: An object-oriented approach. In *Proceedings of the 1st International Workshop on Interoperability in Multidatabase Systems*, pages 71–78.

M. Castellanos, F. Saltor and M.García-Solaco. (1991) The development of semantic concepts in BLOOM using an object-oriented metamodel. Report LSI-91-22, Barcelona: U.P.C.

M. Castellanos, F. Saltor, and M. Garcia-Solaco. (1993) A canonical model for the interoperability among object-oriented and relational databases. In this volume.

S. Ceri and S. B. Navathe. (1983) A comprehensive approach to fragmentation and allocation of data in distributed databases. In *Digest of Papers — IEEE COMPCON*, pages 426–431.

S. Ceri and G. Pelagatti. (1984) *Distributed databases: Principles and systems*. New York, NY: McGraw Hill.

S. Ceri, M. Negri, and G. Pelagatti. (1982) Horizontal data partitioning in database design. In *Proceedings of ACM SIGMOD International Conference on Management of Data*, pages 128–136.

S. Ceri, S. B. Navathe, and G. Wiederhold. (1983) Distribution design of logical database schemas. *IEEE Transactions on Software Engineering*, SE-9(5): 487–504.

S. Ceri and J. Widom. (1992) Production rules in parallel and distributed database environments. In *Proceedings of the 18th International Conference on Very Large Data Bases*. San Mateo, CA: Morgan Kaufmann, pages 339–351.

S. Chakravarthy and D. Mishra. (1991) An event specification language (Snoop) for active databases and its detection. Technical Report 91-23, Department of Computer and Information Science, University of Florida.

C. Chambers. (1992) Object-oriented multi-methods in Cecil. In *Proceedings of the European Conference on Object-Oriented Programming (ECOOP)*, pages 33–56.

E. Chang (1989) Effective clustering and buffering in an object-oriented DBMS. Technical Report UCB/CSD/89/515, University of California, Berkeley.

J. Cheng and A. Hurson. (1991) Effective clustering of complex objects in object-oriented databases. In *Proceedings of the ACM SIGMOD International Conference on Management of Data*, pages 22–31.

J. Chomicki and W. Litwin. (1993) Declarative definition of object-oriented multidatabase mappings. In this volume.

P. Christmann, Th. Härder, K. Meyer-Wegener, and A. Sikeler. (1987) Which kinds of OS mechanisms should be provided for database management. In Nehmer, editor, *Experiences with Distributed Systems*, pages 213–251, Berlin: Springer-Verlag.

P.K. Chrysanthis and K. Ramamritham. (1990) ACTA: A framework for specifying and reasoning about transaction structure and behavior. In *Proceedings of ACM SIGMOD International Conference on Management of Data*, pages 194–203.

P.K. Chrysanthis and K. Ramamritham. (1991) A formalism for extended transaction models. In *Proceedings of the 17th International Conference on Very Large Data Bases*. San Mateo, CA: Morgan Kaufmann, pages 103–112.

P.K. Chrysanthis and K. Ramamritham. (1992) ACTA: The SAGA continues. In [Elmagarmid, 1992], pages 349–397.

P.K. Chrysanthis, S. Raghuram, and K. Ramamritham (1991) Extracting concurrency from objects: A methodology. In *Proceedings of the ACM SIGMOD International Conference on Management of Data*, pages 108–117.

P-C. Chu. (1992) A transaction-oriented approach to attribute partitioning. *Information Systems*, 17(4): 329–342.

W. W. Chu and I. T. Ieong. (1991) A transaction-based approach to vertical partitioning for relational databases. Technical report, UCLA.

F.N. Civelek, A. Dogac, and S. Spaccapietra. (1989) An expert system appraoch to view definition and integration. In *Proceedings of the 7th International Conference on Entity-Relationship Approach: A Bridge to the User*, pages 97–117.

S. Cluet, C. Delobel, C. Lécluse, and P. Richard. (1990) RELOOP, an algebra based query language for an object-oriented database system. *Data & Knowledge Engineering*, 5: 333–352.

W. Cockshott, M. Atkinson, K. Chisholm, P. Bailey, and R. Morrison. (1984) Persistent object management system. *Software — Practice and Experience*, 14(1): 49–71.

D. Cohn, P.M. Greenawalt, M.R. Casey, and M.P. Stevenson. (1991) Using kernel-level support for distributed shared data. In *Proceedings of the Symposium on Experiences with Distributed and Multiprocessor Systems*, pages 247–260.

D. Cohn, M. Casey, P. Greenwalt, and J. Saldanha. (1992) A universal distributed programming paradigm for multiple operating systems. In *Proceedings of the Symposium on Experiences with Distributed and Multiprocessor Systems*, pages 191–203.

R. Cole. (1990) A model for security in distributed systems. *Computers & Security*, 9(4): 319–330.

R.C.H. Connor. (1991) *Types and polymorphism in persistent programming systems*. PhD thesis, Department of Computational Science, University of St Andrews.

R.C.H. Connor and R. Morrison. (1992) Subtyping without tears. In *Proceedings of the 15th Australian Computing Science Conference-ACSC-13*, pages 209–225.

R.C.H. Connor, A. Dearle, R. Morrison, and A.L. Brown. (1989) An object addressing mechanism for statically typed languages with multiple inheritance. In *Proceedings of the OOPSLA '89 Conference*, pages 279–285.

R.C.H. Connor, A.L. Brown, Q. Cutts, A. Dearle, R. Morrison, and J. Rosenberg. (1990a) Type equivalence checking in persistent object systems. In [Dearle et al., 1990], pages 154–167.

R.C.H. Connor, A. Dearle, R. Morrison, and A.L. Brown. (1990b) Existentially quantified types as a database viewing mechanism. In *Proceedings of the 2nd International Conference on Extending Database Technology*, pages 301–315.

R.C.H. Connor, D. McNally, and R. Morrison. (1991) Subtyping and assignment in database programming languages. In [Kanellakis and Schmidt, 1991], pages 305–324.

R.C.B. Cooper and K.G. Hamilton. (1985) Preserving abstraction in concurrent programming. Technical Report 76, University of Cambridge Computer Laboratory.

G. Copeland, M. Franklin, and G. Weikum. (1990) Uniform object management. In *Proceedings of the International Conference on Extended Database Technology*, pages 253–268.

D. W. Cornell and P. S. Yu. (1987) A vertical partitioning algorithm for relational databases. In *Proceedings of the 4th International Conference on Data Engineering*, pages 30–35.

H. Corporaal, T. Veldman, and A.J. van de Goor. (1990) An efficient, reference weight–based garbage collection method for distributed systems. In *Proceedings of the International Conference on Databases, Parallel Architectures, and Their Applications (PARBASE-90)*, pages 463–465.

P.L. Curien and G. Ghelli.(1992) Coherence of subsumption. *Mathematical Structures in Computer Science*, 2(1): 55–91.

A. Dan and P. Yu. (1992) Performance analysis of coherency control policies through lock retention. In *Proceedings of the ACM SIGMOD International Conference on Management of Data*, pages 114–123.

S. Danforth and C. Tomlinson. (1988) Type theories and object-oriented programming. *ACM Computing Surveys*, 20(1): 29–72.

S. D. Daniels. (1990) Speaking in tongues: The language of Revelation. Technical Report CSE-91-007, Oregon Graduate Institute.

M. Day. (1993) *Managing a Cache of Swizzled Objects and Surrogates*, Ph.D. Thesis, Department of Electrical Engineering and Computer Science, Massachusetts Institute of Technology (forthcoming).

U. Dayal. (1983) Processing queries over generalization hierarchies in a multidatabase system. In *Proceedings of the 9th International Conference on Very Large Data Bases*. San Mateo, CA: Morgan Kaufmann, pages 342–353.

U. Dayal, B. Blaustein, A. Buchmann, U. Chakravarthy, M. Hsu, R. Ladin, D. McCarthy, A. Rosenthal, S. Sarin, M.J. Carey, M. Livny, and R. Jauhari. (1988a) The HiPAC project: Combining active databases and timing constraints. *ACM SIGMOD Record*, 17(1): 51–70.

U. Dayal, A. Buchmann, and D. McCarthy. (1988b) Rules are objects too: A knowledge model for an active, object-oriented database management system. In [Dittrich, 1988].

U. Dayal. (1989) Queries and views in an object-oriented data model. In *Proceedings of the 2nd International Workshop on Database Programming Languages*, pages 80–102.

U. Dayal., M. Hsu, and R. Ladin. (1990a) Organizing long-running activities with triggers and transactions. In *Proceedings of the ACM SIGMOD International Conference on Management of Data*, pages 204–214.

U. Dayal, F. Manola, A. Buchmann, U. Chakravarthy, D. Goldhirsch, S. Heiler, J. Orenstein, and A. Rosenthal. (1990b) Simplifying complex objects: The PROBE approach to modelling and querying them. In [Zdonik and Maier, 1990], pages 390–399.

U. Dayal, M. Hsu, and R. Ladin. (1991) A transactional model for long-running activities. In *Proceedings of the 17th International Conference on Very Large Data Bases*. San Mateo, CA: Morgan Kaufmann, pages 113–122.

U. Dayal. (1993) Activity/transaction management for a distributed multi-service system. In this volume

A. Dearle. (1989) Environments: A flexible binding mechanism to support system evolution. In *Proceedings of the 22nd Annual Hawaii International Conference on System Sciences*, pages 46–45.

A. Dearle and A.L. Brown. (1988) Safe browsing in a strongly typed persistent environment. *The Computer Journal*, 31(6): 540–544.

A. Dearle, G.M. Shaw, and S.B. Zdonik, editors. (1991) *Implementing Persistent Object Bases: Principles and Practice. Proceedings of the 4th International Workshop on Persistent Object Bases*. San Mateo, CA: Morgan Kaufmann.

A. Dearle, J. Rosenberg, F. Henskens, F. Vaughan, and K. Maciunas. (1992) An examination of operating system support for persistent object systems. In *Proceedings of the 24th Hawaii International Conference on System Sciences*, pages 779–789.

D. Decouchant. (1986), Design of a distributed object manager for the Smalltalk-80 system. In *Proceedings of the OOPSLA '86 Conference*, pages 444–452.

Defence Research Agency. (1991) TDF specification part I. Technical report, United Kingdom's Defence Research Agency.

Defence Research Agency. (1992) TDF facts & figures. Technical report, United Kingdom's Defence Research Agency.

W. Delaney. (1989) *The ARCADE distributed environment: Design, implementation and analysis*. Ph.D. dissertation, Department of Computer Science, University of Notre Dame.

L. DeMichiel and R. Gabriel. (1987) The common Lisp object system: An overview. In *Proceedings of the European Conference on Object-Oriented Programming (ECOOP)*, pages 151–170.

Department of Defence. (1985) *Computer system evaluation criteria DoD 5200-28-STD*. Department of Defence.

O. Deux et al. (1990) The Story of O_2. *IEEE Transactions on Knowledge and Data Engineering*, 2(1): 91–108. [Also appears in Banilhon et al., 1992].

O. Deux et al. (1991) The O_2 system. *Communications of the ACM*, 34(10): 34–48. [Also appears in Banilhon et al., 1992].

D. DeWitt. (1991) Personal communication.

D. DeWitt, P. Futtersack, D. Maier, and F. Velez. (1990) A study of three alternative workstation-server architectures for object-oriented database systems. In *Proceedings of the 16th International Conference on Very Large Data Bases*. San Mateo, CA: Morgan Kaufmann, pages 107–121.

P. Dickman. (1991) Effective load balancing in a distributed object-support operating system. In *Proceedings of the International Workshop on Object Orientation in Operating Systems*, pages 147–153.

P. Dickman. (1992) *Distributed object management in a non-small graph of autonomous networks with few failures*. PhD thesis, University of Cambridge Computer Laboratory.

P. Dickman. (1993a) Optimising weighted reference counts for scalable fault-tolerant distributed object-support systems. In preparation.

P. Dickman. (1993b) The Bellerophon Project: A scalable object- support architecture suitable for a large OODBMS? In this volume.

E. Dijkstra, L. Lamport, A. Martin, and C. Scholten. (1978) On-the-fly garbage collection: An exercise in cooperation. *Communications of the ACM*, 21(11): 966-975.

K.R. Dittrich, editor. (1988) *Advances in object-oriented database systems. Proceedings of the 2nd International Workshop on Object-Oriented Database Systems*. Berlin: Springer-Verlag.

K.R. Dittrich and U. Dayal. (1991) Active database systems (Tutorial Notes). *The 17th International Conference on Very Large Data Bases*.

K. Dittrich, M. Hartig, and H. Pfefferle. (1989) Discretionary access control in structurally object oriented database systems. In C. Landwehr, editor, *Database Security II: Status & Prospects*, pages 105–121, North-Holland.

J. Dollimore, S. Min, E. Miranda, C. Nascimento, D. Steel and W. Xu. (1990) Communicating distributed persistent objects in Smalltalk. *QMW CS Report No. 504*.

J. Dollimore, C. Nascimento, and W. Xu. (1993) Fine grained object migration. In this volume.

W. Du and A. K. Elmagarmid. (1989) Quasi-serializability: A correctness criterion for global concurrency control in InterBase. In *Proceedings of the 15th International Conference on Very Large Data Bases*. San Mateo, CA: Morgan Kaufmann, pages 347–355.

ECMA. (1990) Portable common tool environment — Abstract specification (Standard ECMA-149). Geneva: European Computer Manufacturers Association.

ECMA. (1991) Portable common tool environment — C bindings (Standard ECMA–158). Geneva: European Computer Manufacturers Association.

A. El Abbadi, D. Skeen, and F. Cristian. (1985) An efficient fault-tolerant protocol for replicated data management. In *Proceedings of the 4th Symposium on Principles of Database Systems*, pages 215–219.

A. El Abbadi and S. Toueg. (1986) Maintaining availability in partitioned replicated databases. In *Proceedings of the 5th Symposium on Principles of Database Systems*, pages 240–251.

A. Elmagarmid, editor. (1991) *Bulletin of the IEEE Technical Committee on Data Engineering*, 14(1) (special issue on unconventional transaction management).

A.K. Elmagarmid, editor. (1992) *Database Transaction Models for Advanced Applications*. San Mateo, CA: Morgan Kaufmann.

A.K. Elmagarmid, Y. Leu, W. Litwin, and M. Rusinkiewicz. (1990) A Multidatabase Transaction Model for InterBase. In *Proceedings of the 16th International Conference on Very Large Data Bases*. San Mateo, CA: Morgan Kaufmann, pages 507–518.

R. Elmasri and S. B. Navathe. (1989) *Fundamentals of database systems*. Menlo Park, CA: Benjamin-Cummings.

E.A. Emerson. (1990) Temporal and modal logic. In *Handbook of Theoretical Computer Science, Volume B*, pages 995–1072.

K. Eswaran, J. Gray, R. Lorie, and I. Traiger. (1976) The notion of consistency and predicate locks in a database system. *Communications of the ACM*, 19(11): 624–633.

EXODUS Project. (1991) *EXODUS Storage Manager Architectural Overview*. Univ. of Wisconsin-Madison.

D. Fang and D. McLeod. (1992) A testbed and mechanism for object-based sharing in federated database systems. Technical Report USC-CS-92-507, Computer Science Department, University of Southern California, Los Angeles, California.

D. Fang, J. Hammer, D. McLeod, and A. Si. (1991) Remote-exchange: An approach to controlled sharing among autonomous, heterogenous database systems. In *Digest of papers — IEEE COMPCON*, pages 510–515.

D. Fang, J. Hammer, and D. McLeod. (1993) An approach to behavior sharing in federated database systems. In this volume.

A. Farkas, A. Dearle, G. Kirby, Q. Cutts, R. Morrison, and R. Connor. (1992) Persistent program construction – A new paradigm. In [Albano and Morrison, 1993].

D.H. Fishman, J. Annevelink, D. Beech, E. Chow, T. Connors, J.W. Davis, W. Hasan, C.G. Hoch, W. Kent, S. Leichner, P. Lyngbaek, B. Mahbod, M.A. Neimat, M.C. Risch, T. Shan, and W.K. Wilkinson. (1991) Overview of the Iris DBMS. In W. Kim and F. Lochovsky, editors, *Object-Oriented Concepts, Databases and Applications*, Reading, MA: Addison-Wesley.

D. Fishman, D. Beech, H. Cate, E. Chow, T. Connors, T. Davis, N. Derrett, C. Hoch, W. Kent, P. Lyngbaek, B. Mahbod, M. Neimat, T. Ryan, and M. Shan. (1987) Iris: An object-oriented database management system. *ACM Transactions on Office Information Systems*, 5(1): 48–69.

E. Fong, W. Kent, K. Moore, and C. Thompson, editors. (1991) X3/PARC/DBSSG/OODBTG Final Report. 17 September 1991.

G. Foster and D. Tatar. (1988) Experiments in computer support for teamwork — Colab (Video), Technical Reports, Xerox PARC.

R.J Fowler. (1985) Decentralized object finding using forwarding addresses. Technical Report 85-12-1, Department of Computer Science, University of Washington.

R.J. Fowler. (1986) The complexity of using forwarding addresses for decentralised object finding. In *Proceedings of the 5th Annual ACM Symposium on Principles of Distributed Computing*, pages 108–120.

P. Franaszek and J. T. Robinson. (1985) Limitations of concurrency in transaction processing. *ACM Transactions on Database Systems*, 10(1): 1–28.

M. J. Franklin and M. J. Carey (1993) Client-server caching revisited. In this volume.

M. Franklin, M. Carey, and M. Livny. (1992a) Global memory management in client-server DBMS architectures. In *Proceedings of the 18th International Conference on Very Large Data Bases*. San Mateo, CA: Morgan Kaufmann, pages 596–609.

M. Franklin, M. Zwilling, C. Tan, M. Carey, and D. DeWitt. (1992b) Crash recovery in client-server EXODUS. In *Proceedings of the ACM SIGMOD International Conference on Management of Data*, pages 165–174.

H. Garcia-Molina. (1983) Using semantic knowledge for transaction processing in a distributed database. *ACM Transactions on Database Systems*, 8(2): 186–213.

H. Garcia-Molina and K. Salem. (1987) Sagas. In *Proceedings of ACM SIGMOD International Conference on Management of Data*, pages 249–259.

H. Garcia-Molina, D. Gawlick, J. Klein, C. Kleissner, K. Salem. (1990) Coordinating Multi-Transaction Activities. Technical Report CS-TR-247-90, Department of Computer Science, Princeton University.

H. Garcia-Molina, D. Gawlick, J. Klein, K. Kleissner, and K. Salem. (1991) Modeling Long-Running Activities as Nested Sagas. *Bulletin of the IEEE Technical Committee on Data Engineering*, 14(1): 14–18.

M. García-Solaco and F. Saltor. (1991) Discriminated operations for interoperable databases. In *Proceedings of the 1st International Workshop on Interoperability in Multidatabase Systems*, pages 222–225.

M. García-Solaco, M. Castellanos and F. Saltor. (1992) Discovering interdatabase resemblance of classes for interoperable databases. In *Proceedings of the RIDE-IMS '93 Workshop*.

D. Garvin. (1987) Competing on the eight dimensions of quality. *Harvard Business Review*, 65:101–109.

P. Gautron. (1990) Experience in programming with C++ parameterized types. Technical Report LITP 90.45 RXF, Rank Xerox, Laboratoire Informatique Théorique et Programmation, Université Paris VI, Paris, France.

P. Gautron and M. Shapiro. (1987) Two extensions to C++: A dynamic link editor and inner data. In *Proceedings and Additional papers, C++ Workshop*, pages 23–34.

N.H. Gehani and H.V. Jagadish. (1991) Ode as an active database: Constraints and triggers. In *Proceedings of the 17th International Conference Very Large Data Bases*. San Mateo, CA: Morgan Kaufmann, pages 327–336.

N.H. Gehani, H.V. Jagadish, and O. Shmueli (1992a) Event specification in an active object-oriented database. In *Proceedings of the ACM SIGMOD International Conference on Management of Data*, pages 81–90.

N.H. Gehani, H.V. Jagadish, and O. Shmueli. (1992b) Composite event specification in active databases: Model & implementation. In *Proceedings of the 18th International Conference on Very Large Data Bases*. San Mateo, CA: Morgan Kaufmann, pages 327–338.

J. Geller, Y. Perl, and E.J. Neuhold. (1991) Structural schema integration in heterogeneous multi-database systems using the dual model. In *Proceedings of the 1st International Workshop on Interoperability in Multidatabase Systems*, pages 200–203.

D. Georgakopoulos, M. Hornick, and P. Krychniak. (1992) An environment for specification and management of extended transactions in DOMS. In *Proceedings of the 3rd International RIDE-IMS'93 Workshop*.

S. Ghandeharizadeh, et al. (1991) Design and implementation of OMEGA object-based system. Technical Report USC-CS, Computer Science Department, University of Southern California, Los Angeles, California.

I. Goldstein and D. Bobrow. (1981) An experimental description-based programming environment: Four reports. Technical Report CSL-81-3, Palo Alto, CA: Xerox Palo Alto Research Center.

Y. Gourhant and M. Shapiro. (1990) FOG/C++: A fragmented-object generator. In *Proceedings of the C++ Conference*, pages 63–74.

G. Graefe. (1990a) Volcano, an extensible and parallel dataflow query processing system. Computer Science Technical Report 481, University of Colorado-Boulder. To appear in shortened form in *IEEE Transactions on Knowledge and Data Engineering*.

G. Graefe. (1990b) Encapsulation of parallelism in the Volcano query processing system. In *Proceedings of the 1990 ACM SIGMOD International Conference on Management of Data*, pages 102–111.

G. Graefe and D. DeWitt. (1987) The EXODUS optimizer generator. In *Proceedings of the ACM SIGMOD International Conference on Management of Data*, pages 160–171.

G. Graefe and W. J. McKenna. (1991) The Volcano optimizer generator. Computer Science Technical Report 563, University of Colorado-Boulder.

J. N. Gray. (1979) Notes on database operating systems. In R. Bayer, R. M. Graham, and G. Seegmuller, editors, *Operating Systems — An Advanced Course*, pages 393–481, New York, NY: Springer-Verlag.

J. N. Gray. (1981) Transaction concepts: Virtues and limitations. In *Proceedings of the 7th International Conference on Very Large Data Bases*. San Mateo, CA: Morgan Kaufmann, pages 144–154.

J.N. Gray, R.A. Lorie, G.R. Putzulo, and I.L. Traiger. (1976) Granularity of locks and degrees of consistency in a shared database. In G. M. Nijssen, editor, *Modelling in Data Base Management Systems*, pages 365–394, Amsterdam: North Holland.

J.N. Gray and A. Reuter. (1992) *Transaction Processing: Concepts and Techniques*, San Mateo, CA: Morgan Kaufmann.

O. Gruber and L. Amsaleg. (1993) Object grouping in Eos. In this volume.

O. Gruber, L. Amsaleg, L. Daynès, and P. Valduriez. (1992) EOS, An environment for object-based systems. In *Proceedings of the 25th Hawaii International Conference on System Sciences*, Volume 1, pages 757–768.

A. Gupta, editor. (1989) *Integration of information systems: Bridging heterogeneous databases*. IEEE Press.

J. Guttag. (1980) Notes on type abstraction. *IEEE Transactions on Software Engineering*, 6(1): 13–23.

L. Haas, W. Chang, G. Lohman, J. McPherson, P. F. Wilms, G. Lapis, B. Lindsay, H. Pirahesh, M. J. Carey and E. Shekita. (1990) Starburst mid-flight: As the dust clears. *IEEE Transactions on Knowledge and Data Engineering*, 2(1): 143–160.

S. Habert, L. Mosseri, and V. Abrossimov. (1990) COOL: Kernel support for object-oriented environments. In *Proceedings of the Joint ECOOP/OOPSLA Conference*, pages 269–277.

T. Haerder, K. Meyer-Wegner, K. Mitschang, and A. Sikeler. (1987) PRIMA : A DBMS prototype supporting engineering applications. *In Proceedings of the 7th International Conference on Very Large Data Bases*. San Mateo, CA: Morgan Kaufmann, pages 433–442.

K. G. Hamilton. (1984) *A remote procedure call system*. PhD thesis, University of Cambridge Computer Laboratory.

M. Hammer and D. McLeod. (1981) Database description with SDM: A semantic data model. *ACM Transactions on Database Systems*, 6(3): 351–386.

R. Haskin, Y. Malachi, W. Sawdon, and G. Chan. (1987) Recovery management in Quicksilver. *ACM Transactions on Computer Systems* 6(1): 82–108.

J. Hauser and D. Clausing. (1988) The house of quality. *Harvard Business Review*, 66(3): 63–73.

K.J. Hebel and R.E. Johnson. (1990) Arithmetic and Double Dispatching in Smalltalk-80. *Journal of Object-Oriented Programming*, 2(6): 40–44.

S. Heiler and S. Zdonik. (1990) Object views: Extending the vision. In *Proceedings of the 6th International Conference on Data Engineering*, pages 86–93.

A. Herbert, editor. (1989) *The ANSA reference manual (Release 01.00)*. Architecture Projects Management.

M. Herlihy. (1986) Optimistic concurrency control for abstract data types. In *Proceedings of the ACM Symposium of Principle of Distributed Computing*, pages 206–217.

M. Herlihy. (1987) Extending multiversion time-stamping protocols to exploit type information. *IEEE Transactions on Computers,* 36(4): 443-448.

M.P. Herlihy and W. Weihl. (1988) Hybrid concurrency control for abstract data types. In *Proceedings of the 7th ACM SIGACT-SIGMOD-SIGART Symposium on Principles of Database Systems*, pages 201–210.

M.P. Herlihy and J.M. Wing. (1987) Axioms for concurrent objects. In *Proceedings of the 14th ACM Symposium on Principles of Programming Languages*, pages 13–26.

C.A.R. Hoare. (1975) Recursive data structures. *International Journal of Computer and Information Science*, 4(2): 105–132.

J. A. Hoffer and D. G. Severance. (1975) The use of cluster analysis in physical database design. In *Proceedings of the 1st International Conference on Very Large Data Bases*, pages 69–86.

M. Hornick and S. Zdonik. (1987) A shared, segmented memory system for an object-oriented database. *ACM Transactions on Office Information Systems* 5(1) 70–95:

W. Hou, G. Ozsoyoglu, and B.K. Taneja. (1989) Processing aggregate relational queries with hard time constraints. In *Proceedings of the ACM SIGMOD International Conference on Management of Data*, pages 68–67.

J. Howard, M. Kazar, S. Menees, D. Nichols, M. Satyanarayanan, R. Sidebotham, and M. West. (1988) Scale and performance in a distributed file system. *ACM Transactions on Computer Systems* 6(1): 51–81.

M. Hsu, R. Ladin, and D. McCarthy. (1988) An Execution Model for Active Database Management System. In *Proceedings of the 3rd International Conference on Data and Knowledge Bases*, pages 171–179.

M. Hsu, A. Ghoneimy, and C. Kleissner. (1991) An Execution Model for an Activity Management System. In *Proceedings of the Workshop on High Performance Transaction Systems..*

S. Hudson and R. King. (1989) CACTIS : A self-adaptative, concurrent implementation of an object-oriented database management system. *ACM Transactions on Database Systems*, 14(3): 291–321.

J. Hughes. (1985) A distributed garbage collection algorithm. In *Proceedings of the Conference on Functional Languages and Computer Architecture*, pages 256–271.

R. Hull and R. King. (1987) Semantic database modeling: Survey, applications, and research issues. *ACM Computing Surveys*, 19(3): 201–260.

R. Hull, R. Morrison and D. Stemple, editors. (1989). *Database Programming Languages. Proceedings of the Second International Workshop on Database Programming Languages.* San Mateo, CA: Morgan Kaufmann.

R. Hull and M. Yoshikawa. (1990) ILOG: Declarative creation and manipulation of object identifiers. In *Proceedings of the International Conference on Very Large Data Bases*, pages 455–468.

D. J. Hwang. (1987) Constructing a highly-available location service for a distributed environment. Technical Report MIT/LCS/TR-410, M.I.T. Laboratory for Computer Science.

D. J. Hwang. (1993) *Indexing for fast associative access to large object sets.* Ph.D. Thesis, Department of Electrical Engineering and Computer Science, Massachusetts Institute of Technology (forthcoming).

IBM. (1991) *OS/2 2.0 Technical library, system object model guide and reference*, IBM.

H.V. Jagadish and X. Qian. (1992) Integrity maintenance in an object-oriented database. In *Proceedings of the 18th International Conference on Very Large Data Bases.* San Mateo, CA: Morgan Kaufmann, pages 469–480.

J.V. Jagadish and O. Shmueli. (1993) Synchronizing trigger events in a distributed object-oriented database. In this volume.

J.B. Johnston. (1971) The contour model of block structure processes. *ACM SIGPLAN Notices*, 6(2): 56–82.

E. Jul, H. Levy, N. Hutchinson, and A. Black. (1988) Fine-grained mobility in the Emerald system. *ACM Transactions on Computer Systems*, 6(1): 109–133.

T. Kaehler and G. Krasner. (1990) LOOM-Large object-oriented memory for Smalltalk-80 systems. In [Zdonik and Maier, 1990], pages 298–307,

K. Kahn and M. Miller. (1988) Language design and open systems, In B. Huberman, editor, *The Ecology of Computation.* North Holland.

P. Kanellakis and J. W. Schmidt, editors. (1991) *Database Programming Languages: Bulk Types & Persistent Data. Proceedings of the 3rd International Workshop on Database Programming Languages*, San Mateo, CA: Morgan Kaufmann.

K. Karlapalem, S.B. Navathe, and M.M.A. Morsi. (1993) Issues in distribution design of object-oriented databases. In this volume.

M. Kaul, K. Drosten, and E. J. Neuhold. (1990) ViewSystem: Integrating heterogeneous information bases by object-oriented views. In *Proceedings of the 6th International Conference on Data Engineering*, pages 2–10.

T. F. Keefe, W.T. Tsai, and M.B. Thuraisingham. (1989) SODA: A secure object oriented database system. *Computers & Security*, 8(6): 517–533.

T. Keller, G. Graefe and D. Maier. (1991) Efficient assembly of complex objects. In *Proceedings of the 1991 ACM SIGMOD International Conference on Management of Data*, pages 148–157.

U. Kelter. (1990) Group-oriented discretionary access controls for distributed structurally object-oriented database Systems. In *Proceedings of the European Symposium on Research in Computer Security*, pages 23–33.

U. Kelter. (1992a) H-PCTE — A high-performance object management system for system development environments. In *Proceedings of the COMPSAC'92 Conference*, pages 45–50.

U. Kelter. (1992b) Type-level access controls for distributed structurally object-oriented database systems. In *Proceedings of the European Symposium on Research in Computer Security*, to appear.

U. Kelter. (1993) Distribution of schemata in H-PCTE. In this volume.

G. Kelley. (1991) Personal communication.

W. Kent. (1991a) The breakdown of the information model in multi-database systems. *ACM SIGMOD Record*, 20(4): 10–15.

W. Kent. (1991b) Solving domain mismatch and schema mismatch problems with an object-oriented database programming language. In *Proceedings of the International Conference on Very Large Data Bases*, pages 147–160.

M.L. Kersten. (1990) Large scale handling of complex objects. In *Proceedings of the International AI Symposium 90*, pages 151–158

M.L. Kersten. (1991) Goblin: A DBPL designed for advanced database applications. In *Proceedings of the 2nd International Conference on Database and Expert Systems Applications*, pages 345–349.

M.L. Kersten. (1992) A modular conditional term rewriter for compiling DBPL programs. In *Proceedings of the International Workshop on Compiler Construction*, in press.

M.L. Kersten, P.M.G. Apers, M.A.W. Houtsma, E.J.A. van Kuyk, and R.L.W. van de Weg. (1988) A distributed, main-memory database machine; Research Issues and a preliminary architecture. In M. Kitsuregawa and H. Janakal, editors, *Database Machines and Knowledge Base Machines*, pages 353–369, North-Holland.

M.L. Kersten, S. Shair-Ali, and C.A. vd Berg. (1990) Performance analysis of a dynamic query processing scheme. Tecnical Report CS-R9050, CWI, Amsterdam.

M.L. Kersten, M.H. vd Voort, C.A. vd Berg, A.P.J.M. Siebes, C. Thieme, and S. Plomp. (1992) The goblin database programming language. Technical Report CS-R9209, CWI, Amsterdam.

M.L. Kersten, S. Plomp, and C.A. van der Berg. (1993) Object management in Goblin. In this volume.

S. Khoshafian, G. Copeland, T. Jadodits, H. Boral, and P. Valduriez. (1987) A query processing strategy for the decomposed storage model. In *Proceedings of the 3rd International Conference on Data Engineering*, pages 636–643.

G. Kiczales, J. des Rivières, and D. G. Bobrow. (1991) *The art of the metaobject protocol*, Cambridge, MA: MIT Press.

G. Kiczales, M. Theimer, and B. Welch. (1992) A new model of abstraction for operating system design. In*Proceedings of the 2nd International Workshop on Object Orientation in Operating Systems*, pages 346–349.

M. Kifer and G. Lausen. (1989) F-Logic: A higher-order language for reasoning about object, inheritance, and scheme. In *Proceedings of the ACM SIGMOD International Conference on Management of Data*, pages 134–146.

M. Kifer and J. Wu. (1989) A logic for object-oriented programming (Maier's O-Logic: Revisited). In *Proceedings of the ACM SIGACT-SIGMOD-SIGART Symposium on Principles of Database Systems*, pages 379–393.

M. Kifer, G. Lausen, and J. Wu. (1990) Logical foundations of object-oriented and frame-based languages. Technical Report, Department of Computer Science, SUNY at Stony Brook. (To appear in *Journal of the ACM*).

M. Kifer, W. Kim, and Y. Sagiv. (1992) Querying object-oriented databases. In *Proceedings of the ACM SIGMOD International Conference on Management of Data*, pages 393–402.

W. Kim. (1989) A model of queries for object-oriented databases. In *Proceedings of the 15th International Conference on Very Large Databases.* San Mateo, CA: Morgan Kaufmann, pages 423–432.

W. Kim. (1990) *Introduction to object-oriented databases.* Cambridge, MA: MIT Press.

W. Kim and J. Seo. (1991) Classifying schematic and data heterogeneity in multidatabase systems. *Computer*, 24(12): 12–18.

W. Kim, J. Banerjee, H. Chou, J. Garza, and D. Woelk. (1987) Composite objects support in an object-oriented database system. In *Proceedings of the OOPSLA'87 Conference*, pages 118–125.

W. Kim, E. Bertino, and J. Garza. (1989) Composite objects revisited. In *Proceedings of ACM SIGMOD International Conference on Management of Data*, pages 423–432.

W. Kim, J. Garza, N. Ballou, and D. Woelk. (1990) Architecture of the ORION next-generation database system. *IEEE Transactions on Knowledge Data Engineering*, 2(1): 109– 117.

W.F. King. (1980) Future directions in data base management systems. In B. Shaw, editor, *Data Base Systems. Proceedings of the Joint IBM/University of Newcastle upon Tyne Seminar*, page 129.

G. Kirby. (1992) Persistent programming with type-safe linguistic reflection. In *Proceedings of the 25th Hawaii International Conference on System Sciences*, pages 820–831.

G. Kirby, R. Connor, Q. Cutts, A. Dearle, A. Farkas, and R. Morrison. (1992) Persistent hyper-programs. In [Albano and Morrison, 1993].

W. Klas, E. Neuhold and M. Schrefl. (1990) Metaclasses in VODAK and their application in database integration. In *Arbeitspapiere der GMD No.462*, GMD.

J. Klein. (1991) Advanced Rule Driven Transaction Management. In *Digest of Papers — IEEE COMPCON*, pages 562–567.

J. Klein and A. Reuter (1988) Migrating transactions. In *Proceedings of the Future Trends in Distributed Computer Systems in the '90s Conference.*

H.F. Korth. (1983) Locking primitives in a database system. *Journal of the ACM*, 30(1): 55–79.

H.F. Korth and G. Speegle. (1988) Formal models of correctness without serializability. In *Proceedings of the ACM SIGMOD International Conference on Management of Data*, pages 379–386.

H.F. Korth and G. Speegle. (1990) Encapsulation of transaction management in object databases. In *Proceedings of the OOPSLA/ECOOP'90 Workshop on Transactions and Objects*, pages 27–32.

H.F. Korth, W. Kim, and F. Bancilhon. (1988) On long-duration CAD transactions. *Information Sciences*, 46(1-2): 73–107.

H.F. Korth, E. Levy, and A. Silberschatz. (1990a) Compensating transactions: A new recovery paradigm. In *Proceedings of the 16th International Conference on Very Large Data Bases.* San Mateo, CA: Morgan Kaufmann, pages 95–106.

H.F. Korth, N. Soparkar, and A. Silberschatz. (1990b) Triggered real-time databases with consistency constraints. In *Proceedings of the 16th International Conference on Very Large Data Bases.* San Mateo, CA: Morgan Kaufmann, pages 71–82.

R. Krishnamurthy, W. Litwin, and W. Kent. (1991) Language features for interoperability of databases with schematic discrepancies. In *Proceedings of the ACM SIGMOD International Conference on Management of Data*, pages 40–49.

D. Kulkarni. (1991) *Nested Transaction Support for Reliable Distributed Applications.* MS Thesis, Department of Computer Science, University of Notre Dame.

D. Kulkarni, A. Banerji, M.R. Casey and D.L. Cohn. (1992) Distribution and persistence: Natural outgrowths of the ARCADE data model. In *Proceedings of the International Workshop on Object-Oriented Operating Systems*, pages 311–318.

D.C. Kulkarni, A. Banerji and D.L. Cohn. (1993) Operating System Support for Cooperation in Distributed OODBs. In this volume.

H.T. Kung and J.T. Robinson. (1981) On optimistic methods for concurrency control. *ACM Transactions on Database Systems*, 6(2): 213–226.

C. Laasch and M.H. Scholl. (1992) Generic update operations keeping object-oriented databases consistent. In *Proceedings of the 2nd GI Workshop on Information Systems and Artificial Intelligence (IS/KI)*, pages 40–55.

C. Lamb, G. Landis, J. Orenstein, and D. Weinreb. (1991) The ObjectStore database system, *Communications of the ACM*, 34(10): 34–48.

R. Ladin. (1989) *A method for constructing highly available services and a technique for distributed garbage collection.* Ph.D. Thesis, Department of Electrical Engineering and Computer Science, Massachusetts Institute of Technology.

R. Ladin and B. Liskov. (1986) Highly-available distributed services and fault-tolerant distributed garbage collection. *In Proceedings of the 5th ACM Symposium on Principles of Distributed Computing*, pages 29–39.

L. Lamport. (1983) Specifying concurrent program module. *ACM Transactions on Programming Languages and Systems*, 5(2): 190–222.

L. Lamport. (1986) *LaTeX: A document preparation system.* Reading, MA: Addison-Wesley.

T. Landers and R.L. Rosenberg. (1982) An overview of Multibase. In H.-J. Schneider, editor, *Distributed Databases*, pages 153–184, North-Holland.

P. LaRowe, C. Ellis, and L. Kaplan. (1991) The robustness of NUMA memory management. In *Proceedings of the 13th ACM Symposium on Operating System Principles*, pages 137–151.

J. A. Larson, S. B. Navathe, and R. Elmasri. (1989) A theory of attribute equivalence in databases with applications to schema integration. *IEEE Transactions on Software Engineering*, 15(4): 449–463.

R. Lea, P. Amaral, and C. Jaquemot. (1991) COOL-2: An object oriented support platform built above the Chorus micro-kernel. In *Proceedings of the International Workshop on Object Orientation in Operating Systems*, pages 68–72.

C. Lecluse, P. Richard, and F. Velez. (1988) 0_2, An object-oriented data model. In *Proceedings of the ACM SIGMOD International Conference on Management of Data*, pages 424–433.

B. Lewis and D. LaLiberte. (1990) *GNU Emacs Lisp reference manual.* Cambridge, MA: Free Software Foundation.

K. Li and P. Hudak. (1989) Memory coherence in shared virtual memory systems. *ACM Transactions on Computer Systems*, 7(4): 321–359.

S. Lippman. (1991) *C++ Primer*. Reading, MA: Addison-Wesley.

B. Liskov. (1984) Overview of the ARGUS language and system. Technical Report MIT Programming Methodology Group Memo 40, MIT.

B. Liskov. (1988) Distributed programming in Argus. *Communications of the ACM*, 31(3): 300–312.

B. Liskov. (1991) Challenges in distributed systems. In A. Meyer et. al., editors, *Research Directions in Computer Science: An MIT Perspective*, pages 52–74, Cambridge, MA: MIT Press.

B. Liskov. (1992) Preliminary design of the Thor object-oriented database system. Programming Methodology Group Memo 74, MIT Laboratory for Computer Science.

B. Liskov and W. Weihl. (1986) Specifications of distributed programs. *Distributed Computing*, 1(2): 102–118.

B. Liskov, R. Atkinson, T. Bloom, E. Moss, J.C. Schaffert, R. Scheifler, and A. Snyder. (1981) *CLU reference manual*, New York, NY: Springer-Verlag.

B. Liskov, D. Curtis, P. Johnson and R. Scheifler. (1987) Implementation of Argus. In *Proceedings of the 11th ACM Symposium on Operating Systems Principles*, pages 111–122.

B. Liskov, T. Bloom, D. Gifford, R. Scheifler, W. Weihl. (1988) Communication in the Mercury system. In *Proceedings of the 21st Hawaii International Conference on System Sciences*, pages 178–187.

B. Liskov, S. Ghemawat, R. Gruber, P. Johnson, L. Shrira, and M. Williams. (1991a) Replication in the Harp file system. In *Proceedings of the 13th ACM Symposium on Operating Systems Principles,* pages 226–238.

B. Liskov, L. Shrira, and J. Wroclawski. (1991b) Efficient at-most-once messages based on synchronous clocks. *ACM Transactions on Computer Systems*, 9(2): 125–142.

B. Liskov, M. Day, and L. Shrira. (1993) Distributed object management in Thor. In this volume.

W. Litwin, L. Mark, and N. Roussopoulos. (1990) Interoperability of multiple autonomous databases. *ACM Computing Surveys*, 22(3): 267–293.

M. Livny. (1988) *DeNet User's Guide*, Version 1.0, Computer Science Department, University of Wisconsin-Madison.

G.M. Lohman, B. Lindsay, H. Pirahesh, and B. Schiefer. (1991) Extensions to Starburst: Objects, types, functions, and rules. *Communications of the ACM*, 34(10): 94–109.

T.F. Lunt. (1990) Multilevel security for object oriented database systems. In D. L. Spooner and C. E. Landwehr, editors, *Database Security III: Status & Prospects*, pages 190–209, North-Holland.

N.A. Lynch. (1983) Multilevel atomicity — A new correctness for database concurrency control. *ACM Transactions on Database Systems*, 8(4): 484–502.

G.H. MacEwen. (1987) Effects of distributed system technology on database security: A survey. In C. E. Landwehr, editor, *Database Security & Prospects*, pages 253–261, North Holland.

P. Madany and R. Campbell. (1992) Organizing and typing persistent objects within an object-oriented framework. In *Proceedings of the 25th Hawaii International Conference on System Sciences*, pages 800–809.

P. Maes. (1987) *Computational reflection.* Ph.D. Dissertation, Vrije Universiteit.

U. Maheshwari. (1992) *Distributed garbage collection in a client-server transaction system.* Master's Thesis, Department of Electrical Engineering and Computer Science, Massachusetts Institute of Technology (forthcoming).

D. Maier. (1986) A logic of objects. In *Proceedings of the Workshop on Deductive Databases and Logic Programming*.

D. Maier and J. Stein. (1986) Indexing in an object-oriented DBMS. In *Proceedings of the International Workshop on Object-Oriented Database Systems*, pages 171–182.

D. Maier, J. Stein, A. Otis, and A. Purdy. (1986) Development of an object-oriented DBMS. In *Proceedings of the OOPSLA '86 Conference*, pages 472–482.

D. Maier, G. Graefe, L. Shapiro, S. Daniels, T. Keller, and B. Vance. (1993) Issues in distributed object assembly. In this volume.

M. Makpangou, Y. Gourhant, and M. Shapiro. (1991a) BOAR: A library of fragmented object types for distributed abstractions. In *Proceedings of the International Workshop on Object-Orientation in Operating Systems*, pages 164–168.

M. Makpangou, et. al. (1991b) *Structuring distributed applications as fragmented objects.* Technical Report 1404, INRIA.

M. Makpangou, Y. Gourhant, J. Le Narzul, and M. Shapiro. (1992) Fragmented objects for distributed abstractions. *IEEE Transactions on Software Engineering*, to appear.

M. Makpangou, Y. Gourhant, J.P Le Narzul, and M. Shapiro. (1993) Fragmented objects for distributed abstractions. In T. L. Casavant and M. Singhal, editors, *Advances in Distributed Computing: Concepts and Design*. IEEE Computer Society Press.

F. Manola. (1988) Distributed object management technology. Technical Report TM-0014-06-88-165, Waltham, MA: GTE Laboratories Incorporated.

F. Manola. (1989) Object model capabilities for distributed object management. Technical Report TM-0149-06-89-165, Waltham, MA: GTE Laboratories Incorporated.

F. Manola and U. Dayal. (1990) PDM: An object-oriented data model. In [Zdonik and Maier, 1990], pages 209–215.

F. Manola, S. Heiler, D. Georgakopoulos, M. Hornick, and M. Brodie. (1992) Distributed object management. *International Journal of Intelligent and Cooperative Information Systems*, 1(1): 5–42.

F. Manola and S. Heiler. (1993) An approach to interoperable object models. In this volume.

A. Margaret and B. Stroustrup. (1990) *The annotated C++ reference manual*. Reading, MA: Addison-Wesley.

B. Martin. (1987) Modeling concurrent activities with nested objects. In *Proceedings of the 7th International Conference on Distributed Computing Systems*, pages 432–439.

B. Martin. (1988a) *Concurrent nested object computations*. PhD thesis, University of California at San Diego, La Jolla, California.

B.E. Martin. (1988b) Scheduling protocols for nested objects. Technical Report CS-094, Department of Computer Science and Engineering, University of California, San Diego.

B.E. Martin and C. Pedersen. (1993) Long-lived concurrent activities. In this volume.

H.H. Mashburn and M. Satyanarayanan. (1992) RVM: Recoverable virtual memory. Technical Report, School of Computer Science, Carnegie Mellon University.

F. Mattern. (1988) Timestamps in message-passing systems that preserve the partial ordering. In *Proceedings of the International Conference on Parallel and Distributed Algorithms*, pages .

F. Matthes. (1992) *Generic database programming: A linguistic and architectural framework*. PhD thesis, Fachbereich Informatik, Universität Hamburg, Germany (in German).

F. Matthes and J.W. Schmidt. (1991) Bulk data types; built-in or added-on? In [Kanellakis and Schmidt, 1991], pages 33–54.

F. Matthes and J.W. Schmidt. (1992) Preliminary definition of the Tycoon language TL. DBIS Tycoon Report 062-92, Fachbereich Informatik, Universität Hamburg, Germany.

S. Mehrotra, R. Rastogi, H. Korth, and A. Silberschatz. (1991) Non-serializable executions in heterogeneous distributed database systems. In *Proceedings of the 1st International Conference on Parallel and Distributed Information Systems*, pages 245–252.

B. Meyer. (1988) *Object-oriented software construction*. Englewood Cliffs, NJ: Prentice Hall.

D. L. Mills. (1988) Network time protocol (version 1) specification and implementation. RFC 1059, DARPA-Internet.

R. Milner, M. Tofte, and R. Harper. (1990) *The definition of standard ML*, Cambridge, MA: MIT Press.

E. Miranda. (1987) BrouHaHa — A portable Smalltalk interpreter. In *Proceedings of OOPSLA Conference*, pages 354–365.

R. Morrison, A.L. Brown, R. Carrick, R.C.H. Connor, A. Dearle, and M.P. Atkinson. (1990) The Napier type system. In [Rosenberg and Koch, 1990], pages 3–18.

R. Morrison, A. Dearle, R.C.H. Connor, and A.L. Brown. (1991) An ad hoc approach to the implementation of polymorphism. *ACM Transactions on Programming Languages and Systems*, 13(3): 342–371.

M. Morsi, S. Navathe, and H.-J. Kim. (1991) A schema management and prototyping interface for an object-oriented database environment. In *Proceedings of the IFIP Working Conference on the Object Oriented Approach in Information Systems*, pages 157–181.

M. Morsi, S. Navathe, and H.-J. Kim. (1992) An extensible object-oriented database testbed. In *Proceedings of the 8th International Conference on Data Engineering*, pages 150–157.

J.E.B. Moss. (1985) *Nested transactions: An approach to reliable distributed computing.* Cambridge, MA: The MIT Press.

J.E.B. Moss. (1989) Addressing large distributed collections of persistent objects: The Mneme project's approach. In [Hull, et al., 1989], pages 358–374.

J.E.B. Moss. (1990) Design of the Mneme persistent object store. *ACM Transactions on Information Systems* 8(2): 103–139.

J.E.B. Moss. (1991) Simple and flexible consistency management in distributed persistent object systems. Unpublished position paper presented at the *Workshop on Objects in Large Distributed Applications* held at OOPSLA'91.

J.E.B. Moss, N. Griffeth, and M. Graham. (1986) Abstraction in recovery management. In *Proceedings of the ACM SIGMOD International Conference on Management of Data*, pages 72–83.

A. Motro. (1987) Superviews: virtual integration of multiple databases. *IEEE Transactions on Software Engineering*, 13(7) 785–798:

S.J. Mullender and A.S. Tanenbaum. (1986) The Design of a capability-based distributed operating system. *The Computer Journal*, 29(4): 289–300.

J. Muthuraj, S. Chakravarthy, R. Varadarajan, and S. B. Navathe. (1993) A formal approach to the vertical partitioning problem in distributed database design. In *Proceedings of the 2nd International Conference on Parallel and Distributed Information Systems*, pages .

T. Nakajima. (1990) *Atomicity in multiversion objects.* Ph.D Thesis, Keio University.

T. Nakajima and H. Tokuda. (1992) Implementation of scheduling policies in real-time Mach. In *Proceeding of the 2nd International Workshop on Object-Oriented Operating Systems*, pages 165–169.

T. Nakajima. (1993) Commutativity-based concurrency control and recovery for multiversion objects. In this volume.

S. B. Navathe and M. Ra. (1989) Vertical partitioning for database design: A graphical algorithm. In *Proceedings of ACM SIGMOD International Conference on Management of Data*, pages 440–450.

S. B. Navathe, S. Ceri, G. Wiederhold, and J. Dou. (1984) Vertical partitioning algorithms for database design. *ACM Transactions on Database Systems*, 9(4): 680–710.

S. B. Navathe, M. Ra, R. Varadarajan, K. Karlapalem, and K. Sreewastav. (1990) A mixed partitioning methodology for distributed database design. Technical Report, University of Florida.

M. Nelson, B. Welch, and J. Ousterhout. (1988) Caching in the Sprite network file system. *ACM Transactions on Computer Systems*, 6(1): 135–154.

S.M. Nettles and J.M. Wing. (1992) Persistence + Undoability = Transactions. In *Proceedings of the 25th Annual Hawaii International Conference on System Sciences, Vol. II*, pages 832–843.

E.J. Neuhold and M. Schrefl. (1988) Dynamic derivation of personalized views. In *Proceedings of the 14th International Conference on Very Large Data Bases*. San Mateo, CA: Morgan Kaufmann, pages 183–194.

T.P. Ng. (1989) Using histories to implement atomic objects. *ACM Transactions on Computer Systems*, 7(4): 360–393.

R.S. Nikhil. (1988) Functional databases, functional languages. In M.P. Atkinson, O.P. Buneman, and R. Morrison, editors, *Data Types and Persistence*, pages 51–67, New York, NY: Springer-Verlag, .

W. Nitzberg and V. Lo. (1991) Distributed shared memory: A survey of issues and algorithms. *Computer*, 24(8): 52–60.

G.M. Nyanchama and S.L. Osborn. (1991) Orthogonal views in object oriented database security. Technical Report # 308, Department of Computer Science, The University of Western Ontario, London, Canada.

A. Ohori, I. Tabkha, R.C.H. Connor, and P.C. Philbrow. (1990) Persistence and type abstraction revisited. In [Dearle, et al., 1990], pages 141–153.

B.M. Oki and B. Liskov. (1988) Viewstamped replication: A new primary copy method to support highly-available distributed systems. In *Proceedings of the 7th ACM Symposium on Principles of Distributed Computing*, pages 8–17.

OMG. (1991) The common object request broker: Architecture and specification. OMG Document Number 91.12.1, Rev. 1.1, Framingham, MA: Object Management Group.

P.E. O'Neil. (1986) The escrow transactional method. *ACM Transactions on Database Systems*, 11(4): 405–430.

M.T. Özsu and P. Valduriez. (1991a) *Principles of distributed database systems*. Englewood Cliffs, NJ: Prentice-Hall.

M. T. Özsu and P. Valduriez. (1991b) Distributed database systems: Where are we now? *Computer*, 24(8): 68–78.

M.T. Özsu and P. Valduriez. (1993) Distributed data management: Unsolved problems and new issues. In T. Casavant and M. Singhal, editors, *Readings in Distributed Computing Systems*, IEEE Computer Society Press.

M. Palmer and S. Zdonik. (1990) Predictive caching. Report CS-90-29, Department of Computer Science, Brown University, Providence, RI.

Perihelion. (1992) *Polyhedra application generation environment, Version 2.0*. Somerset, England: Perihelion Technology Ltd.

G. Pernul, K. Karlapalem and S.B. Navathe. (1991) Relational database organization based on views and fragments. In *Proceedings of the 2nd International Conference on Data and Expert Systems Applications (DEXA'91)*.

R.J. Peters, M.T. Özsu, and D. Szafron. (1992) TIGUKAT: An object model for query and view support in object database systems. Technical Report TR92-14, University of Alberta, Edmonton, Canada.

L.L. Peterson, N.C. Bucholz, and R.D. Schlichting. (1989) Preserving and using context information in interprocess communication. *ACM Transactions on Computer Systems*, 7(3): 217–246.

M.M.L. Petrie, E. Gudes, H. Song, and E. Fernandez. (1990) Security in object oriented database systems. In D. L. Spooner and C. E. Landwehr, editors, *Database Security III: Status & Prospects*, pages 257–268, North-Holland.

J.M. Piquer. (1991) Indirect reference-counting, a distributed garbage collection algorithm. In *Proceedings of the PARLE'91 Conference, Vol. I*, pages 150–165.

C. Pu and A. Leff. (1991) Replica control in distributed systems: An asynchronous approach. In *Proceedings of the ACM SIGMOD International Conference on Management of Data*, pages 377–386.

C. Pu, G.E. Kaiser, and N. Hutchinson. (1988) Split-transactions for open-ended activities. In *Proceedings of the 14th International Conference on Very Large Data Bases*. San Mateo, CA: Morgan Kaufmann, pages 26–37.

F. Rabitti, E. Bertino, D. Woelk, and W. Kim. (1991) A model of authorization for next generation database systems. *ACM Transactions on Database Systems*, 16(1): 88–131.

K. Ramamritham. (1993) Real-time databases. *Distributed and Parallel Databases*, 1(2): 199–226.

K. Ramamritham and P.K. Chrysanthis. (1993) In search of acceptability criteria: Database consistency requirements and transaction correctness properties. In this volume.

K. Ramamritham and C. Pu. (1992) A formal characterization of epsilon serializability. Technical Report 92-21, Department of Computer and Information Science, University of Massachusetts.

K. Ramamritham, P.K. Chrysanthis, and A. Buchmann. (1991) Degrees of consistency — Specification and maintenance. Technical Report, Computer Science Department, University of Massachusetts.

A. Reuter. (1989) Contracts: A Means for Extending Control Beyond Transaction Boundaries. In *Proceedings of the International Workshop on High Performance Transaction Systems*.

J. Richardson and M. Carey (1987) Programming constructs for database system implementation in EXODUS. In *Proceedings of the ACM SIGMOD International Symposium on Management of Data*, pages 208–219.

J. Richardson and P. Schwartz. (1991) Aspects: Extending objects to support multiple, independent roles. In *Proceedings of the ACM SIGMOD International Conference on Management of Data*, pages 298–307.

D. Ritchie and K. Thompson. (1974) The UNIX time-sharing system. *Communications of the ACM*, 17(7): 365–375.

M. Riveill. (1992) An overview of the Guide language. In *Proceedings of the 2nd Workshop on Objects in Large Distributed Applications*.

J. Rosenberg and D. Koch, editors. (1990) *Persistent Object Systems: Their Design, Implementation and Use. Proceedings of the 3rd International Workshop on Persistent Object Systems*. Springer-Verlag.

L. A. Rowe and M. Stonebraker. (1987) The POSTGRES data model. In *Proceedings of the 13th International Conference on Very Large Data Bases*. San Mateo, CA: Morgan Kaufmann, pages 83–96.

J. Richardson and P. Schwartz. (1991) Aspects: Extending objects to support multiple, independent roles. In *Proceedings of the ACM SIGMOD International Conference on Management of Data*, pages 298–307.

J. Rosenberg and J.L. Keedy, editors. (1990) *Security and Persistence. Proceedings of the International Workshop on Computer Architectures to Support Security and Persistence of Information*. New York, NY: Springer-Verlag.

M. Ruffin. (1992) Kitlog: A generic logging service. Rapport de Recherche 1678, INRIA, Rocquencourt, France.

M. Rusinkiewicz, A. Elmagarmid, Y. Leu, and W. Litwin. (1990) Extending the transaction model to capture more meaning. *ACM SIGMOD Record*, 19(1): 3–7.

M. Rusinkiewicz, A. Sheth, and G. Karabatis. (1991) Specification of dependencies for the management of interdependent data. *Computer*, 12(12): 46–54.

F. Saltor, M. Castellanos and M. García–Solaco. (1991) Suitability of data models as canonical models for federated databases. *ACM SIGMOD Record*, 20(4): 44–48.

F. Saltor, M. Castellanos and M. García-Solaco. (1992) Overcoming schematic discrepancies in interoperable databases. In *Proceedings of the DS-5 Semantics of Interoperable Database Systems*, pages 185–198.

R. W. Scheifler and J. Gettys. (1983) The X window system. *ACM Transactions on Graphics*, 16(8): 57–69.

M.H. Scholl and H.-J. Schek. (1990) A relational object model. In *Proceedings of the International Conference on Database Theory*, pages 89–105, Berlin: Springer-Verlag

426 M.H. Scholl, C. Laasch, and M. Tresch. (1991) Updatable views in object-oriented databases. In *Proceedings of the 2nd Int'l Conf. on Deductive and Object-Oriented Databases*, pages 189–207, Berlin: Springer-Verlag.

M.H. Scholl, C. Laasch, C. Rich, H.-J. Schek, and M. Tresch. (1992) The COCOON object model. Technical report, ETH Zürich, Deptartment of Computer Science.

H. Schorr and W. Waite. (1967) An efficient machine-independent procedure for garbage collection in various list structures. *Communications of the ACM*, 10(8): 501–506.

M. Schrefl. (1988) *Object-Oriented Database Integration.* PhD thesis, Technische Universität Wien, Österreich.

M. Schrefl and E. Neuhold. (1988) Object class definition by generalization using upward inheritance. In *Proceedings of the 4th International Conference on Data Engineering*, pages 4–13.

P. Z. Schwartz. (1984) Transactions on typed object. Technical Report CMU-CS-82-143, Carnegie Mellon University.

P. Schwarz and A. Spector. (1984) Synchronizing shared abstract types. *ACM Transactions on Computer Systems*, 2(3): 223–250.

L. Sha. (1985) *Modular concurrency control and failure recovery — Consistency, correctness and optimality.* PhD thesis, Department of Computer and Electrical Engineering, Carnegie-Mellon University.

K. Shannon and R. Snodgrass. (1991) Semantic clustering. In [Dearle et al., 1991], pages 389–402.

M. Shapiro. (1986) Structure and encapsulation in distributed systems: The proxy principle. In *Proceedings of the 6th International Conference on Distributed Computer Systems*, pages 198–204.

M. Shapiro. (1990) Object-support operating systems. In *Proceedings of the Workshop on Operating Systems and Object Orientation at ECOOP/OOPSLA 1990.*

M. Shapiro. (1991) Soul: An object-oriented OS framework for object support. In *Proceedings of the Workshop on Operating Systems for the Nineties and Beyond*, Springer-Verlag, pages 251–255.

M. Shapiro. (1993) Operating system support for distributed and persistent objects. In this volume.

M. Shapiro, P. Gautron, and L. Mosseri. (1989a) Persistence and migration for C++ objects. In *Proceedings of the European Conference on Object-oriented Programming (ECOOP)*, pages 191–204.

M. Shapiro, Y. Gourhant, S. Habert, L. Mosseri, M. Ruffin, and C. Valot. (1989b) SOS: An object-oriented operating system — Assessment and perspectives. *Computing Systems*, 2(2): 287–338.

M. Shapiro, O. Gruber, and D. Plainfossé. (1990) A garbage detection protocol for a realistic distributed object-support system. Research Report 1320, Rocquencourt, France: INRIA.

M. Shapiro, P. Dickman, and D. Plainfossé. (1992) Robust, distributed references and acyclic garbage collection. In *Proceedings of the 11th Annual ACM Symposium on Principles of Distributed Computing*, pages 135–146. Superceded by "SSP chains: Robust, distributed references supporting acyclic garbage collection", Research Report 1799, INRIA.

G.M. Shaw and S.B. Zdonik. (1989) An object-oriented query algebra. *Bulletin of the IEEE Technical Committee on Data Engineering*, 12(3).

E. Shekita. (1991) High-performance implementation techniques for next-generation database systems. Technical Report 1026, University of Wisconsin, Madison.

E. J. Shekita and M. J. Carey. (1990) A performance evaluation of pointer-based joins. In *Proceedings of the ACM SIGMOD International Conference on Management of Data*, pages 300–311.

A. P. Sheth. (1991) Semantic issues in multidatabase systems. *ACM SIGMOD Record*, 20(4): 5–9.

A. Sheth and J. Larson. (1990) Federated database systems for managing distributed, heterogeneous, and autonomous databases. *ACM Computing Surveys*, 22(3): 183–236.

A. Sheth and M. Rusinkiewicz. (1990) Management of interdependent data: Specifying dependency and consistency requirements. In *Proceedings of the Workshop on the Management of Replicated Data*, pages 133–136.

A. Sheth, Y. Leu, and A. Elmagarmid. (1991) Maintaining consistency of interdependent data in multidatabase systems. Technical Report CSD-TR-91-016, Computer Science Department, Purdue University.

A. Sheth, M. Rusinkiewicz, and G. Karabatis. (1992) Using polytransactions to manage interdependent data. In [Elmagarmid, 1992], pages 555–581.

J. Shilling and P. Sweeney. (1989) Three steps to views: Extending the object-oriented paradigm. In *Proceedings of the OOPSLA '89 Conference*, pages 353–361.

D. Shin and K. B. Irani. (1991) Fragmenting relations horizontally using a knowledge-based approach. *IEEE Transactions on Software Engineering*, 17(9): 872–883.

D. Shipman. (1981) The functional data model and the data language DAPLEX. *ACM Transactions on Database Systems*, 2(3): 140–173.

S.K. Shrivastava and S.M. Wheater. (1990) Implementing fault-tolerant distributed applications using objects and multi-coloured actions. In *Proceedings of the 10th International Conference on Distributed Computing Systems*, pages .

N.C. Shu, B.C. Housel, R.W. Taylor, S.P. Ghosh, and V.Y. Lum. (1977) EXPRESS: A data EXtraction, Processing, and REStructuring System. *ACM Transactions on Database Systems*, 2(2): 134–174.

A.P.J.M. Siebes and M.H. vd Voort. (1992) A design theory for active objects. In *Proceedings of Third International Conference on Database and Expert Systems Applications*, pages 338–344.

A. Silberschatz, M. Stonebraker, and J. Ullman. (1991) Database systems: Achievements and opportunities. *Communications of the ACM*, 34(10): 110–120.

D. Sjøberg. (1992a) Measuring name and identifier usage in Napier88 applications. Technical Report FIDE/92/37, ESPRIT Basic Research Action, Project Number 3070-FIDE.

D. Sjøberg. (1992b) Measuring schema evolution. Technical Report FIDE/92/36, ESPRIT Basic Research Action, Project Number 3070-FIDE.

A. Skarra. (1991) Localized correctness specifications for cooperating transactions in an object-oriented database. *IEEE Bulletin on Office and Knowledge Engineering*, 4(1): 79–106.

A. Skarra and S. Zdonik. (1986) The management of changing types in an object-oriented database. In *Proceedings of the OOPSLA '86 Conference*, pages 483–495.

A.H. Skarra and S.B. Zdonik. (1989) Concurrency control and object-oriented databases. In W. Kim and F. H. Lochovsky, editors, *Object-Oriented Languages, Applications, and Databases*, Reading, MA: Addison-Wesley.

J. Smith and D. Smith. (1977) Database abstractions: Aggregation and generalization. *ACM Transactions on Database Systems*, 2(2): 105–133.

W. Smith and R. Welland. (1992) A model for address-oriented software and hardware. In *Proceedings of the 25th Hawaii International Conference on Systems Science*, pages 720–729.

R. Soley, editor. (1990) *Object management architecture guide*. Framingham, MA: Object Management Group.

S. Spaccapietra, C. Parent, and Y. Dupont. (1992) Model Independent Assertions for Integration of Heterogeneous Schemas. *The VLDB Journal*, 1(1): 81–126.

A. Z. Spector and P. Z. Schwartz. (1983) Transactions: A construct for reliable distributed computing. Technical Report CMU-CS-82-143, Carnegie Mellon University.

J. Stamos. (1984) Static grouping of small objects to enhance performance of a paged virtual memory. *ACM Transactions on Computer Systems*, 2(2): 155–180.

T. Standish. (1980) *Data structure techniques*. Reading, MA : Addison-Wesley.

J.A. Stankovic. (1982) Software communication mechanisms: Procedure calls versus messages. *Computer*, 15(4): 19–25.

G. Steele. (1975) Multiprocessing compactifying garbage collection. *Communications of the ACM*, 18(9): 495–508. (Corrigendum: *Communications of the ACM*, 19(6): 354.)

G. Steele. (1990) *Common Lisp*. Maynard, MA: Digital Press.

J.G. Steiner, C. Neuman, and J.I. Schiller. (1988) Kerberos: An authentication service for open network systems. Project Athena Report, MIT, Cambridge, MA.

D. Stemple and R. Morrison. (1992) Specifying flexible concurrency control schemes: An abstract operational approach. Technical Report FIDE/92/35, ESPRIT Basic Research Action, Project Number 3070-FIDE.

D. Stemple, R.B. Stanton, T. Sheard, P.C. Philbrow, R. Morrison, G.N.C. Kirby, L. Fegaras, R.L. Cooper, R.C.H. Connor, M.P. Atkinson, and S. Alagic. (1992) Type-safe linguistic reflection: A generator technology. Technical Report FIDE/92/49, ESPRIT Basic Research Action, Project Number 3070-FIDE.

M. Stonebraker. (1979) Concurrency control and consistency of multiple copies of data in distributed INGRES. *IEEE Transactions Software Engineering* SE-5(3): 188–194.

M. Stonebraker. (1981) Operating system support for database management. *Communications of the ACM*, 24(7):412–418.

M. Stonebraker and G. Kemnitz. (1991) The POSTGRES next-generation database management system. *Communications of the ACM*, 34(10): 78–93.

M. Stonebraker and L. Rowe. (1990) The POSTGRES System. *IEEE Transactions on Knowledge and Data Engineering*, 2(1): 77–90.

M. Stonebraker, L. Rowe, and M. Hirohama. (1990) The implementation of POSTGRES. *IEEE Transactions on Knowledge and Data Engineering* 2(1): 125–142.

M. Stonebraker, A. Jhingran, J. Goh, and S. Potamianos. (1990a) On rules, procedures, caching, and views in database systems. In *Proceedings of ACM SIGMOD International Conference on Management of Data*, pages 281–290.

D.D. Straube and M.T. Özsu. (1990) Queries and query processing in object-oriented database systems. *ACM Transactions on Information Systems*, 8(4): 387–430.

R. Strom and S. Yemini. (1985) The NIL distributed systems programming language: A status report. *ACM SIGPLAN Notices*, 20(5): 36–43.

R.E. Strom, D.F. Bacon, A.P. Goldberg, A. Lowry, D.M. Yellin, and S.A. Yemini. (1991) *Hermes: A language for distributed computing*. Englewood Cliffs, NJ: Prentice-Hall.

B. Stroustrup. (1987) *The C++ programming language*. Reading, MA: Addison-Wesley.

L. Sullivan. (1986) Quality function deployment. *Quality Progress*, :39.

K. Sullivan and D. Notkin. (1991) *Behavioral relationships in object oriented analysis*. Technical Report 91-09-03, Department of Computer Science, University of Washington.

Sun Microsystems. (1988) *Network programming*.

K. Tanaka, M. Yoshikawa, and K. Ishihara. (1988) Schema virtualization in object-oriented databases. In *Proceedings of the 4th International Conference on Data Engineering*, pages 23–30.

A. S. Tanenbaum, S. J. Mullender, G. Rossu, and R. Renesse. (1990) Amoeba: A distributed operating system for the 1990s. *Computer*, 23(5): 44–53.

M.B. Thuraisingham. (1989) Mandatory security in object oriented database systems. In *Proceedings of the OOPSLA '89 Conference*, pages 203–210.

H. Tirri, J. Srinivasan, and B. Bhargava. (1991) Transactions for fragmented composite objects. Technical Report CSD-TR-91-083, Purdue University.

H.R. Tirri, J. Srinivasan, and B. Bhargava. (1993) Integrating distributed data sources using federated objects. In this volume.

K. Tracey. (1991) *Processor sharing for cooperative multi-task applications*. Ph.D. Dissertation, Department of Computer Science, University of Notre Dame.

I. Traiger. (1982) Virtual memory management for database systems. *ACM Operating Systems Review*, 16(10): 26–48.

M. Tresch and M.H. Scholl. (1992) Meta object management and its application to database evolution. In *Proceedings of the 11th International Conference on Entity-Relationship Approach*, pages 299–321.

P.W. Trinder. (1991) Comprehensions, a query notation for DBPLs. In [Kanellakis and Schmidt, 1991], pages 55–68.

M. Tsangaris and J. Naughton. (1991) A stochastical approach for clustering in object bases. In *Proceedings of ACM SIGMOD International Conference on Management of Data*, pages 12–21.

M. Tsangaris and J. Naughton. (1992) On the performances of object clustering techniques. In *Proceedings of ACM SIGMOD International Conference on Management of Data*, pages 144–153.

D. Turner. (1979) A new implementation technique for applicative languages. *Software — Practice and Experience*, 9:31–49.

D. Ungar. (1984) Generation scavenging: a non-disruptive high performance storage reclaimation algorithm. *ACM SIGPLAN Notices*, 19(5): 157–167.

P. Valduriez. (1987) Join indices. *ACM Transactions on Database Systems*, 12(2): 218–246.

P. Valduriez, S. Khoshafian, and G. Copeland. (1986) Implementation techniques of complex objects. In *Proceedings of the 12th International Conference on Very Large Data Bases*. San Mateo, CA: Morgan Kaufmann, pages 101-109.

B. Vance. (1992) Towards an object-oriented query algebra. Technical Report CSE-91-008, Oregon Graduate Institute.

V. Varadharan and S. Black. (1991) Multilevel security in a distributed object-oriented system. *Computers & Security*, 10(1): 51–68.

F. Vaughan and A. Dearle. (1992) Supporting large persistent stores using conventional hardware. In [Albano and Morrison, 1993].

S.R. Vegdahl. (1986) Moving structures between Smalltalk images. In *Proceedings of the OOPSLA'86 Conference*, pages 466–471.

M.H. vd Voort and M.L. Kersten. (1990) The facets of database triggers, Technical Report CS-9122, CWI, Amsterdam.

M.H. vd Voort, A. Siebes, and M.L. Kersten. (1991) A framework for the formalisation of active objects. In *Proceedings of Computer Science in the Netherlands 1991*, pages 484–498.

Y. Wang and L. Rowe. (1991) Cache consistency and concurrency control in a client/server DBMS architecture. In *Proceedings of the ACM SIGMOD International Conference on Management of Data*, pages 367–376.

I. Watson and P. Watson. (1987) An efficient garbage collection scheme for parallel computer architectures. In *Proceedings of the PARLE'87 Conference, Vol. II*, pages 432–443.

W. Weihl. (1988) Commutativity-based concurrency control for abstract data types. *IEEE Transactions on Computers*, 33(12): 1488–1505.

W. Weihl. (1989a) Local atomicity properties: Modular concurrency control for abstract data types. *ACM Transactions on Programming Languages and Systems*, 11(4): 249–281.

W. Weihl. (1989b) The impact of recovery on concurrency control. In *Proceedings of the 8th ACM Symposium on Principles of Database Systems*, pages 259–269.

W. Weihl and B. Liskov. (1985) Implementation of resilient, atomic data types. *ACM Transactions on Programming Languages and Systems* 7(2): 244–269.

G. Weikum and H.-J. Schek. (1992) Concepts and applications of multilevel transactions and open nested transactions. In [Elmagarmid, 1992], pages 515–553.

D. Weinreb, D. Gerson, and C. Lamb. (1988) An object oriented system to support an integrated programming environment. *IEEE Transactions on Data Engineering* 11(2): 33–43.

J. Weizenbaum. (1969) Recovery of reentrant list structures in SLIP. *Communications of the ACM*, 12(7): 370–372.

D. L. Wells. (1991a) DARPA Open object-oriented database architecture specification. Technical Report Version 6, Computer Science Laboratory, Texas Instruments, Inc.

D.L. Wells. (1991b) DARPA Open object-oriented database persistence policy manager specification. Technical Report Version 2, Computer Science Laboratory, Texas Instruments, Inc.

D. Wells and J. Blakeley. (1993) Distribution and persistence in the open object-oriented database system. In this volume.

D.L. Wells, J.A. Blakeley, and C.W. Thompson. (1992) Architecture of an open object-oriented database management system. *Computer*, 25(10);74–82.

J. Widom and S.J. Finkelstein. (1990) Set-oriented production rules in relational database systems. *Proceedings of the ACM SIGMOD International Conference on Management of Data*, pages 259–270.

W. Wilkinson, and M. Neimat. (1990) Maintaining consistency of client cached data. In *Proceedings of the 16th International Conference on Very Large Data Bases*. San Mateo, CA: Morgan Kaufmann, pages 122–133.

K. Wilkinson, P. Lyngbaek, and W. Hasan. (1990) The Iris architecture and implementation. *IEEE Transactions on Knowledge and Data Engineering*, 2(1): 63–75.

P. Wilson, R. Bayardo, A. Chaudhry, S. Kakkad, S. Krishnamoorthy, R. Kumar, and R. Singhal. (1992) TEXAS: An efficient, portable persistent store. In [Albano and Morrison, 1993].

M. Wolczko. (1992) Multi-level garbage collection in a high-performance persistent object system. In [Albano and Morrison, 1993].

M. Wolfe. (1990) A Hypertext based decision support system to support team decision making. In *Proceedings of the International Conference on Systems, Man, and Cybernetics*, pages 884–888.

M. Yannakakis. (1984) Serializability by locking. *Journal of the ACM*, 31(2): 227–244.

Y. Yokote, F. Teraoka, and M. Tokoro. (1989) A reflective architecture for an object-oriented distributed operating system. In *Proceedings of the European Conference on Object-Oriented Programming (ECOOP) Conference*, pages 89–106.

Y. Yokote, F. Teraoka, A. Mitsuzawa, N. Fujinami, and M. Tokora. (1991) The Muse object architecture: A new operating system structuring concept. *Operating Systems Review*, 25(2): 22–46.

A. Yonezawa and M. Tokoro. (1987) *Object oriented concurrent programming*. Cambridge, MA: The MIT Press.

S. Zdonik. (1988) Data abstraction and query optimization. In [Dittrich, 1988], pages 368–373.

S.B. Zdonik and D. Maier editors. (1990) *Readings in Object-Oriented Database Systems*. San Mateo, CA: Morgan Kaufmann.

P. Zezula and F. Rabitti. (1992) An efficient store for object bases. In *Proceedings of the 25th Hawaii International Conference on System Sciences*, pages 756–765.

J. Zhu and D. Maier. (1989) Computational objects in object-oriented data models. In [Hull, et al., 1989], pages 138–160.

Index